Lecture Notes in Computer Science 10342

Commenced Publication in 1973
Founding and Former Series Editors:
Gerhard Goos, Juris Hartmanis, and Jan van Leeuwen

Editorial Board

David Hutchison
Lancaster University, Lancaster, UK
Takeo Kanade
Carnegie Mellon University, Pittsburgh, PA, USA
Josef Kittler
University of Surrey, Guildford, UK
Jon M. Kleinberg
Cornell University, Ithaca, NY, USA
Friedemann Mattern
ETH Zurich, Zurich, Switzerland
John C. Mitchell
Stanford University, Stanford, CA, USA
Moni Naor
Weizmann Institute of Science, Rehovot, Israel
C. Pandu Rangan
Indian Institute of Technology, Madras, India
Bernhard Steffen
TU Dortmund University, Dortmund, Germany
Demetri Terzopoulos
University of California, Los Angeles, CA, USA
Doug Tygar
University of California, Berkeley, CA, USA
Gerhard Weikum
Max Planck Institute for Informatics, Saarbrücken, Germany

More information about this series at http://www.springer.com/series/7410

Josef Pieprzyk · Suriadi Suriadi (Eds.)

Information Security and Privacy

22nd Australasian Conference, ACISP 2017
Auckland, New Zealand, July 3–5, 2017
Proceedings, Part I

 Springer

Editors
Josef Pieprzyk (iD)
Queensland University of Technology
Brisbane, QLD
Australia

Suriadi Suriadi (iD)
Queensland University of Technology
Brisbane, QLD
Australia

ISSN 0302-9743   ISSN 1611-3349   (electronic)
Lecture Notes in Computer Science
ISBN 978-3-319-60054-3   ISBN 978-3-319-60055-0   (eBook)
DOI 10.1007/978-3-319-60055-0

Library of Congress Control Number: 2017943039

LNCS Sublibrary: SL4 – Security and Cryptology

Printed on acid-free paper

This Springer imprint is published by Springer Nature
The registered company is Springer International Publishing AG
The registered company address is: Gewerbestrasse 11, 6330 Cham, Switzerland

Preface

The 22nd Australasian Conference on Information Security and Privacy was organized in beautiful New Zealand on the Massey University campus in Auckland, July 3–5, 2017. This was the first time that the conference was organized outside Australia.

This year we received 150 submissions. Each paper got assigned to four referees. In the first stage of the review process, the submitted papers were read and evaluated by the Program Committee members. In the second stage, the papers were scrutinized during an extensive discussion. Finally, the Program Committee chose 45 regular and ten short papers to be included in the conference program. The authors of the accepted papers had ten days for revision and preparation of final versions. The revised papers were not subject to editorial review and the authors bear full responsibility for their contents. The submission and review process was supported by the EasyChair conference submission server. We thank the EasyChair people for letting us use it.

The Program Committee voted for the best paper using the Doodle software. We nominated four papers with best reviews. Out of the four, two papers were the preferred options with no clear winner. We decided to award the ACISP2017 Best Paper Award to the two papers:

- "Dynamic Searchable Symmetric Encryption with Physical Deletion and Small Leakage" by Peng Xu, Shuai Liang, Wei Wang, Willy Susilo, Qianhong Wu and Hai Jin
- "Multi-user Cloud-Based Secure Keyword Search" by Shabnam Kasra Kermanshahi, Joseph K. Liu and Ron Steinfeld

The awards were handed during the conference dinner.

The Jennifer Seberry Lecture this year was delivered by Clark Thomborson from the University of Auckland, New Zealand. The keynote lecture was presented by L. Jean Camp from Indiana University, USA. The program also included invited talks by well-known researchers working in different areas of cybersecurity. They were Dong Seong Kim, University of Canterbury, New Zealand; Dongxi Liu, CSIRO/Data61, Australia; Surya Nepal, CSIRO/Data61, Australia; Paul Pang, Unitec Institute of Technology, New Zealand; Peter Pilley, Department of Internal Affairs, New Zealand; Ian Welch, Victoria University of Wellington, New Zealand and Henry B. Wolfe, University of Otago, New Zealand.

We would like to thank the Program Committee members and the external reviewers for their effort and time to evaluate the submissions. Big thanks go to Julian Jang-Jaccard and Paul Watters for their excellent job in the organization of the conference. We are indebted to the team at Springer for their continuous support of the conference and for their help in the production of the conference proceedings.

July 2017

Josef Pieprzyk
Suriadi Suriadi

ACISP 2017

The 22nd Australasian Conference on Information Security
and Privacy

Massey University, Auckland, New Zealand
July 3–5, 2017

In Co-operation with IACR

Sponsored by Massey University

General Co-chairs

Julian Jang-Jaccard   Massey University, New Zealand
Paul Watters   La Trobe University, Australia

Program Co-chairs

Josef Pieprzyk   Queensland University of Technology, Australia
Suriadi Suriadi   Queensland University of Technology, Australia

Program Committee

Cristina Alcaraz   University of Malaga, Spain
Claudio Agostino Ardagna Università degli Studi di Milano, Italy
Giuseppe Ateniese   Stevens Institute of Technology, USA
Man Ho Au   Hong Kong Polytechnic University, SAR China
Milton Baar   Macquarie University, Australia
Joonsang Baek   Khalifa University of Science, UAE
Lynn Batten   Deakin University, Australia
Colin Boyd   Norwegian University of Science and Technology,
                            Norway
Serdar Boztas   RMIT University, Australia
Alvaro Cardenas   University of Texas at Dallas, USA
Aniello Castiglione   University of Salerno, Italy
Ebrima Ceesay   Leidos and Johns Hopkins University, USA
Jinjun Chen   University Technology Sydney, Australia

Shiping Chen	Data61 - CSIRO, Australia
Xiaofeng Chen	Xidian University, China
Kim-Kwang Raymond Choo	University of Texas at San Antonio, USA
Christophe Doche	Macquarie University, Australia
Ernest Foo	Queensland University of Technology, Australia
David Galindo	University of Birmingham, UK
Colm Gannon	DCET - Internal Affairs, New Zealand
Swee-Huay Heng	Multimedia University, Malaysia
Andreas Holzer	Google Inc., USA
Xinyi Huang	Fujian Normal University, China
Mitsugu Iwamoto	University of Electro-Communications, Japan
Sanjay Jha	University of New South Wales, Australia
Akinori Kawachi	The University of Tokushima, Japan
Peter Kieseberg	SBA Research, Austria
Dong Seong Kim	University of Canterbury, New Zealand
Howon Kim	Pusan National University, South Korea
Jongkil Kim	Data61 - CSIRO, Australia
Ryan Ko	University of Waikato, New Zealand
Marina Krotofil	Hamburg University of Technology, Germany
Noboru Kunihiro	University of Tokyo, Japan
Mirosław Kutyłowski	Wrocław University of Science and Technology, Poland
Junzuo Lai	Singapore Management University, Singapore
Shujun Li	University of Surrey, UK
Kaitai Liang	Aalto University, Finland
Dongxi Liu	Data61 - CSIRO, Australia
Joseph Liu	Monash University, Australia
Shengli Liu	Shanghai Jiao Tong University, China
Javier Lopez	University of Malaga, Spain
Jiqiang Lu	Institute for Infocomm Research, Singapore
Rongxing Lu	University of New Brunswick, Canada
Félix Gómez Mármol	University of Murcia, Spain
Weizhi Meng	Technical University of Denmark, Denmark
Kazuhiko Minematsu	NEC Corporation, Japan
Chris Mitchell	Royal Holloway - University of London, UK
Paweł Morawiecki	Polish Academy of Sciences, Poland
Kirill Morozov	Tokyo Institute of Technology, Japan
Yi Mu	University of Wollongong, Australia
Surya Nepal	Data61 - CSIRO, Australia
Ivica Nikolić	Nanyang Technological University, Singapore
Thomas Peyrin	Nanyang Technological University, Singapore
Man Qi	Canterbury Christ Church University, UK
Kenneth Radke	Queensland University of Technology and CERT Australia, Australia
Reza Reyhanitabar	NEC Laboratories Europe, Germany

Jun Shao	Zhejiang Gongshang University, China
Taeshik Shon	Ajou University, South Korea
Haya Shulman	Fraunhofer SIT, Germany
Tony Skjellum	Auburn University, USA
Ron Steinfeld	Monash University, Australia
Chunhua Su	Japan Advanced Institute of Science and Technology, Japan
Willy Susilo	University of Wollongong, Australia
Shaohua Tang	South China University of Technology, China
Juan Tapiador	Universidad Carlos III de Madrid, Spain
Clark Thomborson	University of Auckland, New Zealand
Fergus Toolan	UCD School of Computer Science, Ireland
Petros Wallden	University of Edinburgh, UK
Cong Wang	City University of Hong Kong, SAR China
Huaxiong Wang	Nanyang Technological University, Singapore
Yu Wang	Deakin University, Australia
George Weir	University of Strathclyde, UK
Sheng Wen	Deakin University, Australia
Henry B. Wolfe	University of Otago, New Zealand
Chi Yang	Unitec Institute of Technology, New Zealand
Guomin Yang	University of Wollongong, Australia
Yanjiang Yang	Huawei Singapore Research Center, Singapore
Wun-She Yap	Universiti Tunku Abdul Rahman, Malaysia
Xun Yi	RMIT University, Australia
Tsz Hon Yuen	Huawei Singapore Research Center, Singapore
Aaram Yun	Ulsan National Institute of Science and Technology, South Korea
Xuyun Zhang	University of Auckland, New Zealand

Additional Reviewers

Fatma Al Maqbali	Ed Dawson	Andrei Kelarev
Janaka Alawatugoda	Nabil El Ioini	Jeongsu Kim
Yoshinori Aono	Gerardo Fernandez	Jianchang Lai
Shahriar Badsha	Filippo Gaudenzi	Anna Lauks-Dutka
Anubhab Baksi	Junqing Gong	Hyung Tae Lee
Arcangelo Castiglione	Zheng Gong	Nan Li
Luigi Catuogno	Fuchun Guo	Xiaoyu Li
Claire Che	Jian Guo	Xingye Lu
Jiahui Chen	Jingjing Guo	Lin Lyu
Jie Chen	Felix Günther	Jinhua Ma
Rongmao Chen	Jinguang Han	Moesfa Soeheila
Ji-Jian Chin	Shuai Han	Mohamad
Craig Costello	Yasufumi Hashimoto	Mihai Moraru
Hui Cui	Shoichi Hirose	Khoa Nguyen

Abstracts of Invited Talks

Jennifer Seberry Lecture: Contextual Privacy

Clark Thomborson

Computer Science Department
University of Auckland, Auckland, New Zealand
cthombor@cs.auckland.ac.nz

Abstract. Could you design a computer system which respects all forms of privacy that are relevant to its users? What forms of privacy are important to you personally, and in what contexts are they important? How can a user obtain a "private place" in a computerised system? Is it feasible and economic for a system to afford a particular form of privacy to its users? Is it socially appropriate, or legal, for a system to grant a privacy request? Which privacy requests should be denied? Can you identify all of the "assets at risk" in a privacy-protective system? I won't attempt to answer any of these questions fully! However I will get you started on finding your own answers, for the next system you design, for the next privacy analysis you perform, and for the next system you use. My explanations are grounded in Lawrence Lessig's taxonomy of control and liberty, in Alan Westin's taxonomy of private states, in Helen Nissenbaum's legal theory of contextual integrity, and in the Jericho Forum's Identity Commandments. I'll draw examples from commonly-encountered systems such as Facebook.

Key Note Lecture: Security as Risk Communication

L. Jean Camp

School of Informatics
Indiana University, Indianapolis, USA
ljcamp@indiana.edu

Abstract. In usable security design, opaque designs enable the user take an action seamlessly rather than requiring some understanding of the underlying system design. However, security choices inherently require some information, or the default option is to prevent all risky behaviors without interaction. In fact, blocking desired action without communication is one reason that individuals may abandon security technologies even when the risks these technologies mitigate are known.

Incentives cannot work unless there are two conditions. First, the incentives must be visible. Second, there must be a clear action to take in response to the incentives. Both of these outcomes are the goal of translucent design. A truly transparent design can overwhelm and under-inform the user with information about configuration, the nature of the security technology, and the elements of a risk that are mitigated.

Risk communication allows individuals to easily see the consequences of their action. The ideal design, of making visible user-action-system-consequence, may be overwhelming or context-dependent. Risk communication is neither transparent nor opaque; but rather consists of security technologies that are easy to use, communicate risk choices only to the degree necessary to avoid inadvertent fatal choices, can be overcome in a straight-forward manner if the individual chooses to take a risk, or if the system is in error.

Key Note Lecture: I Was Sure that Was My Password... and Other Just so Law Enforcement Stories

Peter Pilley

Department of Internal Affairs, Manukau, New Zealand

Abstract. With the advent of communications devices and software being encrypted by design there is now a number of new risks presenting themselves some predicted and some only becoming apparent now.

Who owns the data that is encrypted? What right or access does a family have to the encrypted data of a sibling or Son/Daughter at the time of their death? How can law enforcement be seen to be able to successfully investigate a suspect if they have taken steps to encrypt their communications platform or device?

These are not new fears or technologies but they do raise some interesting questions and scenarios. Encrypted networks such as TOR and platforms such as WhatsApp are potentially removing the traditional investigation methods from the investigator Agencies are turning to, and in some instances failing in the use of., more advanced interception techniques. How do we as Law Enforcement manage this, and more importantly how as a community do we need to see it managed?

Graphical Security Models

Dong Seong Kim

Department of Computer Science and Software Engineering
University of Canterbury, Christchurch, New Zealand
dongseong.kim@canterbury.ac.nz

Abstract. Graphical security models can be used to assess the network security. Purely graph based (e.g., Attack Graphs) security models have a state-space explosion problem. Tree-based models (e.g., Attack Trees) cannot capture the attack paths information explicitly. In this talk, we briefly introduce a scalable security model named hierarchical attack representation models (HARM) to deal with the above mentioned issues. First, I present how the HARM with other methods to evaluate the effectiveness of Moving Target Defenses. Second, I present how the HARM can be used to evaluate the security of Internet of Things. Finally, research revenues in the graphical security modeling and assessment will be discussed in brief.

Compact-LWE for Lightweight Public Key Encryption and Leveled IoT Authentication

Dongxi Liu

CSIRO, Data61, Melbourne, Australia
Dongxi.Liu@data61.csiro.au

Abstract. Leveled authentication allows resource-constrained IoT devices to be authenticated at different strength levels according to the particular types of communication. To achieve efficient leveled authentication, a lightweight public key encryption scheme is introduced in this talk, which can produce very short ciphertexts without sacrificing its security.

The semantic security of this scheme is based on the Learning With Secretly Scaled Errors in Dense Lattice (referred to as Compact-LWE) problem designed in CSIRO. This problem is a variant of the Learning With Errors (LWE) problem, but with two improvements (i.e., secretly scaled errors, which can be very big, and dense lattice, which has small fundamental parallelepiped) that make Compact-LWE resistant against well-known lattice-based attacks to LWE. In addition to the security proof, we verify, with a public attack tool, that the lattice-based attacks, which are successful on LWE, cannot succeed on Compact-LWE even for a small dimension parameter (e.g., a lattice of dimension 13).

The evaluation of our scheme and a leveled Needham-Schroeder-Lowe public key authentication protocol on the Contiki operating system and Sky motes will also be introduced.

Orchestration and Automation of Cybersecurity: Issues and Challenges

Surya Nepal

Data61 CSIRO, Canberra, Australia
surya.nepal@data61.csiro.au

Abstract. Almost all present cybersecurity expenditure and activities (85%) focuses on designing solutions to prevent known cybersecurity threats. No matter how much efforts are put in preparation and prevention, these solutions are not working and cyberattacks and data breaches are inevitable. Current compromise-to-discovery time can be 30 to 60 days. One the one hand, the number of incidents of cyberattacks and data breaches are increasing every year; the increase in time required to detect cyberattacks and data breaches is causing higher reputational, operational and economic loss due to the impact on the continuity of the business. On the other hand, we have a limited pool of security experts who can focus on human-intensive tasks such as analysing programs/ protocols, designing patches, understanding a compromise and responding/ recovering from a compromise. Current approaches are mostly manual, signature base, reactive and not robust and resilient. Furthermore, the increasing complexity of the cyberspace and its dynamic nature makes it impossible for humans to effectively secure and protect the cyber system. These space requires a paradigm shift towards more orchestrated and automated cybersecurity solutions so security experts could be more efficiently utilised and small-to-medium businesses can have access to more advanced cybersecurity capabilities through software-as-a-service. A number of organisations have already started taking some actions to automate and orchestrate incident response processes, while researchers have started to explore the coordinated response of the human body immune system towards building autonomic, resilient cyber systems. This talk explores the potential opportunities and issues to automate and orchestrate cybersecurity solutions.

UniteCloud: A Resilient Private Cloud Platform for Education and Research Service

Paul S. Pang

High Tech Transdisciplinary Research Network
and Department of Computer Science
Unitec Institute of Technology, Auckland, New Zealand
ppang@unitec.ac.nz

Abstract. UniteCloud is a cloud-computing platform developed in Unitec Institute of Technology to provide a solution to resilient infrastructure and data services. UniteCloud has been constructed using OpenStack with its peak computational capability up to 500 virtual machines and maximum storage allocation 64 tera-bytes per virtual machine. The resiliency of UniteCloud is achieved by three novel components. CloudViz-3D is a top-level interactive cloud monitoring system that monitors the running status of cloud and notifies users before any disaster occurs. rRVM is a low latency and high consistency high availability system that generates real time backup and disaster recovery. CRaaSH is an offline disaster recovery system that provides decentralized service checkpoint/restart over commodity networks. In addition, the platform supports group collaborative working, editing, big data processing and machine learning algorithmic experiments with its open source implementation of Gitlab, ShareLatex, HadoopDataCenter and TensorFlow. With all its resilient service features, UniteCloud is specializing in supplying eLearning and eResearch services for New Zealand tertiary students and staffs.

Software Defined Networking as a Security Enabler for Enterprises

Ian Welch

School of Engineering and Computer Science
Victoria University of Wellington, Wellington
New Zealand
ian.welch@vuw.ac.nz

Abstract. Industry commentators have raised concerns about software-defined networking (SDN) as looking "like a nice squishy target to spies and crooks" and a "nightmare" from a risk assessment point-of-view. Security concerns include worries that it will be impossible to secure the perimeter because the network architecture is no longer fixed, the controller managing the control plane is centralised, and a single point of failure and the software-centric approach is highly vulnerable to exploitation as opposed to current hardware-based approaches.

We argue that some of these concerns are not new and software defined network provides an approach to implementing secure enterprise networks that can lead to better enforcement and greater assurance. This talk will address concerns and explain how we are working with other academics and commercial partners on the development of a software defined security platform that leverages these advantages over traditional approaches.

Mobile Phone Security Issues

Henry B. Wolfe

Department of Information Science
University of Otago, Dunedin, New Zealand
hank.wolfe@otago.ac.nz

Abstract. We take for granted every day that we are safe from any given risk because we are protected by various standards, statutes, and laws. The mobile phone has become ubiquitous and there are currently more than 8 billion connections and almost 5 billion mobile phones in use around the world. It is really nothing more than a small computer with a radio transmitter and receiver and other communications devices (Wi/Fi, Bluetooth, etc) integrated into it. Smart phones may also have the ability to record photos, videos and sound. Most have a built in Global Positioning Satellite System capability. Some phones may also have Near Field Communications (NFC). Each of these capabilities may result in various risks. Every generation of mobile phone has expanded its capabilities and we are now able to communicate with the Internet in addition to normal telephone activity.

A long with these capabilities come a number of risks. Some of these are normally associated with using the Internet, so mobile users are exposed to malware of various kinds from that source. However, there are other more insidious risks that are less known. The purpose of this presentation is to discuss the current risks associated with mobile phone use including malware; loss, theft, seizure; communications interception, loss of privacy; location logging and tracking; and bugging. Most people are not aware of these threats. They assume that their service provider has put in place measures to eliminate any risks as well as protect their privacy (by the use of cryptography). 100% safe mobile phone use will unlikely ever be possible. This presentation will cover mitigating alternatives that can be put in place to reduce the identified mobile phone risks. These will be graphically portrayed and clearly described and defined in terms and language that non-technical people will understand.

Contents – Part I

Searchable Encryption

Cryptanalysis

Digital Signatures

Contents – Part II

Privacy

Authentication

Elliptic Curve Cryptography

Short Papers

Public Key Encryption

Tightly-Secure Encryption in the Multi-user, Multi-challenge Setting with Improved Efficiency

Puwen Wei[1(✉)], Wei Wang[1(✉)], Bingxin Zhu[1], and Siu Ming Yiu[2]

[1] Key Laboratory of Cryptologic Technology and Information Security, Ministry of Education, Shandong University, Jinan, China
{pwei,weiwangsdu}@sdu.edu.cn, bingxinzhu@mail.sdu.edu.cn
[2] The University of Hong Kong, Pokfulam, Hong Kong
smyiu@cs.hku.hk

Abstract. We construct a compact public-key encryption with tight CCA security in the multi-user, multi-challenge setting, where the reduction loss is a constant. Our scheme follows the Hofheinz-Jager framework but is compressed in the sense that only one of the underlying two-tier signatures needs to be committed. Considering the virtually unbounded simulations, e.g., 2^{80}, the ciphertext size of our scheme decreases to about 256 group elements, whereas the best known solution provided by Blazy et al. required about 625 group elements under the same standard assumptions. In particular, we formalize a new notion called simulatable two-tier signature, which plays a central role in the construction of our tree-based signature and public-key encryption. Combining simulatable two-tier signatures with additional "ephemeral" signatures, we provide a method of constructing commitments to a tree-based signature, where most parts of the tree-based signature can be simulated and sent in the clear. Our method can reduce the length of the commitments and the related proofs of knowledge in previous works by 60%.

Keywords: Multi-user · Multi-challenge · Public-key encryption · Tight security

1 Introduction

Standard security notions for public-key encryptions (PKE) only consider one user and one challenge ciphertext, e.g., IND-CCA security [27]. The realistic setting for PKE, however, usually involves more users and ciphertexts, which is called multi-user, multi-challenge setting. General result [7] shows that one-user, one-ciphertext security implies security in the multi-user, multi-challenge setting, and the reduction loss of the proof is $n_u \cdot n_c$, where n_u and n_c denote the number of users and the number of challenge ciphertexts per user, respectively. In that sense, if a PKE which is secure in a one-user, one-challenge setting is deployed in a multi-user, multi-challenge setting, its security may significantly

© Springer International Publishing AG 2017
J. Pieprzyk and S. Suriadi (Eds.): ACISP 2017, Part I, LNCS 10342, pp. 3–22, 2017.
DOI: 10.1007/978-3-319-60055-0_1

deteriorate in the number of users or ciphertexts. In fact, the choice of the size of cryptographic parameters depends on the concrete loss of the reduction. That is, the larger the security loss requires, the larger the parameters are. The following example given by [5] illustrates the relation above. Suppose a RSA-based digital signature with reduction loss $n_u \cdot n_s$ is deployed in a large-scale setting, such as TLS protocol on the internet, where the number of users and signatures are $n_u = 2^{20}$ and $n_s = 2^{20}$, respectively. If we want to achieve a security level of 100 "bits of security", the RSA-modulus size of the digital signature needs to be greater than 4000 bits, which means much more running time than that of current schemes with 2048-bit modulus. What is worse, the number of users, signatures or ciphertexts is usually not clear at deployment time. Hence, it is necessary to consider tight security for the multi-user/-challenge setting, where "tight" means the reduction loss is a constant.

Bellare et al. [7] proved the tight IND-CPA security of ElGamal encryption [15] in the multi-user/-challenge setting. However, the problem of constructing tightly IND-CCA secure PKE in the same setting from standard assumptions was left open for many years. The important development was made by Hofheinz and Jager [19]. They showed the first IND-CCA secure PKE in the multi-user/-challenge setting, the security of which tightly relates to the decision linear (DLIN) assumption. Abe et al. [1] improved Hofheinz and Jager's scheme by introducing an efficient tagged one-time signature, while the ciphertext of the resulting scheme still requires many hundreds of group elements. Another line of research concentrates on the construction of primitives with *almost* tight security, where "almost tight security" means that the reduction loss depends only on the security parameter and not the number of adversarial queries. Chen and Wee [13] presented the first fully secure identity-based encryption (IBE) with almost tight security from the standard assumptions. Subsequently, Blazy, Kiltz and Pan [9] provided IBE with "somewhat" tight security from affine message authentication. Although the IBE schemes in [9,13] are not proved secure in a multi-user/-challenge setting, their schemes imply almost tightly secure PKE in the multi-user/-challenge setting. Then Hofheinz, Koch and Striecks [21] extended Chen and Wee's proof technique and constructed an IBE that is almost tightly secure in the multi-user/-challenge setting, which can be converted to an almost tightly CCA secure PKE in the same setting via the Canetti-Halevi-Katz paradigm [12]. Considering the large ciphertexts size in previous works, Libert et al. [24] showed an almost tightly CCA secure PKE, the ciphertext size of which decreases to 69 group elements under the DLIN assumption. Subsequent works [3,20,25] were devoted to further reducing the ciphertexts size. Very recently, Gay et al. [16] constructed an almost tightly CCA-secure encryption scheme from the DDH assumption without pairings, where the ciphertext overhead is only 3 group elements.

Nevertheless, current PKEs with tight CCA security in the multi-user/-challenge setting (under standard assumptions) are not as compact as their counterparts with *almost* tight security. They are more feasibility results than practical solutions. So far as we know, Blazy et al. [10] provided the most efficient PKE schemes with tight CCA security in the multi-user/-challenge setting.

They gave a new framework for obtaining tightly secure signatures from standard assumptions, which leads to a tightly CCA-secure encryption using the framework of [19]. The ciphertext size of their PKE is about 625 group elements[1].

The difficulty in reducing ciphertext size. Current tightly CCA-secure encryptions [1,10,19] based on standard assumptions all rely on tightly simulation-sound non-interactive zero-knowledge proof system (SS-NIZK), where the central building block is the tightly secure tree-based signature. Due to the tree structure, the tree-based signature mainly consists of lots of underlying one-time signatures, the number of which is linear with the depth of the tree. More importantly, the prover has to commit to all those underlying signatures in the construction of SS-NIZK, which results in the large size of SS-NIZK even if the underlying signatures size can be made very small, say, only one element as in [10]. Essentially, any further improvements on the size of the underlying signatures cannot help in reducing the size of current SS-NIZK dramatically.

Our contribution. In this paper, we focus on the construction of tightly secure encryptions in the multi-user/-challenge setting and provide a new method of reducing the size of the commitment to a tree-based signature, which yields a more compact tightly CCA-secure PKE in the multi-user/-challenge setting based on standard assumptions. The resulting ciphertext is only of $5\lambda/(1 + \log d) + d/f + 54$ group elements in $\mathbb{G}$, 1 element in $\mathbb{Z}_p$ and 1 scalar. For $d = 2$, $f = 1$ and 2^λ simulations, the ciphertext of our construction requires only about $2.5\lambda + 56$ group elements, which is much less than that of [10] (about $7\lambda + 65$ group elements) under the same assumptions. In particular, if $\lambda = 80$ (which allows almost unbounded simulations, suggested by [19]), our ciphertext consists of 256 group elements, 1 element in $\mathbb{Z}_p$ and 1 scalar, which reduces the ciphertext size of Blazy et al.'s scheme [10] (roughly 625 group elements) by about 60%.

As a main tool to achieve our construction, we introduce the notion of simulatable two-tier signatures[2], which captures the property of the simulation of two-tier signatures and the corresponding secondary public keys. Actually, such property was implicitly used in the security proof of the signatures in previous works [10,19,22]. Here, we take advantage of this property in a different way: Without using Groth-Sahai commitments, the simulated two-tier signatures are directly applied to construction of the simulation extractable NIZK. However, to generate a commitment to a tree-based signature, simulatable two-tier signatures needs to be combined with properly embedded ephemeral two-tier signatures, which is crucial to the shrinking of the ciphertexts. Indeed, the combination of simulatable two-tier signatures and ephemeral two-tier signatures provide a new

---

[1] The concrete ciphertext size of PKE in [10] is not explicit in their paper. We compute the ciphertext size according to the appendix of [10] when $d = 2$, $f = 1$ and $\lambda = 80$. Note that (d, f) are the parameters related to the underlying d-time two-tier signatures and 2^λ denotes the maximal number of signatures.

[2] The simulatable two-tier signature is different from the notion simulatable signature introduced in [2]. The latter is defined in the common reference string (CRS) model and allows to create valid signatures using the trapdoor associated with the CRS, while our simulatable two-tier signature does not require the CRS and the trapdoor.

method of reducing the size of tightly SS-NIZK, which can be applied in the construction of other tightly secure cryptographic primitives, such as tightly secure authenticated key exchange [4], leakage resistant public key encryption [14] and delegatable anonymous credentials [6]. Although the resulting schemes are still not practical due to hundreds of elements, the concrete efficiency assessment of theoretical constructions should serve as a reference for more efficient ones as mentioned in [1].

2   Preliminaries

Digital signatures. A digital signature scheme $\mathsf{Sig} = (\mathsf{Gen}, \mathsf{Sign}, \mathsf{Vrfy})$ consists of three algorithms. The key generation algorithm Gen on input parameter λ outputs a public/private key pair $(\mathsf{pk}, \mathsf{sk})$. The signing algorithm Sign takes the signing key sk and a massage m as input and outputs a signature σ. The verification algorithm Vrfy on inputs the verification pk, a message m and the corresponding signature σ outputs $b \in \{0,1\}$. The security of the signature schemes can be defined by the following experiment played between a challenger and a adversary $\mathcal{A}$.

$\mathsf{Exp}_{\mathsf{Sig},\mathcal{A},q}^{\mathsf{EUF\text{-}NCMA}}(\lambda)$

- $(m_1, \ldots, m_q) \leftarrow \mathcal{A}(1^\lambda)$;
- $(\mathsf{pk}, \mathsf{sk}) \leftarrow \mathsf{Gen}(1^\lambda)$, $\sigma_i \leftarrow \mathsf{Sign}(\mathsf{sk}, m_i)$, for $i = 1, \ldots, q$;
- $(m^*, \sigma^*) \leftarrow \mathcal{A}(\mathsf{pk}, \sigma_1, \ldots, \sigma_q)$;
- If $\mathsf{Vrfy}(\mathsf{pk}, m^*, \sigma^*) = 1$ and $m^* \notin (m_1, \ldots, m_q)$, then return 1. Otherwise, return 0.

We say Sig is (ϵ, t, q)-existentially unforgeable against non-adaptive chosen message attacks (EUF-NCMA) if $\Pr[\mathsf{Exp}_{\mathsf{Sig},\mathcal{A},q}^{\mathsf{EUF\text{-}NCMA}}(\lambda) = 1] \leq \epsilon$ holds for any PPT adversary $\mathcal{A}$ with running time at most t and at most q chosen-message queries. Additional state information usually needs to be added to the inputs of Sign and Vrfy when we deal with stateful signatures. For convenience, the stateful tree-based signatures in [10,19] as well as this paper follow the above definitions of ordinary signatures, where the state information is not explicitly taken as inputs of Sign and Vrfy.

Two-Tier Signatures. Two-tier signature schemes, introduced by Bellare and Shoup [8], have a primary key and a secondary key. The primary key is a long-time key, which can be used for all signatures, while the secondary key is a one-time key, which is usually used for only one message. Blazy et al. [10] presented a generalization of two-tier signature schemes and introduce the notion of d-time two-tier signature, which allows the secondary key to sign at most d messages. We follow the definition of d-time two-tier signatures in [10].

Definition 1 (*d-time two-tier signature scheme*). *A d-time two-tier signature TTSig consists of four probabilistic algorithms ($\mathsf{PriGen}, \mathsf{SecGen}, \mathsf{TTSign}, \mathsf{TTVrfy}$).*

- $PriGen(1^\lambda, d)$ generates a primary verification key ppk and signing key psk.
- $SecGen(ppk, psk)$ generates a secondary verification key and signing key pair (spk, ssk).
- $TTSign(psk,ssk, m)$ outputs a signature σ for message m. For a stateful $TTSign$, it takes as input the state in addition to (psk,ssk, m). That is, $\sigma \leftarrow TTSign(psk,ssk, m; j)$, where j is the state.
- $TTVrfy(ppk, spk, m, \sigma)$ deterministically outputs 1 for acceptance, or 0 for rejection. The stateful version is denoted as $TTVrfy(ppk, spk, m, \sigma; j)$, where j is the state.

The security of d-time two-tier signatures is defined by the following experiment.

$Exp_{TTSig,\mathcal{A},q}^{TT\text{-}EUF\text{-}NCMA}(\lambda, d)$
- $(ppk, psk) \leftarrow PriGen(1^\lambda, d)$;
- $(m^*, \sigma^*, i^*) \leftarrow \mathcal{A}^{\mathcal{O}_{Sig}(\cdot)}(ppk)$;
- If $TTVrfy(ppk, spk_{i^*}, m^*, \sigma^*) = 1$ and $m^* \notin \mathcal{Q}_{i^*}$, then return 1. Otherwise, return 0.

$\mathcal{O}_{Sig}(\cdot)$ is the signing oracle, which on receiving i-th query $\mathcal{Q}_i = (m_1, \ldots, m_d)$, computes $(spk_i, ssk_i) \leftarrow SecGen(ppk, psk)$ and $\sigma_j \leftarrow TTSign(psk,ssk_i, m_j)$ for $j = 1, \ldots, d$, and returns $(spk_i, \sigma_1, \ldots, \sigma_d)$. Note that the adversary submits a list of messages $(m_1, \ldots, m_d)$ as the i-th query before he sees the i-th secondary public key. In addition, a valid forgery σ^* is a signature of the message m^* under a secondary public key spk_{i^*} generated by $\mathcal{O}_{Sig}$ during the query phase.

The security model of the stateful d-time two-tier signatures below is defined in a similar way, except that the state j_i is taken as part of the inputs of $TTSign$ and $TTVrfy$.

$Exp_{TTSig,\mathcal{A},q}^{TT\text{-}EUF\text{-}NCMA}(\lambda, d)$
- $(ppk, psk) \leftarrow PriGen(1^\lambda, d)$;
- $(m^*, \sigma^*, i^*, j_{i^*}^*) \leftarrow \mathcal{A}^{\mathcal{O}_{Sig}(\cdot)}(ppk)$;
- If $TTVrfy(ppk, spk_{i^*}, m^*, \sigma^*; j_{i^*}^*) = 1$ and $m^* \notin \mathcal{Q}_{i^*}$, then return 1. Otherwise, return 0.

$\mathcal{O}_{Sig}(\cdot)$ which on receiving i-th query $\mathcal{Q}_i = (m_1, \ldots, m_d)$ computes $(spk_i, ssk_i) \leftarrow SecGen(ppk, psk)$ and $\sigma_j \leftarrow TTSign(psk,ssk_i, m_j; j_i)$ for $j = 1, \ldots, d$, and returns $(spk_i, \sigma_1, \ldots, \sigma_d)$. In this paper, we consider the case that $j_i = j$.

Definition 2 (Existential unforgeability against non-adaptive chosen-message attacks). A d-time two-tier signature $TTSig$ is a (t, q, d, ϵ)-existentially unforgeable under non-adaptive chosen message attacks (EUF-NCMA) if for any PPT adversary $\mathcal{A}$ with running time t and q chosen-message queries the probability $\Pr[Exp_{TTSig,\mathcal{A},q}^{TT\text{-}EUF\text{-}NCMA}(\lambda, d) = 1] \leq \epsilon$.

Chameleon Hash Functions. Chameleon hash functions [23] are a special type of collision resistant hash functions with public/private keys. Anyone who knows the private key of a chameleon hash function can easily find collisions for every given input. Formally, a chameleon hash function CHF=(CHGen,CHash,Coll) consists of three algorithms. CHGen takes as input 1^λ and outputs the hash key chk and the trapdoor td. CHash on inputs chk, a message $m \in \mathcal{M}_{CH}$ and a randomness $r \in \mathcal{R}_{CH}$ outputs the hash value $h \in \mathcal{Y}_{CH}$, where $\mathcal{M}_{CH}$, $\mathcal{R}_{CH}$ and $\mathcal{Y}_{CH}$ denotes the message space, the randomness space and the range of CHash, respectively. Coll on inputs $(td, (m, r), \tilde{m})$ outputs a randomness $\tilde{r}$ such that CHash(chk, m, r) = CHash(chk, $\tilde{m}, \tilde{r}$). The security of CHF satisfies following requirements.

- **Collision resistance.** CHF is (t, ϵ)-collision resistance if the following holds for any PPT adversary $\mathcal{A}$ with running time t:

$$\Pr\left[\begin{array}{c} (\text{chk,td}) \leftarrow \text{CHGen}(1^\lambda); ((m, r), (\tilde{m}, \tilde{r})) \leftarrow \mathcal{A}(\text{chk}) \\ \wedge \text{CHash}(\text{chk}, m, r) = \text{CHash}(\text{chk}, \tilde{m}, \tilde{r}) \wedge (m, r) \neq (\tilde{m}, \tilde{r}) \end{array} \right] \leq \epsilon.$$

- **Uniformity.** For all $m \in \mathcal{M}_{CH}$, the distributions of (chk, CHash(chk, m, r)) and (chk, y) are computationally indistinguishable, where $r \xleftarrow{R} \mathcal{R}_{CH}$, $y \xleftarrow{R} \mathcal{Y}_{CH}$ and (chk,td) $\leftarrow$ CHGen (1^λ).

3 Simulatable Two-Tier Signatures

The security of two-tier signatures requires that it is difficult for any PPT adversary to generate a forgery under any secondary public key generated by the oracle. We note that in some two-tier signature schemes, however, it may be easy for the adversary to output a forgery under a secondary public key generated by the adversary himself. Since this property can be used in the simulation of signatures, we call a two-tier signature with such kind of property a simulatable two-tier signature.

Definition 3 *(Simulatable two-tier signature). A two-tier signature TTSig is simulatable if there exists an efficient algorithm SimTTSign which takes as input (ppk, m) and outputs (spk$'$, σ') such that*

- *TTVrfy(ppk, spk$'$, m, σ') = 1;*
- *the distribution of (spk$'$, σ') is computationally indistinguishable from that of (spk, σ), where (spk, ssk) $\leftarrow$ SecGen(ppk, psk) and $\sigma \leftarrow$ TTSign(psk, ssk, m). Formally, for all probabilistic polynomial time distinguisher $\mathcal{D}$, there exists a negligible function $\epsilon(\lambda)$ such that*

$$\Pr[\mathcal{D}^{\mathcal{O}_{STT}(\cdot)}(ppk) = 1] - \Pr[\mathcal{D}^{\mathcal{O}_{TT}(\cdot)}(ppk) = 1] \leq \epsilon(\lambda),$$

where (ppk, psk) $\leftarrow$ PriGen(1^λ, d), $\mathcal{O}_{STT}(\cdot)$ takes as input m and returns SimTTSign(ppk, m) and $\mathcal{O}_{TT}(\cdot)$ takes as input m, computes (spk, ssk) $\leftarrow$ SecGen(ppk, psk), $\sigma \leftarrow$ TTSign(psk, ssk, m) and returns (spk, σ).

for any message m in the message space of TTSig.

There are many two-tier signatures which are simulatable. For instance, the two-tier signature based on chameleon hash in [10], which is described below. Other examples of simulatable two-tier signatures under concrete computational assumptions are shown in Appendix A.

Two-tier signature based on chameleon hash [10]
- PriGen(1^λ): (chk, td) ← CHGen(1^λ). Output ppk = chk, psk = td.
- SecGen(ppk,psk): h = CHash(ppk, $\hat{m}, \hat{\sigma}$), where $\hat{m}$ is an arbitrary public element in $\mathcal{M}_{CH}$ and $\hat{\sigma} \xleftarrow{R} \mathcal{R}_{CH}$. Output spk = h and ssk = $\hat{\sigma}$.
- TTSign(psk,ssk,m): Output σ = Coll(psk, $\hat{m}, \hat{\sigma}, m$).
- TTVrfy(ppk, spk, m, σ): Output 1 if CHash(ppk, m, σ) = spk; Otherwise, 0.

We can construct the corresponding SimTTSign as follows.

SimTTSign(ppk, m):
1. On inputs ppk=chk and m, compute spk′ ← CHash(ppk, m, σ'), where $\sigma' \xleftarrow{R} \mathcal{R}_{CH}$;
2. Output (spk′, σ').

Claim 1. *The two-tier signature based on chameleon hash function is simulatable if the underlying Coll(td, $\hat{m}, \cdot, m$) is a bijection function from $\mathcal{R}_{CH}$ to $\mathcal{R}_{CH}$ for any td generated by CHGen and any $\hat{m}, m \in \mathcal{M}_{CH}$.*

The proof of Claim 1 proceeds via a sequence of games, where the signing oracle is gradually modified. The indistinguishability between adjacent games relies on the properties of the underlying chameleon hash. The proof is omitted due to lack of space and will be described in the full paper.

4   Tightly Secure Signatures

The tree-based signature schemes of [10,19] cannot be simulated by replacing the underlying two-tier signatures with simulatable TTSig directly. The main difficulty is that different secondary public keys of sibling nodes cannot be mapped to the same secondary public key of their parent using SimTTSign, since SimTTSign on different inputs will generate different secondary public keys. To solve this problem, we insert additional "ephemeral" d-time two-tier signatures $\widehat{TTSig}$ into each level of the tree, where the primary public/secret key pair $(\widehat{ppk}, \widehat{psk})$ of $\widehat{TTSig}$ are generated during the signing phase of the tree-based signature. In particular, there are two "ephemeral" secondary public/secret key pairs associated with each internal node N_{v_i}. More precisely, each internal node N_{v_i} lying on the path $(v_0, v_1, \ldots, v_h)$ has secondary public keys $(\text{spk}_{v_i}, \widehat{\text{spk}}_{v_i||0}, \widehat{\text{spk}}_{v_i||1})$, where spk_{v_i} denotes the secondary public key of TTSig, and $\widehat{\text{spk}}_{v_i||0}$ and $\widehat{\text{spk}}_{v_i||1}$ denote the secondary public keys of $\widehat{TTSig}$. See Fig. 1 in Appendix B for an illustration, where spk_{v_i} is associated with $\widehat{\text{spk}}_{v_i||0}$ and $\widehat{\text{spk}}_{v_i||1}$ for $i = 0, \ldots, h-1$, and the resulting tree has $(2d)^h$ leafs. The signer can be viewed as maintaining a

$2d$-ary tree of depth h. In the simulation phase, the secondary public/secret key pairs $(\widehat{\mathsf{spk}}_{v_i||0}, \widehat{\mathsf{ssk}}_{v_i||0})$ and $(\widehat{\mathsf{spk}}_{v_i||1}, \widehat{\mathsf{ssk}}_{v_i||1})$ can be generated using $(\widehat{\mathsf{ppk}}, \widehat{\mathsf{psk}})$. Hence, spk_{v_i}s and the corresponding signature σ_{v_i}s in different levels (except for the root) can be simulated independently by SimTTSign.

TreeSig. Let $\mathsf{TTSig} = (\mathsf{PriGen}, \mathsf{SecGen}, \mathsf{TTSign}, \mathsf{TTVrfy})$ be a simulatable one-time two-tier signature and $\widehat{\mathsf{TTSig}} = (\widehat{\mathsf{PriGen}}, \widehat{\mathsf{SecGen}}, \widehat{\mathsf{TTSign}}, \widehat{\mathsf{TTVrfy}})$ be a d-time two-tier signature. Our stateful tree-based scheme $\mathsf{TreeSig} = (\mathsf{TreeSig.Gen},$ $\mathsf{TreeSig.Sign}, \mathsf{TreeSig.Vrfy})$ is defined as follows.

- $\mathsf{TreeSig.Gen}(1^\lambda)$: Compute $(\mathsf{ppk}, \mathsf{psk}) \leftarrow \mathsf{PriGen}(1^\lambda)$ and $(\mathsf{spk}_{v_0}, \mathsf{ssk}_{v_0}) \leftarrow \mathsf{SecGen}(\mathsf{ppk}, \mathsf{psk})$. Let the verification key $\mathsf{vk}_{tree} = (\mathsf{ppk}, \mathsf{spk}_{v_0})$ and the signing key $\mathsf{sk}_{tree} = (\mathsf{psk}, \mathsf{ssk}_{v_0})$. Let N_{v_0} be the root of the tree, where $v_0 = \epsilon$.
- $\mathsf{TreeSig.Sign}(\mathsf{sk}_{tree}, m)$: Suppose N_{v_h} is the leftmost unused leaf and $(v_0, \ldots, v_h)$ is the path, where $v_i = v_{i-1}||\beta_{i-1}j_{i-1}$ for $i \in \{1, \ldots, h\}$, $\beta_{i-1} \in \{0, 1\}$ and $j_{i-1} \in \{1, \ldots, d\}$.
  - **Nodes generation.** If $(\widehat{\mathsf{spk}}_{v_0||0}, \widehat{\mathsf{spk}}_{v_0||1})$ has not been defined, generate $(\widehat{\mathsf{ppk}}, \widehat{\mathsf{psk}}) \leftarrow \widehat{\mathsf{PriGen}}(1^\lambda)$, $(\widehat{\mathsf{spk}}_{v_0||0}, \widehat{\mathsf{ssk}}_{v_0||0}) \leftarrow \widehat{\mathsf{SecGen}}(\widehat{\mathsf{ppk}}, \widehat{\mathsf{psk}})$ and $(\widehat{\mathsf{spk}}_{v_0||1}, \widehat{\mathsf{ssk}}_{v_0||1}) \leftarrow \widehat{\mathsf{SecGen}}(\widehat{\mathsf{ppk}}, \widehat{\mathsf{psk}})$.
    For $i = 1, \ldots, h - 1$, if the related keys associated to N_{v_i} are not defined, compute $(\mathsf{spk}_{v_i}, \mathsf{ssk}_{v_i}) \leftarrow \mathsf{SecGen}(\mathsf{ppk}, \mathsf{psk})$, $(\widehat{\mathsf{spk}}_{v_i||0}, \widehat{\mathsf{ssk}}_{v_i||0}) \leftarrow \widehat{\mathsf{SecGen}}(\widehat{\mathsf{ppk}}, \widehat{\mathsf{psk}})$ and $(\widehat{\mathsf{spk}}_{v_i||1}, \widehat{\mathsf{ssk}}_{v_i||1}) \leftarrow \widehat{\mathsf{SecGen}}(\widehat{\mathsf{ppk}}, \widehat{\mathsf{psk}})$. For the leaf N_{v_h}, compute $(\mathsf{spk}_{v_h}, \mathsf{ssk}_{v_h}) \leftarrow \mathsf{SecGen}(\mathsf{ppk}, \mathsf{psk})$.
  - **Path authentication.** For $i = 0, 1, \ldots, h - 1$, if $N_{v_{i+1}}$ has not been authenticated, compute $\sigma_{v_i} \leftarrow \mathsf{TTSign}(\mathsf{psk}, \mathsf{ssk}_{v_i}, \widehat{\mathsf{spk}}_{v_i||0}||\widehat{\mathsf{spk}}_{v_i||1}||\widehat{\mathsf{ppk}})$ and $\widehat{\sigma}_{v_i||\beta_i} \leftarrow \widehat{\mathsf{TTSign}}(\widehat{\mathsf{psk}}, \widehat{\mathsf{ssk}}_{v_i||\beta_i}, \mathsf{spk}_{v_{i+1}}; j_i)$, where $v_{i+1} = v_i||\beta_i j_i$. Finally, $\sigma_{v_h} \leftarrow \mathsf{TTSign}(\mathsf{psk}, \mathsf{ssk}_{v_h}, m)$.
  The signature σ is $(v_h; (\widehat{\mathsf{ppk}}, \widehat{\mathsf{spk}}_{v_0||0}, \widehat{\mathsf{spk}}_{v_0||1}); (\mathsf{spk}_{v_1}, \widehat{\mathsf{spk}}_{v_1||0}, \widehat{\mathsf{spk}}_{v_1||1}), \ldots,$ $(\mathsf{spk}_{v_{h-1}}, \widehat{\mathsf{spk}}_{v_{h-1}||0}, \widehat{\mathsf{spk}}_{v_{h-1}||1}), \mathsf{spk}_{v_h}; (\sigma_{v_0}, \widehat{\sigma}_{v_0||\beta_0}), (\sigma_{v_1}, \widehat{\sigma}_{v_1||\beta_1}), \ldots, (\sigma_{v_{h-1}},$ $\widehat{\sigma}_{v_{h-1}||\beta_{h-1}}); \sigma_{v_h})^3$.
- $\mathsf{TreeSig.Vrfy}(\mathsf{vk}_{tree}, m, \sigma)$:
  - Parse v_h as $v_0||\beta_0 j_0||\beta_1 j_1||\ldots||\beta_{h-1}j_{h-1}$. For $i = 0, 1, \ldots, h - 1$, check if $\mathsf{TTVrfy}(\mathsf{ppk}, \mathsf{spk}_{v_i}, \widehat{\mathsf{spk}}_{v_i||0}||\widehat{\mathsf{spk}}_{v_i||1}||\widehat{\mathsf{ppk}}, \sigma_{v_i}) = 1$ and $\widehat{\mathsf{TTVrfy}}(\widehat{\mathsf{ppk}}, \widehat{\mathsf{spk}}_{v_i||\beta_i}, \mathsf{spk}_{v_{i+1}}, \widehat{\sigma}_{v_i||\beta_i}; j_i) = 1$.
  - Check if $\mathsf{TTVrfy}(\mathsf{ppk}, \mathsf{spk}_{v_h}, m, \sigma_{v_h}) = 1$.
  If all the above equations hold, return 1; Otherwise, 0.

Theorem 1. *TreeSig is $(\epsilon_{Tree}, t_{Tree}, q_{Tree})$-EUF-NCMA secure, if TTSig is $(\epsilon_{TTSig}, t_{TTSig}, q_{TTSig})$-EUF-NCMA secure and $\widehat{TTSig}$ is d-time $(\epsilon_{\widehat{TTSig}}, t_{\widehat{TTSig}}, q_{\widehat{TTSig}})$-EUF -NCMA secure, where $\epsilon_{Tree} \le \epsilon_{TTSig} + \epsilon_{\widehat{TTSig}}$, $t_{Tree} = \max\{t_{TTSig}, t_{\widehat{TTSig}}\} - O(hq_{Tree})$ and $q_{Tree} \le \max\{q_{TTSig}, q_{\widehat{TTSig}}\}$.*

---

[3] For simplicity, we omit the description of state information. Indeed, we need to store the state information, such as v_h, $(\widehat{\mathsf{ppk}}, \widehat{\mathsf{psk}})$, and the secondary public/secret key pairs and corresponding two-tier signatures generated so far.

The proof of Theorem 1 is shown in Appendix C.

Simulation of TreeSig. This section shows a PPT algorithm SimTree which can simulate most parts of the signature σ generated by TreeSig. (Note that the TreeSig is not simulatable.) SimTree takes as input (vk_{tree}, m) and works in a bottom-up fashion to reconstruct secondary keys and signatures associated to the nodes (except for the root) on the path. More details are as follows.

1. Choose the leftmost unused leaf N_{v_h}.
2. If $\widehat{\mathsf{ppk}}$ has not been defined, run $(\widehat{\mathsf{ppk}}, \widehat{\mathsf{psk}}) \leftarrow \widehat{\mathsf{PriGen}}(1^\lambda)$. Compute $(\widehat{\mathsf{spk}}_{v_h}, \sigma_{v_h}) \leftarrow \mathsf{SimTTSign}(\widehat{\mathsf{ppk}}, m)$.
3. For $i = h - 1, \ldots, 1$, if $\widehat{\sigma}_{v_i \| \beta_i}$ has not been generated, conduct the following steps.
   (a) If $(\widehat{\mathsf{spk}}_{v_i \| 0}, \widehat{\mathsf{spk}}_{v_i \| 1})$ are not defined, compute $(\widehat{\mathsf{spk}}_{v_i \| 0}, \widehat{\mathsf{ssk}}_{v_i \| 0}) \leftarrow \widehat{\mathsf{SecGen}}$
   $(\widehat{\mathsf{ppk}}, \widehat{\mathsf{psk}})$, $(\widehat{\mathsf{spk}}_{v_i \| 1}, \widehat{\mathsf{ssk}}_{v_i \| 1}) \leftarrow \widehat{\mathsf{SecGen}}(\widehat{\mathsf{ppk}}, \widehat{\mathsf{psk}})$ and

   $$(\widehat{\mathsf{spk}}_{v_i}, \sigma_{v_i}) \leftarrow \mathsf{SimTTSign}(\widehat{\mathsf{ppk}}, \widehat{\mathsf{spk}}_{v_i \| 0} \| \widehat{\mathsf{spk}}_{v_i \| 1} \| \widehat{\mathsf{ppk}}).$$

   (b) Compute $\widehat{\sigma}_{v_i \| \beta_i} \leftarrow \widehat{\mathsf{TTSign}}(\widehat{\mathsf{psk}}, \widehat{\mathsf{ssk}}_{v_i \| \beta_i}, \widehat{\mathsf{spk}}_{v_{i+1}}; j_i)$, where $v_{i+1} = v_i \| \beta_i j_i$.
4. If $\widehat{\sigma}_{v_0 \| \beta_0}$ has not been generated, conduct the following steps.
   (a) If $(\widehat{\mathsf{spk}}_{v_0 \| 0}, \widehat{\mathsf{spk}}_{v_0 \| 1})$ are not defined, run $(\widehat{\mathsf{spk}}_{v_0 \| 0}, \widehat{\mathsf{ssk}}_{v_0 \| 0}) \leftarrow \widehat{\mathsf{SecGen}}$
   $(\widehat{\mathsf{ppk}}, \widehat{\mathsf{psk}})$ and $(\widehat{\mathsf{spk}}_{v_0 \| 1}, \widehat{\mathsf{ssk}}_{v_0 \| 1}) \leftarrow \widehat{\mathsf{SecGen}}(\widehat{\mathsf{ppk}}, \widehat{\mathsf{psk}})$.
   (b) Compute $\widehat{\sigma}_{v_0 \| \beta_0} \leftarrow \widehat{\mathsf{TTSign}}(\widehat{\mathsf{psk}}, \widehat{\mathsf{ssk}}_{v_0 \| \beta_0}, \widehat{\mathsf{spk}}_{v_1}; j_0)$.
5. Store $(v_h; (\widehat{\mathsf{ppk}}, \widehat{\mathsf{psk}}); (\widehat{\mathsf{spk}}_{v_0 \| 0}, \widehat{\mathsf{ssk}}_{v_0 \| 0}), (\widehat{\mathsf{spk}}_{v_0 \| 1}, \widehat{\mathsf{ssk}}_{v_0 \| 1}), \ldots, (\widehat{\mathsf{spk}}_{v_{h-1} \| 0},$
   $\widehat{\mathsf{ssk}}_{v_{h-1} \| 0}), (\widehat{\mathsf{spk}}_{v_{h-1} \| 1}, \widehat{\mathsf{ssk}}_{v_{h-1} \| 1}); \widehat{\mathsf{spk}}_{v_1}, \ldots, \widehat{\mathsf{spk}}_{v_h}; \widehat{\sigma}_{v_0 \| \beta_0}, (\sigma_{v_1}, \widehat{\sigma}_{v_1 \| \beta_1}), \ldots,$
   $(\sigma_{v_{h-1}}, \widehat{\sigma}_{v_{h-1} \| \beta_{h-1}}); \sigma_{v_h})$ in the record. Output the signature σ_{Sim}, which is
   $(v_h; (\widehat{\mathsf{ppk}}, \widehat{\mathsf{spk}}_{v_0 \| 0}, \widehat{\mathsf{spk}}_{v_0 \| 1}); (\widehat{\mathsf{spk}}_{v_1}, \widehat{\mathsf{spk}}_{v_1 \| 0}, \widehat{\mathsf{spk}}_{v_1 \| 1}), \ldots, (\widehat{\mathsf{spk}}_{v_{h-1}}, \widehat{\mathsf{spk}}_{v_{h-1} \| 0},$
   $\widehat{\mathsf{spk}}_{v_{h-1} \| 1}), \widehat{\mathsf{spk}}_{v_h}; \widehat{\sigma}_{v_0 \| \beta_0}, (\sigma_{v_1}, \widehat{\sigma}_{v_1 \| \beta_1}), \ldots, (\sigma_{v_{h-1}}, \widehat{\sigma}_{v_{h-1} \| \beta_{h-1}}); \sigma_{v_h})$.

Remark. Note that the only difference between a real signature σ and σ_{Sim} is that the latter does not have σ_{v_0}. Due to the property of SimTTSig, the distribution of σ_{Sim} is computationally indistinguishable from that of the corresponding parts of the real σ. Indeed, SimTTSig can perfectly simulate the corresponding parts of σ if TTSig and $\widehat{\mathsf{TTSig}}$ are chosen properly, e.g., two-tier signatures based on f-CDHI [10]. Furthermore, it is known that a stateful tree-based signature can be made stateless using pseudorandom functions (PRF) [17]. The same technique can be also applied to our scheme, where PRFs are used to determine the path and to generate the randomness used in TreeSig.Sign and SimTree.

5   Tight Simulation Extractable NIZK (SE-NIZK)

In this section, we show how to apply our TreeSig to the construction of SE-NIZK [1]. For more details on the related definitions of SS-NIZK including simulation sound extractability, we refer to [1,18,19].

To construct tight simulation sound NIZK proof, previous works [1,10,19] generate a GS proof π stating that either $x \in \mathcal{L}$ (which means the simultaneous satisfiability of a set of PPEs) or it knows a valid signature σ of the public key of a one-time signature, say opk, where the signature is instantiated with the tree-based signature. During the proof, the prover needs to compute a tree-based pseudo-signature σ and generates a commitment $Com(\sigma)$ to σ. Since a tree-based signature mainly consists of the related public keys and signatures of nodes on the path from the root to a leaf, the prover needs to commit to all the pseudo-signatures of nodes along the path, say, σ_{v_i}s. [1,10] find that some parts of a signature σ_{v_i} which do not require the knowledge of the secret key do not need to be committed and can be sent in the clear. Although such optimization leads to considerable savings of elements, the number of the commitments to signatures still grows linearly with the depth of the tree.

Our construction. To further reduce the number of commitments, we replace the tree-based signature of SE-NIZK in [1] with our TreeSig. Recall that the signature σ consists of $(v_h; (\widehat{\mathsf{ppk}}, \widehat{\mathsf{spk}}_{v_0||0}, \widehat{\mathsf{spk}}_{v_0||1}); (\mathsf{spk}_{v_1}, \widehat{\mathsf{spk}}_{v_1||0}, \widehat{\mathsf{spk}}_{v_1||1}), \ldots,$ $(\mathsf{spk}_{v_{h-1}}, \widehat{\mathsf{spk}}_{v_{h-1}||0}, \widehat{\mathsf{spk}}_{v_{h-1}||1}), \mathsf{spk}_{v_h}; (\sigma_{v_0}, \widetilde{\sigma}_{v_0||\beta_0}), (\sigma_{v_1}, \widetilde{\sigma}_{v_1||\beta_1}), \ldots, (\sigma_{v_{h-1}},$ $\widetilde{\sigma}_{v_{h-1}||\beta_{h-1}}); \sigma_{v_h})$. In our SE-NIZK, the only part of σ that needs to be committed is σ_{v_0}, while other parts can be simulated using SimTree and sent in the clear. More details of our SE-NIZK are described below.

Let R be a binary relation, $\mathcal{L} = \{x : \exists w \text{ s.t. } R(x,w) = 1\}$, POK=(POK.Crs, POK.Prv, POK.Vrfy, POK.Ext) be a NIZK proof of knowledge system and OTSig=(OTSig.Gen, OTSig.Sign, OTSig.Vrfy) be a one-time signature. Our SE-NIZK for a relation R consists of the following algorithms.

- SE-NIZK.Crs(gk): Run $(\mathsf{crs}_{\mathsf{pok}}, \tau_{\mathsf{ex}}) \leftarrow$ POK.Crs(gk) and $(\mathsf{vk}_{tree}, \mathsf{sk}_{tree}) \leftarrow$ TreeSig.Gen(gk), where gk denotes the global parameter. Let $\mathsf{crs} = (gk, \mathsf{crs}_{\mathsf{pok}}, \mathsf{vk}_{tree})$ and $\tau_{\mathsf{zk}} = \mathsf{sk}_{tree}$. Output crs, τ_{ex} and τ_{zk}.
- SE-NIZK.Prv(crs, x, w): Parse crs as $(gk, \mathsf{crs}_{\mathsf{pok}}, \mathsf{vk}_{tree})$. Compute $(\mathsf{opk}, \mathsf{osk}) \leftarrow$ OTSig.Gen(gk). Let $x_{\mathsf{se}} = (x, \mathsf{opk})$, $\sigma = \bot$, $w_{\mathsf{se}} = (w, \sigma)$ and relation R_{se} be $R_{\mathsf{se}}(x_{\mathsf{se}}, w_{\mathsf{se}}) = (R(x,w) = 1) \vee (\mathsf{TreeSig.Vrfy}(\mathsf{vk}_{tree}, \mathsf{opk}, \sigma) = 1)$. Here, $\sigma = \bot$ denotes a pseudo-signature, which is not a valid signature. Generate $\pi \leftarrow$ POK.Prv($\mathsf{crs}_{\mathsf{pok}}, x_{\mathsf{se}}, w_{\mathsf{se}}$) and $\sigma_{\mathsf{OT}} \leftarrow$ OTSig.Sign(osk, π), where POK.Prv is similar to that of [1], except the following modifications for the commitment $Com(\sigma)$: Compute $\sigma_{\mathsf{Sim}} \leftarrow$ SimTree($\mathsf{vk}_{tree}, \mathsf{opk}$) and generate a pseudo-signature $\widetilde{\sigma}_{v_0}$ and the commitment $Com(\widetilde{\sigma}_{v_0})$. Let $Com(\sigma) = (\sigma_{\mathsf{Sim}}, Com(\widetilde{\sigma}_{v_0}))$. When $Com(\sigma)$ are used in the OR proof, we only need to consider the proof of knowledge for $\widetilde{\sigma}_{v_0}$ instead of σ. Output $\pi_{\mathsf{se}} = (\pi, \mathsf{opk}, \sigma_{\mathsf{OT}})$.

- SE-NIZK.Vrfy(crs, x, π_{se}): Parse π_{se} as $(\pi, \text{opk}, \sigma_{OT})$. Verify σ_{OT} and check π as a GS proof for R_{se}. If the above checks are passed, output 1; Otherwise, 0.
- SE-NIZK.PrvSim(crs, τ_{zk}, x): Parse crs as $(gk, \text{crs}_{pok}, \text{vk}_{tree})$. Compute (opk, osk) $\leftarrow$ OTSig.Gen(gk) and generate $Com(\sigma)$ as follows: Compute $\sigma_{Sim} \leftarrow$ SimTree $(\text{vk}_{tree}, \text{opk})$, a real signature $\sigma_{v_0} \leftarrow$ TTSign$(\text{psk}, \text{ssk}_{v_0}, \widehat{\text{spk}}_{v_0||0}|| \ \widehat{\text{spk}}_{v_0||1}||\widehat{\text{ppk}})$ and the commitment $Com(\sigma_{v_0})$ to σ_{v_0}. Let $Com(\sigma) = (\sigma_{Sim}, Com(\sigma_{v_0}))$, where $\sigma = (\sigma_{Sim}, \sigma_{v_0})$. Similarly, only $Com(\sigma_{v_0})$ needs to be taken into account in the following proof of knowledge. Let $w_{se} = \{\bot, \sigma\}$. Generate $\pi \leftarrow$ POK.Prv$(\text{crs}_{pok}, x_{se}, w_{se})$ and $\sigma_{OT} \leftarrow$ OTSig.Sign(osk, π). Output $\pi_{se} = (\pi, \text{opk}, \sigma_{OT})$.
- SE-NIZK.Ext(crs, τ_{ex}, x, π_{se}): Parse crs as $(gk, \text{crs}_{pok}, \text{vk}_{tree})$ and π_{se} as $(\pi, \text{opk}, \sigma_{OT})$. Compute $w_{se} \leftarrow$ POK.Ext$(\text{crs}_{pok}, \tau_{ex}, \pi, (x, \text{opk}))$. Output w in $w_{se} = (w, \sigma)$.

Remark. The distribution of $\sigma = (\sigma_{Sim}, \sigma_{v_0})$ in SE-NIZK.PrvSim may be not identical to the real tree signature due to the quality of the underlying simulatable two-tier signatures. To decrease the reduction loss, we choose proper TTSig, e.g., TTSig based on f-CDHI [10] (See Appendix A), such that the distributions of σ_{Sim} and σ are identical to that of real one. Another method of generating a real tree signature σ in SE-NIZK.PrvSim is to run TreeSig.Sign$(\text{sk}_{tree}, \text{opk})$ directly. Although the latter method is much easier to understand, the corresponding security proof is a bit more complex than that of the former one. A concrete instantiation of our SE-NIZK will be provided in the description of encryption algorithm Enc in Sect. 6, where more details of SE-NIZK.Prv are shown. Details of other sub-algorithms of SE-NIZK are easy to follow and thus omitted.

Let 2^λ denote the number of messages which can be signed by TreeSig. When instantiated with d-time two-tier signatures of [10], TreeSig requires $5\lambda/(1 + \log d) + (d/f) + 2$ group elements and one scalar for v_h. Since only one element needs to be committed, with the GS proof over the DLIN setting, the commitment and the corresponding proof for the linear pairing-product equation requires 6 group elements. Hence, the overall cost for the committed signature is $5\lambda/(1 + \log d) + (d/f) + 7$ group elements and 1 scalar.

The completeness of our scheme is easy to verify. Due to Theorem 1 and witness indistinguishability of POK, Theorem 6 in [1] still holds for our construction. So we have

Theorem 2. *Our SE-NIZK preserves zero-knowledge and simulation extractability, if POK is a witness indistinguishable proof of knowledge system with knowledge-soundness error ϵ_{ks}, TreeSig is unforgeable against non-adaptive chosen message attacks (EUF-NCMA) with advantage ϵ_{Tree}, and OTSig is strongly one-time unforgeable against chosen message attacks with advantage ϵ_{OTSig}. In particular, the zero-knowledge distinguishing advantage $\epsilon_{zk} \leq 2\epsilon_{GS}$ and the simulation-extraction error $\epsilon_{se} \leq \epsilon_{OTSig} + \epsilon_{ks} + \epsilon_{Tree}$, where ϵ_{GS} denotes the distinguishing advantage between hiding and binding GS CRSs.*

The proof follows that of [1,19], and more details will be shown in the full paper.

Remark. Theorem 2 are proven in the "one instance, one prover setting", where the CRS and the prover are fixed, and the adversary can query the corresponding oracles many times. Since there is only one prover in our setting, the simulator can generate consistent distributions of simulated tree-based signatures for the same party. Such properties, however, only can be used to construct tightly secure PKE in the single user, multi-challenge setting. To extend the tight security of PKE to the multi-user, multi-challenge setting, we need the "μ-fold" tightly secure SE-NIZK. That is, the SE-NIZK is tightly secure in the "multi-instance, multi-prover setting", where there are μ SE-NIZK instances (CRSs) and each instance corresponds to a CRS and a prover. As in [1], it is easy for our scheme to preserve tightness when extending the security to the multi-instance, multi-prover setting, since no secret information is shared between different instances and the underlying complexity assumptions are random self reducible. In particular, the underlying assumptions of POK, TreeSig and OTSig in our SE-NIZK are DLIN, f-CDHI and DLOG, respectively, all of which are random self reducible.

6 Tightly IND-CCA Secure PKE in the Multi-User/-challenge Setting

To construct tightly IND-CCA secure encryption scheme[4], we follow the construction of [1,14], which is an efficient variant of the Naor-Yung paradigm [10,19,26]. The basic idea is to prove that either we know a TreeSig signature for the public key of an one-time signature or we know the plaintext and the randomness corresponding to the ciphertext. On the NIZK for the above OR relation during encryption phase, we use SimTree to generate most parts of the commitment to the (pseudo-)TreeSig signature. The underlying public-key encryption $\mathsf{PKE_{cpa}}$ is instantiated with linear encryption scheme [11], which is proven to be tightly IND-CPA secure in the multi-user/-challenge setting [19]. The underlying TTSig and $\widehat{\mathsf{TTSig}}$ in TreeSig are instantiated with the d-time two-tier signature scheme based on f-CDHI [10], where $d = 1$ for TTSig. The underlying one-time signature OTSig in SE-NIZK is instantiated with the one-time two-tier signature scheme based on DLOG. (All the above signatures are described in Appendix A.) Note that these underlying schemes can share some parameters, say, the generator g.

Our PKE=(ParGen, KeyGen, Enc, Dec) consists of the following algorithms.

- ParGen(1^λ): Generate the common public parameters $\mathbf{par} = (\mathbb{G}, \mathbb{G}_T, g)$, where $(\mathbb{G}, \mathbb{G}_T)$ are bilinear groups of prime order p and g is the generator of $\mathbb{G}$. Let $\mathsf{H} : \{0,1\}^* \to \mathbb{Z}_p^*$ be a hash function, which is used in the underlying signatures.
- KeyGen($\mathbf{par}$): Run the key generation algorithm of the underlying public-key encryption $\mathsf{PKE_{cpa}}$ to generate (pk, sk). That is, randomly choose $k \in \mathbb{G}$, $x_0, x_1 \in \mathbb{Z}_p$ and compute $y_0 = k^{x_0}, y_1 = k^{x_1}$. Let sk = (x_0, x_1) and pk =

---

[4] For more details on the definition of IND-CCA security in the multi-user/-challenge setting, we refer to [19].

(y_0, y_1, k). Run TreeSig.Gen to generate $\mathsf{vk}_{tree} = (\mathsf{ppk}, \mathsf{spk}_{v_0})$ and $\mathsf{sk}_{tree} = (\mathsf{psk}, \mathsf{ssk}_{v_0})$, where $x \stackrel{R}{\leftarrow} \mathbb{Z}_p$, $\mathsf{psk} = x$, $\mathsf{ppk} = h = g^x$, ssk_{v_0} is empty and $\mathsf{spk}_{v_0} = u_{v_0}$ for a random element $u_{v_0} \in \mathbb{G}$. Choose a perfectly witness indistinguishable Groth-Sahai CRS crs. The public key is $\mathbf{PK} = (\mathsf{pk}, \mathsf{vk}_{tree}, \mathsf{crs})$ and the private key is $\mathbf{SK} = (\mathsf{sk}, \mathsf{sk}_{tree})$.

- $\mathsf{Enc}(\mathbf{PK}, m)$:

1. Compute $c_0 = y_0^{r_0}, c_1 = y_1^{r_1}$ and $c_2 = mk^{r_0+r_1}$, where $r_0, r_1 \stackrel{R}{\leftarrow} \mathbb{Z}_p$.
2. SE-NIZK for relation $R((\mathsf{pk}, c), (m, r_0, r_1))$, where $c = (c_0, c_1, c_2)$.
   (a) **Generate a public/secret key pair $(\mathbf{opk}, \mathbf{osk})$ of a one-time signature OTSig.** Concretely, compute $\mathsf{psk}_{\mathsf{OT}} = x_{\mathsf{OT}}$, $\mathsf{ppk}_{\mathsf{OT}} = y_{\mathsf{OT}} = g^{x_{\mathsf{OT}}}$, $\mathsf{ssk}_{\mathsf{OT}} = r_{\mathsf{OT}}$ and $\mathsf{spk}_{\mathsf{OT}} = y_{\mathsf{OT}}^0 g^{r_{\mathsf{OT}}}$, where $x_{\mathsf{OT}}, r_{\mathsf{OT}} \stackrel{R}{\leftarrow} \mathbb{Z}_p$. Let $\mathsf{opk} = (\mathsf{ppk}_{\mathsf{OT}}, \mathsf{spk}_{\mathsf{OT}})$ and $\mathsf{osk} = (\mathsf{psk}_{\mathsf{OT}}, \mathsf{ssk}_{\mathsf{OT}})$. Next, we will provide the OR proof for the relation

   $$(R((\mathsf{pk}, c), (m, r_0, r_1)) = 1) \vee (\mathsf{TreeSig}.\mathsf{Vrfy}(\mathsf{vk}_{tree}, \sigma, \mathsf{opk}) = 1).$$

   (b) **Generate a commitment to the pseudo-signature on $\mathbf{opk}$.**
   - Suppose N_{v_h} is the leftmost unused leaf. Compute $\sigma_{\mathsf{Sim}} \leftarrow \mathsf{SimTree}\,(\mathsf{vk}_{tree}, \mathsf{opk})$. Note that $\sigma_{\mathsf{Sim}} = (v_h; (\widehat{\mathsf{ppk}}, \widehat{\mathsf{spk}_{v_0||0}}, \widehat{\mathsf{spk}_{v_0||1}});$ $(\mathsf{spk}_{v_1}, \widehat{\mathsf{spk}_{v_1||0}}, \widehat{\mathsf{spk}_{v_1||1}}), \cdots, (\mathsf{spk}_{v_{h-1}}, \widehat{\mathsf{spk}_{v_{h-1}||0}}, \widehat{\mathsf{spk}_{v_{h-1}||1}}),$ $\mathsf{spk}_{v_h}; \widehat{\sigma_{v_0||\beta_0}}, (\sigma_{v_1}, \widehat{\sigma_{v_1||\beta_1}}), \cdots, (\sigma_{v_{h-1}}, \widehat{\sigma_{v_{h-1}||\beta_{h-1}}}); \sigma_{v_h}), \widehat{\mathsf{ppk}} = (\widehat{h_0}, \widehat{h_1}, \dots, \widehat{h_c}) \in \mathbb{G}^{c+1}$ and $c \cdot f = d$.
   - σ_{v_0} is set to the identity element $1 \in \mathbb{G}$ and generate a commitment $Com(\sigma_{v_0})$. Hence, the committed pseudo-signature for $\mathsf{spk}_{\mathsf{OT}}$ is $(\sigma_{\mathsf{Sim}}, Com(\sigma_{v_0}))$.

   (c) **Provide the OR proof.** We need additional variable s for the switcher, variable w_k for the constant k in Eqs. (4), (5) and (6)[5] and variable w_g for the constant g in the right side of (7), where s, w_k and w_g satisfy the following equations.

   $$e(s, s) = e(s, g) \tag{1}$$
   $$e(w_k, g) = e(k, s) \tag{2}$$
   $$e(w_g, g) = e(g, s^{-1}g) \tag{3}$$

   Set $s = g$. So we have $w_k = k$ and $w_g = 1$ due to Eqs. (2) and (3). Compute the commitments $Com(s)$, $Com(w_k)$ and $Com(w_g)$ to s, w_k and w_g, respectively. Let π_s, π_k and π_g denote the proofs for Eqs. (1), (2) and (3), respectively. To prove the well-formness of (c_0, c_1, c_2), we need additional variables a_0, a_1 and w_m satisfying that $a_0 = k^{r_0}$, $a_1 = k^{r_1}$ and $w_m = m$. Let $Com(a_0), Com(a_1), Com(w_m)$ be the corresponding commitments to a_0, a_1 and w_m, respectively. To prove that the committed variables (w_k, a_0, a_1) satisfy the following equations, generate NIWI proofs $\pi_{a_0}, \pi_{a_1}, \pi_m$ for Eqs. (4), (5) and (6), respectively.

---

[5] k in the left side of Eq. (6).

$$e(c_0, \underline{w_k}) = e(y_0, \underline{a_0}) \tag{4}$$

$$e(c_1, \underline{w_k}) = e(y_1, \underline{a_1}) \tag{5}$$

$$e(c_2, \underline{w_k})e(\underline{w_m^{-1}}, k) = e(k, \underline{a_0 a_1}) \tag{6}$$

Next, in order to prove the "knowledge" of a signature σ_{v_0} on message $\widehat{\mathsf{spk}_{v_0||0}}||\widehat{\mathsf{spk}_{v_0||1}}||\widehat{\mathsf{ppk}}$ under vk_{tree} satisfying

$$e(\underline{\sigma_{v_0}}, h) = e(g^{H(\widehat{\mathsf{spk}_{v_0||0}}||\widehat{\mathsf{spk}_{v_0||1}}||\widehat{\mathsf{ppk}})}u_{v_0}, \underline{w_g}), \tag{7}$$

compute a NIWI proof $\pi_{\sigma_{v_0}}$ that the committed variables (σ_{v_0}, w_g) satisfy Eq. (7). Note that the underlined $w_k, a_0, a_1, w_m, \sigma_{v_0}$ and w_g in the above equations are variables.

Let $\pi_{GS} = (\pi_s, \ \pi_k, \ \pi_g, \ \pi_{a_0}, \pi_{a_1}, \ \pi_m, \ \pi_{\sigma_{v_0}})$ and $Com = (Com(s), Com(w_k), Com(w_g), Com(a_0), Com(a_1), Com(w_m), Com(\sigma_{v_0}))$.

3. Compute $\sigma_{\mathsf{OT}} \leftarrow \mathsf{OTSign}(\mathsf{osk}, \sigma_{\mathsf{Sim}}||Com||\pi_{GS})$. That is, $\sigma_{\mathsf{OT}} = r_{\mathsf{OT}} - x_{\mathsf{OT}} \cdot H(\sigma_{\mathsf{Sim}}||Com||\pi_{GS})$.
4. Let $\pi = (\sigma_{\mathsf{Sim}}; Com; \pi_{GS}; \mathsf{opk}, \sigma_{\mathsf{OT}})$. The final ciphertext $c = (c_0, c_1, c_2; \pi)$.
- $\mathsf{Dec}(\mathbf{SK}, c)$: Parse $(c_0, c_1, c_2, ; \pi) \leftarrow c$. Check whether π is valid. That is, check the validity of σ_{OT} and σ_{Sim}, and check the validity of Groth-Sahai proofs π_{GS}. If π is valid, decrypt (c_0, c_1, c_2) using sk. Otherwise, return $\perp$.

With a Groth-Sahai proof system based on DLIN in symmetric pairing configurations, the commitment to a variable requires 3 group elements, the proofs for linear pairing product equations cost 3 group elements and proofs for quadratic equations cost 9 group elements. So we have $|(c_0, c_1, c_2)| = 3_{\mathbb{G}}$, $|\sigma_{\mathsf{Sim}}| = 5\lambda/(1+\log d)_{\mathbb{G}} + d/f_{\mathbb{G}} + 1_{\mathbb{G}} + 1_s$, $|Com| = 3 \times 7 = 21_{\mathbb{G}}$, $|\pi_{GS}| = 9 \times 1 + 3 \times 6 = 27_{\mathbb{G}}$, $|\mathsf{opk}| = 2_{\mathbb{G}}$ and $|\sigma_{\mathsf{OT}}| = 1_{\mathbb{Z}_p}$, where the subscripts $\mathbb{G}$ and $\mathbb{Z}_p$ denote elements in corresponding groups and subscript $_s$ means "scalar". Hence, the total size of the ciphertext is $3_{\mathbb{G}} + (5\lambda/(1+\log d)_{\mathbb{G}} + d/f_{\mathbb{G}} + 1_{\mathbb{G}} + 1_s) + 21_{\mathbb{G}} + 27_{\mathbb{G}} + 2_{\mathbb{G}} + 1_{\mathbb{Z}_p} = 5\lambda/(1+\log d)_{\mathbb{G}} + d/f_{\mathbb{G}} + 54_{\mathbb{G}} + 1_{\mathbb{Z}_p} + 1_s$. Since the public key size of our PKE scheme is similar to that of [10], we only compare the ciphertexts size between [10] and this paper in Table 1, where $f = 1$. Note that $f = 1$ corresponds to the 1-CDHI assumption, which is equivalent to the CDH assumption. Considering the tradeoff between the efficiency and the reduction loss, we recommend that $f = 1$ and $d = 2$.

Security. Due to Theorem 7 of [1][6], our PKE is still IND-CCA secure in the multi-user/-challenge setting. Combining with Theorems 1 and 2, we have the following theorem. The proof is similar to that of Theorem 7 and Theorem 6 of [1] and is omitted due to lack of space.

Theorem 3. *If the underlying encryption PKE_{cpa} is (μ, q)-IND-CPA secure encryption scheme with advantage ϵ_{cpa} and SE-NIZK is simulation-extractable*

---

[6] Theorem 7 in [1] states that their scheme is IND-CCA secure in the multi-challenge setting. As explained in [1] it is trivial to preserve tightness when extending the security reduction from the single user setting to the multi-user setting.

Table 1. Comparison of ciphertext size between [10] and this paper when $f = 1$. "$|Sim|$" denotes the number of simulations which the underlying NIZK allows.

	$|Sim|$	$d = 16$	$d = 2$	$d = 1$
Blazy et al. [10]	2^λ	$1.75\lambda_G + 65_G + 1_{Z_p} + 1_s$	$7\lambda_G + 65_G + 1_{Z_p} + 1_s$	$8\lambda_G + 65_G + 1_{Z_p} + 1_s$
This paper	2^λ	$\lambda_G + 70_G + 1_{Z_p} + 1_s$	$2.5\lambda_G + 56_G + 1_{Z_p} + 1_s$	$5\lambda_G + 55_G + 1_{Z_p} + 1_s$
Blazy et al. [10]	2^{80}	$205_G + 1_{Z_p} + 1_s$	$625_G + 1_{Z_p} + 1_s$	$705_G + 1_{Z_p} + 1_s$
This paper	2^{80}	$150_G + 1_{Z_p} + 1_s$	$256_G + 1_{Z_p} + 1_s$	$455_G + 1_{Z_p} + 1_s$
Blazy et al. [10]	2^{20}	$100_G + 1_{Z_p} + 1_s$	$205_G + 1_{Z_p} + 1_s$	$225_G + 1_{Z_p} + 1_s$
This paper	2^{20}	$90_G + 1_{Z_p} + 1_s$	$106_G + 1_{Z_p} + 1_s$	$155_G + 1_{Z_p} + 1_s$

NIZK with zero-knowledge error ϵ_{zk} and simulation-extraction error ϵ_{se}, then PKE is (μ, q)-IND-CCA secure with advantage $\epsilon_{cca} \leq 2(\epsilon_{zk} + \epsilon_{se}) + \epsilon_{cpa}$. In particular, $\epsilon_{cca} \leq 5\epsilon_{dlin} + 2(d + 1)\epsilon_{cdhi} + 2\epsilon_{dlog} + 6\epsilon_H - \mu/p$, where ϵ_{dlin} denotes the distinguishing advantage for DLIN assumption, ϵ_{cdhi} denotes the advantage for CDHI assumption, ϵ_{dlog} denotes the advantage of DLOG assumption and ϵ_H denotes the advantage for finding collisions of the underlying hash function H.

Acknowledgements. We would like to thank the reviewers for helpful comments. Puwen Wei and Wei Wang were supported by NSFC (No. 61502276 and No. 61672019) and the Foundation of Science and Technology on Communication Security Laboratory (No. 9140c110207150c11050). Bingxin Zhu was supported by the Fundamental Research Funds of Shandong University (No. 2016JC029).

A   Examples of Simulatable Two-Tier Signatures

In this section, we briefly describe some examples of simulatable two-tier signatures based on schemes in [10]. The validity proof of the corresponding SimTTSign algorithms is easy to check and thus omitted.

Simulatable two-tier signatures based on f-CDHI [10]

- PriGen($1^\lambda, d$): $g \xleftarrow{R} G$, $(x_0, \ldots, x_c) \xleftarrow{R} Z_p$, psk $= (x_0, \ldots, x_c)$, ppk $= (g, (h_0, \ldots, h_c))$, where $c \cdot f = d$ and $h_i = g^{x_i}$ for $i = 0, \ldots, c$.
- SecGen(ppk, psk): $k \xleftarrow{R} G$, spk $= k$, ssk is empty.
- TTSign(psk, ssk, m, j): $j = \alpha f + \beta$, where $j \in \{1, \ldots, d\}, \alpha \in \{0, \ldots, c\}$ and $\beta \in \{0, \ldots, f - 1\}$. Output $\sigma = (g^m k)^{1/(x_\alpha + \beta)}$.
- TTVrfy(ppk,spk,m,σ; j): Check if $e(\sigma, h_\alpha g^\beta) = e(g^m k, g)$.
- SimTTSign(ppk, m): $r \xleftarrow{R} Z_p$, $\sigma' \leftarrow g^r$ and spk$' = (h_\alpha g^\beta)^r g^{-m}$, where $j = \alpha f + \beta$. Output (spk$'$, σ').

Simulatable two-tier signatures based on DLOG [10]

- PriGen(1^λ): $x \xleftarrow{R} Z_p$, $g \in G$, psk $= x$, ppk $= y = g^x$.
- SecGen(ppk, psk): $r \xleftarrow{R} Z_p$, ssk $= r$, spk $= y^0 g^r$.
- TTSign(psk, ssk, m): Output $\sigma = r - xm$.

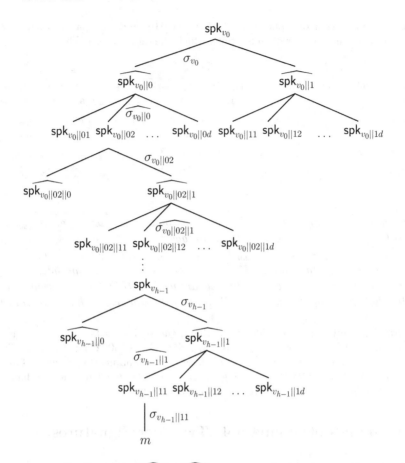

Fig. 1. Structure of TreeSig. $(\widehat{\mathsf{spk}_{v_i||0}}, \widehat{\mathsf{spk}_{v_i||1}})$ are authenticated by signature σ_{v_i} that verifies under spk_{v_i}, and $\mathsf{spk}_{v_{i+1}}$ with $v_{i+1} = v_i||\beta_i j_i$ is authenticated by signature $\widehat{\sigma_{v_i||\beta_i}}$ that verifies under $\widehat{\mathsf{spk}_{v_i||\beta_i}}$.

- TTVrfy(ppk, spk, m, σ): Check if $y^m g^\sigma = \mathsf{spk}$.
- SimTTSign(ppk, m): $\sigma' \xleftarrow{R} \mathbb{Z}_p$ and $\mathsf{spk}' = y^m g^{\sigma'}$. Output (spk', σ').

B   Illustration of **TreeSig**

C   Proof of Theorem 1

Proof. Suppose $\mathcal{A}$ is a PPT adversary that $(\epsilon_{\mathsf{Tree}}, t_{\mathsf{Tree}}, q_{\mathsf{Tree}})$-breaks the EUF-NCMA security of TreeSig. We show how to construct a PPT algorithm $\mathcal{B}$ that $(\epsilon_{\mathsf{TTSig}}, t_{\mathsf{TTSig}}, q_{\mathsf{TTSig}})$-breaks the EUF-NCMA security of TTSig or a PPT algorithm $\hat{\mathcal{B}}$ that $(\epsilon_{\widehat{\mathsf{TTSig}}}, t_{\widehat{\mathsf{TTSig}}}, q_{\widehat{\mathsf{TTSig}}})$-breaks the EUF-NCMA security of $\widehat{\mathsf{TTSig}}$.

Construction of $\mathcal{B}$. When receiving $(m^{(1)}, \ldots, m^{(q)})$, $\mathcal{B}$ computes $(\widehat{\mathsf{ppk}}, \widehat{\mathsf{psk}}) \leftarrow \widehat{\mathsf{PriGen}}(1^\lambda)$ and generates the signature $\sigma^{(j)}$ on $m^{(j)}$ as below, for $j = 1, \ldots, q$.

- **Authentication for $\widehat{\mathsf{spk}}_{v_i \| \beta_i}$ and nodes generation.** Choose the leftmost unused leaf N_{v_h}. For $i = 0, 1, \ldots, h-1$, if the related keys associated to N_{v_i} have not been defined, compute $(\widehat{\mathsf{spk}}_{v_i \| 0}, \widehat{\mathsf{ssk}}_{v_i \| 0}) \leftarrow \widehat{\mathsf{SecGen}}(\widehat{\mathsf{ppk}}, \widehat{\mathsf{psk}})$ and $(\widehat{\mathsf{spk}}_{v_i \| 1}, \widehat{\mathsf{ssk}}_{v_i \| 1}) \leftarrow \widehat{\mathsf{SecGen}}(\widehat{\mathsf{ppk}}, \widehat{\mathsf{psk}})$, query the signing oracle $\mathcal{O}_{\mathsf{TTSig}}(\cdot)$ with message $\widehat{\mathsf{spk}}_{v_i \| 0} \| \widehat{\mathsf{spk}}_{v_i \| 1} \| \widehat{\mathsf{ppk}}$ and get $(\mathsf{spk}_{v_i}, \sigma_{v_i})$. For the leaf N_{v_h}, query the signing oracle $\mathcal{O}_{\mathsf{TTSig}}(\cdot)$ with message $m^{(j)}$, and get $(\mathsf{spk}_{v_h^{(j)}}, \sigma_{v_h^{(j)}})$.
- **Authentication for $\mathsf{spk}_{v_{i+1}}$.** For $i = 0, 1, \ldots, h-1$, if $\mathsf{spk}_{v_{i+1}}$ has not been authenticated, compute $\widehat{\sigma}_{v_i \| \beta_i} \leftarrow \widehat{\mathsf{TTSign}}(\widehat{\mathsf{psk}}, \widehat{\mathsf{ssk}}_{v_i \| \beta_i}, \mathsf{spk}_{v_{i+1}}; j_i)$, where $v_{i+1} = v_i \| \beta_i j_i$.

Hence the signature $\sigma^{(j)}$ on message $m^{(j)}$ can be generated without knowing sk_{tree}. Return $\mathsf{vk}_{tree} = (\mathsf{ppk}, \mathsf{spk}_{v_0})$ and $(\sigma^{(1)}, \ldots, \sigma^{(q)})$ to $\mathcal{A}$. Note that $\mathcal{B}$ perfectly simulates the signing oracle of $\mathsf{TreeSig}$ and the resulting distribution is identical to that of the real one. Suppose $\mathcal{A}$ outputs a forgery $(m^*, \sigma^{(*)})$ and δ is the largest index such that $\mathsf{spk}_{v_\delta^{(*)}} = \mathsf{spk}_{v_\delta^{(i)}}$ for some (i). Here, variables with $(*)$ (or (i)) denote the corresponding parts of $\sigma^{(*)}$ (or $\sigma^{(i)}$). Consider the following cases.

- If $\widehat{\mathsf{ppk}}^{(*)} \neq \widehat{\mathsf{ppk}}$, $\mathcal{B}$ outputs $(\widehat{\mathsf{spk}}_{v_0 \| 0^{(*)}} \| \widehat{\mathsf{spk}}_{v_0 \| 1^{(*)}} \| \widehat{\mathsf{ppk}}^{(*)}, \sigma_{v_0^{(*)}}, i_{v_0})$, where i_{v_0} denotes the i_{v_0}-th query to $\mathcal{O}_{\mathsf{TTSig}}$ and corresponds to the secondary public key spk_{v_0}.
- If $\widehat{\mathsf{ppk}}^{(*)} = \widehat{\mathsf{ppk}}$,
  - $\delta = h$. $\mathcal{B}$ outputs $(m^*, \sigma_{v_h^{(*)}}, i_{v_h^{(i)}})$, where $i_{v_h^{(i)}}$ denotes the $i_{v_h^{(i)}}$-th query to $\mathcal{O}_{\mathsf{TTSig}}$ and corresponds to $\mathsf{spk}_{v_h^{(i)}}$.
  - $\delta < h$.
    * $\beta_\delta^{(*)} \neq \beta_\delta^{(i)}$ and $\widehat{\mathsf{spk}}_{v_\delta \| \beta_\delta^{(*)}} \neq \widehat{\mathsf{spk}}_{v_\delta \| (\beta_\delta^{(i)} \oplus 1)}$. $\mathcal{B}$ outputs $(\widehat{\mathsf{spk}}_{v_\delta \| 0^{(*)}} \| \widehat{\mathsf{spk}}_{v_\delta \| 1^{(*)}} \| \widehat{\mathsf{ppk}}^{(*)}, \sigma_{v_\delta^{(*)}}, i_{v_\delta^{(i)}})$, where $i_{v_\delta^{(i)}}$ denotes the $i_{v_\delta^{(i)}}$-th query to $\mathcal{O}_{\mathsf{TTSig}}$ and corresponds to $\mathsf{spk}_{v_\delta^{(i)}}$.
    * $\beta_\delta^{(*)} = \beta_\delta^{(i)}$ and $\widehat{\mathsf{spk}}_{v_\delta \| \beta_\delta^{(*)}} \neq \widehat{\mathsf{spk}}_{v_\delta \| \beta_\delta^{(i)}}$. $\mathcal{B}$ outputs $(\widehat{\mathsf{spk}}_{v_\delta \| 0^{(*)}} \| \widehat{\mathsf{spk}}_{v_\delta \| 1^{(*)}} \| \widehat{\mathsf{ppk}}^{(*)}, \sigma_{v_\delta^{(*)}}, i_{v_\delta^{(i)}})$.
    * Otherwise, $\mathcal{B}$ aborts. More precisely, $\mathcal{B}$ aborts if $((\beta_\delta^{(*)} \neq \beta_\delta^{(i)}) \wedge (\widehat{\mathsf{spk}}_{v_\delta \| \beta_\delta^{(*)}} = \widehat{\mathsf{spk}}_{v_\delta \| (\beta_\delta^{(i)} \oplus 1)}))$ or $((\beta_\delta^{(*)} = \beta_\delta^{(i)}) \wedge (\widehat{\mathsf{spk}}_{v_\delta \| \beta_\delta^{(*)}} = \widehat{\mathsf{spk}}_{v_\delta \| \beta_\delta^{(i)}}))$. Denote this event as Bad.

By the perfect simulation of $\mathcal{B}$,

$$\Pr[\mathsf{Exp}_{\mathsf{TreeSig}, \mathcal{A}, q_{\mathsf{Tree}}}^{\mathsf{EUF\text{-}NCMA}}(\lambda) = 1 \wedge \neg \mathsf{Bad}] = \Pr[\mathsf{Exp}_{\mathsf{TTSig}, \mathcal{B}, q_{\mathsf{TTSig}}}^{\mathsf{TT\text{-}EUF\text{-}NCMA}}(\lambda) = 1 \wedge \neg \mathsf{Bad}],$$

where $q_{\mathsf{Tree}} = q$. So we have

$$\Pr[\mathsf{Exp}_{\mathsf{TreeSig},\mathcal{A},q_{\mathsf{Tree}}}^{\mathsf{EUF\text{-}NCMA}}(\lambda) = 1]$$
$$\leq \Pr[\mathsf{Exp}_{\mathsf{TreeSig},\mathcal{A},q_{\mathsf{Tree}}}^{\mathsf{EUF\text{-}NCMA}}(\lambda) = 1 \wedge \mathsf{Bad}] + \Pr[\mathsf{Exp}_{\mathsf{TTSig},\mathcal{B},q_{\mathsf{TTSig}}}^{\mathsf{TT\text{-}EUF\text{-}NCMA}}(\lambda) = 1]. \quad (8)$$

Construction of $\hat{\mathcal{B}}$. Next, we will show that $\Pr[\mathsf{Exp}_{\mathsf{TreeSig},\mathcal{A},q_{\mathsf{Tree}}}^{\mathsf{EUF\text{-}NCMA}}(\lambda) = 1 \wedge \mathsf{Bad}] \leq \epsilon_{\widetilde{\mathsf{TTSig}}}$ by constructing a PPT algorithm $\hat{\mathcal{B}}$, which breaks the security of $\widetilde{\mathsf{TTSig}}$. $\hat{\mathcal{B}}$ takes as input $\widehat{\mathsf{ppk}}$ and simulates $\mathsf{Exp}_{\mathsf{TreeSig},\mathcal{A},q_{\mathsf{Tree}}}^{\mathsf{EUF\text{-}NCMA}}(\lambda)$ as follows. Upon receiving $m^{(1)}, \ldots, m^{(q)}$, $\hat{\mathcal{B}}$ compute $(\mathsf{vk}_{tree}, \mathsf{sk}_{tree}) \leftarrow \mathsf{TreeSig.Gen}(1^\lambda)$ where $\mathsf{vk}_{tree} = (\mathsf{ppk}, \mathsf{spk}_{v_0})$ and $\mathsf{sk}_{tree} = (\mathsf{psk}, \mathsf{ssk}_{v_0})$.

1. **Authentication for spk_{v_i} and nodes generation.** Choose the leftmost unused node N_{v_h}. For $i = 1, \ldots, h$, if the related keys associated to the node N_{v_i} have not been defined, run $\mathsf{SecGen}(\mathsf{ppk}, \mathsf{psk})$ $2d$ times to generate $(\mathsf{spk}_{v_{i-1}\|01}, \mathsf{ssk}_{v_{i-1}\|01}), \ldots, (\mathsf{spk}_{v_{i-1}\|0d}, \mathsf{ssk}_{v_{i-1}\|0d})$ and $(\mathsf{spk}_{v_{i-1}\|11}, \mathsf{ssk}_{v_{i-1}\|11}), \ldots, (\mathsf{spk}_{v_{i-1}\|1d}, \mathsf{ssk}_{v_{i-1}\|1d})$, query $\mathcal{O}_{\widetilde{\mathsf{TTSig}}}(\cdot)$ with $(\mathsf{spk}_{v_{i-1}\|01}, \ldots, \mathsf{spk}_{v_{i-1}\|0d})$ and $(\mathsf{spk}_{v_{i-1}\|11}, \ldots, \mathsf{spk}_{v_{i-1}\|1d})$ respectively, and get $(\widehat{\mathsf{spk}}_{v_{i-1}\|0}; \widehat{\sigma_{v_{i-1}\|01}}^1, \ldots, \widehat{\sigma_{v_{i-1}\|0d}}^d)$ and $(\widehat{\mathsf{spk}}_{v_{i-1}\|1}; \widehat{\sigma_{v_{i-1}\|11}}^1, \ldots, \widehat{\sigma_{v_{i-1}\|1d}}^d)$. Then, $(\mathsf{spk}_{v_{i-1}\|01}, \ldots, \mathsf{spk}_{v_{i-1}\|0d})$ and $(\mathsf{spk}_{v_{i-1}\|11}, \ldots, \mathsf{spk}_{v_{i-1}\|1d})$ are assigned to nodes $N_{v_{i-1}\|01}, \ldots, N_{v_{i-1}\|0d}$ and $N_{v_{i-1}\|11}, \ldots, N_{v_{i-1}\|1d}$, respectively. For message $m^{(j)}$, compute $\sigma_{v_h} \leftarrow \mathsf{TTSign}(\mathsf{psk}, \mathsf{ssk}_{v_h}, m^{(j)})$.
2. **Authentication for $\widehat{\mathsf{spk}}_{v_i\|0}$ and $\widehat{\mathsf{spk}}_{v_i\|1}$.** For $i = 0, 1, \ldots, h-1$, if $\widehat{\mathsf{spk}}_{v_i\|0}$ and $\widehat{\mathsf{spk}}_{v_i\|1}$ has not been authenticated, compute $\sigma_{v_i} \leftarrow \mathsf{TTSign}(\mathsf{psk}, \mathsf{ssk}_{v_i}, \widehat{\mathsf{spk}}_{v_i\|0}\|\widehat{\mathsf{spk}}_{v_i\|1}\|\widehat{\mathsf{ppk}})$.

So the signature $\sigma^{(j)}$ on message $m^{(j)}$ can be generated for $j = 1, \ldots, q$. Note that, for simplicity, we denote $\widehat{\sigma_{v_i}}$ as the corresponding signature of N_{v_i}, where $v_i = v_{i-1}\|\beta_{i-1}j_{i-1}$. $\hat{\mathcal{B}}$ returns $\mathsf{vk}_{tree} = (\mathsf{ppk}, \mathsf{spk}_{v_0})$ and $(\sigma^{(1)}, \ldots, \sigma^{(q)})$ to $\mathcal{A}$.

Finally, $\mathcal{A}$ outputs a forgery $(m^*, \sigma^{(*)})$. Suppose δ is the largest index such that $\mathsf{spk}_{v_\delta^{(*)}} = \mathsf{spk}_{v_\delta^{(i)}}$ for some $i \in \{1, \ldots, q\}$. $\hat{\mathcal{B}}$ outputs $(\mathsf{spk}_{v_{\delta+1}^{(*)}}, \widehat{\sigma_{v_\delta\|\beta_\delta^{(*)}}}, i_{v_\delta\|\beta_\delta^{(*)}}, j_\delta^{(*)})$ if either one of the following conditions holds:

- $(\beta_\delta^{(*)} \neq \beta_\delta^{(i)}) \wedge (\widehat{\mathsf{spk}}_{v_\delta\|\beta_\delta^{(*)}} = \mathsf{spk}_{v_\delta\|(\beta_\delta^{(i)}\oplus 1)})$,
- $(\beta_\delta^{(*)} = \beta_\delta^{(i)}) \wedge (\widehat{\mathsf{spk}}_{v_\delta\|\beta_\delta^{(*)}} = \mathsf{spk}_{v_\delta\|\beta_\delta^{(i)}})$,

where $i_{v_\delta\|\beta_\delta^{(*)}}$ denotes the $i_{v_\delta\|\beta_\delta^{(*)}}$-th query to $\mathcal{O}_{\widetilde{\mathsf{TTSig}}}$ and corresponds to $\widehat{\mathsf{spk}}_{v_\delta\|\beta_\delta^{(*)}}$. Otherwise, $\hat{\mathcal{B}}$ aborts. Note that the above conditions correspond to the event Bad. Since $\hat{\mathcal{B}}$ perfectly simulates $\mathsf{Exp}_{\mathsf{TreeSig},\mathcal{A},q_{\mathsf{Tree}}}^{\mathsf{EUF\text{-}NCMA}}(\lambda)$, we have

$$\Pr[\mathsf{Exp}_{\mathsf{TreeSig},\mathcal{A},q_{\mathsf{Tree}}}^{\mathsf{EUF\text{-}NCMA}}(\lambda) = 1 \wedge \mathsf{Bad}] = \Pr[\mathsf{Exp}_{\widetilde{\mathsf{TTSig}},\hat{\mathcal{B}},q_{\widetilde{\mathsf{TTSig}}}}^{\mathsf{TT\text{-}EUF\text{-}NCMA}}(\lambda, d) = 1], \quad (9)$$

where $q_{\mathsf{Tree}} = q$. By (8) and (9), we have $\epsilon_{\mathsf{Tree}} \le \epsilon_{\mathsf{TTSig}} + \epsilon_{\widehat{\mathsf{TTSig}}}$. Since $\mathcal{B}$ has to make at most $h + 1$ queries to $\mathcal{O}_{\mathsf{TTSig}}(\cdot)$ for each $m^{(j)}$, we have $t_{\mathsf{Tree}} = t_{\mathsf{TTSig}} - O(hq_{\mathsf{Tree}})$, $q_{\mathsf{Tree}} \le q_{\mathsf{TTSig}}$. Similarly, for the construction of $\hat{\mathcal{B}}$, $t_{\mathsf{Tree}} = t_{\widehat{\mathsf{TTSig}}} - O(hq_{\mathsf{Tree}})$, $q_{\mathsf{Tree}} \le q_{\widehat{\mathsf{TTSig}}}$. Therefore, $t_{\mathsf{Tree}} = \max\{t_{\mathsf{TTSig}}, t_{\widehat{\mathsf{TTSig}}}\} - O(hq_{\mathsf{Tree}})$ and $q_{\mathsf{Tree}} \le \max\{q_{\mathsf{TTSig}}, q_{\widehat{\mathsf{TTSig}}}\}$.

References

1. Abe, M., David, B., Kohlweiss, M., Nishimaki, R., Ohkubo, M.: Tagged one-time signatures: tight security and optimal tag size. In: Kurosawa, K., Hanaoka, G. (eds.) PKC 2013. LNCS, vol. 7778, pp. 312–331. Springer, Heidelberg (2013). doi:10.1007/978-3-642-36362-7_20

2. Abe, M., Fuchsbauer, G., Groth, J., Haralambiev, K., Ohkubo, M.: Structure-preserving signatures and commitments to group elements. In: Rabin, T. (ed.) CRYPTO 2010. LNCS, vol. 6223, pp. 209–236. Springer, Heidelberg (2010). doi:10.1007/978-3-642-14623-7_12

3. Attrapadung, N., Hanaoka, G., Yamada, S.: A framework for identity-based encryption with almost tight security. In: Iwata, T., Cheon, J.H. (eds.) ASIACRYPT 2015. LNCS, vol. 9452, pp. 521–549. Springer, Heidelberg (2015). doi:10.1007/978-3-662-48797-6_22

4. Bader, C., Hofheinz, D., Jager, T., Kiltz, E., Li, Y.: Tightly-secure authenticated key exchange. In: Dodis, Y., Nielsen, J.B. (eds.) TCC 2015. LNCS, vol. 9014, pp. 629–658. Springer, Heidelberg (2015). doi:10.1007/978-3-662-46494-6_26

5. Bader, C., Jager, T., Li, Y., Schäge, S.: On the impossibility of tight cryptographic reductions. In: Fischlin, M., Coron, J.-S. (eds.) EUROCRYPT 2016. LNCS, vol. 9666, pp. 273–304. Springer, Heidelberg (2016). doi:10.1007/978-3-662-49896-5_10

6. Belenkiy, M., Camenisch, J., Chase, M., Kohlweiss, M., Lysyanskaya, A., Shacham, H.: Randomizable proofs and delegatable anonymous credentials. In: Halevi, S. (ed.) CRYPTO 2009. LNCS, vol. 5677, pp. 108–125. Springer, Heidelberg (2009). doi:10.1007/978-3-642-03356-8_7

7. Bellare, M., Boldyreva, A., Micali, S.: Public-key encryption in a multi-user setting: security proofs and improvements. In: Preneel, B. (ed.) EUROCRYPT 2000. LNCS, vol. 1807, pp. 259–274. Springer, Heidelberg (2000). doi:10.1007/3-540-45539-6_18

8. Bellare, M., Shoup, S.: Two-tier signatures, strongly unforgeable signatures, and fiat-shamir without random oracles. In: Okamoto, T., Wang, X. (eds.) PKC 2007. LNCS, vol. 4450, pp. 201–216. Springer, Heidelberg (2007). doi:10.1007/978-3-540-71677-8_14

9. Blazy, O., Kiltz, E., Pan, J.: (Hierarchical) identity-based encryption from affine message authentication. In: Garay, J.A., Gennaro, R. (eds.) CRYPTO 2014. LNCS, vol. 8616, pp. 408–425. Springer, Heidelberg (2014). doi:10.1007/978-3-662-44371-2_23

10. Blazy, O., Kakvi, S.A., Kiltz, E., Pan, J.: Tightly-secure signatures from chameleon hash functions. In: Katz, J. (ed.) PKC 2015. LNCS, vol. 9020, pp. 256–279. Springer, Heidelberg (2015). doi:10.1007/978-3-662-46447-2_12

11. Boneh, D., Boyen, X., Shacham, H.: Short group signatures. In: Franklin, M. (ed.) CRYPTO 2004. LNCS, vol. 3152, pp. 41–55. Springer, Heidelberg (2004). doi:10.1007/978-3-540-28628-8_3

12. Canetti, R., Halevi, S., Katz, J.: Chosen-ciphertext security from identity-based encryption. In: Cachin, C., Camenisch, J.L. (eds.) EUROCRYPT 2004. LNCS, vol. 3027, pp. 207–222. Springer, Heidelberg (2004). doi:10.1007/978-3-540-24676-3_13
13. Chen, J., Wee, H.: Fully, (almost) tightly secure IBE and dual system groups. In: Canetti, R., Garay, J.A. (eds.) CRYPTO 2013. LNCS, vol. 8043, pp. 435–460. Springer, Heidelberg (2013). doi:10.1007/978-3-642-40084-1_25
14. Dodis, Y., Haralambiev, K., López-Alt, A., Wichs, D.: Efficient public-key cryptography in the presence of key leakage. In: Abe, M. (ed.) ASIACRYPT 2010. LNCS, vol. 6477, pp. 613–631. Springer, Heidelberg (2010). doi:10.1007/978-3-642-17373-8_35
15. ElGamal, T.: A public key cryptosystem and a signature scheme based on discrete logarithms. IEEE Trans. Inf. Theor. **IT–31**(4), 469–472 (1985)
16. Gay, R., Hofheinz, D., Kiltz, E., Wee, H.: Tightly CCA-secure encryption without pairings. In: Fischlin, M., Coron, J.-S. (eds.) EUROCRYPT 2016. LNCS, vol. 9665, pp. 1–27. Springer, Heidelberg (2016). doi:10.1007/978-3-662-49890-3_1
17. Goldreich, O.: Two remarks concerning the goldwasser-micali-rivest signature scheme. In: Odlyzko, A.M. (ed.) CRYPTO 1986. LNCS, vol. 263, pp. 104–110. Springer, Heidelberg (1987). doi:10.1007/3-540-47721-7_8
18. Groth, J.: Simulation-sound NIZK proofs for a practical language and constant size group signatures. In: Lai, X., Chen, K. (eds.) ASIACRYPT 2006. LNCS, vol. 4284, pp. 444–459. Springer, Heidelberg (2006). doi:10.1007/11935230_29
19. Hofheinz, D., Jager, T.: Tightly secure signatures and public-key encryption. In: Safavi-Naini, R., Canetti, R. (eds.) CRYPTO 2012. LNCS, vol. 7417, pp. 590–607. Springer, Heidelberg (2012). doi:10.1007/978-3-642-32009-5_35
20. Hofheinz, D.: Algebraic partitioning: fully compact and (almost) tightly secure cryptography. In: Kushilevitz, E., Malkin, T. (eds.) TCC 2016. LNCS, vol. 9562, pp. 251–281. Springer, Heidelberg (2016). doi:10.1007/978-3-662-49096-9_11
21. Hofheinz, D., Koch, J., Striecks, C.: Identity-based encryption with (almost) tight security in the multi-instance, multi-ciphertext setting. In: Katz, J. (ed.) PKC 2015. LNCS, vol. 9020, pp. 799–822. Springer, Heidelberg (2015). doi:10.1007/978-3-662-46447-2_36
22. Kiltz, E., Pan, J., Wee, H.: Structure-preserving signatures from standard assumptions, revisited. In: Gennaro, R., Robshaw, M. (eds.) CRYPTO 2015. LNCS, vol. 9216, pp. 275–295. Springer, Heidelberg (2015). doi:10.1007/978-3-662-48000-7_14
23. Krawczyk, H., Rabin, T.: Chameleon hashing and signatures. In: Proceedings of NDSS 2000, pp. 143–154 (2000)
24. Libert, B., Joye, M., Yung, M., Peters, T.: Concise multi-challenge CCA-secure encryption and signatures with almost tight security. In: Sarkar, P., Iwata, T. (eds.) ASIACRYPT 2014. LNCS, vol. 8874, pp. 1–21. Springer, Heidelberg (2014). doi:10.1007/978-3-662-45608-8_1
25. Libert, B., Peters, T., Joye, M., Yung, M.: Compactly hiding linear spans. In: Iwata, T., Cheon, J.H. (eds.) ASIACRYPT 2015. LNCS, vol. 9452, pp. 681–707. Springer, Heidelberg (2015). doi:10.1007/978-3-662-48797-6_28
26. Naor, M., Yung, M.: Public-key cryptosystems provably secure against chosen cipher-text attacks. In: STOC 1990, pp. 427–437. ACM, New York (1990)
27. Rackoff, C., Simon, D.R.: Non-interactive zero-knowledge proof of knowledge and chosen ciphertext attack. In: Feigenbaum, J. (ed.) CRYPTO 1991. LNCS, vol. 576, pp. 433–444. Springer, Heidelberg (1992). doi:10.1007/3-540-46766-1_35

Hierarchical Functional Encryption
for Linear Transformations

Shiwei Zhang[1]([✉]), Yi Mu[1], Guomin Yang[1], and Xiaofen Wang[2,3]

[1] Institute of Cybersecurity and Cryptology, School of Computing
and Information Technology, University of Wollongong, Wollongong, Australia
{sz653,ymu,gyang}@uow.edu.au
[2] The Center for Cyber Security, University of Electronic Science
and Technology of China, Chengdu 611731, Sichuan, China
wangxuedou@sina.com
[3] Guangxi Key Laboratory of Trusted Software,
Guilin University of Electronic Technology, Guilin 541004, Gunagxi, China

Abstract. In contrast to the conventional all-or-nothing encryption, functional encryption (FE) allows partial revelation of encrypted information based on the keys associated with different functionalities. Extending FE with key delegation ability, hierarchical functional encryption (HFE) enables a secret key holder to delegate a portion of its decryption ability to others and the delegation can be done hierarchically. All HFE schemes in the literature are for general functionalities and not very practical. In this paper, we focus on the functionality of linear transformations (i.e. matrix product evaluation). We refine the definition of HFE and further extend the delegation to accept multiple keys. We also propose a generic HFE construction for linear transformations with IND-CPA security in the standard model from hash proof systems. In addition, we give two instantiations from the DDH and DCR assumptions which to the best of our knowledge are the first practical concrete HFE constructions.

Keywords: Hierarchical · Functional encryption · Matrix product · Hash proof system

1 Introduction

Encryption can provide confidentiality and privacy for our sensitive information in a variety of ways. Typically, conventional encryption is in an all-or-nothing fashion that an entity is able to either access all the encrypted information or nothing, excepting the message length. In contrast, functional encryption [8] allows partial revelation of encrypted information based on the keys associated with different functionalities. Precisely, Alice can encrypt some message m under Bob's public key, and send the ciphertext to a public domain where Charlie can access. Later, Bob issues a secret key for a function f to Charlie using a master secret key corresponding to Bob's public key. As a result, Charlie is able to learn

© Springer International Publishing AG 2017
J. Pieprzyk and S. Suriadi (Eds.): ACISP 2017, Part I, LNCS 10342, pp. 23–43, 2017.
DOI: 10.1007/978-3-319-60055-0_2

$f(m)$ from the ciphertext and the secret key received from Bob but nothing else. Usually, the function f is a universal function for a function class $\mathcal{F}$ indexed by a function key k from a key space K s.t. $\mathcal{F} = \{f_k \mid k \in K\}$. In this case, Bob sends a secret key for a function key k to Charlie who learns $f(k, m)$ or simply $f_k(m)$.

When Bob can control the amount of the information that Charlie can reveal, it leads to a natural question of whether Charlie is able to further let other people (e.g. David) obtain a narrower portion of his decryption ability. Hierarchical functional encryption (HFE) [5,9,11] gives an affirmative answer. In HFE, Charlie with a secret key associated with a function f is able to generate a new secret key associated with a composed function $f' \circ f$ for David without the help of Bob. Upon receiving the key from Charlie, David can learn $f'(f(m))$ but nothing else of the original message m. It is worth noting that the above delegation process is repeatable that David can delegate a portion of his decryption ability to other people, making the hierarchy grow deeper and deeper.

In this paper, we focus on HFE for the functionality of matrix product evaluation, which implies the function class of linear transformation via transformation matrices. More precisely, the functionality is defined as $f(\mathbf{A}, \mathbf{X}) = f_\mathbf{A}(\mathbf{X}) = \mathbf{A}\mathbf{X}$ where the matrix $\mathbf{A}$ is the transformation matrix (i.e. the function key) and the matrix $\mathbf{X}$ is the message to be encrypted. It is easy to see that such a functionality is a natural generalisation of the functionality of inner product evaluation [1,2,4,19].

There are a few practical applications of HFE for the functionality of matrix product evaluation, including but not limited to descriptive statistics. Differing from the functional encryption for inner product evaluation [1,2,4,19], our proposed HFE allows the evaluation to be done in a levelled manner. We take the calculation of the weighted sum as an example. Suppose Alice is a researcher in a consulting firm conducting marketing research on the demand of various products and the company will sell Alice's results to different clients. Once the research results are ready, Alice encrypts the demand level of different areas for each product (e.g. $\mathbf{X} = \begin{bmatrix} 2 \ 1 \ 9 \ 0 \ 6 \ 2 \ 5 \ 6 \ 1 \end{bmatrix}^\top$ for the demand of coffee in different regions) under her company's public key. As the manager of Alice's company, Bob has the master secret key and decides to sell Alice's result in different levels and at different prices. Suppose Charlie wants to buy from Bob some information he is interested in. He does not want all the details but a overall score for the demand of coffee, and he is more interested in the areas near his store, i.e. those areas will have a higher weight. Hence, Charlie buys a secret key of a weighted matrix (e.g. $\mathbf{A} = \begin{bmatrix} 0 \ 1 \ 2 \ 3 \ 4 \ 3 \ 2 \ 1 \ 0 \end{bmatrix}$) from Bob for a low price so that he can learn a summary of the market demand (e.g. $\mathbf{A}\mathbf{X} = 65$ for coffee).

With HFE, Bob is also able to sell Alice's result to some regional resellers (or proxies), e.g. David. Unlike Charlie, David wants the details of some regions and a summary for other regions. Thus he buys a secret key of a weighted matrix (e.g. $\mathbf{A} = \left[\begin{array}{c|c} \mathbf{I}_5 & \mathbf{0}_{5,4} \\ \hline \mathbf{0}_{1,5} & 5 \ 4 \ 1 \ 2 \end{array} \right]$) from Bob for a higher price so that he learns Alice's partial result (e.g. $\mathbf{A}\mathbf{X} = \begin{bmatrix} 2 \ 1 \ 9 \ 0 \ 6 \ 38 \end{bmatrix}^\top$ for coffee). Later, David can resell what he obtained from Bob to other clients in his region. For example, another store manager Eve in David's region is interested in Alice's result, and decides to buy some market information for her nearby regions from David. In the reselling process, David uses his secret key for $\mathbf{A}$ to generate a new secret key for $\mathbf{C} = \mathbf{BA}$ based on Eve's demand (e.g. $\mathbf{B} = \begin{bmatrix} 20 & 15 & 10 & 5 & 2 & 0 \end{bmatrix}$ and thus $\mathbf{C} = \begin{bmatrix} 20 & 15 & 10 & 5 & 2 & 0 & 0 & 0 & 0 \end{bmatrix}$). Once Eve gets the key, she can learn $\mathbf{CX}$ from Alice's research (e.g. $\mathbf{CX} = 157$ for coffee). On the other hand, David can also resell his data obtained from Bob to other resellers in different levels and at different prices.

There are many potential applications of HFE for linear transformation, such as those related to descriptive statistics as demonstrated above. In this paper, we introduce and formalise this useful cryptographic primitive and present a generic construction of it. We also show two practical instantiations of the generic construction based on some standard assumptions.

1.1 Related Work

The formal study of functional encryption (FE) was initiated by Boneh et al. [8] with syntax and security model defined for general functionality. In this paper, we focus on the public-key FE. Other than predicate encryption [15] (a subclass of FE) and theoretical constructions [14] for arbitrary functionality, Abdalla et al. [2] focused on the functionality of inner product evaluation that only the inner product $\langle x, y \rangle$ of the encrypted vector y is revealed with a secret key for the vector x. Furthermore, the authors challenged to construct practical schemes with such a functionality, and proposed an s-IND-CPA secure generic construction from any s-IND-CPA public key encryption (PKE) schemes with the properties of randomness reuse, linear key homomorphism, and linear ciphertext homomorphism under shared randomness. Precisely, s-IND-CPA (or selective IND-CPA) is a weaker notion of the standard indistinguishability under chosen plaintext attacks (IND-CPA) where the adversary is required to submit the target plaintexts before receiving the public key from the challenger. Based on [2], Abdalla et al. [1] enhanced their previous generic construction [2] to the standard IND-CPA security from any s-IND-CPA PKE schemes with the properties of linear key homomorphism, linear ciphertext homomorphism under shared randomness, ℓ-public-key reproducibility, and ℓ-ciphertext reproducibility. The authors also showed several instantiations from various s-IND-CPA PKE schemes based on Decisional Diffie-Hellman (DDH) assumption [13], Decisional Composite Residuosity (DCR) assumption [10,17], and Learning With Error (LWE) assumption [18]. Independent from [1], Agrawal et al. [4] constructed function encryption schemes for inner products directly from DDH, DCR, and LWE assumptions instead of a generic construction, and obtained better efficiency. It is worth noting that the proofs of the DDH construction and the DCR construction in [4] are implicitly built on Hash Proof System (HPS) [12] as the HPS makes the secret keys simulatable and IND-CPA security achievable. In contrast to [4], Zhang et al. [19] recently provided another framework of constructing functional encryption for inner products (FE-IP) explicitly from HPS with the properties of key linearity, hash linearity and diversity. Also, the authors further improved the security from IND-CPA to indistinguishability under adaptive chosen ciphertext attacks (IND-CCA).

There are several extension works [3,5,6] on functional encryption. As one of those extensions, Hierarchical functional encryption (HFE) enables delegation capability, which is initially mentioned in [5], generalising the notions of hierarchical identity-based encryption [7] and hierarchical predicate encryption [16] for more expressive access controls. In particular, [5,9,11] define HFE as a normal FE with an extra delegation algorithm that takes a function key SK_f and a function f' and outputs a function key $SK_{f' \circ f}$. As mentioned above, the newly generated key $SK_{f' \circ f}$ allows revelation of $f'(f(m))$ but nothing else from the encrypted message m. In the literature, Ananth et al. [5] and Chandran et al. [11] purposed general purpose HFE constructions direct from indistinguishable obfuscation ($i\mathcal{O}$) with fixed depth where the delegation process can only be proceeded for a fixed number of times. As an improvement, Brakerski et al. [9] proposed a generic transformation from any general purpose FE to a general purpose HFE with unbounded depth. The transformation requires a private-key encryption scheme and a puncturable pseudorandom function family, and does not rely on $i\mathcal{O}$. As far as we know, all the HFE schemes in the literature are general purposed and not very practical.

1.2 Our Contribution

In this paper, we refine and simplify the definition of *hierarchical functional encryption* (HFE) originally from [5,9,11]. We merge the delegation algorithm $SK_{f' \circ f} \leftarrow \mathsf{Delegate}(SK_f, f')$ with the key generation algorithm $SK_{f_k} \leftarrow \mathsf{KeyGen}(MSK, k)$ to form a new key generation algorithm $SK_{f' \circ f} \leftarrow \mathsf{KeyGen}(SK_f, f')$, making the master secret key equivalent to a secret key of an identity function $MSK \stackrel{\text{def}}{=} SK_{\mathsf{id}}$. As a result, our definition of HFE consists of four algorithms instead of five algorithms, and it is compatible with the IND-CPA security model defined for the normal functional encryption, which is much simpler than the previously defined model for HFE. In terms of the evolution of encryption, our definition of HFE is a more natural generalisation of hierarchical identity-based encryption (HIBE) [7].

As an extension of HFE, we introduce the notion of *extended hierarchical functional encryption* (eHFE), allowing delegation from multiple secret keys. Precisely, in eHFE, the key generation algorithm takes n secret keys $SK_{f_1}, \ldots, SK_{f_n}$ for functions $f_1, \ldots, f_n$ correspondingly and a delegation function f', and it generates a new secret key SK_f for a function f such that $f(x) = f'(f_1(x), \ldots, f_n(x))$.

We derive the definition of *hierarchical function encryption for linear transformation* (HFE-LT) from HFE (similarly, eHFE-LT from eHFE) for the functionality of matrix product evaluation. Different from the previous general results which are of theoretical interest, we propose a generic and practical construction of HFE-LT. It is worth noting that our construction has unbounded depth in delegation (Table 1). Since the HFE-LT scheme cannot be trivially constructed from function encryption for inner products, our generic construction is explicitly built from hash proof systems (HPS) with key linearity, hash linearity and diversity, and achieves IND-CPA security in the standard model. As an extension, we also adapt our generic HFE-LT construction to a generic eHFE-LT construction. We provide two practical HFE-LT instantiations based on the Decisional Diffie-Hellman (DDH) assumption and the Decisional Composite Residuosity (DCR) assumption. In the DDH instantiation, the decryption space is limited to be of polynomial size so that the decryption can be done in polynomial time. However, in the DCR instantiation, there is no such limitation. In addition, both instantiations can be extended to the eHFE-LT setting.

Table 1. Comparison of different schemes

Scheme	Functionality	Assumption	Hierarchical	Depth	Multi-key
[5]	Generic	$i\mathcal{O}$	Yes	Constant	No
[11]	Generic	$i\mathcal{O}$ + HIBE	Yes	Fixed	No
[9]	Generic	Generic FE	Yes	Unbounded	No
[1]	Inner product	s-IND-CPA PKE: DDH/DCR/LWE	No	×	No
[4]	Inner product	DDH/DCR/LWE	No	×	No
Our HFE-LT	Matrix product	Diverse HPS: DDH/DCR	Yes	Unbounded	No
Our eHFE-LT	Matrix product	Diverse HPS	Yes	Unbounded	Yes

1.3   Paper Organisation

The rest of this paper is organised as follows. It is strongly suggested to read the preliminaries in Sect. 2, especially the notations used in this paper. In Sect. 3, we review the subset membership problems, hash proof system, and functional encryption. As our main contribution, we refine HFE and define HFE-LT in Sect. 3.1. The generic construction from HPS is proposed in Sect. 3.2 and follows the security proof in Sect. 3.3. In Sect. 3.4, we adapt HFE to eHFE in terms of the definition, the generic construction, and the security proof. After that, we propose our concrete HFE-LT constructions instantiated from DDH and DCR assumptions in Sect. 4. Finally, the conclusion is addressed in Sect. 5.

2   Preliminaries

2.1   Notations

Let $\in_R$ denote random sampling that $x \in_R X$ means that x is uniformly and randomly chosen from a set or distribution X. Let $\circ$ denote the function composition that $(g \circ f)(x) = g(f(x))$, and id denote the identity function that $\mathsf{id}(x) = x$ and $f \circ \mathsf{id} = f$. Let $\lfloor x \rfloor$ denote the floor function of a real number x.

In the group computation, the function sca denotes the inverse operation to the scalar multiplication that $a = \text{sca}_x(b) \iff b = ax$ where X is an additive group generated by x, $a \in \mathbb{Z}_{|X|}$, and $b \in X$. It is an analogue of the logarithm operation in a multiplicative group.

In the matrix computation, let $\mathbf{X}_{m \times n}$ be a matrix of size $m \times n$, and $\mathbf{I}_n$ be the identity matrix of size n. If the size is clear in the context, $\mathbf{X}$ and $\mathbf{I}$ are used for short with size omitted. Let $\top$ denote matrix transpose. In addition to the standard matrix addition and multiplication operations, we define the following notations for better representations. Let f be a function that takes an element from X with other fixed parameters as input, $\mathbf{X} \in X^{m \times n}$ be a matrix, and $\stackrel{\text{def}}{=}$ denote equal by definition. We define that

$$
\mathbf{X} \stackrel{\text{def}}{=} \begin{bmatrix} X_{1,1} & \cdots & X_{1,n} \\ \vdots & \ddots & \vdots \\ X_{m,1} & \cdots & X_{m,n} \end{bmatrix}, \quad f(\mathbf{X}, \ldots) \stackrel{\text{def}}{=} \begin{bmatrix} f(X_{1,1}, \ldots) & \cdots & f(X_{1,n}, \ldots) \\ \vdots & \ddots & \vdots \\ f(X_{m,1}, \ldots) & \cdots & f(X_{m,n}, \ldots) \end{bmatrix}.
$$

If f is an additive homomorphism that $f(a) + f(b) = f(a+b)$, we have $f(\mathbf{A}) + f(\mathbf{B}) = f(\mathbf{A} + \mathbf{B})$ where $\mathbf{A}$ and $\mathbf{B}$ are two matrices with the same size. Besides that, we can have more complex scalar multiplication as

$$
\begin{aligned}
\mathbf{A}f(\mathbf{B}) &= \begin{bmatrix} A_{1,1} & \cdots & A_{1,n} \\ \vdots & \ddots & \vdots \\ A_{m,1} & \cdots & A_{m,n} \end{bmatrix} \begin{bmatrix} f(B_{1,1}) & \cdots & f(B_{1,l}) \\ \vdots & \ddots & \vdots \\ f(B_{n,1}) & \cdots & f(B_{n,l}) \end{bmatrix} \\
&= \begin{bmatrix} \sum_{i=1}^n A_{1,i}f(B_{i,1}) & \cdots & \sum_{i=1}^n A_{1,i}f(B_{i,l}) \\ \vdots & \ddots & \vdots \\ \sum_{i=1}^n A_{m,i}f(B_{i,1}) & \cdots & \sum_{i=1}^n A_{m,i}f(B_{i,l})) \end{bmatrix} \\
&= \begin{bmatrix} f(\sum_{i=1}^n A_{1,i}B_{i,1}) & \cdots & f(\sum_{i=1}^n A_{1,i}B_{i,l}) \\ \vdots & \ddots & \vdots \\ f(\sum_{i=1}^n A_{m,i}B_{i,1}) & \cdots & f(\sum_{i=1}^n A_{m,i}B_{i,l})) \end{bmatrix} = f(\mathbf{AB})
\end{aligned}
$$

where $\mathbf{A}$ is an $m \times n$ matrix and $\mathbf{B}$ is an $n \times l$ matrix. Similarly, we have $f(\mathbf{A})\mathbf{B} = f(\mathbf{AB})$. In addition, the symbol $(\mathbf{A} \mid \mathbf{B})$ denotes an argumented matrix of two matrices $\mathbf{A}$ and $\mathbf{B}$ with the same row size. It can be generalised as $(\mathbf{A}_1 \mid \cdots \mid \mathbf{A}_n) \stackrel{\text{def}}{=} ((\cdots ((\mathbf{A}_1 \mid \mathbf{A}_2) \mid \mathbf{A}_3) \mid \cdots) \mid \mathbf{A}_n)$.

2.2   Subset Membership Problems

Subset Membership Problem (SMP) is a problem class introduced by Cramer and Shoup [12]. Many standard problems can be classified to SMP, including DDH and DCR problems.

Definition 1 (Subset Membership Problem). *Let $L \subset X, W$ be three nonempty sets, and $R = \{(x, w) \mid x \in L\} \subset X \times W$ be a binary relation where w is a witness of a word x in the language L. Let $\Lambda = (X, L, W, R)$ be a problem* *instance,* $x \in_R L$, *and* $x' \in_R X \setminus L$. *Given two probability distributions* $\mathcal{D}_L = \{(\Lambda, x)\}$ *and* $\mathcal{D}_{X \setminus L} = \{(\Lambda, x')\}$, *there is an algorithm* $\mathcal{A}$ *that distinguishes* $\mathcal{D}_L$ *and* $\mathcal{D}_{X \setminus L}$ *with advantage:*

$$\mathsf{Adv}_{\mathcal{A}}^{\mathrm{SMP}} = \left| \Pr[1 \leftarrow \mathcal{A}(D \in_R \mathcal{D}_L)] - \Pr[1 \leftarrow \mathcal{A}(D \in_R \mathcal{D}_{X \setminus L})] \right|$$

An SMP is computational hard if and only if the advantage $\mathsf{Adv}_{\mathcal{A}}^{\mathrm{SMP}}$ is negligible for any probabilistic polynomial time (PPT) algorithm $\mathcal{A}$.

2.3 Hash Proof System

In this subsection, the hash proof system introduced by Cramer and Shoup [12] and extended by Zhang et al. [19] is reviewed.

Definition 2 (Hash Proof System). *A hash proof system (HPS) associated with subset membership problems consists of the following five polynomial time algorithms:*

- param $\leftarrow$ Setup(1^λ): *The randomised system setup algorithm takes a security parameter* 1^λ *as input, and specifies an SMP instance* $\Lambda = (X, L, W, R)$ *where the hash domain is* X. *The algorithm further specifies a secret hash key space* K, *a public hash key space* S, *and a hash codomain* Π. *After that, the algorithm packs all above descriptions and publishes a system-wide parameter* param = (X, L, W, R, K, S, Π).
- SK $\leftarrow$ SKGen(param): *The randomised secret hash key generation algorithm takes a system parameter* param, *and generates a random hash key* SK $\in_R K$.
- PK $\leftarrow$ PKGen(SK): *The deterministic public hash key generation algorithm takes a secret hash key* SK $\in K$ *as input, and maps it to a public hash key* PK $\in S$.
- $\pi \leftarrow$ Hash(SK, x): *The deterministic private evaluation algorithm takes a secret hash key* SK $\in K$ *and a word* $x \in X$ *as inputs, and outputs a hash value* $\pi \in \Pi$ *of* x.
- $\pi \leftarrow$ PHash(PK, x, w): *The deterministic public evaluation algorithm takes a public hash key* PK $\in S$ *and a word* x *in the language* L *along with a corresponding witness* $w \in W$ *such that* $(x, w) \in R$, *and output a hash value* $\pi \in \Pi$ *of* x.

A HPS is required to be correct that the private evaluation algorithm Hash and the public evaluation algorithm PHash are equivalent when $x \in L$.

Definition 3 (Correctness). *A HPS is correct if*

$$\forall \mathsf{param} \leftarrow \mathsf{Setup}(1^\lambda), \quad \forall \mathsf{SK} \leftarrow \mathsf{SKGen}(\mathsf{param}), \quad \mathsf{PK} \leftarrow \mathsf{PKGen}(\mathsf{SK}),$$
$$\forall (x, w) \in R, \quad \mathsf{Hash}(\mathsf{SK}, x) = \mathsf{PHash}(\mathsf{PK}, x, w).$$

The original definition of HPS from [12] is not sufficient for our schemes, and the following extended properties introduced by [19] are required.

Definition 4 (Key Linearity). *A HPS is linear key homomorphic if K and S are additive abelian groups and*

$$\forall a, b \in K, \quad \mathsf{PKGen}(a) + \mathsf{PKGen}(b) = \mathsf{PKGen}(a + b) \in S.$$

Definition 5 (Hash Linearity). *A HPS is linear hash homomorphic if K and Π are additive abelian groups and*

$$\forall a, b \in K, \quad \forall x \in X, \quad \mathsf{Hash}(a, x) + \mathsf{Hash}(b, x) = \mathsf{Hash}(a + b, x) \in \Pi.$$

Definition 6 (Diversity). *A HPS is diverse if*

$$\exists \pi \in \Pi \setminus \{0\}, \quad \forall x \in X \setminus L, \quad \exists \mathsf{SK} \in K, \quad \mathsf{PKGen}(\mathsf{SK}) = 0 \wedge \mathsf{Hash}(\mathsf{SK}, x) = \pi$$

We call such a element π as an element derived from the diversity.

2.4 Functional Encryption

The definition and the security model of functional encryption by Boneh et al. [8] are reviewed as follows.

Definition 7 (Functional Encryption). *Let $f : K \times X \to Y$ be a universal function for a function class $\mathcal{F} = \{f_k \mid k \in K\}$ indexed by a function key space K, mapping the message space X to the revelation space Y. A functional encryption (FE) for a function class $\mathcal{F}$ consists of the following four polynomial time algorithms:*

- *$(\mathsf{PK}, \mathsf{MSK}) \leftarrow \mathsf{Setup}(1^\lambda)$: The randomised system setup algorithm takes a security parameter 1^λ as input, and generates system-wide parameters and a random pair of a master secret key MSK and a public key PK.*
- *$\mathsf{SK} \leftarrow \mathsf{KeyGen}(\mathsf{MSK}, k)$: The (probably) randomised secret key generation algorithm takes a master secret key MSK and a function key $k \in K$ as inputs, and computes a secret key SK for the function f_k.*
- *$C \leftarrow \mathsf{Encrypt}(\mathsf{PK}, x)$: The randomised encryption algorithm takes a public key PK and a message $x \in X$ as inputs, and generates a ciphertext C of the message x.*
- *$y \leftarrow \mathsf{Decrypt}(\mathsf{SK}, C)$: The (probably) deterministic decryption algorithm takes a secret key SK for a function f_k and a ciphertext C of a message x as inputs. The algorithm reveals $y = f_k(x) \in Y$ from the ciphertext C, and outputs it.*

Indistinguishability-based security is considered in this paper. Precisely, we consider the Indistinguishability under Chosen Plaintext Attacks (IND-CPA security) formulated by Boneh et al. [8]. In the IND-CPA game formally defined as follows, an adaptive adversary $\mathcal{A}$ tries to distinguish a target ciphertext from two messages x_0 and x_1 chosen by $\mathcal{A}$.

Setup phase. The challenger $\mathcal{S}$ runs the system setup algorithm $\mathsf{Setup}(1^\lambda)$ to generate a key pair $(\mathsf{MSK}, \mathsf{PK})$, and passes the public key PK to $\mathcal{A}$.

Pre-challenge phase. $\mathcal{A}$ can adaptively query the key generation oracle $\mathcal{O}_{\mathsf{KeyGen}}$ with a function key $k \in K$ to obtain a secret key SK for the function f_k. At the same time, $\mathcal{S}$ stores the queried function key k in the list $\mathcal{K}$. The restriction is that $\mathcal{A}$ can only query the function key k such that $f_k(x_0) = f_k(x_1)$ where x_0 and x_1 are the messages chosen by $\mathcal{A}$ in the challenge phase. Otherwise, winning the game is trivial since $\mathsf{Decrypt}(\mathsf{SK}, C) \neq f_k(x_{1-b})$.

Challenge phase. At some point, $\mathcal{A}$ outputs two messages x_0 and x_1. $\mathcal{S}$ randomly picks $b \in_R \{0,1\}$, and generates a target ciphertext $C \leftarrow \mathsf{Encrypt}(\mathsf{PK}, x_b)$. After that, $\mathcal{S}$ passes the target ciphertext C to $\mathcal{A}$.

Post-challenge phase. $\mathcal{A}$ can further query the oracle $\mathcal{O}_{\mathsf{KeyGen}}$ as in the pre-challenge phase with the same restriction.

Guessing phase. Eventually, $\mathcal{A}$ outputs an educated guess b'. If $b = b'$, $\mathcal{A}$ wins.

The advantage of the adversary $\mathcal{A}$ winning the IND-CPA game is

$$\mathsf{Adv}_{\mathcal{A}}^{\mathrm{IND\text{-}CPA}} = \left| \Pr\left[b = b' \mid \forall k \in \mathcal{K},\ f_k(x_0) = f_k(x_1) \right] - \frac{1}{2} \right|$$

Definition 8 (IND-CPA Security). *An FE scheme is Indistinguishable under Chosen Plaintext Attacks (IND-CPA) if the advantage $\mathsf{Adv}_{\mathcal{A}}^{\mathrm{IND\text{-}CPA}}$ for all adversary $\mathcal{A}$ winning the IND-CPA game in the polynomial time is a negligible function.*

3 Hierarchical Functional Encryption for Linear Transformations

3.1 Definition

In [5,9,11], the hierarchical functional encryption (HFE) is defined as a normal functional encryption with an extra delegation algorithm Delegate. The (probably) randomised algorithm $\mathsf{SK}_{f'\circ f} \leftarrow \mathsf{Delegate}(\mathsf{SK}_f, f')$ takes a secret key SK_f for a function $f : X \to Z \subset Y$, and an another function $f' : Z \to Z' \subset Y$ as inputs where Z, Z' are the images of the functions f, f' correspondingly. It generates a new secret key $\mathsf{SK}_{f'\circ f}$ for the composed function $f' \circ f : X \to Z' \subset Y$. By observing the key generation algorithm $\mathsf{SK}_{f_k} \leftarrow \mathsf{KeyGen}(\mathsf{MSK}, k)$ and the delegation algorithm $\mathsf{SK}_{f'\circ f} \leftarrow \mathsf{Delegate}(\mathsf{SK}_f, f')$, we find that the algorithm KeyGen is actually a special case of the algorithm Delegate when the master secret key MSK is considered as a secret key $\mathsf{SK}_{\mathsf{id}}$ of an identity function. More precisely, we have $\mathsf{KeyGen}(\mathsf{MSK}, k) \overset{\mathrm{def}}{=} \mathsf{Delegate}(\mathsf{SK}_{\mathsf{id}}, f_k) \to \mathsf{SK}_{f_k \circ \mathsf{id}} = \mathsf{SK}_{f_k}$ with $\mathsf{MSK} \overset{\mathrm{def}}{=} \mathsf{SK}_{\mathsf{id}}$. Therefore, the duplicated algorithm can be removed, and it becomes a more natural generalisation of hierarchical identity based encryption (HIBE) [7] as there is no Delegate algorithm in HIBE. The refined HFE is formalised as follows.

Definition 9 (Hierarchical Functional Encryption). *A hierarchical functional encryption (HFE) for a function class* $\mathcal{F} = \{f_k : X \to Y \mid k \in K\}$ *consists of the following four polynomial time algorithms:*

$$(\mathsf{PK}, \mathsf{MSK}) \leftarrow \mathsf{Setup}(1^\lambda), \qquad \mathsf{SK}_{f' \circ f} \leftarrow \mathsf{KeyGen}(\mathsf{SK}_f, f'),$$
$$C \leftarrow \mathsf{Encrypt}(\mathsf{PK}, x), \qquad y = f(x) \leftarrow \mathsf{Decrypt}(\mathsf{SK}_f, C).$$

While other three algorithms work as in Definition 7, the refined key generation algorithm KeyGen *takes a secret key for function* $f \in \mathcal{F} : X \to Z \subset Y$, *and a function* $f' : Z \to Z' \subset Y$ *as inputs such that* $f_k = f' \circ f \in \mathcal{F}$ *for some* $k \in K$. *The algorithm* KeyGen *outputs a secret key for the function* f_k. *The master secret key is defined as a secret key for the identity function (*$\mathsf{MSK} \overset{\text{def}}{=} \mathsf{SK}_{\mathsf{id}}$*) and thus it can be directly used in the decryption algorithm* $\mathsf{Decrypt}$.

Remark 1. The secret key holders should be careful in the secret key generation. If the delegation function f' is invertible, the newly generated secret key $\mathsf{SK}_{f' \circ f} \leftarrow \mathsf{KeyGen}(\mathsf{SK}_f, f')$ is equivalent to the original secret key SK_f since

$$\mathsf{KeyGen}(\mathsf{SK}_{f' \circ f}, f'^{-1}) = \mathsf{SK}_{f'^{-1} \circ f' \circ f} = \mathsf{SK}_{\mathsf{id} \circ f} = \mathsf{SK}_f.$$

As the above operations can be done in the ideal world, it is not considered as a security issue in the real world, even with a secure scheme.

Since the syntax is similar to the normal FE, the definition of the IND-CPA security (Definition 8) can be re-used for HFE. When the adversary $\mathcal{A}$ query the key generation oracle $\mathcal{O}_{\mathsf{KeyGen}}$ for functions f and f' to obtain a new secret key $\mathsf{SK}_{f' \circ f}$ in HFE, it can be resolved by querying the original oracle $\mathcal{O}_{\mathsf{KeyGen}}$ with a function key k since $f_k = f' \circ f \in \mathcal{F}$ for some $k \in K$. Using the security model of FE for HFE, we implicitly require that the secret key and the delegated key have the same distribution.

With the refined definition of HFE, we derive the syntax of our HFE for Linear Transformations.

Definition 10 (Hierarchical Functional Encryption for Linear Transformations). *Let* $\mathbb{R}$ *be a ring,* $K = \{\mathbf{A} \mid \mathbf{A} \in \mathbb{R}^{i \times \delta}, i \in \mathbb{Z}^+\}$, $X = \mathbb{R}^{\delta \times \gamma}$, *and* $Y = \{\mathbf{Y} \mid \mathbf{Y} \in \mathbb{R}^{i \times \gamma}, i \in \mathbb{Z}^+\}$. *The universal function* $f : K \times X \to Y$ *is defined as* $f_{\mathbf{A}} : \mathbf{X} \mapsto \mathbf{A}\mathbf{X}$. *In short, the transformation function* $f_{\mathbf{A}}$ *is simply denoted by the internal transformation matrix* $\mathbf{A}$. *A hierarchical functional encryption for linear transformation (HFE-LT) is an HFE for a function class* $\mathcal{F} = \{f_k : X \to Y \mid k \in K\}$, *consisting of the following four polynomial time algorithms:*

$$(\mathsf{PK}, \mathsf{MSK}) \leftarrow \mathsf{Setup}(1^\lambda, 1^\delta, 1^\gamma), \qquad \mathsf{SK}_{\mathbf{BA}} \leftarrow \mathsf{KeyGen}(\mathsf{SK}_{\mathbf{A}}, \mathbf{B}),$$
$$C \leftarrow \mathsf{Encrypt}(\mathsf{PK}, \mathbf{X}), \qquad \mathbf{Y} = \mathbf{A}\mathbf{X} \leftarrow \mathsf{Decrypt}(\mathsf{SK}_{\mathbf{A}}, C).$$

It is clear that the system setup algorithm Setup specifies the dimensions of K, X, and Y by the extra inputs δ and γ. Again, the master secret key is a secret key for the identity matrix that $\mathsf{MSK} \stackrel{\text{def}}{=} \mathsf{SK_I}$. Since the properties of ring are not fully used in matrix multiplication, the above definition can be extended to any algebraic structure (even different structures for K, X, and Y) as long as $(\mathbf{BA})\mathbf{X} = \mathbf{B}(\mathbf{AX})$ with all operations valid. In addition to the key generation algorithm KeyGen, if the delegation matrix $\mathbf{B}$ is invertible, the newly generated key is equivalent to the original key since $\mathsf{KeyGen}(\mathsf{KeyGen}(\mathsf{SK_A}, \mathbf{B}), \mathbf{B}^{-1}) = \mathsf{SK_{B^{-1}BA}} = \mathsf{SK_A}$.

3.2 Construction

In this subsection, we propose a generic construction of HFE-LT from HPS. It is strongly recommended that the readers should read Sect. 2.1 in advance since our construction is based on the notations defined in Sect. 2.1.

Let $\varXi = (\mathsf{Setup}, \mathsf{SKGen}, \mathsf{PKGen}, \mathsf{Hash}, \mathsf{PHash})$ be a diverse HPS associated with an SMP instance $\varLambda = (X, L, W, R)$ and further spaces $(K, S, \varPi)$. The HPS $\varXi$ is required to have hash linearity for completeness and key linearity for soundness. Let $\xi \in \varPi \setminus \{0\}$ be an element derived from the diversity of the HPS $\varXi$, and n be the order of the group $\varPi' = \{a\xi \mid a \in \mathbb{Z}\}$. Our hierarchical functional encryption for linear transformation with $\mathbb{R} = \mathbb{Z}_n$ works as follows[1].

- $(\mathsf{PK}, \mathsf{MSK}) \leftarrow \mathsf{Setup}(1^\lambda, 1^\delta, 1^\gamma)$: Given a security parameter 1^λ and the size $\delta \times \gamma$ of message matrices, the system setup algorithm generates a system-wide parameter $\mathsf{param} \leftarrow \varXi.\mathsf{Setup}(1^\lambda)$. Then the algorithm generates a key matrix $\mathbf{K_I}$ of size $\delta \times \gamma$ as the core part of the secret key of the identity matrix $\mathbf{I}_\delta \in \mathbb{Z}_n^{\delta \times \delta}$ by invoking $\varXi.\mathsf{SKGen}(\mathsf{param})$ for $\delta \times \gamma$ times. After that, the algorithm generates the corresponding public keys $\mathbf{P} = \varXi.\mathsf{PKGen}(\mathbf{K_I})$. The full secret key for the identity matrix is packed as $\mathsf{SK_I} = (\mathbf{I}_\delta, \mathbf{K_I})$. Finally, the algorithm publishes $\mathbf{P}$ as the public key PK, and keeps $\mathsf{SK_I}$ as the master secret key MSK.

$$\mathsf{param} \leftarrow \varXi.\mathsf{Setup}(1^\lambda), \quad k_{i,j} \leftarrow \varXi.\mathsf{SKGen}(\mathsf{param}),$$

$$\mathbf{K_I} = \begin{bmatrix} k_{1,1} & \cdots & k_{1,\gamma} \\ \vdots & \ddots & \vdots \\ k_{\delta,1} & \cdots & k_{\delta,\gamma} \end{bmatrix} \in K^{\delta \times \gamma}, \quad \mathbf{P} = \varXi.\mathsf{PKGen}(\mathbf{K_I}), \quad \mathsf{SK_I} = (\mathbf{I}_\delta, \mathbf{K_I}).$$

return $(\mathsf{PK}, \mathsf{MSK}) = (\mathbf{P}, \mathsf{SK_I})$.

- $\mathsf{SK_{BA}} \leftarrow \mathsf{KeyGen}(\mathsf{SK_A}, \mathbf{B})$: In the key generation algorithm, the algorithm recognises the secret key $\mathsf{SK_A}$ for the matrix $\mathbf{A}$. If the secret key is not in the form of $\mathsf{SK_A} = (\mathbf{A}, \mathbf{K_A}) \in \mathbb{Z}_n^{m \times \delta} \times K^{m \times \gamma}$ for some $m \in \mathbb{Z}^+$, the algorithm returns $\bot$ for failure indication. The algorithm also checks the validity of the parameter $\mathbf{B} \in \mathbb{Z}_n^{m' \times m}$ for some $m' \in \mathbb{Z}^+$. If all parameters are valid and compatible, the algorithm computes and returns a secret key

---

[1] From the key linearity and hash linearity, we have that $|K| \geq |\varPi| \geq |\varPi'| = n$, and n could be maximised by summing two or more elements derived from the diversity if those elements generate different groups.

$\mathsf{SK_{BA}} = (\mathbf{BA}, \mathbf{BK_A}) \in \mathbb{Z}_n^{m' \times \delta} \times K^{m' \times \gamma}$ for the matrix $\mathbf{BA}$. Remark that $\mathbf{BK_A} = \mathbf{BAK_I}$.

- $C \leftarrow \mathsf{Encrypt}(\mathsf{PK}, \mathbf{X})$: To encrypt a matrix $\mathbf{X} \in \mathbb{Z}_n^{\delta \times \gamma}$, the algorithm randomly samples a word x in the language L with a witness w such that $(x, w) \in R$. After that, the algorithm computes the core part of the ciphertext $\mathbf{C} = \mathbf{X}\xi + \Xi.\mathsf{PHash}(\mathbf{P}, x, w) \in \varPi^{\delta \times \gamma}$. The full ciphertext is $C = (x, \mathbf{C})$.

$$(x, w) \in_R R, \quad \mathbf{C} = \mathbf{X}\xi + \Xi.\mathsf{PHash}(\mathbf{P}, x, w).$$

return $C = (x, \mathbf{C})$.

- $\mathbf{Y} \leftarrow \mathsf{Decrypt}(\mathsf{SK_A}, C)$: To decrypt a ciphertext $C = (x, \mathbf{C}) \in X \times \varPi^{\delta \times \gamma}$ with a secret key $\mathsf{SK_A} = (\mathbf{A}, \mathbf{K_A}) \in \mathbb{Z}_n^{m \times \delta} \times K^{m \times \gamma}$, the algorithm computes an intermediate value $\mathbf{D} = \mathbf{AC} - \Xi.\mathsf{Hash}(\mathbf{K_A}, x) \in \varPi^{m \times \gamma}$. After that, the algorithm find the scalar of $\mathbf{D}$ with the base ξ as the final decryption result $\mathbf{Y} = \mathrm{sca}_\xi(\mathbf{D}) \in \mathbb{Z}_n^{m \times \gamma}$.

$$\mathbf{D} = \mathbf{AC} - \Xi.\mathsf{Hash}(\mathbf{K_A}, x).$$

return $\mathbf{Y} = \mathrm{sca}_\xi(\mathbf{D})$.

We show that our construction is complete by verifying the decryption algorithm. Starting from the intermediate value $\mathbf{D}$, we have

$$\begin{aligned} \mathbf{D} = \mathbf{AC} - \Xi.\mathsf{Hash}(\mathbf{K_A}, x) &= \mathbf{A}(\mathbf{X}\xi + \Xi.\mathsf{PHash}(\mathbf{P}, x, w)) - \Xi.\mathsf{Hash}(\mathbf{K_A}, x) \\ &= \mathbf{AX}\xi + \mathbf{A}\Xi.\mathsf{PHash}(\mathbf{P}, x, w) - \Xi.\mathsf{Hash}(\mathbf{K_A}, x) \\ &= \mathbf{AX}\xi + \mathbf{A}\Xi.\mathsf{Hash}(\mathbf{K_I}, x) - \Xi.\mathsf{Hash}(\mathbf{K_A}, x) \\ &= \mathbf{AX}\xi + \Xi.\mathsf{Hash}(\mathbf{AK_I}, x) - \Xi.\mathsf{Hash}(\mathbf{AK_I}, x) = \mathbf{AX}\xi. \end{aligned}$$

Then the completeness of our construction is verified by

$$\mathbf{Y} = \mathrm{sca}_\xi(\mathbf{D}) = \mathrm{sca}_\xi(\mathbf{AX}\xi) = \mathbf{AX}.$$

3.3 Security Proof

Theorem 1. *The HFE-LT construction in Sect. 3.2 is IND-CPA secure if the SMP instance Λ associated with the underlying diverse HPS Ξ is hard.*

Proof. In this proof, we require the underlying HPS Ξ to have diversity instead of smoothness introduced by Cramer and Shoup [12], which is used to prove the security of an IND-CPA public key encryption scheme. The reason is that the smoothness only prevents the information leakage of the hashing value from the public hash keys but not from the secret hash keys. In other words, the adversary may be able to distinguish ciphertexts via secret keys obtained from the key generation algorithm KeyGen of the HFE-LT scheme. If we follow the proof in [12] that the hash values are replaced with random values, the adversary can recognise this game modification with overwhelming probability by running the decryption algorithm since the adversary finds that $\mathsf{Decrypt}(\mathsf{SK_A}, C) \neq \mathbf{AX_0}$ and $\mathsf{Decrypt}(\mathsf{SK_A}, C) \neq \mathbf{AX_1}$ where C is the challenge ciphertext of $\mathbf{X_0}$ or $\mathbf{X_1}$.

To prove the theorem, we show that an simulator $\mathcal{S}$ can be constructed to solve the SMP instance $\Lambda = (X, L, W, R)$ in polynomial time with non-negligible probability if an adversary $\mathcal{A}$ can win the IND-CPA game with non-negligible probability.

Let (Λ, x^*) be the actual subset membership problem challenged to the simulator $\mathcal{S}$. The objective of the simulator $\mathcal{S}$ is to distinguish whether $x^* \in L$ or $x^* \in X \backslash L$ with x^* sampled from L or $X \backslash L$ with equal probability. Following the IND-CPA game (defined in Sect. 2.4), the simulator $\mathcal{S}$ runs the system setup algorithm Setup to generate a key pair $(\mathsf{PK}, \mathsf{MSK}) = (\mathbf{P}, \mathsf{SK_I})$, and passes the public key PK to the adversary $\mathcal{A}$ in the setup phase. During the pre-challenge phase, the simulator $\mathcal{S}$ invokes the key generation algorithm KeyGen with the master secret key $\mathsf{MSK} = \mathsf{SK_I}$ to answer the key generation oracle $\mathcal{O}_{\mathsf{KeyGen}}$ directly. The restriction for the adversary $\mathcal{A}$ is that $\mathcal{A}$ can only query the secret keys for $\mathbf{A}$ such that $\mathbf{AX_0} = \mathbf{AX_1}$ where $\mathbf{X_0}$ and $\mathbf{X_1}$ are the target message matrices output by $\mathcal{A}$ in the challenge phase.

At some point, the adversary $\mathcal{A}$ outputs two target message matrices $\mathbf{X_0}$ and $\mathbf{X_1}$, changing the game state to the challenge phase. The simulator $\mathcal{S}$ tosses a random coin $b \in_R \{0, 1\}$, and computes the target ciphertext $C^* = (x^*, \mathbf{C}^*)$ different to the encryption algorithm Encrypt where

$$\mathbf{C}^* = \mathbf{X}_b \xi + \Xi.\mathsf{Hash}(\mathbf{K_I}, x^*).$$

After that, the target ciphertext C^* is sent to the adversary $\mathcal{A}$. In the post-challenge phase, the adversary $\mathcal{A}$ is allowed to access the oracle $\mathcal{O}_{\mathsf{KeyGen}}$ as before with the same restriction. Eventually, the adversary $\mathcal{A}$ outputs a bit b' in the guessing phase. If $b = b'$, the adversary $\mathcal{A}$ wins, and the simulator $\mathcal{S}$ outputs 1. Otherwise, the simulator $\mathcal{S}$ outputs 0 instead. Finally, the simulator $\mathcal{S}$ halts and completes the simulation.

After the simulation, we analyse the probabilities in the style of [12, 19]. Let E_L be the event that $\mathcal{S}$ outputs 1 conditioned on $x^* \in L$, and $E_{X \backslash L}$ be the event that $\mathcal{S}$ outputs 1 conditioned on $x^* \in X \backslash L$. The advantage $\mathsf{Adv}_\mathcal{S}^{\mathsf{SMP}}$ of solving the subset membership problem is

$$\mathsf{Adv}_\mathcal{S}^{\mathsf{SMP}} \geq |\Pr[1 \leftarrow \mathcal{S} \mid x^* \in L] - \Pr[1 \leftarrow \mathcal{S} \mid x^* \in X \backslash L]| = \left|\Pr[E_L] - \Pr[E_{X \backslash L}]\right| \tag{1}$$

For the case of $x^* \in L$, the simulation is perfect since the algorithms $\Xi.\mathsf{Hash}$ and $\Xi.\mathsf{PHash}$ are equivalent. From the IND-CPA game, we have

$$\mathsf{Adv}_\mathcal{A}^{\mathsf{IND\text{-}CPA}} = \left|\Pr[E_L] - \frac{1}{2}\right|. \tag{2}$$

For the case of $x^* \in X \backslash L$, we show that the hidden bit b is independent from the adversary $\mathcal{A}$'s view that

$$\Pr[E_{X \backslash L}] = \frac{1}{2} \tag{3}$$

Since the element ξ is an element derived from the the diversity of the HPS Ξ, we have that there exists a $k \in K$ such that $\mathsf{PKGen}(k) = 0$ and $\Xi.\mathsf{Hash}(k, x^*) = \xi$

where k is not required to be efficiently computable. Let $\mathbf{\Gamma} = (\mathbf{X}_b - \mathbf{X}_{1-b}) \cdot k \in K^{\delta \times \gamma}$. We have

$$\Xi.\mathsf{Hash}(\mathbf{\Gamma}, x^*) = \Xi.\mathsf{Hash}((\mathbf{X}_b - \mathbf{X}_{1-b}) \cdot k, x^*) = (\mathbf{X}_b - \mathbf{X}_{1-b}) \cdot \Xi.\mathsf{Hash}(k, x^*)$$
$$= (\mathbf{X}_b - \mathbf{X}_{1-b})\xi = \mathbf{X}_b\xi - \mathbf{X}_{1-b}\xi.$$

Based on $\Xi.\mathsf{Hash}(\mathbf{\Gamma}, x^*) = \mathbf{X}_b\xi - \mathbf{X}_{1-b}\xi$, we argue that the target ciphertext C^* is not only a valid ciphertext of the message $\mathbf{X}_b$ under the key $\mathbf{K_I}$ but also a valid ciphertext of the message $\mathbf{X}_{1-b}$ under the key $\mathbf{K_I^*} = \mathbf{K_I} + \mathbf{\Gamma}$. More precisely, we have

$$C^* = \mathbf{X}_{1-b}\xi + \Xi.\mathsf{Hash}(\mathbf{K_I} + \mathbf{\Gamma}, x^*) = \mathbf{X}_{1-b}\xi + \Xi.\mathsf{Hash}(\mathbf{K_I}, x^*) + \Xi.\mathsf{Hash}(\mathbf{\Gamma}, x^*)$$
$$= \mathbf{X}_{1-b}\xi + \Xi.\mathsf{Hash}(\mathbf{K_I}, x^*) + \mathbf{X}_b\xi - \mathbf{X}_{1-b}\xi = \mathbf{X}_b\xi + \Xi.\mathsf{Hash}(\mathbf{K_I}, x^*).$$

Furthermore, we show that it is impossible for the adversary $\mathcal{A}$ to distinguish $\mathbf{K_I}$ and $\mathbf{K_I^*}$ from the public key $\mathbf{P}$ or the secret keys $\mathbf{K_A}$ obtained from the key generation oracle $\mathcal{O}_{\mathsf{KeyGen}}$. Since $\Xi.\mathsf{PKGen}(k) = 0$ from the diversity, the keys $\mathbf{K_I}$ and $\mathbf{K_I^*}$ have the same public key

$$\mathbf{P} = \Xi.\mathsf{PKGen}(\mathbf{K_I} + \mathbf{\Gamma}) = \Xi.\mathsf{PKGen}(\mathbf{K_I}) + \Xi.\mathsf{PKGen}(\mathbf{\Gamma})$$
$$= \Xi.\mathsf{PKGen}(\mathbf{K_I}) + \Xi.\mathsf{PKGen}((\mathbf{X}_b - \mathbf{X}_{1-b}) \cdot k)$$
$$= \Xi.\mathsf{PKGen}(\mathbf{K_I}) + (\mathbf{X}_b - \mathbf{X}_{1-b}) \cdot \Xi.\mathsf{PKGen}(k) = \Xi.\mathsf{PKGen}(\mathbf{K_I}).$$

Since the adversary $\mathcal{A}$ is restricted that $\mathcal{A}$ can only query the secret keys for $\mathbf{A}$ such that $\mathbf{AX}_0 = \mathbf{AX}_1 \iff \mathbf{A}(\mathbf{X}_0 - \mathbf{X}_1) = 0$, the keys $\mathbf{K_I}$ and $\mathbf{K_I^*}$ generate the same secret key $\mathbf{K_A}$ for such a matrix $\mathbf{A}$ for the adversary $\mathcal{A}$ as

$$\mathbf{K_A} = \mathbf{A}(\mathbf{K_I} + \mathbf{\Gamma}) = \mathbf{AK_I} + \mathbf{A\Gamma} = \mathbf{AK_I} + \mathbf{A}(\mathbf{X}_b - \mathbf{X}_{1-b}) \cdot k = \mathbf{AK_I}.$$

Hence, the hidden bit b is independent from the adversary $\mathcal{A}$'s view.

By combining Eqs. (1), (2) and (3), we have the following inequality and complete the proof.

$$\mathsf{Adv}_{\mathcal{A}}^{\text{IND-CPA}} \leq \mathsf{Adv}_{\mathcal{S}}^{\text{SMP}}.$$

3.4   Extensions

In the Definition 9, the delegation is performed by one party with a secret key SK_f and a delegation function f' so that the delegated party can learn $f'(f(x))$. In order not to be restricted to nested hierarchy, the HFE can be extended to allow delegation performed by multiple parties. Precisely, n secret key holders with $\mathsf{SK}_{f_1}, \dots, \mathsf{SK}_{f_n}$ can work together to generate a secret key SK_{f^*} for a function f^* defined as $f^*(x) = f'(f_1(x), \dots, f_n(x))$ where f' is a delegation function, which takes n inputs. The extended HFE is formalised as follows.

Definition 11 (Extended Hierarchical Functional Encryption). *An extended hierarchical functional encryption (eHFE) for a function class* $\mathcal{F} = \{f_k : X \to Y \mid k \in K\}$ *consists of the following four polynomial time algorithms:*

$$(\mathsf{PK}, \mathsf{MSK}) \leftarrow \mathsf{Setup}(1^\lambda), \qquad \mathsf{SK}_{f_k} \leftarrow \mathsf{KeyGen}(\mathsf{SK}_{f_{k_1}}, \ldots \mathsf{SK}_{f_{k_n}}, f'),$$

$$C \leftarrow \mathsf{Encrypt}(\mathsf{PK}, x), \quad y = f(x) \leftarrow \mathsf{Decrypt}(\mathsf{SK}_f, C).$$

While all other components work as in Definition 9, the extended key generation algorithm KeyGen *takes* n *secret keys for function* $f_{k_i} \in \mathcal{F} : X \to Z_i \subset Y$, *and a function* $f' : Z_1 \times \cdots \times Z_n \to Z' \subset Y$ *as inputs such that* $f_k(x) \stackrel{\text{def}}{=} f'(f_{k_1}(x), \ldots, f_{k_2}(x))$ *and* $f_k \in \mathcal{F}$ *for some* $k \in K$. *The algorithm* KeyGen *outputs a secret key for the function* f_k. *It is worth noting the number* n *of parameters of the algorithm* KeyGen *is not fixed by the system setup algorithm* Setup.

Similar to HFE, the definition of the IND-CPA security (Definition 8) can also be applied to eHFE with the same method to resolve the queries to the key generation oracle $\mathcal{O}_{\mathsf{KeyGen}}$. Based on Definitions 10 and 11, we derive the syntax of our extended HFE-LT.

Definition 12 (Extended HFE-LT). *Let* $\mathbb{R}$ *be a ring,* $K = \{\mathbf{A} \mid \mathbf{A} \in \mathbb{R}^{i \times \delta}, i \in \mathbb{Z}^+\}$, $X = \mathbb{R}^{\delta \times \gamma}$, *and* $Y = \{\mathbf{Y} \mid \mathbf{Y} \in \mathbb{R}^{i \times \gamma}, i \in \mathbb{Z}^+\}$. *The universal function* $f : K \times X \to Y$ *is defined as* $f_{\mathbf{A}} : \mathbf{X} \mapsto \mathbf{AX}$. *An extended hierarchical functional encryption for linear transformation (eHFE-LT) is an eHFE for a function class* $\mathcal{F} = \{f_k : X \to Y \mid k \in K\}$, *consisting of the following four polynomial time algorithms:*

$$(\mathsf{PK}, \mathsf{MSK}) \leftarrow \mathsf{Setup}(1^\lambda, 1^\delta, 1^\gamma), \qquad \mathsf{SK}_{\mathbf{B}} \leftarrow \mathsf{KeyGen}(\mathsf{SK}_{\mathbf{A}_1}, \ldots, \mathsf{SK}_{\mathbf{A}_n}, \mathbf{T}),$$

$$C \leftarrow \mathsf{Encrypt}(\mathsf{PK}, \mathbf{X}), \quad \mathbf{Y} = \mathbf{AX} \leftarrow \mathsf{Decrypt}(\mathsf{SK}_{\mathbf{A}}, C).$$

In the key generation algorithm KeyGen, *the resulted transformation matrix is calculated as*

$$\mathbf{B} = \mathbf{T} \left(\mathbf{A}_1^\top \mid \cdots \mid \mathbf{A}_n^\top \right)^\top.$$

The construction of our eHFE-LT scheme is exactly the same as the HFE-LT scheme in Sect. 3.2 except the key generation algorithm. The idea of constructing the new key generation algorithm is simple due to the special structure of the secret keys that we combine the keys $\mathsf{SK}_{\mathbf{A}_1}, \ldots, \mathsf{SK}_{\mathbf{A}_\ell}$ to be a new key $\mathsf{SK}_{\mathbf{A}}$ where $\mathbf{A} = \left(\mathbf{A}_1^\top \mid \cdots \mid \mathbf{A}_\ell^\top \right)^\top$, and then runs the original key generation algorithm $\mathsf{KeyGen}(\mathsf{SK}_{\mathbf{A}}, \mathbf{T})$ to obtain the final key $\mathsf{SK}_{\mathbf{B}}$. More precisely, we have

- $\mathsf{SK}_{\mathbf{B}} \leftarrow \mathsf{KeyGen}(\mathsf{SK}_{\mathbf{A}_1}, \ldots, \mathsf{SK}_{\mathbf{A}_\ell}, \mathbf{T})$: Given ℓ secret keys for $\mathbf{A}_i \in \mathbb{Z}_n^{m_i \times \delta}$, the algorithm checks the validity of $\mathbf{T} \in \mathbb{Z}_n^{m' \times \sum_{i=1}^{\ell} m_i}$ for some $m' \in \mathbb{Z}^+$. Then it computes

$$\mathbf{B} = \mathbf{T} \left(\mathbf{A}_1^\top \mid \cdots \mid \mathbf{A}_\ell^\top \right)^\top, \quad \mathbf{K}_{\mathbf{B}} = \mathbf{T} \left(\mathbf{K}_{\mathbf{A}_1}^\top \mid \cdots \mid \mathbf{K}_{\mathbf{A}_\ell}^\top \right)^\top.$$

return $\mathsf{SK}_{\mathbf{B}} = (\mathbf{B}, \mathbf{K}_{\mathbf{B}}) \in \mathbb{Z}_n^{m' \times \delta} \times K^{m' \times \gamma}$.

Theorem 2. *The proposed eHFE-LT construction in Sect. 3.4 is IND-CPA secure if the SMP instance Λ associated with the underlying diverse HPS Ξ is hard.*

Proof. The proof follows the same lines as in Sect. 3.3 and is omitted.

4   Instantiations

In this section, we instantiate our generic HFE-LT construction from the Decisional Diffie-Hellman (DDH) problem and from the Decisional Composite Residuosity (DCR) problem. Remark that the HFE-LT instantiations can be easily converted to eHFE-LT instantiations as discussed in Sect. 3.4. For better readability, we use multiplication in this section instead of addition in the previous sections for the group operations related to HPS. Therefore, all scalar multiplications on groups related to HPS are replaced by exponentiations.

4.1   HFE-LT from DDH

Definition 13 (Decisional Diffie-Hellman problem). *Let $\mathbb{G}$ be a cyclic multiplicative group of prime order p where $|p| = \lambda$ and λ is the security parameter. Let $a, b \in_R \mathbb{Z}_p$, $g, Z \in_R \mathbb{G}$. Given two probability distributions $\mathcal{D}_{\mathrm{DDH}} = \{(g, g^a, g^b, g^{ab})\}$ and $\mathcal{D}_R = \{(g, g^a, g^b, Z)\}$, there is an algorithm $\mathcal{A}$ that distinguishes $\mathcal{D}_{\mathrm{DDH}}$ and $\mathcal{D}_R$ with advantage:*

$$\mathsf{Adv}_{\mathcal{A}}^{\mathrm{DDH}} = |\Pr[1 \leftarrow \mathcal{A}(D \in_R \mathcal{D}_{\mathrm{DDH}})] - \Pr[1 \leftarrow \mathcal{A}(D \in_R \mathcal{D}_R \setminus \mathcal{D}_{\mathrm{DDH}})]|$$

Let $g_1, g_2, x_1, x_2 \in_R \mathcal{D}, w \in_R \mathbb{Z}_p$. The above distributions can be represented as $\mathcal{D}_{\mathrm{DDH}} = \{(g_1, g_2, g_1^w, g_2^w)\}$ and $\mathcal{D}_R = \{g_1, g_2, x_1, x_2\}$. Thus fixed on g_1, g_2, the DDH problem is an SMP problem where $X = \mathbb{G}^2$, $L = \{g_1^w, g_2^w\} \subset X$, and $W = \mathbb{Z}_p$. The DDH problem is assumed hard that $\mathsf{Adv}_{\mathcal{A}}^{\mathrm{DDH}}$ is negligible. From [12], we review the corresponding HPS construction as follows with $K = \mathbb{Z}_p^2$, $S = \Pi = \mathbb{G}$.

- param $\leftarrow$ Setup(1^λ): $g_1, g_2 \in_R \mathbb{G}$, return param $= (\mathbb{G}, g_1, g_2)$.
- SK $\leftarrow$ SKGen(param): return SK $= (k_1, k_2) \in_R \mathbb{Z}_p^2$.
- PK $\leftarrow$ PKGen(SK): return PK $= g_1^{k_1} g_2^{k_2}$.
- $\pi \leftarrow$ Hash(SK, x): $(x_1, x_2) \leftarrow x$, return $\pi = x_1^{k_1} x_2^{k_2}$.
- $\pi \leftarrow$ PHash(PK, x, w): return $\pi = $ PK^w.

From [19], the above HPS construction has key linearity, hash linearity, and diversity with g_1 as a derived element[2].

---

[2] All elements in $\mathbb{G}$ are elements derived from the diversity.

Let $\xi = g_1$. Our HFE-LT instantiation of $\mathbb{R} = \mathbb{Z}_p$ works as follows.

- $(\mathsf{PK}, \mathsf{MSK}) \leftarrow \mathsf{Setup}(1^\lambda, 1^\delta, 1^\gamma)$:

$$g_1, g_2 \in \mathbb{G}, \quad \mathbf{K_I} = \begin{bmatrix} (k_{1,1,1}, k_{1,1,2}) & \cdots & (k_{1,\gamma,1}, k_{1,\gamma,2}) \\ \vdots & \ddots & \vdots \\ (k_{\delta,1,1}, k_{\delta,1,2}) & \cdots & (k_{\delta,\gamma,1}, k_{\delta,\gamma,2}) \end{bmatrix} \in_R (\mathbb{Z}_p^2)^{\delta \times \gamma},$$

$$\mathbf{P} = \begin{bmatrix} P_{1,1} & \cdots & P_{1,\gamma} \\ \vdots & \ddots & \vdots \\ P_{\delta,1} & \cdots & P_{\delta,\gamma} \end{bmatrix} \text{ s.t. } P_{i,j} = g_1^{k_{i,j,1}} g_2^{k_{i,j,2}}, \quad \mathsf{SK_I} = (\mathbf{I_\delta}, \mathbf{K_I}).$$

  return $(\mathsf{PK}, \mathsf{MSK}) = ((g_1, g_2, \mathbf{P}), \mathsf{SK_I})$.
- $\mathsf{SK_{BA}} \leftarrow \mathsf{KeyGen}(\mathsf{SK_A}, \mathbf{B})$: return $\mathsf{SK_{BA}} = (\mathbf{BA}, \mathbf{BK_A})$.
- $C \leftarrow \mathsf{Encrypt}(\mathsf{PK}, \mathbf{X})$:

$$w \in_R \mathbb{Z}_p, \quad x = (x_1, x_2) = (g_1^w, g_2^w), \quad \begin{bmatrix} X_{1,1} & \cdots & X_{1,\gamma} \\ \vdots & \ddots & \vdots \\ X_{\delta,1} & \cdots & X_{\delta,\gamma} \end{bmatrix} \leftarrow \mathbf{X} \in \mathbb{Z}_p^{\delta \times \gamma},$$

$$\mathbf{C} = \begin{bmatrix} C_{1,1} & \cdots & C_{1,\gamma} \\ \vdots & \ddots & \vdots \\ C_{\delta,1} & \cdots & C_{\delta,\gamma} \end{bmatrix} \text{ s.t. } C_{i,j} = \xi^{X_{i,j}} P_{i,j}^w = g_1^{X_{i,j}} P_{i,j}^w.$$

  return $C = (x, \mathbf{C})$.
- $\mathbf{Y} \leftarrow \mathsf{Decrypt}(\mathsf{SK_A}, C)$:

$$\begin{bmatrix} (k_{1,1,1}, k_{1,1,2}) & \cdots & (k_{1,\gamma,1}, k_{1,\gamma,2}) \\ \vdots & \ddots & \\ (k_{m,1,1}, k_{m,1,2}) & \cdots & (k_{m,\gamma,1}, k_{m,\gamma,2}) \end{bmatrix} \leftarrow \mathbf{K_A} \in (\mathbb{Z}_p^2)^{m \times \gamma},$$

$$\begin{bmatrix} A_{1,1} & \cdots & A_{1,\delta} \\ \vdots & \ddots & \vdots \\ A_{m,1} & \cdots & A_{m,\delta} \end{bmatrix} \leftarrow \mathbf{A} \in \mathbb{Z}_p^{m \times \delta},$$

$$\mathbf{D} = \begin{bmatrix} D_{1,1} & \cdots & D_{1,\gamma} \\ \vdots & \ddots & \vdots \\ D_{m,1} & \cdots & D_{m,\gamma} \end{bmatrix} \text{ s.t. } D_{i,j} = \frac{\prod_{l=1}^\delta C_{l,j}^{A_{i,l}}}{x_1^{k_{i,j,1}} x_2^{k_{i,j,2}}}.$$

  return $\mathbf{Y} = \log_\xi \mathbf{D} = \log_{g_1} \mathbf{D}$.

Remark the calculation of $\log_{g_1} \mathbf{D}$ can be done in polynomial time if the decryption space $\{\mathbf{Y}\}$ is polynomial sized.

4.2   HFE-LT Instantiation from DCR

Definition 14 (Decisional Composite Residuosity problem). *Let p, q be two safe primes such that $p = 2p' + 1$ and $q = 2q' + 1$ where p', q' are two primes of length λ bites and λ is the security parameter. Let $N = pq$, and $N' = p'q'$. We have that $\mathbb{Z}_{N^2}^* = \mathbb{G}_N \mathbb{G}_{N'} \mathbb{G}_2 \mathbb{G}_T$ where $\mathbb{G}_T$ is a group generated by $-1 \pmod{N^2}$. Let $P = \mathbb{G}_{N'} \mathbb{G}_2 \mathbb{G}_T \subset \mathbb{Z}_{N^2}^*$, $x \in_R P$, and $x' \in_R \mathbb{Z}_{N^2}^* \setminus P$. Given two probability distributions $\mathcal{D}_P = \{(N, x)\}$ and $\mathcal{D}_{\mathbb{Z}_{N^2}^* \setminus P} = \{(N, x')\}$, there is an algorithm $\mathcal{A}$ that distinguishes $\mathcal{D}_P$ and $\mathcal{D}_{\mathbb{Z}_{N^2}^* \setminus P}$ with advantage:*

$$\mathsf{Adv}_{\mathcal{A}}^{\mathrm{DCR}} = \left| \Pr[1 \leftarrow \mathcal{A}(D \in_R \mathcal{D}_P)] - \Pr[1 \leftarrow \mathcal{A}(D \in_R \mathcal{D}_{\mathbb{Z}_{N^2}^* \setminus P})] \right|$$

The DCR problem is assumed to be hard with negligible advantage $\mathsf{Adv}_{\mathcal{A}}^{\mathrm{DCR}}$. However, we do not use $(\mathbb{Z}_{N^2}^*, P)$ as (X, L) for several technical reasons. Instead, we set $X = \mathbb{G}_N \mathbb{G}_{N'}$ and $L = \mathbb{G}_{N'} \subset X$. According to the full version of [12], the resulted SMP problem with (X, L) is at least hard as the DCR problem. Slightly different from [12], we have the corresponding HPS construction as follows with $W = \{0, \ldots, \lfloor N/4 \rfloor\}$, $K = \{0, \ldots, \lfloor N^2/2 \rfloor\}$, $S = L = \mathbb{G}_{N'}$, and $\Pi = X = \mathbb{G}_N \mathbb{G}_{N'}$.

- param $\leftarrow$ Setup(1^λ): $\mu \in_R \mathbb{Z}_{N^2}^*, g = \mu^{2N} \pmod{N^2}$, return param $= (N, g)$.
- SK $\leftarrow$ SKGen(param): return SK $= k \in_R \{0, \ldots, \lfloor N^2/2 \rfloor\}$.
- PK $\leftarrow$ PKGen(SK): return PK $= g^k \pmod{N^2}$.
- $\pi \leftarrow$ Hash(SK, x): return $\pi = x^k \pmod{N^2}$.
- $\pi \leftarrow$ PHash(PK, $x = g^w, w$): return $\pi = \mathsf{PK}^w \pmod{N^2}$.

Remark that the value N in Setup is generated as described in Defintion 14 and g is a generator of $L = \mathbb{G}_{N'}$ with overwhelming probability.

The key linearity and hash linearity of the above HPS can be easily verified as $g^{k_1} g^{k_2} = g^{k_1 + k_2}$ and $x^{k_1} x^{k_2} = x^{k_1 + k_2}$. Let $\xi = 1 + N \pmod{N^2}$, which is a generator of $\mathbb{G}_N$ of order N. It is worth noting that $\xi^a = 1 + aN \pmod{N^2}$ and $\log_\xi x = \frac{x - 1 \bmod N^2}{N}$ for all $a \in \mathbb{Z}_N$ and $x \in \mathbb{G}_N$ where the division does not mean the multiplicative inverse but the division of integers. We show that the above HPS has diversity and ξ is a derived element such that $\forall x \in X \setminus L, \exists k \in K, \mathsf{PKGen}(k) = 1 \wedge \mathsf{Hash}(k, x) = \xi$ where 1 is the identity element 0 in Definition 6. Let $r = \left(\log_\xi x^{N'} \right)^{-1} \bmod N$ where $x^{N'} \in \mathbb{G}_N$ and the multiplicative inverse is computable for all $x \in \mathbb{G}_N \mathbb{G}_{N'}$ with overwhelming probability. Let $k = rN'$. Since g is a generator of $\mathbb{G}_{N'}$ of order N', we have $\mathsf{PKGen}(k) = g^k = g^{rN'} = 1 \pmod{N^2}$. Since $r^{-1} = \log_\xi x^{N'} \iff x^{N'} = \xi^{r^{-1}}$, we have $\mathsf{Hash}(k, x) = x^{rN'} = (x^{N'})^r = (\xi^{r^{-1}})^r = \xi$. Hence, the diversity is verified with the derived element $\xi = 1 + N \pmod{N^2}$.

Our HFE-LT instantiation of $\mathbb{R} = \mathbb{Z}_N$ works as follows[3]. Let $\xi = 1 + N \pmod{N^2}$.

---

[3] We do not fully use the key space (i.e. $|K| = \lfloor N^2/2 \rfloor > N$).

- $(\mathsf{PK}, \mathsf{MSK}) \leftarrow \mathsf{Setup}(1^\lambda, 1^\delta, 1^\gamma)$:

$$\mu \in_R \mathbb{Z}_{N^2}^*, \ g = \mu^{2N} \ (\mathrm{mod} \ N^2), \ \mathbf{K_I} = \begin{bmatrix} k_{1,1} \cdots k_{1,\gamma} \\ \vdots \ \ddots \ \vdots \\ k_{\delta,1} \cdots k_{\delta,\gamma} \end{bmatrix} \in_R \{0, \ldots, \lfloor N^2/2 \rfloor\}^{\delta \times \gamma},$$

$$\mathbf{P} = \begin{bmatrix} P_{1,1} \cdots P_{1,\gamma} \\ \vdots \ \ddots \ \vdots \\ P_{\delta,1} \cdots P_{\delta,\gamma} \end{bmatrix} \ \text{s.t.} \ P_{i,j} = g^{k_{i,j}} \ (\mathrm{mod} \ N^2), \quad \mathsf{SK_I} = (\mathbf{I_\delta}, \mathbf{K_I}).$$

  return $(\mathsf{PK}, \mathsf{MSK}) = ((N, g, \mathbf{P}), \mathsf{SK_I})$.
- $\mathsf{SK_{BA}} \leftarrow \mathsf{KeyGen}(\mathsf{SK_A}, \mathbf{B})$: return $\mathsf{SK_{BA}} = (\mathbf{BA}, \mathbf{BK_A})$ where $\mathbf{BK_A}$ is computed over $\mathbb{Z}$.
- $C \leftarrow \mathsf{Encrypt}(\mathsf{PK}, \mathbf{X})$:

$$w \in_R \{0, \ldots, \lfloor N/4 \rfloor\}, \quad x = g^w \ (\mathrm{mod} \ N^2), \quad \begin{bmatrix} X_{1,1} \cdots X_{1,\gamma} \\ \vdots \ \ddots \ \vdots \\ X_{\delta,1} \cdots X_{\delta,\gamma} \end{bmatrix} \leftarrow \mathbf{X} \in \mathbb{Z}_N^{\delta \times \gamma},$$

$$\mathbf{C} = \begin{bmatrix} C_{1,1} \cdots C_{1,\gamma} \\ \vdots \ \ddots \ \vdots \\ C_{\delta,1} \cdots C_{\delta,\gamma} \end{bmatrix} \ \text{s.t.} \ C_{i,j} = \xi^{X_{i,j}} P_{i,j}^w = (1 + X_{i,j} N) P_{i,j}^w \ (\mathrm{mod} \ N^2).$$

  return $C = (x, \mathbf{C})$.
- $\mathbf{Y} \leftarrow \mathsf{Decrypt}(\mathsf{SK_A}, C)$:

$$\begin{bmatrix} A_{1,1} \cdots A_{1,\delta} \\ \vdots \ \ddots \ \vdots \\ A_{m,1} \cdots A_{m,\delta} \end{bmatrix} \leftarrow \mathbf{A} \in \mathbb{Z}_N^{m \times \delta}, \quad \begin{bmatrix} k_{1,1} \cdots k_{1,\gamma} \\ \vdots \ \ddots \ \vdots \\ k_{m,1} \cdots k_{m,\gamma} \end{bmatrix} \leftarrow \mathbf{K_A} \in \mathbb{Z}^{m \times \gamma},$$

$$\mathbf{D} = \begin{bmatrix} D_{1,1} \cdots D_{1,\gamma} \\ \vdots \ \ddots \ \vdots \\ D_{m,1} \cdots D_{m,\gamma} \end{bmatrix} \ \text{s.t.} \ D_{i,j} = \frac{\prod_{l=1}^\delta C_{l,j}^{A_{i,l}}}{x^{k_{i,j}}} \ (\mathrm{mod} \ N^2),$$

$$\mathbf{Y} = \log_\xi \mathbf{D} = \begin{bmatrix} Y_{1,1} \cdots Y_{1,\gamma} \\ \vdots \ \ddots \ \vdots \\ Y_{m,1} \cdots Y_{m,\gamma} \end{bmatrix} \ \text{s.t.} \ Y_{i,j} = \frac{D_{i,j} - 1 \ \ \mathrm{mod} \ N^2}{N}.$$

  return $\mathbf{Y}$.

5   Conclusion

In this paper, we revisited and simplified the definition of HFE, and further extended it to eHFE. We derived the notion of HFE-LT from HFE (and eHFE-LT from eHFE), allowing matrix product evaluation. Furthermore, we proposed a generic construction of HFE-LT (and eHFE-LT) with IND-CPA security in the standard model from Hash Proof Systems with key and hash linearity, and diversity. To illustrate that our scheme is practical, we presented two concrete HFE-LT instantiations from the DDH and DCR assumptions.

This paper proposed a practical HFE construction for matrix product evaluation. It is still an open problem whether we could build a practical HFE for other functionalities and we leave it as our future work.

Acknowledgements. This work is supported by the National Natural Science Foundation of China under Grants 61502086 and 61572115, the foundation from Guangxi Colleges and Universities Key Laboratory of Cloud Computing and Complex Systems (No. YF16202) and the foundation from Guangxi Key Laboratory of Trusted Software (No. PF16116X).

References

1. Abdalla, M., Bourse, F., Caro, A.D., Pointcheval, D.: Better security for functional encryption for inner product evaluations. Cryptology ePrint Archive, Report 2016/011 (2016)
2. Abdalla, M., Bourse, F., Caro, A., Pointcheval, D.: Simple functional encryption schemes for inner products. In: Katz, J. (ed.) PKC 2015. LNCS, vol. 9020, pp. 733–751. Springer, Heidelberg (2015). doi:10.1007/978-3-662-46447-2_33
3. Abdalla, M., Raykova, M., Wee, H.: Multi-input inner-product functional encryption from pairings. Cryptology ePrint Archive, Report 2016/425 (2016)
4. Agrawal, S., Libert, B., Stehlé, D.: Fully secure functional encryption for inner products, from standard assumptions. In: Robshaw, M., Katz, J. (eds.) CRYPTO 2016. LNCS, vol. 9816, pp. 333–362. Springer, Heidelberg (2016). doi:10.1007/978-3-662-53015-3_12
5. Ananth, P., Boneh, D., Garg, S., Sahai, A., Zhandry, M.: Differing-inputs obfuscation and applications. Cryptology ePrint Archive, Report 2013/689 (2013)
6. Bishop, A., Jain, A., Kowalczyk, L.: Function-hiding inner product encryption. In: Iwata, T., Cheon, J.H. (eds.) ASIACRYPT 2015. LNCS, vol. 9452, pp. 470–491. Springer, Heidelberg (2015). doi:10.1007/978-3-662-48797-6_20
7. Boneh, D., Boyen, X., Goh, E.-J.: Hierarchical identity based encryption with constant size ciphertext. In: Cramer, R. (ed.) EUROCRYPT 2005. LNCS, vol. 3494, pp. 440–456. Springer, Heidelberg (2005). doi:10.1007/11426639_26
8. Boneh, D., Sahai, A., Waters, B.: Functional encryption: definitions and challenges. In: Ishai, Y. (ed.) TCC 2011. LNCS, vol. 6597, pp. 253–273. Springer, Heidelberg (2011). doi:10.1007/978-3-642-19571-6_16
9. Brakerski, Z., Segev, G.: Hierarchical functional encryption. Cryptology ePrint Archive, Report 2015/1011 (2015)
10. Bresson, E., Catalano, D., Pointcheval, D.: A simple public-key cryptosystem with a double trapdoor decryption mechanism and its applications. In: Laih, C.-S. (ed.) ASIACRYPT 2003. LNCS, vol. 2894, pp. 37–54. Springer, Heidelberg (2003). doi:10.1007/978-3-540-40061-5_3
11. Chandran, N., Goyal, V., Jain, A., Sahai, A.: Functional encryption: Decentralised and delegatable. Cryptology ePrint Archive, Report 2015/1017 (2015)
12. Cramer, R., Shoup, V.: Universal hash proofs and a paradigm for adaptive chosen ciphertext secure public-key encryption. In: Knudsen, L.R. (ed.) EUROCRYPT 2002. LNCS, vol. 2332, pp. 45–64. Springer, Heidelberg (2002). doi:10.1007/3-540-46035-7_4

13. Diffie, W., Hellman, M.: New directions in cryptography. IEEE Trans. Inf. Theor. **22**(6), 644–654 (1976)
14. Garg, S., Gentry, C., Halevi, S., Raykova, M., Sahai, A., Waters, B.: Candidate indistinguishability obfuscation and functional encryption for all circuits. Cryptology ePrint Archive, Report 2013/451 (2013)
15. Katz, J., Sahai, A., Waters, B.: Predicate encryption supporting disjunctions, polynomial equations, and inner products. In: Smart, N. (ed.) EUROCRYPT 2008. LNCS, vol. 4965, pp. 146–162. Springer, Heidelberg (2008). doi:10.1007/978-3-540-78967-3_9
16. Lewko, A., Okamoto, T., Sahai, A., Takashima, K., Waters, B.: Fully secure functional encryption: attribute-based encryption and (hierarchical) inner product encryption. In: Gilbert, H. (ed.) EUROCRYPT 2010. LNCS, vol. 6110, pp. 62–91. Springer, Heidelberg (2010). doi:10.1007/978-3-642-13190-5_4
17. Paillier, P.: Public-key cryptosystems based on composite degree residuosity classes. In: Stern, J. (ed.) EUROCRYPT 1999. LNCS, vol. 1592, pp. 223–238. Springer, Heidelberg (1999). doi:10.1007/3-540-48910-X_16
18. Regev, O.: On lattices, learning with errors, random linear codes, and cryptography. In: ACM Symposium on Theory of Computing - STOC 2005, pp. 84–93 (2005)
19. Zhang, S., Mu, Y., Yang, G.: Achieving IND-CCA security for functional encryption for inner products. In: Chen, K., Lin, D., Yung, M. (eds.) Inscrypt 2016. LNCS, vol. 10143, pp. 119–139. Springer, Cham (2017). doi:10.1007/978-3-319-54705-3_8

KDM-Secure Public-Key Encryption from Constant-Noise LPN

Shuai Han[1,2] and Shengli Liu[1,2,3($\boxtimes$)]

[1] Department of Computer Science and Engineering,
Shanghai Jiao Tong University, Shanghai 200240, China
{dalen17,slliu}@sjtu.edu.cn
[2] State Key Laboratory of Cryptology, P.O. Box 5159, Beijing 100878, China
[3] Westone Cryptologic Research Center, Beijing 100070, China

Abstract. The Learning Parity with Noise (LPN) problem has found many applications in cryptography due to its conjectured post-quantum hardness and simple algebraic structure. Over the years, constructions of different public-key primitives were proposed from LPN, but most of them are based on the LPN assumption with *low noise* rate rather than *constant noise* rate. A recent breakthrough was made by Yu and Zhang (Crypto'16), who constructed the first Public-Key Encryption (PKE) from constant-noise LPN. However, the problem of designing a PKE with *Key-Dependent Message* (KDM) security from constant-noise LPN is still open.

In this paper, we present the first PKE with KDM-security assuming certain sub-exponential hardness of constant-noise LPN, where the number of users is predefined. The technical tool is two types of *multi-fold LPN on squared-log entropy*, one having *independent secrets* and the other *independent sample subspaces*. We establish the hardness of the multi-fold LPN variants on constant-noise LPN. Two squared-logarithmic entropy sources for multi-fold LPN are carefully chosen, so that our PKE is able to achieve correctness and KDM-security simultaneously.

Keywords: Learning parity with noise · Key-dependent message security · Public-key encryption

1 Introduction

The search Learning Parity with Noise (LPN) problem asks to recover a random secret binary vector $\mathbf{s} \in \mathbb{F}_2^n$ from noisy linear samples of the form $(\mathbf{a}, \langle \mathbf{a}, \mathbf{s} \rangle + e)$, where $\mathbf{a} \in \mathbb{F}_2^n$ is chosen uniformly at random and $e \in \mathbb{F}_2$ follows the Bernoulli distribution $\mathcal{B}_\mu$ with parameter μ (i.e., $\Pr[\mathcal{B}_\mu = 1] = \mu$). The decisional LPN problem simply asks to distinguish the samples $(\mathbf{a}, \langle \mathbf{a}, \mathbf{s} \rangle + e)$ from uniform. The two versions of LPN turn out to be polynomially equivalent [BFKL93, KS06].

From a theoretical point, LPN offers a very strong security guarantee. The LPN problem can be formulated as a well-investigated NP-complete problem,

© Springer International Publishing AG 2017
J. Pieprzyk and S. Suriadi (Eds.): ACISP 2017, Part I, LNCS 10342, pp. 44–64, 2017.
DOI: 10.1007/978-3-319-60055-0_3

the problem of decoding random linear codes [BMT78]. An efficient algorithm for LPN would imply a major breakthrough in coding theory. LPN also becomes a central hub in learning theory: an efficient algorithm for it could be used to learn several important concept classes such as 2-DNF formulas, juntas and any function with a sparse Fourier spectrum [FGKP06]. Until now, the best known LPN solvers require sub-exponential time. Further, there are no quantum algorithms known to have any advantage over classic ones in solving it. This makes LPN a promising candidate for post-quantum cryptography.

From a practical point, LPN-based schemes are often extremely efficient. The operations of LPN are simply bitwise exclusive OR (XOR) between binary strings, which are more efficient than other quantum-secure candidates like the learning with errors (LWE) assumption [Reg05]. Consequently, LPN-based schemes are very suitable for weak-power devices like RFID tags.

Low-Noise LPN vs. Constant-Noise LPN. Obviously, with the noise rate μ decreasing, the LPN problem can only become easier. Under a *constant noise* rate $0 < \mu < 1/2$, the best known algorithms for solving LPN require $2^{O(n/\log n)}$ time and samples [BKW03, LF06]. The time complexity goes up to $2^{O(n/\log\log n)}$ when given only polynomially many $\mathsf{poly}(n)$ samples [Lyu05], and even $2^{O(n)}$ when given only linearly many $O(n)$ samples [Ste88, MMT11]. Under a *low noise* rate $\mu = O(n^{-c})$ (typically $c = 1/2$), the best LPN solvers need only $2^{O(n^{1-c})}$ time when given $O(n)$ samples [Ste88, CC98, BLP11, Kir11, BJMM12].

The low-noise LPN is mostly believed to be a stronger assumption than constant-noise LPN. Moreover, low-noise LPN results in less efficient schemes than constant-noise LPN. For example, to achieve a same security level, the secret length n of low-noise LPN for noise rate $\mu = O(1/\sqrt{n})$ has to be squared compared with constant-noise LPN [DMN12], according to the time complexity of the attack algorithms.

For public-key primitives, Alekhnovich [Ale03] constructed a chosen-plaintext (IND-CPA) secure public-key encryption (PKE) scheme based on low-noise LPN for noise rate $\mu = O(1/\sqrt{n})$. Recently, Döttling et al. [DMN12] provided a chosen-ciphertext (IND-CCA2) secure PKE scheme from low-noise LPN, and Kiltz et al. [KMP14] improved the efficiency of the PKE scheme significantly. David et al. [DDN14] proposed a universally composable oblivious transfer (OT) protocol from low-noise LPN. All the above schemes are based on LPN for noise rate $\mu = O(1/\sqrt{n})$ or even $\mu = O(n^{-1/2-\epsilon})$ with some $\epsilon > 0$.

Though constant-noise LPN provides more security confidence and efficiency than low-noise LPN, it had been a long-standing open problem to construct public-key primitives based on constant-noise LPN since Alekhnovich's work [Ale03]. This problem was not resolved until the recent work of Yu and Zhang [YZ16], who designed the first IND-CPA secure PKE scheme, the first IND-CCA2 secure PKE scheme and the first OT protocol from constant-noise LPN.

Key-Dependent Message Security. The traditional IND-CPA (or even IND-CCA2) security might be sufficient for some scenarios, but not strong enough for high-level systems like hard disk encryptions [BHHO08] and anonymous credential systems [CL01], where messages are closely dependent on the secret keys. Such an issue was first identified by Goldwasser and Micali [GM84], and appropriate security notion for key-dependent messages was formalized as KDM-security by Black et al. [BRS02]. Over the years, more and more counterexamples were found, suggesting that IND-CPA/IND-CCA2 security does not imply KDM-security (see [ABBC10, CGH12, MO14, BHW15, KRW15, KW16, AP16, GKW17], to name a few).

Roughly speaking, a PKE scheme is called KDM-secure, if for any PPT adversary who is given public keys $(\mathsf{pk}_1, \cdots, \mathsf{pk}_l)$ of l users, it is hard to distinguish encryptions of functions of secret keys $f(\mathsf{sk}_1, \cdots, \mathsf{sk}_l)$ from encryptions of a constant say $\mathbf{0}$, where the functions f are adaptively chosen by the adversary. In this work, we focus on KDM-CPA security, where the adversary has no access to a decryption oracle.

The first KDM-secure PKE scheme in the standard model (i.e., without using random oracles) was proposed by Boneh et al. [BHHO08] and based on the decisional Diffie-Hellman (DDH) assumption. Later, more KDM-secure PKE schemes were constructed from a variety of assumptions, such as the DDH [CCS09, BHHI10, BGK11, GHV12], the quadratic residuosity (QR) [BG10] and the decisional composite residuosity (DCR) [BG10, MTY11, Hof13, LLJ15, HLL16] assumptions. However, these number-theoretic assumptions are succumb to known quantum algorithms. The only exceptions are the KDM-secure PKE designed by Applebaum et al. [ACPS09] from LWE and the one proposed by Döttling [Döt15] from low-noise LPN. Until now, the problem of constructing KDM-secure PKE from constant-noise LPN has remained open.

Applebaum [App11] provided a generic KDM amplification for boosting any KDM-secure PKE for affine functions to a KDM-secure PKE for arbitrary (bounded size) circuits. Thus it suffices to construct KDM-secure PKE schemes for affine functions to obtain schemes with KDM-security against more general class of functions.

Our Contributions. In this paper, we present the first KDM-secure PKE scheme for affine functions from *constant-noise LPN*, where the number l of users is predefined. Our construction is neat and enjoys roughly the same efficiency as the IND-CPA secure PKE scheme proposed by Yu and Zhang [YZ16]. We show a comparison in Table 1.

The starting point of our work is a variant of the LPN problem called *LPN on squared-log entropy*, which was developed by Yu and Zhang [YZ16] as a technical tool in their IND-CPA/IND-CCA2 secure PKE construction. Different from standard LPN, the secret $\mathbf{s}$ is not necessarily uniform but only required to have some squared-logarithmic entropy, and the linear samples $\mathbf{a}$ are no longer uniformly chosen but sampled from a random subspace of sublinear-sized dimension.

We introduce two types of *multi-fold version* of LPN on squared-log entropy, one having *independent secrets* and the other *independent sample subspaces*. Informally speaking, it stipulates that the samples $(\mathbf{a}_i, \langle \mathbf{a}_i, \mathbf{s}_i \rangle + e_i)$ are computationally indistinguishable from uniform, even given multiple instances $i = 1, \cdots, k$ for any polynomial k. In the version with independent secrets, $\mathbf{s}_i$ are independently distributed; in the version with independent sample subspaces, $\mathbf{a}_i$

Table 1. Comparison among known PKE schemes either based on LPN or achieving KDM-security in the standard model under standard assumptions. "KDM?" asks whether the security is proved in the KDM setting. We kindly note that, the operations of LWE (i.e., modular additions and multiplications over a large ring) are less efficient than that of LPN (i.e., bit operations), while low-noise LPN is mostly believed to be a stronger assumption than constant-noise LPN.

Scheme	KDM?	Assumption	Quantum resistance?
[Ale03, DMN12, KMP14]	✗	Low-noise LPN	✓
[YZ16]	✗	Constant-noise LPN	✓
[BHHO08, CCS09, BHHI10, BGK11, GHV12]	✓	DDH	✗
[BG10]	✓	QR	✗
[BG10, MTY11]	✓	DCR	✗
[Hof13, LLJ15, HLL16]	✓	DDH & DCR	✗
[ACPS09]	✓	LWE	✓
[Döt15]	✓	Low-noise LPN	✓
Ours	✓	Constant-noise LPN	✓

are uniformly chosen from independent subspaces. We establish the hardness of the multi-fold LPN variants on constant-noise LPN.

Then we construct a PKE scheme and reduce the KDM-security to the multi-fold LPN variants, which are in turn implied by constant-noise LPN. In contrast to LPN-based PKE constructions in prior works like [Ale03, DMN12, YZ16], our PKE makes a novel use of two *different* squared-logarithmic entropy distributions for LPN secrets in a delicate combination, one of which is employed in the key generation algorithm and the other is employed in the encryption algorithm. This is crucial to achieving correctness and KDM-security of our PKE scheme simultaneously.

2 Preliminaries

Let $n \in \mathbb{N}$ denote the security parameter. For $i \in \mathbb{N}$, define $[i] := \{1, 2, \cdots, i\}$. Vectors are used in the column form. Denote by $x \leftarrow_\$ X$ the operation of picking an element x according to the distribution X. If X is a set, then this denotes that x is sampled uniformly at random from X. For an algorithm $\mathscr{A}$, denote by $y \leftarrow_\$ \mathscr{A}(x; r)$, or simply $y \leftarrow_\$ \mathscr{A}(x)$, the operation of running $\mathscr{A}$ with input x and randomness r and assigning output to y. Denote by $|\mathbf{s}|$ the Hamming weight of a binary string $\mathbf{s}$. For a random variable X and a distribution D, let $X \sim D$ denote that X is distributed according to D. "PPT" is short for Probabilistic Polynomial-Time. Denote by poly an unspecified polynomial function, and negl an unspecified negligible function. For random variables X and Y, the min-entropy of X is defined as $\mathbf{H}_\infty(X) := -\log(\max_x \Pr[X = x])$, and the statistical distance between X and Y is defined by $\Delta(X,Y) := \frac{1}{2} \cdot \sum_x \left| \Pr[X = x] - \Pr[Y = x] \right|$. For probability ensembles $X = \{X_n\}_{n \in \mathbb{N}}$ and $Y = \{Y_n\}_{n \in \mathbb{N}}$, X and Y are called statistically indistinguishable, denoted by $X \overset{s}{\sim} Y$, if $\Delta(X_n, Y_n) \leq \mathsf{negl}(n)$; X and Y are called computationally indistinguishable, denoted by $X \overset{c}{\sim} Y$, if for any PPT distinguisher $\mathscr{D}$, $\left| \Pr[\mathscr{D}(X_n) = 1] - \Pr[\mathscr{D}(Y_n) = 1] \right| \leq \mathsf{negl}(n)$.

2.1 Useful Distributions and Lemmas

For $0 < \mu, \mu_1 < 1$ and integers $n, m, q, \lambda \in \mathbb{N}$, we define some useful distributions as follows.

- Let $\mathcal{B}_\mu$ denote the Bernoulli distribution with parameter μ, i.e., $\Pr[\mathcal{B}_\mu = 1] = \mu$ and $\Pr[\mathcal{B}_\mu = 0] = 1 - \mu$, and $\mathcal{B}_\mu^n$ the concatenation of n independent copies of $\mathcal{B}_\mu$.
- Let $\widetilde{\mathcal{B}}_{\mu_1}^n$ denote the distribution $\mathcal{B}_{\mu_1}^n$ conditioned on $(1 - \frac{\sqrt{6}}{3})\mu_1 n \leq |\mathcal{B}_{\mu_1}^n| \leq 2\mu_1 n$, and $(\widetilde{\mathcal{B}}_{\mu_1}^n)^q$ an $n \times q$ matrix distribution where each column is an independent copy of $\widetilde{\mathcal{B}}_{\mu_1}^n$.
- Let χ_m^n denote the uniform distribution over the set $\{\mathbf{s} \in \mathbb{F}_2^n \mid |\mathbf{s}| = m\}$.
- Let $\mathcal{U}_n$ (resp., $\mathcal{U}_{q \times n}$) denote the uniform distribution over $\mathbb{F}_2^n$ (resp., $\mathbb{F}_2^{q \times n}$).
- Let $\mathcal{D}_\lambda^{q \times n} := \mathcal{U}_{q \times \lambda} \cdot \mathcal{U}_{\lambda \times n}$.
- Let $\mathcal{P}_n$ denote the uniform distribution over the set of all $n \times n$ permutation matrices, i.e., matrices that have exactly one entry of 1 in each row and each column and 0s elsewhere.

The distribution $\widetilde{\mathcal{B}}_{\mu_1}^n$ was introduced by Yu and Zhang [YZ16] as a very important distribution in the context of constant-noise LPN. $\widetilde{\mathcal{B}}_{\mu_1}^n$ are efficiently sampleable, e.g., by sampling $\mathbf{s} \leftarrow_\$ \mathcal{B}_{\mu_1}^n$ repeatedly and outputting $\mathbf{s}$ until the condition $(1 - \frac{\sqrt{6}}{3})\mu_1 n \leq |\mathbf{s}| \leq 2\mu_1 n$ is met.

Remark 1. In this work, we are mostly interested in $\widetilde{\mathcal{B}}_{\mu_1}^n$ and $\chi_{\mu_1 n}^n$ for $\mu_1 = \Theta(\log n / n)$, both of which have *square-logarithmic entropy*, i.e., $\mathbf{H}_\infty(\widetilde{\mathcal{B}}_{\mu_1}^n) = \Theta(\log^2 n)$ and $\mathbf{H}_\infty(\chi_{\mu_1 n}^n) = \Theta(\log^2 n)$, as shown in [YZ16].

Lemma 1 (Chernoff Bound [KMP14, YZ16]**).** *For any $0 < \mu < 1$ and any $\delta > 0$, we have*

$$\Pr\left[|\mathcal{B}_\mu^n| > (1 + \delta)\mu n\right] < e^{-\frac{\min(\delta, \delta^2)}{3}\mu n}.$$

In particular, for any $0 < \mu \leq (\frac{1}{2} - p)$ with $0 < p < 1/2$, we have

$$\Pr\left[|\mathcal{B}_\mu^n| > (\frac{1}{2} - \frac{p}{2})n\right] < e^{-\frac{p^2 n}{8}}.$$

Lemma 2 (Piling-up Lemma [Mat93]**).** *For independent random variables $e_i \sim \mathcal{B}_{\mu_i}$, $i \in [q]$, we have $\sum_{i=1}^{q} e_i \sim \mathcal{B}_\sigma$ with $\sigma = \frac{1}{2} - \frac{1}{2} \cdot \prod_{i=1}^{q}(1 - 2\mu_i)$.*

Lemma 3 ([YZ16, Lemmas 4.3 and 4.4]). *For any $0 < \mu \leq 1/10$, any $\mu_1 = \Theta(\log n/n) \leq 1/8$, any $\mathbf{e} \in \mathbb{F}_2^n$ with $|\mathbf{e}| \leq 1.01\mu n$, and any $\mathbf{s} \in \mathbb{F}_2^n$ with $|\mathbf{s}| \leq 2\mu_1 n$, it holds that*

$$\Pr\left[\hat{\mathbf{s}}^\top \mathbf{e} = 1\right] \leq 1/2 - 2^{-\mu_1 n/2} \qquad and \qquad \Pr\left[\hat{\mathbf{e}}^\top \mathbf{s} = 1\right] \leq 1/2 - 2^{-\mu_1 n - 1},$$

where $\hat{\mathbf{s}} \sim \widetilde{\mathcal{B}}_{\mu_1}^n$ and $\hat{\mathbf{e}} \sim \mathcal{B}_\mu^n$.

We state a simplified version of the leftover hash lemma, by adopting a specific family of universal hash functions $\mathcal{H} = \{H_{\mathbf{U}} : \mathbb{F}_2^n \longrightarrow \mathbb{F}_2^l \mid \mathbf{U} \in \mathbb{F}_2^{l \times n}\}$, where $H_{\mathbf{U}}(\mathbf{x}) := \mathbf{U} \cdot \mathbf{x} \in \mathbb{F}_2^l$ for any $\mathbf{x} \in \mathbb{F}_2^n$.

Lemma 4 (Leftover Hash Lemma [HILL99]). *For any random variable X on $\mathbb{F}_2^n$ with min-entropy $\mathbf{H}_\infty(X) \geq k$, we have $\Delta\big((\mathbf{U}, \mathbf{U} \cdot \mathbf{x}), (\mathbf{U}, \mathcal{U}_l)\big) \leq 2^{-(k-l)/2}$, where $\mathbf{U} \sim \mathcal{U}_{l \times n}$ and $\mathbf{x} \sim X$.*

2.2 Learning Parity with Noise

Definition 1 (Learning Parity with Noise). *Let $0 < \mu < 1/2$. The decisional LPN problem $\mathsf{LPN}_{\mu,n}$ with secret length n and noise rate μ is hard, if for any $q = \mathsf{poly}(n)$, it holds that*

$$(\mathbf{A}, \mathbf{A} \cdot \mathbf{s} + \mathbf{e}) \overset{c}{\sim} (\mathbf{A}, \mathcal{U}_q), \tag{1}$$

where $\mathbf{A} \sim \mathcal{U}_{q \times n}$, $\mathbf{s} \sim \mathcal{U}_n$ and $\mathbf{e} \sim \mathcal{B}_\mu^q$.

We say that $\mathsf{LPN}_{\mu,n}$ is T-hard, if for any $q \leq T$, any probabilistic distinguisher of running time T, the distinguishing advantage in (1) is upper bounded by $1/T$.

A central tool for constructing IND-CPA/IND-CCA2 secure PKE in [YZ16] is a variant of the LPN problem, called *LPN on squared-log entropy*. There are two main differences: (i) the secret $\mathbf{s}$ is not necessarily uniform, but only required to have some squared-logarithmic entropy; (ii) the rows of $\mathbf{A}$ are no longer uniformly chosen, but sampled from a *random subspace* of squared-logarithmic dimension. It was shown in [YZ16] that under constant-noise LPN with certain sub-exponential hardness, the LPN problem on squared-log entropy is hard even given some log-sized auxiliary input about the secret and noise. Formally, we have the following theorem.

Theorem 1 (LPN on Squared-log Entropy [YZ16, Theorem 4.1]). *Let $0 < \mu < 1/2$ be any constant. Assume that $\mathsf{LPN}_{\mu,n}$ is $2^{\omega(n^{\frac{1}{2}})}$-hard, then for any $\lambda = \Theta(\log^2 n)$, $q = \mathsf{poly}(n)$, any polynomial-time sampleable distribution $\mathcal{S}$ on $\mathbb{F}_2^n$ with $\mathbf{H}_\infty(\mathcal{S}) \geq 2\lambda$, and any polynomial-time computable function $f : (\mathbb{F}_2^n \times \mathbb{F}_2^q) \times \mathcal{Z} \longrightarrow \mathbb{F}_2^{O(\log n)}$ with public coins Z, we have*

$$(\mathbf{A}, \mathbf{A} \cdot \mathbf{s} + \mathbf{e}, Z, f(\mathbf{s}, \mathbf{e}; Z)) \overset{c}{\sim} (\mathbf{A}, \mathcal{U}_q, Z, f(\mathbf{s}, \mathbf{e}; Z)),$$

where $\mathbf{A} \sim \mathcal{D}_\lambda^{q \times n}$, $\mathbf{s} \sim \mathcal{S}$ and $\mathbf{e} \sim \mathcal{B}_\mu^q$.

By Remark 1, $\widetilde{\mathcal{B}}_{\mu_1}^n$ and $\chi_{\mu_1 n}^n$ with $\mu_1 = \Theta(\log n / n)$ are suitable candidate distributions for $\mathcal{S}$, as long as the constant hidden in $\lambda = \Theta(\log^2 n)$ is small enough such that $\mathbf{H}_\infty(\widetilde{\mathcal{B}}_{\mu_1}^n) \geq 2\lambda$ and $\mathbf{H}_\infty(\chi_{\mu_1 n}^n) \geq 2\lambda$ hold.

2.3 Public-Key Encryption and Key-Dependent Message Security

A public-key encryption (PKE) scheme $\mathsf{PKE} = (\mathsf{KeyGen}, \mathsf{Enc}, \mathsf{Dec})$ with secret key space $\mathcal{SK}$ and message space $\mathcal{M}$ consists of a tuple of PPT algorithms: (i) the key generation algorithm $\mathsf{KeyGen}(1^n)$ outputs a public key pk and a secret key $\mathsf{sk} \in \mathcal{SK}$; (ii) the encryption algorithm $\mathsf{Enc}(\mathsf{pk}, \mathsf{m})$ takes as input a public key pk and a message $\mathsf{m} \in \mathcal{M}$, and outputs a ciphertext c; (iii) the decryption algorithm $\mathsf{Dec}(\mathsf{sk}, \mathsf{c})$ takes as input a secret key sk and a ciphertext c, and outputs either a message m or a failure symbol $\perp$. Correctness of PKE requires that, for all messages $\mathsf{m} \in \mathcal{M}$, we have

$$\Pr\left[(\mathsf{pk}, \mathsf{sk}) \leftarrow_\$ \mathsf{KeyGen}(1^n) : \mathsf{Dec}(\mathsf{sk}, \mathsf{Enc}(\mathsf{pk}, \mathsf{m})) \neq \mathsf{m}\right] \leq \mathsf{negl}(n),$$

where the probability is over the inner coin tosses of KeyGen and Enc.

Definition 2 (KDM-Security for PKE). *Let $l \in \mathbb{N}$ denote the number of users, and let $\mathcal{F}$ be a family of functions from $(\mathcal{SK})^l$ to $\mathcal{M}$. A PKE scheme PKE is called l-KDM[$\mathcal{F}$]-CPA secure, if for any PPT adversary $\mathscr{A}$, in the following l-kdm[$\mathcal{F}$]-cpa game played between $\mathscr{A}$ and a challenger $\mathscr{C}$, the advantage of $\mathscr{A}$ is negligible in n.*

KEYGEN. *$\mathscr{C}$ picks $b \leftarrow_\$ \{0, 1\}$ as a challenge bit, and proceeds as follows.*
  (a) For each user $i \in [l]$, invoke $(\mathsf{pk}_i, \mathsf{sk}_i) \leftarrow_\$ \mathsf{KeyGen}(1^n)$.
  Finally, $\mathscr{C}$ sends the public keys $(\mathsf{pk}_1, \cdots, \mathsf{pk}_l)$ to $\mathscr{A}$.
CHAL($j \in [l], f \in \mathcal{F}$). *$\mathscr{A}$ can query this oracle $\mathsf{poly}(n)$ times. Each time, $\mathscr{A}$ sends a user identity $j \in [l]$ and a function $f \in \mathcal{F}$ to $\mathscr{C}$, and $\mathscr{C}$ proceeds as follows.*
  (a) Set $f \leftarrow \mathbf{0}$ (the zero function) if $b = 0$. Then compute a message $\mathsf{m} := f(\mathsf{sk}_1, \cdots, \mathsf{sk}_l) \in \mathcal{M}$.
  (b) Compute the encryption of m under the public key pk_j of the j-th user, i.e., $\mathsf{c} \leftarrow_\$ \mathsf{Enc}(\mathsf{pk}_j, \mathsf{m})$.
  Finally, $\mathscr{C}$ returns the challenge ciphertext c to $\mathscr{A}$.
GUESS. *$\mathscr{A}$ outputs a guessing bit $b' \in \{0, 1\}$. The advantage of $\mathscr{A}$ is defined as $\left| \Pr[b' = b] - \frac{1}{2} \right|$.*

3 Multi-fold LPN on Squared-Log Entropy

In this section, we present the technical tools used in our construction of KDM-secure PKE from constant-noise LPN. We develop two types of *multi-fold version* of LPN on squared-log entropy: one has *independent secrets* and the other has *independent sample subspaces*.

3.1 Multi-fold LPN on Squared-Log Entropy with Independent Secrets

Firstly, we state a k-fold version of LPN on squared-log entropy with independent secrets and noise vectors, where the auxiliary input per fold is a 2-bit linear leakage of the secret and noise.

Lemma 5. *Let $0 < \mu < 1/2$ be any constant. Assume that $\mathsf{LPN}_{\mu,n}$ is $2^{\omega(n^{\frac{1}{2}})}$-hard, then for any $\mu_1 = \Theta(\log n/n)$ and $\lambda = \Theta(\log^2 n)$ such that $\mathbf{H}_\infty(\widetilde{\mathcal{B}}_{\mu_1}^n) \geq 2\lambda$, and any $k = \mathsf{poly}(n)$, it holds that*

$$(\mathbf{A}, \hat{\mathbf{S}}^\top \mathbf{A} + \hat{\mathbf{E}}^\top, (\mathbf{e}, \mathbf{s}, \mathbf{P}), (\hat{\mathbf{S}}^\top \mathbf{e}, \hat{\mathbf{E}}^\top \mathbf{P} \mathbf{s})) \overset{c}{\sim} (\mathbf{A}, \mathcal{U}_{k \times n}, (\mathbf{e}, \mathbf{s}, \mathbf{P}), (\hat{\mathbf{S}}^\top \mathbf{e}, \hat{\mathbf{E}}^\top \mathbf{P} \mathbf{s})), \tag{2}$$

where $\mathbf{A} \sim \mathcal{D}_\lambda^{n \times n}$, $\hat{\mathbf{S}} \sim (\widetilde{\mathcal{B}}_{\mu_1}^n)^k$, $\hat{\mathbf{E}} \sim \mathcal{B}_\mu^{n \times k}$, $\mathbf{e} \sim \mathcal{B}_\mu^n$, $\mathbf{s} \sim \chi_{\mu_1 n}^n$ and $\mathbf{P} \sim \mathcal{P}_n$.

Proof. By instantiating a transposed version of Theorem 1 with $q = n$, $\mathcal{S} = \widetilde{\mathcal{B}}_{\mu_1}^n$ and $f : (\mathbb{F}_2^n \times \mathbb{F}_2^n) \times (\mathbb{F}_2^n \times \mathbb{F}_2^n \times \mathbb{F}_2^{n \times n}) \longrightarrow \mathbb{F}_2^2$ being $f(\hat{\mathbf{s}}, \hat{\mathbf{e}}; (\mathbf{e}, \mathbf{s}, \mathbf{P})) = (\hat{\mathbf{s}}^\top \mathbf{e}, \hat{\mathbf{e}}^\top \mathbf{P} \mathbf{s})$, we obtain

$$(\mathbf{A}, \hat{\mathbf{s}}^\top \mathbf{A} + \hat{\mathbf{e}}^\top, (\mathbf{e}, \mathbf{s}, \mathbf{P}), (\hat{\mathbf{s}}^\top \mathbf{e}, \hat{\mathbf{e}}^\top \mathbf{P} \mathbf{s})) \overset{c}{\sim} (\mathbf{A}, \mathcal{U}_{1 \times n}, (\mathbf{e}, \mathbf{s}, \mathbf{P}), (\hat{\mathbf{s}}^\top \mathbf{e}, \hat{\mathbf{e}}^\top \mathbf{P} \mathbf{s})), \tag{3}$$

where $\mathbf{A} \sim \mathcal{D}_\lambda^{n \times n}$, $\hat{\mathbf{s}} \sim \widetilde{\mathcal{B}}_{\mu_1}^n$, $\hat{\mathbf{e}} \sim \mathcal{B}_\mu^n$, and $(\mathbf{e} \sim \mathcal{B}_\mu^n, \mathbf{s} \sim \chi_{\mu_1 n}^n, \mathbf{P} \sim \mathcal{P}_n)$ are public coins. Observe that (2) is k-fold version of (3), thus a standard hybrid argument leads to Lemma 5. ∎

We also develop a k-fold version of LPN on squared-log entropy with independent secrets and noise vectors, where the auxiliary input per fold is a 1-bit linear leakage of a special form. We show that *the auxiliary input is also computationally indistinguishable from uniform.*

Lemma 6. *Let $0 < \mu < 1/2$ be any constant. Assume that $\mathsf{LPN}_{\mu,n}$ is $2^{\omega(n^{\frac{1}{2}})}$-hard, then for any $\mu_1 = \Theta(\log n/n)$ and $\lambda = \Theta(\log^2 n)$ such that $\mathbf{H}_\infty(\widetilde{\mathcal{B}}_{\mu_1}^n) \geq 2\lambda$, and any $k = \mathsf{poly}(n)$, it holds that*

$$(\mathbf{A}, \hat{\mathbf{S}}^\top \mathbf{A} + \hat{\mathbf{E}}^\top, \mathbf{y}, \hat{\mathbf{S}}^\top \mathbf{y} + \mathbf{e}) \overset{c}{\sim} (\mathbf{A}, \mathcal{U}_{k \times n}, \mathbf{y}, \mathcal{U}_k), \tag{4}$$

where $\mathbf{A} \sim \mathcal{D}_\lambda^{n \times n}$, $\hat{\mathbf{S}} \sim (\widetilde{\mathcal{B}}_{\mu_1}^n)^k$, $\hat{\mathbf{E}} \sim \mathcal{B}_\mu^{n \times k}$, $\mathbf{y} \sim \mathcal{U}_n$ and $\mathbf{e} \sim \mathcal{B}_\mu^k$.

Proof. By instantiating a transposed version of Theorem 1 with $q = n$, $\mathcal{S} = \widetilde{\mathcal{B}}_{\mu_1}^n$ and $f : (\mathbb{F}_2^n \times \mathbb{F}_2^n) \times (\mathbb{F}_2^n \times \mathbb{F}_2) \longrightarrow \mathbb{F}_2$ being $f(\hat{\mathbf{s}}, \hat{\mathbf{e}}; (\mathbf{y}, e)) = \hat{\mathbf{s}}^\top \mathbf{y} + e$, we have

$$(\mathbf{A}, \hat{\mathbf{s}}^\top \mathbf{A} + \hat{\mathbf{e}}^\top, (\mathbf{y}, e), \hat{\mathbf{s}}^\top \mathbf{y} + e) \overset{c}{\sim} (\mathbf{A}, \mathcal{U}_{1 \times n}, (\mathbf{y}, e), \hat{\mathbf{s}}^\top \mathbf{y} + e)$$

$$\Rightarrow (\mathbf{A}, \hat{\mathbf{s}}^\top \mathbf{A} + \hat{\mathbf{e}}^\top, \mathbf{y}, \hat{\mathbf{s}}^\top \mathbf{y} + e) \overset{c}{\sim} (\mathbf{A}, \mathcal{U}_{1 \times n}, \mathbf{y}, \hat{\mathbf{s}}^\top \mathbf{y} + e), \tag{5}$$

where $\mathbf{A} \sim \mathcal{D}_\lambda^{n \times n}$, $\hat{\mathbf{s}} \sim \tilde{\mathcal{B}}_{\mu_1}^n$, $\hat{\mathbf{e}} \sim \mathcal{B}_\mu^n$, and $(\mathbf{y} \sim \mathcal{U}_n, e \sim \mathcal{B}_\mu)$ are public coins. Again, by instantiating a transposed version of Theorem 1 with $q = 1$, $\mathcal{S} = \tilde{\mathcal{B}}_{\mu_1}^n$ and f that always outputs nothing, we get

$$(\mathbf{y}, \hat{\mathbf{s}}^\top \mathbf{y} + e) \overset{c}{\sim} (\mathbf{y}, \mathcal{U}_1)$$

$$\Rightarrow (\mathbf{A}, \mathcal{U}_{1 \times n}, \mathbf{y}, \hat{\mathbf{s}}^\top \mathbf{y} + e) \overset{c}{\sim} (\mathbf{A}, \mathcal{U}_{1 \times n}, \mathbf{y}, \mathcal{U}_1), \qquad (6)$$

where $\mathbf{A} \sim \mathcal{D}_\lambda^{n \times n}$, $\mathbf{y} \sim \mathcal{D}_\lambda^{n \times 1} = \mathcal{U}_n$, $\hat{\mathbf{s}} \sim \tilde{\mathcal{B}}_{\mu_1}^n$ and $e \sim \mathcal{B}_\mu$.

By combining (5) with (6), we immediately obtain

$$(\mathbf{A}, \hat{\mathbf{s}}^\top \mathbf{A} + \hat{\mathbf{e}}^\top, \mathbf{y}, \hat{\mathbf{s}}^\top \mathbf{y} + e) \overset{c}{\sim} (\mathbf{A}, \mathcal{U}_{1 \times n}, \mathbf{y}, \mathcal{U}_1). \qquad (7)$$

Observe that (4) is k-fold version of (7), thus a standard hybrid argument leads to Lemma 6. ∎

3.2   Multi-fold LPN on Squared-Log Entropy with Independent Sample Subspaces

We introduce an l-fold version of LPN on squared-log entropy, with independent sample subspaces and noise vectors, but shared a same secret $\mathbf{s}$, i.e.,

$$(\mathbf{A}_i, \mathbf{A}_i \cdot \mathbf{s} + \mathbf{e}_i, Z, f(\mathbf{s}, \mathbf{e}_i; Z))_{i \in [l]} \overset{c}{\sim} (\mathbf{A}_i, \mathcal{U}_q, Z, f(\mathbf{s}, \mathbf{e}_i; Z))_{i \in [l]}. \qquad (8)$$

The name of "sample subspaces" originates from the fact that, each $\mathbf{A}_i \sim \mathcal{D}_\lambda^{q \times n}$ is associated with a random *subspace* of dimension λ, from which the rows of $\mathbf{A}_i$ are sampled.

We stress that this cannot be implied by Theorem 1, for two reasons: (i) for l independent $\mathbf{A}_i \sim \mathcal{D}_\lambda^{q \times n}$, the distribution of their concatenation $\begin{pmatrix} \mathbf{A}_1 \\ \vdots \\ \mathbf{A}_l \end{pmatrix}$ does not follow the form of $\mathcal{D}_\lambda^{lq \times n}$ any more; (ii) we cannot resort to a hybrid argument since the secret $\mathbf{s}$ is shared by the l folds and unknown to the simulator.

For our KDM-secure PKE, it suffices to consider the case free of auxiliary input.

Theorem 2. *Let $0 < \mu < 1/2$ and $l \in \mathbb{N}$ be any constant. Assume that $\mathsf{LPN}_{\mu,n}$ is $2^{\omega(n^{\frac{1}{2}})}$-hard, then for any $\mu_1 = \Theta(\log n / n)$ and $\lambda = \Theta(\log^2 n)$ such that $\mathbf{H}_\infty(\chi_{\mu_1 n}^n) \geq (l+1)\lambda$, it holds that*

$$(\mathbf{A}_i, \mathbf{A}_i \cdot \mathbf{s} + \mathbf{e}_i)_{i \in [l]} \overset{c}{\sim} (\mathbf{A}_i, \mathbf{u}_i)_{i \in [l]},$$

where $\mathbf{s} \sim \chi_{\mu_1 n}^n$, $\mathbf{A}_i \sim \mathcal{D}_\lambda^{n \times n}$, $\mathbf{e}_i \sim \mathcal{B}_\mu^n$ and $\mathbf{u}_i \sim \mathcal{U}_n$ for $i \in [l]$.

Proof. Since $\mathbf{H}_\infty(\chi_{\mu_1 n}^n) \geq (l+1)\lambda$, by the leftover hash lemma (i.e., Lemma 4), we have

$$(\mathbf{V}, \mathbf{V} \cdot \mathbf{s}) \overset{s}{\sim} (\mathbf{V}, \mathbf{y}),$$

where $\mathbf{V} \sim \mathcal{U}_{l\lambda \times n}$, $\mathbf{s} \sim \chi^n_{\mu_1 n}$ and $\mathbf{y} \sim \mathcal{U}_{l\lambda}$.

By expressing $\mathbf{V} = \begin{pmatrix} \mathbf{V}_1 \\ \vdots \\ \mathbf{V}_l \end{pmatrix}$ with $\mathbf{V}_i \sim \mathcal{U}_{\lambda \times n}$ and $\mathbf{y} = \begin{pmatrix} \mathbf{y}_1 \\ \vdots \\ \mathbf{y}_l \end{pmatrix}$ with $\mathbf{y}_i \sim \mathcal{U}_\lambda$,

we get

$$(\mathbf{V}_i, \mathbf{V}_i \cdot \mathbf{s})_{i \in [l]} \overset{s}{\sim} (\mathbf{V}_i, \mathbf{y}_i)_{i \in [l]}$$

$$\Rightarrow ((\mathbf{U}_i, \mathbf{V}_i), \mathbf{U}_i \cdot \mathbf{V}_i \cdot \mathbf{s} + \mathbf{e}_i)_{i \in [l]} \overset{s}{\sim} ((\mathbf{U}_i, \mathbf{V}_i), \mathbf{U}_i \cdot \mathbf{y}_i + \mathbf{e}_i)_{i \in [l]}, \quad (9)$$

where $\mathbf{U}_i \sim \mathcal{U}_{n \times \lambda}$, and $\mathbf{e}_i \sim \mathcal{B}^n_\mu$.

Next, consider the $\mathsf{LPN}_{\mu, \lambda}$ problem on uniform string $\mathbf{y}_i$ of length λ (instead of n), which is assumed to be $2^{\omega(\lambda^{\frac{1}{2}})}$ $(= n^{\omega(1)})$-hard. It implies that

$$(\mathbf{U}_i, \mathbf{U}_i \cdot \mathbf{y}_i + \mathbf{e}_i) \overset{c}{\sim} (\mathbf{U}_i, \mathbf{u}_i),$$

where $\mathbf{u}_i \sim \mathcal{U}_n$, for any $i \in [l]$. Through a standard hybrid argument, we have

$$(\mathbf{U}_i, \mathbf{U}_i \cdot \mathbf{y}_i + \mathbf{e}_i)_{i \in [l]} \overset{c}{\sim} (\mathbf{U}_i, \mathbf{u}_i)_{i \in [l]}$$

$$\Rightarrow ((\mathbf{U}_i, \mathbf{V}_i), \mathbf{U}_i \cdot \mathbf{y}_i + \mathbf{e}_i)_{i \in [l]} \overset{c}{\sim} ((\mathbf{U}_i, \mathbf{V}_i), \mathbf{u}_i)_{i \in [l]}. \quad (10)$$

Finally, by combining (9) with (10) and setting $\mathbf{A}_i := \mathbf{U}_i \cdot \mathbf{V}_i \sim \mathcal{D}^{n \times n}_\lambda$, Theorem 2 follows. ∎

4 KDM-Secure PKE from Constant-Noise LPN

In this section, we present a PKE scheme with KDM-security for affine functions assuming certain sub-exponential hardness (i.e., $2^{\omega(n^{\frac{1}{2}})}$ for secret length n) of constant-noise LPN.

4.1 The Construction

Our PKE scheme uses the following parameters and building blocks.

- Let $0 < \mu \leq 1/10$, $\alpha > 0$ and $l \in \mathbb{N}$ be any constants, and let $\mu_1 = \alpha \log n / n$.
- Let $\lambda = \beta \log^2 n$ with a constant $\beta > 0$ such that both $\mathbf{H}_\infty(\widetilde{\mathcal{B}}^n_{\mu_1}) \geq 2\lambda$ and $\mathbf{H}_\infty(\chi^n_{\mu_1 n}) \geq (l+1)\lambda$ holds. By Remark 1, such a λ can be easily found by setting β small enough.
- Let $\mathbf{G} \in \mathbb{F}^{k \times n}_2$ be the generator matrix of a binary linear error-correcting code together with an efficient decoding algorithm Decode, which can correct at least $(\frac{1}{2} - \frac{2}{5n^{3\alpha/2}}) \cdot k$ errors. Such a code exists for $k = O(n^{3\alpha+1})$, and explicit constructions of the code can be found in [For66].

We present the construction of $\mathsf{PKE} = (\mathsf{KeyGen}, \mathsf{Enc}, \mathsf{Dec})$ with secret key space $\mathbb{F}^n_2$ and message space $\mathbb{F}^n_\mu$ in Fig. 1.

$(\mathsf{pk}, \mathsf{sk}) \leftarrow_\$ \mathsf{KeyGen}(1^n)$:	$\mathsf{c} \leftarrow_\$ \mathsf{Enc}(\mathsf{pk}, \mathsf{m})$: // $\mathsf{m} \in \mathbb{F}_2^n$	
$\mathbf{A} \leftarrow_\$ \mathcal{D}_\lambda^{n \times n}$.	Parse $\mathsf{pk} = (\mathbf{A}, \mathbf{y})$.	$\mathsf{m} \leftarrow \mathsf{Dec}(\mathsf{sk}, \mathsf{c})$:
$\mathbf{s} \leftarrow_\$ \chi_{\mu_1 n}^n$.	$\hat{\mathbf{S}} \leftarrow_\$ (\widetilde{\mathcal{B}}_{\mu_1}^n)^k$.	Parse $\mathsf{sk} = \mathbf{s}$.
$\mathbf{e} \leftarrow_\$ \mathcal{B}_\mu^n$.	$\hat{\mathbf{E}} \leftarrow_\$ \mathcal{B}_\mu^{n \times k}$.	Parse $\mathsf{c} = (\mathbf{C}_1, \mathbf{c}_2)$.
$\mathbf{y} := \mathbf{A}\mathbf{s} + \mathbf{e} \in \mathbb{F}_2^n$.	$\mathbf{C}_1 := \hat{\mathbf{S}}^\top \mathbf{A} + \hat{\mathbf{E}}^\top \in \mathbb{F}_2^{k \times n}$.	$\mathbf{z} := \mathbf{c}_2 - \mathbf{C}_1 \mathbf{s} \in \mathbb{F}_2^k$.
Return $\mathsf{pk} := (\mathbf{A}, \mathbf{y})$,	$\hat{\mathbf{e}} \leftarrow_\$ \mathcal{B}_\mu^k$.	$\mathsf{m} := \mathsf{Decode}(\mathbf{z}) \in \mathbb{F}_2^n$.
$\mathsf{sk} := \mathbf{s} \in \mathbb{F}_2^n$.	$\mathbf{c}_2 := \hat{\mathbf{S}}^\top \mathbf{y} + \hat{\mathbf{e}} + \mathbf{G}\mathsf{m} \in \mathbb{F}_2^k$.	Return m.
	Return $\mathsf{c} := (\mathbf{C}_1, \mathbf{c}_2)$.	

Fig. 1. Construction of PKE with KDM-security from constant-noise LPN.

Remark 2. In contrast to LPN-based PKE constructions in prior works like [Ale03, DMN12, YZ16], our PKE scheme makes a novel use of two squared-log entropy distributions for LPN secrets in a delicate combination, i.e., $\chi_{\mu_1 n}^n$ in the KeyGen algorithm and $\widetilde{\mathcal{B}}_{\mu_1}^n$ in the Enc algorithm. This is crucial to achieving correctness and KDM-security of our scheme simultaneously. Jumping ahead,

- For KDM-security, the distribution $\chi_{\mu_1 n}^n$ employed in KeyGen allows us to express secret keys of l users, $\mathbf{s}_i \sim \chi_{\mu_1 n}^n$ with $i \in [l]$, as random permutations of a base secret key $\mathbf{s}^* \sim \chi_{\mu_1 n}^n$, i.e., $\mathbf{s}_i := \mathbf{P}_i \cdot \mathbf{s}^*$ for $\mathbf{P}_i \sim \mathcal{P}_n$. Then we are able to reduce KDM-security for l users to that for a single user. This approach makes the KDM-security proof possible. (See Subsect. 4.3 for the formal security proof.)

- For correctness, the distribution $\widetilde{\mathcal{B}}_{\mu_1}^n$ employed in Enc helps us to use Lemma 3 to bound the error term $\hat{\mathbf{S}}^\top \mathbf{e}$ in decryption, where $\hat{\mathbf{S}} \sim (\widetilde{\mathcal{B}}_{\mu_1}^n)^k$, and decode the message m successfully. (See Subsect. 4.2 for the formal correctness analysis.)

We stress that $\chi_{\mu_1 n}^n$ and $\widetilde{\mathcal{B}}_{\mu_1}^n$ are carefully selected so that both the correctness and KDM-security can be satisfied. If $\chi_{\mu_1 n}^n$ is adopted in both KeyGen and Enc, it will be hard for us to show the correctness; if $\widetilde{\mathcal{B}}_{\mu_1}^n$ is adopted in both KeyGen and Enc, it will be hard for us to prove the KDM-security.

4.2 Correctness

Theorem 3. *Our PKE scheme* PKE *in Fig. 1 is correct.*

Proof. For $(\mathsf{pk}, \mathsf{sk}) \leftarrow_\$ \mathsf{KeyGen}(1^n)$ and $\mathsf{c} \leftarrow_\$ \mathsf{Enc}(\mathsf{pk}, \mathsf{m})$, we have

$$\mathsf{pk} = (\mathbf{A}, \mathbf{y}) = (\mathbf{A}, \mathbf{A}\mathbf{s} + \mathbf{e}) \quad \text{and} \quad \mathsf{c} = (\mathbf{C}_1, \mathbf{c}_2) = (\hat{\mathbf{S}}^\top \mathbf{A} + \hat{\mathbf{E}}^\top, \hat{\mathbf{S}}^\top \mathbf{y} + \hat{\mathbf{e}} + \mathbf{G}\mathsf{m}),$$

where $\mathbf{s} \sim \chi^n_{\mu_1 n}$, $\mathbf{e} \sim \mathcal{B}^n_\mu$, $\hat{\mathbf{S}} \sim (\widetilde{\mathcal{B}}^n_{\mu_1})^k$, $\hat{\mathbf{E}} \sim \mathcal{B}^{n \times k}_\mu$ and $\hat{\mathbf{e}} \sim \mathcal{B}^k_\mu$. Then in $\mathsf{Dec}(\mathsf{sk}, \mathbf{c})$, it follows that

$$\mathbf{z} = \mathbf{c}_2 - \mathbf{C}_1 \mathbf{s} = \hat{\mathbf{S}}^\top \mathbf{y} + \hat{\mathbf{e}} + \mathbf{Gm} - (\hat{\mathbf{S}}^\top \mathbf{A} + \hat{\mathbf{E}}^\top) \cdot \mathbf{s}$$
$$= \hat{\mathbf{S}}^\top \cdot (\mathbf{As} + \mathbf{e}) + \hat{\mathbf{e}} + \mathbf{Gm} - (\hat{\mathbf{S}}^\top \mathbf{A} + \hat{\mathbf{E}}^\top) \cdot \mathbf{s}$$
$$= \mathbf{Gm} + \hat{\mathbf{e}} + \hat{\mathbf{S}}^\top \mathbf{e} - \hat{\mathbf{E}}^\top \mathbf{s}.$$

We analyze the error term $\hat{\mathbf{e}} + \hat{\mathbf{S}}^\top \mathbf{e} - \hat{\mathbf{E}}^\top \mathbf{s}$. By the Chernoff bound (i.e., Lemma 1), $|\mathbf{e}| \leq 1.01\mu n$ holds except with negligible probability $2^{-\Omega(n)}$. Besides, $|\mathbf{s}| = \mu_1 n \leq 2\mu_1 n$. Thus, by Lemma 3, we have $\hat{\mathbf{S}}^\top \mathbf{e} \sim \mathcal{B}^k_{\sigma_1}$ for $\sigma_1 \leq 1/2 - 2^{-\mu_1 n/2} = 1/2 - n^{-\alpha/2}$, and $\hat{\mathbf{E}}^\top \mathbf{s} \sim \mathcal{B}^k_{\sigma_2}$ for $\sigma_2 \leq 1/2 - 2^{-\mu_1 n - 1} = 1/2 - n^{-\alpha}/2$. Then by the Piling-up Lemma (i.e., Lemma 2), $\hat{\mathbf{e}} + \hat{\mathbf{S}}^\top \mathbf{e} - \hat{\mathbf{E}}^\top \mathbf{s} \sim \mathcal{B}^k_\sigma$ for $\sigma \leq 1/2 - \frac{4}{5} \cdot n^{-3\alpha/2}$. Finally, by Lemma 1,

$$\Pr\left[\left| \hat{\mathbf{e}} + \hat{\mathbf{S}}^\top \mathbf{e} - \hat{\mathbf{E}}^\top \mathbf{s} \right| \leq (\tfrac{1}{2} - \tfrac{2}{5n^{3\alpha/2}}) \cdot k \right] \geq 1 - 2^{-\Omega(n^{-3\alpha}k)} = 1 - 2^{-\Omega(n)}.$$

Therefore, with overwhelming probability, it holds that $\left| \hat{\mathbf{e}} + \hat{\mathbf{S}}^\top \mathbf{e} - \hat{\mathbf{E}}^\top \mathbf{s} \right| \leq (\tfrac{1}{2} - \tfrac{2}{5n^{3\alpha/2}}) \cdot k$, and in this case, Decode will be able to decode $\mathbf{m}$ from $\mathbf{z}$. ∎

4.3 KDM-Security for Affine Functions

Theorem 4. *Let $\mathcal{F}_{aff} = \{ f : (\mathbb{F}^n_2)^l \longrightarrow \mathbb{F}^n_2 \}$ be a family of affine functions. Assume that $\mathsf{LPN}_{\mu,n}$ is $2^{\omega(n^{\frac{1}{2}})}$-hard, then our PKE scheme PKE in Fig. 1 is l-KDM[$\mathcal{F}_{aff}$]-CPA secure.*

Proof. Suppose that $\mathscr{A}$ is a PPT adversary against the l-KDM[$\mathcal{F}_{aff}$]-CPA security of PKE with advantage ϵ. We prove the theorem by defining a sequence of games G_1–G_{12} and showing that ϵ is negligible in n. The changes between adjacent games will be highlighted by underline. In the sequel, by $a \overset{\mathsf{G}_i}{=} b$ we mean that a equals b or is computed as b in game G_i, and by $\Pr_i[\cdot]$ we denote the probability of a particular event occurring in game G_i.

Game G_1. This is the l-kdm[$\mathcal{F}_{aff}$]-cpa security game of PKE, which is played between $\mathscr{A}$ and a challenger $\mathscr{C}$.

KeyGen. $\mathscr{C}$ picks $b \leftarrow_\$ \{0, 1\}$ as the challenge bit, and generates the public keys of l users as follows.
 (a) For each user $i \in [l]$, choose $\mathbf{A}_i \leftarrow_\$ \mathcal{D}^{n \times n}_\lambda$, $\mathbf{s}_i \leftarrow_\$ \chi^n_{\mu_1 n}$, $\mathbf{e}_i \leftarrow_\$ \mathcal{B}^n_\mu$, and compute $\mathbf{y}_i := \mathbf{A}_i \mathbf{s}_i + \mathbf{e}_i \in \mathbb{F}^n_2$.
 Finally, $\mathscr{C}$ sends the public keys $\mathsf{pk}_i := (\mathbf{A}_i, \mathbf{y}_i)$, $i \in [l]$, to $\mathscr{A}$.
Chal($j \in [l], f \in \mathcal{F}_{aff}$). $\mathscr{A}$ can query this oracle $Q = \mathsf{poly}(n)$ times. Each time, $\mathscr{A}$ sends a user identity $j \in [l]$ and an affine function $f \in \mathcal{F}_{aff}$ to $\mathscr{C}$, and $\mathscr{C}$ proceeds as follows.
 (a) Set $f \leftarrow \mathbf{0}$ (the zero function) if $b = 0$. Then compute the message $\mathbf{m} := f(\mathsf{sk}_1, \cdots, \mathsf{sk}_l) \in \mathbb{F}^n_2$, which essentially is $\mathbf{m} := \sum_{i \in [l]} \mathbf{T}_i \mathbf{s}_i + \mathbf{t} \in \mathbb{F}^n_2$, where $\mathbf{T}_i \in \mathbb{F}^{n \times n}_2$ and $\mathbf{t} \in \mathbb{F}^n_2$ are $\mathbf{0}$s in the case of $b = 0$ and are specified by $\mathscr{A}$ as the description of the affine function f in the case of $b = 1$.

(b) Compute the encryption of m under the public key $\mathsf{pk}_j = (\mathbf{A}_j, \mathbf{y}_j)$ of the j-th user, i.e., choose $\hat{\mathbf{S}} \leftarrow_\$ (\widetilde{\mathcal{B}}^n_{\mu_1})^k$, $\hat{\mathbf{E}} \leftarrow_\$ \mathcal{B}^{n \times k}_\mu$, $\hat{\mathbf{e}} \leftarrow_\$ \mathcal{B}^k_\mu$, and compute $\mathbf{C}_1 := \hat{\mathbf{S}}^\top \mathbf{A}_j + \hat{\mathbf{E}}^\top \in \mathbb{F}^{k \times n}_2$ and $\mathbf{c}_2 := \hat{\mathbf{S}}^\top \mathbf{y}_j + \hat{\mathbf{e}} + \mathbf{G}\mathsf{m} \in \mathbb{F}^k_2$.

Finally, $\mathscr{C}$ returns the challenge ciphertext $\mathsf{c} := (\mathbf{C}_1, \mathbf{c}_2)$ to $\mathscr{A}$.

GUESS. $\mathscr{A}$ outputs a guessing bit $b' \in \{0, 1\}$.

Let Win denote the event that $b' = b$. Then by definition, $\epsilon = \left| \Pr_1[\mathsf{Win}] - \frac{1}{2} \right|$.

Game G_2. This game is the same as G_1, except that, the oracle KEYGEN is changed as follows.

KEYGEN. $\mathscr{C}$ picks $b \leftarrow_\$ \{0, 1\}$ uniformly, and proceeds as follows.
(a) Choose a master secret $\mathsf{s}^* \leftarrow_\$ \chi^n_{\mu_1 n}$.
(b) For each user $i \in [l]$, choose $\mathbf{A}_i \leftarrow_\$ \mathcal{D}^{n \times n}_\lambda$, $\mathbf{P}_i \leftarrow_\$ \mathcal{P}_n$, $\mathbf{e}_i \leftarrow_\$ \mathcal{B}^n_\mu$, and compute $\mathsf{s}_i := \mathbf{P}_i \mathsf{s}^* \in \mathbb{F}^n_2$ and $\mathbf{y}_i := \mathbf{A}_i \mathbf{P}_i \mathsf{s}^* + \mathbf{e}_i \in \mathbb{F}^n_2$.

Finally, $\mathscr{C}$ sends the public keys $\mathsf{pk}_i := (\mathbf{A}_i, \mathbf{y}_i)$, $i \in [l]$, to $\mathscr{A}$.

Claim 1. $\Pr_1[\mathsf{Win}] = \Pr_2[\mathsf{Win}]$.

Proof of Claim 1. Since $\mathsf{s}^* \sim \chi^n_{\mu_1 n}$, we have $|\mathsf{s}^*| = \mu_1 n$. Then as $\mathbf{P}_i \sim \mathcal{P}_n$, $\mathsf{s}_i = \mathbf{P}_i \mathsf{s}^*$ follows the distribution $\chi^n_{\mu_1 n}$ and is independent of s^*, the same as that in game G_1. Besides, $\mathbf{y}_i \overset{\mathsf{G}_1}{=} \mathbf{A}_i \mathsf{s}_i + \mathbf{e}_i \overset{\mathsf{G}_2}{=} \mathbf{A}_i \mathbf{P}_i \mathsf{s}^* + \mathbf{e}_i$. Consequently, the changes are just conceptual, and $\Pr_1[\mathsf{Win}] = \Pr_2[\mathsf{Win}]$. ∎

Game G_3. This game is the same as G_2, except that, the oracle CHAL is changed as follows.

CHAL$(j \in [l], f \in \mathcal{F}_{aff})$. $\mathscr{C}$ proceeds as follows.
(a) Set $f \leftarrow \mathbf{0}$ if $b = 0$. Then compute $\mathbf{T}_f := \sum_{i \in [l]} \mathbf{T}_i \mathbf{P}_i \in \mathbb{F}^{n \times n}_2$ and $\mathsf{m} := \mathbf{T}_f \mathsf{s}^* + \mathbf{t} \in \mathbb{F}^n_2$.
(b) Choose $\hat{\mathbf{S}} \leftarrow_\$ (\widetilde{\mathcal{B}}^n_{\mu_1})^k$, $\hat{\mathbf{E}} \leftarrow_\$ \mathcal{B}^{n \times k}_\mu$, $\hat{\mathbf{e}} \leftarrow_\$ \mathcal{B}^k_\mu$, and compute $\mathbf{C}_1 := \hat{\mathbf{S}}^\top \mathbf{A}_j + \hat{\mathbf{E}}^\top \in \mathbb{F}^{k \times n}_2$ and $\mathbf{c}_2 := (\mathbf{C}_1 \mathbf{P}_j + \mathbf{G}\mathbf{T}_f) \cdot \mathsf{s}^* - \hat{\mathbf{E}}^\top \mathbf{P}_j \mathsf{s}^* + \hat{\mathbf{S}}^\top \mathbf{e}_j + \hat{\mathbf{e}} + \mathbf{G}\mathbf{t} \in \mathbb{F}^k_2$.

Finally, $\mathscr{C}$ returns the challenge ciphertext $\mathsf{c} := (\mathbf{C}_1, \mathbf{c}_2)$ to $\mathscr{A}$.

Claim 2. $\Pr_2[\mathsf{Win}] = \Pr_3[\mathsf{Win}]$.

Proof of Claim 2. Observe that $\mathsf{m} \overset{\mathsf{G}_2}{=} \sum_{i \in [l]} \mathbf{T}_i \mathsf{s}_i + \mathbf{t} = \sum_{i \in [l]} \mathbf{T}_i \cdot (\mathbf{P}_i \mathsf{s}^*) + \mathbf{t} \overset{\mathsf{G}_3}{=} \mathbf{T}_f \mathsf{s}^* + \mathbf{t}$, and

$$
\begin{aligned}
\mathbf{c}_2 &\overset{\mathsf{G}_2}{=} \hat{\mathbf{S}}^\top \mathbf{y}_j + \hat{\mathbf{e}} + \mathbf{G}\mathsf{m} = \hat{\mathbf{S}}^\top \cdot (\mathbf{A}_j \mathbf{P}_j \mathsf{s}^* + \mathbf{e}_j) + \hat{\mathbf{e}} + \mathbf{G} \cdot (\mathbf{T}_f \mathsf{s}^* + \mathbf{t}) \\
&= (\hat{\mathbf{S}}^\top \mathbf{A}_j \mathbf{P}_j + \mathbf{G}\mathbf{T}_f) \cdot \mathsf{s}^* + \hat{\mathbf{S}}^\top \mathbf{e}_j + \hat{\mathbf{e}} + \mathbf{G}\mathbf{t} \\
&= ((\mathbf{C}_1 - \hat{\mathbf{E}}^\top)\mathbf{P}_j + \mathbf{G}\mathbf{T}_f) \cdot \mathsf{s}^* + \hat{\mathbf{S}}^\top \mathbf{e}_j + \hat{\mathbf{e}} + \mathbf{G}\mathbf{t} \\
&\overset{\mathsf{G}_3}{=} (\mathbf{C}_1 \mathbf{P}_j + \mathbf{G}\mathbf{T}_f) \cdot \mathsf{s}^* - \hat{\mathbf{E}}^\top \mathbf{P}_j \mathsf{s}^* + \hat{\mathbf{S}}^\top \mathbf{e}_j + \hat{\mathbf{e}} + \mathbf{G}\mathbf{t},
\end{aligned}
$$

where the penultimate equality is due to $\mathbf{C}_1 = \hat{\mathbf{S}}^\top \mathbf{A}_j + \hat{\mathbf{E}}^\top$. Thus, the changes are just conceptual.   ∎

Game G_4. This game is the same as G_3, except that, the oracle CHAL is changed as follows.

CHAL$(j \in [l], f \in \mathcal{F}_{aff})$. $\mathscr{C}$ proceeds as follows.
   (a) Set $f \leftarrow \mathbf{0}$ if $b = 0$. Then compute $\mathbf{T}_f := \sum_{i \in [l]} \mathbf{T}_i \mathbf{P}_i \in \mathbb{F}_2^{n \times n}$.
   (b) Choose $\hat{\mathbf{S}} \leftarrow_s (\widetilde{\mathcal{B}}_{\mu_1}^n)^k$, $\hat{\mathbf{E}} \leftarrow_s \mathcal{B}_\mu^{n \times k}$, $\hat{\mathbf{e}} \leftarrow_s \mathcal{B}_\mu^k$, $\underline{\mathbf{U} \leftarrow_s \mathbb{F}_2^{k \times n}}$, and compute
   $\underline{\mathbf{C}_1 := \mathbf{U} \in \mathbb{F}_2^{k \times n}}$ and $\mathbf{c}_2 := (\mathbf{C}_1 \mathbf{P}_j + \mathbf{GT}_f) \cdot \mathbf{s}^* - \hat{\mathbf{E}}^\top \mathbf{P}_j \mathbf{s}^* + \hat{\mathbf{S}}^\top \mathbf{e}_j + \hat{\mathbf{e}} + \mathbf{Gt} \in$
   $\mathbb{F}_2^k$.
   Finally, $\mathscr{C}$ returns the challenge ciphertext $\mathbf{c} := (\mathbf{C}_1, \mathbf{c}_2)$ to $\mathscr{A}$.

Claim 3. If $\mathsf{LPN}_{\mu,n}$ is $2^{\omega(n^{\frac{1}{2}})}$-hard, then $\left| \Pr_3[\mathsf{Win}] - \Pr_4[\mathsf{Win}] \right| \leq \mathsf{negl}(n)$.

Proof sketch of Claim 3. The only difference between game G_3 and game G_4 is the distribution of $\mathbf{C}_1$ in the CHAL$(j \in [l], f \in \mathcal{F}_{aff})$ queries: in game G_3, $\mathbf{C}_1 = \hat{\mathbf{S}}^\top \mathbf{A}_j + \hat{\mathbf{E}}^\top$; in game G_4, $\mathbf{C}_1 = \mathbf{U}$.

We can construct a PPT distinguisher $\mathscr{D}$ to solve the multi-fold LPN problem described in Lemma 5 by simulating game G_3 or game G_4 for $\mathscr{A}$, such that the distinguishing advantage is at least $\frac{1}{Ql} \cdot \left| \Pr_3[\mathsf{Win}] - \Pr_4[\mathsf{Win}] \right|$. Due to lack of space, we present the construction and analysis of $\mathscr{D}$ in the full version [HL17].

Consequently, by Lemma 5, $\frac{1}{Ql} \cdot \left| \Pr_3[\mathsf{Win}] - \Pr_4[\mathsf{Win}] \right|$ is negligible in n, and so is $\left| \Pr_3[\mathsf{Win}] - \Pr_4[\mathsf{Win}] \right|$.   ∎

Game G_5. This game is the same as G_4, except that, the oracle CHAL is changed as follows.

CHAL$(j \in [l], f \in \mathcal{F}_{aff})$. $\mathscr{C}$ proceeds as follows.
   (a) Set $f \leftarrow \mathbf{0}$ if $b = 0$. Then compute $\mathbf{T}_f := \sum_{i \in [l]} \mathbf{T}_i \mathbf{P}_i \in \mathbb{F}_2^{n \times n}$.
   (b) Choose $\hat{\mathbf{S}} \quad \leftarrow \quad_s (\widetilde{\mathcal{B}}_{\mu_1}^n)^k$, $\hat{\mathbf{E}} \quad \leftarrow \quad_s \mathcal{B}_\mu^{n \times k}$,
   $\hat{\mathbf{e}} \leftarrow_s \mathcal{B}_\mu^k$, $\mathbf{U} \leftarrow_s \mathbb{F}_2^{k \times n}$, and compute $\underline{\mathbf{C}_1 := \mathbf{U} - \mathbf{GT}_f \mathbf{P}_j^{-1} \in \mathbb{F}_2^{k \times n}}$ and
   $\mathbf{c}_2 := (\mathbf{C}_1 \mathbf{P}_j + \mathbf{GT}_f) \cdot \mathbf{s}^* - \hat{\mathbf{E}}^\top \mathbf{P}_j \mathbf{s}^* + \hat{\mathbf{S}}^\top \mathbf{e}_j + \hat{\mathbf{e}} + \mathbf{Gt} \in \mathbb{F}_2^k$.
   Finally, $\mathscr{C}$ returns the challenge ciphertext $\mathbf{c} := (\mathbf{C}_1, \mathbf{c}_2)$ to $\mathscr{A}$.

Claim 4. $\Pr_4[\mathsf{Win}] = \Pr_5[\mathsf{Win}]$.

Proof of Claim 4. Since $\mathbf{U}$ is uniformly chosen and independent of other parts of the game, $\mathbf{C}_1 = \mathbf{U}$ in game G_4 has the same distribution as $\mathbf{C}_1 = \mathbf{U} - \mathbf{GT}_f \mathbf{P}_j^{-1}$ in game G_5. Thus, this change is just conceptual, and $\Pr_4[\mathsf{Win}] = \Pr_5[\mathsf{Win}]$.   ∎

Game G_6. This game is the same as G_5, except that, the oracle CHAL is changed as follows.

CHAL$(j \in [l], f \in \mathcal{F}_{aff})$. $\mathscr{C}$ proceeds as follows.

(a) Set $f \leftarrow \mathbf{0}$ if $b = 0$. Then compute $\mathbf{T}_f := \sum_{i \in [l]} \mathbf{T}_i \mathbf{P}_i \in \mathbb{F}_2^{n \times n}$.

(b) Choose $\hat{\mathbf{S}} \leftarrow_s (\widetilde{\mathcal{B}}_{\mu_1}^n)^k$, $\hat{\mathbf{E}} \leftarrow_s \mathcal{B}_\mu^{n \times k}$, $\hat{\mathbf{e}} \leftarrow_s \mathcal{B}_\mu^k$, and compute $\underline{\mathbf{C}_1 := \hat{\mathbf{S}}^\top \mathbf{A}_j}$ $\underline{+\hat{\mathbf{E}}^\top - \mathbf{GT}_f \mathbf{P}_j^{-1} \in \mathbb{F}_2^{k \times n}}$ and $$\underline{\mathbf{c}_2 := (\mathbf{C}_1 \mathbf{P}_j + \mathbf{GT}_f) \cdot \mathbf{s}^* - \hat{\mathbf{E}}^\top \mathbf{P}_j \mathbf{s}^* + \hat{\mathbf{S}}^\top \mathbf{e}_j + \hat{\mathbf{e}} + \mathbf{Gt} \in \mathbb{F}_2^k.}$$

Finally, $\mathscr{C}$ returns the challenge ciphertext $\mathsf{c} := (\mathbf{C}_1, \mathbf{c}_2)$ to $\mathscr{A}$.

Claim 5. If $\mathsf{LPN}_{\mu,n}$ is $2^{\omega(n^{\frac{1}{2}})}$-hard, then $\big| \Pr_5[\mathsf{Win}] - \Pr_6[\mathsf{Win}] \big| \leq \mathsf{negl}(n)$.

The proof of Claim 5 is essentially the same as that for Claim 3, since the change from game G_5 to game G_6 is symmetric to the change from game G_3 to game G_4. For completeness, we put the proof in the full version [HL17].

Game G_7. This game is the same as G_6, except that, the oracle CHAL is changed as follows.

$\underline{\mathrm{CHAL}(j \in [l], f \in \mathcal{F}_{aff})}$. $\mathscr{C}$ proceeds as follows.

(a) Set $f \leftarrow \mathbf{0}$ if $b = 0$. Then compute $\mathbf{T}_f := \sum_{i \in [l]} \mathbf{T}_i \mathbf{P}_i \in \mathbb{F}_2^{n \times n}$.

(b) Choose $\hat{\mathbf{S}} \leftarrow_s (\widetilde{\mathcal{B}}_{\mu_1}^n)^k$, $\hat{\mathbf{E}} \leftarrow_s \mathcal{B}_\mu^{n \times k}$, $\hat{\mathbf{e}} \leftarrow_s \mathcal{B}_\mu^k$, and compute $\mathbf{C}_1 := \hat{\mathbf{S}}^\top \mathbf{A}_j + \hat{\mathbf{E}}^\top - \mathbf{GT}_f \mathbf{P}_j^{-1} \in \mathbb{F}_2^{k \times n}$ and $\underline{\mathbf{c}_2 := \hat{\mathbf{S}}^\top \mathbf{y}_j + \hat{\mathbf{e}} + \mathbf{Gt} \in \mathbb{F}_2^k}$.

Finally, $\mathscr{C}$ returns the challenge ciphertext $\mathsf{c} := \underline{(\mathbf{C}_1, \mathbf{c}_2)}$ to $\mathscr{A}$.

Claim 6. $\Pr_6[\mathsf{Win}] = \Pr_7[\mathsf{Win}]$.

Proof of Claim 6. Observe that

$$
\begin{aligned}
\mathbf{c}_2 &\overset{\mathsf{G}_6}{=} (\mathbf{C}_1 \mathbf{P}_j + \mathbf{GT}_f) \cdot \mathbf{s}^* - \hat{\mathbf{E}}^\top \mathbf{P}_j \mathbf{s}^* + \hat{\mathbf{S}}^\top \mathbf{e}_j + \hat{\mathbf{e}} + \mathbf{Gt} \\
&= ((\hat{\mathbf{S}}^\top \mathbf{A}_j + \hat{\mathbf{E}}^\top) \mathbf{P}_j) \cdot \mathbf{s}^* - \hat{\mathbf{E}}^\top \mathbf{P}_j \mathbf{s}^* + \hat{\mathbf{S}}^\top \mathbf{e}_j + \hat{\mathbf{e}} + \mathbf{Gt} \\
&= \hat{\mathbf{S}}^\top \cdot (\mathbf{A}_j \mathbf{P}_j \mathbf{s}^* + \mathbf{e}_j) + \hat{\mathbf{e}} + \mathbf{Gt} \overset{\mathsf{G}_7}{=} \hat{\mathbf{S}}^\top \mathbf{y}_j + \hat{\mathbf{e}} + \mathbf{Gt},
\end{aligned}
$$

where the second equality follows from the fact that $\mathbf{C}_1 = \hat{\mathbf{S}}^\top \mathbf{A}_j + \hat{\mathbf{E}}^\top - \mathbf{GT}_f \mathbf{P}_j^{-1}$. Therefore, this change is just conceptual, and $\Pr_6[\mathsf{Win}] = \Pr_7[\mathsf{Win}]$. ∎

Game G_8. This game is the same as G_7, except that, the oracle KEYGEN is changed as follows.

$\underline{\mathrm{KEYGEN}}$. $\mathscr{C}$ picks $b \leftarrow_s \{0, 1\}$ uniformly, and proceeds as follows.

(a) Choose a master secret $\mathbf{s}^* \leftarrow_s \chi_{\mu_1 n}^n$.

(b) For each user $i \in [l]$, choose $\underline{\mathbf{B}_i \leftarrow_s \mathcal{D}_\lambda^{n \times n}}$, $\mathbf{P}_i \leftarrow_s \mathcal{P}_n$, $\mathbf{e}_i \leftarrow_s \mathcal{B}_\mu^n$, and compute $\mathbf{A}_i := \mathbf{B}_i \mathbf{P}_i^{-1} \in \mathbb{F}_2^{n \times n}$ and $\mathbf{y}_i := \mathbf{B}_i \mathbf{s}^* + \mathbf{e}_i \in \mathbb{F}_2^n$.

Finally, $\mathscr{C}$ sends the public keys $\mathsf{pk}_i := (\mathbf{A}_i, \mathbf{y}_i)$, $i \in [l]$, to $\mathscr{A}$.

Claim 7. $\Pr_7[\mathsf{Win}] = \Pr_8[\mathsf{Win}]$.

Proof of Claim 7. For each $i \in [l]$, the permutation $\mathbf{P}_i \sim \mathcal{P}_n$ is invertible. Then as $\mathbf{B}_i \sim \mathcal{D}_\lambda^{n \times n}$, $\mathbf{A}_i = \mathbf{B}_i \mathbf{P}_i^{-1}$ also follows the distribution $\mathcal{D}_\lambda^{n \times n}$ and is independent of $\mathbf{P}_i$. The reason is as follows. $\mathbf{B}_i \sim \mathcal{D}_\lambda^{n \times n}$ basically means that $\mathbf{B}_i = \mathbf{U}_i \mathbf{V}_i$ for $\mathbf{U}_i \sim \mathcal{U}_{n \times \lambda}$ and $\mathbf{V}_i \sim \mathcal{U}_{\lambda \times n}$. Then $\mathbf{A}_i = \mathbf{B}_i \mathbf{P}_i^{-1} = \mathbf{U}_i(\mathbf{V}_i \mathbf{P}_i^{-1})$, where $\mathbf{V}_i \mathbf{P}_i^{-1}$ follows the distribution $\mathcal{U}_{\lambda \times n}$ since $\mathbf{V}_i$ is. Consequently, $\mathbf{A}_i$ is distributed according to $\mathcal{D}_\lambda^{n \times n}$, the same as that in game G_7.

Besides, $\mathbf{y}_i \overset{\mathsf{G}_7}{=} \mathbf{A}_i \mathbf{P}_i \mathbf{s}^* + \mathbf{e}_i = (\mathbf{B}_i \mathbf{P}_i^{-1}) \cdot \mathbf{P}_i \mathbf{s}^* + \mathbf{e}_i \overset{\mathsf{G}_8}{=} \mathbf{B}_i \mathbf{s}^* + \mathbf{e}_i$. Thus, the changes are just conceptual, and $\mathrm{Pr}_7[\mathsf{Win}] = \mathrm{Pr}_8[\mathsf{Win}]$. ∎

Game G_9. This game is the same as G_8, except that, the oracle KEYGEN is changed as follows.

KEYGEN. $\mathscr{C}$ picks $b \leftarrow_\$ \{0,1\}$ uniformly, and proceeds as follows.
 (a) For each user $i \in [l]$, choose $\mathbf{B}_i \leftarrow_\$ \mathcal{D}_\lambda^{n \times n}$, $\mathbf{P}_i \leftarrow_\$ \mathcal{P}_n$, and compute $\mathbf{A}_i :=$ $\mathbf{B}_i \mathbf{P}_i^{-1} \in \mathbb{F}_2^{n \times n}$ and $\mathbf{y}_i \leftarrow_\$ \mathbb{F}_2^n$.
 Finally, $\mathscr{C}$ sends the public keys $\mathsf{pk}_i := (\mathbf{A}_i, \mathbf{y}_i)$, $i \in [l]$, to $\mathscr{A}$.

Claim 8. If $\mathsf{LPN}_{\mu,n}$ is $2^{\omega(n^{\frac{1}{2}})}$-hard, then $\big| \mathrm{Pr}_8[\mathsf{Win}] - \mathrm{Pr}_9[\mathsf{Win}] \big| \leq \mathsf{negl}(n)$.

Proof sketch of Claim 8. The only difference between game G_8 and game G_9 is that $\mathbf{y}_i = \mathbf{B}_i \mathbf{s}^* + \mathbf{e}_i$ in G_8 is replaced by $\mathbf{y}_i \leftarrow_\$ \mathbb{F}_2^n$ in G_9. Observe that the master secret key $\mathbf{s}^*$ and the noise vectors $\mathbf{e}_i$, $i \in [l]$, are never used in the CHAL oracle in both G_8 and G_9. Therefore, we can directly bound the difference by constructing a PPT distinguisher to solve the multi-fold LPN problem described in Theorem 2, such that the distinguishing advantage is at least $\big| \mathrm{Pr}_8[\mathsf{Win}] - \mathrm{Pr}_9[\mathsf{Win}] \big|$. (For completeness, we show the distinguisher in the full version [HL17].) Consequently, by Theorem 2, $\big| \mathrm{Pr}_8[\mathsf{Win}] - \mathrm{Pr}_9[\mathsf{Win}] \big|$ is negligible in n. ∎

Game G_{10}. This game is the same as G_9, except that, the oracle KEYGEN is changed as follows.

KEYGEN. $\mathscr{C}$ picks $b \leftarrow_\$ \{0,1\}$ uniformly, and proceeds as follows.
 (a) For each user $i \in [l]$, choose $\mathbf{A}_i \leftarrow_\$ \mathcal{D}_\lambda^{n \times n}$, $\mathbf{P}_i \leftarrow_\$ \mathcal{P}_n$, and $\mathbf{y}_i \leftarrow_\$ \mathbb{F}_2^n$.
 Finally, $\mathscr{C}$ sends the public keys $\mathsf{pk}_i := (\mathbf{A}_i, \mathbf{y}_i)$, $i \in [l]$, to $\mathscr{A}$.

Claim 9. $\mathrm{Pr}_9[\mathsf{Win}] = \mathrm{Pr}_{10}[\mathsf{Win}]$.

Proof of Claim 9. The proof is essentially the same as that for Claim 7. The key observation is that $\mathbf{A}_i = \mathbf{B}_i \mathbf{P}_i^{-1}$ in game G_9 is distributed according to $\mathcal{D}_\lambda^{n \times n}$ and independent of $\mathbf{P}_i$, the same as that in game G_{10}. Thus, this change is just conceptual, and $\mathrm{Pr}_9[\mathsf{Win}] = \mathrm{Pr}_{10}[\mathsf{Win}]$. ∎

Game G_{11}. This game is the same as G_{10}, except that, the oracle CHAL is changed as follows.

CHAL$(j \in [l], f \in \mathcal{F}_{aff})$. $\mathscr{C}$ proceeds as follows.
 (a) Set $f \leftarrow \mathbf{0}$ if $b = 0$. Then compute $\mathbf{T}_f := \sum_{i \in [l]} \mathbf{T}_i \mathbf{P}_i \in \mathbb{F}_2^{n \times n}$.

(b) Choose $\mathbf{U} \leftarrow_\$ \mathbb{F}_2^{k \times n}$, $\mathbf{u} \leftarrow_\$ \mathbb{F}_2^k$, and compute $\underline{\mathbf{C}_1 := \mathbf{U} - \mathbf{GT}_f \mathbf{P}_j^{-1}} \in \mathbb{F}_2^{k \times n}$
and $\mathbf{c}_2 := \mathbf{u} + \mathbf{Gt} \in \mathbb{F}_2^k$.
Finally, $\mathscr{C}$ returns the challenge ciphertext $\mathsf{c} := (\mathbf{C}_1, \mathbf{c}_2)$ to $\mathscr{A}$.

Claim 10. If $\mathsf{LPN}_{\mu,n}$ is $2^{\omega(n^{\frac{1}{2}})}$-hard, then $\left| \Pr_{10}[\mathsf{Win}] - \Pr_{11}[\mathsf{Win}] \right| \leq \mathsf{negl}(n)$.

Proof sketch of Claim 10. The only difference between game G_{10} and game G_{11} is the distribution of $\mathbf{C}_1$ and $\mathbf{c}_2$ in the CHAL$(j \in [l], f \in \mathcal{F}_{\text{aff}})$ queries: in game G_{10}, $\mathbf{C}_1 = \hat{\mathbf{S}}^\top \mathbf{A}_j + \hat{\mathbf{E}}^\top - \mathbf{GT}_f \mathbf{P}_j^{-1}$ and $\mathbf{c}_2 = \hat{\mathbf{S}}^\top \mathbf{y}_j + \hat{\mathbf{e}} + \mathbf{Gt}$; in game G_{11}, $\mathbf{C}_1 = \mathbf{U} - \mathbf{GT}_f \mathbf{P}_j^{-1}$ and $\mathbf{c}_2 = \mathbf{u} + \mathbf{Gt}$.

We can construct a PPT distinguisher $\mathscr{D}$ to solve the multi-fold LPN problem described in Lemma 6, by simulating game G_{10} or game G_{11} for $\mathscr{A}$. The construction of $\mathscr{D}$ is analogous to that in the proof of Claim 3. Similarly, $\mathscr{D}$'s distinguishing advantage is at least $\frac{1}{Ql} \cdot \left| \Pr_{10}[\mathsf{Win}] - \Pr_{11}[\mathsf{Win}] \right|$. For lack of space, we present the construction and analysis of $\mathscr{D}$ in the full version [HL17].

Consequently, by Lemma 6, $\frac{1}{Ql} \cdot \left| \Pr_{10}[\mathsf{Win}] - \Pr_{11}[\mathsf{Win}] \right|$ is negligible in n, and so is $\left| \Pr_{10}[\mathsf{Win}] - \Pr_{11}[\mathsf{Win}] \right|$. ∎

Game G_{12}. This game is the same as G_{11}, except that, the oracle CHAL is changed as follows.

CHAL$(j \in [l], f \in \mathcal{F}_{aff})$. $\mathscr{C}$ proceeds as follows.

(a) Choose $\mathbf{U} \leftarrow_\$ \mathbb{F}_2^{k \times n}$, $\mathbf{u} \leftarrow_\$ \mathbb{F}_2^k$, and compute $\underline{\mathbf{C}_1 := \mathbf{U}} \in \mathbb{F}_2^{k \times n}$ and $\mathbf{c}_2 := \underline{\mathbf{u}} \in \mathbb{F}_2^k$.
Finally, $\mathscr{C}$ returns the challenge ciphertext $\mathsf{c} := (\mathbf{C}_1, \mathbf{c}_2)$ to $\mathscr{A}$.

Claim 11. $\Pr_{11}[\mathsf{Win}] = \Pr_{12}[\mathsf{Win}] = \frac{1}{2}$.

Proof of Claim 11. Since $\mathbf{U}$ and $\mathbf{u}$ are uniformly chosen and independent of other parts of the game, $\mathbf{C}_1 = \mathbf{U} - \mathbf{GT}_f \mathbf{P}_j^{-1}$ and $\mathbf{C}_2 = \mathbf{u} + \mathbf{Gt}$ in game G_{11} have the same distributions as $\mathbf{C}_1 = \mathbf{U}$ and $\mathbf{C}_2 = \mathbf{u}$ in game G_{12}, respectively. Therefore, the changes are just conceptual, and $\Pr_{11}[\mathsf{Win}] = \Pr_{12}[\mathsf{Win}]$.

Moreover, the challenge bit b is never used in game G_{12}, thus completely hidden from $\mathscr{A}$'s view. Consequently, we have $\Pr_{12}[\mathsf{Win}] = \frac{1}{2}$. ∎

Taking all things together, by Claims 1–11, it follows that $\epsilon = \left| \Pr_1[\mathsf{Win}] - \frac{1}{2} \right| \leq \mathsf{negl}(n)$. This completes the proof of Theorem 4. ∎

Acknowledgments. We would like to thank Yunhua Wen for a careful proofreading, and the reviewers for valuable comments. The authors are supported by the National Natural Science Foundation of China Grant (Nos. 61672346, 61373153).

References

[ABBC10] Acar, T., Belenkiy, M., Bellare, M., Cash, D.: Cryptographic agility and its relation to circular encryption. In: Gilbert, H. (ed.) EUROCRYPT 2010. LNCS, vol. 6110, pp. 403–422. Springer, Heidelberg (2010). doi:10.1007/978-3-642-13190-5_21

[ACPS09] Applebaum, B., Cash, D., Peikert, C., Sahai, A.: Fast cryptographic primitives and circular-secure encryption based on hard learning problems. In: Halevi, S. (ed.) CRYPTO 2009. LNCS, vol. 5677, pp. 595–618. Springer, Heidelberg (2009). doi:10.1007/978-3-642-03356-8_35

[Ale03] Alekhnovich, M.: More on average case vs approximation complexity. In: FOCS 2003, pp. 298–307. IEEE Computer Society (2003)

[AP16] Alamati, N., Peikert, C.: Three's compromised too: circular insecurity for any cycle length from (Ring-)LWE. In: Robshaw, M., Katz, J. (eds.) CRYPTO 2016. LNCS, vol. 9815, pp. 659–680. Springer, Heidelberg (2016). doi:10.1007/978-3-662-53008-5_23

[App11] Applebaum, B.: Key-dependent message security: generic amplification and completeness. In: Paterson, K.G. (ed.) EUROCRYPT 2011. LNCS, vol. 6632, pp. 527–546. Springer, Heidelberg (2011). doi:10.1007/978-3-642-20465-4_29

[BFKL93] Blum, A., Furst, M., Kearns, M., Lipton, R.J.: Cryptographic primitives based on hard learning problems. In: Stinson, D.R. (ed.) CRYPTO 1993. LNCS, vol. 773, pp. 278–291. Springer, Heidelberg (1994). doi:10.1007/3-540-48329-2_24

[BG10] Brakerski, Z., Goldwasser, S.: Circular and leakage resilient public-key encryption under subgroup indistinguishability. In: Rabin, T. (ed.) CRYPTO 2010. LNCS, vol. 6223, pp. 1–20. Springer, Heidelberg (2010). doi:10.1007/978-3-642-14623-7_1

[BGK11] Brakerski, Z., Goldwasser, S., Kalai, Y.T.: Black-box circular-secure encryption beyond affine functions. In: Ishai, Y. (ed.) TCC 2011. LNCS, vol. 6597, pp. 201–218. Springer, Heidelberg (2011). doi:10.1007/978-3-642-19571-6_13

[BHHI10] Barak, B., Haitner, I., Hofheinz, D., Ishai, Y.: Bounded key-dependent message security. In: Gilbert, H. (ed.) EUROCRYPT 2010. LNCS, vol. 6110, pp. 423–444. Springer, Heidelberg (2010). doi:10.1007/978-3-642-13190-5_22

[BHHO08] Boneh, D., Halevi, S., Hamburg, M., Ostrovsky, R.: Circular-secure encryption from decision Diffie-Hellman. In: Wagner, D. (ed.) CRYPTO 2008. LNCS, vol. 5157, pp. 108–125. Springer, Heidelberg (2008). doi:10.1007/978-3-540-85174-5_7

[BHW15] Bishop, A., Hohenberger, S., Waters, B.: New circular security counterexamples from decision linear and learning with errors. In: Iwata, T., Cheon, J.H. (eds.) ASIACRYPT 2015. LNCS, vol. 9453, pp. 776–800. Springer, Heidelberg (2015). doi:10.1007/978-3-662-48800-3_32

[BJMM12] Becker, A., Joux, A., May, A., Meurer, A.: Decoding random binary linear codes in $2^{n/20}$: How 1+1=0 improves information set decoding. In: Pointcheval, D., Johansson, T. (eds.) EUROCRYPT 2012. LNCS, vol. 7237, pp. 520–536. Springer, Heidelberg (2012). doi:10.1007/978-3-642-29011-4_31

[BKW03] Blum, A., Kalai, A., Wasserman, H.: Noise-tolerant learning, the parity problem, and the statistical query model. J. ACM **50**(4), 506–519 (2003)

[BLP11] Bernstein, D.J., Lange, T., Peters, C.: Smaller decoding exponents: ball-collision decoding. In: Rogaway, P. (ed.) CRYPTO 2011. LNCS, vol. 6841, pp. 743–760. Springer, Heidelberg (2011). doi:10.1007/978-3-642-22792-9_42

[BMT78] Berlekamp, E.R., McEliece, R.J., van Tilborg, H.C.A.: On the inherent intractability of certain coding problems. IEEE Trans. Inf. Theor. **24**(3), 384–386 (1978)

[BRS02] Black, J., Rogaway, P., Shrimpton, T.: Encryption-scheme security in the presence of key-dependent messages. In: Nyberg, K., Heys, H. (eds.) SAC 2002. LNCS, vol. 2595, pp. 62–75. Springer, Heidelberg (2003). doi:10.1007/3-540-36492-7_6

[CC98] Canteaut, A., Chabaud, F.: A new algorithm for finding minimum-weight words in a linear code: application to mceliece's cryptosystem and to narrow-sense BCH codes of length 511. IEEE Trans. Inf. Theor. **44**(1), 367–378 (1998)

[CCS09] Camenisch, J., Chandran, N., Shoup, V.: A public key encryption scheme secure against key dependent chosen plaintext and adaptive chosen ciphertext attacks. In: Joux, A. (ed.) EUROCRYPT 2009. LNCS, vol. 5479, pp. 351–368. Springer, Heidelberg (2009). doi:10.1007/978-3-642-01001-9_20

[CGH12] Cash, D., Green, M., Hohenberger, S.: New definitions and separations for circular security. In: Fischlin, M., Buchmann, J., Manulis, M. (eds.) PKC 2012. LNCS, vol. 7293, pp. 540–557. Springer, Heidelberg (2012). doi:10.1007/978-3-642-30057-8_32

[CL01] Camenisch, J., Lysyanskaya, A.: An efficient system for non-transferable anonymous credentials with optional anonymity revocation. In: Pfitzmann, B. (ed.) EUROCRYPT 2001. LNCS, vol. 2045, pp. 93–118. Springer, Heidelberg (2001). doi:10.1007/3-540-44987-6_7

[DDN14] David, B., Dowsley, R., Nascimento, A.C.A.: Universally composable oblivious transfer based on a variant of LPN. In: Gritzalis, D., Kiayias, A., Askoxylakis, I. (eds.) CANS 2014. LNCS, vol. 8813, pp. 143–158. Springer, Cham (2014). doi:10.1007/978-3-319-12280-9_10

[DMN12] Döttling, N., Müller-Quade, J., Nascimento, A.C.A.: IND-CCA secure cryptography based on a variant of the LPN problem. In: Wang, X., Sako, K. (eds.) ASIACRYPT 2012. LNCS, vol. 7658, pp. 485–503. Springer, Heidelberg (2012). doi:10.1007/978-3-642-34961-4_30

[Döt15] Döttling, N.: Low noise LPN: KDM secure public key encryption and sample amplification. In: Katz, J. (ed.) PKC 2015. LNCS, vol. 9020, pp. 604–626. Springer, Heidelberg (2015). doi:10.1007/978-3-662-46447-2_27

[FGKP06] Feldman, V., Gopalan, P., Khot, S., Ponnuswami, A.K.: New results for learning noisy parities and halfspaces. In: FOCS 2006, pp. 563–574. IEEE Computer Society (2006)

[For66] Forney, G.D.: Concatenated Codes. MIT Press, Cambridge (1966)

[GHV12] Galindo, D., Herranz, J., Villar, J.: Identity-based encryption with master key-dependent message security and leakage-resilience. In: Foresti, S., Yung, M., Martinelli, F. (eds.) ESORICS 2012. LNCS, vol. 7459, pp. 627–642. Springer, Heidelberg (2012). doi:10.1007/978-3-642-33167-1_36

[GKW17] Goyal, R., Koppula, V., Waters, B.: Separating IND-CPA and circular security for unbounded length key cycles. In: Fehr, S. (ed.) PKC 2017. LNCS, vol. 10174, pp. 232–246. Springer, Heidelberg (2017). doi:10.1007/978-3-662-54365-8_10

[GM84] Goldwasser, S., Micali, S.: Probabilistic encryption. J. Comput. Syst. Sci. **28**(2), 270–299 (1984)

[HILL99] Håstad, J., Impagliazzo, R., Levin, L.A., Luby, M.: A pseudorandom generator from any one-way function. SIAM J. Comput. **28**(4), 1364–1396 (1999)

[HL17] Han, S., Liu, S.: KDM-secure public-key encryption from constant-noise LPN. IACR Cryptology ePrint Archive, Report 2017/310 (2017)

[HLL16] Han, S., Liu, S., Lyu, L.: Efficient KDM-CCA secure public-key encryption for polynomial functions. In: Cheon, J.H., Takagi, T. (eds.) ASIACRYPT 2016. LNCS, vol. 10032, pp. 307–338. Springer, Heidelberg (2016). doi:10.1007/978-3-662-53890-6_11

[Hof13] Hofheinz, D.: Circular chosen-ciphertext security with compact ciphertexts. In: Johansson, T., Nguyen, P.Q. (eds.) EUROCRYPT 2013. LNCS, vol. 7881, pp. 520–536. Springer, Heidelberg (2013). doi:10.1007/978-3-642-38348-9_31

[Kir11] Kirchner, P.: Improved generalized birthday attack. IACR Cryptology ePrint Archive, Report 2011/377 (2011)

[KMP14] Kiltz, E., Masny, D., Pietrzak, K.: Simple chosen-ciphertext security from low-noise LPN. In: Krawczyk, H. (ed.) PKC 2014. LNCS, vol. 8383, pp. 1–18. Springer, Heidelberg (2014). doi:10.1007/978-3-642-54631-0_1

[KRW15] Koppula, V., Ramchen, K., Waters, B.: Separations in circular security for arbitrary length key cycles. In: Dodis, Y., Nielsen, J.B. (eds.) TCC 2015. LNCS, vol. 9015, pp. 378–400. Springer, Heidelberg (2015). doi:10.1007/978-3-662-46497-7_15

[KS06] Katz, J., Shin, J.S.: Parallel and concurrent security of the HB and HB+ protocols. In: Vaudenay, S. (ed.) EUROCRYPT 2006. LNCS, vol. 4004, pp. 73–87. Springer, Heidelberg (2006). doi:10.1007/11761679_6

[KW16] Koppula, V., Waters, B.: Circular security separations for arbitrary length cycles from LWE. In: Robshaw, M., Katz, J. (eds.) CRYPTO 2016. LNCS, vol. 9815, pp. 681–700. Springer, Heidelberg (2016). doi:10.1007/978-3-662-53008-5_24

[LF06] Levieil, É., Fouque, P.-A.: An improved LPN algorithm. In: Prisco, R., Yung, M. (eds.) SCN 2006. LNCS, vol. 4116, pp. 348–359. Springer, Heidelberg (2006). doi:10.1007/11832072_24

[LLJ15] Lu, X., Li, B., Jia, D.: KDM-CCA security from RKA secure authenticated encryption. In: Oswald, E., Fischlin, M. (eds.) EUROCRYPT 2015. LNCS, vol. 9056, pp. 559–583. Springer, Heidelberg (2015). doi:10.1007/978-3-662-46800-5_22

[Lyu05] Lyubashevsky, V.: The parity problem in the presence of noise, decoding random linear codes, and the subset sum problem. In: Chekuri, C., Jansen, K., Rolim, J.D.P., Trevisan, L. (eds.) APPROX/RANDOM -2005. LNCS, vol. 3624, pp. 378–389. Springer, Heidelberg (2005). doi:10.1007/11538462_32

[Mat93] Matsui, M.: Linear cryptanalysis method for DES cipher. In: Helleseth, T. (ed.) EUROCRYPT 1993. LNCS, vol. 765, pp. 386–397. Springer, Heidelberg (1994). doi:10.1007/3-540-48285-7_33

[MMT11] May, A., Meurer, A., Thomae, E.: Decoding random linear codes in $\tilde{O}(2^{0.054n})$. In: Lee, D.H., Wang, X. (eds.) ASIACRYPT 2011. LNCS, vol. 7073, pp. 107–124. Springer, Heidelberg (2011). doi:10.1007/978-3-642-25385-0_6

[MO14] Marcedone, A., Orlandi, C.: Obfuscation $\Rightarrow$ (IND-CPA Security !$\Rightarrow$ Circular Security). In: Abdalla, M., Prisco, R. (eds.) SCN 2014. LNCS, vol. 8642, pp. 77–90. Springer, Cham (2014). doi:10.1007/978-3-319-10879-7_5

[MTY11] Malkin, T., Teranishi, I., Yung, M.: Efficient circuit-size independent public key encryption with KDM security. In: Paterson, K.G. (ed.) EUROCRYPT 2011. LNCS, vol. 6632, pp. 507–526. Springer, Heidelberg (2011). doi:10.1007/978-3-642-20465-4_28

[Reg05] Regev, O.: On lattices, learning with errors, random linear codes, and cryptography. In: Gabow, H.N., Fagin, R. (eds.) STOC 2005, pp. 84–93. ACM (2005)

[Ste88] Stern, J.: A method for finding codewords of small weight. In: Cohen, G., Wolfmann, J. (eds.) Coding Theory 1988. LNCS, vol. 388, pp. 106–113. Springer, Heidelberg (1989). doi:10.1007/BFb0019850

[YZ16] Yu, Y., Zhang, J.: Cryptography with auxiliary input and trapdoor from constant-noise LPN. In: Robshaw, M., Katz, J. (eds.) CRYPTO 2016. LNCS, vol. 9814, pp. 214–243. Springer, Heidelberg (2016). doi:10.1007/978-3-662-53018-4_9

Long-Term Secure Commitments
via Extractable-Binding Commitments

Ahto Buldas[1,2], Matthias Geihs[3]([⊠]), and Johannes Buchmann[3]

[1] Tallinn University of Technology, Tallinn, Estonia
[2] Cybernetica AS, Tallinn, Estonia
[3] Darmstadt University of Technology, Darmstadt, Germany
mgeihs@cdc.informatik.tu-darmstadt.de

Abstract. Cryptographic commitments are either unconditionally hiding or unconditionally binding, but cannot be both. As a consequence, the security of commonly used commitment schemes is threatened in the long-term, when adversaries become computationally much more powerful. We improve over this situation by putting forward a new notion of commitment schemes, so called *long-term commitment schemes*. These schemes allow for long-term protection because they allow to adjust the protection level after the initial commitment. We also present a construction of a long-term commitment scheme. Unfortunately, it seems impossible to prove the security of such a scheme using the traditional commitment binding definition. Therefore, we put forward a new notion of binding commitments, so called *extractable-binding commitments*, and use this notion to establish a security proof for our proposed long-term commitment scheme.

1 Introduction

During the last decades, we have witnessed a fast growth of computer- and network technology that is expected to continue in the foreseeable future. The rapid growth of informational assets that require long-term protection poses a challenge to the cryptographic protection mechanisms. Most of the cryptographic mechanisms used in practical solutions only provide *computational security* (i.e., security against attackers with limited computational resources). This means that their security needs to be adjusted over time to protect against attackers with increasing computational resources.

Commitment schemes are important building blocks in many cryptographic protocols and also important mechanisms in secure electronic archival storage [7]. Commitment schemes enable a party to commit to (potentially) secret data, so that the commitment procedure reveals no useful information about the data (the *hiding property*) and the party cannot later deny or modify the already

---

This work has been co-funded by the DFG as part of project S6 within the CRC 1119 CROSSING.

J. Pieprzyk and S. Suriadi (Eds.): ACISP 2017, Part I, LNCS 10342, pp. 65–81, 2017.
DOI: 10.1007/978-3-319-60055-0_4

committed data (the *binding property*). As it is a well-known fact that no commitment scheme can simultaneously be hiding and binding against an adversary with unlimited computational resources, commitment schemes used in long-term archives certainly need periodic renewal.

While the precise mathematical security conditions for commitment schemes have been extensively studied in various contexts and security models, the exact mathematical security notions for renewable commitments have not been studied so far. There has been some progress though in the field of digital *time-stamping*. Bayer et al. [2] proposed a renewal mechanism for time stamps and recently, Geihs et al. [14] gave a formal security proof for a timestamp renewal scheme. An important conclusion of their work was that the overall cryptographic strength of renewed timestamps tends to decrease gradually when renewed many times. Hence, for choosing proper security parameters of long-term archives, one has to know how much extra security we need to compensate the gradual security decrease.

The renewal method of [2,14] can be adapted for commitment schemes. A document X and its commitment $c = C(X)$ is renewed by creating (at time t) a new commitment $c^* = C^*(X, c)$. If later (say, at $t' > t$) the cryptographic mechanisms of C are broken but those of C^* are still secure, and it is believed that the mechanisms in C were secure at t, then after opening the *renewed commitment* (c, c^*) (and seeing X), it is still reasonable to believe that X was indeed the committed message.

To formalize this as a reduction-type security proof, we have to show that if there exists an adversary A' that creates a double-opening of c at time t', i.e., two commitments $c_1^* = C^*(X, c)$ and $c_2^* = C^*(X', c)$ such that c opens to both X and X', then there exists an adversary A that breaks the binding property of C at t. Therefore, we introduce the notion of physical time and assume that the class $\mathcal{M}_t$ of computing technology available at time t widens when t increases, i.e., $\mathcal{M}_t \subseteq \mathcal{M}_{t'}$ if $t < t'$. We assume that the adversary is able to increment the time-reading t of the clock. The adversary can send commitments to the receiver at any time. The commitment receiver stores all the received commitments together with the times that they were received. In such a model, for having the reduction above, we cannot use the classical security definition for binding because as $A' \in \mathcal{M}_{t'}$, we are not able to use the code of A' to construct an $A \in \mathcal{M}_t$ for breaking C. Instead, we have to use *extraction-based* binding conditions, i.e., we assume for every committing adversary $A_1 \in \mathcal{M}_t$ the existence of an extractor $\mathcal{E}_t \in \mathcal{M}_t$ that, having as input the random coins of A_1, outputs the committed message X, such that no $A_2 \in \mathcal{M}_t$ is able to open the commitment with a different message X'.

In Sect. 2 of this paper, we provide the reader with preliminary notions. In Sect. 3, we give a formal definition for *extractable binding* and study its relation with the existing notions of binding. We show that extractable binding implies classical binding and we can also show with a quadratic loss of security that classical binding implies extractable binding. In Sect. 4, we define the notion of long-term secure renewable commitments and give a construction that uses unconditionally hiding and extractable binding commitment schemes. In Sect. 5, we present a security proof and in Sect. 6, we draw practical conclusions by giving the exact security evaluation of the scheme under a set of reasonable assumptions.

2 Preliminaries

Exact Security Model. The traditional provable security model is asymptotic and only guarantees that security reductions have practical conclusions for sufficiently large values of the security parameter. In practice, we would like to have security reductions for particular choices of the security parameter. Such an approach is called *exact security* (or *concrete security*) and was first proposed by Bellare et al. [3,4]. In such a model, all the resources of the adversary should be taken into account. For example, it is insufficient to deal with t-time (p-step) adversaries without considering their number of states (the code-size). For example, in the model with adversaries with unlimited (but still finite!) number of states any instance of the modular exponent function $g^x \bmod n$ can be inverted by an $O(|x|)$-time adversary (where $|x|$ is the bit-size of x). To avoid such an unintuitive (and impractical) conclusion, we assume that the adversary is forced to load (read) its code, which means that the code-size of the adversary cannot exceed its running time (the number of computational steps).

We use the following conventions. A cryptographic adversary $\mathcal{A}$ can be thought of as a computer running an algorithm, where the step count of that computer is the number of operations performed by the CPU. These concepts are formalized using a computational model, e.g., Turing Machines [1,17]. If $\mathcal{A}$ is finished after at most p steps, we say $\mathcal{A}$ is a p-step adversary. An adversary may use random coins during a computation. We write $y \xleftarrow{\omega} \mathcal{A}$, if $\mathcal{A}$ uses random coins ω and outputs y. We describe the concrete security of a cryptographic scheme in terms of a success bound $\epsilon : \mathcal{R} \to [0,1]$, which is a function that maps computational resources $R \in \mathcal{R}$ to a success probability $\epsilon(R) \in [0,1]$. We say a cryptographic scheme is ϵ-secure if for every adversary with computational resources R, the probability that the adversary breaks the computational security of the scheme is at most $\epsilon(R)$.

Commitment Schemes. A commitment scheme is the cryptographic equivalent of a sealed envelope. It allows for committing to some message m which will only later be revealed, where it is guaranteed that the committer cannot change his mind about the committed message and the receiver does not learn the message before the commitment is opened. More formally, a commitment scheme is defined as follows.

Definition 1 (Commitment scheme). *A commitment scheme is defined by a triple of algorithms* Setup, Commit, *and* Verify.

– Setup *gets no input and outputs a commitment parameter* ck.

- Commit *gets as input a commitment parameter ck, and a message m. It outputs a commitment c and a witness w.*
- Verify *gets as input a commitment parameter ck, a message m, a commitment c, and a witness w. It outputs a boolean b, where b = 1 means that the commitment is valid and b = 0 means the commitment is invalid.*

We remark that in this work we consider commitment schemes that allow messages of arbitrary length, i.e., with message space $\{0,1\}^*$. Next, we define the security properties of commitment schemes, which are *hiding* and *binding*. Hiding means that the commitment receiver does not learn the message in the commitment phase. If this properties holds for commitment receivers with unlimited computational resources, then we say the scheme is unconditional hiding.

Definition 2 (Hiding). *A commitment scheme* CS *is unconditionally hiding if for any adversary* $\mathcal{A}$: $\quad \mathbf{Adv}_{\mathsf{CS}}^{\mathrm{Hide}}(\mathcal{A}) = \Pr\left[\mathbf{Exp}_{\mathsf{CS}}^{\mathrm{Hide}}(\mathcal{A}) = 1\right] = \frac{1}{2}$.

A commitment scheme is binding if the committer cannot change his mind about the committed message. Here, we only allow computationally bounded committers. We remark that commitment schemes cannot be unconditionally binding and unconditionally hiding at the same time [6].

Definition 3 (Classical binding). *Let* $\epsilon : \mathbb{N} \to [0, 1]$. *A commitment scheme is* ϵ-*classical-binding if for every integer p, for every p-step adversary* $\mathcal{A}$:

$$\mathbf{Adv}_{\mathsf{CS}}^{\mathrm{Bind}}(\mathcal{A}) = \Pr\left[\mathbf{Exp}_{\mathsf{CS}}^{\mathrm{Bind}}(\mathcal{A}) = 1\right] \leq \epsilon(p) .$$

Algorithm 1. The hiding experiment $\mathbf{Exp}_{\mathsf{CS}}^{\mathrm{Hide}}(\mathcal{A})$.

$ck \leftarrow$ CS.Setup;
$(m_0, m_1, s) \leftarrow \mathcal{A}(ck)$;
$b \leftarrow_\$ \{0, 1\}$;
$c \leftarrow$ CS.Commit(ck, m_b);
$b' \leftarrow \mathcal{A}(s, c)$;
if $b = b'$ **then**
$\quad\mid$ **return** 1;
else
$\quad\lfloor$ **return** 0;

Although the classical binding definition presented in this section is the traditionally most commonly used one, there exist many alternative definitions for commitment binding. It occurs that the classical binding definition is insufficient for certain scenarios such as in the Universal Composability Framework [11], for Quantum Commitments [18], and also for proving the security of long-term commitments. Thus, in the next section we introduce a new notion for commitment binding called *extractable-binding*.

Algorithm 2. The binding experiment $\mathbf{Exp}_{CS}^{Bind}(\mathcal{A})$.

$ck \leftarrow$ CS.Setup;
$(c, m, w, m', w') \leftarrow \mathcal{A}(ck)$;
if CS.Verify$(ck, m, c, w) =$ CS.Verify$(ck, m', c, w') = 1$ **and** $m \neq m'$ **then**
  | **return** 1;
else
  | **return** 0;

---

3 Extractable-Binding Commitments

For extractable-binding commitments we require that the committer, who produces a commitment and later opens the commitment to some message, must already know the message at the time of the commitment. This notion allows us to prove the security of long-term commitment schemes (Sects. 4 and 5).

Extractable-binding is defined in experiment $\mathbf{Exp}^{ExtBind}$ with a two staged adversary $(\mathcal{A}_1, \mathcal{A}_2)$ and an extractor $\mathcal{E}$. Here, $\mathcal{A}_1$ is the committing algorithm who outputs a commitment c and an advice string s that contains information how to open c. The extractor $\mathcal{E}$ gets as input the random coins ω of $\mathcal{A}_1$ and the advice string s. It outputs a message m^* which is the extracted message. Afterwards, the second stage adversary $\mathcal{A}_2$ is run on input of advice string s and outputs a commitment opening (m, w). A commitment scheme is extractable-binding if there exists an extractor such that for any commitment opening, the extracted message equals the opened message.

Definition 4 (Extractable binding). *Let* $\epsilon : \mathbb{N}^3 \to [0, 1]$. *A commitment scheme* CS *is* ϵ-*extractable-binding, if for every integers* p_1 *and* p_2, *for every* p_1-*step adversary* $\mathcal{A}_1$, *there exists a* $p_{\mathcal{E}}$-*step extractor* $\mathcal{E}$, *such that for every* p_2-*step adversary* $\mathcal{A}_2$:

$$\mathbf{Adv}_{CS}^{ExtBind}(\mathcal{A}_1, \mathcal{E}, \mathcal{A}_2) = \Pr\left[\mathbf{Exp}_{CS}^{ExtBind}(\mathcal{A}_1, \mathcal{E}, \mathcal{A}_2) = 1\right] \leq \epsilon(p_1, p_{\mathcal{E}}, p_2) .$$

Algorithm 3. The extractable-binding experiment $\mathbf{Exp}_{CS}^{ExtBind}(\mathcal{A}_1, \mathcal{E}, \mathcal{A}_2)$.

$ck \leftarrow$ CS.Setup;
$(s, c) \xleftarrow{\omega} \mathcal{A}_1(ck)$;
$m^* \leftarrow \mathcal{E}(ck, \omega)$;
$(m, w) \leftarrow \mathcal{A}_2(s)$;
if CS.Verify$(ck, m, c, w) = 1 \wedge m \neq m^*$ **then**
  | **return** 1;
else
  | **return** 0;

Algorithm 4. The single-message knowledge-binding experiment $\mathbf{Exp}_{CS}^{KBind}(\mathcal{A}, \mathcal{E}, a)$.

$ck \leftarrow \mathsf{CS.Setup};$
$(s, c) \overset{\omega_1}{\longleftarrow} \mathcal{A}_1(ck);$
$m' \leftarrow \mathcal{E}(ck, \omega_1);$
$(m, w) \leftarrow \mathcal{A}_2(a, s);$
if $\mathsf{CS.Verify}(ck, m, c, w) = 1 \wedge m \neq m'$ then
  | return 1;
else
  | return 0;

Related Notions

In the following we discuss other notions of commitment binding that are related to extractable-binding.

Classical-Binding. It turns out that every extractable-binding commitment scheme is classical-binding and every classical-binding commitment scheme is extractable-binding. Theorem 1 shows that extractable binding implies classical binding. Later, with Theorems 2 and 3 we also show that classical binding implies extractable binding, though with a significant security loss.

Theorem 1 (EB⇒CB). *If* CS *is ϵ-extractable binding, then* CS *is ϵ'-classical-binding, where $\epsilon'(p) = \inf\{2 \cdot \epsilon(p, p_\mathcal{E}) : p_\mathcal{E} \in \mathbb{N}\}$.*

Proof Let $\mathcal{A}$ be a p-step Bind-adversary and let $\mathcal{E}$ be any extractor guaranteed by the assumption. We construct an ExtBind adversary $(\mathcal{A}_1, \mathcal{A}_2)$ as follows. The first stage $\mathcal{A}_1(ck)$ runs $\mathcal{A}(ck)$ (with random string ω) to obtain (c, m, w, m', w') and returns (s, c), where $s = (ck, \omega, m, w, m', w')$. The second stage $\mathcal{A}_2(s)$ parses s to obtain $(ck, \omega, m, w, m', w')$, tosses a coin $b \leftarrow \{0, 1\}$, and outputs (m, w) if $b = 0$, and otherwise outputs (m', w'). If $\mathcal{A}$ is successful in $\mathbf{Exp}_{CS}^{Bind}$, then $(\mathcal{A}_1, \mathcal{A}_2)$ is successful in $\mathbf{Exp}_{CS}^{ExtBind}$ with probability $\frac{1}{2}$ independent of the extractor $\mathcal{E}$. As the running time of $(\mathcal{A}_1, \mathcal{A}_2)$ is about p ($\mathcal{A}_2$ just parses and tosses a coin), we have $\mathbf{Adv}_{CS}^{ExtBind}(\mathcal{A}_1, \mathcal{E}, \mathcal{A}_2) \geq \frac{1}{2}\mathbf{Adv}_{CS}^{Bind}(\mathcal{A})$ and hence,

$$\mathbf{Adv}_{CS}^{Bind}(\mathcal{A}) \leq 2 \cdot \mathbf{Adv}_{CS}^{ExtBind}(\mathcal{A}_1, \mathcal{E}, \mathcal{A}_2) \leq 2 \cdot \epsilon(p, p_\mathcal{E}) \ ,$$

where $p_\mathcal{E}$ is the step count of $\mathcal{E}$. □

Knowledge-Binding. Knowledge-binding commitments were proposed by Buldas and Laur [8] as a new security notion for time-stamping. In comparison to extractable-binding, knowledge-binding is defined for multi-message commitments (e.g., list commitments or set commitments) and the extractor depends on the second stage adversary A_2, but A_2 gets an additional advice string which is not available to the extractor. Theorem 2 implies that the single-message variant of knowledge-binding (Definition 5, Algorithm 4) implies extractable-binding up to a small security loss due to the reduction.

Definition 5 (Knowledge binding). *Let* $\epsilon : \mathbb{N}^2 \rightarrow [0, 1]$. *A commitment scheme* CS *is* ϵ-*knowledge-binding, if for all integers* p *and* $p_{\mathcal{E}}$, *for every* p-*step adversary* $\mathcal{A} = (\mathcal{A}_1, \mathcal{A}_2)$, *there exists a* $p_{\mathcal{E}}$-*step extractor* $\mathcal{E}$, *such that for every advice string* $a \in \{0, 1\}^p$:

$$\mathbf{Adv}_{\mathsf{CS}}^{\mathrm{KBind}}(\mathcal{A}, \mathcal{E}, a) = \Pr\left[\mathbf{Exp}_{\mathsf{CS}}^{\mathrm{KBind}}(\mathcal{A}, \mathcal{E}, a) = 1\right] \leq \epsilon(p, p_{\mathcal{E}}) .$$

Theorem 2 (KB⇒EB). *If* CS *is* ϵ-*knowledge-binding, then* CS *is* ϵ'-*extractable-binding with* $\epsilon'(p_1, p_{\mathcal{E}}, p_2) = \epsilon(p_1 + \alpha \cdot p_2 \log p_2, p_{\mathcal{E}})$, *for some constant* α.

Proof. Consider an arbitrary p_1-step adversary $\mathcal{A}_1$ that acts in terms of the extractable binding experiment. We define $\mathcal{A}_2'(a, s)$ as a universal probabilistic Turing machine that uses the first argument a as a program for an arbitrary p_2-step machine $\mathcal{A}_2(s)$. According to [1], $\mathcal{A}_2'$ runs in $O(p_2 \log p_2)$ steps, say $\alpha \cdot p_2 \log p_2$ for some constant α. Consider the KBind-adversary $\mathcal{A} = (\mathcal{A}_1, \mathcal{A}_2')$ that runs in $(p_1 + \alpha \cdot p_2 \log p_2)$ steps and let $\mathcal{E}$ be a $p_{\mathcal{E}}$-step KBind-extractor. Note that $\mathcal{E}$ can also be considered as an ExtBind-extractor. We observe that $\mathcal{A}$ succeeds in the KBind-experiment if and only if $(\mathcal{A}_1, \mathcal{A}_2)$ succeeds in the ExtBind-experiment and hence,

$$\mathbf{Adv}_{\mathsf{CS}}^{\mathrm{ExtBind}}(\mathcal{A}_1, \mathcal{E}, \mathcal{A}_2) = \mathbf{Adv}_{\mathsf{CS}}^{\mathrm{KBind}}(\mathcal{A}, \mathcal{E}, a) \leq \epsilon(p_1 + \alpha \cdot p_2 \log p_2, p_{\mathcal{E}}) .$$

□

Theorem 3 (CB⇒KB). *If* CS *is* ϵ-*binding then it is also* ϵ'-*knowledge-binding, where* $\epsilon'(p, p_{\mathcal{E}}) = \epsilon(p_{\mathcal{E}}) + \alpha \cdot \frac{p}{p_{\mathcal{E}}}$, *for some constant* α. *(from Theorem 5 of [8])*

Corollary 1 (CB⇒EB). *If* CS *is* ϵ-*binding then it is also* ϵ'-*extractable-binding, where* $\epsilon'(p_1, p_{\mathcal{E}}, p_2) = \epsilon(p_{\mathcal{E}}) + \alpha \cdot \frac{p_1 + p_2 \log p_2}{p_{\mathcal{E}}}$, *for some constant* α.

This corollary is a direct consequence of Theorems 2 and 3. As a conclusion, if a commitment scheme is ϵ-binding with $\epsilon(p) = \frac{p}{S}$, with $S \geq \alpha \cdot (S')^2$ (where α is an overhead constant), then the commitment scheme is also $\epsilon'(p_1, p_{\mathcal{E}}, p_2)$-binding with $\epsilon'(p_1, p_{\mathcal{E}}, p_2) = \frac{p_1 + p_2}{S'}$, i.e., we have a quadratic security loss.

Other Related Notions. In [12], Crescenzo proposes an extractable commitment scheme in the public random string model. There, the extractor prepares the public string such that it can extract the committed message from a commitment. This idea was before used by Canetti and Fischlin to achieve universally composable commitments [11].

In [13], Dodis et al. propose the notion of preimage-aware hash functions. Preimage-aware is defined in an idealized model where oracle access to an idealized primitive is globally available. In comparison, our notion is defined in the standard model and no such ideal assumptions are made.

In [15], Pass and Wee propose an extractable commitment scheme in the standard model. However, their scheme is only computationally hiding whereas for long-term secrecy we require commitments to be unconditionally hiding.

In [10], Canetti and Dakdouk generalize the notion of extractable functions. Building on this work, Bitansky et al. formulate the notion of extractable collision-resistant hash functions [5] in a setting where adversaries have auxiliary input. In their work, they show how to construct an extractable collision-resistant hash function from the Knowledge of Exponent Assumption.

In [18], Unruh proposes collapse-binding commitments as a strengthened security notion for commitments in the quantum setting. Collapse-binding commitments seem conceptually similar to extractable-binding commitments. It is an interesting open question what is the relation between extractable-binding and collapse-binding.

4   Long-Term Commitments

4.1   Scheme Description

A long-term secure commitment scheme allows to generate commitments that remain binding for long periods of time, e.g., decades or even centuries. Such a commitment is generated in an initial commitment generation procedure and needs to be updated periodically in order to remain valid. For initial commitment and also for updating a commitment, a short-term secure commitment scheme is chosen whose security must be provided until the next update.

The following definition captures long-term commitment schemes more formally. Here, by a *a reference to a commitment function* we mean a pointer to the commitment algorithm of a chosen commitment scheme. A commitment function Com gets as input a message m and outputs a commitment c. By a *trusted commitment verification function* we mean a function that allows to verify commitments that have been generated in the past. A commitment verification function Ver gets as input a message m, a commitment c, a witness w, and a time t. It outputs 1 if (m, w) is a valid opening for commitment c at time t and it outputs 0 in any other case.

Definition 6 (Long-term commitment scheme). *A long-term commitment scheme is a triple of algorithms* Commit, Recommit, Verify, *where:*

- Commit *gets as input a reference to a commitment function* Com, *and a message* m. *It outputs a state* S, *a witness* W, *and a commitment* c.
- Recommit *gets as input a state* S *and a reference to a commitment function* Com. *It outputs a state* S', *a renewed witness* W, *and a commitment* c.
- Verify *gets as input a reference to a trusted commitment verification function* Ver, *a message* m, *a list of commitments* C, *and a witness* W. *It outputs a boolean* b, *where* $b = 1$ *if* C *is a valid long-term commitment for* m *and* $b = 0$ *if* C *is invalid.*

Protocol. In the following, we describe how a long-term commitment scheme (Commit, Recommit, Verify) is used by a committer $\mathcal{A}$ for committing to a message m in the presence of a verifier $\mathcal{B}$. In this protocol, the verifier $\mathcal{B}$ maintains a list of commitment values C.

Initial commitment. The committer $\mathcal{A}$ chooses a secure commitment scheme CS, generates the initial commitment $(S, W, c) \leftarrow$ Commit(CS.Com, m) and sends the commitment c to the verifier $\mathcal{B}$. When $\mathcal{B}$ receives c, it reads the current time t and sets $C \leftarrow [(t, c)]$.

Recommitment. $\mathcal{A}$ chooses a new commitment scheme CS, generates a new commitment by running $(S, W, c) \leftarrow$ Recommit(CS.Com, S), and sends c to $\mathcal{B}$. When $\mathcal{B}$ receives c, it reads the current time t and appends (t, c) to C.

Verification. $\mathcal{A}$ sends the witness W to $\mathcal{B}$. When $\mathcal{B}$ receives W, it uses a trusted commitment verification function Ver and runs $b \leftarrow$ Verify(Ver, m, C, W). The verifier $\mathcal{B}$ accepts the commitment if $b = 1$, otherwise $\mathcal{B}$ rejects.

Construction (LtCom). We describe a simple long-term commitment scheme which we refer to by LtCom. The algorithms Commit, Recommit, and Verify of LtCom are defined as follows.

- Commit(Com, m): Run $(c, w) \leftarrow$ Com(m). Set $W = [w]$ and $S = [m, W]$. Output S, W, and c.
- Recommit(S, Com): Run $(c, w) \leftarrow$ Com(S). Let $S = [m, [w_1, \ldots, w_i]]$. Set $W = [w_1, \ldots, w_i, w]$ and $S' = [m, W]$. Output S', W, and c.
- Verify(Ver, m, C, W): Let $C = [(c_1, t_1), \ldots, (c_n, t_n)]$ and $W = [w_1, \ldots, w_n]$. Compute $b \leftarrow \bigwedge_{i=1}^{n}$ Ver($m \| [w_1, \ldots, w_{i-1}], c_i, w_i, t_{i+1}$), where t_{n+1} is the current time. Output b.

4.2 Security Model

In order to model long-term adversaries whose computational power increases over time, we assume that the class $\mathcal{M}_t$ of computing machines available at time t widens when t increases, i.e., $\mathcal{M}_t \subseteq \mathcal{M}_{t'}$ whenever $t < t'$. This model captures that possibly much more powerful computing architectures may become available in the future, like quantum computers. Quantum communication is not considered in this model.

Model of real time. Modeling real time is a delicate issue and different approaches for modeling time have been proposed. In [14,16] a global clock mechanism is used in a computational model that only allows for sequential computation and interaction. In [9], another approach for modeling time in model of concurrent computation is described. We use a time formalism based on the global clock mechanism. More precisely, in our security experiments we consider a global clock Clock that holds a state time, which is initialized to 0. The adversary is given the power to advance time, but never go backwards, that is, it may call the oracle Clock to set the time forward.

Adversaries and extractors. We define adversaries with increasing computational power over time. Such an adversary $\mathcal{A}^{\mathsf{Clock}}$ is defined as a sequence $(\mathcal{A}_{(0)}, \mathcal{A}_{(1)}, \mathcal{A}_{(2)}, \ldots)$ of machines. When $\mathcal{A}$ is started, then actually the component $\mathcal{A}_{(0)}$ is run. Whenever a component $\mathcal{A}_{(t)}$ advances to a future time t' by calling Clock, then the control is given to $\mathcal{A}_{(t')}$, where we assume that $\mathcal{A}_{(t')}$ gets as input the state of $\mathcal{A}_{(t)}$. Extractors may also be sequences $(\mathcal{E}_{(0)}, \mathcal{E}_{(1)}, \mathcal{E}_{(2)}, \ldots)$ such that $\mathcal{E}_t \in \mathcal{M}_t$. That is, running an extractor $\mathcal{E}$ at time t means running $\mathcal{E}_{(t)}$. We remark that the extractor components do not have access to the clock oracle.

Real time computational bounds. Let $\mathcal{A}^{\mathsf{Clock}}$ be a computing machine that is associated with clock Clock and let $\rho : \mathbb{N} \to \mathbb{N}$ and $q : \mathbb{N} \to \mathbb{N}$ be functions. We say $\mathcal{A}$ is *ρ-bounded* if for every time t, the aggregated step count of the components of $\mathcal{A}$ until time t is at most $\rho(t)$. We say $\mathcal{A}$ is *q-call-bounded* if for every time t, it has done at most $q(t)$ oracle calls until time t.

Commitment scheme instances. In the following security definitions we define experiments that involve a set of commitment scheme instances $\mathcal{C} = \{\mathsf{CS}_1, \mathsf{CS}_2, \ldots\}$. Each instance CS_i is associated with a start time t_i^s and an end time t_i^b. At the start time, public commitment parameters are generated and after the end time, commitments generated using this instance are considered invalid (e.g. not considered secure anymore).

Security Definitions. In the following, we present definitions of binding and hiding for long-term commitment schemes.

Clock oracle. The following long-term experiments use the clock oracle described by Algorithm 5. This oracle, in addition to defining the time, also checks whether new commitment instances have become available and generates and outputs the public commitment parameters accordingly.

Algorithm 5. The clock oracle $\mathtt{Clock}(t)$.

$CK \leftarrow [\,]$;
if $t > \mathtt{time}$ **then**
    $\mathtt{time} \leftarrow t$;
    forall the $i \in \{j : t_j^s = t\}$ **do**
        $ck \leftarrow \mathsf{CS}_i.\mathsf{Setup}$;
        $\mathtt{CK}[i] \leftarrow ck$;
        $CK \leftarrow CK \| (i, ck)$;

return CK;

Hiding. The unconditionally hiding experiment $\mathbf{Exp}^{\mathrm{LtHide}}$ for long-term commitment schemes (Algorithm 6) is defined similar to the unconditionally hiding experiment $\mathbf{Exp}^{\mathrm{Hide}}$ for (short-term) commitment schemes. It considers an unbounded adversary $\mathcal{A}$ which is given access to oracle $\mathtt{Clock}$. The adversary $\mathcal{A}$ generates two messages (m_0, m_1) and an advice string s. Then, a coin is flipped

$b \leftarrow_\$ \{0, 1\}$ and the adversary may call oracles Com and ReCom. If the Com oracle is called, an initial long-term commitment to m_b is generated and returned to the adversary. When the ReCom oracle is called, a chosen long-term commitment is renewed and the adversary gets the renewed commitment value. At some point in time, the adversary $\mathcal{A}$ guesses which message has been committed to by outputting a bit b' and wins if it guesses correctly, i.e. if $b' = b$. Unconditional hiding for long-term commitment schemes is defined as follows.

Definition 7 (Long-Term Hiding). *A long-term commitment scheme* LCS *is unconditionally hiding if for any set* $\mathcal{C}$ *of unconditionally hiding commitment schemes, for any adversary* $\mathcal{A}$:

$$\mathbf{Adv}_{\mathsf{LCS}, \mathcal{C}}^{\mathrm{LtHide}}(\mathcal{A}) = \Pr\left[\mathbf{Exp}_{\mathsf{LCS}, \mathcal{C}}^{\mathrm{LtHide}}(\mathcal{A}) = 1\right] = \frac{1}{2}.$$

Algorithm 6. The long-term hiding experiment $\mathbf{Exp}_{\mathsf{LCS}, \mathcal{C}}^{\mathrm{LtHide}}(\mathcal{A})$.

$(m_0, m_1, s) \leftarrow \mathcal{A}^{\texttt{Clock}};$		
$b \leftarrow_\$ \{0, 1\};$	**oracle**Com(i, j):	**oracle** Recom(i, j):
$b' \leftarrow \mathcal{A}^{\texttt{Clock},\texttt{Com},\texttt{Recom}}(s);$	$(S_i, W_i, c) \leftarrow$	$(S_i, W_i, c) \leftarrow$
if $b' = b$ **then**	LCS.Commit(Com$_j, m_b$);	LCS.Recommit(S_i, Com$_j$);
$\quad$ **return** 1;	**return** c;	**return** c;
else		
$\quad$ **return** 0;		

Binding. The binding experiment $\mathbf{Exp}^{\mathrm{LtExtBind}}$ for long-term commitment schemes (Algorithm 7) considers a two-staged long-term adversary $(\mathcal{A}_1, \mathcal{A}_2)$, which is given access to an oracle Clock, and an extractor $\mathcal{E}$. The first-stage adversary $\mathcal{A}_1$ outputs an initial commitment c and an advice string s using random coins ω. The extractor $\mathcal{E}$ then gets the public commitment parameters CK and random coins ω and outputs an extracted message m'. The initial commitment c is recorded by running Rec(c). Afterwards, the second-stage adversary $\mathcal{A}_2$ gets the advice string s, runs the long-term commitment protocol (during which he may call Rec several times), and finally outputs a message m and a long-term witness W. The adversary wins if it is finished early enough (time $\leq \tau$), (m, W) is a valid opening for the commitment sequence C, and m differs from the extracted message m'.

Definition 8 (Long-Term Binding). *Let* $\mathcal{M}$ *describe the available machine classes and* $\mathcal{C}$ *describe the available commitment scheme instances. Let* $\epsilon : \mathbb{N}^5 \rightarrow [0, 1]$. *A long-term commitment scheme* LCS *is* ϵ-*binding (for* $\mathcal{M}$ *and* $\mathcal{C}$*) if for any bounds* $\rho_1, \rho_\mathcal{E}, \rho_2,$ *and* q, *for any* ρ_1-*bounded deterministic adversary* $\mathcal{A}_1 \in \mathcal{M}$, *there exists a* $\rho_\mathcal{E}$-*bounded extractor* $\mathcal{E} \in \mathcal{M}$, *such that for any* ρ_2-*bounded* $\mathcal{A}_2 \in \mathcal{M}$ *that is* q-*call-bounded, and any time* t:

$$\mathbf{Adv}_{\mathsf{LCS}, \mathcal{C}}^{\mathrm{LtExtBind}}(\mathcal{A}_1, \mathcal{E}, \mathcal{A}_2, t) = \Pr\left[\mathbf{Exp}_{\mathsf{LCS}, \mathcal{C}}^{\mathrm{LtExtBind}}(\mathcal{A}_1, \mathcal{E}, \mathcal{A}_2, t) = 1\right] \leq \epsilon(\rho_1, \rho_\mathcal{E}, \rho_2, q, t).$$

Algorithm 7. The experiment $\mathbf{Exp}_{\mathsf{LCS},\mathcal{C}}^{\mathrm{LtExtBind}}(\mathcal{A}_1, \mathcal{E}, \mathcal{A}_2, t)$ of long-term extractable-binding.

$(s, c) \xleftarrow{\omega} \mathcal{A}_1^{\mathrm{Clock}}$;
$m' \leftarrow \mathcal{E}(\mathsf{CK}, \omega)$;
$\mathsf{Rec}(c)$;
$(m, W) \leftarrow \mathcal{A}_2^{\mathrm{Clock},\mathrm{Rec}}(s)$;
if time $\leq t$ and $m \neq m'$ and
$\mathsf{LCS.Verify}(\mathsf{Ver}, m, \mathsf{C}, W) = 1$
then
$\quad$| return 1;
else
$\quad$| return 0;

---

oracle $\mathsf{Rec}(c)$:
$t \leftarrow \texttt{time}$;
$\mathsf{C} \leftarrow \mathsf{C}\|(t, c)$;

---

function $\mathsf{Ver}(m, c, w, t)$:
$c = (i, c')$;
if $t_i^s \leq \texttt{time}$ and $t < t_i^b$ then
$\quad$| $b \leftarrow \mathsf{CS}_i.\mathsf{Verify}(\mathsf{CK}[i], m, c, w)$;
$\quad$| return b;
else
$\quad$| return 0;

---

5   Security Analysis

In this section we analyze the security of the scheme LtCom described in Sect. 4. First, we note that LtCom is unconditionally hiding, because if we assume that the committed messages and the random strings of the individual commitments are independent, then the commitments are also independent (of each other and of the committed messages) and contain no information about the committed messages. We prove that LtCom is long-term binding, given that the accumulated security level of the used short-term commitment schemes is sufficiently small. For the long-term binding security analysis we first refine the extractable-binding definition for short-term commitment schemes to make it meaningful in the long-term security model. More specifically, we refine the definition such that the computational models of the adversary and the extractor may be restricted to a certain class of machines. With Theorem 4, we obtain a bound on the binding security of the long-term commitment scheme LtCom in terms of the binding security of each of the chosen short-term commitment schemes.

Definition 9 (Extractable-binding (refined)). *Let* $\mathcal{M}_{\mathcal{A}}$ *and* $\mathcal{M}_{\mathcal{E}}$ *be machine classes and* $\epsilon : \mathbb{N}^3 \rightarrow [0, 1]$. *We say a commitment scheme* CS *is* ϵ-*extractable-binding for adversaries of* $\mathcal{M}_{\mathcal{A}}$ *and extractors of* $\mathcal{M}_{\mathcal{E}}$ *if for every integers* p_1 *and* p_2, *for every* p_1-*step adversary* $\mathcal{A}_1 \in \mathcal{M}_{\mathcal{A}}$, *there exists a* $p_{\mathcal{E}}$-*step extractor* $\mathcal{E} \in \mathcal{M}_{\mathcal{E}}$, *such that for every* p_2-*step adversary* $\mathcal{A}_2 \in \mathcal{M}_{\mathcal{A}}$:

$$\mathbf{Adv}_{\mathsf{CS}}^{\mathrm{ExtBind}}(\mathcal{A}_1, \mathcal{E}, \mathcal{A}_2) \leq \epsilon(p_1, p_{\mathcal{E}}, p_2) \ .$$

Theorem 4. *Let* $\mathcal{M}$ *describe the available machine classes and* $\mathcal{C} = \{\mathsf{CS}_i\}_i$ *describe the available commitment scheme instances. For every* i, *assume that the commitment scheme* CS_i *is* ϵ_i-*extractable-binding for adversaries of* $\mathcal{M}_{t_i^b}$ *and extractors of* $\mathcal{M}_{t_i^s}$. *Then,* LtCom *is* ϵ-*binding with*

$$\epsilon(p_1, p_{\mathcal{E}}, p_2, q, t) = \sum_{i \in \{i : t_i^b \leq t\}} \epsilon_i \left(\rho_{\mathcal{A}}(t_i^b), \rho_{\mathcal{E}}(t_i^b), \alpha \right)$$

and $\rho_{\mathcal{A}}(t) = \rho_1(t) + \rho_2(t) + q(t) * \rho_{\mathcal{E}}(t)$, for a constant α.

Proof. To prove the theorem, we first describe the extractor algorithm that extracts the committed message from the first commitment of a long-term adversary in $\mathbf{Exp}^{\mathrm{LtExtBind}}$. Then we describe a reduction from the security of the long-term commitment scheme to the aggregated security of the commitment schemes $\mathcal{C}$.

We start by describing the long-term extractor $\mathcal{E}$ (Algorithm 8) that we construct using the first-stage adversary $\mathcal{A}_1$ and the short-term extractors $\{\mathcal{E}_i\}_i$ corresponding to commitment schemes $\{\mathsf{CS}_i\}_i$. When the long-term extractor is called with input (CK, ω), it runs $\mathcal{A}_1$ using commitment parameters CK and random coins ω for obtaining the commitment c. The extractor then decomposes c into a commitment scheme identifier i and a commitment value c'. Afterwards, it checks if scheme i is currently usable and if this is the case, it runs the extractor $\mathcal{E}_i$, corresponding to scheme i, with input the corresponding key $\mathsf{CK}[i]$ and random coins ω. The long-term extractor outputs the message m returned by the short-term extractor $\mathcal{E}_i$.

Algorithm 8. Long-term extractor $\mathcal{E}(\mathsf{CK}, \omega)$

Simulate $\mathcal{A}_1$ using commitment parameters CK and random coins ω to obtain commitment c;

$c = (i, c')$;

if $t_i^s \leq \mathtt{time} < t_i^b$ **then**
$\quad \mid \quad m \leftarrow \mathcal{E}_i(\mathsf{CK}[i], \omega)$;
else
$\quad \mid \quad m \leftarrow \perp$;

return m;

Next, we describe the reduction from a successful long-term adversary to a set of short-term commitment adversaries, of which at least one is successful. Let $(\mathcal{A}_1, \mathcal{A}_2)$ be an adversary pair that participates in $\mathbf{Exp}^{\mathrm{LtExtBind}}$. For each commitment scheme $\mathsf{CS}_i \in \mathcal{C}$, we construct a corresponding short-term adversary pair $(\mathcal{B}_{i,1}, \mathcal{B}_{i,2})$ that participates in $\mathbf{Exp}^{\mathrm{ExtBind}}$. The adversary $\mathcal{B}_{i,1}$ (Algorithm 9) simulates the experiment $\mathbf{Exp}^{\mathrm{LtExtBind}}$ with $(\mathcal{A}_1, \mathcal{A}_2)$ until it successfully obtains two different message-witness pairs which are valid for the same commitment with respect to commitment scheme CS_i, or the lifetime of the commitment scheme CS_i is over. It passes the two different message-witness pairs (m_0, w_0, m_1, w_1) to $\mathcal{B}_{i,2}$ and commits c. The adversary $\mathcal{B}_{i,2}$ (Algorithm 10) gets as input the message-witness pairs, flips a coin $b \leftarrow_{\$} \{0,1\}$, and outputs (m_b, w_b).

For every time t, define $I_t = \{i : t_i^b \leq t\}$ as the set of indices of the schemes whose lifetime expires until time t. We observe that for every successful run of the long-term adversary $(\mathcal{A}_1, \mathcal{A}_2)$, there is $i \in I_t$ such that the run of the short-term adversary $(\mathcal{B}_{i,1}, \mathcal{B}_{i,2})$ is successful. It follows that

$$\mathbf{Adv}_{\mathsf{LtCom}, \mathcal{C}}^{\mathrm{LtExtBind}}(\mathcal{A}_1, \mathcal{E}, \mathcal{A}_2, t) \leq \sum_{i \in I_t} \mathbf{Adv}_{\mathsf{CS}_i}^{\mathrm{ExtBind}}(\mathcal{B}_{i,1}, \mathcal{E}_i, \mathcal{B}_{i,2}) \, .$$

Assume $\mathcal{A}_1$ is ρ_1-bounded, $\mathcal{A}_2$ is ρ_2-bounded, and $\mathcal{E}$ is $\rho_{\mathcal{E}}$-bounded. Additionally assume that $\mathcal{A}_2$ makes at most $q(t)$ receiver oracle calls until time t. Define $\rho_{\mathcal{B}}(t) := \rho_1(t) + \rho_2(t) + q(t) * \rho_{\mathcal{E}}(t)$. The step count of $\mathcal{B}_{i,1}$ is bounded by $\rho_{\mathcal{B}}(t_i^b)$. It follows that for every t,

$$\mathbf{Adv}_{\mathsf{LtCom},\mathcal{C}}^{\mathsf{LtExtBind}}(\mathcal{A}_1, \mathcal{E}, \mathcal{A}_2, t) \leq \sum_{i \in I_t} \mathbf{Adv}_{\mathsf{CS}_i}^{\mathsf{ExtBind}}(\mathcal{B}_{i,1}, \mathcal{E}_i, \mathcal{B}_{i,2})$$

$$\leq \sum_{i \in I_t} \epsilon_i \left(\rho_{\mathcal{B}}(t_i^b), \rho_{\mathcal{E}}(t_i^b), 1 \right). \qquad \square$$

6   Evaluation

We evaluate the security loss over time for the long-term commitment scheme described in Sect. 4. For our evaluation we consider a scenario where a commitment should last for a time period t. The security level of the long-term commitment scheme is evaluated in terms of the security level of the short-term commitment schemes that are used. For convenience, we assume that all used commitment schemes have the same security level before they become insecure. Here, by the security level we mean a bound on the success probability of the adversary. Concretely, consider a long-term commitment scheme that uses short-term commitment schemes $\mathcal{C} = \{\mathsf{CS}_i\}_i$. We assume that the extractable-binding security of a commitment scheme derives from the ratio of the adversary power p_A and the extractor power $p_{\mathcal{E}}$, multiplied by a base security level δ. Hence, we assume each CS_i is ϵ-secure extractable-binding before its breakage time t_i^b with $\epsilon(p_1, p_{\mathcal{E}}, p_2) = \frac{p_1 + p_2}{p_{\mathcal{E}}} \delta$. By Theorem 4, we obtain that the long-term commitment scheme is ϵ'-secure extractable-binding with

$$\epsilon'(\rho_1, \rho_{\mathcal{E}}, \rho_2, q, t) = \delta * \sum_{i \in \{i : t_i^b \leq t\}} \frac{\rho_1(t_i^b) + \rho_2(t_i^b) + q(t_i^b) * \rho_{\mathcal{E}}(t_i^b) + \alpha}{\rho_{\mathcal{E}}(t_i^b)}$$

for some constant α. Let the unit of time be years and assume that the number of commitment schemes that become available during each year is at most L and the number of renewals that are done per year is at most R, i.e., $|I_t| = |\{i : t_i^b \leq t\}| \leq t * L$ and $q(t) \leq t * R$. We suggest that it is reasonable that the computational power of the adversary is comparable to the computational power of the extractor. Hence, we assume that $\frac{\rho_1(t)}{\rho_{\mathcal{E}}} = \frac{\rho_2(t)}{\rho_{\mathcal{E}}} = 1$. We also observe that the step count α of the very simple second-stage adversary described in Algorithm 10 should be smaller than $\rho_{\mathcal{E}}$, hence, we assume $\frac{\alpha}{\rho_{\mathcal{E}}(t)} \leq 1$. We obtain the following bound on the long-term security level:

$$\epsilon'(\rho_1, \rho_{\mathcal{E}}, \rho_2, q, t) \leq 3 * t^2 * LR\delta .$$

Algorithm 9. ExtBind adversary $\mathcal{B}_{\underline{i},1}(\underline{ck})$ constructed from long-term adversary $(\mathcal{A}_1, \mathcal{A}_2)$ and long-term extractor $\mathcal{E}$.

---

run

    $(s^*, c^*) \xleftarrow{\omega^*} \mathcal{A}_1^{\mathtt{Clock}}$;

    $\mathtt{C} \leftarrow \mathtt{C} \cup \{c^*\}$;

    $m^* \leftarrow \mathcal{E}(\mathtt{CK}, \omega^*)$;

    $\mathtt{M} \leftarrow \mathtt{M} \cup \{m^*\}$;

    $(m^{**}, W^{**}) \leftarrow \mathcal{A}_2^{\mathtt{Clock}, \mathtt{Rec}}(s^*)$;

    $\mathtt{M} \leftarrow \mathtt{M} \cup \{m^{**}\}$;

    $\mathtt{W} \leftarrow \mathtt{W} \cup W^{**}$;

until $(\mathtt{time} \geq t_{\underline{i}}^b)$ **or**

$(\exists m, m' \in \mathtt{M}, w, w' \in \mathtt{W}, (\underline{i}, c) \in \mathtt{C} :$

$\mathtt{CS}_{\underline{i}}.\mathsf{Verify}(\mathtt{CK}[\underline{i}], m, c, w) = \mathtt{CS}_{\underline{i}}.\mathsf{Verify}(\mathtt{CK}[\underline{i}], m', c, w') = 1)$;

return $((m, w, m', w'), c)$;

---

simulator $\underline{\mathtt{Clock}}(t)$:

$CK \leftarrow []$;

if $t > \mathtt{time}$ **then**

    forall the $i \in \{j : \mathtt{time} < t_j^s \leq t\}$ **do**

        if $i = \underline{i}$ **then**

            $ck \leftarrow \underline{ck}$;

        else

            $ck \leftarrow \mathtt{CS}_i.\mathsf{Setup}$;

        $\mathtt{CK}[i] \leftarrow ck$;

        $CK \leftarrow CK \| (i, ck)$;

    $\mathtt{time} \leftarrow t$;

return CK;

---

simulator $\underline{\mathtt{Rec}}(c)$:

$\mathtt{C} \leftarrow \mathtt{C} \cup \{c\}$;

$c = (i, c')$;

if $t_i^s \leq \mathtt{time}$ **then**

    Let ω be the random coins consumed by $\mathcal{A}_1$ and $\mathcal{A}_2$ until this point;

    $m \leftarrow \mathcal{E}_i(\mathtt{CK}[i], \omega, c')$;

    $m = (m', w')$;

    $\mathtt{M} \leftarrow \mathtt{M} \cup \{m'\}$;

    $\mathtt{W} \leftarrow \mathtt{W} \cup \{w'\}$;

Algorithm 10. ExtBind adversary $\mathcal{B}_{\underline{i},2}(s)$.

$s = (m_0, w_0, m_1, w_1)$;

$b \leftarrow_\$ \{0, 1\}$;

return (m_b, w_b);

In Fig. 1, we show how the long-term security level develops over time and for different choices of the base security level δ. We observe that after 100 years the security level drops from 2^{-182} to 2^{-175} (for $R = 1$, $L = 5$, and $\delta = 2^{-192}$). We also observe that there is a constant difference of roughly 2^{18} between the base security level δ and the long-term security level ϵ' if the time period is kept fixed.

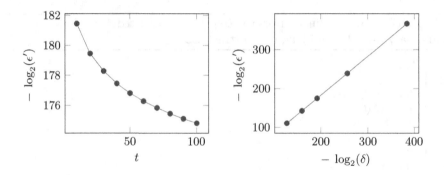

Fig. 1. Evaluation of the security level ϵ' of the long-term commitment scheme LtCom in terms of time t and short-term commitment security level δ. Here, we assume $R = 1$, $L = 5$, and we choose $\delta = 2^{-192}$ for evaluating over time t and we choose $t = 100$ for evaluating over δ.

7   Conclusions and Open Questions

We presented a simple construction of a long-term renewable commitment scheme based on extractable-binding commitment schemes. Our security proofs have security loss that gradually increases when the renewing procedure is applied many times and there is no obvious way to avoid it. This suggests that such a decrease has to be taken into account and the systems that rely on long-term digital evidence have to be designed with a certain security margin. An interesting open question is whether secure long-term renewable commitment schemes can be efficiently constructed from commitment schemes with weaker notions of secure binding. For example, though classical binding implies extractable binding, the security reductions would double the commitment size.

References

1. Arora, S., Barak, B.: Computational Complexity: A Modern Approach. Cambridge University Press, Cambridge (2009)
2. Bayer, D., Haber, S., Stornetta, W.S.: Improving the efficiency and reliability of digital time-stamping. In: Capocelli, R., De Santis, A., Vaccaro, U. (eds.) Sequences II: Methods in Communication, Security, and Computer Science, pp. 329–334. Springer, New York (1993)
3. Bellare, M., Desai, A., Jokipii, E., Rogaway, P.: A concrete security treatment of symmetric encryption. In: 38th Annual Symposium on Foundations of Computer Science, FOCS 1997, Miami Beach, Florida, 19–22 October 1997, pp. 394–403 (1997)
4. Bellare, M., Rogaway, P.: The exact security of digital signatures - how to sign with RSA and rabin. In: Proceedings of the International Conference on the Theory and Application of Cryptographic Techniques, Advances in Cryptology - EUROCRYPT 1996, Saragossa, Spain, 12–16 May 1996, pp. 399–416 (1996)

5. Bitansky, N., Canetti, R., Chiesa, A., Goldwasser, S., Lin, H., Rubinstein, A., Tromer, E.: The hunting of the SNARK. J. Cryptol. 1–78 (2016). doi:10.1007/s00145-016-9241-9

6. Brassard, G., Crépeau, C., Mayers, D., Salvail, L.: A brief review on the impossibility of quantum bit commitment. arXiv preprint quant-ph/9712023 (1997)

7. Braun, J., Buchmann, J., Demirel, D., Geihs, M., Fujiwara, M., Moriai, S., Sasaki, M., Waseda, A.: LINCOS: A storage system providing long-term integrity, authenticity, and confidentiality. In: Proceedings of the 2017 ACM on Asia Conference on Computer and Communications Security, ASIA CCS 2017, pp. 461–468. ACM, New York (2017)

8. Buldas, A., Laur, S.: Knowledge-binding commitments with applications in time-stamping. In: Okamoto, T., Wang, X. (eds.) PKC 2007. LNCS, vol. 4450, pp. 150–165. Springer, Heidelberg (2007). doi:10.1007/978-3-540-71677-8_11

9. Canetti, R., Cheung, L., Kaynar, D., Lynch, N., Pereira, O.: Modeling computational security in long-lived systems. In: Breugel, F., Chechik, M. (eds.) CONCUR 2008. LNCS, vol. 5201, pp. 114–130. Springer, Heidelberg (2008). doi:10.1007/978-3-540-85361-9_12

10. Canetti, R., Dakdouk, R.R.: Towards a theory of extractable functions. In: Reingold, O. (ed.) TCC 2009. LNCS, vol. 5444, pp. 595–613. Springer, Heidelberg (2009). doi:10.1007/978-3-642-00457-5_35

11. Canetti, R., Fischlin, M.: Universally composable commitments. In: Kilian, J. (ed.) CRYPTO 2001. LNCS, vol. 2139, pp. 19–40. Springer, Heidelberg (2001). doi:10.1007/3-540-44647-8_2

12. Crescenzo, G.D.: Equivocable and extractable commitment schemes. In: Cimato, S., Persiano, G., Galdi, C. (eds.) SCN 2002. LNCS, vol. 2576, pp. 74–87. Springer, Heidelberg (2003). doi:10.1007/3-540-36413-7_6

13. Dodis, Y., Ristenpart, T., Shrimpton, T.: Salvaging merkle-damgård for practical applications. In: Joux, A. (ed.) EUROCRYPT 2009. LNCS, vol. 5479, pp. 371–388. Springer, Heidelberg (2009). doi:10.1007/978-3-642-01001-9_22

14. Geihs, M., Demirel, D., Buchmann, J.: A security analysis of techniques for long-term integrity protection. In: 2016 14th Annual Conference on Privacy, Security and Trust (PST) (2016)

15. Pass, R., Wee, H.: Black-box constructions of two-party protocols from one-way functions. In: Reingold, O. (ed.) TCC 2009. LNCS, vol. 5444, pp. 403–418. Springer, Heidelberg (2009). doi:10.1007/978-3-642-00457-5_24

16. Schwenk, J.: Modelling time for authenticated key exchange protocols. In: Kutyłowski, M., Vaidya, J. (eds.) ESORICS 2014. LNCS, vol. 8713, pp. 277–294. Springer, Cham (2014). doi:10.1007/978-3-319-11212-1_16

17. Turing, A.M.: On computable numbers, with an application to the entscheidungsproblem. Proc. London Math. Soc. 2(1), 230–265 (1937)

18. Unruh, D.: Computationally binding quantum commitments. In: Fischlin, M., Coron, J.-S. (eds.) EUROCRYPT 2016. LNCS, vol. 9666, pp. 497–527. Springer, Heidelberg (2016). doi:10.1007/978-3-662-49896-5_18

Attribute-Based Encryption

New Proof Techniques for DLIN-Based Adaptively Secure Attribute-Based Encryption

Katsuyuki Takashima[✉]

Mitsubishi Electric, Kamakura, Japan
Takashima.Katsuyuki@aj.MitsubishiElectric.co.jp

Abstract. We propose *adaptively secure* attribute-based encryption (ABE) schemes for boolean formulas over large universe attributes from the *decisional linear (DLIN) assumption*, which allow *attribute reuse* in an available formula *without the previously employed redundant multiple encoding technique*. Thus our KP-(resp. CP-)ABE has non-redundant ciphertexts (resp. secret keys). For achieving the results, we develop a new encoding method for access policy matrix for ABE, by *decoupling linear secret sharing (LSS)* into its matrix and randomness, and *partially randomizing* the LSS shares in simulation. The new techniques are of independent interest and we expect it will find another application than ABE.

Keywords: Attribute-based encryption · Multi-use attributes in policy · Adaptive security · Static assumption

1 Introduction

1.1 Backgrounds

Attribute-based encryption (ABE) introduced by Sahai and Waters [21] presents an advanced vision for encryption and provides more flexible and fine-grained access control in sharing and distributing sensitive data than traditional symmetric and public-key encryption as well as recent identity-based encryption. In ABE systems, either one of the parameters for encryption and secret key is a set of attributes, and the other is an access policy (structure) over a universe of attributes, e.g., a secret key for a user is associated with an access policy and a ciphertext is associated with a set of attributes. A secret key with a policy can decrypt a ciphertext associated with a set of attributes, iff the attribute set satisfies the policy. If the access policy is for a secret key (resp. for encryption), it is called key-policy ABE (KP-ABE) (resp. ciphertext-policy ABE (CP-ABE)).

All the existing *practical* ABE schemes have been constructed by (bilinear) pairing groups, and the largest class of relations supported by the ABE schemes is (non-monotone or arithmetic) span programs [3,9,12,13] (or (non-monotone) span programs with inner-product relations [18]). While general polynomial size circuits are supported [8,11] recently, they are much less efficient than the

© Springer International Publishing AG 2017
J. Pieprzyk and S. Suriadi (Eds.): ACISP 2017, Part I, LNCS 10342, pp. 85–105, 2017.
DOI: 10.1007/978-3-319-60055-0_5

pairing-based ABE schemes and non-practical when the relations are limited to span programs. Hereafter, we focus on pairing-based ABE with span program access structures. An example of such span program predicate over attributes is given by (Institute = Univ. A) AND ((Department = Biology) OR (Position = Professor)), which we simply denote by $\mathcal{X}_1 \wedge (\mathcal{X}_2 \vee \mathcal{X}_3)$ where $\mathcal{X}_1 :=$ Univ. A, $\mathcal{X}_2 :=$ Biology and $\mathcal{X}_3 :=$ Professor. We define attribute-multiplicity k for a predicate as the maximum number of appearances of attribute variables, i.e., $k = 2$ for predicate $(\mathcal{X}_1 \wedge \mathcal{X}_2) \vee (\mathcal{X}_1 \wedge \mathcal{X}_3) \vee (\mathcal{X}_2 \wedge \mathcal{X}_4)$ since $\mathcal{X}_1$ and $\mathcal{X}_2$ appear twice and others appear just once. While adaptive security for ABE is the standard, realistic and desirable security notion, previously, either efficiency or security is sacrificed for achieving the "multi-use" property in adaptively secure ABE. See adaptively secure ABE in Tables 1 and 2. Our aim is to achieve *short (i.e., non-redundant) ciphertexts (resp. keys)* in *adaptively secure multi-use* KP-ABE (resp. CP-ABE) from *static assumptions*.

In previous *static* assumption based schemes [9,14,18], for allowing reuse of attributes in a policy in the adaptive security setting, for example, in KP-ABE, multiple ciphertext components whose number is linear in the product kn' of the number n' of attributes for the ciphertext and the attribute multiplicity k for available policies are necessary, which leads to a very long ciphertext. More precisely, the same information representing attribute set Γ is duplicated over *multiple* ciphertext components depending linearly on the multiplicity k. (See OT10 and CGW15 KP-ABE schemes in Table 1.)

Lewko-Waters [16] first constructed adaptively-secure CP-ABE and KP-ABE schemes for span programs with allowing reuse of attributes in a policy *without the above redundant multiple encoding technique*. While Lewko-Waters's (CP-) ABE scheme ([16] and subsequent work [2,3] in Table 1) shows an interesting approach to allowing reuse of attributes in a policy, the security is proven only based on *q-type assumptions* with q the maximum number of attribute-multiplicities in access structures. However, the assumptions (and also the associated schemes) suffered a special attack which was presented by Cheon [10] at Eurocrypt 2006, which leads to inefficiency. Consequently, it is very desirable that the q-type assumption should be replaced by a *static* (non-q type) assumption with keeping compact ciphertexts.

Moreover, we note that there exist *no multi-use* CP-ABE scheme with short, i.e., non-redundant, secret keys *even in the selective security setting* from *a static assumption* (Table 2). Now, an important open question is:

Is there an adaptively secure KP-(resp. CP-)ABE scheme for span programs from a static (standard) assumption whose ciphertext (resp. secret key) size is not linear in kn' for the attribute number n' in ciphertext (resp. secret key) and the maximum attribute-multiplicity k of available policies ?

This work makes a significant step for addressing the problem.

1.2   Our Results

We obtain the following results.

Table 1. Comparison with the existing pairing-based multi-use KP-ABE schemes, where PK, SK, CT stand for public key, secret key, ciphertext, respectively, and n' represents the number of attributes in CT, n the max of n', ℓ the number of rows in access matrix in SK, r the max of the number of columns in access matrix in SK, k (the max of) the "attribute-multiplicity" of an access matrix in SK, respectively. The fourth row describes the warm-up scheme in Sect. 5.3.

	Security	Assump.	PK size	SK size	CT size
GPSW06 [12]	Selective	DBDH	$O(n)|\mathbb{G}|$	$O(\ell)|\mathbb{G}|$	$O(n')|\mathbb{G}|$
Tak14 [22]	Semi-adaptive	DLIN	$O(n)|\mathbb{G}|$	$O(\ell n)|\mathbb{G}|$	$O(1)|\mathbb{G}|$
(Warm-up)				$O(\ell)|\mathbb{G}|$	$O(n)|\mathbb{G}|$
OT10 [18]	Adaptive	DLIN	$O(n)|\mathbb{G}|$	$O(\ell)|\mathbb{G}|$	$O(kn')|\mathbb{G}|$
LW12 [16]		ℓ-Parallel BDHE $(+\alpha)$	$O(n)|\mathbb{G}|$	$O(\ell)|\mathbb{G}|$	$O(n')|\mathbb{G}|$
Att15 [2,3]		EDHE3 & 4 parametrized by n, ℓ, r	$O(n)|\mathbb{G}|$	$O(\ell n)|\mathbb{G}|$	$O(1)|\mathbb{G}|$
CGW15 [9]		s-Lin for $\forall s$	$O(n)\,|\mathbb{G}|$ for $s=2$	$O(\ell)|\mathbb{G}|$ for $s=2$	$O(kn')|\mathbb{G}|$ for $s=2$
Proposed	Adaptive	DLIN	$O(n+r)|\mathbb{G}|$	$O(\ell)|\mathbb{G}|$	$O(n+r)|\mathbb{G}|$

- We propose an adaptively secure *multi-use* KP-ABE construction for boolean formulas (or span programs) over large universe attribute matching predicates *with non-redundant ciphertexts from the DLIN assumption* (in Sect. 5). The size of a ciphertext for attributes *is not linear in the product kn' of the number of ciphertext attributes n' and the attribute multiplicity k in available access structures,* but has only a linear dependence on some size parameter r of access structures. For comparison with existing ones, refer to Table 1.
- We also propose an adaptively secure multi-use CP-ABE construction for the same access structures as the above KP-ABE with short (non-redundant) keys from DLIN. The CP-ABE scheme is obtained from the above KP-ABE by the natural dual conversion, in particular, the key size *is not linear in kn' for the number n' of key attributes and the attribute multiplicity k in available access structures.* We note that it is *the first multi-use CP-ABE construction with short keys from a static assumption even including the selective secure schemes* (Table 2). For the concrete scheme, see Appendix B.

We used two techniques, decoupling of linear secret sharing (LSS) into two (dual) components, i.e., span program matrix and randomness, and the partial randomization of LSS. A new sparse matrix machinery (Sect. 4) underlies them. The techniques can be extended naturally to arithmetic span programs (ASP), then, our results can be extended to ASP based ABE proposed by Ishai and Wee [13].

Table 2. Comparison with the existing pairing-based multi-use CP-ABE schemes, where PK, SK, CT stand for public key, secret key, ciphertext, respectively, and n' represents the number of attributes in SK, n the max of n', ℓ the number of rows in access matrix in CT, r the max of the number of columns in access matrix in CT, k (the max of) the "attribute-multiplicity" of an access matrix in CT, respectively.

	Security	Assump.	PK size	SK size	CT size
Wat11 [25] Scheme 2	Selective	ν-BDHE	$O(n)\|\mathbb{G}\|$	$O(kn')\|\mathbb{G}\|$	$O(\ell)\|\mathbb{G}\|$
Wat11 [25] Scheme 3		DBDH	$O(nr)\|\mathbb{G}\|$	$O(kn'+r)\|\mathbb{G}\|$	$O(\ell^2)\|\mathbb{G}\|$
AHY15 [4][a]		Parameterized	$O((n\ell)^2\lambda)\|\mathbb{G}\|$	$O((n\ell)^4\lambda^2)\|\mathbb{G}\|$	$O(1)\|\mathbb{G}\|$
OT10 [18]	Adaptive	DLIN	$O(n)\|\mathbb{G}\|$	$O(kn')\|\mathbb{G}\|$	$O(\ell)\|\mathbb{G}\|$
LW12 [16]		ℓ-Parallel BDHE $(+\alpha)$	$O(n)\|\mathbb{G}\|$	$O(n')\|\mathbb{G}\|$	$O(\ell)\|\mathbb{G}\|$
CGW15 [9]		s-Lin for $\forall s$	$O(n)\|\mathbb{G}\|$ for $s=2$	$O(kn')\|\mathbb{G}\|$ for $s=2$	$O(\ell)\|\mathbb{G}\|$ for $s=2$
Proposed	Adaptive	DLIN	$O(n+r)\|\mathbb{G}\|$	$O(n+r)\|\mathbb{G}\|$	$O(\ell)\|\mathbb{G}\|$

[a] Since $k \leq \ell$, the size of secret keys of the AHY15 scheme [4] is very large compared with others. Also, in [1], a *selective-secure* constant-size ciphertext, but, large secret keys CP-ABE scheme was proposed, recently

1.3 Key Techniques

Our results are related to KP- and CP-ABEs, however, for simplicity, we mainly treat on KP-ABE. According to a new framework introduced by Attrapadung, doubly selective security (i.e., selective and co-selective) leads to achieving adaptive one. Since selective security is easily obtained in KP-ABE, we should concentrate on achieving *co-selectively* secure KP-ABE below.

Based on the technique in [5,22], we have DLIN-based, multi-use and *semi-adaptively* secure KP-ABE with short ciphertext size. We give the underlying scheme in Sect. 5.3 (as a warm-up) and extend it to our adaptive one. Here, access structure $\mathbb{S}$ is given by $\ell \times r$ matrix M and each row $M_i \in \mathbb{F}_q^r$ of the matrix is associated to an attribute value by a map ρ, i.e., labeled with attributes $v_i := \rho(i)$. An attribute set Γ satisfies $\mathbb{S}$ iff $\vec{1} \in \mathsf{span}\langle M_i \mid v_i \in \Gamma\rangle$ for a fixed special (all-one) vector $\vec{1}$. First, to achieve short ciphertexts in the underlying KP-ABE, attributes $\Gamma := \{x_j\}_{j=1,\ldots,n'}$ are encoded in an n-dimensional (with $n \geq n'+1$) vector $\vec{y} := (y_1, \ldots, y_n)$ such that $\sum_{j=0}^{n-1} y_{n-j} z^j = z^{n-1-n'} \prod_{j=1}^{n'}(z - x_j)$. Each (non-zero) attribute value v_i (for $i = 1, \ldots, \ell$) associated with a row of access structure matrix M (in $\mathbb{S}$) is encoded as $\vec{v}_i := (v_i^{n-1}, \ldots, v_i, 1)$, so $\vec{y} \cdot \vec{v}_i = v_i^{n-1-n'} \prod_{j=1}^{n'}(v_i - x_j)$, and the value of inner product is equal to zero if and only if $v_i = x_j$ for some j, i.e., $v_i \in \Gamma$. Here, the relation between $\mathbb{S}$ and Γ is determined by the multiple inner product values $\vec{y} \cdot \vec{v}_i$ for one vector $\vec{y}$ which is equivalent to Γ. As in previous works (e.g., [5,22]), a ciphertext element c_1 is encoded with $\omega\vec{y}$ (for random ω), and key elements $\boldsymbol{k}_i^*$ are encoded with $\vec{v}_i$ and shared secret values $M_i \cdot \vec{f}$ $(i = 1, \ldots, \ell)$ for a central secret $\vec{1} \cdot \vec{f}$ with uniformly random $\vec{f}$, respectively. We change the encoding method for our new proof method as indicated below.

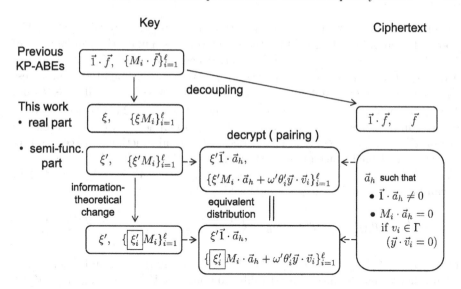

Fig. 1. Decoupling of LSS matrix from randomness and partial LSS randomization in semi-functional parts. Here, $(M = (M_i), \rho)$ is an access structure, uniformly random $\vec{f} \xleftarrow{\mathsf{U}} \mathbb{F}_q^r, \xi, \xi', \xi'_i, \theta'_i \xleftarrow{\mathsf{U}} \mathbb{F}_q, \vec{y} := (y_1, \ldots, y_n)$ such that $\sum_{j=0}^{n-1} y_{n-j} z^j = z^{n-1-n'} \prod_{j=1}^{n'} (z - x_j)$, and $\vec{v}_i := (v_i^{n-1}, \ldots, v_i, 1)$ for $v_i := \rho(i)$.

Basic Idea: Decoupling of LSS Matrix from Randomness. Secret keys in all previous KP-ABE schemes contain shared secret values $s_0 := \vec{1} \cdot \vec{f}$ and $s_i := M_i \cdot \vec{f}$, which means that randomness $\vec{f}$ is fixed at the key generation phase. Moreover, since, for *pre-challenge* queried keys (in simulation), the challenge $\vec{y}$ is not yet revealed to the challenger, i.e., simulator, at the query phase, we have never had a co-selective simulation strategy for achieving compact ciphertexts together with multi-use leaf attributes v_i in the queried access matrix.

For addressing the problem, we change an encoding method of LSS (Fig. 1). First, we decouple LSS encoding into LSS matrix and randomness, and randomness is encoded on the ciphertext side. (Then, the simulation of the randomness is delayed until the challenge phase.) Precisely, in the secret key, concatenated $V_i := (\theta_i \vec{v}_i, \xi M_i) \in \mathbb{F}_q^{n+r}$ are encoded in the i-th component k_i^* for $i = 1, .., \ell$ with random θ_i, ξ. We note that the key component k_i^* has no randomness for LSS (except for connecting randomness ξ), instead, LSS matrix $M := (M_i)_{i=1}^\ell$ is directly encoded in $\{k_i^*\}$. In ciphertext, $Y := (\omega \vec{y}, \vec{f}) \in \mathbb{F}_q^{n+r}$ is encoded. Hence, in decryption, inner-product values are

$$Y \cdot V_i = \omega \theta_i (\vec{y} \cdot \vec{v}_i) + \xi M_i \cdot \vec{f} = \omega \theta_i (\vec{y} \cdot \vec{v}_i) + \xi s_i \quad \text{for } i = 1, \ldots, \ell,$$

therefore, if $\vec{y} \cdot \vec{v}_i = 0$, secret share ξs_i for central secret ξs_0 is obtained, and if $\vec{y} \cdot \vec{v}_i \neq 0$, s_i is totally hidden from the decryptor since θ_i is freshly random.

New Proof Techniques: Partial LSS Randomization in Simulation and New Underlying Lemma. At the top level of strategy of the security proof, we follow the dual system encryption methodology proposed by Waters [24]. The above change of encoding enables the simulator to simulate the randomness of LSS depending on both of the h-th queried access structure $\mathbb{S} := (M, \rho)$ and attributes $\Gamma := \{x_t\}$ (equivalently, vector $\vec{y}$). We use the simulated randomness $\vec{a}_h$, which is *not fully random* in $\mathbb{F}_q^r$, but satisfies $M_i \cdot \vec{a}_h = 0$ if $v_i \in \Gamma$ and $\vec{1} \cdot \vec{a}_h \neq 0$. Such a vector exists since Γ does not satisfy $\mathbb{S}$, and it has been used for security in previous works, for example, in [12]. In ciphertext, the concatenated vector $Y' := (\omega' \vec{y}, \vec{a}_h) \in \mathbb{F}_q^{n+r}$ is encoded in the semi-functional space. And, in the semi-functional space of the h-th queried key, $V_i' := (\theta_i' \vec{v}_i, \xi' M_i) \in \mathbb{F}_q^{n+r}$ are encoded in the i-th component $\boldsymbol{k}_i^*$ for $i = 1, .., \ell$. Since V_i' is *independent of Γ*, it can be simulated for the *pre-challenge* key. Then,

$$Y' \cdot V_i' = \omega' \theta_i' (\vec{y} \cdot \vec{v}_i) + \xi' M_i \cdot \vec{a}_h = \begin{cases} 0 & \text{if } \vec{y} \cdot \vec{v}_i = 0, \\ \omega' \theta_i' (\vec{y} \cdot \vec{v}_i) + \xi' M_i \cdot \vec{a}_h & \text{if } \vec{y} \cdot \vec{v}_i \neq 0, \end{cases}$$

for $i = 1, \ldots, \ell$. Here, if $\vec{y} \cdot \vec{v}_i \neq 0$, $Y' \cdot V_i'$ is uniformly random and independent from other variables since θ_i' are freshly random. Let $V_i'' := (\theta_i' \vec{v}_i, \xi_i' M_i) \in \mathbb{F}_q^{n+r}$ with uniformly random ξ_i' which are independent of each other for $i = 1, \ldots, \ell$.

$$Y' \cdot V_i'' = \omega' \theta_i' (\vec{y} \cdot \vec{v}_i) + \xi_i' M_i \cdot \vec{a}_h = \begin{cases} 0 & \text{if } \vec{y} \cdot \vec{v}_i = 0, \\ \omega' \theta_i' (\vec{y} \cdot \vec{v}_i) + \xi_i' M_i \cdot \vec{a}_h & \text{if } \vec{y} \cdot \vec{v}_i \neq 0, \end{cases}$$

for $i = 1, \ldots, \ell$. Again, if $\vec{y} \cdot \vec{v}_i \neq 0$, $Y' \cdot V_i''$ is uniformly random and independent of other variables. That is, $Y' \cdot V_i'$ and $Y' \cdot V_i''$ are equivalently distributed. Therefore, we can conceptually change V_i' which contains variable ξ' to V_i'' with *no ξ'* by using the pairwise independence lemma (Lemma 3) as in the previous dual system encryption proofs. We stress that V_i'' *are also independent of the challenge attributes* Γ, and then can be used in the pre-challenge key simulation. In this way, we can sequentially eliminate the randomness ξ' from all key components, $\boldsymbol{k}_i^*$ for $i = 1, .., \ell$, *except for $\boldsymbol{k}_0^*$*, and finally, ξ' remains only in the central element $\boldsymbol{k}_0^*$, and the inner-product of the semi-functional parts of $\boldsymbol{k}_0^*$ and the corresponding ciphertext component is uniformly random value $\xi' \vec{1} \cdot \vec{a}_h$ since $\vec{1} \cdot \vec{a}_h \neq 0$. So, the proof proceeds successfully (See Sect. 5.4 for proof outline).

We extend the sparse matrix technique on dual pairing vector spaces (DPVS) developed in [19, 22] for achieving compact ciphertexts. Refer to Sect. 5.1 for the details.

1.4 Notations

When A is a random variable or distribution, $y \xleftarrow{\mathsf{R}} A$ denotes that y is randomly selected from A according to its distribution. When A is a set, $y \xleftarrow{\mathsf{U}} A$ denotes that y is uniformly selected from A. We denote the finite field of order q by $\mathbb{F}_q$, and $\mathbb{F}_q \setminus \{0\}$ by $\mathbb{F}_q^\times$. A vector symbol denotes a vector representation over $\mathbb{F}_q$, e.g., $\vec{y}$ denotes $(y_1, \ldots, y_n) \in \mathbb{F}_q^n$. For two vectors $\vec{y} = (y_1, \ldots, y_n)$ and $\vec{v} = (v_1, \ldots, v_n)$, $\vec{y} \cdot \vec{v}$ denotes the inner-product $\sum_{i=1}^n y_i v_i$. X^{T} denotes the transpose of matrix X. A bold face letter denotes an element of vector space $\mathbb{V}$, e.g.,

$x \in \mathbb{V}$. When $b_i \in \mathbb{V}$ $(i = 1, \ldots, n)$, $\mathrm{span}\langle b_1, \ldots, b_n \rangle \subseteq \mathbb{V}$ (resp. $\mathrm{span}\langle \vec{x}_1, \ldots, \vec{x}_n \rangle$) denotes the subspace generated by $b_1, \ldots, b_n$ (resp. $\vec{x}_1, \ldots, \vec{x}_n$). For bases $\mathbb{B} := (b_1, \ldots, b_N)$ and $\mathbb{B}^* := (b_1^*, \ldots, b_N^*)$, $(x_1, \ldots, x_N)_{\mathbb{B}} := \sum_{i=1}^{N} x_i b_i$ and $(y_1, \ldots, y_N)_{\mathbb{B}^*} := \sum_{i=1}^{N} y_i b_i^*$. $\vec{e}_j$ denotes the canonical basis vector $(\overbrace{0 \cdots 0}^{j-1}, 1, \overbrace{0 \cdots 0}^{n+r-j}) \in \mathbb{F}_q^{n+r}$ for positive integers n and r. $GL(n, \mathbb{F}_q)$ denotes the general linear group of degree n over $\mathbb{F}_q$.

2 Dual Pairing Vector Spaces (DPVS)

In this paper, for simplicity of description, we will present the proposed schemes on the symmetric version of dual pairing vector spaces (DPVS) [17] constructed using symmetric bilinear pairing groups given in Definition 1. Owing to the abstraction of DPVS, the presentation and the security proof of the proposed schemes are essentially the same as those on the asymmetric version of DPVS.

Definition 1. *"Symmetric bilinear pairing groups"* $(q, \mathbb{G}, \mathbb{G}_T, G, e)$ *are a tuple of a prime q, cyclic additive group $\mathbb{G}$ and multiplicative group $\mathbb{G}_T$ of order q, $G \neq 0 \in \mathbb{G}$, and a polynomial-time computable nondegenerate bilinear pairing $e : \mathbb{G} \times \mathbb{G} \to \mathbb{G}_T$ i.e., $e(sG, tG) = e(G, G)^{st}$ and $e(G, G) \neq 1$. Let $\mathcal{G}_{\mathsf{bpg}}$ be an algorithm that takes input 1^λ and outputs a description of bilinear pairing groups $(q, \mathbb{G}, \mathbb{G}_T, G, e)$ with security parameter λ.*

"Dual pairing vector spaces (DPVS)" of dimension N by a direct product of symmetric pairing groups $(q, \mathbb{G}, \mathbb{G}_T, G, e)$ are given by prime q, N-dimensional vector space $\mathbb{V} := \overbrace{\mathbb{G} \times \cdots \times \mathbb{G}}^{N}$ over $\mathbb{F}_q$, cyclic group $\mathbb{G}_T$ of order q, and pairing $e : \mathbb{V} \times \mathbb{V} \to \mathbb{G}_T$. The pairing is defined by $e(x, y) := \prod_{i=1}^{N} e(G_i, H_i) \in \mathbb{G}_T$ where $x := (G_1, \ldots, G_N) \in \mathbb{V}$ and $y := (H_1, \ldots, H_N) \in \mathbb{V}$. This is nondegenerate bilinear i.e., $e(sx, ty) = e(x, y)^{st}$ and if $e(x, y) = 1$ for all $y \in \mathbb{V}$, then $x = 0$.

3 Definition of KP-ABE

3.1 Span Programs and Access Structures

Definition 2 (Span Programs [6] and Access Structures). $\mathcal{U}$ $(\subset \{0,1\}^*)$ *is a universe, a set of attributes, which is expressed by a value of attribute, i.e., $v \in \mathbb{F}_q^\times (:= \mathbb{F}_q \setminus \{0\})$. A span program over $\mathbb{F}_q$ is a labeled matrix $\mathbb{S} := (M, \rho)$ where M is a $(\ell \times r)$ matrix over $\mathbb{F}_q$ and ρ is a labeling of the rows of M by literals from $\{v, v', \ldots\}$ (every row is labeled by one literal), i.e., $\rho : \{1, \ldots, \ell\} \to \{v, v', \ldots\}$. A span program accepts or rejects an input by the following criterion. Let Γ be a set of attributes, i.e., $\Gamma := \{x_j\}_{1 \le j \le n'}$ $(x_j \in \mathbb{F}_q^\times)$. The span program $\mathbb{S}$ accepts Γ if and only if $\vec{1} \in \mathsf{span}\langle (M_i)_{\rho(i)=v_i \in \Gamma} \rangle$, i.e., some linear combination of the rows $(M_i)_{\rho(i) \in \Gamma}$ gives the all one vector $\vec{1}$.*

No row M_i $(i = 1, \ldots, \ell)$ of the matrix M is $\vec{0}$.

We now construct a secret-sharing scheme for a (monotone) span program.

Definition 3. *A secret-sharing scheme for span program* $\mathbb{S} := (M, \rho)$ *is:*

1. *Let* M *be* $\ell \times r$ *matrix. Let column vector* $\vec{f} := (f_1, \ldots, f_r) \xleftarrow{\mathsf{U}} \mathbb{F}_q^r$. *Then,* $s_0 := \vec{1} \cdot \vec{f} = \sum_{k=1}^{r} f_k$ *is the secret to be shared, and* $\vec{s} := (s_1, \ldots, s_\ell)^{\mathrm{T}} := M \cdot \vec{f}^{\mathrm{T}}$ *is the* ℓ *shares of the secret* s_0 *and the share* s_i *belongs to* $\rho(i)$.
2. *If span program* $\mathbb{S} := (M, \rho)$ *accepts* Γ, *i.e.,* $\vec{1} \in \mathrm{span}\langle (M_i)_{\rho(i) \in \Gamma} \rangle$, *there exist constants* $\{\alpha_i \in \mathbb{F}_q \mid i \in I\}$ *such that* $I \subseteq \{i \in \{1, \ldots, \ell\} \mid \rho(i) \in \Gamma\}$ *and* $\sum_{i \in I} \alpha_i s_i = s_0$. *Furthermore, these constants* $\{\alpha_i\}$ *can be computed in time polynomial in the size of the matrix* M.

3.2 Key-Policy Attribute-Based Encryption (KP-ABE)

In key-policy attribute-based encryption (KP-ABE), encryption (resp. a secret key) is associated with attributes Γ (resp. access structure $\mathbb{S}$). Relation R for KP-ABE is defined as $R(\mathbb{S}, \Gamma) = 1$ iff access structure $\mathbb{S}$ accepts Γ.

Definition 4 (Key-Policy Attribute-Based Encryption: KP-ABE). *A key-policy attribute-based encryption scheme consists of probabilistic polynomial-time algorithms* Setup, KeyGen, Enc *and* Dec. *They are given as follows:*

Setup *takes as input security parameter* 1^λ, *a bound* n *on the number of attributes per ciphertext and a bound* r *on the number of columns of an access matrix in a secret key. It outputs public parameters* pk *and master secret key* sk.

KeyGen *takes as input public parameters* pk, *master secret key* sk, *and access structure* $\mathbb{S} := (M, \rho)$. *It outputs a corresponding secret key* $\mathsf{sk}_\mathbb{S}$.

Enc *takes as input public parameters* pk, *message* m *in some associated message space* msg, *and a set of attributes,* $\Gamma := \{x_j\}_{j=1}^{n'}$. *It outputs a ciphertext* ct_Γ.

Dec *takes as input public parameters* pk, *secret key* $\mathsf{sk}_\mathbb{S}$ *for access structure* $\mathbb{S}$, *and ciphertext* ct_Γ *that was encrypted under a set of attributes* Γ. *It outputs either* $m' \in$ msg *or the distinguished symbol* $\bot$.

A KP-ABE scheme should have the correctness: for all $(\mathsf{pk}, \mathsf{sk}) \xleftarrow{\mathsf{R}} \mathsf{Setup}(1^\lambda, n, r)$, all access structures $\mathbb{S}$, all secret keys $\mathsf{sk}_\mathbb{S} \xleftarrow{\mathsf{R}} \mathsf{KeyGen}(\mathsf{pk}, \mathsf{sk}, \mathbb{S})$, all messages m, all attribute sets Γ, all ciphertexts $\mathsf{ct}_\Gamma \xleftarrow{\mathsf{R}} \mathsf{Enc}(\mathsf{pk}, m, \Gamma)$, it holds that $m = \mathsf{Dec}(\mathsf{pk}, \mathsf{sk}_\mathbb{S}, \mathsf{ct}_\Gamma)$ if $\mathbb{S}$ accepts Γ. Otherwise, it holds with negligible probability.

Definition 5 (Adaptive Security). *The model for defining the adaptively payload-hiding security of KP-ABE under chosen plaintext attack is given by the following game:*

Setup. *In the adaptive security, the challenger runs the setup,*

$(\mathsf{pk}, \mathsf{sk}) \xleftarrow{\mathsf{R}} \mathsf{Setup}(1^\lambda, n, r)$, *and gives public parameters* pk *to the adversary.*

Phase 1. *The adversary is allowed to adaptively issue a polynomial number of key queries, $\mathbb{S}$, to the challenger. The challenger gives $\mathsf{sk}_{\mathbb{S}} \xleftarrow{\mathsf{R}}$ KeyGen(pk, sk, $\mathbb{S}$) to the adversary.*

Challenge. *The adversary submits two messages $m^{(0)}, m^{(1)}$, and a challenge attribute set, Γ, provided that no $\mathbb{S}$ queried to the challenger in Phase 1 accepts Γ. The challenger flips a coin $b \xleftarrow{\mathsf{U}} \{0,1\}$, and computes $\mathsf{ct}_{\Gamma}^{(b)} \xleftarrow{\mathsf{R}}$ Enc(pk, $m^{(b)}, \Gamma$). It gives $\mathsf{ct}_{\Gamma}^{(b)}$ to the adversary.*

Phase 2. *Phase 1 is repeated with the restriction that no queried $\mathbb{S}$ accepts challenge Γ.*

Guess. *The adversary outputs a guess b' of b, and wins if $b' = b$.*

The advantage of adversary $\mathcal{A}$ in the adaptive game is defined as $\mathsf{Adv}_{\mathcal{A}}^{\mathsf{KP\text{-}ABE}}(\lambda) := \Pr[\mathcal{A} \text{ wins}] - 1/2$ for any λ. A KP-ABE scheme is adaptively payload-hiding secure if all poly-time adversaries have at most a negligible advantage in the game.

Remark 1. The challenge Γ is declared by the adversary just before **Phase 1** (resp. before **Setup**) in the semi-adaptive (resp. selective) game, and the corresponding security notions are defined in the similar manner as above.

4   Special Matrix Subgroups

Let $n \geq 2$ and $\tilde{n} := n + r$. Lemmas 1, 2 and 3 are key lemmas for the security proof for our KP- and CP-ABE schemes.

We start by a motivational argument for introducing our new sparse matrix technique. Previous sparse matrices in DPVS [19,22] are given by the form whose diagonal element except for the first one is the same denoted by u. (For the sparse-matrix DPVS and modified pairwise independence lemma, refer to Sect. 5.4 in [20].) For achieving our information theoretical change from (Y', V_i') to (Y', V_i'') described in Sect. 1.3, we use one more randomness in diagonal elements, i.e., two random u_1 and u_2, as given in Eq. (1). More precisely, random $U \xleftarrow{\mathsf{U}} \mathcal{H}(n, r, \mathbb{F}_q)$ acts on $\mathbb{F}_q^{n+r} = \mathbb{F}_q^n \times \mathbb{F}_q^r$ by using different scalars u_1 and u_2 on the first $\mathbb{F}_q^n$ and the second $\mathbb{F}_q^r$ respectively. The new sparse matrix action is the key fact for proving Lemma 3. For positive integers n and r, let

$$
\mathcal{H}(n, r, \mathbb{F}_q) := \left\{ \begin{pmatrix} u'_1 & & & & \\ u'_2 & u_1 & & & \\ \vdots & & \ddots & & \\ u'_n & & & u_1 & \\ u'_{n+1} & & & & u_2 \\ \vdots & & & & & \ddots \\ u'_{n+r} & & & & & & u_2 \end{pmatrix} \middle| \begin{array}{l} u_1, u_2, u'_l \in \mathbb{F}_q \\ \text{for } l = 1, \ldots, n+r, \\ \text{a blank element} \\ \text{in the matrix} \\ \text{denotes } 0 \in \mathbb{F}_q \end{array} \right\}, \quad (1)
$$

and $\mathcal{H}(n, r, \mathbb{F}_q)^{\times} := \mathcal{H}(n, r, \mathbb{F}_q) \cap GL(\tilde{n}, \mathbb{F}_q)$.

Lemma 1. $\mathcal{H}(n, r, \mathbb{F}_q)^\times$ *is a subgroup of* $GL(\tilde{n}, \mathbb{F}_q)$, *where* $\tilde{n} := n + r$.

Lemma 1 is directly verified from the definition of groups.   □
Let

$$X_{i,j} := \begin{pmatrix} \mu'_{i,j,1} & & & & \\ \mu'_{i,j,2} & \mu_{i,j,1} & & & \\ \vdots & & \ddots & & \\ \mu'_{i,j,n} & & & \mu_{i,j,1} & \\ \mu'_{i,j,n+1} & & & & \mu_{i,j,2} \\ \vdots & & & & & \ddots \\ \mu'_{i,j,n+r} & & & & & & \mu_{i,j,2} \end{pmatrix} \begin{array}{l} \in \mathcal{H}(n, r, \mathbb{F}_q) \\ \text{for } i, j = \\ 1, \ldots, 5 \end{array} \quad (2)$$

and using $X_{i,j}$, we define

$$\mathcal{L}(5, n, r, \mathbb{F}_q) := \left\{ X := \begin{pmatrix} X_{1,1} & \cdots & X_{1,5} \\ \vdots & & \vdots \\ X_{5,1} & \cdots & X_{5,5} \end{pmatrix} \middle| \begin{array}{l} X_{i,j} \in \mathcal{H}(n, r, \mathbb{F}_q) \\ \text{for } i, j = 1, \ldots, 5 \end{array} \right\} \bigcap GL(5\tilde{n}, \mathbb{F}_q). \quad (3)$$

Lemma 2. $\mathcal{L}(5, n, r, \mathbb{F}_q)$ *is a subgroup of* $GL(5\tilde{n}, \mathbb{F}_q)$.

Lemma 2 is given in a similar manner as Lemma 2 in the full version of [19]. For the proof, see the full version of this paper [23]. Next is a generalization of Lemma 6 in [19].

Lemma 3. *Let* $\vec{e}_j := (0, \ldots, 0, \overset{j}{1}, 0, \ldots, 0) \in \mathbb{F}_q^{n+r}$.
For all $\vec{v} = (v_1, \ldots, v_n, 0, \ldots, 0) \in \mathsf{span}\langle \vec{e}_1, .., \vec{e}_n \rangle \setminus \mathsf{span}\langle \vec{e}_1 \rangle$,
$\vec{\kappa} = (0, \ldots, 0, \kappa_1, \ldots, \kappa_r) \in \mathsf{span}\langle \vec{e}_{n+1}, .., \vec{e}_{n+r} \rangle$ *and* $\pi \in \mathbb{F}_q$, *let*

$$W_{\vec{v}, \vec{\kappa}, \pi} := \{ (\vec{w}, \vec{z}) \in (\mathsf{span}\langle \vec{e}_1, \vec{v}, \vec{\kappa} \rangle \setminus \mathsf{span}\langle \vec{e}_1 \rangle) \times (\mathbb{F}_q^{n+r} \setminus \mathsf{span}\langle \vec{e}_1 \rangle^\perp) \mid \vec{w} \cdot \vec{z} = \pi \}.$$

For all $(\vec{v}, \vec{\kappa}, \vec{x}) \in (\mathsf{span}\langle \vec{e}_1, .., \vec{e}_n \rangle \setminus \mathsf{span}\langle \vec{e}_1 \rangle) \times \mathsf{span}\langle \vec{e}_{n+1}, .., \vec{e}_{n+r} \rangle \times (\mathbb{F}_q^{n+r} \setminus \mathsf{span}\langle \vec{e}_1 \rangle^\perp)$, *and* $U \xleftarrow{\mathsf{U}} \mathcal{H}(n, r, \mathbb{F}_q)^\times$, $Z := (U^{-1})^\mathrm{T}$, *the pair* $((\vec{v} + \vec{\kappa})U, \vec{x}Z)$ *is uniformly distributed in* $W_{\vec{v}, \vec{\kappa}, (\vec{v} + \vec{\kappa}) \cdot \vec{x}}$ *except with negligible probability.*

For the proof, see the full version of this paper [23].

5   Adaptively Secure Multi-Use KP-ABE Scheme with Short Ciphertexts

5.1   Key Ideas in Constructing the Proposed KP-ABE Scheme

We extend the techniques developed in [22], where the author presented a semi-adaptively secure KP-ABE with constant-size ciphertexts by using sparse matrix DPVS approach. An underlying construction of our proposed one is given in Sect. 5.3, which is a dual form of the scheme in [22] since the $5n \times 5n$ sparse basis matrix is used in a dual manner. Hence, while [22] scheme has size $O(1)$

ciphertexts and size $O(\ell n)$ keys, the underlying one has size $O(n)$ ciphertexts and size $O(\ell)$ keys (Table 1), where ℓ, n are the number of rows in access structure matrix M and the max of the number of attributes in Γ, respectively. In other words, the dual conversion of the scheme in [22] to the underlying scheme increases ciphertext size $O(n)$-times and then decreases key size $O(n)$-times.

As mentioned in Introduction, the top level idea of our construction is the decoupling technique of LSS encoding. The underlying scheme has a usual encoding of LSS, i.e., encoding a central secret s_0 and shares s_i. Therefore, the comprehension of the construction idea of the underlying one is necessary for understanding our proposed one. In this section, we will explain key ideas of constructing the underlying and our KP-ABE schemes. First, we will show how size $O(n)$ ciphertexts and size $O(\ell)$ keys can be achieved in the underlying scheme, where the IPE scheme given in [19] is used as a building block. Here, we will use a simplified (or toy) version of the underlying KP-ABE scheme, for which the security is no more ensured in the standard model under the DLIN assumption.

A ciphertext in the simplified KP-ABE scheme consists of two vector elements, $(\boldsymbol{c}_0, \boldsymbol{c}_1) \in \mathbb{G}^5 \times \mathbb{G}^n$, and $c_T \in \mathbb{G}_T$. A secret key consists of $\ell + 1$ vector elements, $(\boldsymbol{k}_0^*, \boldsymbol{k}_1^*, \ldots, \boldsymbol{k}_\ell^*) \in \mathbb{G}^5 \times (\mathbb{G}^n)^\ell$ for access structure $\mathbb{S} := (M, \rho)$, where the number of rows of M is ℓ and $\boldsymbol{k}_i^*$ with $i \geq 1$ corresponds to the i-th row. Therefore, to achieve shorter secret keys, we have to compress $\boldsymbol{k}_i^* \in \mathbb{G}^n$ to a constant size in n. We now employ a special form of basis generation matrix, $X :=$
$$\begin{pmatrix} \mu_1' & & \\ \mu_2' & \mu & \\ \vdots & & \ddots \\ \mu_n' & & \mu \end{pmatrix} \in \mathcal{H}(n, 0, \mathbb{F}_q)$$
of Eq. (1) in Sect. 4, where $\mu, \mu_1', \ldots, \mu_n' \xleftarrow{\mathsf{U}} \mathbb{F}_q$ and a blank in the matrix denotes $0 \in \mathbb{F}_q$. The master secret key (DPVS basis) is $\mathbb{B}^* :=$
$$\begin{pmatrix} \boldsymbol{b}_1^* \\ \vdots \\ \boldsymbol{b}_n^* \end{pmatrix} := \begin{pmatrix} \mu_1' G & & \\ \mu_2' G & \mu G & \\ \vdots & & \ddots \\ \mu_n' G & & \mu G \end{pmatrix}.$$
Let the i-th component of a secret key associated with $\mathbb{S} := (M := (M_i)_{i=1}^\ell, \rho)$ consists of $\boldsymbol{k}_i^* := (\theta_i v_i^{n-1} + s_i, \theta_i v_i^{n-2}, \ldots, \theta_i v_i, \theta_i)_{\mathbb{B}^*} = (\theta_i v_i^{n-1} + s_i)\boldsymbol{b}_1^* + \theta_i(v_i^{n-2}\boldsymbol{b}_2^* + \cdots + v_i \boldsymbol{b}_{n-1}^* + \boldsymbol{b}_n^*) = \left(\left(\theta_i(\sum_{j=1}^n v_i^{n-j}\mu_j') + s_i \mu_1' \right) G, v_i^{n-2}\theta_i \mu G, \ldots, \theta_i \mu G \right)$, where $v_i := \rho(i), \theta_i \xleftarrow{\mathsf{U}} \mathbb{F}_q, \vec{f} \xleftarrow{\mathsf{U}} \mathbb{F}_q^r$ and $s_i := M_i \cdot \vec{f}$. Then, $\boldsymbol{k}_i^*$ can be compressed to only *two* group elements $\left(K_{i,1}^* := \left(\theta_i(\sum_{j=1}^n v_i^{n-j}\mu_j') + s_i \mu_1' \right) G, K_{i,2}^* := \theta_i \mu G \right)$ as well as v_i, since $\boldsymbol{k}_i^*$ can be obtained by $(K_{i,1}^*, v_i^{n-2} K_{i,2}^*, \ldots, v_i K_{i,2}^*, K_{i,2}^*)$ (note that $v_i^j K_{i,2}^* = v_i^j \theta_i \mu G$ for $j = 0, \ldots, n-2$). That is, the i-th component of a secret key (excluding v_i) can be just two group elements, or the size is constant in n, then $(\boldsymbol{k}_i^*)_{i=0}^\ell$ can be compressed into size $O(\ell)$.

Let $\mathbb{B} := (\boldsymbol{b}_i)$ be the dual orthonormal basis of $\mathbb{B}^* := (\boldsymbol{b}_i^*)$, and $\mathbb{B}$ be the public key in the simplified KP-ABE scheme. We specify $(\boldsymbol{c}_0, \boldsymbol{k}_0^*, c_T)$ such that $e(\boldsymbol{c}_0, \boldsymbol{k}_0^*) = g_T^{\zeta - \xi s_0}$ and $c_T := g_T^\zeta m \in \mathbb{G}_T$ with s_0 is a center secret of shares $\{s_i\}_{i=1,\ldots,\ell}$ associated with access structure $\mathbb{S}$, which are embedded into

$\{k_i^*\}_{i=1,\ldots,\ell}$ as indicated above. We also set a ciphertext for $\Gamma := \{x_1, \ldots, x_{n'}\}$ as $c_1 := (\omega \vec{y})_{\mathbb{B}}$ where $\vec{y} := (y_1, \ldots, y_n)$ such that $\sum_{j=0}^{n-1} y_{n-j} z^j = z^{n-1-n'} \prod_{j=1}^{n'} (z - x_j)$, and $\omega \xleftarrow{\mathsf{U}} \mathbb{F}_q$. From the dual orthonormality of $\mathbb{B}$ and $\mathbb{B}^*$, if $\mathbb{S}$ accepts Γ, there exists a system of coefficients $\{\alpha_i\}_{\rho(i) \in \Gamma}$ such that $e(c_1, k'^*) = g_T^{\xi s_0}$, where $k'^* := \sum_{\rho(i) \in \Gamma} \alpha_i k_i^*$. Hence, a decryptor can compute $g_T^{\xi s_0}$ if and only if $\mathbb{S}$ accepts Γ, i.e., can obtain plaintext m. We can extend the simplified KP-ABE to a *semi-adaptively* secure KP-ABE scheme under the DLIN assumption just by enlarging the dimension of the underlying vector space, which is shown in Sect. 5.3. The security proof is based on the Waters's dual system technique and given in a similar manner to [22]. The provably secure scheme has the same asymptotic sizes of keys and ciphertexts, i.e., $O(\ell)$-sized keys and $O(n)$-sized ciphertexts.

Our goal is to construct an *adaptively* secure KP-ABE with a comparable asymptotic data sizes, i.e., $O(\ell)$-sized keys and $O(n+r)$-sized ciphertexts, from the underlying one. We use a decoupling technique of LSS matrix from randomness for achieving the goal. First, we enlarge the space from $O(n)$ to $O(n+r)$ dimension. As described in Fig. 1, a uniformly random vector $\vec{f} \in \mathbb{F}_q^r$ for LSS is encoded on the ciphertext component c_1. In the simplified scheme, $c_1 := (\omega \vec{y}, \vec{f})_{\mathbb{B}} \in \mathbb{G}^{n+r}$ where $\vec{y} \in \mathbb{F}_q^r$ is defined as above. For encoding each row M_i of access matrix M on k_i^*, the above matrix X is extended to a $(n+r) \times (n+r)$ matrix in $\mathcal{H}(n, r, \mathbb{F}_q)$ (Eq. (1)), then the master secret key is given by

$$
\mathbb{B}^* := \begin{pmatrix} b_1^* \\ \vdots \\ b_n^* \\ b_{n+1}^* \\ \vdots \\ b_{n+r}^* \end{pmatrix} := \begin{pmatrix} \mu_1' G & & & & \\ \mu_2' G & \mu_1 G & & & \\ \vdots & & \ddots & & \\ \mu_n' G & & & \mu_1 G & \\ \mu_{n+1}' G & & & & \mu_2 G \\ \vdots & & & & & \ddots \\ \mu_{n+r}' G & & & & & & \mu_2 G \end{pmatrix} \quad \text{where}
$$

$\mu_1, \mu_2, \mu_1', \ldots, \mu_{n+r}' \xleftarrow{\mathsf{U}} \mathbb{F}_q$. Here, note that two independent diagonal elements μ_1, μ_2 are used for the first n-dimension and the second r-dimension. (Refer to the argument given in the beginning of Sect. 4.) Hence, k_i^* is given by $k_i^* := (\theta_i \vec{v}_i, \xi M_i)_{\mathbb{B}^*}$. We note k_i^* is compressed to three group elements as before, i.e., $K_{i,1}^* := (\theta_i (\sum_{l=1}^{n} v_i^{n-l} \mu_l') + \xi(\sum_{l=1}^{r} M_{i,l} \mu_{n+l}')) G$, $K_{i,2}^* := \theta_i \mu_1 G$, $K_{i,3}^* := \xi \mu_2 G$ for $i = 1, .., \ell$, and the secret key size is $O(\ell)$. The pairing value of c_1 and k_i^* is $e(c_1, k_i^*) = g_T^{\omega \theta_i \vec{y} \cdot \vec{v}_i + \xi M_i \cdot \vec{f}} = g_T^{\omega \theta_i \vec{y} \cdot \vec{v}_i + \xi s_i}$ where $s_i := M_i \cdot \vec{f}$. These values are equivalent to the previous underlying scheme. Therefore, the decryption algorithm is the same as before.

We then explain how our *full* KP-ABE scheme is constructed on the above-mentioned simplified KP-ABE scheme. The target of designing the full KP-ABE scheme is to achieve the adaptive security *under the DLIN assumption*. Here, we adopt and extend a strategy initiated in [18], in which the dual system encryption methodology is employed in a modular or hierarchical manner. That is, three top level assumptions, the security of Problems 1–3, are directly used in the dual system encryption methodology and the assumptions are reduced to a primitive assumption, the DLIN assumption. To meet the requirements for applying to the dual system encryption methodology and reducing to the DLIN assumption, the underlying vector space is five times greater than that of the above-mentioned simplified scheme. For example, $k_i^* := (\ \theta_i \vec{v}_i,\ \xi M_i,\ 0^{2n+2r},\ \psi_i \vec{v}_i,\ \eta_i M_i,\ 0^{n+r}\ )_{\mathbb{B}^*}$ for $\rho(i) = v_i$, $c_1 = (\ \omega \vec{y},\ \vec{f},\ 0^{2n+2r},\ 0^{n+r},\ \vec{\varphi}_1\ )_{\mathbb{B}}$ with $\vec{\varphi}_1 \xleftarrow{\mathsf{U}} \mathbb{F}_q^{n+r}$, and

$$X := \begin{pmatrix} X_{1,1} & \cdots & X_{1,5} \\ \vdots & & \vdots \\ X_{5,1} & \cdots & X_{5,5} \end{pmatrix} \in \mathcal{L}(5,n,r,\mathbb{F}_q) \text{ of Eq. (3) in Sect. 4, where each } X_{i,j} \text{ is}$$

of the form of $X \in \mathcal{H}(n,r,\mathbb{F}_q)$ in the simplified scheme. The vector space consists of four orthogonal subspaces, i.e., real encoding part, hidden part, secret key randomness part, and ciphertext randomness part. The simplified KP-ABE scheme corresponds to the first real encoding part.

A key fact in the security reduction is that $\mathcal{L}(5,n,r,\mathbb{F}_q)$ is a *subgroup* of $GL(5(n+r),\mathbb{F}_q)$ (Lemma 2), which enables a *random-self-reducibility* argument for reducing the intractability of Problems 1–3 to the DLIN assumption. For the reduction, see [19]. We employ a new simulation technique in dual system encryption using random vector $\vec{f}$ in c_1. For the details, refer to the proof outline in Sect. 5.4.

5.2   Dual Orthonormal Basis Generator

We describe random dual orthonormal basis generator $\mathcal{G}_{\mathsf{ob}}^{\mathsf{KP}}$ below, which is used as a subroutine in the proposed KP-ABE scheme.

$\mathcal{G}_{\mathsf{ob}}^{\mathsf{KP}}(1^\lambda, 5, (n,r)) : \mathsf{param}_{\mathbb{G}} := (q, \mathbb{G}, \mathbb{G}_T, G, e) \xleftarrow{\mathsf{R}} \mathcal{G}_{\mathsf{bpg}}(1^\lambda), N_0 := 5, N_1 := 5(n+r),$

$\quad \mathsf{param}_{\mathbb{V}_t} := (q, \mathbb{V}_t, \mathbb{G}_T, \mathbb{A}_t, e) := \mathcal{G}_{\mathsf{dpvs}}(1^\lambda, N_t, \mathsf{param}_{\mathbb{G}}) \text{ for } t = 0,1,$

$\quad \psi \xleftarrow{\mathsf{U}} \mathbb{F}_q^\times,\ g_T := e(G,G)^\psi,\ \mathsf{param}_{(n,r)} := ((n,r), \{\mathsf{param}_{\mathbb{V}_t}\}_{t=0,1}, g_T),$

$\quad X_0 := (\chi_{0,i,j})_{i,j=1,\dots,5} \xleftarrow{\mathsf{U}} GL(N_0, \mathbb{F}_q),\ X_1 \xleftarrow{\mathsf{U}} \mathcal{L}(5,n,r,\mathbb{F}_q), \text{ hereafter,}$

$\quad \{\mu_{i,j,\iota}, \mu'_{i,j,l}\}_{l=1,\dots,n+r}^{i,j=1,\dots,5;\iota=1,2} \text{ denotes non-zero entries of } X_1 \text{ as in Eq. (2),}$

$\quad b_{0,i}^* := (\chi_{0,i,1}, \dots, \chi_{0,i,5})\mathbb{A} = \sum_{j=1}^5 \chi_{0,i,j} a_j \text{ for } i = 1,..,5,\ \mathbb{B}_0^* := (b_{0,1}^*, .., b_{0,5}^*),$

$\quad B_{i,j,\iota}^* := \mu_{i,j,\iota} G,\ B_{i,j,l}'^* := \mu'_{i,j,l} G \text{ for } i,j = 1,\dots,5; \iota = 1,2; l = 1,\dots,n+r,$

$\quad \text{for } t = 0,1,\ (\vartheta_{t,i,j})_{i,j=1,\dots,N_t} := \psi \cdot (X_t^{\mathsf{T}})^{-1},$

$\quad b_{t,i} := (\vartheta_{t,i,1}, .., \vartheta_{t,i,N_t})\mathbb{A} = \sum_{j=1}^{N_t} \vartheta_{t,i,j} a_j \text{ for } i = 1,..,N_t,\ \mathbb{B}_t := (b_{t,1}, .., b_{t,N_t}),$

$\quad \text{return } (\mathsf{param}_{(n,r)}, \mathbb{B}_0, \mathbb{B}_0^*, \mathbb{B}_1, \{B_{i,j,\iota}^*, B_{i,j,l}'^*\}_{l=1,\dots,n+r}^{i,j=1,\dots,5;\iota=1,2}).$

Remark 2. Let sparse block matrix $\begin{pmatrix} b_{1,(i-1)(n+r)+1}^* \\ \vdots \\ b_{1,i(n+r)}^* \end{pmatrix} := (X_{i,1} \cdot G \cdots X_{i,5} \cdot G)$

for $i = 1,\dots,5$, and $\mathbb{B}_1^* := (b_{1,1}^*, \dots, b_{1,5(n+r)}^*)$, where $X_{i,j} \cdot G$ means the componentwise multiplication. $\mathbb{B}_1$ is the dual orthonormal basis of $\mathbb{B}_1^*$, i.e., $e(b_{1,i}, b_{1,i}^*) = g_T$ and $e(b_{1,i}, b_{1,j}^*) = 1$ for $1 \le i \ne j \le 5(n+r)$.

5.3 Warm-Up: Underlying Semi-adaptively Secure Construction

As a warm-up, we describe a semi-adaptively secure KP-ABE scheme, which is a dual construction of [22] whose secret keys are compressed by using a sparse matrix while [22] scheme has compressed ciphertexts. Namely, we use the sparse matrix in a dual manner of [22]. We refer to Sect. 1.4 for notations on DPVS.

$\mathsf{Setup}(1^\lambda, n) : / * \ N_0 := 5, \ N_1 := 5n \ */$

$\quad (\mathsf{param}_n, \mathbb{B}_0, \mathbb{B}_0^*, \mathbb{B}_1, \{B_{i,j,\iota}^*, B_{i,j,l}'^*\}_{l=1,..,n}^{i,j=1,...,5; \iota=1,2}) \xleftarrow{\mathsf{R}} \mathcal{G}_{\mathsf{ob}}^{\mathsf{KP}}(1^\lambda, 5, (n, 0)),$

$\quad \widehat{\mathbb{B}}_0 := (\boldsymbol{b}_{0,1}, \boldsymbol{b}_{0,2}, \boldsymbol{b}_{0,5}), \ \ \widehat{\mathbb{B}}_0^* := (\boldsymbol{b}_{0,1}^*, \boldsymbol{b}_{0,2}^*, \boldsymbol{b}_{0,4}^*),$

$\quad \widehat{\mathbb{B}}_1 := (\boldsymbol{b}_{1,1}, .., \boldsymbol{b}_{1,n}, \boldsymbol{b}_{1,4n+1}, .., \boldsymbol{b}_{1,5n}),$

$\quad \text{return } \mathsf{pk} := (1^\lambda, \mathsf{param}_n, \{\widehat{\mathbb{B}}_t\}_{t=0,1}), \ \ \mathsf{sk} := (\widehat{\mathbb{B}}_0^*, \{B_{i,j,\iota}^*, B_{i,j,l}'^*\}_{\iota=1,2; l=1,...,n}^{i=1,4; j=1,...,5}).$

$\mathsf{KeyGen}(\mathsf{pk}, \mathsf{sk}, \mathbb{S} := (M, \rho)) : \ \vec{f} \xleftarrow{\mathsf{U}} \mathbb{F}_q^r, \ s_0 := \vec{1} \cdot \vec{f}, \ \eta_0 \xleftarrow{\mathsf{U}} \mathbb{F}_q,$

$\quad \boldsymbol{k}_0^* := (1, \ s_0, \ 0, \ \eta_0, \ 0)_{\mathbb{B}_0^*},$

$\quad \text{for } i = 1, \ldots, \ell, \ \text{if } \rho(i) = v_i, \ \vec{v}_i := (v_{i,l})_{l=1}^n := (v_i^{n-1}, .., v_i, 1),$

$\qquad s_i := M_i \cdot \vec{f}, \ \theta_i, \psi_i, \eta_i \xleftarrow{\mathsf{U}} \mathbb{F}_q,$

$\qquad \text{for } j = 1, \ldots, 5, \ K_{i,1,j}^* := \sum_{l=1}^n v_{i,l}(\theta_i B_{1,j,l}'^* + \psi_i B_{5,j,l}'^*) + s_i B_{1,j,1}'^* + \eta_i B_{5,j,1}'^*,$

$\qquad K_{i,2,j}^* := \theta_i B_{1,j,1}^* + \psi_i B_{5,j,1}^*,$

$\quad \text{return } \mathsf{sk}_\mathbb{S} := (\mathbb{S}, \ \boldsymbol{k}_0^*, \ \{K_{i,1,j}^*, K_{i,2,j}^*\}_{i=1,...,\ell; j=1,...,5}).$

$\mathsf{Enc}(\mathsf{pk}, m, \ \Gamma := \{x_1, \ldots, x_{n'} \mid x_j \in \mathbb{F}_q^\times, n' \le n - 1\}) :$

$\quad \vec{y} := (y_1, \ldots, y_n) \text{ such that } \sum_{j=0}^{n-1} y_{n-j} z^j = z^{n-1-n'} \prod_{j=1}^{n'}(z - x_j),$

$\quad \omega, \varphi_0, \zeta \xleftarrow{\mathsf{U}} \mathbb{F}_q, \ \vec{\varphi}_1 \xleftarrow{\mathsf{U}} \mathbb{F}_q^n, \ \ \boldsymbol{c}_0 := (\zeta, \ \omega, \ 0, \ 0, \ \varphi_0)_{\mathbb{B}_0},$

$$\boldsymbol{c}_1 := (\ \overbrace{\omega\vec{y},}^{n} \ \overbrace{0^{2n},}^{2n} \ \overbrace{0^n,}^{n} \ \overbrace{\vec{\varphi}_1}^{n} \ )_{\mathbb{B}_1}$$

$\quad c_T := g_T^\zeta m, \ \ \mathsf{ct}_\Gamma := (\Gamma, \boldsymbol{c}_0, \boldsymbol{c}_1, c_T), \ \ \text{return } \mathsf{ct}_\Gamma.$

$\mathsf{Dec}(\mathsf{pk}, \mathsf{sk}_\mathbb{S} := (\mathbb{S}, \ \boldsymbol{k}_0^*, \{K_{i,1,j}^*, K_{i,3,j}^*\}_{j=1,...,5}^{i=1,...,\ell}), \mathsf{ct}_\Gamma := (\Gamma, \boldsymbol{c}_0, \boldsymbol{c}_1, c_T)) :$

$\quad \text{If } \mathbb{S} := (M, \rho) \text{ accepts } \Gamma, \text{ then compute } I \text{ and } \{\alpha_i\}_{i \in I} \text{ such that}$

$\qquad \vec{1} = \sum_{i \in I} \alpha_i M_i, \text{ where } M_i \text{ is the } i\text{-th row of } M, \text{ and}$

$\qquad I \subseteq \{i \in \{1, \ldots, \ell\} \ \mid \ [\rho(i) = v_i \ \wedge \ v_i \in \Gamma] \}.$

$\quad \text{for } i \in I, \ \ \text{if } \rho(i) = v_i, \ \vec{v}_i := (v_{i,l})_{l=1}^n := (v_i^{n-1}, \ldots, v_i, 1),$

$$\boldsymbol{k}_i^* := (\ \overbrace{K_{i,1,1}^*, \ v_{i,2}K_{i,2,1}^*, .., v_{i,n}K_{i,2,1}^*,}^{n} \ \cdots \ \overbrace{K_{i,1,5}^*, \ v_{i,2}K_{i,2,5}^*, .., v_{i,n}K_{i,2,5}^*}^{n}),$$

$$\text{that is, } \boldsymbol{k}_i^* := (\ \overbrace{\theta_i\vec{v}_i + s_i\vec{e}_1,}^{n} \ \overbrace{0^{2n},}^{2n} \ \overbrace{\psi_i\vec{v}_i + \eta_i\vec{e}_1,}^{n} \ \overbrace{0^n}^{n} \ )_{\mathbb{B}_1^*},$$

$\quad \boldsymbol{k}'^* := \sum_{i \in I} \alpha_i \boldsymbol{k}_i^*, \ \ K := e(\boldsymbol{c}_0, \boldsymbol{k}_0^*) \cdot e(\boldsymbol{c}_1, \boldsymbol{k}'^*), \ \ \text{return } m' := c_T/K.$

[**Correctness**] If $\mathbb{S} := (M, \rho)$ accepts Γ, $K = e(\boldsymbol{c}_0, \boldsymbol{k}_0^*) \cdot e(\boldsymbol{c}_1, \boldsymbol{k}'^*) = g_T^{-\omega s_0 + \zeta} g_T^{\omega \sum_{i \in I} \alpha_i s_i} = g_T^{\zeta}$ where $s_0 := \vec{1} \cdot \vec{f}$, $s_i := M_i \cdot \vec{f}$ for $i = 1, \ldots, \ell$.

We note that secret key $\mathsf{sk}_{\mathbb{S}}$ consists of $5\ell + 5$ group elements and ciphertext ct_{Γ} consists of $5n + 5$ group elements (and one $\mathbb{G}_T$ element).

The standard DLIN assumption is defined in Appendix A.

Theorem 1. *The above multi-use KP-ABE scheme is semi-adaptively payload-hiding against chosen plaintext attacks under the DLIN assumption.*

Theorem 1 is proven in a similar manner as in [22].

In the semi-adaptive security model, the challenge attribute set Γ is declared by the adversary at the start of the game, but after receiving the public key pk from the challenger. Therefore, for each key query $\mathbb{S} := (M, \rho)$, the challenger can determine whether $\rho(i) \in \Gamma$ or not for $i = 1, \ldots, \ell$. The challenger in the security proof makes use of this information to simulate a component $\boldsymbol{k}_i^*$ of a queried key for each $i = 1, \ldots, \ell$ in a refined dual system encryption proof. The main part of the game sequence is similar (but not equal) to the Game 3 sequence in the proof of Theorem 2 below.

5.4 Proposed Adaptively Secure Construction

By decoupling LSS coefficients $s_i := M_i \cdot \vec{f} \in \mathbb{F}_q$ to $M_i \in \mathbb{F}_q^r$ in the key side and $\vec{f} \in \mathbb{F}_q^r$ in the ciphertext side (of the underlying scheme in Sect. 5.3), we obtain our proposed adaptively secure KP-ABE scheme.

$\mathsf{Setup}(1^\lambda,\ (n, r)) : /\ast\ N_0 := 5,\ N_1 := 5(n + r)\ \ast/$

$\quad (\mathsf{param}_{(n,r)}, \mathbb{B}_0, \mathbb{B}_0^*, \mathbb{B}_1, \{B_{i,j,\iota}^*, B_{i,j,l}'^*\}_{l=1,\ldots,n+r}^{i,j=1,\ldots,5;\ \iota=1,2}) \xleftarrow{\mathsf{R}} \mathcal{G}_{\mathsf{ob}}^{\mathsf{KP}}(1^\lambda, 5, (n, r)),$

$\quad \widehat{\mathbb{B}}_0 := (\boldsymbol{b}_{0,1}, \boldsymbol{b}_{0,2}, \boldsymbol{b}_{0,5}),\ \widehat{\mathbb{B}}_0^* := (\boldsymbol{b}_{0,1}^*, \boldsymbol{b}_{0,2}^*, \boldsymbol{b}_{0,4}^*),$

$\quad \widehat{\mathbb{B}}_1 := (\boldsymbol{b}_{1,1}, .., \boldsymbol{b}_{1,n+r}, \boldsymbol{b}_{1,4(n+r)+1}, .., \boldsymbol{b}_{1,5(n+r)}),$

$\quad \mathsf{return}\ \ \mathsf{pk} := (1^\lambda, \mathsf{param}_{(n,r)}, \{\widehat{\mathbb{B}}_t\}_{t=0,1}),$

$\qquad\ \ \mathsf{sk} := (\widehat{\mathbb{B}}_0^*, \{B_{i,j,\iota}^*, B_{i,j,l}'^*\}_{\iota=1,2;\ l=1,..,n+r}^{i=1,4;j=1,..,5}).$

$\mathsf{KeyGen}(\mathsf{pk}, \mathsf{sk}, \mathbb{S} := (M, \rho)) :\quad \xi, \eta_0 \xleftarrow{\mathsf{U}} \mathbb{F}_q,\qquad \boldsymbol{k}_0^* := (1,\ \xi,\ 0,\ \eta_0,\ 0)_{\mathbb{B}_0^*},$

$\quad \mathsf{for}\ i = 1, .., \ell,\ \ \mathsf{if}\ \rho(i) = v_i,\ \vec{v}_i := (v_{i,l})_{l=1}^n := (v_i^{n-1}, .., v_i, 1),\ \theta_i, \psi_i, \eta_i \xleftarrow{\mathsf{U}} \mathbb{F}_q,$

$\qquad \mathsf{for}\ j = 1, \ldots, 5,$

$\quad K_{i,1,j}^* := \sum_{l=1}^n v_{i,l}(\theta_i B_{1,j,l}'^* + \psi_i B_{5,j,l}'^*) + \sum_{l=1}^r M_{i,l}(\xi B_{1,j,n+l}'^* + \eta_i B_{5,j,n+l}'^*),$

$\quad K_{i,2,j}^* := \theta_i B_{1,j,1}^* + \psi_i B_{5,j,1}^*,\quad K_{i,3,j}^* := \xi B_{1,j,2}^* + \eta_i B_{5,j,2}^*,$

$\quad \mathsf{return}\ \ \mathsf{sk}_{\mathbb{S}} := (\mathbb{S},\ \boldsymbol{k}_0^*,\ \{K_{i,1,j}^*, K_{i,2,j}^*, K_{i,3,j}^*\}_{i=1,\ldots,\ell; j=1,\ldots,5}).$

$\mathsf{Enc}(\mathsf{pk},\ m,\ \Gamma := \{x_1,\ldots,x_{n'} \mid x_j \in \mathbb{F}_q^\times, n' \leq n-1\})$:

$$\vec{y} := (y_1,\ldots,y_n) \text{ such that } \sum_{j=0}^{n-1} y_{n-j}z^j = z^{n-1-n'} \prod_{j=1}^{n'}(z - x_j),$$

$$\vec{f} \xleftarrow{\mathsf{U}} \mathbb{F}_q^r,\ \omega,\varphi_0,\zeta \xleftarrow{\mathsf{U}} \mathbb{F}_q,\ \vec{\varphi}_1 \xleftarrow{\mathsf{U}} \mathbb{F}_q^{n+r},\quad \boldsymbol{c}_0 := (\zeta,\ \vec{1}\cdot\vec{f},\ 0,\ 0,\ \varphi_0)_{\mathbb{B}_0},$$

$$\boldsymbol{c}_1 := (\ \overbrace{\omega\vec{y},\ \vec{f}}^{n+r},\ \overbrace{0^{2n+2r}}^{2n+2r},\ \overbrace{0^{n+r}}^{n+r},\ \overbrace{\vec{\varphi}_1}^{n+r}\ )_{\mathbb{B}_1}$$

$$c_T := g_T^\zeta m,\quad \mathsf{ct}_\Gamma := (\Gamma, \boldsymbol{c}_0, \boldsymbol{c}_1, c_T),\quad \text{return } \mathsf{ct}_\Gamma.$$

$\mathsf{Dec}(\mathsf{pk}, \mathsf{sk}_{\mathbb{S}} := (\mathbb{S}, \boldsymbol{k}_0^*, \{K_{i,1,j}^*, K_{i,2,j}^*, K_{i,3,j}^*\}_{j=1,\ldots,5}^{i=1,\ldots,\ell}), \mathsf{ct}_\Gamma := (\Gamma, \boldsymbol{c}_0, \boldsymbol{c}_1, c_T))$:

If $\mathbb{S} := (M, \rho)$ accepts Γ, then compute I and $\{\alpha_i\}_{i \in I}$ such that

$$\vec{1} = \sum_{i \in I} \alpha_i M_i, \text{ where } M_i \text{ is the } i\text{-th row of } M, \text{ and}$$

$$I \subseteq \{i \in \{1,..,\ell\} \mid [\rho(i) = v_i \wedge v_i \in \Gamma]\ \}.$$

$$\text{for } i \in I, \quad \text{if } \rho(i) = v_i,\quad \vec{v}_i := (v_{i,l})_{l=1}^n := (v_i^{n-1},\ldots,v_i,1),$$

$$\boldsymbol{k}_i^* := (\ \overbrace{K_{i,1,1}^*,\ v_{i,2}K_{i,2,1}^*,..,v_{i,n}K_{i,2,1}^*,\ M_{i,1}K_{i,3,1}^*,..,M_{i,r}K_{i,3,1}^*,\ \cdots}^{n+r}$$
$$K_{i,1,5}^*,\ v_{i,2}K_{i,2,5}^*,..,v_{i,n}K_{i,2,5}^*,\ M_{i,1}K_{i,3,5}^*,..,M_{i,r}K_{i,3,5}^*\ ),$$

$$\text{that is, } \boldsymbol{k}_i^* := (\ \overbrace{\theta_i\vec{v}_i,\ \xi M_i,}^{n+r}\ \overbrace{0^{2n+2r},}^{2n+2r}\ \overbrace{\psi_i\vec{v}_i,\ \eta_i M_i,}^{n+r}\ \overbrace{0^{n+r}}^{n+r}\ )_{\mathbb{B}_1^*},$$

$$\boldsymbol{k}'^* := \sum_{i \in I} \alpha_i \boldsymbol{k}_i^*,\quad K := e(\boldsymbol{c}_0, \boldsymbol{k}_0^*) \cdot e(\boldsymbol{c}_1, \boldsymbol{k}'^*),\quad \text{return } m' := c_T/K.$$

[Correctness] If $\mathbb{S} := (M, \rho)$ accepts Γ, $K = e(\boldsymbol{c}_0, \boldsymbol{k}_0^*) \cdot e(\boldsymbol{c}_1, \boldsymbol{k}'^*) = g_T^{-\xi s_0 + \zeta} g_T^{\xi \sum_{i \in I} \alpha_i s_i} = g_T^\zeta$ where $s_0 := \vec{1}\cdot\vec{f}$, $s_i := M_i \cdot \vec{f}$ for $i = 1,\ldots,\ell$.

We note that secret key $\mathsf{sk}_{\mathbb{S}}$ consists of $5\ell + 5$ group elements and ciphertext ct_Γ consists of $5(n + r) + 5$ group elements (and one $\mathbb{G}_T$ element).

While our adaptively secure KP- and CP-ABE schemes have the maximum of size r as one of public parameters, they allow several useful class of access structures. According to the explicit construction of span programs from boolean formulas (e.g., Appendix of [15]), while appending AND gate gets r (and ℓ) larger, appending OR gate gets only ℓ larger. Therefore, for example, available access structures for our adaptive ABE include any r-CNF formula with any arbitrarily long disjunctions (for a bounded r), i.e., length r conjunctions of length $t_1,\ldots,t_r$ disjunctions for arbitrarily large $t_1,\ldots,t_r$ like $(\mathcal{X}_1 \vee \overset{\text{arb. long}}{\cdots\cdots} \vee \mathcal{X}_{t_1}) \wedge \cdots \wedge (\mathcal{Z}_1 \vee \overset{\text{arb. long}}{\cdots\cdots} \vee \mathcal{Z}_{t_r})$, where multi-use of attributes for $\mathcal{X}_1,\ldots,\mathcal{X}_{t_1},\ldots,\mathcal{Z}_1,\ldots,\mathcal{Z}_{t_r}$ is allowed. The j-th column of the LSS matrix M is given by $(0,\ldots,0,\overbrace{1,\ldots,1}^{t_j},0,\ldots,0)^{\mathrm{T}}$ with length $\ell = \sum_{\iota=1}^r t_\iota$ for $j = 1,\ldots,r$ (where the first group has length $\sum_{\iota=1}^{j-1} t_\iota$) when the target is all 1 vector $\vec{1} \in \mathbb{F}_q^r$.

The standard DLIN assumption is defined in Appendix A.

Theorem 2. *The proposed multi-use KP-ABE scheme is adaptively payload-hiding against chosen plaintext attacks under the DLIN assumption.*

The proof of Theorem 2 is given in the full version of this paper [23].

Acknowledgement. This work was supported by JST CREST Grant Number JPMJCR14D6.

A Decisional Linear (DLIN) Assumption

Definition 6 (DLIN: Decisional Linear Assumption [7]). *The DLIN problem is to guess* $\beta \in \{0,1\}$, *given* $(\mathsf{param}_\mathbb{G},\ G, \xi G, \kappa G, \delta\xi G, \sigma\kappa G, S_\beta) \xleftarrow{\mathsf{R}}$ $\mathcal{G}_\beta^{\mathsf{DLIN}}(1^\lambda)$, *where* $\mathcal{G}_\beta^{\mathsf{DLIN}}(1^\lambda) : \mathsf{param}_\mathbb{G} := (q, \mathbb{G}, \mathbb{G}_T, G, e) \xleftarrow{\mathsf{R}} \mathcal{G}_{\mathsf{bpg}}(1^\lambda), \kappa, \delta, \xi, \sigma \xleftarrow{\mathsf{U}}$ $\mathbb{F}_q, S_0 := (\delta + \sigma)G, S_1 \xleftarrow{\mathsf{U}} \mathbb{G}, \text{return } (\mathsf{param}_\mathbb{G},\ G, \xi G, \kappa G, \delta\xi G, \sigma\kappa G, S_\beta), \text{ for}$ $\beta \xleftarrow{\mathsf{U}} \{0,1\}.$ *For a probabilistic machine* $\mathcal{E}$, *we define the advantage of* $\mathcal{E}$ *for the DLIN problem as:* $\mathsf{Adv}_\mathcal{E}^{\mathsf{DLIN}}(\lambda) := \left| \Pr\left[\mathcal{E}(1^\lambda, \varrho) \to 1 \,\middle|\, \varrho \xleftarrow{\mathsf{R}} \mathcal{G}_0^{\mathsf{DLIN}}(1^\lambda)\right] - \Pr\left[\mathcal{E}(1^\lambda, \varrho) \to 1 \,\middle|\, \varrho \xleftarrow{\mathsf{R}} \mathcal{G}_1^{\mathsf{DLIN}}(1^\lambda)\right]\right|.$ *The DLIN assumption is: For any probabilistic polynomial-time adversary* $\mathcal{E}$, *the advantage* $\mathsf{Adv}_\mathcal{E}^{\mathsf{DLIN}}(\lambda)$ *is negligible in* λ.

B Adaptively Secure Multi-Use CP-ABE Scheme with Short Secret Keys

B.1 Definition of CP-ABE

Definition 7 (Ciphertext-Policy Attribute-Based Encryption: CP-ABE). *A ciphertext-policy attribute-based encryption scheme consists of four algorithms.*

Setup *takes as input security parameter. It outputs the public parameters* pk *and a master key* sk.

KeyGen *takes as input a set of attributes,* $\Gamma := \{x_j\}_{1 \le j \le n'}$, pk *and* sk. *It outputs a decryption key.*

Enc *takes as input public parameters* pk, *message* m *in some associated message space* msg, *and access structure* $\mathbb{S} := (M, \rho)$. *It outputs the ciphertext.*

Dec *takes as input public parameters* pk, *decryption key* sk_Γ *for a set of attributes* Γ, *and ciphertext* $\mathsf{ct}_\mathbb{S}$ *that was encrypted under access structure* $\mathbb{S}$. *It outputs either* $m' \in$ msg *or the distinguished symbol* $\perp$.

A CP-ABE scheme should have the correctness property: for all $(\mathsf{pk}, \mathsf{sk}) \xleftarrow{\mathsf{R}}$ $\mathsf{Setup}(1^\lambda)$, all attribute sets Γ, all decryption keys $\mathsf{sk}_\Gamma \xleftarrow{\mathsf{R}} \mathsf{KeyGen}(\mathsf{pk}, \mathsf{sk}, \Gamma)$, all messages m, all access structures $\mathbb{S}$, all ciphertexts $\mathsf{ct}_\mathbb{S} \xleftarrow{\mathsf{R}} \mathsf{Enc}(\mathsf{pk}, m, \mathbb{S})$, it holds that $m = \mathsf{Dec}(\mathsf{pk}, \mathsf{sk}_\Gamma, \mathsf{ct}_\mathbb{S})$ with overwhelming probability, if $\mathbb{S}$ accepts Γ.

Definition 8. *The model for proving the adaptively payload-hiding security of CP-ABE under chosen plaintext attack is:*

Setup. *The challenger runs the setup algorithm,* $(\mathsf{pk}, \mathsf{sk}) \xleftarrow{\mathsf{R}} \mathsf{Setup}(1^\lambda)$, *and gives the public parameters* pk *to the adversary.*

Phase 1. *The adversary is allowed to issue a polynomial number of queries,* Γ, *to the challenger or oracle* $\mathsf{KeyGen}(\mathsf{pk}, \mathsf{sk}, \cdot)$ *for private keys,* sk_Γ *associated with* Γ.

Challenge. *The adversary submits two messages* $m^{(0)}, m^{(1)}$ *and an access structure,* $\mathbb{S} := (M, \rho)$, *provided that the* $\mathbb{S}$ *does not accept any* Γ *sent to the challenger in Phase 1. The challenger flips a random coin* $b \xleftarrow{\mathsf{U}} \{0, 1\}$, *and computes* $\mathsf{ct}_{\mathbb{S}}^{(b)} \xleftarrow{\mathsf{R}} \mathsf{Enc}(\mathsf{pk}, m^{(b)}, \mathbb{S})$. *It gives* $\mathsf{ct}_{\mathbb{S}}^{(b)}$ *to the adversary.*

Phase 2. *The adversary is allowed to issue a polynomial number of queries,* Γ, *to the challenger or oracle* $\mathsf{KeyGen}(\mathsf{pk}, \mathsf{sk}, \cdot)$ *for private keys,* sk_Γ *associated with* Γ, *provided that* $\mathbb{S}$ *does not accept* Γ.

Guess. *The adversary outputs a guess* b' *of* b.

The advantage of an adversary $\mathcal{A}$ *in the above game is defined as* $\mathsf{Adv}_{\mathcal{A}}^{\mathsf{CP\text{-}ABE,PH}}(\lambda)$ $:= \Pr[b' = b] - 1/2$ *for any security parameter* λ. *A CP-FE scheme is adaptively payload-hiding secure if all polynomial time adversaries have at most a negligible advantage in the above game.*

B.2 Dual Orthonormal Basis Generator

We describe random dual orthonormal basis generator $\mathcal{G}_{\mathsf{ob}}^{\mathsf{CP}}$ below, which is used as a subroutine in the proposed CP-ABE scheme, where $\mathcal{G}_{\mathsf{ob}}^{\mathsf{KP}}$ is defined in Sec. 5.2.

$\mathcal{G}_{\mathsf{ob}}^{\mathsf{CP}}(1^\lambda, 5, (n, r))$:

$$(\mathsf{param}_{(n,r)}, \mathbb{D}_0, \mathbb{D}_0^*, \mathbb{D}_1, \{D_{i,j,\iota}^*, D_{i,j,l}'^*\}_{l=1,\ldots,n+r}^{i,j=1,\ldots,5; \iota=1,2}) \xleftarrow{\mathsf{R}} \mathcal{G}_{\mathsf{ob}}^{\mathsf{KP}}(1^\lambda, 5, (n, r)),$$

$$\mathbb{B}_0 := \mathbb{D}_0^*, \ \mathbb{B}_0^* := \mathbb{D}_0, \ \mathbb{B}_1^* := \mathbb{D}_1, \ B_{i,j,\iota} := D_{i,j,\iota}^*, \ B_{i,j,l}' := D_{i,j,l}'^* \text{ for all } i, j, l, \iota,$$

$$\text{return } (\mathsf{param}_{(n,r)}, \mathbb{B}_0, \mathbb{B}_0^*, \mathbb{B}_1^*, \{B_{i,j,\iota}, B_{i,j,l}'\}_{l=1,\ldots,n+r}^{i,j=1,\ldots,5; \iota=1,2}).$$

B.3 Construction

$\mathsf{Setup}(1^\lambda, (n, r)) : / * \ N_0 := 5, \ N_1 := 5(n + r) \ * /$

$$(\mathsf{param}_{(n,r)}, \mathbb{B}_0, \mathbb{B}_0^*, \mathbb{B}_1^*, \{B_{i,j,\iota}, B_{i,j,l}'\}_{l=1,\ldots,n+r}^{i,j=1,\ldots,5; \iota=1,2}) \xleftarrow{\mathsf{R}} \mathcal{G}_{\mathsf{ob}}^{\mathsf{CP}}(1^\lambda, 5, (n, r)),$$

$$\widehat{\mathbb{B}}_0 := (\boldsymbol{b}_{0,1}, \boldsymbol{b}_{0,2}, \boldsymbol{b}_{0,4}), \ \widehat{\mathbb{B}}_0^* := (\boldsymbol{b}_{0,1}^*, \boldsymbol{b}_{0,2}^*, \boldsymbol{b}_{0,5}^*),$$

$$\widehat{\mathbb{B}}_1^* := (\boldsymbol{b}_{1,1}^*, .., \boldsymbol{b}_{1,n+r}^*, \boldsymbol{b}_{1,3(n+r)+1}^*, .., \boldsymbol{b}_{1,4(n+r)}^*),$$

$$\text{return } \mathsf{pk} := (1^\lambda, \mathsf{param}_{(n,r)}, \widehat{\mathbb{B}}_0, \{B_{i,j,\iota}, B_{i,j,l}'\}_{\iota=1,2; \, l=1,\ldots,n+r}^{i=1,4; j=1,\ldots,5}),$$

$$\mathsf{sk} := \{\widehat{\mathbb{B}}_t^*\}_{t=0,1}.$$

$\mathsf{KeyGen}(\mathsf{pk}, \mathsf{sk}, \Gamma := \{x_1, \ldots, x_{n'} \mid x_j \in \mathbb{F}_q^\times, n' \le n - 1\})$:

$\vec{y} := (y_1, \ldots, y_n)$ such that $\sum_{j=0}^{n-1} y_{n-j} z^j = z^{n-1-n'} \prod_{j=1}^{n'} (z - x_j)$,

$\vec{f} \xleftarrow{\mathsf{U}} \mathbb{F}_q^r$, $\omega, \varphi_0 \xleftarrow{\mathsf{U}} \mathbb{F}_q$, $\vec{\varphi}_1 \xleftarrow{\mathsf{U}} \mathbb{F}_q^{n+r}$, $\boldsymbol{k}_0^* := (1, \ \vec{1} \cdot \vec{f}, \ 0, \ \varphi_0)_{\mathbb{B}_0^*}$,

$$\boldsymbol{k}_1^* := (\quad \overbrace{\omega \vec{y}, \ \vec{f},}^{n+r} \quad \overbrace{0^{2n+2r},}^{2n+2r} \quad \overbrace{0^{n+r},}^{n+r} \quad \overbrace{\vec{\varphi}_1}^{n+r} \quad)_{\mathbb{B}_1^*}$$

$\mathsf{sk}_\Gamma := (\Gamma, \boldsymbol{k}_0^*, \ \boldsymbol{k}_1^*)$.   return sk_Γ.

$\mathsf{Enc}(\mathsf{pk}, \ m, \ \mathbb{S} := (M, \rho)) :$ $\zeta, \xi, \eta_0 \xleftarrow{\mathsf{U}} \mathbb{F}_q$, $\boldsymbol{c}_0 := (\zeta, \ \xi, \ 0, \ \eta_0, \ 0)_{\mathbb{B}_0}$,

for $i = 1, \ldots, \ell$, if $\rho(i) = v_i$, $\vec{v}_i := (v_{i,l})_{l=1}^n := (v_i^{n-1}, .., v_i, 1)$, $\theta_i, \psi_i, \eta_i \xleftarrow{\mathsf{U}} \mathbb{F}_q$,

for $j = 1, \ldots, 5$,

$C_{i,1,j} := \sum_{l=1}^n v_{i,l}(\theta_i B'_{1,j,l} + \psi_i B'_{4,j,l}) + \sum_{l=1}^r M_{i,l}(\xi B'_{1,j,n+l} + \eta_i B'_{4,j,n+l})$,

$C_{i,2,j} := \theta_i B_{1,j,1} + \psi_i B_{4,j,1}$, $C_{i,3,j} := \xi B_{1,j,2} + \eta_i B_{4,j,2}$,

$c_T := g_T^\zeta m$,   return $\mathsf{cts} := (\mathbb{S}, \boldsymbol{c}_0, \{C_{i,1,j}, C_{i,2,j}, C_{i,3,j}\}_{j=1,\ldots,5}^{i=1,\ldots,\ell}, c_T)$.

$\mathsf{Dec}(\mathsf{pk}, \mathsf{sk}_\Gamma := (\Gamma, \boldsymbol{k}_0^*, \ \boldsymbol{k}_1^*), \ \mathsf{cts} := (\mathbb{S}, \boldsymbol{c}_0, \{C_{i,1,j}, C_{i,2,j}, C_{i,3,j}\}_{j=1,\ldots,5}^{i=1,\ldots,\ell}, c_T)) :$

If $\mathbb{S} := (M, \rho)$ accepts Γ, then compute I and $\{\alpha_i\}_{i \in I}$ such that

$\vec{1} = \sum_{i \in I} \alpha_i M_i$, where M_i is the i-th row of M, and

$I \subseteq \{i \in \{1, \ldots, \ell\} \mid \rho(i) \in \Gamma \}$.

for $i \in I$,   if $\rho(i) = v_i$, $\vec{v}_i := (v_{i,l})_{l=1}^n := (v_i^{n-1}, \ldots, v_i, 1)$,

$$\boldsymbol{c}_i := (\overbrace{\begin{array}{l} C_{i,1,1}, \ v_{i,2} C_{i,2,1}, .., v_{i,n} C_{i,2,1}, \ M_{i,1} C_{i,3,1}, .., M_{i,r} C_{i,3,1}, \quad \cdots \\ C_{i,1,5}, \ v_{i,2} C_{i,2,5}, .., v_{i,n} C_{i,2,5}, \ M_{i,1} C_{i,3,5}, .., M_{i,r} C_{i,3,5} \end{array}}^{n+r}),$$

that is, $\boldsymbol{c}_i := (\quad \overbrace{\theta_i \vec{v}_i, \ \xi M_i,}^{n+r} \quad \overbrace{0^{2n+2r},}^{2n+2r} \quad \overbrace{\psi_i \vec{v}_i, \ \eta_i M_i,}^{n+r} \quad \overbrace{0^{n+r}}^{n+r} \quad)_{\mathbb{B}_1}$,

$\boldsymbol{c}' := \sum_{i \in I} \alpha_i \boldsymbol{c}_i$, $K := e(\boldsymbol{c}_0, \boldsymbol{k}_0^*) \cdot e(\boldsymbol{c}', \boldsymbol{k}_1^*)$,   return $m' := c_T / K$.

[**Correctness**] If Γ satisfies $\mathbb{S}$, $K = e(\boldsymbol{c}_0, \boldsymbol{k}_0^*) \cdot e(\boldsymbol{c}', \boldsymbol{k}_1^*) = g_T^{-\xi s_0 + \zeta} g_T^{\xi \sum_{i \in I} \alpha_i s_i} = g_T^\zeta$ where $s_0 := \vec{1} \cdot \vec{f}$, $s_i := M_i \cdot \vec{f}$ for $i = 1, \ldots, \ell$.

Theorem 3. *The proposed multi-use CP-ABE scheme is adaptively payload-hiding against chosen plaintext attacks under the DLIN assumption.*

Theorem 3 is similarly proven to Theorem 2.

References

1. Agrawal, S., Chase, M.: A study of pair encodings: predicate encryption in prime order groups. In: Kushilevitz, E., Malkin, T. (eds.) TCC 2016. LNCS, vol. 9563, pp. 259–288. Springer, Heidelberg (2016). doi:10.1007/978-3-662-49099-0_10
2. Attrapadung, N.: Dual system encryption via doubly selective security: framework, fully secure functional encryption for regular languages, and more. In: Nguyen, P.Q., Oswald, E. (eds.) EUROCRYPT 2014. LNCS, vol. 8441, pp. 557–577. Springer, Heidelberg (2014). doi:10.1007/978-3-642-55220-5_31

3. Attrapadung, N.: Dual system encryption framework in prime-order groups via computational pair encodings. In: Cheon, J.H., Takagi, T. (eds.) ASIACRYPT 2016. LNCS, vol. 10032, pp. 591–623. Springer, Heidelberg (2016). doi:10.1007/978-3-662-53890-6_20

4. Attrapadung, N., Hanaoka, G., Yamada, S.: Conversions among several classes of predicate encryption and applications to ABE with various compactness tradeoffs. In: Iwata, T., Cheon, J.H. (eds.) ASIACRYPT 2015. LNCS, vol. 9452, pp. 575–601. Springer, Heidelberg (2015). doi:10.1007/978-3-662-48797-6_24

5. Attrapadung, N., Libert, B., Panafieu, E.: Expressive key-policy attribute-based encryption with constant-size ciphertexts. In: Catalano, D., Fazio, N., Gennaro, R., Nicolosi, A. (eds.) PKC 2011. LNCS, vol. 6571, pp. 90–108. Springer, Heidelberg (2011). doi:10.1007/978-3-642-19379-8_6

6. Beimel, A.: Secure schemes for secret sharing and key distribution. Ph.D. thesis, Israel Institute of Technology, Technion, Haifa (1996)

7. Boneh, D., Boyen, X., Shacham, H.: Short group signatures. In: Franklin, M. (ed.) CRYPTO 2004. LNCS, vol. 3152, pp. 41–55. Springer, Heidelberg (2004). doi:10.1007/978-3-540-28628-8_3

8. Boneh, D., Gentry, C., Gorbunov, S., Halevi, S., Nikolaenko, V., Segev, G., Vaikuntanathan, V., Vinayagamurthy, D.: Fully key-homomorphic encryption, arithmetic circuit ABE and compact garbled circuits. In: Nguyen, P.Q., Oswald, E. (eds.) EUROCRYPT 2014. LNCS, vol. 8441, pp. 533–556. Springer, Heidelberg (2014). doi:10.1007/978-3-642-55220-5_30

9. Chen, J., Gay, R., Wee, H.: Improved dual system ABE in prime-order groups via predicate encodings. In: Oswald, E., Fischlin, M. (eds.) EUROCRYPT 2015. LNCS, vol. 9057, pp. 595–624. Springer, Heidelberg (2015). doi:10.1007/978-3-662-46803-6_20

10. Cheon, J.H.: Security analysis of the strong diffie-hellman problem. In: Vaudenay, S. (ed.) EUROCRYPT 2006. LNCS, vol. 4004, pp. 1–11. Springer, Heidelberg (2006). doi:10.1007/11761679_1

11. Gorbunov, S., Vaikuntanathan, V., Wee, H.: Attribute-based encryption for circuits. In: STOC 2013, pp. 545–554 (2013)

12. Goyal, V., Pandey, O., Sahai, A., Waters, B.: Attribute-based encryption for fine-grained access control of encrypted data. In: ACM CCS 2006, pp. 89–98 (2006)

13. Ishai, Y., Wee, H.: Partial garbling schemes and their applications. In: Esparza, J., Fraigniaud, P., Husfeldt, T., Koutsoupias, E. (eds.) ICALP 2014. LNCS, vol. 8572, pp. 650–662. Springer, Heidelberg (2014). doi:10.1007/978-3-662-43948-7_54

14. Lewko, A., Okamoto, T., Sahai, A., Takashima, K., Waters, B.: Fully secure functional encryption: attribute-based encryption and (hierarchical) inner product encryption. In: Gilbert, H. (ed.) EUROCRYPT 2010. LNCS, vol. 6110, pp. 62–91. Springer, Heidelberg (2010). doi:10.1007/978-3-642-13190-5_4

15. Lewko, A., Waters, B.: Decentralizing attribute-based encryption. In: Paterson, K.G. (ed.) EUROCRYPT 2011. LNCS, vol. 6632, pp. 568–588. Springer, Heidelberg (2011). doi:10.1007/978-3-642-20465-4_31

16. Lewko, A., Waters, B.: New proof methods for attribute-based encryption: achieving full security through selective techniques. In: Safavi-Naini, R., Canetti, R. (eds.) CRYPTO 2012. LNCS, vol. 7417, pp. 180–198. Springer, Heidelberg (2012). doi:10.1007/978-3-642-32009-5_12

17. Okamoto, T., Takashima, K.: Hierarchical predicate encryption for inner-products. In: Matsui, M. (ed.) ASIACRYPT 2009. LNCS, vol. 5912, pp. 214–231. Springer, Heidelberg (2009). doi:10.1007/978-3-642-10366-7_13

18. Okamoto, T., Takashima, K.: Fully secure functional encryption with general relations from the decisional linear assumption. In: Rabin, T. (ed.) CRYPTO 2010. LNCS, vol. 6223, pp. 191–208. Springer, Heidelberg (2010). doi:10.1007/978-3-642-14623-7_11

19. Okamoto, T., Takashima, K.: Achieving short ciphertexts or short secret-keys for adaptively secure general inner-product encryption. Des. Codes Crypt. **77**(2–3), 725–771 (2015). the preliminary version appeared in CANS 2011

20. Okamoto, T., Takashima, K.: Dual pairing vector spaces and their applications. In: IEICE Transactions 98-A(1), pp. 3–15 (2015)

21. Sahai, A., Waters, B.: Fuzzy identity-based encryption. In: Cramer, R. (ed.) EUROCRYPT 2005. LNCS, vol. 3494, pp. 457–473. Springer, Heidelberg (2005). doi:10.1007/11426639_27

22. Takashima, K.: Expressive attribute-based encryption with constant-size ciphertexts from the decisional linear assumption. In: Abdalla, M., Prisco, R. (eds.) SCN 2014. LNCS, vol. 8642, pp. 298–317. Springer, Cham (2014). doi:10.1007/978-3-319-10879-7_17

23. Takashima, K.: New proof techniques for DLIN-based adaptively secure attribute-based encryption. IACR Cryptology ePrint Archive 2015, 1021 (2015)

24. Waters, B.: Dual system encryption: realizing fully secure IBE and HIBE under simple assumptions. In: Halevi, S. (ed.) CRYPTO 2009. LNCS, vol. 5677, pp. 619–636. Springer, Heidelberg (2009). doi:10.1007/978-3-642-03356-8_36

25. Waters, B.: Ciphertext-policy attribute-based encryption: an expressive, efficient, and provably secure realization. In: Catalano, D., Fazio, N., Gennaro, R., Nicolosi, A. (eds.) PKC 2011. LNCS, vol. 6571, pp. 53–70. Springer, Heidelberg (2011). doi:10.1007/978-3-642-19379-8_4

Attribute-Based Encryption with Expressive and Authorized Keyword Search

Hui Cui[1(✉)], Robert H. Deng[1], Joseph K. Liu[2], and Yingjiu Li[1]

[1] School of Information Systems, Singapore Management University,
Singapore, Singapore
{hcui,robertdeng,yli}@smu.edu.sg
[2] Faculty of Information Technology, Monash University, Melbourne, Australia
joseph.liu@monash.edu

Abstract. To protect data security and privacy in cloud storage systems, a common solution is to outsource data in encrypted forms so that the data will remain secure and private even if storage systems are compromised. The encrypted data, however, must be pliable to search and access control. In this paper, we introduce a notion of attribute-based encryption with expressive and authorized keyword search (ABE-EAKS) to support both expressive keyword search and fine-grained access control over encrypted data in the cloud. In ABE-EAKS, every data user is associated with a set of attributes and is issued a private attribute-key corresponding to his/her attribute set, and each data owner encrypts the message using attribute-based encryption and attaches the encrypted message with encrypted keywords related with the message, and then uploads the encrypted message and keywords to the cloud. To access encrypted messages containing certain keywords satisfying a search policy, a data user generates a trapdoor for the search policy using his/her private attribute-key and sends it to the cloud server equipped to the cloud. The cloud server searches over encrypted data stored in the cloud for the encrypted messages containing keywords satisfying the search policy and sends back the results to the data user who then decrypts the returned ciphertexts to obtain the underlying messages. We present a generic construction for ABE-EAKS, formally prove its security, give a concrete construction, and then extend the concrete ABE-EAKS scheme to support user revocation. Also, we implement the proposed ABE-EAKS scheme and its extension and study their performance through experiments.

Keywords: Cloud storage · Data security and privacy · Keyword search · Attribute-based encryption · Access control

1 Introduction

Consider a cloud storage system (e.g., [21,29,31]) that keeps personal health records (PHRs) provided by various medical institutions (i.e., data owners), in which all PHRs are stored in encrypted forms to protect data security and

© Springer International Publishing AG 2017
J. Pieprzyk and S. Suriadi (Eds.): ACISP 2017, Part I, LNCS 10342, pp. 106–126, 2017.
DOI: 10.1007/978-3-319-60055-0_6

privacy [30]. In order to facilitate data sharing, it is important for a cloud storage system to support powerful keyword search and scalable access control over the encrypted PHRs [46]. A straightforward approach meeting this requirement is to combine public key encryption mechanism and public-key based keyword search[1] such as public-key encryption with keyword search (PEKS) put forward by Boneh et al. [8], which allows a cloud server (equipped to the cloud) to search over encrypted PHRs on behalf of authorized data users (e.g., doctors, scientists) without learning any information about the underlying PHRs. Informally, in this combined approach, a PHR is encrypted using a public-key encryption scheme, the keywords associated with the PHR are encrypted using PEKS, and the ciphertext uploaded to the cloud is a concatenation of the "ciphertext" on the PHR and the "PEKS ciphertext" on the keywords associated with the PHR. To retrieve all encrypted PHRs containing certain keywords, a data user generates a "trapdoor" corresponding to the keywords and sends it to the cloud server such that the cloud server is able to spot and return all encrypted PHRs containing the specified keywords but learns nothing about the underlying PHRs.

However, a traditional public-key encryption scheme is a one-to-one encryption scheme targeted for decryption by a single data user, while encrypted messages in the cloud storage scenarios are expected to be accessed by groups of data users. Attribute-based encryption (ABE) [28,37,43,44] is widely believed as a promising solution for accomplishing fine-grained access control over encrypted data. In an ABE scheme, every data user is identified by a set of attributes and issued a private attribute-key associated with his/her attributes, every message is encrypted under an access structure, and any data user whose set of attribute satisfies the access structure ascribed to a ciphertext can decrypt this ciphertext.

Ideally, search policies should be expressive such that it can be expressed as conjunction, disjunction or any Boolean formulas. For example, in the aforementioned cloud storage system for PHRs, to find the relationship between "diabetes" and "age" or "weight", a researcher may submit a keyword search request with a search policy such as "(Illness: Diabetes AND (Age: 30 OR Weight: 100–200))"[2]. Unfortunately, most of the existing PEKS schemes only support single keyword search as in [8]. Though there are efforts in designing expressive keyword search (EKS) schemes that allows expressive keyword search policies (e.g., [10,13,24,32]), in all existing EKS schemes, data users need to send trapdoor generation requests on search policies to a trusted third party such as the key generation center (KGC), and then forward the trapdoors given by the KGC to the cloud server to conduct search over encrypted data. Relying on the KGC to generate trapdoors is not consistent with the standard PEKS notion in which trapdoors are generated by each data user himself/herself, and makes the KGC a bottleneck for both security and performance as it requires the KGC to be online all the time to answer requests of data users. There are authorized keyword

---

[1] In this paper, unless otherwise specified, all keyword search schemes we talk about are in the public-key setting.

[2] Note that in this paper, each keyword is divided into two parts N_i: W_i, where the former is the keyword name and the latter is the keyword value, e.g., Illness, Age, Weight are keyword names and Diabetes, 30, 100–200 are keyword values.

search (AKS) schemes (e.g., [20, 39–41]) which authorize data users the capabilities of generating trapdoors by themselves, but existing solutions on AKS either lack the expressiveness in search polices or is inefficient due to the use of bilinear pairings over the composite-order groups. We note that most of the previous keyword search schemes are designed without taking message encryption into consideration, and yet it is known that simply combining a public-key encryption scheme for the message encryption and a keyword search scheme for the encryption of keywords may result in a solution subject to severe attacks [3].

Contributions. Motivated by the above observations, we propose a notion of attribute-based encryption with expressive and authorized keyword search (ABE-EAKS) to better meet the needs of cloud storage, which supports keyword search and access control over encrypted data in the setting of multiple data owners and multiple data users such as the cloud-based PHR system. Our goal is to design an ABE-EAKS scheme which simultaneously enables fine-grained access control and expressive keyword search over encrypted data without depending on a trusted third party to generate trapdoors. We compare our proposed ABE-EAKS scheme with existing constructions on AKS in Table 1.

Table 1. Comparison of properties among the AKS schemes.

	Expressiveness	Authorized keyword search	Bilinear group	Construction
AKS [39]	AND, OR gates	✓	Composite-Order	Concrete
AKS [40]	AND gates	✓	Prime-Order	Concrete
AKS [41]	AND gates	✓	Prime-Order	Concrete
AKS [20]	Single Keyword	✓	Prime-Order	Concrete
ABE-EAKS	AND, OR gates	✓	Composite-Order Prime-Order	Generic

We briefly summarize our contributions in this paper as follows.

- Firstly, we propose the notion of ABE-EAKS, which allows fine-grained access control and expressive keyword search over encrypted messages without relying on a trusted third party for the trapdoor generation.
- Secondly, we give a generic construction of ABE-EAKS which can be applied to transform ABE scheme and EKS scheme into a secure ABE-EAKS scheme, and formally prove its security. The main potential security vulnerability of an integrated ABE and EAKS scheme is the "swapping attack" [3] where an attacker can tamper with the ciphertext (which could be either the part on message encryption or the part on keyword encryption) stored in the cloud without being detected so that a privileged data user will not obtain the correct message. Thanks to the generic technique introduced by Fujisaki and

Okamoto [15] to achieve security in the integrated public-key and symmetric encryption schemes, we protect ABE-EAKS from swapping attacks by applying a similar approach as in [15] such that a data user can check whether a ciphertext has been modified when performing decryption operation on the ciphertext.

- Thirdly, we describe an instantiation of ABE-EAKS by applying concrete ABE and EKS schemes into the generic transformation, and extend the instantiation with an efficient user revocation mechanism which simultaneously improves decryption efficiency.
- Fourthly, we implement the instantiation and its extension to assess their performance.

1.1   Related Work

Attribute-Based Encryption. Sahai and Waters [37] first introduced attribute-based encryption (ABE). Later, Goyal et al. [17] formulated two complimentary forms of ABE: key-policy ABE (KP-ABE) and ciphertext-policy ABE (CP-ABE). In CP-ABE, a private attribute-key is associated with a set of attributes and a ciphertext is associated with an access structure, while the situation is reversed in KP-ABE. Nevertheless, we believe that KP-ABE is less flexible than CP-ABE because the access structure is determined once a data user's private attribute-key is issued[3]. Bethencourt, Sahai and Waters [7] proposed the first CP-ABE scheme, but it was secure under the generic group model. Cheung and Newport [11] presented a CP-ABE scheme secure under the standard model, but it only allowed the access structures in AND gates. A CP-ABE scheme with expressive access structures was put forth by Goyal et al. [16] based on the number theoretic assumption. Lewko et al. [25] put forward the first fully secure CP-ABE scheme, but it was in the composite-order groups. Rouselakis and Waters [36] gave a large universe CP-ABE scheme in the prime-order groups to improve the efficiency of ABE built from the composite-order groups while overcoming the limitation of bounded attribute space, but it was selectively secure.

Public-Key Encryption with Keyword Search. Since Boneh et al. [8] initiated the study of public-key encryption with keyword search (PEKS), many solutions [3,4,6,10,18,19,24,27,32,34,35,39,42,48–50] were proposed focusing on addressing three limitations in PEKS: (1) how to make PEKS secure against offline keyword dictionary guessing attacks; (2) how to support expressive search policies; and (3) how to achieve security in the integrated public-key encryption (PKE) and keyword search in the public-key setting. For the security against offline keyword dictionary guessing attacks, it requires that no adversary (including the cloud server) can learn keywords from a given trapdoor. To the best of our knowledge, such a security notion is very hard to be achieved in the public-key setting [38]. In terms of the expressive search policies, there are only a few expressive keyword search (EKS) schemes [10,14,24,32,39], but they either are

---

[3] In the rest of the paper, unless otherwise specified, what we talk about is CP-ABE.

expensive in implementations (e.g., [10,24,32,39]) or have limitations in security (e.g., [14]). Concerning the security of the integrated PKE scheme with keyword search scheme, there are solutions such as [3,50], but they only consider the security in the setting of the traditional public-key encryption schemes.

Authorized Keyword Search. Narayan, Gagné and Safavi-Naini [33] combined PEKS and ABE to create a secure electronic health record system, which provided both keyword search and access control mechanisms, but it failed to address the privacy issue of access control policies. Li et al. [27] put forth a notion of authorized private keyword search (APKS) in the setting of cloud storage and presented two concrete constructions on APKS, but their schemes were limited in applications since the search policies were defined and maintained by the trusted authorities. Sun et al. [40,41] proposed an attribute-based keyword search with fine-grained owner-enforced search authorization scheme, but it only supported access structures expressed in "AND" gates and search policies with conjunctive keywords. Shi et al. [39] presented a searchable encryption based on ABE to support fine-grained search and access control, but their scheme required each data user to ask a trusted trapdoor generation center to create trapdoors on search policies on behalf of himself/herself. Jiang et al. [20] introduced the notion of public-key encryption with authorized keyword search (PEAKS), but their construction of PEAKS could only be applied to single keyword search.

1.2 Organization

The remainder of this paper is organized as follows. In Sect. 2, we revisit the definitions to be used in this paper. In Sect. 3, after depicting the system architecture for ABE-EAKS, we present its security definition. In Sect. 4, we give a generic construction of ABE-EAKS, and prove its security. We conclude this paper in Sect. 5.

2   Preliminaries

In this section, we review some basic cryptographic notions and definitions that are to be used in this paper.

2.1   Bilinear Pairings

Let G be a group of a prime order p with a generator g. We define $\hat{e} : G \times G \rightarrow G_1$ to be a bilinear map if it has the following properties [9].

- Bilinear: for all $g \in G$, and $a, b \in Z_p$, we have $\hat{e}(g^a, g^b) = \hat{e}(g, g)^{ab}$.
- Non-degenerate: $\hat{e}(g, g) \neq 1$.

We say that G is a bilinear group if the group operation in G is efficiently computable and there exists a group G_1 and an efficiently computable bilinear map $\hat{e} : G \times G \rightarrow G_1$ as above.

2.2   Access Structure and Linear Secret Sharing

Definition 1 *Access Structures* [26,45]. *Let* $\{P_1, ..., P_n\}$ *be a set of parties.* *A collection* $\mathbb{A} \subseteq 2^{\{P_1,...,P_n\}}$ *is monotone if* $\forall B, C :$ *if* $B \in \mathbb{A}$ *and* $B \subseteq C$, *then* $C \subseteq \mathbb{A}$. *An (monotone) access structure is a (monotone) collection* $\mathbb{A}$ *of non-empty subsets of* $\{P_1, ..., P_n\}$, *i.e.,* $\mathbb{A} \subseteq 2^{\{P_1,...,P_n\}} \setminus \{\emptyset\}$. *The sets in* $\mathbb{A}$ *are called the authorized sets, and the sets not in* $\mathbb{A}$ *are called the unauthorized sets.*

Definition 2 *Linear Secret Sharing Schemes* [26,45]. *Let* P *be a set of parties,* $\mathbb{M}$ *be a matrix of size* $l \times n$, *and* $\rho : \{1, ..., l\} \to P$ *be a function mapping a row to a party for labeling. A secret sharing scheme* Π *over a set of parties* P *is a linear secret-sharing scheme (LSSS) over* Z_p *if*

1. *The shares for each party form a vector over* Z_p.
2. *There exists a matrix* $\mathbb{M}$ *which has* l *rows and* n *columns called the share-generating matrix for* Π. *For* $i = 1, ..., l$, *the* x-*th row of matrix* $\mathbb{M}$ *is labeled by a party* $\rho(i)$, *where* $\rho : \{1, ..., l\} \to P$ *is a function that maps a row to a party for labeling. Considering that the column vector* $v = (\mu, r_2, ..., r_n)$, *where* $\mu \in Z_p$ *is the secret to be shared and* $r_2, ..., r_n \in Z_p$ *are randomly chosen, then* $\mathbb{M}v$ *is the vector of* l *shares of the secret* μ *according to* Π. *The share* $(\mathbb{M}v)_i$ *belongs to a party* $\rho(i)$.

It has been noted in [26] that every LSSS also enjoys the linear reconstruction property. Suppose that Π is an LSSS for access structure $\mathbb{A}$. Let $\mathbf{A}$ be an authorized set, and define $I \subseteq \{1, ..., l\}$ as $I = \{i | \rho(i) \in \mathbf{A}\}$. Then the vector $(1, 0, ..., 0)$ is in the span of rows of matrix $\mathbb{M}$ indexed by I, and there exist constants $\{w_i \in Z_p\}_{i \in I}$ such that, for any valid shares $\{v_i\}$ of a secret μ according to Π, $\sum_{i \in I} w_i v_i = \mu$. These constants $\{w_i\}$ can be found in polynomial time with respect to the size of the share-generating matrix $\mathbb{M}$ [5].

Boolean Formulas [26]. Access structures can also be described in terms of monotonic boolean formulas. LSSS access structures are more general, and can be derived from representations as boolean formulas. There are standard techniques to convert any monotonic boolean formula into a corresponding LSSS matrix. The boolean formula can be represented as an access tree, where the interior nodes are AND and OR gates, and the leaf nodes correspond to attributes. The number of rows in the corresponding LSSS matrix will be the same as the number of leaf nodes in the access tree.

2.3   Attribute-Based Encryption

An attribute-based encryption (ABE) scheme $\mathcal{ABE}$ [37] consists of a setup algorithm $\mathcal{ABE}.\mathrm{Set}(1^\lambda)$ which outputs the public parameter *par* and the master private key *msk* on input a security parameter λ, a key generation algorithm $\mathcal{ABE}.\mathrm{KG}(par, msk, \mathbf{A})$ which outputs a private attribute-key $sk_{\mathbf{A}}$ on input the public parameter *par*, the master private key *msk* and an attribute set $\mathbf{A}$, an encryption algorithm $\mathcal{ABE}.\mathrm{Enc}(par, \mathbb{A}\ m)$ which outputs a ciphertext CT on input the public parameter par, an access structure $\mathbb{A}$ and a message m, and a decryption algorithm $\mathcal{ABE}$.Dec(par, $sk_{\mathbb{A}}$, CT) which outputs a message m or a failure symbol $\perp$ on input the public parameter par, a private key $sk_{\mathbb{A}}$ and a ciphertext CT.

An ABE scheme $\mathcal{ABE}$ is indistinguishable under chosen plaintext attacks (IND-CPA secure) if for any probabilistic polynomial time (PPT) adversary $\mathcal{A}$ = $(\mathcal{A}_1, \mathcal{A}_2)$, the advantage function

$$\mathbf{Adv}_{\mathcal{ABE},\mathcal{A}}^{\text{IND-CPA}}(\lambda) = \Pr\left[b' = b \left| \begin{array}{l} (par, msk) \leftarrow \mathcal{ABE}.\text{Set}(1^\lambda); \; b \leftarrow \{0,1\} \\ (m_0, m_1, \mathbb{A}^*, st) \leftarrow \mathcal{A}_1^{\mathcal{ABE}.\text{KG}(msk,\cdot)}(par) \\ \text{CT}^* \leftarrow \mathcal{ABE}.\text{Enc}(par, \mathbb{A}^*, m_b) \\ b' \leftarrow \mathcal{A}_2^{\mathcal{ABE}.\text{KG}(msk,\cdot)}(par, m_0, m_1, \mathbb{A}^*, st, \text{CT}^*) \end{array} \right. \right]$$
$$- 1/2$$

is negligible in the security parameter λ, where $|m_0| = |m_1|$, st is the state information, and adversary $\mathcal{A}$ is not allowed to make key generation queries on attributes that can satisfy the challenge access structure $\mathbb{A}^*$.

2.4   Symmetric Encryption

A symmetric encryption (SE) scheme $\mathcal{SE}$ with a key space $\mathcal{K}$ is composed of an encryption algorithm $\mathcal{SE}$.Enc(K, m) which outputs a ciphertext CT on input a key K and a message m, and a decryption algorithm $\mathcal{SE}$.Dec(K, CT) which outputs m or a failure symbol $\perp$ on input a key K and a ciphertext CT [15].

Let st be the state information. A symmetric encryption scheme $\mathcal{SE}$ is secure under chosen plaintext attacks (IND-CPA secure), if for any PPT adversary $\mathcal{A}$ = $(\mathcal{A}_1, \mathcal{A}_2)$, the advantage function

$$\mathbf{Adv}_{\mathcal{SE},\mathcal{A}}^{\text{IND-CPA}}(\lambda) = \Pr\left[b' = b \left| \begin{array}{l} K \leftarrow \mathcal{K}; b \leftarrow \{0,1\} \\ (m_0, m_1, st) \leftarrow \mathcal{A}_1(1^\lambda) \\ \text{CT}^* \leftarrow \mathcal{SE}.\text{Enc}(K, m_b) \\ b' \leftarrow \mathcal{A}_2(par, m_0, m_1, st, \text{CT}^*) \end{array} \right. \right] - 1/2$$

is negligible in the security parameter λ, where $|m_0| = |m_1|$.

2.5   Expressive Keyword Search

An expressive keyword search (EKS) scheme $\mathcal{EKS}$ [24] consists of a setup algorithm $\mathcal{EKS}$.Set(1^λ) which outputs the public parameter par and the master private key msk on input a security parameter λ, a trapdoor generation algorithm $\mathcal{EKS}$.Trd(par, msk, $\mathbb{S}$) which outputs a trapdoor $T_{\mathbb{S}}$ on input the public parameter par, the master private key msk and a search policy $\mathbb{S}$, an encryption algorithm $\mathcal{EKS}$.Enc(par, $\mathbf{W}$) which outputs a ciphertext CT on input the public parameter par and a set of keywords $\mathbf{W}$, and a test algorithm $\mathcal{EKS}$.Tst(par, $T_{\mathbb{S}}$, CT) which outputs 1 or 0 on input the public parameter par, a trapdoor $T_{\mathbb{S}}$ and a ciphertext CT.

Denote by st the state information. An expressive keyword search scheme $\mathcal{EKS}$ is indistinguishable under chosen keyword-set attacks (IND-CKA secure) if for any PPT adversary $\mathcal{A} = (\mathcal{A}_1, \mathcal{A}_2)$, the advantage function

$$\mathbf{Adv}_{\mathcal{EKS},\mathcal{A}}^{\text{IND-CKA}}(\lambda) = \Pr\left[b' = b \left| \begin{array}{l} (par, msk) \leftarrow \mathcal{EKS}.\text{Set}(1^\lambda); \; b \leftarrow \{0,1\} \\ (\mathbf{W}_0^*, \mathbf{W}_1^*, st) \leftarrow \mathcal{A}_1^{\mathcal{EKS}.\text{Trd}(msk,\cdot)}(par) \\ \text{CT}^* \leftarrow \mathcal{EKS}.\text{Enc}(par, \mathbf{W}_b^*) \\ b' \leftarrow \mathcal{A}_2^{\mathcal{EKS}.\text{Trd}(msk,\cdot)}(par, \mathbf{W}_0^*, \mathbf{W}_1^*, st, \text{CT}^*) \end{array} \right. \right]$$
$$- 1/2$$

is negligible in the security parameter λ, where $|\mathbf{W}_0^*| = |\mathbf{W}_1^*|$, and adversary $\mathcal{A}$ is not allowed to make trapdoor generation queries on keywords that can be satisfied by the challenge keyword set $\mathbf{W}_0^*$ or $\mathbf{W}_1^*$.

3 System Architecture and Security Model

In this section, we describe the framework and security definition of attribute-based encryption with expressive and authorized keyword search (ABE-EAKS).

3.1 System Architecture

The architecture of an ABE-EAKS scheme is shown in Fig. 1, which consists of data owners who outsource encrypted data and the associated keywords to the cloud, data users who are identified by different attributes and are privileged to access data in the cloud, a key generation center (KGC) who holds the master private key and publishes the public parameter and is responsible for generating private attribute-keys for data users in terms of their attributes, and a cloud for data storage which is equipped with a cloud server who executes search operations over encrypted data for data users. Suppose that a data owner Bob uploads to the cloud an encrypted document M along with m encrypted keywords N_1: W_1, ..., N_m: W_m (here N_i is the keyword name and W_i is the keyword value) using the public parameter, and an authorized data user Alice, who is issued with a private attribute-key generated by the KGC in terms of her attributes, wants to search for documents containing keywords that satisfy a search policy $\mathbb{S}$. In order to do so, Alice generates a trapdoor over the search policy $\mathbb{S}$ using her private attribute-key. Then, Alice forwards this trapdoor to the cloud server such that the cloud server is able to spot all ciphertexts that contain the keywords which satisfy the search policy $\mathbb{S}$ and can be decrypted by Alice. Finally, the cloud server sends the relevant ciphertexts back to Alice.

We assume that the KGC is a trusted entity. The cloud is pubic, and thus any ciphertexts stored in the cloud might be tampered with by any malicious party. The cloud server is assumed to be "honest-but-curious", i.e., it honestly follows the protocol but it is curious to learn the data stored in the cloud. Data owners are assumed to honestly encrypt their data as well as the associated keywords and upload the corresponding ciphertext to the cloud. Data users are not trusted, and

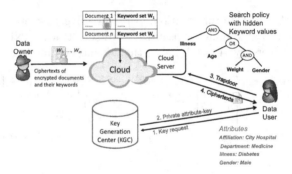

Fig. 1. System architecture of ABE-EAKS.

they may even collude with other participants in order to discover information beyond their privileges. We assume that the trusted KGC is equipped with a separate authentication mechanism to verify data users before issuing private attribute-keys to them.

3.2   Framework

Formally, an ABE-EAKS scheme consists of the following algorithms: setup algorithm Setup, user key generation algorithm KeyGen, trapdoor generation algorithm Trapdoor, encryption algorithm Encrypt, testing algorithm Test and decryption algorithm Decrypt. In an ABE-EAKS scheme, the KGC is given the public parameter and master private key generated from the Setup algorithm, and runs the KeyGen algorithm to generate each data user a private attribute-key in terms of his/her attributes. A data owner runs the Encrypt algorithm on the document and the relevant keywords using the public parameter, and uploads the corresponding ciphertext to the cloud. A data user can create a trapdoor on a search policy over a set of keywords by running the Trapdoor algorithm using his/her private attribute-key. Given a trapdoor, the cloud server runs the Test algorithm to determine whether an encrypted document contains the keywords satisfying the specified search policy and its access structure can be satisfied by the attributes associated with the trapdoor. After receiving the results from the cloud server, the data user runs the Decrypt algorithm on the ciphertexts to obtain the underlying document.

- Setup(1^λ) $\rightarrow$ (par, msk). Taking the security parameter λ as the input, this algorithm outputs the public parameter par and the master private key msk.
- KeyGen(par, msk, **A**) $\rightarrow$ $sk_\mathbf{A}$. Taking the public parameter par, the master private key msk and an attribute set **A** of a data user as the input, this algorithm outputs a private attribute-key $sk_\mathbf{A}$ for this data user.
- Trapdoor(par, $sk_\mathbf{A}$, $\mathbb{S}$) $\rightarrow$ $T_{\mathbf{A},\mathbb{S}}$. Taking the public parameter par, the private attribute-key $sk_\mathbf{A}$ of a data user and a search policy $\mathbb{S}$ over a set of keywords as the input, this algorithm outputs a trapdoor $T_{\mathbf{A},\mathbb{S}}$.

- Encrypt$(par, (M, \mathbb{A}), \mathbf{W}) \rightarrow$ CT. Taking the public parameter par, a message M and an access structure $\mathbb{A}$, and a set of keywords $\mathbf{W}$ as the input, this algorithm outputs a ciphertext CT which consists of CT_M (an encryption of M under $\mathbb{A}$), $CT_{\mathbf{W}}$ (an encryption of $\mathbf{W}$) and τ (a tag binding CT_M and $CT_{\mathbf{W}}$ to prevent them from being tampered with).
- Test$(par,$ CT$, T_{\mathbf{A},\mathbb{S}}) \rightarrow 1/0$. Taking the public parameter par, a ciphertext CT and a trapdoor $T_{\mathbf{A},\mathbb{S}}$ as the input, this algorithm outputs either 1 if the keywords associated with CT satisfies the search policy of $T_{\mathbf{A},\mathbb{S}}$ and the access structure ascribed to CT can be satisfied by the attributes of $T_{\mathbf{A},\mathbb{S}}$ or 0 otherwise, i.e., the Test algorithm outputs 1 if (1) the attributes associated with the trapdoor satisfy the access structure of the ciphertext; and (2) the ciphertext contains the keywords satisfying the search policy of the trapdoor.
- Decrypt$(par, sk_{\mathbf{A}},$ CT$) \rightarrow M/\perp$. Taking the public parameter par, a private attribute-key $sk_{\mathbf{A}}$ over an attribute set $\mathbf{A}$ and a ciphertext CT as the input. This algorithm parses CT $= (CT_M, CT_{\mathbf{W}}, \tau)$, and checks whether the tag τ is valid for CT_M and $CT_{\mathbf{W}}$. If so, it decrypts CT_M and outputs the plaintext M when the attributes of $sk_{\mathbf{A}}$ satisfies the access structure of CT_M. Otherwise, it outputs a failure symbol $\perp$.

We require that an ABE-EAKS scheme is correct, meaning that for all keyword sets $\mathbf{W}$ satisfying search policies $\mathbb{S}$, and attribute sets $\mathbf{A}$ satisfying access structures $\mathbb{A}$, if $(par, msk) \leftarrow$ Setup(1^λ), $sk_{\mathbf{A}} \leftarrow$ KeyGen$(par, msk, \mathbf{A})$, $T_{\mathbf{A},\mathbb{S}} \leftarrow$ Trapdoor$(par, sk_{\mathbf{A}}, \mathbb{S})$, CT $\leftarrow$ Encrypt$(par, (M, \mathbb{A}), \mathbf{W})$, then Test$(par,$ CT$, T_{\mathbf{A},\mathbb{S}}) = 1$, Decrypt$(par, sk_{\mathbf{A}},$ CT$) = M$.

Notice that in the concrete construction, the input $\mathbb{A}$ in the Encrypt algorithm will be set to be $(\mathbb{M}_{\mathbb{A}}, \rho_{\mathbb{A}})$ where $\mathbb{M}_{\mathbb{A}}$ is a matrix, and $\rho_{\mathbb{A}}$ is a function maps the rows of $\mathbb{M}_{\mathbb{A}}$ to attributes. In addition, the input $\mathbb{S}$ in the Trapdoor algorithm will be set to be $(\mathbb{M}_{\mathbb{S}}, \rho_{\mathbb{S}}, \{\rho_{\mathbb{S}}(i)\})$, where $\mathbb{M}_{\mathbb{S}}$ is a matrix, and $\rho_{\mathbb{S}}$ is a function that associates the rows of $\mathbb{M}_{\mathbb{S}}$ to keyword names, and $\{\rho_{\mathbb{S}}(i)\}$ are the corresponding keyword values.

3.3   Security Definitions

In addition to provide the confidentiality of the encrypted data (i.e., data privacy), an ABE-EAKS scheme should ensure that any private information about the keywords will not be revealed from the ciphertext (i.e., keyword privacy). Also, it should guarantee that a ciphertext that encrypts a message and a set of keywords cannot be tampered with without being detected. Below we describe the security game called indistinguishability under chosen-ciphertext attacks (i.e., IND-CCA security) for ABE-EAKS to meet these requirements, which is defined between a challenger algorithm $\mathcal{C}$ and an adversary algorithm $\mathcal{A}$.

- Setup. Algorithm $\mathcal{C}$ runs the Setup algorithm to obtain the public parameter par and the master private key msk, and gives par to algorithm $\mathcal{A}$.
- Phase 1. Algorithm $\mathcal{A}$ adaptively issues the following queries.

1. Algorithm $\mathcal{A}$ issues queries for the private attribute-keys corresponding to the attribute sets $\mathbf{A}_1$, ..., $\mathbf{A}_{q_1}$. For each $\mathbf{A}_i$, $i \in [1, q_1]$, algorithm $\mathcal{C}$ runs the KeyGen algorithm to generate and send $sk_{\mathbf{A}_i}$ to algorithm $\mathcal{A}$.
2. Algorithm $\mathcal{A}$ issues queries for the plaintexts of the ciphertexts CT_1, ..., CT_{q_2}. For each CT_i, $i \in [1, q_2]$, algorithm $\mathcal{C}$ runs the Decrypt algorithm to output and send M_i to algorithm $\mathcal{A}$.

- Challenge. We describe this phase in terms of data privacy and keyword privacy, respectively.

  - Data privacy. Algorithm $\mathcal{A}$ outputs two messages M_0^*, M_1^* of the same size, an access structure $\mathbb{A}^*$ and a keyword set $\mathbf{W}^*$. Algorithm $\mathcal{C}$ randomly chooses $\beta \in \{0, 1\}$, runs the Encrypt algorithm on $(M_\beta^*, \mathbb{A}^*)$, $\mathbf{W}^*$ to obtain and send the challenge ciphertext CT^* to algorithm $\mathcal{A}$.
  - Keyword privacy. Algorithm $\mathcal{A}$ outputs a message M^*, an access structure $\mathbb{A}^*$ and two keyword sets $\mathbf{W}_0^*$, $\mathbf{W}_1^*$ of the same size. Algorithm $\mathcal{C}$ randomly chooses $\beta \in \{0, 1\}$, runs the Encrypt algorithm on $(M^*, \mathbb{A}^*)$, $\mathbf{W}_\beta^*$ to obtain and send the challenge ciphertext CT^* to algorithm $\mathcal{A}$.

- Phase 2. Algorithm $\mathcal{A}$ continues issuing queries to algorithm $\mathcal{C}$ as in Phase 1 except with the following restrictions.

  1. Algorithm $\mathcal{A}$ issues queries for the private attribute-keys corresponding to the attribute sets $\mathbf{A}_{q_1+1}$, ..., $\mathbf{A}_q$ with the restriction that any $\mathbf{A}_i$ for $i \in [q_1 + 1, q]$ cannot satisfy $\mathbb{A}^*$.
  2. Algorithm $\mathcal{A}$ issues queries for the plaintexts of the ciphertexts CT_{q_2+1}, ..., $CT_{q'}$ with the restriction that any CT_i for $i \in [q_2 + 1, q']$ is not equal to CT^*.

- Guess. Algorithm $\mathcal{A}$ outputs its guess $\beta' \in \{0, 1\}$ and wins the game if $\beta' = \beta$.

An ABE-EAKS scheme is IND-CCA secure if the advantage function referring to the security game $\text{Game}_{\Pi, \mathcal{A}}^{\text{IND}}$

$$\mathbf{Adv}_{\Pi, \mathcal{A}}^{\text{IND}}(\lambda) \overset{\text{def}}{=} |\Pr[\beta = \beta'] - 1/2|$$

is negligible in the security parameter λ for any probabilistic polynomial-time (PPT) adversary algorithm $\mathcal{A}$.

In addition, an ABE-EAKS scheme is said to be selectively IND-CCA secure if an Init stage is added before the Setup phase where algorithm $\mathcal{A}$ commits to the challenge access structure $\mathbb{A}^*$ and keyword set $\mathbf{W}^*$ (or keyword sets $\mathbf{W}_0^*$, $\mathbf{W}_1^*$) which it aims to attack.

4   Generic Construction and Its Extensions

In this section, we give a generic construction of attribute-based encryption with expressive and authorized keyword search (ABE-EAKS), and analyze its security.

4.1 Generic Construction

Denote by $\mathcal{M}$ the message space, $\mathcal{K}$ the key space, $\mathcal{R}$ the randomness space. Let $\mathcal{ABE} = (\mathcal{ABE}.\text{Setup}, \mathcal{ABE}.\text{KeyGen}, \mathcal{ABE}.\text{Encrypt}, \mathcal{ABE}.\text{Decrypt})$ be an attribute-based encryption (ABE) scheme (e.g., [36,37]), $\mathcal{EKS} = (\mathcal{EKS}.\text{Setup}, \mathcal{EKS}.\text{Trapdoor}, \mathcal{EKS}.\text{Encrypt}, \mathcal{EKS}.\text{Test})$ be an expressive keyword search (EKS) scheme (e.g., [14,24]), and $\mathcal{SE} = (\mathcal{SE}.\text{Encrypt}, \mathcal{SE}.\text{Decrypt})$ be a symmetric encryption (SE) scheme. Below we describe the generic construction on ABE-EAKS.

- Setup. This algorithm takes the security parameter λ as the input. It runs the $\mathcal{ABE}$.Setup algorithm to obtain the public parameter $par_{\mathcal{ABE}}$ and the master private key $msk_{\mathcal{ABE}}$. Then, it runs the $\mathcal{EKS}$.Setup algorithm to obtain the public parameter $par_{\mathcal{EKS}}$ and the master private key $msk_{\mathcal{EKS}}$. Also, it randomly chooses two hash functions $H_0 : \mathcal{M} \to \mathcal{K}$, $H_1 : \mathcal{M} \to \mathcal{R}$. It outputs the public parameter $par = (par_{\mathcal{ABE}}, par_{\mathcal{EKS}}, H_0, H_1)$ and the master private key $msk = (msk_{\mathcal{ABE}}, msk_{\mathcal{EKS}})$.

  Remarks. For the correctness of the proposed generic construction on ABE-EAKS, we require that the schemes $\mathcal{EKS}$ and $\mathcal{ABE}$ share most elements in their public parameters such that $msk_{\mathcal{ABE}} \subseteq msk_{\mathcal{EKS}}$ (or $msk_{\mathcal{EKS}} \subseteq msk_{\mathcal{ABE}}$) holds. Note that this is possible since there exist techniques to convert a CP-ABE scheme to a KP-ABE scheme, and vice versa [2], and an EKS scheme can be obtained from a KP-ABE scheme [14,23]. Therefore, $ct_{\mathbf{W}}$ and ct_1 (to be defined below) generated using the same randomness have several elements in common.

- KeyGen. This algorithm takes the public parameter par, the master private key msk and a data user's attribute set $\mathbf{A}$ as the input. It runs the $\mathcal{ABE}$.KeyGen algorithm on the attribute set $\mathbf{A}$ and outputs $sk_{\mathbf{A}}$ as the private attribute-key.

- Trapdoor. This algorithm takes the public parameter par, a private attribute-key $sk_{\mathbf{A}}$ and a search policy $\mathbb{S}$ as the input. It runs the $\mathcal{EKS}$.Trapdoor algorithm on the search policy $\mathbb{S}$ by using the private attribute-key $sk_{\mathbf{A}}$ in place of the master private key $msk_{\mathcal{EKS}}$ to generate the trapdoor $T_{\mathbf{A},\mathbb{S}} = (T_{\mathbf{A}}, T_{\mathbb{S}})$, where $T_{\mathbf{A}}$ is associated with attributes of the data user, and $T_{\mathbb{S}}$ is associated with the search policy.

  Remarks. Notice that there exists a twist here for running the $\mathcal{EKS}$.Trapdoor algorithm using the private attribute-key $sk_{\mathbf{A}}$ in place of the required master private key. Firstly, the Trapdoor algorithm randomly chooses a value s, and binds the value s to $sk_{\mathbf{A}}$ to obtain $T_{\mathbf{A}}$ by performing certain operations. Then it runs the $\mathcal{EKS}$.Trapdoor algorithm on the search policy $\mathbb{S}$ using the secret value s in place of the required master private key $msk_{\mathcal{EKS}}$ to obtain $T_{\mathbb{S}}$. Finally, it outputs the trapdoor $T_{\mathbf{A},\mathbb{S}} = (T_{\mathbf{A}}, T_{\mathbb{S}})$.

- Encrypt. This algorithm takes the public parameter par, a message M, an access structure $\mathbb{A}$ and a keyword set $\mathbf{W}$ as the input. Firstly, it randomly chooses $R \in \mathcal{M}$, and runs the $\mathcal{ABE}$.Encrypt algorithm on the "message" R and the access structure $\mathbb{A}$ to generate CT_R. Secondly, it computes CT_M by running the $\mathcal{SE}$.Encrypt algorithm on the message M using the key $H_0(R)$.

Thirdly, it computes $r = H_1(M, R)$, and runs the $\mathcal{EKS}$.Encrypt algorithm on the keyword set $\mathbf{W}$ using the randomness r to generate $ct_{\mathbf{W}}$. Fourthly, it runs the $\mathcal{ABE}$.Encrypt algorithm on an identity element $\mathbf{1}$ under the access structure $\mathbb{A}$ using the randomness r to generate ct_1. Finally, it outputs the ciphertext $CT = (CT_R, CT_M, CT_{\mathbf{W}})$ for $CT_{\mathbf{W}} = (ct_{\mathbf{W}}, ct_1)$, where (CT_R, CT_M) is the encryption of the message M, $CT_{\mathbf{W}}$ is the encryption of the keywords $\mathbf{W}$, which also implicitly plays the role of the tag τ.

- Test. This algorithm takes the public parameter par, a trapdoor $T_{\mathbb{A},\mathbb{S}}$ and a ciphertext CT as the input. It parses $T_{\mathbb{A},\mathbb{S}}$ as $(T_{\mathbb{A}}, T_{\mathbb{S}})$, and CT as $(CT_R, CT_M, (ct_{\mathbf{W}}, ct_1))$. Firstly, it runs the $\mathcal{ABE}$.Decrypt algorithm on the ciphertext ct_1 using $T_{\mathbb{A}}$ as the private attribute-key to obtain an intermediate value X_0. Then, it runs the $\mathcal{EKS}$.Test algorithm on the trapdoor $T_{\mathbb{S}}$ and the ciphertext $(X_0, ct_{\mathbf{W}})$. If the keywords and access structure ascribed to $CT_{\mathbf{W}}$ satisfy the search policy and attributes associated with $T_{\mathbb{A},\mathbb{S}}$, it outputs 1. Otherwise, it outputs 0.

  Remarks. Since the attributes associated with the private attribute-key of each data user are embedded in the trapdoor, the Test algorithm also excludes those ciphertexts whose access structures cannot be satisfied by the attributes of the data user.

- Decrypt. This algorithm takes the public parameter par, a private attribute-key $sk_{\mathbf{A}}$ and a ciphertext CT as the input. It parses CT as $(CT_R, CT_M, CT_{\mathbf{W}})$. It runs the $\mathcal{ABE}$.Decrypt algorithm on the ciphertext CT_R using the private attribute-key $sk_{\mathbf{A}}$ to obtains R'. Then, it computes M' by running the $\mathcal{SE}$.Decrypt algorithm on the ciphertext CT_M using the key $H_0(R')$. Finally, it computes $r' = H_1(M', R')$, and runs the Encrypt algorithm on using the randomness r' to obtain $CT'_{\mathbf{W}}$. If $CT'_{\mathbf{W}}$ is equal to $CT_{\mathbf{W}}$, it outputs M. Otherwise, it outputs $\perp$.

4.2   Security Proof

Theorem 1. *Assuming that the underlying $\mathcal{ABE}$ is IND-CPA secure, $\mathcal{SE}$ is IND-CPA secure, and $\mathcal{EKS}$ is IND-CKA secure, then the proposed construction on ABE-EAKS is IND-CCA secure in the random oracle model.*

Proof. Assuming that there exists an adversary algorithm $\mathcal{A}$ that breaks the IND-CCA security of the proposed ABE-EAKS scheme, then we can build an adversary algorithm $\mathcal{A}'$ that breaks the IND-CPA security of the underlying schemes $\mathcal{ABE}$, $\mathcal{SE}$ or $\mathcal{EKS}$. Denote by $\mathcal{B}_0$, $\mathcal{B}_1$, $\mathcal{B}_2$ the challenger algorithms in the IND-CPA security games of the schemes $\mathcal{ABE}$, $\mathcal{SE}$, $\mathcal{EKS}$, respectively.

- Setup. Algorithm $\mathcal{A}'$ is given $par_{\mathcal{ABE}}$ from algorithm $\mathcal{B}_0$ of $\mathcal{ABE}$, and $par_{\mathcal{EKS}}$ from the algorithm $\mathcal{B}_1$ of $\mathcal{EKS}$. Algorithm $\mathcal{A}'$ sends $par = (par_{\mathcal{ABE}}, par_{\mathcal{EKS}}, H_0, H_1)$ to algorithm $\mathcal{A}$, where H_0, H_1 are random oracles controlled by algorithm $\mathcal{A}'$.
- H_0, H_1-queries. At any time, algorithm $\mathcal{A}$ can query the random oracle H_0 (or H_1). To respond to these queries, algorithm $\mathcal{A}'$ keeps an initially empty list L_{H_0} (or L_{H_1}) of tuples (R_i, k_i) (or $((M_i, R_i), r_i)$).

- If the query R_i (or (M_i, R_i)) already exists in the list L_{H_0} (or L_{H_1}), algorithm $\mathcal{A}'$ responds with $k_i = H_0(R_i)$ (or $r_i = H_1(M_i, R_i)$).
- Otherwise, it randomly chooses k_i (or r_i), sets $k_i = H_0(R_i)$ (or $r_i = H_1(M_i, R_i)$), and stores k_i (or r_i) to the list L_{H_0} (or L_{H_1}).
- Phase 1. Algorithm $\mathcal{A}$ adaptively issue the following queries to algorithm $\mathcal{A}'$.
  - Algorithm $\mathcal{A}$ issues private attribute-key queries on attribute sets $\mathbf{A}_i$. Algorithm $\mathcal{A}'$ forwards each private attribute-key query on $\mathbf{A}_i$ to algorithm $\mathcal{B}_0$, and sends the corresponding private attribute-key obtained from algorithm $\mathcal{B}_0$ to algorithm $\mathcal{A}$.
  - Algorithm $\mathcal{A}$ issues decryption queries on ciphertexts CT_i. If algorithm $\mathcal{A}'$ does not have the private attribute-key to decrypt the ciphertext, it issues a private attribute-key query on an attribute set satisfying the access structure of CT_i to algorithm $\mathcal{B}_0$, and then uses the returned private attribute-key to decrypt CT_i and sends the result to algorithm $\mathcal{A}$. Otherwise, algorithm $\mathcal{A}'$ runs the $\mathcal{ABE}$.Decrypt algorithm on CT_i and sends the result to algorithm $\mathcal{A}$.
- Challenge. We discuss this phase in terms of data privacy and key privacy, respectively.
  - Data privacy. Algorithm $\mathcal{A}$ outputs two messages M_0^*, M_1^* of the same size, an access structure $\mathbb{A}^*$ and a keyword set $\mathbf{W}^*$. Algorithm $\mathcal{A}'$ sends R_0^*, R_1^* and $\mathbb{A}^*$ to algorithm $\mathcal{B}_0$ to obtain $CT_{R_\beta^*}$, and M_0^*, M_1^* to algorithm $\mathcal{B}_1$ to obtain $CT_{M_\beta^*}$. Also, it randomly chooses $k \in \mathcal{K}$, $r \in \mathcal{R}$, $\beta \in \{0,1\}$, sets $k = H_0(R_\beta^*)$, $r = H_1(M_\beta^*, R_\beta^*)$ (note that because of random oracle, adversary $\mathcal{A}'$ can easily perform this setting), and runs the $\mathcal{EKS}$.Encrypt algorithm on $\mathbf{W}^*$ to obtain $CT_{\mathbf{W}^*}$ using the randomness r. Algorithm $\mathcal{A}'$ sends the challenge ciphertext $CT^* = (CT_{R_\beta^*}, CT_{M_\beta^*}, CT_{\mathbf{W}}^*)$ to algorithm $\mathcal{A}$.
  - Keyword privacy. Algorithm $\mathcal{A}$ outputs a message M^*, an access structure $\mathbb{A}^*$ and two keyword sets $\mathbf{W}_0^*$, $\mathbf{W}_1^*$ of the same size. Algorithm $\mathcal{A}'$ sends $\mathbf{W}_0^*$, $\mathbf{W}_1^*$ to algorithm $\mathcal{B}_2$ to obtain $CT_{\mathbf{W}_\beta^*}$. Also, it randomly chooses $R^* \in \mathcal{M}$, $r \in \mathcal{R}$, sets $r = H_1(M^*, R^*)$ (assuming that r is the randomness used in generating $CT_{\mathbf{W}_\beta^*}$), and runs the $\mathcal{ABE}$.Encrypt algorithm on R^* and $\mathbb{A}^*$ to obtain CT_{R^*}, the $\mathcal{SE}$.Encrypt algorithm on M^* using the key $H_0(R^*)$ to obtain CT_{M^*}. Algorithm $\mathcal{A}'$ sends the challenge ciphertext $CT^* = (CT_{R^*}, CT_{M^*}, CT_{\mathbf{W}_\beta}^*)$ to algorithm $\mathcal{A}$.
- Phase 2. Algorithm $\mathcal{A}$ continues issuing queries to algorithm $\mathcal{A}'$ as in Phase 1, following the restrictions defined in the security model.
- Guess. Algorithm $\mathcal{A}$ makes a guess β' for β, algorithm $\mathcal{A}'$ forwards β' to algorithm $\mathcal{B}_0$, $\mathcal{B}_1$, $\mathcal{B}_2$ as the guesses to the IND-CPA security games for the schemes $\mathcal{ABE}$, $\mathcal{SE}$ and $\mathcal{KS}$.

In the view of algorithm $\mathcal{A}$, the simulation is the same as the real security game except that algorithm $\mathcal{A}$ issues R_β^* for $\beta \in \{0,1\}$ or R^* (or (M_β^*, R_β^*) for $\beta \in \{0,1\}$ or (M^*, R^*)) to the random oracle H_0 (or H_1). Notice that algorithm $\mathcal{A}$ has negligible probability in outputting such queries; otherwise, it helps algorithm $\mathcal{A}'$ directly break the IND-CPA security of the underlying attribute-based encryption scheme $\mathcal{ABE}$, symmetric encryption scheme $\mathcal{SE}$ or expressive keyword search scheme $\mathcal{EKS}$.

To conclude, if algorithm $\mathcal{A}$ can win the IND-CCA game of ABE-EAKS, then algorithm $\mathcal{A}'$ can win the IND-CPA game of the underlying schemes $\mathcal{ABE}$, $\mathcal{SE}$ or $\mathcal{EKS}$. This completes the proof of Theorem 1.

4.3 Extensions

The proposed generic construction on ABE-EAKS can be extended as follows.

- Standard model. Due to the efficiency purpose, the proposed ABE-EAKS scheme is secure in the random oracle model. There exist generic methodologies (e.g., [22]) to achieve security in the standard model, which can be applied to build a generic construction on ABE-EAKS that is secure in the standard model. Thus, we can replace the symmetric encryption scheme and random oracles in the proposed ABE-EAKS scheme by the tag-based encryption as introduced in [22], thereby resulting in a generic construction on ABE-EAKS that is secure in the standard model.
- User revocation. As a cloud storage system may involve a large number of data users whose access rights may change with time, it is important to equip it with an efficient user revocation mechanism. Taking efficiency into consideration, techniques utilizing a third party to achieve user revocation (e.g., [12,47]) might be desirable solutions, which can simultaneously reduce data users' computational overheads in decryption. It is possible to incorporate such techniques into ABE-EAKS to additionally achieve efficient user revocation in the cloud storage system. We detail how to accomplish it in full version[4] of this paper using a concrete construction as an example.

4.4 Performance Analysis

Let $l_{\mathbb{S}}$ be the number of keywords in a search policy, $l_{\mathbb{M}}$ be the number of attributes in an access structure, k be the size of an attribute set associated with a private attribute-key, and m be the size of a keyword set ascribed to a ciphertext. In Table 2, we summarize the computational overheads incurred in the instantiation of ABE-EAKS (given in the full version) and its extension supporting user revocation. Denote "NA" as not applicable, "E" as an exponentiation operation, "P" as a pairing operation, $I_{\mathbb{S}} = \{I_1, ..., I_{\chi_1}\}$ as a set of minimum keyword subsets satisfying a search policy $\mathbb{S}$, χ_2 as $|I_1| + ... + |I_{\chi_1}|$.

We implement the instantiation of ABE-EAKS and its extension in Charm [1]. We use Charm of version Charm-0.43 and Python 3.4 in our implementation. Along with Charm-0.43, we install the PBC library for the underlying cryptographic operations. Our experiments are run on a laptop with Intel Core i5-4210U CPU @ 1.70 GHz and 8.00 GB RAM running 64-bit Ubuntu 16.04. We conduct the experiments over the elliptic curves: SS512 and MNT159 to provide

---

[4] Please contact the authors for the full version.

Table 2. Computational overhead of the instantiation and its extension.

	Trapdoor	Encrypt	Test (per search)	Transform server	Decrypt user
Instantiation on ABE-EAKS	$(4k + 3) \cdot$ E $+ 13l_S \cdot$ E	$(4 + 10l_M) \cdot$ E $+ 7m \cdot$ E	$\leq (k + \chi_2) \cdot$ E $+ (3k + 1 + 6\chi_2) \cdot$ P	NA	$\geq 4 \cdot$ P $+ 2 \cdot$ E
Extension	$(4k + 3) \cdot$ E $+ 13l_S \cdot$ E	$(4 + 10l_M) \cdot$ E $+ 7m \cdot$ E	$\leq (k + \chi_2) \cdot$ E $+ (3k + 1 + 6\chi_2) \cdot$ P	$\geq 4 \cdot$ P $+$ E	$2 \cdot$ E

security level of 80-bit, where SS512 is a supersingular elliptic curve with the symmetric Type 1 pairing on it, and MNT159 is an asymmetric Type 3 pairing.

To begin with, we test the performance of the search function in the instantiation. In the experiments, each keyword contains a keyword name such as "Illness", "Position" and a keyword value such as "Diabetes", "Doctor", and we generate a random set of keywords containing 10 to 50 keywords, and use them to create 5,000 ciphertexts with access structures composed of 10 attributes. Thereafter, we create a set of search policies containing 2 to 10 keywords, and use them to yield trapdoors under the assumption that the data user is given a private attribute-key associated with 20 attributes. Finally, we run the test algorithm on the ciphertexts and the trapdoors.

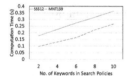 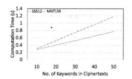 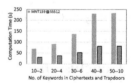

(a) Average time for one trapdoor generation.

(b) Average time for one encryption operation.

(c) Average time for testing among 5,000 cipher-texts.

Fig. 2. Computation time of the Trapdoor, Encrypt and Test algorithms.

Figure 2 shows the average computation time of running the Trapdoor, Encrypt and Test algorithms, respectively. In terms of the trapdoor generation (See Fig. 2-(a)), the computation time of a data user in creating a trapdoor over a search policy of 2 to 10 keywords ranges from 0.2 s and 0.4 s for the SS512 curve, and 0.1 s to 0.3 s for the MNT159 curve, respectively. For the data encryption (See Fig. 2-(b)), the computation time of generating a ciphertext having 10 to 50 keywords and an access structure with 10 attributes is 0.3 s to 0.8 s for the SS512 curve, and 0.4 s to 1.2 s for the MNT159 curve, respectively. The computation time of the Test algorithm increases as the number of keywords involved in the trapdoor and the ciphertext raises (See Fig. 2-(c)). Regarding the 2 curves used in our experiments, given a trapdoor for a search policy composed of 10 keywords, the computation time of searching over 5,000 encrypted documents each having 50 keywords is about 82 s and 233 s, respectively.

In addition, we test the computation time of a data user with 10 to 50 attributes in decrypting a ciphertext with an access structure composed of 2 to 10 attributes in the instantiation on ABE-EAKS and its extension in Fig. 3. In the instantiation of ABE-EAKS (See Fig. 3-(a)), the computation time of decrypting ciphertexts for access structures with 2 to 10 attributes using attribute-keys of 10 to 50 attributes ranges from 6.5 ms to 17 ms for the SS512 curve and 19 ms to 34 ms for the MNT159 curve, respectively, while in the extension (See Fig. 3-(b)), the computation time of decrypting ciphertexts for access structures with 2 to 10 attributes using attribute-keys of 10 to 50 attributes is about 0.6 ms in terms of the SS512 curve and 1.6 ms in terms of the MNT159 curve, respectively.

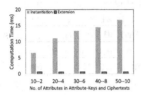

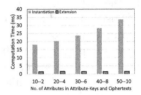

(a) Average time for the SS512 curve.

(b) Average time for the MNT159 curve.

Fig. 3. Computation time of decrypting a ciphertext by a data user.

5   Conclusions

Data encryption is an effective way for protecting data security and privacy in the cloud; however, in order for encrypted data to be useful, encryption mechanisms must be amenable to search and access control. In this paper, we introduced a notion of attribute-based encryption with expressive and authorized keyword search (ABE-EAKS) to support both expressive keyword search and fine-grained access control over encrypted data in cloud-based storage systems. We first presented the framework of ABE-EAKS and gave its security definition, and then provided a generic construction on ABE-EAKS which is able to transform any IND-CPA secure ABE scheme and IND-CKA secure EKS scheme into an IND-CCA secure ABE-EAKS scheme. Thereafter, we gave a concrete construction of ABE-EAKS based on the transformation and extended it to support user revocation. Finally, we implemented the concrete ABE-EAKS scheme and its extension, and studied their performance through experiments.

Acknowledgments. This research work is supported by the Singapore National Research Foundation under the NCR Award Number NRF2014NCR-NCR001-012 and the AXA Research Fund.

References

1. Akinyele, J.A., Garman, C., Miers, I., Pagano, M.W., Rushanan, M., Green, M., Rubin, A.D.: Charm: A framework for rapidly prototyping cryptosystems. J. Cryptographic Eng. **3**(2), 111–128 (2013)
2. Attrapadung, N., Yamada, S.: Duality in ABE: Converting attribute based encryption for dual predicate and dual policy via computational encodings. In: Nyberg, K. (ed.) CT-RSA 2015. LNCS, vol. 9048, pp. 87–105. Springer, Cham (2015). doi:10.1007/978-3-319-16715-2_5
3. Baek, J., Safavi-Naini, R., Susilo, W.: On the integration of public key data encryption and public key encryption with keyword search. In: Katsikas, S.K., López, J., Backes, M., Gritzalis, S., Preneel, B. (eds.) ISC 2006. LNCS, vol. 4176, pp. 217–232. Springer, Heidelberg (2006). doi:10.1007/11836810_16
4. Baek, J., Safavi-Naini, R., Susilo, W.: Public key encryption with keyword search revisited. In: Gervasi, O., Murgante, B., Laganà, A., Taniar, D., Mun, Y., Gavrilova, M.L. (eds.) ICCSA 2008. LNCS, vol. 5072, pp. 1249–1259. Springer, Heidelberg (2008). doi:10.1007/978-3-540-69839-5_96
5. Beimel, A.: Secure Schemes for Secret Sharing and Key Distribution. Ph.D. thesis, Israel Institute of Technology, Israel Institute of Technology, June 1996
6. Bellare, M., Boldyreva, A., O'Neill, A.: Deterministic and efficiently searchable encryption. In: Menezes, A. (ed.) CRYPTO 2007. LNCS, vol. 4622, pp. 535–552. Springer, Heidelberg (2007). doi:10.1007/978-3-540-74143-5_30
7. Bethencourt, J., Sahai, A., Waters, B.: Ciphertext-policy attribute-based encryption. In: 2007 IEEE Symposium on Security and Privacy (S& P 2007), pp. 321–334. IEEE Computer Society (2007)
8. Boneh, D., Crescenzo, G., Ostrovsky, R., Persiano, G.: Public key encryption with keyword search. In: Cachin, C., Camenisch, J.L. (eds.) EUROCRYPT 2004. LNCS, vol. 3027, pp. 506–522. Springer, Heidelberg (2004). doi:10.1007/978-3-540-24676-3_30
9. Boneh, D., Franklin, M.: Identity-based encryption from the weil pairing. In: Kilian, J. (ed.) CRYPTO 2001. LNCS, vol. 2139, pp. 213–229. Springer, Heidelberg (2001). doi:10.1007/3-540-44647-8_13
10. Boneh, D., Waters, B.: Conjunctive, subset, and range queries on encrypted data. In: Vadhan, S.P. (ed.) TCC 2007. LNCS, vol. 4392, pp. 535–554. Springer, Heidelberg (2007). doi:10.1007/978-3-540-70936-7_29
11. Cheung, L., Newport, C.C.: Provably secure ciphertext policy ABE. In: ACM Conference on Computer and Communications Security, CCS 2007, pp. 456–465. ACM (2007)
12. Cui, H., Deng, R.H., Li, Y., Qin, B.: Server-aided revocable attribute-based encryption. In: Askoxylakis, I., Ioannidis, S., Katsikas, S., Meadows, C. (eds.) ESORICS 2016. LNCS, vol. 9879, pp. 570–587. Springer, Cham (2016). doi:10.1007/978-3-319-45741-3_29
13. Cui, H., Deng, R.H., Wu, G., Lai, J.: An efficient and expressive ciphertext-policy attribute-based encryption scheme with partially hidden access structures. In: Chen, L., Han, J. (eds.) ProvSec 2016. LNCS, vol. 10005, pp. 19–38. Springer, Cham (2016). doi:10.1007/978-3-319-47422-9_2
14. Cui, H., Wan, Z., Deng, R.H., Wang, G., Li, Y.: Efficient and expressive keyword search over encrypted data in cloud. IEEE Trans. Dependable Secure Comput. **PP**(99), 1 (2016)

15. Fujisaki, E., Okamoto, T.: Secure integration of asymmetric and symmetric encryption schemes. J. Cryptol. **26**(1), 80–101 (2013)
16. Goyal, V., Jain, A., Pandey, O., Sahai, A.: Bounded ciphertext policy attribute based encryption. In: Aceto, L., Damgård, I., Goldberg, L.A., Halldórsson, M.M., Ingólfsdóttir, A., Walukiewicz, I. (eds.) ICALP 2008. LNCS, vol. 5126, pp. 579–591. Springer, Heidelberg (2008). doi:10.1007/978-3-540-70583-3_47
17. Goyal, V., Pandey, O., Sahai, A., Waters, B.: Attribute-based encryption for fine-grained access control of encrypted data. In: ACM Conference on Computer and Communications Security, CCS 2006, pp. 89–98 (2006)
18. Gu, C., Zhu, Y., Pan, H.: Efficient public key encryption with keyword search schemes from pairings. In: Pei, D., Yung, M., Lin, D., Wu, C. (eds.) Inscrypt 2007. LNCS, vol. 4990, pp. 372–383. Springer, Heidelberg (2008). doi:10.1007/978-3-540-79499-8_29
19. Hwang, Y.H., Lee, P.J.: Public key encryption with conjunctive keyword search and its extension to a multi-user system. In: Takagi, T., Okamoto, T., Okamoto, E., Okamoto, T. (eds.) Pairing 2007. LNCS, vol. 4575, pp. 2–22. Springer, Heidelberg (2007). doi:10.1007/978-3-540-73489-5_2
20. Jiang, P., Mu, Y., Guo, F., Wen, Q.: Public key encryption with authorized keyword search. In: Liu, J.K., Steinfeld, R. (eds.) ACISP 2016. LNCS, vol. 9723, pp. 170–186. Springer, Cham (2016). doi:10.1007/978-3-319-40367-0_11
21. Jiang, T., Chen, X., Li, J., Wong, D.S., Ma, J., Liu, J.K.: Towards secure and reliable cloud storage against data re-outsourcing. Future Gener. Comput. Syst. **52**, 86–94 (2015)
22. Kiltz, E.: Chosen-ciphertext security from tag-based encryption. In: Halevi, S., Rabin, T. (eds.) TCC 2006. LNCS, vol. 3876, pp. 581–600. Springer, Heidelberg (2006). doi:10.1007/11681878_30
23. Lai, J., Deng, R.H., Li, Y.: Expressive CP-ABE with partially hidden access structures. In: ASIACCS 2012, pp. 18–19. ACM (2012)
24. Lai, J., Zhou, X., Deng, R.H., Li, Y., Chen, K.: Expressive search on encrypted data. In: ASIACCS 2013, pp. 243–252. ACM (2013)
25. Lewko, A., Okamoto, T., Sahai, A., Takashima, K., Waters, B.: Fully secure functional encryption: attribute-based encryption and (hierarchical) inner product encryption. In: Gilbert, H. (ed.) EUROCRYPT 2010. LNCS, vol. 6110, pp. 62–91. Springer, Heidelberg (2010). doi:10.1007/978-3-642-13190-5_4
26. Lewko, A., Waters, B.: Decentralizing attribute-based encryption. In: Paterson, K.G. (ed.) EUROCRYPT 2011. LNCS, vol. 6632, pp. 568–588. Springer, Heidelberg (2011). doi:10.1007/978-3-642-20465-4_31
27. Li, M., Yu, S., Cao, N., Lou, W.: Authorized private keyword search over encrypted data in cloud computing. In: ICDCS 2011, pp. 383–392. IEEE Computer Society (2011)
28. Liang, K., Au, M.H., Liu, J.K., Susilo, W., Wong, D.S., Yang, G., Yu, Y., Yang, A.: A secure and efficient ciphertext-policy attribute-based proxy re-encryption for cloud data sharing. Future Gener. Comput. Syst. **52**, 95–108 (2015)
29. Liang, K., Susilo, W., Liu, J.K.: Privacy-preserving ciphertext multi-sharing control for big data storage. IEEE Trans. Inf. Forensics Secur. **10**(8), 1578–1589 (2015)
30. Liu, J., Huang, X., Liu, J.K.: Secure sharing of personal health records in cloud computing: Ciphertext-policy attribute-based signcryption. Future Gener. Comput. Syst. **52**, 67–76 (2015)
31. Liu, J.K., Liang, K., Susilo, W., Liu, J., Xiang, Y.: Two-factor data security protection mechanism for cloud storage system. IEEE Trans. Comput. **65**(6), 1992–2004 (2016)

32. Lv, Z., Hong, C., Zhang, M., Feng, D.: Expressive and secure searchable encryption in the public key setting. In: Chow, S.S.M., Camenisch, J., Hui, L.C.K., Yiu, S.M. (eds.) ISC 2014. LNCS, vol. 8783, pp. 364–376. Springer, Cham (2014). doi:10. 1007/978-3-319-13257-0_21

33. Narayan, S., Gagné, M., Safavi-Naini, R.: Privacy preserving EHR system using attribute-based infrastructure. In: ACM CCSW 2010, pp. 47–52. ACM (2010)

34. Rhee, H.S., Park, J.H., Lee, D.H.: Generic construction of designated tester public-key encryption with keyword search. Inf. Sci. **205**, 93–109 (2012)

35. Rhee, H.S., Park, J.H., Susilo, W., Lee, D.H.: Improved searchable public key encryption with designated tester. In: ASIACCS 2009, pp. 376–379. ACM (2009)

36. Rouselakis, Y., Waters, B.: Practical constructions and new proof methods for large universe attribute-based encryption. In: ACM Conference on Computer and Communications Security, CCS 2013, pp. 463–474. ACM (2013)

37. Sahai, A., Waters, B.: Fuzzy identity-based encryption. In: Cramer, R. (ed.) EUROCRYPT 2005. LNCS, vol. 3494, pp. 457–473. Springer, Heidelberg (2005). doi:10. 1007/11426639_27

38. Shen, E., Shi, E., Waters, B.: Predicate privacy in encryption systems. In: Reingold, O. (ed.) TCC 2009. LNCS, vol. 5444, pp. 457–473. Springer, Heidelberg (2009). doi:10.1007/978-3-642-00457-5_27

39. Shi, J., Lai, J., Li, Y., Deng, R.H., Weng, J.: Authorized keyword search on encrypted data. In: Kutyłowski, M., Vaidya, J. (eds.) ESORICS 2014. LNCS, vol. 8712, pp. 419–435. Springer, Cham (2014). doi:10.1007/978-3-319-11203-9_24

40. Sun, W., Yu, S., Lou, W., Hou, Y.T., Li, H.: Protecting your right: Attribute-based keyword search with fine-grained owner-enforced search authorization in the cloud. In: IEEE INFOCOM 2014, pp. 226–234. IEEE (2014)

41. Sun, W., Yu, S., Lou, W., Hou, Y.T., Li, H.: Protecting your right: Verifiable attribute-based keyword search with fine-grained owner-enforced search authorization in the cloud. IEEE Trans. Parallel Distrib. Syst. **27**(4), 1187–1198 (2016)

42. Tang, Q., Chen, L.: Public-key encryption with registered keyword search. In: Martinelli, F., Preneel, B. (eds.) EuroPKI 2009. LNCS, vol. 6391, pp. 163–178. Springer, Heidelberg (2010). doi:10.1007/978-3-642-16441-5_11

43. Wang, S., Liang, K., Liu, J.K., Chen, J., Yu, J., Xie, W.: Attribute-based data sharing scheme revisited in cloud computing. IEEE Trans. Inf. Forensics Secur. **11**(8), 1661–1673 (2016)

44. Wang, S., Zhou, J., Liu, J.K., Yu, J., Chen, J., Xie, W.: An efficient file hierarchy attribute-based encryption scheme in cloud computing. IEEE Trans. Inf. Forensics Secur. **11**(6), 1265–1277 (2016)

45. Waters, B.: Ciphertext-policy attribute-based encryption: An expressive, efficient, and provably secure realization. In: Catalano, D., Fazio, N., Gennaro, R., Nicolosi, A. (eds.) PKC 2011. LNCS, vol. 6571, pp. 53–70. Springer, Heidelberg (2011). doi:10.1007/978-3-642-19379-8_4

46. Xhafa, F., Wang, J., Chen, X., Liu, J.K., Li, J., Krause, P.: An efficient PHR service system supporting fuzzy keyword search and fine-grained access control. Soft Comput. **18**(9), 1795–1802 (2014)

47. Yang, Y., Ding, X., Lu, H., Wan, Z., Zhou, J.: Achieving revocable fine-grained cryptographic access control over cloud data. In: Desmedt, Y. (ed.) ISC 2013. LNCS, vol. 7807, pp. 293–308. Springer, Cham (2015). doi:10.1007/978-3-319-27659-5_21

48. Yau, W., Phan, R.C., Heng, S., Goi, B.: Keyword guessing attacks on secure searchable public key encryption schemes with a designated tester. Int. J. Comput. Math. **90**(12), 2581–2587 (2013)

49. Zhang, B., Zhang, F.: An efficient public key encryption with conjunctive-subset keywords search. J. Netw. Comput. Appl. **34**(1), 262–267 (2011)
50. Zhang, R., Imai, H.: Generic combination of public key encryption with keyword search and public key encryption. In: Bao, F., Ling, S., Okamoto, T., Wang, H., Xing, C. (eds.) CANS 2007. LNCS, vol. 4856, pp. 159–174. Springer, Heidelberg (2007). doi:10.1007/978-3-540-76969-9_11

Towards Revocable Fine-Grained Encryption of Cloud Data: Reducing Trust upon Cloud

Yanjiang Yang[1], Joseph Liu[2,3], Zhuo Wei[1], and Xinyi Huang[4,5(✉)]

[1] Shield Lab, Huawei Singapore Research Center, Singapore, Singapore
{yang.yanjiang,wei.zhuo}@huawei.com
[2] Faculty of Information Technology, Monash University, Melbourne, Australia
joseph.liu@monash.edu.au
[3] College of Information Engineering, Shenzhen University, Shenzhen, China
[4] School of Mathematics and Computer Science, Fujian Normal University,
Fuzhou 350108, China
xyhuang@fjnu.edu.cn
[5] State Key Laboratory of Cryptology, Beijing 100878, China

Abstract. ABE (Attribute-based encryption) is capable of fine-grained data encryption, and thus has been studied for secure cloud data sharing. While a number of efforts have been dedicated to resolving the user revocation issue in the multi-user cloud data sharing setting, the trust assumption placed upon the cloud server is still high. In this work, we identify the necessity of achieving *verifiability of cloud decryption* in the proxy-assisted user revocation approach, so as to weaken the trust assumption on the cloud server. We further formulate a model for the system, and present two independent constructions following the formulation. Experimental results show the practicality of our proposed schemes.

Keywords: ABE (Attribute-Based Encryption) · Cloud computing · Fine-grained encryption · User revocation · Authenticated encryption

1 Introduction

Cloud storage services, e.g., Dropbox, Microsoft's Azure storage, and Amazon's S3, provides a wonderful platform for data sharing, enabling users to upload and store their data remotely in the cloud storage as well as to authorize other users to access and download the remotely stored data in real-time [9,11,12]. It is widely recognized that the user data need to be encrypted in order to safeguard against the cloud provider [16,19]. Under this rationale, there have been a number of work proposing to use attribute-based encryption (ABE) [6,14,15,25] to achieve fine-grained access control over cloud data [18,20,27–29,33,34]. Indeed, ABE is a one-to-many public key encryption mechanism in nature, capable of enforcing fine-grained encryption/decryption. In particular, ABE can be categorized into key policy ABE (KP-ABE) and ciphertext policy ABE (CP-ABE). KP-ABE allows data to be encrypted with a set of *attributes*, and each decryption key is

© Springer International Publishing AG 2017
J. Pieprzyk and S. Suriadi (Eds.): ACISP 2017, Part I, LNCS 10342, pp. 127–144, 2017.
DOI: 10.1007/978-3-319-60055-0_7

associated with an *access policy* (defined in terms of attributes); while CP-ABE is complementary – data are encrypted under an access policy, and a decryption key is associated with a set of *attributes*. In either type, a ciphertext can be decrypted using the corresponding decryption key only if the attributes satisfy the access policy.

In the setting of encrypting cloud data with ABE, *user revocation* has been a primary challenge to be resolved. One approach proposed in e.g., [2,24,26,34], is key-update based revocation, where secret key materials are updated to exclude revoked users. This method suffers from poor scalability as all data must be re-encrypted and all remaining legitimate user keys are to be updated or re-distributed, in which case the cost is tremendously high when the data volume or the number of users scales up.

Another approach is to augment ABE schemes with revocation support by incorporating revocation related mechanisms. The ABE schemes in [6,14] propose to include an "expiry time" attribute in the attribute set such that each decryption key is valid only for a limited period of time. The shortcoming of this method is that it does not allow for immediate revocation. In [22], Ostrovsky et. al. propose to include negative constrains in the access policy, such that a revocation of certain attributes amounts to negating these attributes. This mechanism is not scalable in revoking individual users, as each encryption has to involve information of all revoked users each being treated as a distinctive attribute.

More recently, yet another approach was introduced in [29,33] which implements proxy-assisted user revocation, where the cloud server acts as a proxy, and each user's decryption capability is split and represented by two parts, namely: one part is held by the cloud server (i.e., proxy key), and the other part is held by the user. A decryption requires a partial decryption by the cloud server (i.e., cloud decryption or proxy decryption, interchangeably), and a final decryption by the user. For the purpose of user revocation, the cloud server will simply erase the cloud-held proxy key associated with the user to be revoked. This method is particularly promising, as it instantly nullifies a user's decryption privilege while without affecting the legitimate users, requiring no key update or data re-encryption.

While the proxy-assisted user revocation approach demonstrated enormous potential in attaining revocable attribute-based encryption of cloud data, it has been observed in [32] that the constructions in [29,33] are based on a strong assumption – the cloud server is trusted so as not to disclose the revoked users' proxy keys to the revoked users. Considering the possible compromise of the cloud server or the probable existence of the unscrupulous insiders within the cloud service provider, [32] managed to weaken the strong assumption by extending the proxy-assisted with an "all-or-nothing" strategy, such that the cloud server itself is equipped with a public/private key pair and the private key is required in the partial decryption by the cloud server. This means that it is of no use to a revoked user if the cloud server only reveals to the user his/her proxy key, but not the cloud's private key.

Our Contributions. Going along the line of reducing trust upon the cloud server in the proxy-assisted user revocation approach as in [32], we further observe the necessity to provide verifiability of cloud decryption to the authorized users, i.e., to prevent the cloud server from maliciously manipulating encrypted cloud data. Manipulating cloud data by the cloud server could indeed occur, considering the case that some encrypted data records get crashed/lost on the cloud storage, and the cloud server surreptitiously generates bogus records to fool the data owners. We are thus motivated to achieve verifiability of cloud decryption whereby an authorized user is equipped to check the legitimacy of the result of the partial decryption by the cloud server, leading to a further reduction of the trust assumption upon the cloud server. In particular, our contributions are as follows:

- We give a formulation of revocable cloud data sharing with verifiable cloud decryption.
- We present two concrete schemes under the formulation, by extending and progressing the scheme in [32].
- We implement our schemes for experiments, in order to test the practicality of the proposed schemes.

Organization. The remainder of the paper is as follows. Section 2 presents a formulation of the system, followed by two concrete schemes in Sect. 3. Experimental results are given in Sect. 4, and Sect. 5 reviews related works. Section 6 contains concluding remarks.

2 Description and Formulation of the System

2.1 System Setting

As in the proxy-assisted user revocation approach [29,32,33], we consider a cloud storage system consisting of a data owner, a group of data consumers/users, and a cloud server, depicted in Fig. 1. The data owner needs to store its data records at the cloud server, and authorizes the group of users to access the stored data. An example of the entities would be such that the data owner is a company and the data users are the company's employees. Without fully trusting the cloud server, the data owner encrypts its data to ensure the privacy of the data against the cloud server. Data encryption further serves as a measure of built-in fine-grained access control, in such a way that the users have different decryption capabilities based on a pre-defined need-to-know basis. Particular to this system using ABE for data encryption, a user is specified by a set of attributes, e.g., according to the user's functional role in the company, and the user's decryption capability is thus attached to her attributes. The data owner encrypts each data record under an access control policy (specified in terms of attributes), such that a user can successfully decrypt the encrypted record, if and only if the user's attributes satisfy the access policy. As the system works in a multi-user data sharing setting, user revocation is a critical requirement, e.g. when a user leaves the company. User revocation allows the data owner to revoke a user's ability to decrypt the data (rather than prohibiting the user's access to the encrypted data).

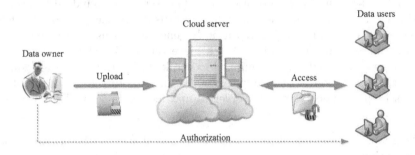

Fig. 1. An overview of the cloud data sharing system

Proxy-assisted User Revocation. To facilitate an understanding of the ensuing formulation of the system, we briefly recall the proxy-assisted user revocation approach [29,32,33]. Specifically, a user's decryption capability is rendered by a proxy key and the user's private key, where the former is held by the cloud server and the latter is possessed by the user. To manage users' proxy keys, the cloud server maintains a list, with each entry containing a user's identity and her corresponding proxy key. When the user requests a data record, the cloud server executes a proxy decryption operation over the data with the user's proxy key (also the cloud's own private key in [32]), generating an intermediate value. The intermediate value is then returned to the user, who gets the plaintext data by a user decryption operation using her private key. As such, to revoke a user it is as simple as to erase the user's proxy key from the cloud server.

2.2   Formulation of the System

As our subsequent constructions will progress the scheme in [32], our formulation extends the model thereof as well by adding in the property of verifiability of cloud/proxy decryption. As such, we first review the formulation in [32], followed by an exposition on the differences incurred due to the addition of verifiability of cloud decryption. Hereafter, familiarity with "attribute" and "access structure" (or "access policy" or "access tree") as introduced in [6,14] is assumed.

Let Λ denote the universe of attributes. A revocable cloud data encryption system specified in [32] comprises the following algorithms:

Setup(1^κ) $\rightarrow$ $(params, msk)$: Taking as input a security parameter 1^κ, the data owner executes the algorithm to set up public parameters $params$, and a master secret key msk. As usual, $params$ is assumed implicit in the input of the below algorithms.

UKGen$(u) \rightarrow (pk_u, sk_u)$: The user key generation algorithm takes as input a user identity, u, and outputs a pair of public/private keys, (pk_u, sk_u), for u. Note that (pk_u, sk_u) is a pair for a standard public key cryptosystem.

PxKGen$(msk, pk_{CS}, pk_u, \mathbb{A}_u) \rightarrow PxK_u$: The proxy key generation algorithm takes as input msk, the cloud server's public key pk_{CS}, a user u's public key pk_u, and the user's attributes, $\mathbb{A}_u \subset \Lambda$, and outputs a proxy key PxK_u for u.

Encrypt$(m, \mathcal{T}) \rightarrow c$: The encryption algorithm takes as input a message m, and an access tree $\mathcal{T}$ which specifies an access policy, and outputs a ciphertext c.

PxDec$(sk_{CS}, PxK_u, c) \rightarrow v$: The proxy/cloud decryption algorithm takes as input the cloud server's private key sk_{CS}, a user's proxy key PxK_u, and a ciphertex, c, and outputs an intermediate value v.

UDec$(sk_u, v) \rightarrow m$: The user decryption algorithm takes as input a user's private key sk_u, and an intermediate value v, and outputs a plaintext message m.

Revoke$(u, \mathcal{L}_{PxK}) \rightarrow \mathcal{L}'_{PxK}$: Taking as input a user identity u, and the Proxy Key list $\mathcal{L}_{PxK}$, the algorithm revokes u's decryption capability by updating and outputting an updated Proxy Key list, $\mathcal{L}'_{PxK}$.

Upon the model, three security requirements, i.e., *Data Privacy Against Cloud Server*, *Data Privacy Against Users* and *User Revocation Support* are specified in [32]. To avoid repetition, we skip the details.

Necessity of Verifiability of Cloud Decryption. In the above formalization, the cloud server is assumed to manage the data owner's data intact and honestly perform the PxDec algorithm. [17,23] studied verifiable outsourced decryption of ABE (where its setting is quite similar to ours if the above PxDec algorithm is understood to be the outsourced decryption of ABE) and identified the necessity of ensuring verifiability of outsourced decryption. We notice that their arguments for the verifiability of outsourced decryption apply to our setting of cloud storage as well, and thus the trust assumption upon the cloud server in the above turns out be a bit strong. This motivates us to investigate providing verifiability to cloud/proxy decryption, reducing the trust assumption on the cloud server.

We further observe that the level of verifiability obtained in [17,23] does not suffice in our setting, and in particular [17,23] did not consider the case where the cloud server who is entrusted for the outsourced decryption to use a bogus but valid ciphertext (in place of the genuine ciphertext) in the outsourced decryption. Note that in [17,23] everyone (including the cloud server) can generate valid ciphertexts (it is public key encryption anyway) and thus the outsourced decryption of these bogus ciphertexts is still valid to the data users; but these ciphertexts are not legitimate, as they are not generated by the data owner. In our setting of cloud data sharing, a higher level of verifiability is desired – it should not only ensure the verifiability as in [17,23], but also enable the data users to verify the legitimacy of the result of cloud decryption. Our idea of formalizing this property is to involve the data owner's master secret key in the Encrypt algorithm.

System Formalization with Verifiability of Cloud Decryption. For brevity, we only highlight the differences that are needed to be imposed to the formulation reviewed above due to the addition of Verifiability of Cloud Decryption. In particular, the changes are restricted to syntax of the Encrypt and UDec algorithms, while other algorithms remain unchanged. Note that in our setting, the verifiability of cloud decryption is checked in the UDec algorithm, rather than the PxDec algorithm.

Encrypt$(msk, m, \mathcal{T}) \to c$: The encryption algorithm takes as input the master secret key msk, message m and an access tree $\mathcal{T}$, and outputs a ciphertext c.

UDec$(sk_u, v) \to \{m, \perp\}$: The user decryption algorithm takes as input a user's private key sk_u, and an intermediate value v, and outputs a plaintext m or $\perp$.

More specifically, the Encrypt algorithm additionally takes as input the master secret key, and the UDec algorithm could output $\perp$ if the verifiability check fails.

Besides the tree security requirements, Data Privacy Against Cloud Server, Data Privacy Against Users and User Revocation Support as defined in [32], one more security requirement, *Verifiability of Cloud Decryption* is to be imposed on the system.

Definition 1 *[Verifiability of Cloud Decryption]. A revocable fine-grained cloud data encryption system satisfies verifiability of cloud decryption if for any PPT adversary, the probability of the adversary winning the following game is $\epsilon(\kappa)$, where $\epsilon(\kappa)$ is a negligible function with respect to the security parameter κ.*

Setup. The challenger runs the Setup algorithm to establish $(params, msk)$, and returns $params$ to the adversary.

Phase 1. The adversary makes a number of data encryption queries, submitting a message m_i and an associated access tree for each query. The challenger executes the Encrypt algorithm and returns the corresponding ciphertexts to the adversary.

Challenge. The adversary submits an attributes set $\mathbb{A}^*$ and a public key pk_u^* (the corresponding private key is sk_u^*), and the challenger returns the corresponding PxK_u^* generated by executing the PxKGen algorithm.

Phase 2. Phase 1 is repeated.

Output. The adversary outputs a ciphertext c^*. The adversary wins the game if $m = \mathsf{UDec}(sk_u^*, \mathsf{PxDec}(PxK_u^*, c^*)) \neq \perp$ and $m \neq m_i$ for any data encryption query m_i the adversary has asked in Phase 1 and 2.

The formalization essentially captures the requirement that no one (including the cloud server) except the data owner can generate genuine encrypted data records.

3   Our Constructions

As argued above, the level of verifiability obtained in [17,23] does not suffice in our setting, and thus the constructions thereof is not directly applicable to us. In this section, we present two independent schemes by working upon the scheme in [32] to additionally satisfy Definition 1, giving rise to "authenticated" revocable fine-grained cloud data encryption. The two constructions will take the scheme in [32] as a building block, which is listed in the Appendix for ease of reference.

3.1 Scheme One

In practice, the actual data encryption in [32] would follow the common practice of key encapsulation + data encapsulation (KEM/DEM), namely, an encryption of a data record m is of the form $(\mathsf{Encrypt}(k, \mathcal{T}), \mathsf{SE}.\mathsf{Enc}_k(m))$, where SE is a symmetric key block cipher and k is a random key for SE. We also present our two scheme to be working in the mode of KEM/DEM.

This first scheme is inspired by [23] to use randomness extractor as a building block to compensate for the loss of entropy of the data encryption key.

Preliminaries. Let $s \in_R S$ denote an element s randomly chosen from a set S. For a discrete distribution X over $\mathcal{X}$, the min-entropy of X is defined to be $\mathsf{H}_\infty(X) = -\log(\max_{x \in \mathcal{X}} \Pr[X = x])$. The average min-entropy of X conditioned on Y (over $\mathcal{Y}$) is defined as $\tilde{\mathsf{H}}_\infty(X|Y) = -\log E_{y \in \mathcal{Y}}(2^{-\mathsf{H}_\infty(X|Y=y)})$. We recall a lemma in [10] that relates to the security of our scheme: *Let X, Y and Z be random variables. If Y has at most 2^r possible values, then $\tilde{\mathsf{H}}_\infty(X|(Y, Z)) \geq \tilde{\mathsf{H}}_\infty(X|Z) - r$.*

Random Extractor: An efficient function $\mathsf{Ext}: \mathcal{X} \times \{0, 1\} \to \mathcal{Y}$ is an average-case (k, ϵ)-strong extractor if for all random variables (X, Z) such that $\tilde{\mathsf{H}}_\infty(X|(Y, Z)) \geq k$, we have $(Z, s, \mathsf{Ext}(X, s)) \approx_\epsilon (Z, s, y \leftarrow_R \mathcal{Y})$, where $s \leftarrow_R \{0, 1\}^t$, and $\approx_\epsilon$ denotes the statistical distance upper-bounding by ϵ.

In [10], it is shown that any family of pairwise independent hash functions $\mathcal{H}$: $\{\hbar : \mathcal{X} \to \mathcal{Y}\}$ is an average-case $(\tilde{\mathsf{H}}_\infty(X|Z), \epsilon)$-strong extractor if $\tilde{\mathsf{H}}_\infty(X|Z) \geq \log|\mathcal{Y}| + 2\log(1/\epsilon)$.

Construction Details. Following the paradigm of constructing "authenticated" public key encryption, e.g., [1], we reasonably assume the data owner to possess a pair of signing key/verification key (sk, vk) for a digital signature scheme Sig. Under the KEM/DEM paradigm, the encryption of a message m would be $(\mathsf{Encrypt}(msk, k, \mathcal{T}), \mathsf{SE}.\mathsf{Enc}_k(m))$. We cannot simply let the data owner sign $\mathsf{SE}.\mathsf{Enc}_k(m)$ with sk to provide verifiability of cloud decryption to the data users. This is because the PxDec algorithm may well output a bogus k'. Thus the legitimacy of k must be verified as well to the data users. To this end, we follow the idea of [23]: $H_0(k)$ is published as the verification data for k, where H_0 is a cryptographic hash function. Since $H_0(k)$ reveals at most $|H_0|$ bits of k, a random extractor $\hbar$ is then applied to k to generate a good random key $\tilde{k}$ for SE. Let $\epsilon_\hbar$ is the upper-bound parameter of the extractor $\hbar$, then the parameters must satisfy $0 \leq |\tilde{k}| \leq |k| - |H_0| - 2\log(1/\epsilon_\hbar)$.

We are ready to show how to extend the scheme in [32] (see Appendix), denoted as Basic, to achieve revocable fine-grained cloud data encryption with verifiability of cloud decryption. To avoid repetition, we only show the algorithms to be modified and highlight the extra operations to be added in each of such algorithms.

Setup(1^κ): On input a security parameter 1^κ, the algorithm does the following:
- execute $(params', msk') = \mathsf{Basic.Setup}(1^\kappa)$;
- select a cryptographic hash functions, $H_0 : G_T \rightarrow \{0,1\}^{\ell_0}$, where G_T is contained in $params'$;
- select a semantically secure block cipher $\mathsf{SE} = (\mathsf{SE.Enc}, \mathsf{SE.Dec})$ with key space $\{0,1\}^{\ell_{\mathsf{SE}}}$;
- select an extractor $\hbar : G_0 \rightarrow \{0,1\}^{\ell_{\mathsf{SE}}}$. Note that let $\epsilon_\hbar$ be the upper-bound parameter of the extractor $\hbar$, then it must satisfy $0 \leq \ell_{\mathsf{SE}} \leq |G_T| - \ell_0 - 2\log(1/\epsilon_\hbar)^1$
- determine a digital signature scheme $\mathsf{Sig} = (\mathsf{Sig.Sign}, \mathsf{Sig.Verify})$, and select a signing/verification key pair (sk, vk) for Sig;
- set $params = params' \cup \{H_0, \mathsf{SE}, \hbar, \mathsf{Sig}, vk\}$ and $msk = msk' \cup \{sk\}$.

Encrypt$(msk, m, \mathcal{T})$: Taking as input the master secret key msk, a message m, and an access tree $\mathcal{T}$, the algorithm works as follows:
- select a random $k \in_R G_T$ and compute $c' = \mathsf{Basic.Encrypt}(k, \mathcal{T})$;
- compute $\tilde{k} = \hbar(k)$, and $\tilde{C} = \mathsf{SE.Enc}_{\tilde{k}}(m)$;
- compute $\sigma = (H_0(k), \mathsf{Sig.Sign}_{sk}(H_0(k)\|\tilde{C}))$, where sk is contained in msk;
- set the ciphertext $c = (c', \tilde{C}, \sigma)$.

PxDec$(sk_{\mathsf{CS}}, PxK_u, c = (c', \tilde{C}, \sigma))$: The algorithm works as follows:
- Compute $v' = \mathsf{Basic.PxDec}(sk_{\mathsf{CS}}, PxK_u, c')$, and set the intermediate value $v = (v', \tilde{C}, \sigma)$.

UDec$(sk_u, v = (v', \tilde{C}, \sigma))$: The algorithm works as follows:
- if $\mathsf{Sig.Verify}_{vk}(\sigma) = 0$, then output $\perp$ and halt;
- compute $k = \mathsf{Basic.UDec}(sk_u, v')$, and test whether $H_0(k)$ equals the corresponding value in σ. If not, then output $\perp$ and halt;
- compute $\tilde{k} = \hbar(k)$ and $m = \mathsf{SE.Dec}_{\tilde{k}}(\tilde{C})$.

Security Analysis. We show that the proposed scheme satisfies the security requirements specified in Sect. 2.

Theorem 1. *The above scheme achieves Data Privacy Against Cloud Server, Data Privacy Against Users, and User Revocation Support, respectively, as specified in [32].*

---

[1] Let's assume to achieve 80-bit security: G_T could be instantiated such that $|G_T| = 512, \ell_0 = 160, \epsilon_\hbar = 2^{-80}$, then $|G_T| - \ell_0 - 2\log(1/\epsilon_\hbar) = 512 - 160 - 160 = 192$. It is thus more than enough to enable 160-bit block cipher, which can work in an appropriate mode to encrypt message of an arbitrary length.

Intuitively, compared to the scheme [32], the only place that reveals more information in terms of data privacy with respect to both the cloud server and the users is $H_0(k)$. However, this leakage has already been accommodated by the use of the random extractor $\hbar$. Hence data privacy of the scheme is warranted. Formally, we can prove Theorem 1 by a series of hybrid arguments, following the rationale in [23], but we omit the details.

Theorem 2. *The above scheme achieves Verifiability of Cloud Decryption as specified in Definition 1, given that* Sig *is universally unforgeable, and H_0 is collisions resistant.*

Proof. Recall that $c^* = (c'^*, \tilde{C}^*, \sigma^* = (H_0^*(k), \mathsf{Sig}.\mathsf{Sign}_{sk}(H_0^*(k)||\tilde{C}^*))$ and the corresponding $v^* = (v'^*, \tilde{C}^*, \sigma^*) = \mathsf{PxDec}(sk_{\mathsf{CS}}, PxK_u^*, c^*)$. If the adversary wins the game, then it means that σ^* is a valid signature, but $\mathsf{SE}.\mathsf{Dec}_{\hbar(k)}(\tilde{C}^*) \neq m_i$ for any asked query m_i. From this, two cases can be derived:

1. $(\tilde{C}^*, \sigma^*)$ is the reply of one of the data encryption queries the adversary has ever asked, or
2. $(\tilde{C}^*, \sigma^*)$ is not the reply of any data encryption queries the adversary has ever asked.

For case 1, it means that the k^* decrypted from v^* is such that $k^* \neq k$, but $H_0(k^*) = H_0(k)$, in which case a collision of H_0 is found.

For case 2, it means that $(\tilde{C}^*, \sigma^*)$ is a forged signature of the underlying digital signature scheme Sig.

The details are tedious and standard, thus omitted. This completes the proof. □

3.2   Scheme Two

The crust of the first scheme is the explicit protection of the authenticity of the data encryption key k used in the symmetric key cipher, resulting in $H_0(k)$ which leaks information on k; to compensate for the leakage, random extractor $\hbar$ is employed. In this section, we present an alternative scheme which is logically simpler. The rationale is to avoid the explicit protection of k (which has led to $H_0(k)$ and the use of random extractor $\hbar$ in the first scheme); instead, authenticated encryption (e.g., [5,7]) keyed by k is used for data encryption, replacing the symmetric key cipher used in the first scheme.

A Review of Authenticated Encryption. Authenticated encryption [5,7] is a well-established symmetric key cryptosystem, simultaneously providing confidentiality and integrity protection of the encrypted messages. Specifically, an authenticated encryption scheme is $\mathsf{AE} = (\mathsf{AE}.\mathsf{Enc}, \mathsf{AE}.\mathsf{Dec})$, where Enc and Dec are encryption algorithm and decryption algorithm, respectively. Compared to symmetric key block cipher, authenticated encryption not only protects the confidentiality/privacy of the messages, but also the integrity of the messages. Concretely, $\mathsf{AE}.\mathsf{Dec}$ could output $\bot$ if the ciphertext to be decrypted is invalid. This property is often naturally formalized as *integrity of ciphertexts*, i.e., AE.Dec checks the integrity of a ciphertext and gives up if the ciphertext is not legitimate/authenticated.

The formalization of confidentiality/privacy protection of authenticated encryption is identical to block cipher, so we do not repeat. For a better understanding of integrity protection, below is a formulation of integrity protection of ciphertexts of authenticated encryption.

1. The challenger chooses a key k for AE.
2. The adversary makes a number of encryption queries, submitting messages $m_1, m_2, \cdots$. For each query m_i, the challenger computes $c_i = \mathsf{AE.Enc}_k(m_i)$ and returns c_i to the adversary.
3. Finally, the adversary outputs a ciphertext c^*. The adversary wins if $\mathsf{AE.Dec}_k(c^*) \neq \perp$ and c^* is not any c_i returned by the challenger in step 2.

Integrity protection of ciphertexts stipulates that the probability of the adversary wins is negligible.

NOTE. We point out that implicit in this formulation is that the adversary cannot make a valid ciphertext under a key k still valid under a different key k'. To see this, in a strive to output a valid v^* under k, the adversary itself can anyway generate a different k' and in turn generate as many valid ciphertexts under k' as it wishes to. So an alternative formalism would be such that at the end, the adversary outputs a key $k^* \neq k$ and a ciphertext $c^* \in \{c_1, c_2, \cdots\}$, and the adversary wins if $\mathsf{AE.Dec}_{k^*}(c^*) \neq \perp$.

Construction Details. Based on the above discussions, encryption of a message m is of the form $(\mathsf{Encrypt}(msk, k, \mathcal{T}), \mathsf{AE.Enc}_k(m))$, where AE is an authenticated encryption scheme. This time, the data owner can simply sign $\mathsf{AE.Enc}_k(m)$ to attain verification of cloud decryption. Since k is directly used to key-up AE, there is no extra leakage of k.

The presentation of the scheme is still in the form of extending Basic, as in the earlier first scheme.

Setup(1^κ): The algorithm does the following:
- execute $(params', msk') = \mathsf{Basic.Setup}(1^\kappa)$;
- select an authenticated encryption scheme $\mathsf{AE} = (\mathsf{AE.Enc}, \mathsf{AE.Dec})$ with key space $\{0,1\}^{\ell_{\mathsf{AE}}}$;
- determine a digital signature scheme $\mathsf{Sig} = (\mathsf{Sig.Sign}, \mathsf{Sig.Verify})$, and select a signing/verification key pair (sk, vk) for Sig;
- set $params = params' \cup \{\mathsf{AE}, \mathsf{Sig}, vk\}$ and $msk = msk' \cup \{sk\}$.

Encrypt($msk, m, \mathcal{T}$): The algorithm works as follows:
- select a random $k \in_R \{0,1\}^{\ell_{\mathsf{AE}}}$ and compute $c' = \mathsf{Basic.Encrypt}(k, \mathcal{T})$;
- compute $\tilde{C} = \mathsf{AE.Enc}_k(m)$;
- compute $\sigma = \mathsf{Sig.Sign}_{sk}(\tilde{C})$);

- set the ciphertext $c = (c', \tilde{C}, \sigma)$.

$\mathbf{PxDec}(sk_{\mathsf{CS}}, PxK_u, c = (c', \tilde{C}, \sigma))$: The algorithm works as follows:

- Compute $v' = \mathsf{Basic.PxDec}(sk_{\mathsf{CS}}, PxK_u, c')$, and set the intermediate value $v = (v', \tilde{C}, \sigma)$.

$\mathbf{UDec}(sk_u, v = (v', \tilde{C}, \sigma))$: The algorithm works as follows:

- if $\mathsf{Sig.Verify}_{vk}(\sigma) = 0$, then output $\perp$ and halt;
- compute $k = \mathsf{Basic.UDec}(sk_u, v')$;
- compute $m = \mathsf{AE.Dec}_k(\tilde{C})$.

Security Analysis. Since authenticated encryption and block cipher is the same in terms of data privacy protection, we only show that this scheme achieves verifiability of cloud decryption.

Theorem 3. *The scheme shown above achieves Verifiability of Cloud Decryption as specified in Definition 1, given that Sig is universally unforgeable and AE satisfies integrity protection of ciphertexts.*

Proof. Recall that $c^* = (c'^*, \tilde{C}^*, \sigma^* = \mathsf{Sig.Sign}_{sk}(\tilde{C}^*))$. If the adversary wins the game, then it means that σ^* is a valid signature upon $\tilde{C}^*$, but $\mathsf{SE.Dec}_k(\tilde{C}^*) \neq m_i$ for any asked query m_i, where $k = \mathsf{Basic.UDec}(sk_u^*, c'^*)$. From this, two cases can be derived:

1. $(\tilde{C}^*, \sigma^*)$ is the reply of one of the data encryption queries the adversary has ever asked, or
2. $(\tilde{C}^*, \sigma^*)$ is not the reply of any data encryption queries the adversary has ever asked.

For case 1, it means that $k = \mathsf{Basic.UDec}(sk_u^*, c'^*)$ is not the same as the original key used to generate $\tilde{C}^*$. This directly contradicts integrity of ciphertexts of authenticated encryption (see the alternative formalism discussed earlier).

For case 2, it means that $(\tilde{C}^*, \sigma^*)$ is a forged signature of the underlying digital signature scheme Sig.

Due to limited space, we omit the details of the proof which will be provided in the full version of this paper. This completes the proof.   □

4   Experimental Results

To evaluate the performance of our proposed schemes, we did extensive experiments. The implementation is based on the Pairing-Based Cryptography (PBC) library (https://crypto.stanford.edu/pbc/). The bilinear map $e : G_0 \times G_0 \rightarrow G_T$ in our schemes is instantiated with a 512-bit supersingular curve of embedding degree, with $|p| = 160$ (p is the prime order of G_0 and G_T). Other cryptographic primitives used include RSA digital signature, AES for block cipher, AES-GCM for authenticated encryption. In addition, SHA256 is used in place of a random extractor.

Experimental Results. In practical cloud storage services, the performance at the cloud server's side and at the user's side is of concern, which directly relates to the PxDec algorithm and the UDec algorithm in our schemes. Our experiments thus mainly gauge the computational performance of these two algorithms in our schemes. Since our schemes are built upon Basic, the scheme in [32], we also implemented Basic as the baseline for comparison.

Performance of Proxy Decryption. We run the PxDec algorithm on a desktop PC with 2.66 GHz Intel Core2Duo and 3.25 GB RAM. The PxDec algorithm is fed a set of all-AND access trees, i.e., an access tree with all non-leaf being "AND" gates. The reason is that an access policy in the form of all-AND tree is expected to impose the heaviest workload in the PxDec algorithm, compared to the access tree with the same number of leaf nodes. The experimental results are shown in Fig. 2, which demonstrates timing (i.e., computational performance of the three schemes) with respect to the number of attributes (leaf nodes). The experimental results are the average of repeating each experiment for 100 times.

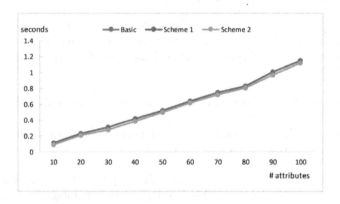

Fig. 2. Computational performance of PxDec of three schemes

As evident from the Figure, (1) the three schemes have identical performance in proxy decryption. This is apparent from the construction of our two schemes; (2) the experimental results show that the PxDec algorithm performs linear computations with respect to the number of attributes; (3) it takes about 1.2 s to perform the PxDec algorithm in case of 100 attributes. Such a performance should be acceptable for practical applications.

Performance of User Decryption. We run the UDec algorithm of the three schemes on a smartphone configured with a 1.2 GHz CPU and 2 GB RAM. The experimental results are depicted in Fig. 3, which indicates that on average, it takes about 50 ms to decrypt a ciphertext in the Basic scheme, and about 110 ms by our two schemes. The extra time taken in our schemes is mainly for digital signature verification. These results suggest that it is indeed affordable for a resource constraint device to perform the UDec algorithm.

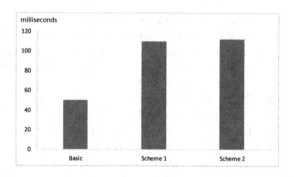

Fig. 3. Computational performance of user decryption

5 Related Work

Cloud Data Encryption with ABE. A large number of cloud data encryption schemes have been proposed in the literature. Of particular relevance to us are those utilizing ABE. As an one-to-many encryption scheme, ABE is required to provide user revocation support if deployed for encryption of cloud data.

Yu et al. [34] suggested adopting KP-ABE to achieve fine-grained data sharing. To support user revocation, they proposed using the proxy re-encryption (PRE) technique [3] to update users' decryption keys. In this approach, the bulk of the computationally expensive operations (e.g. re-generation of encrypted cloud data due to user revocation) are performed by the cloud server. Although a cloud server generally has significantly more computational resources, each user's quota is cost based. Similar limitation is observed in the scheme proposed by Wang et al. [26]. Sahai et al. [24] proposed an attribute revocable CP-ABE scheme, using ciphertext delegation and the piecewise property of private keys. In particular, the system proceeds in epochs, and in each epoch, the attribute authority generates a set of update keys (as the other piece of each private key) according to the revocation list. All the ciphertexts are then re-encrypted with a new access policy (the principal access policy remains unchanged, but the extra access policy changes in each epoch). A similar attribute revocation method has also been explored in the multi-authority setting [30,31], where users' attributes are issued by multiple independent attribute authorities. Similar to other ABE schemes with built-in attribute revocation support (such as expiry time and negative attributes), these schemes face the challenge of transforming attribute revocation into efficient revocation for individual users. For example, the limitation in the scheme proposed by Liu et al. [21] that uses the "expiry time" mechanism for user revocation is the inability to support real-time or immediate revocation. To sum up, the overhead introduced by these schemes in the re-generation of encrypted data and key update is large, although some have managed to push much of the overhead for the cloud server to perform.

Yang et al. [29] were the first to propose proxy-assisted user revocation in using ABE for secure cloud data sharing. The proxy-assisted user revocation approach actually implements decryption capability splitting, where a data user's complete decryption capability is split into two parts – one is taken on by the cloud server as a proxy while the other is taken on by the user herself. Subsequent work such as [32,33] improved over [29] by reducing the strong trust assumption upon the cloud server. Our work in this paper goes along this same line of research, progressing [29,32,33] by further weakening the trust assumption.

We point out that "decryption capability splitting" contrasts with "decryption key splitting" to be reviewed shortly, and the two differ mainly in the way keys are generated: in the latter, the key shares held by the proxy and the user are generated by a single trusted entity; as a result, it suffers from the issue of key escrow, from the user's point of view. In contrast, "decryption capability splitting" does not have the key escrow problem, as a user can generate her own key and does need not disclose it to others. It is expected that "decryption capability splitting" would be advantageous over "decryption key splitting" in many applications.

Key-Split Cryptography. Boneh et al. [4] proposed "mediated RSA" to split the private key of RSA into two shares, such that one share is delegated to an online "mediator" (mediator is a similar concept as proxy in our setting) and the other is given to the user. As RSA decryption and signing require the collaboration of both parties, the user's cryptographic capabilities are immediately revoked if the mediator does not cooperate. Recently, Chen et al. [8] presented a mediated CP-ABE scheme, where the mediator's key is issued over a set of attributes. The scheme in [13] and the follow-up work [17,23] can also be viewed as mediated ABE, although the purpose of these work is to outsource the costly ABE decryption to the mediator, instead of for immediate revocation. As a final note, our work in this paper is inspired by [17,23] to provide verifiability of cloud decryption, but we end up desiring and attaining a higher level of verifiability.

6 Conclusions

In this paper, we went further along the line of reducing trust assumption upon the cloud server in the proxy-assisted user revocation approach. In particular, we first identified the necessity of achieving *verifiability of cloud decryption*, and then gave a formulation of the system; then two concrete schemes were presented; experiments were conducted and promising experimental results were obtained. Our work in this paper walked revocable fine-grained cloud data sharing a step further towards practical deployment.

Acknowledgments. Joseph K. Liu is supported by the Science and Technology Innovation Projects of Shenzhen (GJHZ20160226202520268). Xinyi Huang is supported by the Distinguished Young Scholars Fund of Fujian (2016J06013) and the State Key Laboratory of Cryptology Research Fund.

Appendix: A Review of the Scheme in [32]

The details of the scheme in [32] are as follows.

Setup(1^κ): On input a security parameter 1^κ, the algorithm:
- determines a bilinear map, $e : G_0 \times G_0 \to G_T$, where G_0 and G_T are cyclic groups of κ-bit prime order p;
- selects g, which is a generator of G_0;
- selects a cryptographic hash function, $H : \{0,1\}^* \to G_0$;
- picks $\alpha, \beta \in_R Z_p$, and sets $params = (e, G_0, g, h = g^\beta, \mathcal{G}_\alpha = e(g,g)^\alpha)$ and $msk = (\alpha, \beta)$.

UKGen(u): On input a user identity u, the algorithm chooses $x_u \in_R Z_p$, and sets $(pk_u = g^{x_u}, sk_u = x_u)$. It can be seen that (pk_u, sk_u) is a standard ElGamal type key pair. The cloud server also uses this algorithm to generate a key pair, $(pk_{CS} = g^{x_{CS}}, sk_{CS} = x_{CS})$.

PxKGen($msk, pk_{CS}, pk_u, \mathbb{A}_u$): On input $msk = (\alpha, \beta), pk_{CS} = g^{x_{CS}}, pk_u = g^{x_u}$ and $\mathbb{A}_u$, the algorithm chooses $r_1, r_2, r_i \in_R Z_p, \forall i \in \mathbb{A}_u$, and sets

$$PxK_u = (k = (pk_{CS}^{r_1} pk_u^\alpha g^{r_2})^{\frac{1}{\beta}}, k' = g^{r_1}, \forall i \in \mathbb{A}_u : \{k_{i1} = g^{r_2} H(i)^{r_i}, k_{i2} = g^{r_i}\})$$

Encrypt($m, \mathcal{T}$): Taking as input a message, m, and $\mathcal{T}$, the algorithm works as follows: Firstly, it selects a polynomial, q_n, for each node, n, (including the leaf nodes) in $\mathcal{T}$. These polynomials are chosen in a top-down manner starting from the root node, rt. For each node n, set the degree d_n of the polynomial q_n to be $d_n = t_n - 1$, where t_n is the threshold value of node n. Starting with the root node, rt, the algorithm chooses an $s \in_R Z_p$, and sets $q_{rt}(0) = s$. It next selects d_{rt} other random points to define q_{rt} completely. For any other node n, it sets $q_n(0) = q_{\mathsf{parent}(n)}(\mathsf{index}(n))$, and chooses d_n other points to define q_n. Let L be the set of leaf nodes in $\mathcal{T}$. The algorithm sets the ciphertext, c, as

$$c = (\mathcal{T}, C = m \cdot \mathcal{G}_\alpha^s, C' = h^s, C'' = g^s,$$
$$\forall \ell \in L : \{C_{\ell 1} = g^{q_\ell(0)}, C_{\ell 2} = H(\mathsf{att}(\ell))^{q_\ell(0)}\})$$

PxDec(sk_{CS}, PxK_u, c): On input $sk_{CS} = x_{CS}$, and $PxK_u = (k, k', \forall i \in \mathbb{A}_u : \{k_{i1}, k_{i2}\})$ associating with a set of attributes, $\mathbb{A}_u$, and a ciphertext, $c = (\mathcal{T}, C, C', C'', \forall \ell \in L : \{C_{\ell 1}, C_{\ell 2}\})$, the algorithm outputs an intermediate value, v if $\mathcal{T}(\mathbb{A}_u) = 1$, and $\perp$ otherwise. Specifically, the algorithm is recursive. We first define an algorithm, $\mathsf{DecNd}_n(PxK_u, c)$, on a node, n, of $\mathcal{T}$. If node, n, is a leaf node, we let $z = \mathsf{att}(n)$ and define as follows: $z \notin \mathbb{A}_u$, $\mathsf{DecNd}_n(PxK_u, c) = \perp$; otherwise $\mathsf{DecNd}_n(PxK_u, c) = F_n$, where

$$F_n = \frac{e(k_{z1}, C_{n1})}{e(k_{z2}, C_{n2})} = \frac{e(g^{r_2} H(z)^{r_z}, g^{q_n(0)})}{e(g^{r_z}, H(z)^{q_n(0)})} = e(g,g)^{r_2 \cdot q_n(0)} \qquad (1)$$

We now consider the recursive case when n is a non-leaf node. The algorithm, $\mathsf{DecNd}_n(PxK_u, c)$, then works as follows. For each child node ch of n, it calls $\mathsf{DecNd}_{ch}(PxK_u, c)$, and stores the output as F_{ch}. Let S_n be an arbitrary t_n-sized set of child nodes, ch, such that $F_{ch} \neq \perp$. If such a set does not exist, then the node is not satisfied and $\mathsf{DecNd}_n(PxK_u, c) = F_n = \perp$. Otherwise, we let the Lagrange coefficient, $\triangle_{i,S}$ for $i \in Z_p$, and a set S of elements in Z_p be $\triangle_{i,S}(x) = \prod_{j \in S, j \neq i} \frac{x-j}{i-j}$. We next compute

$$
\begin{aligned}
F_n &= \prod_{ch \in S_n} F_{ch}^{\triangle_{i,S'_n}(0)}, \text{where} \quad \begin{array}{l} i = \text{index}(ch), \\ S'_n = \{\text{index}(ch):ch \in S_n\} \end{array} \\
&= \prod_{ch \in S_n} (e(g,g)^{r_2 \cdot q_{ch}(0)})^{\triangle_{i,S'_n}(0)} \\
&= \prod_{ch \in S_n} (e(g,g)^{r_2 \cdot q_{\text{parent}(ch)}(\text{index}(ch))})^{\triangle_{i,S'_n}(0)} \\
&= \prod_{ch \in S_n} (e(g,g)^{r_2 \cdot q_n(i)})^{\triangle_{i,S'_n}(0)} \\
&= e(g,g)^{r_2 \cdot q_n(0)}
\end{aligned}
\tag{2}
$$

In this way, $\mathsf{DecNd}_{rt}(PxK_u, c)$ for the root node rt can be computed if $\mathcal{T}_{rt}(\mathbb{A}_u) = 1$, where $\mathsf{DecNd}_{rt}(PxK_u, c) = e(g,g)^{r_2 \cdot q_{rt}(0)} = e(g,g)^{r_2 \cdot s} = F_{rt}$. Next, the proxy decryption algorithm computes

$$
\frac{e(k, C')}{e(k', C'')^{x_{\text{CS}}} F_{rt}} = \frac{e((pk_{\text{CS}}^{r_1} pk_u^\alpha g^{r_2})^{\frac{1}{\beta}}, h^s)}{e(g^{r_1}, g^s)^{x_{\text{CS}}} e(g,g)^{r_2 \cdot s}} = e(pk_u, g)^{s \cdot \alpha}.
$$

Finally, it sets $v = (C = m \cdot \mathcal{G}_\alpha^s, e(pk_u, g)^{s \cdot \alpha})$.

$\mathsf{UDec}(sk_u, v)$: On input a user private key, $sk_u = x_u$, and an intermediate value, $v = (C = m \cdot \mathcal{G}_\alpha^s, e(pk_u, g)^{s \cdot \alpha})$, the user decryption algorithm computes $\frac{m \cdot \mathcal{G}_\alpha^s}{(e(pk_u, g)^{s \cdot \alpha})^{x_u^{-1}}} = m$.

$\mathsf{Revoke}(u, \mathcal{L}_{PxK})$: On input a user identity, u, and the Proxy Key list, $\mathcal{L}_{PxK}$, the user revoking algorithm deletes the entry corresponding to u from the list – i.e. $\mathcal{L}'_{PxK} = \mathcal{L}_{PxK} \backslash \{u, PxK_u\}$. In a real world application, an interface should be provided to the data owner for the data owner to perform the update in real-time.

References

1. An, J.H., Dodis, Y., Rabin, T.: On the security of joint signature and encryption. In: Knudsen, L.R. (ed.) EUROCRYPT 2002. LNCS, vol. 2332, pp. 83–107. Springer, Heidelberg (2002). doi:10.1007/3-540-46035-7_6
2. Attrapadung, N., Imai, H.: Attribute-based encryption supporting direct/indirect revocation modes. In: Proceedings of the IMA International Conference on Cryptography and Coding, pp. 278–300 (2009)
3. Blaze, M., Bleumer, G., Strauss, M.: Divertible protocols and atomic proxy cryptography. In: Nyberg, K. (ed.) EUROCRYPT 1998. LNCS, vol. 1403, pp. 127–144. Springer, Heidelberg (1998). doi:10.1007/BFb0054122
4. Boneh, D., Ding, X., Tsudik, G., Wong, C.M.: A method for fast revocation of public key certificates and security capabilities. In: Proceedings of the USENIX Security (2001)

5. Bellare, M., Namprempre, C.: Authenticated encryption: relations among notions and analysis of the generic composition paradigm. In: Okamoto, T. (ed.) ASI-ACRYPT 2000. LNCS, vol. 1976, pp. 531–545. Springer, Heidelberg (2000). doi:10. 1007/3-540-44448-3_41
6. Bethencourt, J., Sahai, A., Waters, B.: Ciphertext-policy attribute-based encryption. In: Proceedings of IEEE S&P (2007)
7. CAESAR: Competition for Authenticated Encryption: Security, Applicability, and Robustness. http://competitions.cr.yp.to/caesar.html
8. Chen, Y., Jiang, L., Yiu, S.M., Au, M., Xuan, W.: Fully-RCCA-CCA-Secure ciphertext-policy attribute based encryption with security mediator. In: Proceedings of the 16th International Conference on Information and Communications Security, ICICS 2014 (2014)
9. Cloud Security Alliance: Security guidance for critical areas of focus in cloud computing (2009). http://www.cloudsecurityalliance.org
10. Dodis, Y., Ostrovsky, R., Reyzin, L., Smith, A.: Fuzzy extractor: how to generate strong keys from biometrics and other noisy data. SIAM J. Comput. **38**(1), 97–139 (2008)
11. Network, E., Agency, I.S.: Cloud computing risk assessment. http://www.enisa. europa.eu/act/rm/_les/deliverables/cloud-computing-risk-assessment
12. Gartner: Don't trust cloud provider to protect your corporate assets, 28 May 2012. http://www.mis-asia.com/resource/cloud-computing/ gartner-dont-trust-cloud-provider-to-protect-your-corporate-assets
13. Green, M., Hohenberger, S., Waters, B.: Outsourcing the decryption of ABE ciphertexts. In: Proceedings of the USENIX Security (2011)
14. Goyal, V., Pandy, O., Sahai, A., Waters, B.: Attribute-based encryption for fine-grained access control of encrypted data. In: Proceedings of the ACM CCS 2006 (2006)
15. Hohenberger, S., Waters, B.: Online/Offline attribute-based encryption. In: Krawczyk, H. (ed.) PKC 2014. LNCS, vol. 8383, pp. 293–310. Springer, Heidelberg (2014). doi:10.1007/978-3-642-54631-0_17
16. Jiang, T., Chen, X., Li, J., Wong, D.S., Ma, J., Liu, J.K.: Towards secure and reliable cloud storage against data re-outsourcing. Future Gener. Comp. Syst. **52**, 86–94 (2015)
17. Lai, J., Deng, R.H., Guan, C., Weng, J.: Attribute-based encryption with verifiable outsourced decryption. IEEE Trans. Inf. Forensics Secur. **8**(8), 1343–1354 (2013)
18. Liang, K., Au, M.H., Liu, J.K., Susilo, W., Wong, D.S., Yang, G., Yu, Y., Yang, A.: A secure and efficient ciphertext-policy attribute-based proxy re-encryption for cloud data sharing. Future Gener. Comp. Syst. **52**, 95–108 (2015)
19. Liang, K., Susilo, W., Liu, J.K.: Privacy-preserving ciphertext multi-sharing control for big data storage. IEEE Trans. Inf. Forensics Secur. **10**(8), 1578–1589 (2015)
20. Liu, Z., Wong, D.S.: Practical attribute based encryption: traitor tracing, revocation, and large universe. https://eprint.iacr.org/2014/616.pdf
21. Liu, J., Wan, Z., Gu, M.: Hierarchical attribute-set based encryption for scalable, flexible and fine-grained access control in cloud computing. In: Proceedings of the 7th Information Security Practice and Experience Conference, ISPEC 2011 (2011)
22. Ostrovsky, R., Sahai, A., Waters, B.: Attribute-based encryption with non-monotonic access structures. In: Proceedings of ACM CCS 2007, pp. 195–203 (2007)
23. Qin, B., Deng, R.H., Liu, S., Ma, S.: Attribute-based encryption with efficient verifiable outsourced decryption. IEEE Trans. Inf. Forensics Secur. **10**(7), 1384–1393 (2015)

24. Sahai, A., Seyalioglu, H., Waters, B.: Dynamic credentials and ciphertext delegation for attribute-based encryption. In: Proceedings of Advances in Cryptology, Crypto 2012, pp. 199–217 (2012)
25. Waters, B.: Ciphertext-policy attribute-Based encryption: an expressive, efficient, and provably secure realization. In: Proceedings of Practice and Theory in Public Key Cryptography, PKC 2011, pp. 53–70 (2011)
26. Wang, G., Liu, Q., Wu, J.: Hierarhical attribute-based encryption for fine-grained access control in cloud storage services. In: Proceedings of ACM CCS 2010 (2010)
27. Wang, S., Zhou, J., Liu, J.K., Yu, J., Chen, J., Xie, W.: An efficient file hierarchy attribute-based encryption scheme in cloud computing. IEEE Trans. Inf. Forensics Secur. $11(6)$, 1265–1277 (2016)
28. Wang, S., Liang, K., Liu, J.K., Chen, J., Yu, J., Xie, W.: Attribute-based data sharing scheme revisited in cloud computing. IEEE Trans. Inf. Forensics Secur. $11(8)$, 1661–1673 (2016)
29. Yang, Y., Ding, X., Lu, H., Wan, Z., Zhou, J.: Achieving revocable fine-grained cryptographic access control over cloud data. In: Proceedings of the 16th Information Security Conference, ISC 2013 (2013)
30. Yang, K., Jia, X.: Expressive, efficient, and revocable data access control for multi-authority cloud storage. IEEE Trans. Parallel Distrib. Syst. $25(7)$, 1735–1744 (2014)
31. Yang, K., Jia, X., Ren, K., Zhang, B., Xie, R.: DAC-MACS: Effective Data Access Control for Multiauthority Cloud Storage Systems. IEEE Trans. Inf. Forensics Secur. $8(11)$, 1790–1801 (2013)
32. Yang, Y., Liu, J.K., Liang, K., Choo, K.-K.R., Zhou, J.: Extended proxy-assisted approach: achieving revocable fine-grained encryption of cloud data. In: Pernul, G., Ryan, P.Y.A., Weippl, E. (eds.) ESORICS 2015. LNCS, vol. 9327, pp. 146–166. Springer, Cham (2015). doi:10.1007/978-3-319-24177-7_8
33. Yang, Y., Lu, H., Weng, J., Zhang, Y., Sakurai, K.: Fine-grained conditional proxy re-encryption and application. In: Chow, S.S.M., Liu, J.K., Hui, L.C.K., Yiu, S.M. (eds.) ProvSec 2014. LNCS, vol. 8782, pp. 206–222. Springer, Cham (2014). doi:10.1007/978-3-319-12475-9_15
34. Yu, S., Wang, C., Ren, K., Lou, W.: Achieving secure, scalable, and fine-grained data access control in cloud computing. In: Proceedings of IEEE INFOCOM 2010 (2010)

Identity-Based Encryption

Mergeable and Revocable Identity-Based Encryption

Shengmin Xu$^{(\boxtimes)}$, Guomin Yang$^{(\boxtimes)}$, Yi Mu$^{(\boxtimes)}$, and Willy Susilo$^{(\boxtimes)}$

School of Computing and Information Technology,
Institute of Cybersecurity and Cryptology, University of Wollongong,
Wollongong, Australia
{sx914,gyang,ymu,wsusilo}@uow.edu.au

Abstract. Identity-based encryption (IBE) has been extensively studied and widely used in various applications since Boneh and Franklin proposed the first practical scheme based on pairing. In that seminal work, it has also been pointed out that providing an efficient revocation mechanism for IBE is essential. Hence, revocable identity-based encryption (RIBE) has been proposed in the literature to offer an efficient revocation mechanism. In contrast to revocation, another issue that will also occur in practice is to combine two or multiple IBE systems into one system, e.g., due to the merge of the departments or companies. However, this issue has not been formally studied in the literature and the naive solution of creating a completely new system is inefficient. In order to efficiently address this problem, in this paper we propose the notion of mergeable and revocable identity-based encryption (MRIBE). Our scheme provides the first solution to efficiently revoke users and merge multiple IBE systems into a single system. The proposed scheme also has several nice features: when two systems are merged, there is no secure channel needed for the purpose of updating user private keys; and the size of the user private key remains unchanged when multiple systems are merged. We also propose a new security model for MRIBE, which is an extension of the security model for RIBE, and prove that the proposed scheme is semantically secure without random oracles.

Keywords: Identity-based encryption · Revocation · Merging

1 Introduction

Public key encryption is the most basic primitive of public key cryptography. However, it suffers from the key distribution and management problem. To overcome this drawback, identity-based encryption (IBE) has been proposed, and it provides a new paradigm for public key encryption [2,3,5,20]. IBE uses the identity string (e.g. emails or IP addresses) of a user as the public key of that user. The sender using an IBE does not need to look up the public keys and the corresponding certificates of the receivers, because the identities together with common public parameters are sufficient for encryption. The private keys of all the users are generated by a private key generator (PKG) which is a fully trusted third party.

© Springer International Publishing AG 2017
J. Pieprzyk and S. Suriadi (Eds.): ACISP 2017, Part I, LNCS 10342, pp. 147–167, 2017.
DOI: 10.1007/978-3-319-60055-0_8

Revocation is an essential requirement in a cryptographic system when a user's key is compromised and/or any misuse is noticed. In PKI, revocation is done via certificate revocation lists (CRLs). However, IBE cannot apply this approach since there is no certificate in the system. Boneh and Franklin provided the first practical IBE scheme, and they also proposed a revocation mechanism by appending the timestamp in each identity string, but the workload of updating the private key is linear to the size of the non-revoked users. To address this issues, some practical Revocable IBE (RIBE) schemes have been proposed [1, 11,15]. Boldyreva et al. [1] proposed the first practical RIBE scheme with the authority's periodic workload to be logarithmic in the number of users while keeping the scheme efficient in both encryption and decryption. However, their RIBE scheme limits the number of users in the system. To overcome this problem, they proposed a method to double the number of users in the system. However, the size of the private key for each user is also increased whenever the size of the system is increased. Some following works [11,15] have focused on improving the security from selective security to adaptive security.

RIBE schemes are useful in many applications such as email systems and data storage systems by disallowing unauthorised or revoked users to access encrypted sensitive information in those systems. However, in practice it is also possible that two or more IBE systems need to be merged due to various reasons. As an example, a university wants to merge two departments: information technology (IT) and computer science (CS). A naive approach to address this issue is creating a completely new system and re-generating the public parameter and private keys for all users. However, this approach is impractical since a new private key needs to be generated for all the users in the combined system and a secure channel needs to be established between each user and the PKG for key distribution.

In this paper, we propose a new notion called mergeable and revocable identity-based encryption (MRIBE) to solve the above problem. Our scheme inherits the advantage of RIBE schemes by allowing the authority (i.e., PKG) to efficiently revoke users. In addition, our scheme allows different systems to be merged into a single system while keeping the size of the user private key unchanged. Also, there is no secure channel needed for updating the user private keys during the merging process.

1.1 Related Work

The concept of identity-based cryptography was introduced by Shamir [19], but the first practical IBE scheme was proposed by Boneh and Franklin in 2001 [3] and the scheme is proved secure in the random oracle model. Since the random oracle model is an idealised model, Boneh and Boyen [2] proposed a selectively security IBE scheme without random oracles in 2004. One year later, Waters [20] proposed a new IBE scheme with adaptive security in the standard model, but the size of the public parameter depends on the length of the user identity. To reduce the size of the public parameter, Gentry [5] proposed another IBE scheme in the standard model, but its security is based on a non-standard assumption.

RIBE is an extension of IBE by providing an efficient revocation mechanism. The issue of revocation in IBE has been pointed out by Boneh and Franklin in their seminal work [3]. They suggested that users renew their private keys periodically by representing an identity as ID‖T where ID is the real identity and T is the current time. However, such an approach is inefficient and not scalable because a secure channel between the PKG and each user needs to be established each time, and the workload of generating new private keys is linear in the number of non-revoked users in each revocation epoch. Hanaoka et al. [8] proposed an approach that the users periodically renew their private keys without interacting with the PKG but each user needs to posses a tamper-resistant hardware device. This assumption makes the solution rather impractical. Boldyreva et al. [1] introduced a scalable but selectively secure RIBE by utilizing several techniques including fuzzy identity-based encryption [13], secret sharing [19] and the tree-based revocation method proposed for broadcast encryption [4,7,10,12,21]. Libert and Vergnaud [11] proposed the first adaptively secure RIBE scheme. Seo and Emura [15] improved the security model in [1] to prevent decryption key exposure attacks. Lee et al. [9] proposed a RIBE scheme by utilizing subset difference (SD) method instead of the Complete Subtree (CS) method which is used in all previous works. Recently, the techniques used in RIBE have also been extended to achieve revocable hierarchical identity-based encryption (RHIBE) [14,16,17].

1.2   Our Contributions

In this work, we propose a new cryptographic notion named mergeable and revocable identity-based encryption (MRIBE), which is an extension of revocable identity-based encryption (RIBE). The proposed MRIBE scheme inherits all the nice properties of RIBE, in particular the property of allowing efficient revocation, and also allows multiple IBE systems to be merged into a single system, which makes it more versatile in handling the dynamics that could occur in real applications.

We also give a new security model for MRIBE by extending of the security model for RIBE and prove that the proposed scheme is semantically secure in the standard model. Our scheme is based on RIBE by introducing several new algorithms to handle the merging functionality. The proposal scheme also has some several nice features: there is no secure channel needed for key update during the merging process; and the size of user private key remains unchanged when multiple systems are merged, which makes the system scalable.

1.3   Paper Organization

Some preliminaries are introduced in the next section. In Sect. 3, we provide definitions for the MRIBE scheme and its security model. We then present our MRIBE construction in Sect. 4. The security proof of the proposed scheme is provided in Sect. 5. Finally, we summarize our result in Sect. 6.

2   Preliminaries

In this section, we introduce the notations used in this paper and review the definitions for bilinear map and pseudorandom function family. We also review some cryptographic primitives, including threshold secret sharing scheme, fuzzy identity-based encryption scheme, and revocable identity-based encryption scheme.

2.1   Notations

Let $\mathbb{N}$ denote the set of all natural numbers, and for $n \in \mathbb{N}$, we define $[n] := \{1, ..., n\}$. "$x \leftarrow y$" denotes that x is chosen uniformly at random from y if y is a finite set, x is output from y if y is a function or an algorithm, or y is assigned to x otherwise. If x and y are strings, then "$|x|$" denotes the bit-length of x, "$x\|y$" denotes the concatenation of x and y. For a finite set S, "$|S|$" denotes its size and $S[i]$ denotes the i-th value in the set S. If $\mathcal{A}$ is a probabilistic algorithm, then "$y \leftarrow \mathcal{A}(x; r)$" denotes that $\mathcal{A}$ computes y as output by taking x as input and using r as randomness, and we just write "$y \leftarrow \mathcal{A}(x)$" if we do not need to make the randomness used by $\mathcal{A}$ explicit. If furthermore $\mathcal{O}$ is a function or an algorithm, then "$\mathcal{A}^{\mathcal{O}}$" means that $\mathcal{A}$ has oracle access to $\mathcal{O}$. A function $\epsilon(k) : \mathbb{N} \rightarrow [0, 1]$ is said to be *negligible* if for all positive polynomials $p(k)$ and all sufficiently large $k \in \mathbb{N}$, we have $\epsilon(k) < 1/p(k)$. Throughout this paper, we use the character "k" to denote a security parameter.

2.2   Bilinear Map

Let $\mathbb{G}$ and $\mathbb{G}_T$ be two cyclic multiplicative groups of prime order p and g be a generator of $\mathbb{G}$. The map $e : \mathbb{G} \times \mathbb{G} \rightarrow \mathbb{G}_T$ is said to be an admissible bilinear pairing if the following properties hold true.

1. Bilinearity: for all $u, v \in \mathbb{G}$ and $a, b \in \mathbb{Z}_p$, $e(u^a, v^b) = e(u, v)^{ab}$.
2. Non-degeneration: $e(g, g) \neq 1$.
3. Computability: it is efficient to compute $e(u, v)$ for any $u.v \in \mathbb{G}$.

We say that $(\mathbb{G}, \mathbb{G}_T)$ are bilinear map groups if there exists a bilinear pairing $e : \mathbb{G} \times \mathbb{G} \rightarrow \mathbb{G}_T$ as above.

2.3   Pseudorandom Function Family

Goldreich, Goldwasser and Micali [6] introduced approaches to constructing random functions in 1984. In this section, we review the definition of pseudorandom function and pseudorandom function family.

Definition 1 (Pseudorandom Function). *Let $k \in \mathbb{N}$ be a security parameter. A function family* F *is associated with* $\{\mathsf{Seed}_k\}_{k\in\mathbb{N}}, \{\mathsf{Dom}_k\}_{k\in\mathbb{N}}$ *and* $\{\mathsf{Rng}_k\}_{k\in\mathbb{N}}$. *Formally, for any* $\sum \leftarrow \mathsf{Seed}_k, \mathcal{D} \leftarrow \sum$ *and* $\mathcal{R} \leftarrow \mathsf{Rng}_k$, $\mathsf{F}_{\omega}^{k,\sum,\mathcal{D},\mathcal{R}}$ *defines a function which maps an element of* $\mathcal{D}$ *to an element of* $\mathcal{R}$. *That is,* $\mathsf{F}_{\omega}^{k,\sum,\mathcal{D},\mathcal{R}}(\rho) \in \mathcal{R}$ *for any* $\rho \in \mathcal{D}$.

Definition 2 (Pseudorandom Function Family). F *is a pseudorandom function family if* $\mathsf{F}_\omega^{k,\Sigma,\mathcal{D},\mathcal{R}}(\rho_i)$ *and* $RF(\rho_i)$ *computational indistinguishability for any* $\rho_i \in \mathcal{D}$ *adaptively chosen by any polynomial time distinguisher, where RF is a truly random function. That is, for any* $\rho \in \mathcal{D}, RF(\rho) \leftarrow \mathcal{R}$.

2.4   Threshold Secret Sharing Scheme

Shamir's secret sharing scheme [18] divides a secret s into n pieces $s_1, ..., s_n$ using a unique polynomial of degree $(t-1)$, any t out of n shares may be used to recover the secret. The details are shown as follow.

Choose a group $\mathbb{Z}_p$ and $p \geq n$. Each user u_i is associated with a public unique number $u_i \in \mathbb{Z}_p$ and the user set $\mathsf{U} = \{u_1, ..., u_n\}$. Choose a random $k-1$ degree polynomial $p(x) = s + \prod_{i=1}^{k-1} a_i x^i$ where $a_i \in \mathbb{Z}_p^*$. Each user in U obtains a share $s_i = p(u_i)$. When k users come together and form a set $\mathsf{J} \subseteq \mathsf{U}$, the secret s can be recovered by utilizing Lagrange coefficient and polynomial interpolation. For $x, i \in \mathbb{Z}$, set $\mathsf{J} \subset \mathbb{Z}$ the *Lagrange coefficient* $\Delta_{i,\mathsf{J}}(x)$ is defined as

$$\Delta_{i,\mathsf{J}}(x) = \prod_{j \in \mathsf{J}, j \neq i} \left(\frac{x-j}{i-j} \right).$$

To recover $p(x)$, we have following equation:

$$p(x) = \sum_{i \in \mathsf{J}} s_i \cdot \Delta_{i,\mathsf{J}}(x).$$

Hence, we can recover the secret key s by setting the element x is equal to 0:

$$s = p(0) = \sum_{i \in \mathsf{J}} s_i \cdot \Delta_{i,\mathsf{J}}(0).$$

2.5   Fuzzy Identity-Based Encryption Scheme

Sahai and Waters [13] proposed a new type of identity-based encryption scheme called fuzzy identity-based encryption. It is the first attribute-based encryption scheme. There are two schemes, one has to define the universe in the setup phase, and the other one has a large universe. In the large universe construction, it utilizes all elements of $\mathbb{Z}_p^*$ as the universe and defines the following function to cooperate Shamir's secret sharing scheme to recover the plaintext from the ciphertext with J attributes. For $x \in \mathbb{Z}; \mathsf{J} \subset \mathbb{Z}; g, h_1, ..., h_{|\mathsf{J}|} \in \mathbb{G}$, we define

$$H_{g,\mathsf{J},h_1,...,h_{|\mathsf{J}|}} \stackrel{\text{def}}{=} g^{x^{|\mathsf{J}|-1}} \prod_{i=1}^{|\mathsf{J}|} \left(h_i^{\Delta_{i,\mathsf{J}}(x)} \right)$$

The large universe construction can be used to build revocable identity-based encryption scheme as follows. The private key generation centre issues the private key for every user based on the identity ω and the time t in each revocation epoch for the non-revoked user. The ciphertext is encrypted under the identity ω and time t. So the revoked users cannot decrypt the ciphertext since they do not have valid time t component.

2.6   Identity-Based Encryption with Revocation Scheme

Boldyreva, Goyal and Kumar [1] points out that the revocation list can be implemented by the complete subtree method [12]. Since our proposed scheme is mergeable, we slightly modify their revocation scheme. Let x_c denote the children of node x. For the root node, it has 2 or more degrees since the mergence, which is differ to the previous work [1]. For the non-root node, it only has two children x_l and x_r. The detail of revocation algorithm is described as follows.

The function KUNodes takes three parameters as input, a binary tree T, revocation list rl and time t. It outputs a set of nodes, which is the minimal set of nodes in the binary tree T such that the non-revoked nodes have at least one ancestor or themselves in the set and none of revoked nodes in revocation list rl have any ancestor or themselves in the set. The function operates as follows. First it marks all the ancestors of revoked nodes as revoked into the set X, then output all the non-revoked children of revoked nodes in the set Y. Here is a formal specification.

$$\text{KUNodes}(\mathsf{T}, rl, t)$$
$$\mathsf{X}, \mathsf{Y} \leftarrow \emptyset$$
$$\forall (v_i, t_i) \in rl \quad \text{if } t_i \leq t \text{ then add } \mathsf{Path}(v_i) \text{ to X}$$
$$\forall x \in \mathsf{X} \qquad \text{if } x_c \notin \mathsf{X} \text{ then add } x_c \text{ to Y}$$
$$\text{If } \mathsf{Y} = \emptyset \text{ then add root to Y}$$
$$\text{Return Y}$$

Our scheme is based on the binary tree except the root node has more than two children. After merging, our revocation tree improves the degree of the root node rather than the depth of the binary tree. Let N denote the number of user for each system and N_S denote the number of systems. Our tree structure keeps the unchanged size of depth $\log_2 N$. Thus the number of the private key for each user remains unchanged $\log_2 N$. After merging all N_S system, the new root node has $2N_S$ degrees. It improves the width N_S times compared to the original revocation tree. However, this tree structure does not reduce the efficient since N_S is not a significant number and we can re-build the whole system if N_S is too large.

3   Formal Definitions and Security Models

3.1   Syntax of Mergeable and Revocable IBE

We start with defining the general syntax of a Mergeable and Revocable IBE scheme. We recall and modify the definition of revocable IBE schemes as defined in [1]. Each algorithm is run by one of following parties - key authority, sender or receiver. The key authority maintains a revocation list rl and state st. We define parameter N_S as the number of system in our proposed scheme and use the Greek characters as the subscript to represent the instantiations of different systems in this section and following sections.

Definition 3 (Mergeable and Revocable IBE). *A mergeable and revocable identity-based encryption scheme* $\mathcal{MRIBE} = (\mathcal{S}, \mathcal{SK}, \mathcal{KU}, \mathcal{DK}, \mathcal{E}, \mathcal{D}, \mathcal{R}, \mathcal{MP}, \mathcal{MSK}, \mathcal{SKU})$ *is defined by ten algorithms and has associated message space* $\mathcal{M}$, *identity space* $\mathcal{I}$ *and time space* $\mathcal{T}$. *In what follows, we call an algorithm stateful only if it updates rl or st.*

The stateful **Setup** *algorithm* $\mathcal{S}$ *is run by the key authority. Given a security parameter* k, *a maximal number of users* N *and a number of systems* N_S, *it outputs one public parameters pp which shares to all* N_S *systems, and generates a public key* pk_i, *a master secret key* msk_i, *a revocation list* rl_i *and a state* st_i *for each system (*$i \in \{1, ..., N_S\}$*).*

The stateful **Private Key Generation** *algorithm* $\mathcal{SK}$ *is run by the key authority. Given the information of the public key, the master secret key and the state* $(pk_i, msk_i, state_i)$ *in system* i *and an identity* $\omega \in \mathcal{I}$, *it outputs private key* $sk_{\omega,i}$ *and an updated state* st_i.

The **Key Update** *algorithm* $\mathcal{KU}$ *is run by the key authority. Given the information of the public key, the master secret key, the revocation list and state* $(pk_i, msk_i, rl_i, st_i)$ *in system* i *and a revocation epoch* $t \in \mathcal{T}$, *it outputs a key update* $ku_{t,i}$.

The **Decryption Key Generation** *algorithm* $\mathcal{DK}$ *is run by the receiver. Given a private key* $sk_{\omega,i}$ *and a key update* $ku_{t,i}$, *it outputs decryption key* $dk_{\omega,t,i}$ *or a special symbol* $\perp$ *indicating that* ω *was revoked.*

The **Encryption** *algorithm* $\mathcal{E}$ *is run by the sender. Given a public key* pk_i *in system* i *and an identity* $\omega \in \mathcal{I}$, *an encryption time* $t \in \mathcal{T}$ *and a message* $m \in \mathcal{M}$, *it outputs a ciphertext* c_i. *For simplicity and w.l.o.g. we assume that* ω *and* t *are efficiently computable from* c_i.

The **Decryption** *algorithm* $\mathcal{D}$ *is run by the receiver. Given a decryption key* $dk_{\omega,t,i}$ *and a ciphertext* c_i, *it outputs a message* $m \in \mathcal{M}$ *or a special symbol* $\perp$ *indicating that the ciphertext is invalid.*

The stateful **Revocation** *algorithm* $\mathcal{R}$ *is run by the key authority. Given an identity to be the revoked* $\omega \in \mathcal{I}$, *revocation list* rl_i *and state* st_i *in system* i *and revocation time* $t \in \mathcal{T}$ *it outputs updated revocation list* rl_i.

The stateful **Merge Parameter** *algorithm* $\mathcal{MP}$ *is run by the key authority. Given the public key* pk_α, *the master key* msk_α, *the revocation list* rl_α *and the state* st_α *in system* α, *the public key* pk_β, *the master key* msk_β, *the revocation list* rl_β *and the state* st_β *in system* β, *it outputs updated revocation list* rl_β *and state* st_β.

The **Merge Private Key** *algorithm* $\mathcal{MSK}$ *is run by the key authority. Given the public key* pk_α, *the master key* msk_α *and the state* st_α *in system* α, *the public key* pk_β, *the master key* mk_β *and the state* st_β *in system* β *and an identity* $\omega \in \mathcal{I}$, *it outputs a mergeable private key* $sk_{\omega,\alpha,\beta}$.

The **Private Key Update** *algorithm* $\mathcal{SKU}$ *is run by the receiver. Given the private key* $sk_{\omega,\alpha}$ *and the mergeable private key* $sk_{\omega,\alpha,\beta}$, *it outputs the private key* $sk_{\omega,\beta}$.

Correctness requires that, for any outputs of $\mathcal{S}$, any $m \in \mathcal{M}$, $\omega \in \mathcal{I}$ and $t \in \mathcal{T}$, all possible states and revocation lists, the following experiments return 1 with probability 1:

– The key authority generates all public parameters for N_S systems:

$$(pp, \{pk_i, msk_i, rl_i, st_i\}_{i \in \{1,...,N_S\}}) \leftarrow \mathcal{S}(k, N, N_S); \alpha, \beta \leftarrow \{1, ..., N_S\}.$$

– ω_1 is a valid user in system α:

$$(sk_{\omega_1,\alpha}, st_\alpha) \leftarrow \mathcal{SK}(pk_\alpha, msk_\alpha, st_\alpha, \omega_1); ku_{t,\alpha} \leftarrow \mathcal{KU}(pk_\alpha, msk_\alpha, rl_\alpha, st_\alpha, t);$$
$$dk_{\omega_1,t,\alpha} \leftarrow \mathcal{DK}(sk_{\omega_1,\alpha}, ku_{t,\alpha}); c_1 \leftarrow \mathcal{E}(pk_\alpha, \omega_1, t, m_1).$$
If $\mathcal{D}(dk_{\omega_1,t,\alpha}, c_1) \neq m_1$ then return 0; else return 1

– ω_2 is a revoked user in system β:

$$(sk_{\omega_2,\beta}, st_\beta) \leftarrow \mathcal{SK}(pk_\beta, msk_\beta, st_\beta, \omega_2); rl_\beta \leftarrow \mathcal{R}(\omega_2, rl_\beta, st_\beta, t);$$
$$ku_{t,\beta} \leftarrow \mathcal{KU}(pk_\beta, msk_\beta, rl_\beta, st_\beta, t).$$
If $\mathcal{DK}(sk_{\omega_2,\beta}, ku_{t,\beta}) \neq \perp$ then return 0; else return 1

– ω_1 is a valid user in system α and merges to system β:

$$(rl_\beta, st_\beta) \leftarrow \mathcal{MP}(\{pk_i, msk_i, rl_i, st_i\}_{i \in \{\alpha,\beta\}});$$
$$sk_{\omega_1,\alpha,\beta} \leftarrow \mathcal{MSK}(\{pk_i, msk_i, st_i\}_{i \in \{\alpha,\beta\}}, \omega_1);$$
$$sk_{\omega_1,\beta} \leftarrow \mathcal{SKU}(sk_{\omega_1,\alpha}, sk_{\omega_1,\alpha,\beta});$$
$$dk_{\omega_1,t,\beta} \leftarrow \mathcal{DK}(sk_{\omega_1,\beta}, ku_{t,\beta}); c_3 \leftarrow \mathcal{E}(pk_\beta, \omega_1, t, m_3).$$
If $\mathcal{D}(dk_{\omega_1,t,\beta}, c_3) = m_3$ then return 1; else return 0.

3.2   Security of Mergeable and Revocable IBE

We define the *selective-mergeable-and-revocable-ID* security for mergeable and revocable IBE scheme. Our security model is based on the model for *selective-revocable-ID security* defined in [1].

Definition 4 (sMRID security). *Let $\mathcal{MRIBE} = (\mathcal{S}, \mathcal{SK}, \mathcal{KU}, \mathcal{DK}, \mathcal{E}, \mathcal{D}, \mathcal{R}, \mathcal{MP}, \mathcal{MSK}, \mathcal{SKU})$ be a mergeable and revocable IBE scheme defined by the security parameter k, the maximum number of user N and the number of systems N_S. The adversary first outputs the challenging identity ω^*, a challenging time t^* and a subscript of challenging public key i^*, and also some state information it wants to preserve. Later it is given access to five oracles that correspond to the algorithms of the scheme. The **Private Key Generation Oracle** $\mathcal{O}_{\mathcal{SK}}(\cdot, \cdot)$ takes a public key pk_i and an identity ω, runs $\mathcal{SK}(pk_i, msk_i, st_i, \omega)$ to return the private key $sk_{\omega,i}$.*

*The **Revocation Oracle** $\mathcal{O}_{\mathcal{R}}(\cdot, \cdot)$ takes input an identity ω and a time t and runs $\mathcal{R}(\omega, rl_i, st_i, t)$ to return the updated revocation list rl_i else return $\perp$ if the identity ω does not exist in any system.*

The **Key Update Oracle** $\mathcal{O}_{\mathcal{KU}}(\cdot, \cdot)$ takes input a public key pk_i and a time t and runs $\mathcal{KU}(pk_i, msk_i, rl_i, st_i, t)$ to return key update $ku_{t,i}$.

The **Merge Parameter Oracle** $\mathcal{O}_{\mathcal{MP}}(\cdot, \cdot)$ takes input public key pk_α and public key pk_β and runs $\mathcal{MP}(\{pk_i, msk_i, rl_i, st_i\}_{i \in \{\alpha, \beta\}})$ to return updated revocation list rl_β and state st_β. The parameters of system α are no longer valid.

The **Merge Private Key Oracle** $\mathcal{O}_{\mathcal{MSK}}(\cdot, \cdot, \cdot)$ takes input an identity ω, a public key pk_α and a public key pk_β and runs $\mathcal{MSK}(\{pk_i, msk_i, st_i\}_{i \in \{\alpha, \beta\}}, \omega)$ to return the mergeable private key $sk_{\omega, \alpha, \beta}$ else return $\perp$ if related $\mathcal{MP}(\cdot, \cdot)$ does not query.

$$\text{Experiment Exp}_{\mathcal{MRIBE}}^{\text{smrid}-\text{cpa}}(k, N, N_S)$$
$$b \leftarrow \{0, 1\}$$
$$(\omega^*, t^*, i^*, state) \leftarrow \mathcal{A}(k, N, N_S)$$
$$(pp, \{pk_i, msk_i, rl_i, st_i\}_{i \in \{1, \ldots, N_S\}}) \leftarrow \mathcal{S}(k, N, N_S)$$
$$(m_0, m_1, state) \leftarrow \mathcal{A}^{\mathcal{O}_{S\mathcal{K}}, \mathcal{O}_\mathcal{R}, \mathcal{O}_{\mathcal{KU}}, \mathcal{O}_{\mathcal{MP}}, \mathcal{O}_{\mathcal{MSK}}}(state)$$
$$c^* \leftarrow \mathcal{E}(pk_{i^*}, \omega^*, t^*, m_b)$$
$$d \xleftarrow{\$} \mathcal{A}^{\mathcal{O}_{S\mathcal{K}}, \mathcal{O}_\mathcal{R}, \mathcal{O}_{\mathcal{KU}}, \mathcal{O}_{\mathcal{MP}}, \mathcal{O}_{\mathcal{MSK}}}(pk_{i^*}, c^*, state)$$
$$\text{If } b = d \text{ return 1 else return 0.}$$

Note that the following conditions must always hold:

1. $m_0, m_1 \in \mathcal{M}$ and $|m_0| = |m_1|$.
2. If $\mathcal{O}_{S\mathcal{K}}(\cdot, \cdot)$ has been queried on message (pk, ω) then the identity ω has been initialized or merged in the system with the public key pk.
3. $\mathcal{O}_{\mathcal{KU}}(\cdot, \cdot)$ and $\mathcal{O}_\mathcal{R}(\cdot, \cdot)$ can be queried on time which is greater than or equal to the time of all previous queries in each system i.e. the adversary is allowed to query only in a non-decreasing order of time. Also, the oracle $\mathcal{O}_\mathcal{R}(\cdot, \cdot)$ cannot be queried on time t if $\mathcal{O}_{\mathcal{KU}}(\cdot, \cdot)$ was queried on t.
4. If $\mathcal{O}_\mathcal{R}(\cdot, \cdot)$ has been queried on (ω^*, t) for any $t \leq t^*$ then $\mathcal{O}_{S\mathcal{K}}(\cdot, \cdot)$ and $\mathcal{O}_{\mathcal{MSK}}(\cdot, \cdot, \cdot)$ can be queried on identity ω^* without constrain. Otherwise, $\mathcal{O}_{S\mathcal{K}}(\cdot, \cdot)$ and $\mathcal{O}_{\mathcal{MSK}}(\cdot, \cdot, \cdot)$ can be queried on identity ω^* but these queries cannot derive the secret key sk_{ω^*, i^*} in a trivial way. The details are described as follows.

The relationships between private key generation oracle $\mathcal{O}_{S\mathcal{K}}(\cdot, \cdot)$ and merge private key generation oracle $\mathcal{O}_{\mathcal{MSK}}(\cdot, \cdot, \cdot)$ has been described in Fig. 1. Suppose the challenging subscript i^* is γ (challenging public key is pk_γ) and the challenging identity ω^* is a non-revoked user, the adversary cannot obtain the secret key $sk_{\omega, \gamma}$ and then there are two situations to be considered.

- $\mathcal{O}_{S\mathcal{K}}(pk_\gamma, \omega^*)$ cannot be queried.
- Any queries are equivalent to $\mathcal{O}_{S\mathcal{K}}(pk_\gamma, \omega^*)$ cannot be queried, e.g. if $\mathcal{O}_{S\mathcal{K}}(pk_\alpha, \omega^*)$ and $\mathcal{O}_{\mathcal{MSK}}(\omega^*, pk_\alpha, pk_\beta)$ have been queried, $\mathcal{O}_{\mathcal{MSK}}(\omega^*, pk_\beta, pk_\gamma)$ cannot be queried since the former two queries are equivalent to the query $\mathcal{O}_{S\mathcal{K}}(pk_\beta, \omega^*)$ and it is trial to gain the private key sk_γ by continually querying $\mathcal{O}_{\mathcal{MSK}}(\omega^*, pk_\beta, pk_\gamma)$.

We use two database called $\mathcal{D}_{\mathcal{SK}}$ and $\mathcal{D}_{\mathcal{MSK}}$ to record the messages queried to the $\mathcal{O}_{\mathcal{SK}}(\omega^*, \cdot)$ and $\mathcal{O}_{\mathcal{MSK}}(\cdot, \cdot, \omega^*)$ oracles, respectively. We can decide if the adversary can recover the secret key sk_{ω^*, i^*} by checking the database $\mathcal{D}_{\mathcal{SK}}$ and $\mathcal{D}_{\mathcal{MSK}}$.

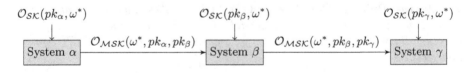

Fig. 1. Relationships of $\mathcal{O}_{\mathcal{SK}}(\cdot, \cdot)$ and $\mathcal{O}_{\mathcal{MSK}}(\cdot, \cdot, \cdot)$

We define the advantage of the adversary $\mathsf{Adv}^{smrid-cpa}_{\mathcal{MRIBE}, \mathcal{A}, N, N_S}(k)$ as

$$2 \cdot \Pr\left[\mathsf{Exp}^{smrid-cpa}_{\mathcal{MRIBE}, \mathcal{A}, N, N_S}(k) = 1\right] - 1$$

The scheme is said to be *sMRID-CPA secure* if the function $\mathsf{Adv}^{smrid-cpa}_{\mathcal{MRIBE}, \mathcal{A}, N, N_S}(k)$ is negligible in k for any efficient algorithm $\mathcal{A}$.

4   The Proposed Schemes

Setup $(pp, \{pk_i, msk_i, rl_i, st_i\}_{i \in \{1,...,N_S\}}) \leftarrow \mathcal{S}(k, N, N_S)$: given a security parameter $k \in \mathbb{N}$, a maximal number of users $N \in \mathbb{N}$ and a maximal number of systems $N_S \in \mathbb{N}$. The key authority defines the valid space of $\mathcal{M}, \mathcal{I}, \mathcal{T}$, define the pseudorandom function $\mathsf{F}_\sigma : \{0,1\}^* \to \mathbb{Z}_p^*$ as well as a complete binary tree T with at least N leaf nodes and does the following.

1. Select bilinear groups $(\mathbb{G}, p, g)$ as the public parameter pp which shares to all systems.
2. For $i \in \{1, ..., N_S\}$ do the following:
   (a) Randomly choose $(a_i, r_i) \leftarrow \mathbb{Z}_p^*$ and set $g_{1,i} \leftarrow g^{a_i}$ as well as randomly choose $g_{2,i}, h_{1,i}, h_{2,i}, h_{3,i} \leftarrow \mathbb{G}$.
   (b) Return public key $pk = (g_{1,i}, g_{2,i}, h_{1,i}, h_{2,i}, h_{3,i})$, master secret key $msk_i = (a_i, r_i)$, revocation list $rl_i = \emptyset$ and state $st_i = \mathsf{T}$.

Private Key Generation $(sk_{\omega, i}, st_i) \leftarrow \mathcal{SK}(pk_i, msk_i, st_i, \omega)$: given an identity $\omega \in \mathcal{I}$, a public key pk_i, a master key msk_i and a state st_i. The key authority generates private key $sk_{\omega, i}$ for the receiver with identity $\omega \in \mathcal{I}$ and the updated state st.

1. Choose an unassigned leaf v from T_i and associate it with $\omega \in \mathcal{I}$.
2. For all node $x \in \mathsf{Path}(v)$ do the following:
   (a) Retrieve a_x from T if it was defined. Otherwise, choose it at random $a_x \leftarrow \mathbb{Z}_p$ and store a_x at node x in $st_i = \mathsf{T}$.

(b) Generate random value $r_x \leftarrow F_{r_i}(\omega \| x)$ bases on random value r_i in master secret key msk, the identity $\omega \in \mathcal{I}$ as well as the label value x and set

$$D_x \leftarrow g_{2,i}^{a_x \omega + a_i} H_{g_{2,i}, \mathsf{J}, h_{1,i}, h_{2,i}, h_{3,i}}(\omega)^{r_x}; d_x \leftarrow g^{r_x}.$$

3. Return private key $sk_{\omega_i} = \{(x, D_x, d_x)\}_{x \in \mathsf{Path}(v)}$ and the updated state $st_i = \mathsf{T}$.

Key Update $ku_{t,i} \leftarrow \mathcal{KU}(pk_i, msk_i, rl_i, st_i, t)$: given a public key pk_i, a master secret key msk_i, a key update time $t \in \mathcal{T}$, a revocation list rl_i and a state st_i. For all nodes $x \in \mathsf{KUNodes}(\mathsf{T}_i, rl_i, t)$.

1. Generate random value $r_x \leftarrow \mathbb{Z}_p$ and set

$$E_x \leftarrow g_{2,i}^{a_x t + a} H_{g_{2,i}, \mathsf{J}, h_{1,i}, h_{2,i}, h_{3,i}}(t)^{r_x}; e_x \leftarrow g^{r_x}.$$

2. Return key update $ku_t = \{(x, E_x, e_x)\}_{x \in \mathsf{KUNodes}(\mathsf{T}_i, rl_i, t)}$.

Decryption Key Generation $dk_{\omega,t,i} \leftarrow \mathcal{DK}(sk_{\omega,i}, ku_{t,i})$: given a private key $sk_{\omega,i}$ and a key update $ku_{t,i}$. The receiver generates the decryption key $dk_{\omega,t,i}$ as follows.

1. Parse $sk_{\omega,i}$ as $\{(j, D_j, d_j)\}_{j \in \vec{j}}$, $ku_{t,i}$ as $\{(k, E_k, e_k)\}_{k \in \vec{k}}$ for some set of nodes $\vec{j}, \vec{k}$. If there exists a pair (j, k) s.t. $j = k$, generate the decryption key

$$dk_{\omega,t,i} \leftarrow (D_j, E_k, d_j, e_k).$$

Otherwise, set the decryption key $dk_{\omega,t,i}$ as $\perp$.
2. Return the decryption key $dk_{\omega,t,i}$.

Encryption $c_i \leftarrow \mathcal{E}(pk_i, \omega, t, m)$: given an identity $\omega \in \mathcal{I}$, a public key pk_i, an encryption time $t \in \mathcal{T}$ and a message $m \in \mathcal{M}$. The sender encrypts the message $m \in \mathcal{M}$ as follows.

1. Randomly choose $z \leftarrow \mathbb{Z}_p$ and generate ciphertext c_1, c_2, c_ω, c_t.

$$c_1 \leftarrow m \cdot e(g_{1,i}, g_{2,i})^z; c_2 \leftarrow g^z;$$
$$c_\omega \leftarrow H_{g_{2,i}, \mathsf{J}, h_{1,i}, h_{2,i}, h_{3,i}}(\omega)^z; c_t \leftarrow H_{g_{2,i}, \mathsf{J}, h_{1,i}, h_{2,i}, h_{3,i}}(t)^z.$$

2. Return ciphertext $c = (\omega, t, c_1, c_2, c_\omega, c_t)$.

Decryption $m \leftarrow \mathcal{D}(dk_{\omega,t,i}, c)$: given a decryption key $dk_{\omega,t,i}$ and a ciphertext c. The receiver decrypts the ciphertext c as follows:

1. Compute the message m:

$$m \leftarrow c_1 \left(\frac{e(d, c_\omega)}{e(D, c_2)} \right)^{\frac{t}{t-\omega}} \left(\frac{e(e, c_t)}{e(E, c_2)} \right)^{\frac{\omega}{\omega - t}}.$$

2. Return the message m.

Revocation $rl_i \leftarrow \mathcal{R}(\omega, rl_i, st_i, t)$: given an identity to be revoked $\omega \in \mathcal{I}$, a revocation list rl_i, a state st_i and a revocation time $t \in \mathcal{T}$. The key authority updates the revocation list rl_i as follows:

1. For all nodes v associated with identity $\omega \in \mathcal{I}$ add (v, t) to rl as follows:

$$rl_i \leftarrow rl_i \cup (v, t).$$

2. Return the updated revocation list rl_i.

Merge Parameter $(rl_\beta, st_\beta) \leftarrow \mathcal{MP}(\{pk_i, msk_i, rl_i, st_i\}_{i \in \{\alpha, \beta\}})$: given all the system parameters $\{pk_i, mk_i, rl_i, st_i\}_{i \in \{\alpha, \beta\}}$ from system α and system β. The key authority generates system parameters which bases on the system parameters in the system β as follows:

1. Update the revocation list rl_β by uniting two revocation lists rl_α and rl_β.

$$rl_\beta \leftarrow rl_\alpha \cup rl_\beta.$$

2. Update the state st_β as follows:
   (a) Let T_α denote the root node in the binary tree in the system α. Remove the T_α in the state st_α. The detail of the tree structure list in system α is in Fig. 2.

$$st_\alpha \leftarrow st_\alpha \setminus \mathsf{T}_\alpha.$$

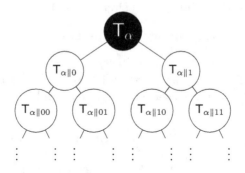

Fig. 2. Tree structure revocation list in System α

   (b) Update the state st_β by uniting it and st_α and the details in the Fig. 3. Note that the new tree is a binary tree except the root node has more than two children.

$$st_\beta \leftarrow st_\alpha \cup st_\beta.$$

3. Return the updated revocation list rl_β and the updated state st_β.

Merge Private Key $sk_{\omega, \alpha, \beta} \leftarrow \mathcal{MSK}(\{pk_i, msk_i, st_i\}_{i \in \{\alpha, \beta\}}, \omega)$: given all the system parameters $\{pk_i, mk_i, st_i\}_{i \in \{\alpha, \beta\}}$ from system α and system β and an identity $\omega \in \mathcal{I}$. The key authority generates the mergeable private key $sk_{\omega, \alpha, \beta}$.

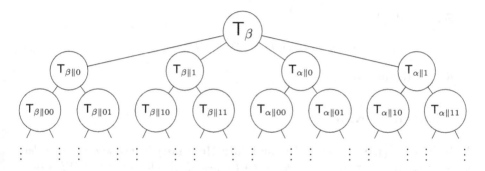

Fig. 3. Tree structure revocation list after merging α and β

1. Parse $pk_i = (g, g_{1,i}, g_{2,i}, h_{1,i}, h_{2,i}, h_{3,i})$ and $mk_i = (a_i, r_i)$ for $i = \alpha, \beta$.
2. Generate system parameters $a_{\alpha,\beta}, g_{1,\alpha,\beta}, g_{2,\alpha,\beta}, h_{1,\alpha,\beta}, h_{2,\alpha,\beta}, h_{3,\alpha,\beta}$ base on the system parameters from the system α and the system β.

$$a_{\alpha,\beta} = a_\beta - a_\alpha \cdot g_{1,\alpha,\beta} = g_{1,\beta}/g_{1,\alpha}; g_{2,\alpha,\beta} = g_{2,\beta}/g_{2,\alpha};$$
$$h_{1,\alpha,\beta} = h_{1,\beta}/h_{1,\alpha}; h_{2,\alpha,\beta} = h_{2,\beta}/h_{2,\alpha}; h_{3,\alpha,\beta} = h_{3,\beta}/h_{3,\alpha}.$$

3. For all node $x \in \mathsf{Path}(v)$ do the following:
   (a) Compute random values $r_{x,\alpha}$, $r_{x,\beta}$ and $r_{x,\alpha,\beta}$.

$$r_{x,\alpha} = \mathsf{F}_{r_\alpha}(\omega\|x); r_{x,\beta} = \mathsf{F}_{r_\beta}(\omega\|x); r_{x,\alpha,\beta} = r_{x,\beta} - r_{x,\alpha}.$$

   (b) Let $a_{x,\alpha}$ and $a_{x,\beta}$ denote the value in node in system α and system β, respectively.
   If x is the root node in system α. Then compute

$$D_{x,\alpha,\beta} = g_{2,\alpha}^{a_{x,\beta}\omega - a_{x,\alpha}\omega + a_{\alpha,\beta}} \cdot g_{2,\alpha,\beta}^{a_{x,\beta}\omega + a_\beta} \cdot H_{g_{2,\alpha},\mathsf{J},h_{1,\alpha},h_{2,\alpha},h_{3,\alpha}}(\omega)^{r_{x,\alpha,\beta}} \cdot$$
$$H_{g_{2,\alpha,\beta},\mathsf{J},h_{1,\alpha,\beta},h_{2,\alpha,\beta},h_{3,\alpha,\beta}}(\omega)^{r_{x,\beta}}.$$
$$d_{x,\alpha,\beta} = g^{r_{x,\alpha,\beta}}.$$

   Else, compute

$$D_{x,\alpha,\beta} = g_{2,\alpha}^{a_{x,\alpha,\beta}} \cdot g_{2,\alpha,\beta}^{a_{x,\alpha}\omega + a_\beta} \cdot H_{g_{2,\alpha},\mathsf{J},h_{1,\alpha},h_{2,\alpha},h_{3,\alpha}}(\omega)^{r_{x,\alpha,\beta}} \cdot$$
$$H_{g_{2,\alpha,\beta},\mathsf{J},h_{1,\alpha,\beta},h_{2,\alpha,\beta},h_{3,\alpha,\beta}}(\omega)^{r_{x,\beta}}.$$
$$d_{x,\alpha,\beta} = g^{r_{x,\alpha,\beta}}.$$

   (c) Return $sk_{\omega,\alpha,\beta} = \{(x, D_{x,\alpha,\beta}, d_{x,\alpha,\beta})\}_{x \in \mathsf{Path}(v)}$.

Private Key Update $sk_{\omega,\beta} \leftarrow \mathcal{SKU}(sk_{\omega,\alpha}, sk_{\omega,\alpha,\beta})$: Parse $sk_{\omega,\alpha}$ as $\{(i, D_{i,\alpha}, d_{i,\alpha})\}_{i \in \vec{i}}$ and $\tilde{sk}_{\omega,\alpha,\beta}$ as $\{(j, D_{j,\alpha,\beta}, d_{j,\alpha,\beta})\}_{j \in \vec{j}}$ for some set of nodes $\vec{i}$ and $\vec{j}$. The receiver generates updated private key $sk_{\omega,\beta}$ as follows.

1. For $i \in \vec{i}$ do the following:

$$sk_{\omega,\beta} \leftarrow (i, D_{i,\alpha} \cdot D_{i,\alpha,\beta}, d_{i,\alpha} \cdot d_{i,\alpha,\beta})$$

2. Return the private key $sk_{\omega,\beta}$.

5   Security Proof

Definition 5 (Decisional Bilinear Diffie-Hellman). *Let $\mathcal{G}$ be a prime order bilinear group generator. The Decisional Bilinear Diffie-Hellman (DBDH) problem is said to be hard for $\mathcal{G}$ if for every efficient adversary $\mathcal{A}$ its advantage* $\mathsf{Adv}_{\mathcal{G},\mathcal{B}}^{dbdh}(k)$ *defined as*

$$\Pr[\mathsf{Exp}_{\mathcal{G},\mathcal{A}}^{dbdh-real}(k) = 1] - \Pr[\mathsf{Exp}_{\mathcal{G},\mathcal{A}}^{dbdh-rand}(k) = 1]$$

is a negligible function in k, and where the experiments are as follows:

Experiment $\mathsf{Exp}_{\mathcal{G},\mathcal{A}}^{dbdh-real}(k)$	Experiment $\mathsf{Exp}_{\mathcal{G},\mathcal{A}}^{dbdh-rand}(k)$
$(\mathcal{G}, p, g) \leftarrow \mathcal{G}(k); x, y, z \leftarrow \mathbb{Z}_p$	$(\mathcal{G}, p, g) \leftarrow \mathcal{G}(k); x, y, z, w \leftarrow \mathbb{Z}_p$
$X \leftarrow g^x; Y \leftarrow g^y; Z \leftarrow g^z;$	$X \leftarrow g^x; Y \leftarrow g^y; Z \leftarrow g^z;$
$W \leftarrow e(g,g)^{xyz}$	$W \leftarrow e(g,g)^w$
$d \leftarrow \mathcal{A}(k, \mathcal{G}, p, g, X, Y, Z, W)$	$d \leftarrow \mathcal{A}(k, \mathcal{G}, p, g, X, Y, Z, W)$
Return d	Return d

Theorem 1. *Let $\mathcal{G}$ be a prime order bilinear group generator and $\mathcal{MRIBE}$ be the associated mergeable and revocable identity-based encryption scheme proposed above. Then for any adversary $\mathcal{A}$ attacking sMRID security (defined in Sect. 3.2) of $\mathcal{MRIBE}$ with N users in each system and N_S systems, and making q_p private key generation queries, q_r revocation queries, q_k key update generation queries, q_m merge parameter queries and q_{mp} merge private key generation queries, there exists an adversary $\mathcal{B}$ solving DBDH problem for $\mathcal{G}$ such that*

$$\mathsf{Adv}_{\mathcal{MRIBE},\mathcal{A},N,N_S}^{smrid-cpa}(k) \leq 4 \cdot \mathsf{Adv}_{\mathcal{G},\mathcal{B}}^{dbdh}(k)$$

Please refer to Appendix A for the detailed proof.

6   Conclusions

In this paper, we proposed a new variant for Revocalbe Identity Based Encryption. Our proposed scheme allows not only efficient revocation but also efficient merging of multiple systems. Compared with all previous RIBE schemes, our construction does not incur any additional cost. Moreover, the size of the user private key remains unchanged when multiple systems are merged and there is no secure channel required for the purpose of key update during the merging process.

A   Security Proof

Proof. The proof is similar to that of [1], except we meed to handle multiple systems and the mergeable algorithms. We construct an adversary $\mathcal{B}$ for the DBDH problem associated with $\mathcal{G}$. $\mathcal{B}$ gets $(k, \mathbb{G}, p, g, X, Y, Z, W)$ as input and it has to return a bit d. It is going to use $\mathcal{A}$. For answering oracles, we define the following four functions. For $i, j, l, r \in \mathbb{Z}_p, S = \{0, j\}$ define

$$F_1(g_2, h_1, h_2, h_3, i, l, r) \overset{\text{def}}{=} g_2^l H_{g_2,h_1,h_2,h_3}(i)^r, \quad F_2(r) \overset{\text{def}}{=} g^r,$$

$$F_3(g_1, g_2, i, j, l, r) \overset{\text{def}}{=} g_2^{l\Delta_{j,s}(i)} \left(g_1^{\frac{-f(i)}{i^2+u(i)}} \left(g_2^{i^2+u(i)} g^{f(i)} \right)^r \right)^{\Delta_{0,s}(i)},$$

$$F_4(g_1, g_2, i, r) \overset{\text{def}}{=} \left(g_1^{\frac{-1}{i^2+u(i)}} g^r \right)^{\Delta_{0,s}(i)}.$$

Setup: $\mathcal{B}$ receives the challenging message $(k, \mathbb{G}, p, g, X, Y, Z, W)$ and sets the system parameters as follows.

- $\mathcal{B}$ chooses the $N, N_S \in \mathbb{N}$ and sends the security parameter (k, N, N_S) to $\mathcal{A}$. $\mathcal{A}$ generates the challenging identity ω^*, the challenging time t^*, the subscript of challenging public key i^* and the *state* for some related information about (ω^*, t^*, i^*), then sends $(\omega^*, t^*, i^*, state)$ to $\mathcal{B}$.
- $\mathcal{B}$ chooses a random bit $b \leftarrow \{0,1\}$ and initializes the database $\mathcal{D}, \mathcal{D}_{SK}, \mathcal{D}_{MSK} \leftarrow \emptyset$, where $\mathcal{D}$ is used to record the historical information of the challenging identity ω^*, and $\mathcal{D}_{SK}, \mathcal{D}_{MSK}$ records information of the challenging identity ω^* to verify whether to abort.
- $\mathcal{B}$ simulates the system parameters for all N_S systems. $\mathcal{B}$ sets public parameter $pp = (\mathbb{G}, p, g)$ and randomly picks a value $i_r \leftarrow \{1, 2, ..., N_S\}$, where the challenging identity ω^* is initialized in the system with public key pk_{i_r}. Then, $\mathcal{B}$ updates the database $\mathcal{D} \leftarrow (\vec{pk}_{\omega^*}, \omega^*)$, where $\vec{pk}_{\omega^*} \leftarrow \vec{pk}_{\omega^*} \cup \{pk_{i_r}\}$. $\forall j \in \{1, 2, ..., N_S\}$ then:
  1. Randomly pick and store $r_j, r_{1,j}, r_{2,j} \leftarrow \mathbb{Z}_p^*$ in the system j and generate the parameters $g_{1,j}$ and $g_{2,j}$.

     $$g_{1,j} \leftarrow X^{r_{1,j}}, g_{2,j} \leftarrow Y^{r_{2,j}}.$$

  2. Pick random second-degree polynomials $f(x), u(x)$ with coefficients in $\mathbb{Z}_p$ s.t. $u(x) = -x^2$ for $x = \omega^*, t^*$, o.w. $u(x) \neq -x^2$. $\forall i = \{1, 2, 3\}$ then: set $h_{i,j} \leftarrow g_{2,j}^{u(i)} g^{f(i)}$.
  3. Set the public key $pk_j \leftarrow (g, g_{1,j}, g_{2,j}, h_{1,j}, h_{2,j}, h_{3,j})$.
- $\mathcal{B}$ sends the public parameter pp and public keys $\{pk_i\}_{i \in \{1,2,...,N_S\}}$ to $\mathcal{A}$.
- $\mathcal{B}$ simulates the revocation list and the binary tree. $\forall j = \{1, 2, ..., N_S\}$ then: let rl_j be an empty set and T_j be a binary tree with at least N leaf nodes. $\mathcal{B}$ picks a leaf node v^* from T_{i_r}, where the challenging identity ω^* is assigned to the leaf v^*, and chooses a random bit $rev \leftarrow \{0,1\}$, where 0 means ω^* is a non-revoked user, otherwise, he is a revoked user.

$\mathcal{O}_{\mathcal{SK}}(pk_i, \omega)$: $\mathcal{A}$ issues up to q_p private key generation queries. $\mathcal{B}$ responds to a query on message (pk_i, ω) as follows.

- If $\omega = \omega^*$, $\mathcal{B}$ simulates the private key $sk_{\omega,i}$ for the challenging identity ω^*.
    1. If $rev = 0$, set $\mathcal{D}_{\mathcal{SK}} \leftarrow \mathcal{D}_{\mathcal{SK}} \cup \{pk_i\}$ and abort if $\mathcal{A}$ is able to obtain the secret key sk_{ω^*, i^*} by checking the transactions in database $\mathcal{D}_{\mathcal{SK}}$ and $\mathcal{D}_{\mathcal{MSK}}$ in Fig. 1.
    2. Else set $v \leftarrow v^*$. $\forall x \in \mathsf{Path}(v)$ then:
        (a) Set $r_x \leftarrow \mathsf{F}_{r_i}(\omega^* \| x)$, where $msk_i = (a_i, r_i)$.
        (b) If $\nexists l_x$ then randomly choose $l_x \leftarrow \mathbb{Z}_p$ and store l_x in node x.
        (c) Set (D_x, d_x) and update private key $sk_{\omega^*,i} \leftarrow sk_{\omega^*,i} \cup (x, D_x, d_x)$.

$$D_x \leftarrow F_1(g_{2,i}, h_{1,i}, h_{2,i}, h_{3,i}, \omega^*, l_x, r_x), d_x \leftarrow F_2(r_x).$$

- If $\omega \neq \omega^*$, $\mathcal{B}$ simulates the private key $sk_{\omega,i}$ for the identity ω. $\forall x \in \mathsf{Path}(v)$ then:
    1. Set $r_x \leftarrow \mathsf{F}_{r_i}(\omega \| x)$, where $msk_i = (a_i, r_i)$.
    2. If $\nexists l_x$ then randomly choose $l_x \leftarrow \mathbb{Z}_p$ and store l_x in node x.
    3. If $rev = 0$, set (D_x, d_x) and update private key $sk_{\omega,i} \leftarrow sk_{\omega,i} \cup (x, D_x, d_x)$.

$$D_x \leftarrow F_3(g_{1,i}, g_{2,i}, \omega, t^*, l_x, r_x), d_x \leftarrow F_4(g_{1,i}, g_{2,i}, \omega, r_x).$$

    4. If $rev = 1$, simulate the private key $sk_{\omega,i}$ depends on the $\mathsf{Path}(v)$ and $\mathsf{Path}(v^*)$.
        (a) $\forall x \in (\mathsf{Path}(v) \setminus \mathsf{Path}(v^*))$ then: set (D_x, d_x) and update private key $sk_{\omega,i} \leftarrow sk_{\omega,i} \cup (x, D_x, d_x)$.

$$D_x \leftarrow F_3(g_{1,i}, g_{2,i}, \omega, t^*, l_x, r_x), d_x \leftarrow F_4(g_{1,i}, g_{2,i}, \omega, r_x).$$

        (b) $\forall x \in (\mathsf{Path}(v) \cap \mathsf{Path}(v^*))$ then: set (D_x, d_x) and update private key $sk_{\omega,i} \leftarrow sk_{\omega,i} \cup (x, D_x, d_x)$.

$$D_x \leftarrow F_3(g_{1,i}, g_{2,i}, \omega, \omega^*, l_x, r_x), d_x \leftarrow F_4(g_{1,i}, g_{2,i}, \omega, r_x).$$

- Return the private key $sk_{\omega,i} = \{(x, D_x, d_x)\}_{x \in \mathsf{Path}(v)}$.

$\mathcal{O}_{\mathcal{R}}(\omega, t)$: $\mathcal{A}$ issues up to q_r revocation queries. $\mathcal{B}$ responds to a query on message (ω, t) as follows. If $(\cdot, \omega) \in \mathcal{D}$, for all leaf nodes v associated with identity ω add (v, t) to revocation list $rl_i \leftarrow rl_i \cup (v, t)$, then return rl_i else return $\perp$.

$\mathcal{O}_{\mathcal{KU}}(pk_i, t)$: $\mathcal{A}$ issues up to q_k key update generation queries. $\mathcal{B}$ responds to a query on message (pk_i, t) as follows.

- If $t \neq t^*$, $\mathcal{B}$ simulates the key update $ku_{t,i}$ for the system i.
    1. If $rev = 0$, $\forall x \in \mathsf{KUNodes}(\mathsf{T}, rl, t)$ then: $r_x \leftarrow \mathbb{Z}_p^*$, set E_x and d_x and update $ku_{t,i} \leftarrow ku_{t,i} \cup (x, E_x, e_x)$.

$$E_x \leftarrow F_3(g_{1,i}, g_{2,i}, t, t^*, l_x, r_x), e_x \leftarrow F_4(g_{1,i}, g_{2,i}, t, r_x).$$

2. If $rev = 1$, simulate the key ku_t depends on the $\mathsf{Path}(v)$ and $\mathsf{Path}(v^*)$.
   (a) $\forall x \in (\mathsf{KUNodes}(\mathsf{T}, rl, t) \setminus \mathsf{Path}(v^*))$ then: $r_x \leftarrow \mathbb{Z}_p^*$, set E_x and d_x and update $ku_{t,i} \leftarrow ku_{t,i} \cup (x, E_x, e_x)$.

   $$E_x \leftarrow F_3(g_{1,i}, g_{2,i}, t, t^*, l_x, r_x), e_x \leftarrow F_4(g_{1,i}, g_{2,i}, t, r_x).$$

   (b) $\forall x \in (\mathsf{KNodes}(\mathsf{T}, rl, t) \cap \mathsf{Path}(v^*))$ then: $r_x \leftarrow \mathbb{Z}_p^*$, set E_x and d_x and update $ku_{t,i} \leftarrow ku_{t,i} \cup (x, E_x, e_x)$.

   $$E_x \leftarrow F_3(g_{1,i}, g_{2,i}, t, \omega^*, l_x, r_x), e_x \leftarrow F_4(g_{1,i}, g_{2,i}, t, r_x).$$

- If $t = t^*$, $\mathcal{B}$ simulates the key update $ku_{t,i}$ in the challenging time t^* for the system i.
  1. If $rev = 1$ and $\forall t \leq t^*$ we have that $(\omega^*, t) \notin rl_{i^*}$ then abort since challenging identity ω^* must be revoked when $rev = 1$.
  2. Else, $\forall x \in \mathsf{KUNodes}(\mathsf{T}, rl, t)$ then: $r_x \leftarrow \mathbb{Z}_p^*$, set E_x and d_x and update $ku_{t,i} \leftarrow ku_{t,i} \cup (x, E_x, e_x)$.

   $$E_x \leftarrow F_1(g_{2,i}, h_{1,i}, h_{2,i}, h_{3,i}, t^*, l_x, r_x), e_x \leftarrow F_2(r_x).$$

- Return the key update $ku_{t,i} = \{(x, E_x, e_x)\}_{x \in \mathsf{KUNodes}(\mathsf{T}, rl, t)}$.

$\mathcal{O}_{\mathcal{MP}}(pk_\alpha, pk_\beta)$: $\mathcal{A}$ issues up to q_m merge parameter generation queries. $\mathcal{B}$ responds to a query on message (pk_α, pk_β) by updating the revocation list rl_β, state st_β and the database $\mathcal{D}$ as follows.

- Update the revocation list and state $rl_\beta \leftarrow rl_\alpha \cup rl_\beta, st_\beta \leftarrow st_\beta \cup st_\alpha \setminus \mathsf{T}_\alpha$.
- If ω^* is involved in the system with pk_α, then updating the database $\mathcal{D}$. $\forall (\vec{pk}, \cdot) \in \mathcal{D}$ then set $len = |\vec{pk}|$, if $pk[len] = pk_\alpha$, $\vec{pk} \leftarrow \vec{pk} \cup pk_\beta$.
- Return the updated revocation list rl_β and state st_β.

$\mathcal{O}_{\mathcal{MSK}}(\omega, pk_\alpha, pk_\beta)$: $\mathcal{A}$ issues up to q_{mp} merge private key generation queries. $\mathcal{B}$ responds to a query on message $(\omega, pk_\alpha, pk_\beta)$.

- If $\omega = \omega^*$, $\mathcal{B}$ simulates the private key $sk_{\omega,\alpha,\beta}$ for challenging identity ω.
  1. If $rev = 0$, set $\mathcal{D}_{\mathcal{MSK}} \leftarrow \mathcal{D}_{\mathcal{MSK}} \cup \{(pk_\alpha, pk_\beta)\}$ and abort if $\mathcal{A}$ is able to obtain the secret key sk_{ω^*, i^*} by checking the transactions in database $\mathcal{D}_{\mathcal{SK}}$ and $\mathcal{D}_{\mathcal{MSK}}$ in Fig. 1.
  2. Else set $v \leftarrow v^*$. $\forall x \in \mathsf{Path}(v)$ then:
     (a) Set $r_{x,\alpha} \leftarrow G_{r_\alpha}(\omega \| x)$ and $r_{x,\beta} \leftarrow F_{r_\beta}(\omega \| x)$.
     (b) Set $(D_{x,\alpha,\beta}, d_{x,\alpha,\beta})$ and update private key $sk_{\omega,\alpha,\beta} \leftarrow sk_{\omega,\alpha,\beta} \cup (x, D_{x,\alpha,\beta}, d_{x,\alpha,\beta})$, where the union symbol is used to combine the secret keys since this algorithm will return secret keys belong to $\mathsf{Path}(v)$.

   $$D_{x,\alpha,\beta} = \frac{F_1(g_{2,\beta}, h_{1,\beta}, h_{2,\beta}, h_{3,\beta}, \omega, l_{x,\beta}, r_{x,\beta})}{F_1(g_{2,\alpha}, h_{1,\alpha}, h_{2,\alpha}, h_{3,\alpha}, \omega, l_{x,\alpha}, r_{x,\alpha})}, d_{x,\alpha,\beta} = \frac{F_2(r_{x,\beta})}{F_2(r_{x,\alpha})}.$$

– If $\omega \neq \omega^*$, $\mathcal{B}$ simulates the private key $sk_{\omega,\alpha,\beta}$ for the identity ω. $\forall x \in \mathsf{Path}(v)$ then:

1. Set $r_{x,\alpha} \leftarrow G_{r_\alpha}(\omega\|x)$ and $r_{x,\beta} \leftarrow G_{r_\beta}(\omega\|x)$.
2. If $rev = 0$, set (D_x, d_x) and update private key $sk_\omega \leftarrow sk_\omega \cup (x, D_x, d_x)$, where the union symbol is used for the same reason in previous section.

$$D_{x,\alpha,\beta} = \frac{F_3(g_{1,\beta}, g_{2,\beta}, \omega, t^*, l_{x,\beta}, r_{x,\beta})}{F_3(g_{1,\alpha}, g_{2,\alpha}, \omega, t^*, l_{x,\alpha}, r_{x,\alpha})}, d_{x,\alpha,\beta} = \frac{F_4(g_{1,\beta}, g_{2,\beta}, \omega, r_{x,\beta})}{F_4(g_{1,\alpha}, g_{2,\alpha}, \omega, r_{x,\alpha})}.$$

3. If $rev = 1$, simulate the private key sk_ω depends on the $\mathsf{Path}(v)$ and $\mathsf{Path}(v^*)$.

   (a) $\forall x \in (\mathsf{Path}(v) \setminus \mathsf{Path}(v^*))$ then: set (D_x, d_x) and update private key $sk_\omega \leftarrow sk_\omega \cup (x, D_x, d_x)$.

$$D_{x,\alpha,\beta} = \frac{F_3(g_{1,\beta}, g_{2,\beta}, \omega, t^*, l_{x,\beta}, r_{x,\beta})}{F_3(g_{1,\alpha}, g_{2,\alpha}, \omega, t^*, l_{x,\alpha}, r_{x,\alpha})}, d_{x,\alpha,\beta} = \frac{F_4(g_{1,\beta}, g_{2,\beta}, \omega, r_{x,\beta})}{F_4(g_{1,\alpha}, g_{2,\alpha}, \omega, r_{x,\alpha})}.$$

   (b) $\forall x \in (\mathsf{Path}(v) \cap \mathsf{Path}(v^*))$ then: set (D_x, d_x) and update private key $sk_\omega \leftarrow sk_\omega \cup (x, D_x, d_x)$.

$$D_{x,\alpha,\beta} = \frac{F_3(g_{1,\beta}, g_{2,\beta}, \omega, \omega^*, l_{x,\beta}, r_{x,\beta})}{F_3(g_{1,\alpha}, g_{2,\alpha}, \omega, \omega^*, l_{x,\alpha}, r_{x,\alpha})}, d_{x,\alpha,\beta} = \frac{F_4(g_{1,\beta}, g_{2,\beta}, \omega, r_{x,\beta})}{F_4(g_{1,\alpha}, g_{2,\alpha}, \omega, r_{x,\alpha})}.$$

4. Return the private key $sk_{\omega,\alpha,\beta} = \{(x, D_{x,\alpha,\beta}, d_{x,\alpha,\beta})\}_{x \in \mathsf{Path}(v)}$.

Output: $\mathcal{A}$ outputs two message m_0 and m_1. $\mathcal{B}$ picks a random bit $b \leftarrow \{0,1\}$ and generates the challenging ciphertext $c^* = (c_1^*, c_2^*, c_{\omega^*}, c_{t^*})$ and then sends c^* to $\mathcal{A}$. $\mathcal{A}$ outputs a bit d. If $b = d$, $\mathcal{B}$ outputs 1 else output 0.

$$c_1^* = m_b \cdot W^{r_{1,\omega^*} \cdot r_{2,\omega^*}}, c_2^* = Z, c_{\omega^*} = Z^{f(\omega^*)}, c_{t^*} = Z^{f(t^*)}.$$

If any oracles abort, $\mathcal{B}$ outputs 1.

A.1   Analysis

Let $\mathsf{sreal}, \mathsf{srand}$ denote the events that none of the oracles abort in $\mathsf{Exp}_{\mathcal{G},\mathcal{B}}^{dbdh-real}(k)$, $\mathsf{Exp}_{\mathcal{G},\mathcal{B}}^{dbdh-rand}(k)$ respectively. Then

$$\Pr[\mathsf{sreal}] = \Pr[\mathsf{srand}] \geq 1/2.$$

The probability that $\mathcal{O}_{\mathcal{SK}}(pk_i, \omega)$, $\mathcal{O}_{\mathcal{MSK}}(\omega, pk_\alpha, pk_\beta)$ and $\mathcal{O}_{\mathcal{KU}}(pk_i, t)$ oracles abort depends on the bit rev which are chosen independently from whether $\mathcal{B}$ is in $\mathsf{Exp}_{\mathcal{G},\mathcal{B}}^{dbdh-real}(k)$ or $\mathsf{Exp}_{\mathcal{G},\mathcal{B}}^{dbdh-rand}(k)$. So, $\Pr[\mathsf{sreal}] = \Pr[\mathsf{srand}]$.

$\mathcal{O}_{\mathcal{SK}}(pk_i, \omega)$ and $\mathcal{O}_{\mathcal{MSK}}(\cdot, \cdot, \omega^*)$ oracles can be queried on ω^* without constrain only if $\mathcal{O}_{\mathcal{R}}(\omega, t)$ oracle was queried on (ω^*, t) for any $t \leq t^*$. Thus, we have

$$\Pr[\omega = \omega^*] \leq \Pr[(\omega^*, t) \in rl_{\omega^*}, \forall t \leq t^*]$$
$$\Rightarrow 1 - \Pr[\omega = \omega^*] \geq \Pr[(\omega^*, t) \notin rl_{\omega^*}, \forall t \leq t^*]$$
$$\Rightarrow 1 - \Pr[\omega = \omega^*] \geq \Pr[(t = t^*) \wedge (\omega^*, t) \notin rl_{\omega^*}, \forall t \leq t^*]$$

We see that $\mathcal{O}_{\mathcal{SK}}(pk_i, \omega)$ oracles abort if $\omega = \omega^*$ and $\mathcal{O}_{\mathcal{KU}}(t)$ oracle aborts if $rev = 1, t = t^*$ and $\exists t \leq t^*$ $(\omega^*, t) \notin rl_{\omega^*}$. Thus,

$$\Pr[\overline{\mathsf{sreal}}] = \Pr[(rev = 0) \wedge (\omega = \omega^*)]$$
$$+ \Pr[(rev = 1) \wedge (t = t^*) \wedge ((\omega^*, t) \notin rl_{\omega^*}, \forall t \leq t^*)]$$
$$= \Pr[rev = 0] \cdot \Pr[\omega = \omega^*]$$
$$+ \Pr[rev = 1] \cdot \Pr[(t = t^*) \wedge ((\omega^*, t) \notin rl_{\omega^*}, \forall t \leq t^*)]$$
$$\leq 1/2 \cdot \Pr[\omega = \omega^*] + \frac{1}{2}(1 - \Pr[\omega = \omega^*]) \leq 1/2$$

$\mathcal{B}$ simulates the exact experiment $\mathsf{Exp}^{smrid-cpa}_{\mathcal{MRIBE}, \mathcal{A}, N, N_S}(k)$ for $\mathcal{A}$ when $\mathcal{B}$ is in $\mathsf{Exp}^{dbdh-real}_{\mathcal{G}, \mathcal{B}}(k)$ and none of the oracles abort. So,

$$\Pr\left[\mathsf{Exp}^{dbdh-real}_{\mathcal{G}, \mathcal{B}}(k) = 1 | \mathsf{sreal}\right] \geq \Pr\left[\mathsf{Exp}^{smrid-cpa}_{\mathcal{MRIBE}, \mathcal{A}, N, N_S}(k) = 1\right].$$

When $\mathcal{B}$ is $\mathsf{Exp}^{dbdh-rand}_{\mathcal{G}, \mathcal{B}}(k)$ and none of the oracles abort then as explained earlier bit b is information-theoretically hidden from $\mathcal{A}$. So,

$$\Pr\left[\mathsf{Exp}^{dbdh-rand}_{\mathcal{G}, \mathcal{B}}(k) = 1 | \mathsf{srand}\right] \leq 1/2.$$

Also, since $\mathcal{B}$ outputs 1 when either of the oracles aborts, so

$$\Pr\left[\mathsf{Exp}^{dbdh-real}_{\mathcal{G}, \mathcal{B}}(k) = 1 | \overline{\mathsf{sreal}}\right] = 1,$$
$$\Pr\left[\mathsf{Exp}^{dbdh-rand}_{\mathcal{G}, \mathcal{B}}(k) = 1 | \overline{\mathsf{srand}}\right] = 1.$$

Thus,

$$\mathsf{Adv}^{dbdh}_{\mathcal{G}, \mathcal{B}}(k) = \Pr\left[\mathsf{Exp}^{dbdh-real}_{\mathcal{G}, \mathcal{B}}(k) = 1\right] - \Pr\left[\mathsf{Exp}^{dbdh-rand}_{\mathcal{G}, \mathcal{B}}(k) = 1\right]$$
$$\geq 1/2 \cdot \left(\Pr\left[\mathsf{Exp}^{dbdh-real}_{\mathcal{G}, \mathcal{B}}(k) = 1 | \mathsf{sreal}\right] - \frac{1}{2}\right)$$
$$\geq 1/2 \cdot \frac{1}{2} \cdot \left(2 \cdot \Pr\left[\mathsf{Exp}^{dbdh-real}_{\mathcal{G}, \mathcal{B}}(k) = 1 | \mathsf{sreal}\right] - 1\right)$$
$$\geq 1/2 \cdot \mathsf{Adv}^{smrid-cpa}_{\mathcal{MRIBE}, \mathcal{A}, N, N_S}(k).$$

References

1. Boldyreva, A., Goyal, V., Kumar, V.: Identity-based encryption with efficient revocation. In: Ning, P., Syverson, P.F., Jha, S. (eds.) CCS, pp. 417–426. ACM (2008)
2. Boneh, D., Boyen, X.: Efficient selective-ID secure identity-based encryption without random oracles. In: Cachin, C., Camenisch, J.L. (eds.) EUROCRYPT 2004. LNCS, vol. 3027, pp. 223–238. Springer, Heidelberg (2004). doi:10.1007/978-3-540-24676-3_14
3. Boneh, D., Franklin, M.: Identity-based encryption from the Weil pairing. In: Kilian, J. (ed.) CRYPTO 2001. LNCS, vol. 2139, pp. 213–229. Springer, Heidelberg (2001). doi:10.1007/3-540-44647-8_13
4. Dodis, Y., Fazio, N.: Public key broadcast encryption for stateless receivers. In: Feigenbaum, J. (ed.) DRM 2002. LNCS, vol. 2696, pp. 61–80. Springer, Heidelberg (2003). doi:10.1007/978-3-540-44993-5_5
5. Gentry, C.: Practical identity-based encryption without random oracles. In: Vaudenay, S. (ed.) EUROCRYPT 2006. LNCS, vol. 4004, pp. 445–464. Springer, Heidelberg (2006). doi:10.1007/11761679_27
6. Goldreich, O., Goldwasser, S., Micali, S.: How to construct random functions (extended abstract). In: FOCS, pp. 464–479. IEEE (1984)
7. Halevy, D., Shamir, A.: The LSD broadcast encryption scheme. In: Yung, M. (ed.) CRYPTO 2002. LNCS, vol. 2442, pp. 47–60. Springer, Heidelberg (2002). doi:10.1007/3-540-45708-9_4
8. Hanaoka, Y., Hanaoka, G., Shikata, J., Imai, H.: Identity-based hierarchical strongly key-insulated encryption and its application. In: Roy, B. (ed.) ASIACRYPT 2005. LNCS, vol. 3788, pp. 495–514. Springer, Heidelberg (2005). doi:10.1007/11593447_27
9. Lee, K., Lee, D.H., Park, J.H.: Efficient revocable identity-based encryption via subset difference methods. IACR, 2014:132 (2014)
10. Liang, K., Liu, J.K., Wong, D.S., Susilo, W.: An efficient cloud-based revocable identity-based proxy re-encryption scheme for public clouds data sharing. In: Kutyłowski, M., Vaidya, J. (eds.) ESORICS 2014. LNCS, vol. 8712, pp. 257–272. Springer, Cham (2014). doi:10.1007/978-3-319-11203-9_15
11. Libert, B., Vergnaud, D.: Adaptive-ID secure revocable identity-based encryption. In: Fischlin, M. (ed.) CT-RSA 2009. LNCS, vol. 5473, pp. 1–15. Springer, Heidelberg (2009). doi:10.1007/978-3-642-00862-7_1
12. Naor, D., Naor, M., Lotspiech, J.: Revocation and tracing schemes for stateless receivers. In: Kilian, J. (ed.) CRYPTO 2001. LNCS, vol. 2139, pp. 41–62. Springer, Heidelberg (2001). doi:10.1007/3-540-44647-8_3
13. Sahai, A., Waters, B.: Fuzzy identity-based encryption. In: Cramer, R. (ed.) EUROCRYPT 2005. LNCS, vol. 3494, pp. 457–473. Springer, Heidelberg (2005). doi:10.1007/11426639_27
14. Seo, J.H., Emura, K.: Efficient delegation of key generation and revocation functionalities in identity-based encryption. In: Dawson, E. (ed.) CT-RSA 2013. LNCS, vol. 7779, pp. 343–358. Springer, Heidelberg (2013). doi:10.1007/978-3-642-36095-4_22
15. Seo, J.H., Emura, K.: Revocable identity-based encryption revisited: security model and construction. In: Kurosawa, K., Hanaoka, G. (eds.) PKC 2013. LNCS, vol. 7778, pp. 216–234. Springer, Heidelberg (2013). doi:10.1007/978-3-642-36362-7_14
16. Seo, J.H., Emura, K.: Adaptive-ID secure revocable hierarchical identity-based encryption. In: Tanaka, K., Suga, Y. (eds.) IWSEC 2015. LNCS, vol. 9241, pp. 21–38. Springer, Cham (2015). doi:10.1007/978-3-319-22425-1_2

17. Seo, J.H., Emura, K.: Revocable hierarchical identity-based encryption: history-free update, security against insiders, and short ciphertexts. In: Nyberg, K. (ed.) CT-RSA 2015. LNCS, vol. 9048, pp. 106–123. Springer, Cham (2015). doi:10.1007/978-3-319-16715-2_6

18. Shamir, A.: How to share a secret. ACM **22**(11), 612–613 (1979)

19. Shamir, A.: Identity-based cryptosystems and signature schemes. In: Blakley, G.R., Chaum, D. (eds.) CRYPTO 1984. LNCS, vol. 196, pp. 47–53. Springer, Heidelberg (1985). doi:10.1007/3-540-39568-7_5

20. Waters, B.: Efficient identity-based encryption without random oracles. In: Cramer, R. (ed.) EUROCRYPT 2005. LNCS, vol. 3494, pp. 114–127. Springer, Heidelberg (2005). doi:10.1007/11426639_7

21. Yang, Y., Liu, J.K., Liang, K., Choo, K.-K.R., Zhou, J.: Extended proxy-assisted approach: achieving revocable fine-grained encryption of cloud data. In: Pernul, G., Ryan, P.Y.A., Weippl, E. (eds.) ESORICS 2015. LNCS, vol. 9327, pp. 146–166. Springer, Cham (2015). doi:10.1007/978-3-319-24177-7_8

ID-Based Encryption with Equality Test Against Insider Attack

Tong Wu[1(✉)], Sha Ma[1,2], Yi Mu[1], and Shengke Zeng[1,3]

[1] School of Computing and Information Technology, Institute of Cybersecurity
and Cryptology, University of Wollongong, Wollongong, NSW, Australia
{tw225,sma,ymu,shengke}@uow.edu.au
[2] College of Mathematics and Informatics, South China Agricultural University,
Guangzhou 510640, Guangdong, China
[3] School of Computer and Software Engineering,
Xihua University, Chengdu 610039, China

Abstract. Testing if two ciphertexts contain the same plaintext is an
interesting cryptographic primitive. It is usually referred to as equality
test of encrypted data or equality test. One of attractive applications
of equality test is for encrypted database systems, where the database
server hosts the encrypted databases and users can query if the plaintext
embedded in a ciphertext on a database is equal to that in the queried
ciphertext without decryption. Although it is not hard to achieve with
the pairing-based cryptography, the security against the insider attack
(by the database server) is a challenging task. In this paper, we propose
a novel equality test scheme aiming to solve the problem. Our scheme
adopts the identity-based cryptography. We prove the security of our
scheme in the random oracle model.

Keywords: ID-Based encryption · Equality test · Insider attack

1 Introduction

The probabilistic public key encryption with equality test (PKEET) [13] is an
interesting technique with wide applications such as in outsourced database systems, which host and manage encrypted data for clients. The merit of the equality test scheme is that one can check whether two ciphertexts contain the same
plaintext without decrypting them.

In the original equality test scheme [13], outsourced database servers are
usually considered to be semi-trusted because of its curiosity on user data. We
call it an "Honest but Curious" (HBC) server. It is practical for the server
to obtain the illegal profit from peddling users' private data by simple brute
force attacks on the encrypted message. Our scheme should resist this kind of
adversaries, even we assume that the adversary has access to all ciphertexts and
can test their equality, which is called "insider attack" [10].

An HBC server (the insider), who runs the test algorithm correctly and
continuously, can perform any polynomial time computation and then obtain

© Springer International Publishing AG 2017
J. Pieprzyk and S. Suriadi (Eds.): ACISP 2017, Part I, LNCS 10342, pp. 168–183, 2017.
DOI: 10.1007/978-3-319-60055-0_9

the information beyond its own. The insider attack on an equality test scheme Ω runs as follows:

Suppose that the adversary has been given the public key and the message space is $\mathcal{M} = \{m_1, m_2, ..., m_{|\mathcal{M}|}\}$. The goal of the adversary is to find out the underlying message of the ciphertext C_{m^*}, where $m^* \in \mathcal{M}$. Run an attack with a binary test function $\mathsf{Test}(m_i, m_j)$:

1: Let $i = 1$;
2: Run Ω to generate the ciphertext of the message m_i as C_{m_i};
3: If $\mathsf{Test}(C_{m_i}, C_{m^*}) = \text{True}$, then return m_i as the result;
4: If $i < |\mathcal{M}|$, set $i = i + 1$ and go to 2, otherwise output $\perp$.

The correctness of the above attack is guaranteed by the consistency of the equality test scheme. In this paper, we propose a novel scheme which resists such attacks.

1.1 Related Work

Boneh et al. first proposed a public key encryption with keyword search scheme (PEKS) in the random oracle model [1]. When a user conducts a search, he can generate a trapdoor with a keyword and his private key. Taking the generated trapdoor and a ciphertext, the test algorithm will output "accept" if they contain the same keyword; otherwise, "reject". Their work provides a solution to the equality test on encrypted keywords in public key encryption.

To provide a general equality test scheme, Yang et al. proposed the first public key encryption with equality test (PKEET) [13]. In PKEET, given two tags T_i and T_j on ciphertexts C_i and C_j generated with PK_i and PK_j corresponding to message M_i and M_j, respectively, there is a function $\mathsf{Test}(\cdot, \cdot)$, which outputs 1 iff $M_i = M_j$. Their work achieves the security against the One-way Chosen Ciphertext Attack (OW-CCA). There are some extensions of PKEET which offer the fine or flexible grain authorization and stronger security [5,7–9,11,12]. To achieve the stronger security, the authorization mechanism is adopted to these PKEET schemes. Some of them utilize trapdoors generated from private keys which are used to the authorization process. As an instance, Ma et al. in [8], proposed a PKEET with the flexible authorization according to four scenarios. In [9], Ma et al. provided a solution to the PKEET in multi-user setting by delegating the equality test to a fully trusted proxy. Later, Ma [7] proposed an identity-based PKEET (IBEET). These works improved the security of PKEET to IND-CCA security, while private keys are kept secret. However, none of their works can resist the insider attack.

Mayer et al. [10] proposed a verifiable private equality test (VPET) for multi-party computation. The protocol resists attacks launched by HBC entities and active malicious entities who can behave active malicious actions. However, it requires that all users are online during testing and generate a proof for each equality test. It is therefore impractical for the cloud storage management and outsourced database services, which require users to be offline. Constructions presented in [2,6] also provide solutions to insider attacks for the PEKS schemes, but not for the general equality test. Chen et al. in [2] proposed a PEKS scheme based on the dual-server framework. Peng et al. [6] proposed a PEKS scheme to prevent the trapdoor generated globally by containing identity set in trapdoors by keeping this set secret, so that the insider attack is eliminated.

Above all, how to achieve a PKEET scheme against insider attacks is still an open problem.

1.2 Our Contribution

The probabilistic public key encryption with equality test was proposed by Yang et al. [13]. However, their scheme is vulnerable to the above insider attack. Since the ciphertext can be generated publicly, the HBC server can test the embedded message in the target ciphertext on its guess. To address this problem, we propose an efficient identity-based equality test scheme with resistance against the insider attack as our contributions. We define a novel security model for the confidentiality of IBEET which allows the adversary to conduct the equality test on all ciphertexts but can not generate ciphertexts. We refer it to as Weak-IND-ID-CCA (W-IND-ID-CCA). Nevertheless, it is stronger than security models for previous works under the same attack.

1.3 Organization

The rest of the paper is organized as follows. In Sect. 2, we provide some preliminaries for our construction. In Sect. 3, we formulate the notion of IBEET-IA. In Sect. 4, we present the construction of IBEET-IA and prove its security in Sect. 5. In Sect. 6, we construct a secure outsourced database application based on IBEET-IA and present the experimental results. In Sect. 7, we conclude our paper.

2 Preliminaries

Before describing our scheme, we introduce some cryptographic preliminaries used in our scheme.

Definition 1 (Bilinear Group [4]). $\mathbb{G}_1$, $\mathbb{G}_2$ and $\mathbb{G}_T$ constitute a bilinear group if there exists a bilinear map $e : \mathbb{G}_1 \times \mathbb{G}_2 \to \mathbb{G}_T$, where $|\mathbb{G}_1| = |\mathbb{G}_2| = |\mathbb{G}_T| = p$.

The bilinear pairing is an operation conducted on bilinear groups. Informally, two elements in such group are linearly related to the pairing result. The formal description of the bilinear paring is given as follows.

Bilinear Pairing. Suppose that $\mathbb{G}_1$, $\mathbb{G}_2$ and $\mathbb{G}_T$ are three cyclic groups with the same prime order p. Suppose that g and h are generators of $\mathbb{G}_1$ and $\mathbb{G}_2$, respectively. A bilinear pairing $e : \mathbb{G}_1 \times \mathbb{G}_2 \to \mathbb{G}_T$ holds properties as follows:

1. Bilinearity: For any $x \in \mathbb{G}_1$, $y \in \mathbb{G}_2$ and $a, b \in \mathbb{Z}_p^*$, $e(x^a, y^b) = e(x, y)^{ab}$.
2. Non-degeneration: $e(g, h) \neq 1_{\mathbb{G}_T}$, where $1_{\mathbb{G}_T}$ is the generator of $\mathbb{G}_T$.
3. Computability: There exists an efficient algorithm to compute $e(x, y)$, for any $x \in \mathbb{G}_1$ and $y \in \mathbb{G}_2$.

We say that a pairing is symmetric if $\mathbb{G}_1 = \mathbb{G}_2$. Our construction is built on such groups.

2.1 Bilinear Diffie-Hellman Problem (BDHP)

Definition 2 (Bilinear Diffie-Hellman Problem (BDHP)). *Let $\mathbb{G}_1$, $\mathbb{G}_2$ be two groups of prime order p. Let $e : \mathbb{G}_1 \times \mathbb{G}_1 \to \mathbb{G}_2$ be a bilinear map and let g be a generator of $\mathbb{G}_1$. The BDH problem in $(\mathbb{G}_1, \mathbb{G}_2, e)$ is as follows: Given (g, g^a, g^b, g^c) for some $a, b, c \in \mathbb{Z}_p^*$ compute $e(g, g)^{abc} \in \mathbb{G}_2$. An polynomial algorithm $\mathcal{A}$ has advantage $\epsilon(\cdot)$ in solving BDH in $(\mathbb{G}_1, \mathbb{G}_2, e)$ if*

$$\Pr[\mathcal{A}(g, g^a, g^b, g^c) = e(g, g)^{abc}] \leq \epsilon(\lambda),$$

where the probability is over the random choice of (a, b, c) in $\mathbb{Z}_p^*$, the random choice of $g \in \mathbb{G}_1$, and the random bits of $\mathcal{A}$.

We say that the BDH assumption holds if for any randomized polynomial time (in λ for some sufficiently large λ) algorithm $\mathcal{A}$ solves the BDH problem with the negligible advantage $\epsilon(\lambda)$. If there exists a bilinear pairing e, then the DDHP is easy to solve in G_1, but the CDHP are still hard in G_1.

3 Definitions

In this section, we give formal definitions of our scheme and security model. Our scheme achieves chosen ciphertext security (i.e. W-IND-ID-CCA) under the defined security model.

3.1 ID-Based Encryption with Equality Test Against Insider Attack

We propose an ID-based encryption with equality test. The scheme Ω consists of a set of algorithms: $\Omega = (\mathsf{Setup}, \mathsf{Extract}, \mathsf{Enc}, \mathsf{Test}, \mathsf{Dec})$.

- $\mathsf{Setup}(1^\lambda)$: It takes the secure parameter λ and outputs the system public parameters pp, the master secret key msk and the master token key mtk.
- $\mathsf{Extract}(\mathsf{ID}, msk, mtk)$: It takes (ID, msk, mtk) and pp and outputs the private key d_{ID} and token $\mathsf{tok}_{\mathsf{ID}}$.
- $\mathsf{Enc}(m, \mathsf{ID}, P_{pub}, \mathsf{tok}_{\mathsf{ID}})$: It takes $(m, \mathsf{ID}, \mathsf{tok}_{\mathsf{ID}}, P_{pub})$ and outputs the ciphertext $C = (c_1, c_2, c_3, c_4)$.

- Test(C_A, C_B): It takes ciphertexts C_A and C_B produced by user A and user B, respectively. It outputs 1 if messages associated with C_A and C_B are equal. Otherwise, it outputs 0.
- Dec(C, d_{ID}, $\mathsf{tok}_{\mathsf{ID}}$): It takes the ciphertext C, d_{ID} and $\mathsf{tok}_{\mathsf{ID}}$ and outputs the message m, if C is a valid ciphertext under ID. Otherwise, it outputs $\bot$.

Note: pp refers to public parameters and hash functions used in our scheme.

3.2   Security Models

Definition 3 (Weak-IND-ID-CCA (W-IND-ID-CCA)). *Let* $\Omega = (\mathsf{Setup}, \mathsf{Extract}, \mathsf{Enc}, \mathsf{Test}, \mathsf{Dec})$ *be the scheme and* $\mathcal{A}$ *be a polynomial time adversary.*

- **Setup:** The challenger runs the Setup algorithm to initialize the system and obtains P_{pub}, msk and mtk. It gives P_{pub} to the adversary $\mathcal{A}$.
- **Phase 1:** The adversary issues queries q_1, q_2, $\cdots$, q_m where q_i is one of:
  - H_1 Query (ID_i). The challenger responds by running $H_1(\cdot)$ to generate g_{ID_i}. It sends g_{ID_i} to the adversary.
  - Extract Query (ID_i). The challenger responds by running Extract algorithm to generate the private key d_{ID_i} corresponding to the public key ID_i. It sends d_{ID_i} to the adversary.
  - H_2 Query ($\mathbb{G}_1^3 \times \mathbb{G}_2$). The challenger responds by running $H_2(\cdot)$ to generate the corresponding hash value. It sends the hash value to the adversary.
  - Encryption Query (m_i, ID_i). The challenger responds by running Enc to generate the ciphertext C_i corresponding to (m_i, ID_i). It sends the ciphertext C_i to the adversary.
  - Decryption Query (C_i, ID_i). The challenger responds by running Extract algorithm to generate d_{ID_i} corresponding to ID_i. It then runs Dec to decrypt the ciphertext C_i using d_{ID_i}. It sends the resulting plaintext to the adversary.
- **Challenge:** Once $\mathcal{A}$ decides the Phase 1 is over, it sends two equal-length messages m_0, m_1 and ID^* to be challenged to the challenger, where both m_0, m_1 are not issued in the Encryption Query and ID^* is not issued in the Extract Query in the Phase 1. The challenger randomly picks $b \in \{0,1\}$, and responds with $C^* \leftarrow \mathsf{Enc}(m_b, \mathsf{ID}^*, P_{pub}, \mathsf{tok}_{\mathsf{ID}^*})$.
- **Phase 2:** The adversary issues queries q_{m+1}, q_{m+2}, $\cdots$, q_n where q_i is one of:
  - H_1 Query (ID_i). The challenger responds as in Phase 1.
  - Extract Query (ID_i) where $\mathsf{ID}_i \neq \mathsf{ID}^*$. The challenger responds as in Phase 1.
  - H_2 Query ($\mathbb{G}_1^3 \times \mathbb{G}_2$). The challenger responds as in Phase 1.
  - Encryption Query (m_i, ID_i) where $m_i \notin \{m_0, m_1\}$. The challenger responds as in Phase 1.
  - Decryption Query (C_i, ID_i) where (C_i, ID_i) $\neq$ (C^*, ID^*). The challenger responds as in Phase 1.
- **Output:** Finally, $\mathcal{A}$ gives a guess b' on b. If $b' = b$, we say $\mathcal{A}$ wins the game.

We define $\mathcal{A}$'s advantage on breaking the scheme as

$$\mathsf{Adv}_{\Omega,\mathcal{A}(H_1,H_2,\mathsf{Extract},\mathsf{Enc},\mathsf{Dec})}^{\text{W-IND-ID-CCA}} = \left| \Pr[b' = b] - \frac{1}{2} \right| = \epsilon(\lambda),$$

where $\epsilon(\lambda)$ is a polynomial of λ. Ω is W-IND-ID-CCA secure if $\epsilon(\lambda)$ is a negligible function. In the W-IND-ID-CCA model, the adversary has access to ciphertexts without any valid tok.

4 The Proposed Scheme

4.1 ID-Based Encryption with Equality Test Against Insider Attack

Our scheme aims to provide the service for designated senders. That is, the receiver and its designated senders form a group of users. $\mathsf{tok_{ID}}$ denotes a secret information shared among group members. The server and other users can only conduct the equality test.

Our protocol consists of the following five algorithms:

- Setup(1^λ): Initially, the system takes a security parameter λ and returns public system parameters pp, the master secret key msk and the master token key mtk.
  1. The system generates two multiplicative groups $\mathbb{G}_1$ and $\mathbb{G}_2$ with the same prime order p of λ-length bits and a bilinear map $e : \mathbb{G}_1 \times \mathbb{G}_1 \to \mathbb{G}_2$. The system selects an arbitrary generator $g \in \mathbb{G}_1$.
  2. The system selects $\alpha, \beta \xleftarrow{\$} \mathbb{Z}_p^*$ as msk and mtk, respectively, and sets $P_{pub} = g^\alpha$.
  3. The system chooses three hash functions:

  $$H : \{0,1\}^t \to \mathbb{Z}_p^*, \quad H_1 : \{0,1\}^* \to \mathbb{G}_1, \quad H_2 : \mathbb{G}_1^3 \times \mathbb{G}_2 \to \{0,1\}^{t+l},$$

  where l is the length of random numbers and t is the length of messages. It publishes pp $= \{\lambda, p, t, l, g, P_{pub}, e, H, H_1, H_2\}$.
- Extract(ID, msk, mtk): PKG generates d_{ID} and $\mathsf{tok_{ID}}$ for each user's ID.

  $$g_{\mathsf{ID}} = H_1(\mathsf{ID}), \quad d_{\mathsf{ID}} = g_{\mathsf{ID}}^\alpha, \quad \mathsf{tok_{ID}} = g_{\mathsf{ID}}^\beta,$$

  where d_{ID} and $\mathsf{tok_{ID}}$ are distributed via a secure channel.
- Enc(m, ID, P_{pub}, $\mathsf{tok_{ID}}$): To encrypt m, it selects two random numbers $r_1, r_2 \xleftarrow{\$} \mathbb{Z}_p^*$, with $|r_1| = l$. Then it computes

  $$c_1 = \mathsf{tok_{ID}}^{r_1 H(m)}, \quad c_2 = g_{\mathsf{ID}}^{r_1}, \quad c_3 = g^{r_2},$$

  $$c_4 = (m \parallel r_1) \oplus H_2(c_1 \parallel c_2 \parallel c_3 \parallel e(P_{pub}, g_{\mathsf{ID}})^{r_2}).$$

  Finally, it returns $C = (c_1, c_2, c_3, c_4)$.

- Test(C_A, C_B): Suppose that

$$C_A \leftarrow \text{Enc}(m_A, \text{ID}_A, P_{pub}, \text{tok}_{\text{ID}_A})$$

and

$$C_B \leftarrow \text{Enc}(m_B, \text{ID}_B, P_{pub}, \text{tok}_{\text{ID}_B})$$

are generated by user A and user B, respectively. With $C_A = (c_{A,1}, c_{A,2}, c_{A,3}, c_{A,4})$ and $C_B = (c_{B,1}, c_{B,2}, c_{B,3}, c_{B,4})$, the test algorithm on C_A and C_B runs as follows:

$$e(c_{A,1}, c_{B,2}) = e(c_{B,1}, c_{A,2}). \tag{1}$$

If the equation holds, it explains the equality between m_A and m_B, then outputs 1. Otherwise, outputs 0.
- Dec$(C, d_{\text{ID}}, \text{tok}_{\text{ID}})$: To decrypt the ciphertext C with d_{ID} and tok_{ID}, it computes:

$$m \parallel r_1 = c_4 \oplus H_2(c_1 \parallel c_2 \parallel c_3 \parallel e(c_3, d_{\text{ID}})).$$

If

$$c_1 = \text{tok}_{\text{ID}}^{r_1 H(m)} \wedge c_2 = g_{\text{ID}}^{r_1},$$

it returns m. Otherwise, $\perp$.

4.2   Correctness

We say that Ω has the ciphertext comparability with error μ, for some function $\mu(\cdot)$. For instance, we run the equality test on $C_A \leftarrow \text{Enc}(m_A, \text{ID}_A, P_{pub}, \text{tok}_{\text{ID}_A})$, $C_B \leftarrow \text{Enc}(m_B, \text{ID}_B, P_{pub}, \text{tok}_{\text{ID}_B})$ generated by user A and user B, respectively.

$$C_A = (c_{A,1}, c_{A,2}, c_{A,3}, c_{A,4}), \quad C_B = (c_{B,1}, c_{B,2}, c_{B,3}, c_{B,4})$$

We compute the left hand side (L) and the right hand side (R) of Eq. (1) in the Test algorithm, respectively. We analyze it in two cases: $m_A = m_B$ and $m_A \neq m_B$.

$$
\begin{aligned}
L &:= e(c_{A,1}, c_{B,2}) & R &:= e(c_{B,1}, c_{A,2}) \\
&= e(\text{tok}_{\text{ID}_A}^{r_{A,1} H(m_A)}, g_{\text{ID}_B}^{r_{B,1}}) & &= e(\text{tok}_{\text{ID}_B}^{r_{B,1} H(m_B)}, g_{\text{ID}_A}^{r_{A,1}}) \\
&= e(g_{\text{ID}_A}^{\beta r_{A,1} H(m_A)}, g_{\text{ID}_B}^{r_{B,1}}) & &= e(g_{\text{ID}_B}^{\beta r_{B,1} H(m_B)}, g_{\text{ID}_A}^{r_{A,1}}) \\
&= e(g_{\text{ID}_A}, g_{\text{ID}_B})^{\beta r_{A,1} r_{B,1} H(m_A)} & &= e(g_{\text{ID}_B}, g_{\text{ID}_A})^{\beta r_{A,1} r_{B,1} H(m_B)}
\end{aligned}
$$

Case 1: If $m_A = m_B$, the equation holds with the probability of 1;
Case 2: If $m_A \neq m_B$, the equation holds when the collision occurs in hash function $H(m)$, that is $H(m_A) = H(m_B)$ while $m_A \neq m_B$. We define $H(m)$ is a collision resistant hash function. $\Pr[H(m_A) = H(m_B)|m_A \neq m_B]$ is a negligible function.

5   Security Analysis

The following theorem shows that our scheme is a chosen ciphertext secure IBEET (i.e. W-IND-ID-CCA), assuming BDH is hard in groups generated by a BDH parameter generator.

Theorem 1. *Let $\mathcal{A}$ be a* W-IND-ID-CCA *adversary on IBEET-IA that making at most q_e times extract queries and q_d times decryption queries achieves advantage at least ϵ. Suppose $\mathcal{A}$ makes at most q_e extraction queries, at most q_d decryption queries. Then there is a BDH algorithm $\mathcal{B}$ solving the BDH problem with the advantage at least $\frac{\epsilon}{e(q_e+q_d+1)}$.*

The hash function $H(\cdot)$ is for mapping and standardizing messages. It can be any qualified hash function.

5.1   W-IND-ID-CCA Security

Suppose there is a probabilistic polynomial time (PPT) adversary $\mathcal{A}$ who achieves the advantage ϵ on breaking $\Omega = (\mathsf{Setup}, \mathsf{Extract}, \mathsf{Enc}, \mathsf{Test}, \mathsf{Dec})$. Given a BDH instance, a PPT adversary $\mathcal{B}$ will take advantage of $\mathcal{A}$ to solve the BDH problem with the probability of ϵ'. Hence, if the BDH assumption holds, then ϵ' is negligible and consequently ϵ must be negligible.

Assume $\mathcal{B}$ holds a BDH tuple (g, U, V, R), where $x = \log_g U$, $y = \log_g V$ and $z = \log_g R$ are unkown. Let g be the generator of $\mathbb{G}_1$. Finally, $\mathcal{B}$ is supposed to output $e(g, g)^{xyz} \in \mathbb{G}_2$. The game between $\mathcal{B}$ and $\mathcal{A}$ runs as follows:

Setup: $\mathcal{B}$ sets $P_{pub} = g^{x \cdot r} = U^r$, where $r \xleftarrow{\$} \mathbb{Z}_p^*$ and sets $mtk = \beta \xleftarrow{\$} \mathbb{Z}_p^*$. $\mathcal{B}$ gives P_{pub} to $\mathcal{A}$.

Phase 1:

- H_1 Query. $\mathcal{A}$ can query the random oracle H_1 at any time. $\mathcal{A}$ queries ID_i to obtain g_{ID_i}. $\mathcal{B}$ responds with g_{ID_i} if ID_i has been in the H_1 table, $(\mathsf{ID}_i, g_{\mathsf{ID}_i}, a_i, \mathsf{coin}_i)$. Otherwise, for each ID_i, $\mathcal{B}$ responds as follows:
  - $\mathcal{B}$ tosses a coin with $\Pr[\mathsf{coin}_i = 0] = \delta$. If $\mathsf{coin}_i = 1$, responds to $\mathcal{A}$ with $g_{\mathsf{ID}_i} = g^{a_i}$, $a_i \xleftarrow{\$} \mathbb{Z}_p^*$. Otherwise, $\mathcal{B}$ sets $g_{\mathsf{ID}_i} = g^{a_i y} = V^{a_i}$.
  - $\mathcal{B}$ responds with g_{ID_i}, then adds $(\mathsf{ID}_i, g_{\mathsf{ID}_i}, a_i, \mathsf{coin}_i)$ in the H_1 table, which is initially empty.
- Extract Query. $\mathcal{A}$ queries the private key of ID_i. $\mathcal{B}$ responds as follows:
  - $\mathcal{B}$ obtains $H_1(\mathsf{ID}_i) = g_{\mathsf{ID}_i}$ in the H_1 table. If $\mathsf{coin}_i = 0$, $\mathcal{B}$ responds with $\perp$ and terminates the game.
  - Otherwise, $\mathcal{B}$ responds with $d_{\mathsf{ID}_i} = P_{pub}^{a_i} = U^{r \cdot a_i}$ and computes $\mathsf{tok}_{\mathsf{ID}_i} = g_{\mathsf{ID}_i}^{\beta}$, where a_i, g_{ID_i} is in the H_1 table.
  - $\mathcal{B}$ sends d_{ID_i} to $\mathcal{A}$, then stores $(d_{\mathsf{ID}_i}, \mathsf{tok}_{\mathsf{ID}_i}, \mathsf{ID}_i)$ in the private key list, which is initially empty.

- H_2 Query. $\mathcal{A}$ queries $D_i \in G_1^3 \times G_2$. $\mathcal{B}$ responds with $W_i \in H_2(D_i)$ in the H_2 table. Otherwise, for every D_i, $\mathcal{B}$ selects a random string $W_i = \{0,1\}^{t+l}$ as the $H_2(D_i)$. $\mathcal{B}$ responds $\mathcal{A}$ with $H_2(D_i)$ and adds (D_i, W_i) in the H_2 table, which is initially empty.
- Encryption Query. $\mathcal{A}$ queries m_i encrypted with ID_i. $\mathcal{B}$ responds as follows:
  - $\mathcal{B}$ searches the H_1 table to obtain the g_{ID_i} and computes $\mathsf{tok}_{\mathsf{ID}_i} = g_{\mathsf{ID}_i}^\beta$.
  - Then $\mathcal{B}$ selects $r_{i,1}, r_{i,2} \overset{\$}{\leftarrow} \mathbb{Z}_p^*$ and computes:

$$c_{i,1} = \mathsf{tok}_{\mathsf{ID}_i}^{r_{i,1} H(m_i)}, \quad c_{i,2} = g_{\mathsf{ID}_i}^{r_{i,1}}, \quad c_{i,3} = g^{r_{i,2}},$$

$$D_i = c_{i,1} \parallel c_{i,2} \parallel c_{i,3} \parallel e(P_{pub}, g_{\mathsf{ID}_i})^{r_{i,2}}.$$

  - $\mathcal{B}$ queries $\mathcal{O}_{H_2}$ to obtain $W_i = H_2(D_i)$.
  - $\mathcal{B}$ computes $c_{i,4} = (m_i \parallel r_{i,1}) \oplus W_i$.

  $\mathcal{B}$ responds with $C_i = (c_{i,1}, c_{i,2}, c_{i,3}, c_{i,4})$.
- Decryption Query. $\mathcal{A}$ queries C_i to be decrypted in ID_i. $\mathcal{B}$ responds as follows:
  - $\mathcal{B}$ searches the H_1 table to obtain the g_{ID_i}. If $\mathsf{coin}_i = 1$, obtain d_{ID_i} of ID_i in the private key list to decrypt C_i. Then $\mathcal{B}$ computes the bilinear map with d_{ID_i}:

$$e(c_{i,3}, d_{\mathsf{ID}_i}) = e(g^{r_{i,2}}, g^{a_i x r}) = e(g, U)^{r_{i,2} a_i r}.$$

  - After that, $\mathcal{B}$ computes $D_i = c_{i,1} \parallel c_{i,2} \parallel c_{i,3} \parallel e(P_{pub}, g_{\mathsf{ID}_i})^{r_{i,2}}$ and obtains W_i in the H_2 table. $\mathcal{B}$ obtains m_i and $r_{i,1}$ by $c_{i,4} \oplus W_i$.
  - Eventually, $\mathcal{B}$ computes $c'_{i,1}, c'_{i,2}$ with m_i and $r_{i,1}$ decrypted from C_i. If it is a valid ciphertext that $c'_{i,1} = c_{i,1}$ and $c'_{i,2} = c_{i,2}$, $\mathcal{B}$ responds with m_i. Otherwise, $\bot$.

Challenge: Once $\mathcal{A}$ decides the Phase 1 is over, $\mathcal{A}$ outputs two equal-length messages m_0, m_1 and ID^* to be challenged, where both m_0, m_1 are not issued in Encryption Query and ID^* is not queried in Extract Query in Phase 1. $\mathcal{B}$ responds as follows:

- $\mathcal{B}$ encrypts m_0 and m_1 and gets C_0 and C_1.
- If $\mathcal{B}$ searches the H_1 table. If $\mathsf{coin}^* = 1$, then $\mathcal{B}$ responds with $\bot$ and terminates the game, since $g_{\mathsf{ID}^*} = g^{a^*}$.
- Otherwise, $\mathcal{B}$ randomly selects $b \in \{0,1\}$. Since $g_{\mathsf{ID}^*} = g^{ya^*} = V^{a^*}$, $\mathcal{B}$ can calculate

$$c_1^* = (\mathsf{tok}_{\mathsf{ID}^*})^{r_1^* H(m_b)}, \quad c_2^* = g_{\mathsf{ID}^*}^{r_1^*}, \quad c_3^* = R = g^z, \quad c_4^* = (m_b \| r_1^*) \oplus W^*,$$

where $W^* = H_2(D^*)$ and $D^* = c_1^* \parallel c_2^* \parallel c_3^* \parallel e(P_{pub}, g_{\mathsf{ID}^*})^z$ (that $e(P_{pub}, g_{\mathsf{ID}^*})^z$ is unknown which $\mathcal{B}$ wants $\mathcal{A}$ to compute). $C^* = (c_1^*, c_2^*, c_3^*, c_4^*)$ is a valid ciphertext for m_b.
- $\mathcal{B}$ responds $\mathcal{A}$ with C^*.

Phase 2:

- H_1 Query. $\mathcal{A}$ queries as in Phase 1.
- Extract Query. $\mathcal{A}$ queries as in Phase 1, except that $\mathsf{ID}_i \neq \mathsf{ID}^*$.
- H_2 Query. $\mathcal{A}$ issues the query as in Phase 1.
- Encryption Query. $\mathcal{A}$ queries as in Phase 1, except that the message $m_i \notin \{m_0, m_1\}$.
- Decryption Query. $\mathcal{A}$ queries as in Phase 1, except that the ciphertext $(C_i, \mathsf{ID}_i) \neq (C^*, \mathsf{ID}^*)$.

Output: $\mathcal{A}$ gives a guess b' on b. If $b' \neq b$, $\mathcal{B}$ responds with failure and terminates the game. If $b' = b$, then $\mathcal{B}$ gets the result of the BDH tuple by guessing the inputs of H_2 Query. Suppose $D_{out} = D^*$, $\mathcal{B}$ obtains $e(P_{pub}, g_{\mathsf{ID}^*})^z$ directly from D_{out} by removing first $3k$ bits (the elements in $\mathbb{G}_1$ and $\mathbb{G}_2$ is k bits length.) that is $c_1^* \parallel c_2^* \parallel c_3^*$. Then $\mathcal{B}$ obtains $e(g,g)^{xyz} = e(P_{pub}, g_{\mathsf{ID}^*})^{z(a^*r)^{-1}} = (e(U,V)^{za^*r})^{(a^*r)^{-1}}$.

Claim. If the algorithm $\mathcal{B}$ does not abort during the simulation then the algorithm $\mathcal{A}$'s view is identical to its view in the real attack. Furthermore, if $\mathcal{B}$ does not abort then $\left|\Pr[b' = b] - \frac{1}{2}\right| \geq \frac{\epsilon}{e(q_e + q_d + 1)}$. The probability over the random bits used by $\mathcal{A}$, $\mathcal{B}$ and the challenger.

Proof. It remains to bound the probability that $\mathcal{B}$ aborts during the simulation. The algorithm $\mathcal{B}$ could abort for three reasons: (1) a bad private key extraction query from $\mathcal{A}$ during the phase 1 or 2, (2) $\mathcal{A}$ chooses a bad ID to be challenged on, or (3) a bad decryption query from $\mathcal{A}$ during the phase 1 or 2. We define three corresponding events:

ε_1: $\mathcal{B}$ aborts at the Extract Query step.
ε_2: $\mathcal{B}$ aborts at the Decryption Query step.
ε_3: $\mathcal{B}$ aborts at the Challenge step.

We have
$$\Pr[\neg\varepsilon_1 \wedge \neg\varepsilon_2 \wedge \neg\varepsilon_3] \geq (1 - \delta)^{q_e + q_d}\delta.$$

We provide the proof on $\Pr[\neg\varepsilon_1 \wedge \neg\varepsilon_2 \wedge \neg\varepsilon_3]$ by induction on the maximum number of queries $q_e + q_d$ made by the adversary. Let $\varepsilon^{0\cdots i}$ be the event that $\varepsilon_1 \vee \varepsilon_2 \vee \varepsilon_3$ happens after $\mathcal{A}$ queries at most i times and let $i = q_e + q_d$. Similarly, let ε^i be the event that $\varepsilon_1 \vee \varepsilon_2 \vee \varepsilon_3$ happens for the first time when $\mathcal{A}$ queries the i_{th} item. For $i = 0$, it is trivial that $\Pr[\neg\varepsilon^{0\cdots 0}] = \delta$. Suppose that for $i - 1$ the $\Pr[\neg\varepsilon^{0\cdots i-1}] = (1 - \delta)^{i-1}\delta$ holds. Then for i, it holds

$$\begin{aligned}
\Pr[\neg\varepsilon^{0\cdots i}] &= \Pr[\neg\varepsilon^{0\cdots i}|\neg\varepsilon^{0\cdots i-1}]\Pr[\neg\varepsilon^{0\cdots i-1}] \\
&= \Pr[\neg\varepsilon^i|\neg\varepsilon^{0\cdots i-1}]\Pr[\neg\varepsilon^{0\cdots i-1}] \\
&\geq \Pr[\neg\varepsilon^i|\neg\varepsilon^{0\cdots i-1}](1 - \delta)^{i-1}\delta.
\end{aligned}$$

Hence, we bound the probability of ε^i not to happen with $\mathcal{A}$'s i_{th} query. The query is either an Extract Query for ID_i or a Decryption Query for (C_i, ID_i). Recall that if $coin_i = 1$ it cannot cause ε_1 and ε_2 to happen. We consider three cases:

Case 1. The i_{th} query is the first time $\mathcal{A}$ queries ID_i. In this case, $\Pr[coin_i = 1] = 1 - \delta$ and hence

$$\Pr[\neg\varepsilon^i|\neg\varepsilon^{0\cdots i-1}] \geq 1 - \delta.$$

Case 2. ID_i was queried in previous Extract Query. Assuming the previous query did not cause $\varepsilon^{0\cdots i-1}$ to happen we have $coin_i = 1$. Hence,

$$\Pr[\neg\varepsilon^i|\neg\varepsilon^{0\cdots i-1}] = 1.$$

Case 3. ID_i was queried in the previous Decryption Query. Similarly to Case 2, we have $coin_i = 1$, Hence,

$$\Pr[\neg\varepsilon^i|\neg\varepsilon^{0\cdots i-1}] = 1.$$

To summarize, we have

$$\Pr[\neg\varepsilon^i|\neg\varepsilon^{0\cdots i-1}] \geq 1 - \delta$$

whatever the i_{th} query is. Therefore,

$$\Pr[\neg\varepsilon^i] \geq (1 - \delta)^i \delta$$

is as required. Since

$$\Pr[\neg\varepsilon_1 \wedge \neg\varepsilon_2 \wedge \neg\varepsilon_3] \geq (1 - \delta)^{q_e + q_d} \delta,$$

the success probability is maximum at δ_{opt}. Using $\delta_{opt} = \frac{1}{q_e + q_d + 1}$, the probability that $\mathcal{B}$ does not abort is at least $\frac{1}{e(q_e + q_d + 1)}$. This shows that $\mathcal{B}$'s advantage is at least $\frac{\epsilon}{e(q_e + q_d + 1)}$ as required.

Remark 1. Responses to H_1 queries are as in the real attack since responses are uniformly and independently distributed in $\mathbb{G}_1^*$. All responses to the private key extraction queries and decryption queries are valid. Finally, the challenge ciphertext C^* given to $\mathcal{A}$ is the encryption of m_b for some random $b \in \{0, 1\}$. Therefore, by the definition of $\mathcal{A}$ we have that

$$\left|\Pr[b' = b] - \frac{1}{2}\right| \geq \frac{\epsilon}{e(q_e + q_d + 1)}.$$

6   Experiments on a Database

6.1   Setup of Experiments

The purpose of our experiments is to demonstrate the efficiency and feasibility of our scheme. The instantiation of our novel IBEET-IA scheme is implemented in Java with the Java Pairing Based Cryptography library (JPBC) [3]. In our experiments, type A pairing is invoked for the configuration of our IBEET-IA program, which is symmetrically built from type A super-singular elliptic curve

Table 1. Experimental environment

Hardware	Parameter
Computer	Mac Pro 13' 2015
Processor	2.7 GHz Intel Core i5
Operation system	OS X El Capitan 10.11.6
Memory	8 GB 1867 MHz DDR3
Cores	2
Software	Parameter
Virtual machine	VMware Fusion 7
VM OS	Ubuntu 14.04.3
VM memory	1024 MB
VM core	1
Database	MySQL
Development	Java 1.8 + Eclipse + JPBC

with the embedding degree of two. Precisely, the length of elements is 512 bits for $\mathbb{G}_1$ and 1024 bits for $\mathbb{G}_2$. For the database, MySQL on a virtual machine with 1024 MB memory and one processing core is used as the experimental environment. Detailed parameters of our experiments are shown in Table 1. In addition, experiments were conducted on the practical database with eight tables, which are constructed with columns over rows on 4×273, 8×23, 6×326, 5×2996, 9×7, 4×273, 8×110 and 3×7, respectively. After running three experiments on three algorithms, Enc, Dec and Test, the efficiency of those algorithms are analyzed. The results are shown in the following subsections.

6.2 Performance Evaluation

In the following three experiments, the total time cost is linear with the size of entities to be encrypted, decrypted or tested. In Enc and Dec algorithms, they conduct a pairing and three exponents, simultaneously. Therefore, the average time consumption is the same, 0.3 s (or 0.3 s) to 0.2 s for each entity in the encryption and the decryption containing the reading and writing time. The average time consumption is 0.1 s for each equality test, which is a reasonable result and can be accepted by practice applications.

Encryption Performance. The encryption encrypted with the user's ID. For the i_{th} encryption on m_i, it inputs ID and the value of the current cell and computes

$$c_1^i = \mathsf{tok}_{\mathsf{ID}}^{r_1^i H(m_i)}, \quad c_2^i = g_{\mathsf{ID}}^{r_1^i}, \quad c_3^i = g^{r_2^i},$$

$$c_4^i = (m_i \parallel r_1^i) \oplus H_2(c_1^i \parallel c_2^i \parallel c_3^i \parallel e(P_{pub}, g_{\mathsf{ID}})^{r_2^i}),$$

Table 2. Encryption performance

Cells	RT [ms]
7	3297
58	19789
183	57940
880	296337
1092	343131
1384	584450
1942	654629
14980	4715098

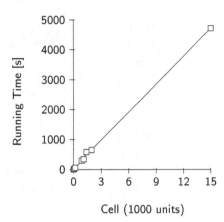

where $r_1^i, r_2^i \xleftarrow{\$} \mathbb{Z}_p^*$, with $|r_1^i| = l$. Finally, it returns $C^i = (c_1^i, c_2^i, c_3^i, c_4^i)$. Results on the total time consumption over the encryption in each experiment are shown as Table 2.

The time consumption of the Enc algorithm is linear with the number of cells to be encrypted. Enc contains one pairing and three exponent computations.

Decryption Performance. We conducted the decryption operation on the random selected column to evaluate the performance of our decryption algorithm. For the i_{th} decryption on captured $(c_1^i, c_2^i, c_3^i, c_4^i)$, it takes ID and the value of the set and computes

$$m_i \parallel r_1^i = c_4^i \oplus H_2(c_1^i \parallel c_2^i \parallel c_3^i \parallel e(c_3, d_{\mathsf{ID}})).$$

If

$$c_1^i = (\mathsf{tok}_{\mathsf{ID}})^{r_1 H(m_i)} \wedge c_2^i = g_{\mathsf{ID}}^{r_1^i},$$

it returns m_i. Otherwise, it returns $\bot$. The results on the total time consumption over the decryption in each experiment are shown as Table 3.

The time consumption of the Dec algorithm is linear with the number of cells to be decrypted. Dec contains one pairing and two exponent computations.

Equality Test Performance. We conducted the equality test between two tables who have the same column. For the i_{th} equality test, it takes IDs and two ciphertexts which are $C^i = (c_1^i, c_2^i, c_3^i, c_4^i)$ and $C^j = (c_1^j, c_2^j, c_3^j, c_4^j)$, respectively, and checks whether $e(c_1^i, c_2^i)$ is equal to $e(c_1^j, c_2^j)$. Results on the total time consumption over the equality test in each experiment are shown in Table 4.

The time consumption of the Test algorithm is linear with the number of cells to be conducted the equality test. Test contains only two pairing computations. The deviation of the performance might be caused by the instability of the CPU used in our simulation.

Table 3. Decryption performance

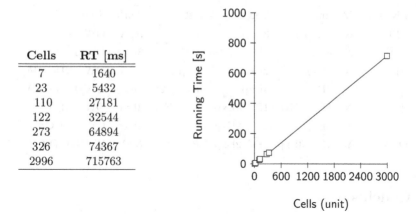

Cells	RT [ms]
7	1640
23	5432
110	27181
122	32544
273	64894
326	74367
2996	715763

Table 4. Equality test performance

Cells	RT [ms]
161	16083
1540	149746
33306	2821123
39772	2898100
329560	23247358

6.3   Comparison

There are some PKEET variants. We made a comparison on the efficiency of
algorithms adopted in these schemes. "Exp" refers to the exponent computation.
"P" refers to the pairing computation. "Auth." refers to the authorization.

The extended PKEET schemes cost three to four steps to conduct the equality test including analyzing trapdoor and inverse-computing trapdoor. In the
contrast, our scheme only needs two pairing computations to conduct the equality test. The results in Table 5 indicate the improvement on efficiency in our
scheme comparing with other schemes. In addition to efficiency, our scheme has
shown the improvement on security and achieved the first W-IND-ID-CCA which
is stronger than OW-ID-CCA.

Table 5. Comparing the efficiency of algorithms of variant PKEETs with our scheme

PKEETs	IA	Enc	Dec	Test	Auth.	Security
[13]	N	3Exp	3Exp	2P	N/A	OW-CCA
[11]	N	4Exp	2Exp	4P	3Exp	OW/IND-CCA
[12]	N	5Exp	2Exp	4Exp	N/A	OW/IND-CCA
[5]	N	4Exp	4Exp	6Exp + 2P	5Exp	OW/IND-CCA
[9]	N	1P + 5Exp	1P + 4Exp	4P + 2Exp	3Exp	OW/IND-CCA
[7]	N	6Exp	2P + 2Exp	4P	2Exp	OW-ID-CCA
Ours	Y	1P + 3Exp	1P + 2Exp	2P	N/A	W-IND-ID-CCA

7   Conclusions

The probabilistic public key encryption with equality test proposed by Yang et al. in 2010 at CT-RSA and its extended works are vulnerable to the insider attack launched by the semi-trusted server by guessing on the embedding message. The server can test whether the guessed message is equal to that contained in the target ciphertext. To solve this problem, we proposed a novel IBEET-IA scheme which a reasonable efficiency. In order to prove that our scheme is chosen ciphertext secure, we proposed a novel W-IND-ID-CCA security model under the defined insider attack. We also demonstrated its efficiency by experiments on a real database.

Acknowledgement. This work was partially supported by the National Natural Science Foundation of China (grant numbers: 61402184 and 61402376).

References

1. Boneh, D., Di Crescenzo, G., Ostrovsky, R., Persiano, G.: Public key encryption with keyword search. In: Cachin, C., Camenisch, J.L. (eds.) EUROCRYPT 2004. LNCS, vol. 3027, pp. 506–522. Springer, Heidelberg (2004). doi:10.1007/978-3-540-24676-3_30
2. Chen, R., Mu, Y., Yang, G., Guo, F., Wang, X.: Dual-server public-key encryption with keyword search for secure cloud storage. IEEE Trans. Inf. Forensics Secur. **11**(4), 789–798 (2016)
3. De Caro, A., Iovino, V.: JPBC: Java pairing based cryptography. In: Proceedings of the 16th IEEE Symposium on Computers and Communications, ISCC 2011, Kerkyra, Corfu, Greece, 28 June–1 July 2011, pp. 850–855. IEEE (2011). http://gas.dia.unisa.it/projects/jpbc/
4. Galbraith, S.D., Paterson, K.G., Smart, N.P.: Pairings for cryptographers. Discrete Appl. Math. **156**(16), 3113–3121 (2008)
5. Huang, K., Tso, R., Chen, Y., Rahman, S.M.M., Almogren, A., Alamri, A.: PKE-AET: public key encryption with authorized equality test. Comput. J. **58**(10), 2686–2697 (2015)

6. Jiang, P., Mu, Y., Guo, F., Wang, X., Wen, Q.: Online/offline ciphertext retrieval on resource constrained devices. Comput. J. **59**(7), 955–969 (2016)
7. Ma, S.: Identity-based encryption with outsourced equality test in cloud computing. Inf. Sci. **328**, 389–402 (2016)
8. Ma, S., Huang, Q., Zhang, M., Yang, B.: Efficient public key encryption with equality test supporting flexible authorization. IEEE Trans. Inf. Forensics Secur. **10**(3), 458–470 (2015)
9. Ma, S., Zhang, M., Huang, Q., Yang, B.: Public key encryption with delegated equality test in a multi-user setting. Comput. J. **58**(4), 986–1002 (2015)
10. Mayer, D.A., Wetzel, S.: Verifiable private equality test: enabling unbiased 2-party reconciliation on ordered sets in the malicious model. In: Proceedings of the 7th ACM Symposium on Information, Computer and Communications Security, ASI-ACCS 2012, Seoul, Korea, 2–4 May 2012, pp. 46–47 (2012)
11. Tang, Q.: Public key encryption schemes supporting equality test with authorization of different granularity. Int. J. Appl. Crypt. **2**(4), 304–321 (2012)
12. Tang, Q.: Public key encryption supporting plaintext equality test and user-specified authorization. Secur. Commun. Netw. **5**(12), 1351–1362 (2012)
13. Yang, G., Tan, C.H., Huang, Q., Wong, D.S.: Probabilistic public key encryption with equality test. In: Pieprzyk, J. (ed.) CT-RSA 2010. LNCS, vol. 5985, pp. 119–131. Springer, Heidelberg (2010). doi:10.1007/978-3-642-11925-5_9

Lattice-Based Revocable Identity-Based Encryption with Bounded Decryption Key Exposure Resistance

Atsushi Takayasu[1,3]([✉]) and Yohei Watanabe[2,3]

[1] The University of Tokyo, Tokyo, Japan
takayasu@mist.i.u-tokyo.ac.jp
[2] The University of Electro-Communications, Tokyo, Japan
[3] National Institute of Advanced Industrial Science and Technology, Tokyo, Japan

Abstract. A revocable identity-based encryption (RIBE) scheme, proposed by Boldyreva et al., provides a revocation functionality for managing a number of users dynamically and efficiently. To capture a realistic scenario, Seo and Emura introduced an additional important security notion, called *decryption key exposure resistance* (DKER), where an adversary is allowed to query short-term decryption keys. Although several RIBE schemes that satisfy DKER have been proposed, all the lattice-based RIBE schemes, e.g., Chen et al.'s scheme, do not achieve DKER, since they basically do not have *the key re-randomization property*, which is considered to be an essential requirement for achieving DKER. In particular, in every existing lattice-based RIBE scheme, an adversary can easily recover plaintexts if the adversary is allowed to issue even a single short-term decryption key query. In this paper, we propose a new lattice-based RIBE scheme secure against exposure of a-priori bounded number of decryption keys (for every identity). We believe that this bounded notion is still meaningful and useful from a practical perspective. Technically, to achieve the bounded security without the key re-randomization property, key updates in our scheme are short vectors whose corresponding syndrome vector changes in each time period. For this approach to work correctly and for the scheme to be secure, *cover free families* play a crucial role in our construction.

1 Introduction

1.1 Background

Identity-based encryption (IBE) is currently one of the central cryptographic primitives. IBE allows any strings to be used as public keys, and therefore is an advanced form of public-key encryption (PKE). The first practical IBE was proposed by Boneh and Franklin [9] from bilinear groups. Since then, several IBE schemes have been proposed including ones from lattices [1,6,10,11,14,20, 24,38–40]. Lattice-based schemes are believed to resist quantum attacks and the average-case security is guaranteed by the worst-case lattice assumptions.

© Springer International Publishing AG 2017
J. Pieprzyk and S. Suriadi (Eds.): ACISP 2017, Part I, LNCS 10342, pp. 184–204, 2017.
DOI: 10.1007/978-3-319-60055-0_10

Although IBE is known as an important cryptographic primitive, IBE itself has not been used that much than PKE in modern society. One main reason for the situation is inefficient revocation procedures of ordinary IBE schemes. Revocation functionality is necessary to handle users in cryptographic schemes since malicious users should be immediately driven out from the schemes, and even honest users should be revoked if their keys get compromised. In the PKE setting, the validity of public keys are guaranteed by certificates issued by public-key infrastructures (PKIs). Therefore, users can be easily revoked by invalidating the corresponding certificate. On the other hand, IBE does not have such a revocation procedure due to the absence of PKIs. Boneh and Franklin [9] mentioned the following naive and inefficient revocation procedure: The lifetime of the system is divided into discrete time periods. In every time period, a key generation center (KGC) generates secret keys for each non-revoked user and sends the new keys to the corresponding users.

Later, Boldyreva et al. [7] proposed a pairing-based IBE scheme with efficient revocation, which is called a *revocable IBE* (RIBE) scheme by utilizing the spirit of fuzzy IBE constructions and a subset cover framework called the complete subtree (CS) method. They significantly improved the efficiency of revocation procedures from linear to logarithmic in the number of all users. Specifically, they considered two kinds of keys: a *long-term secret key* and a *short-term decryption key*. In every time-period, the KGC generates update information called a *key update*, and broadcasts it. Each non-revoked user can derive a decryption key for each time period from his long-term secret key and the key update for the corresponding time period, while revoked users cannot compute their decryption keys. After the proposal, Libert and Vergnaud [28] proposed the first adaptively secure pairing-based RIBE scheme. The first lattice-based RIBE scheme was proposed by Chen et al. [16] in the selective security model. The idea of these constructions follow Boldyreva et al.'s one.

Human errors seem never to be eliminated, and therefore a key exposure problem is unavoidable. In the context of RIBE, Seo and Emura [34] pointed out that Boldyreva et al.'s security model did not capture such a realistic threat, and they first realized an RIBE scheme with *decryption-key exposure resistance* (DKER) from bilinear groups. An RIBE scheme with DKER, DKER RIBE for short, guarantees that the security is not compromised even if polynomially many short-term decryption keys are leaked. Boneh-Franklin's naive solution captures DKER, whereas the previous RIBE schemes [7,16,28] are vulnerable against decryption key exposure. Hence, DKER seems to be a natural security requirement for RIBE. Although the construction idea is almost the same as Boldyreva et al.'s one [7], Seo and Emura [34] made use of *the key re-randomization property* for proving the stronger security (i.e., security with DKER). Since the proposal, DKER has become the standard security notion of RIBE. Indeed, several DKER RIBE schemes [18,23,26,27,33,35,36] have been proposed.

However, no lattice-based DKER RIBE schemes have been proposed thus far; existing lattice-based RIBE schemes [16,17,30][1] do not satisfy DKER. In particular, Chen et al.'s RIBE scheme immediately becomes insecure even with an adversary's single short-term decryption key query. Hence, the limitation does not stem from proof techniques. Actually, all the existing DKER RIBE schemes satisfy the key re-randomization property, which is used for preventing adversaries from obtaining critical information from decryption key queries. Since the current lattice-based RIBE construction does not satisfy the property, we should explore new approaches to construct DKER RIBE schemes.

1.2   Our Contributions

In this paper, we construct the first lattice-based RIBE scheme that is resilient to decryption key exposure. To be precise, we should note that our scheme is secure when adversaries are allowed to query a-priori bounded number of short-term decryption keys, which is denoted by Q, for the target identity. Therefore, we call our proposal *B-DKER RIBE*, where B-DKER stands for *bounded DKER*. Decryption key exposure is mainly caused by human errors. The leakage might happen, however we can assume that it rarely happens. Hence, although the security of B-DKER RIBE is weaker than DKER RIBE, we believe that our security model is sufficient for practical use. Even if a number of decryption keys are exposed, our scheme is secure by setting sufficiently large Q, whereas Chen et al.'s scheme is insecure in such a case (in particular, even in the case that $Q = 1$).

One may think that the notion of B-DKER RIBE is similar to that of bounded-collusion IBE [21] or k-resilient IBE [22]. However, we emphasize that there is a major gap between them from the practical aspect. In the bounded-collusion IBE, the number of secret key extraction queries is a-priori bounded, whereas our definition allows unbounded collusion, i.e., an adversary can unboundedly issue secret key extraction queries and decryption key queries except for the target identity. Practically, in the bounded-collusion IBE scenario, an adversary might collude with the larger number of users than the a-priori bounded number. The KGC may be unaware of the behind-the-scenes collusion, and thus the system would not be refreshed before breaking it. On the one hand, in the B-DKER RIBE scenario, it would appear that decryption key exposures happen only through human errors or some accident. That is, the leakage cannot be controlled by adversaries. The KGC may notice the fact of leakage from users who are honest but leaked their keys, and therefore the KGC can keep the scheme secure by refreshing it at some point.

To obtain (a kind of) DKER for lattice-based RIBE is the main contribution of this paper. Our scheme has a different flavor from the template RIBE construction due to Boldyreva et al. [7] (and therefore Chen et al. [16]) in the sense that

---

[1] Cheng and Zhang [17] proposed the first adaptively secure lattice-based RIBE scheme, however, their security proofs contain unavoidable bugs. Therefore, there are no adaptively secure lattice-based RIBE schemes even without DKER. See Sect. 6 for the detail.

each key update corresponds to distinct syndrome vectors in each time period. Although the modification causes several troubles, cover free families (CFFs) enable us to resolve them with longer secret keys (see Sect. 1.3 for details). For simplicity, we discuss our construction in the selective security model throughout the paper. We believe that it enables readers to understand our technique easily. In addition, as side contributions, we obtain the following improvements although they are not very technical: smaller parameters by utilizing Micciancio-Peikert's gadget matrix [29], the first semi-adaptively secure lattice-based RIBE, the first anonymous RIBE scheme that is resilient to decryption key exposure. They will be discussed in Sect. 6. Notice that in the semi-adaptive security model, the adversary issues the challenge identity and the challenge time period just after receiving a public parameter.

1.3 Our Approach

In this section, we show a brief overview of Chen et al.'s lattice-based RIBE construction [16] and our modification to the scheme to achieve B-DKER. The public parameter of Chen et al.'s RIBE scheme consists of three matrices $\mathbf{A}_0, \mathbf{A}_1, \mathbf{A}_2$ and a syndrome vector $\mathbf{u}$ along with a gadget matrix[2] $\mathbf{G}$ that was introduced in [29]. The ciphertext of a plaintext $M \in \{0, 1\}$ for an identity ID and a time period T is

$$[\mathbf{A}_0 | \mathbf{A}_1 + H(\mathsf{ID})\mathbf{G} | \mathbf{A}_2 + H(\mathsf{T})\mathbf{G}]^T \mathbf{s} + \text{noise} \quad \text{and} \quad \mathbf{u}^T \mathbf{s} + M \left\lfloor \frac{q}{2} \right\rfloor + \text{noise}$$

where $\mathbf{s}$ is a random secret vector and $H()$ is a public hash function. Each user has a long-term secret key $\mathbf{e}'$ whereas KGC broadcasts a key update $\tilde{\mathbf{e}}$ in each time period such that

$$[\mathbf{A}_0 | \mathbf{A}_1 + H(\mathsf{ID})\mathbf{G}] \mathbf{e}' = \mathbf{u}' \quad \text{and} \quad [\mathbf{A}_0 | \mathbf{A}_2 + H(\mathsf{T})\mathbf{G}] \tilde{\mathbf{e}} = \tilde{\mathbf{u}} \quad (1)$$

for some random syndrome vectors $\mathbf{u}'$ and $\tilde{\mathbf{u}}$. If the user is non-revoked, these two syndrome vectors satisfy $\mathbf{u}' + \tilde{\mathbf{u}} = \mathbf{u}$. The short-term decryption key $\mathbf{e}$ for $(\mathsf{ID}, \mathsf{T})$ is their concatenation $\mathbf{e} := (\mathbf{e}', \tilde{\mathbf{e}})$.

As opposed to an ordinary IBE, the RIBE simulator should create a long-term secret key $\mathbf{e}'$ for the target identity ID^* and a key update $\tilde{\mathbf{e}}$ for the challenge time period T^*. Chen et al. resolved the problem by utilizing a Gaussian sampling algorithm in a clever way. If we do not care about DKER, the simulator should create either a secret key $\mathbf{e}'$ for the target identity ID^* or a key update $\tilde{\mathbf{e}}$ for the target time period T^*. Then, the simulator picks $\mathbf{e}'$ or $\tilde{\mathbf{e}}$ in advance and sets $\mathbf{u}'$ or $\tilde{\mathbf{u}}$ according to the Eq. (1). Notice that the simulator can create long-term secret keys and key updates for all the other $\mathsf{ID} \neq \mathsf{ID}^*$ and $\mathsf{T} \neq \mathsf{T}^*$ since it has a trapdoor.

In short, to obtain DKER, the challenge ciphertext for the target $(\mathsf{ID}^*, \mathsf{T}^*)$ should not be decrypted by using a key update for T^* and short-term decryption keys for $(\mathsf{ID}^*, \mathsf{T})$ such that $\mathsf{T} \neq \mathsf{T}^*$. However, since Chen et al.'s short-term

---

[2] Although the gadget matrix was not used by Chen et al. [16], it is well known that the parameters can be reduced by utilizing the matrix.

decryption key is a simple concatenation, the target decryption key for $(\mathsf{ID}^*, \mathsf{T}^*)$ can be recovered even with a single decryption key for $(\mathsf{ID}^*, \mathsf{T})$. Since there is a concrete attack, the limitation is not due to proof techniques but the construction. In other words, the simulator should create both short-term decryption keys $\mathbf{e}'$ for $(\mathsf{ID}^*, \mathsf{T})$ such that $\mathsf{T} \neq \mathsf{T}^*$ and key updates $\tilde{\mathbf{e}}$ for T^* during the simulation. However, once the simulator uses a Gaussian sampling algorithm and sets $\mathbf{e}'$, the corresponding syndrome $\mathbf{u}'$ is fixed. Then, the simulator cannot create $\tilde{\mathbf{e}}$ for $\tilde{\mathbf{u}}$ such that $\mathbf{u}' + \tilde{\mathbf{u}} = \mathbf{u}$. If lattice-based RIBE scheme supports the key re-randomization property, we can avoid the problem as Seo-Emura [34], however, it does not. We will discuss the fact in Sect. 6.

To resolve the problem, we employ a novel RIBE construction. A starting point of our modification is that our key update $\tilde{\mathbf{e}}$ for a time period T satisfies

$$[\mathbf{A}_0 | \mathbf{A}_2 + H(\mathsf{T})\mathbf{G}] \, \tilde{\mathbf{e}} = \tilde{\mathbf{u}}_\mathsf{T}$$

where the corresponding syndrome vector $\tilde{\mathbf{u}}_\mathsf{T}$ changes in each time period. The property directly suggests that decryption keys for $(\mathsf{ID}^*, \mathsf{T})$ such that $\mathsf{T} \neq \mathsf{T}^*$ are useless to recover a decryption key for the target $(\mathsf{ID}^*, \mathsf{T}^*)$. However, a new problem occurs by the construction. Since a secret key $\mathbf{e}'$ corresponds to a fixed syndrome vector $\mathbf{u}'$, even non-revoked users cannot derive well-formed decryption keys such that $\mathbf{u}' + \tilde{\mathbf{u}}_\mathsf{T} = \mathbf{u}$ for all time periods with their secret keys and key updates. To overcome the issue, in our scheme, each user ID has multiple d secret keys $\mathbf{e}'_1, \ldots, \mathbf{e}'_d$ such that

$$[\mathbf{A}_0 | \mathbf{A}_1 + H(\mathsf{ID})\mathbf{G}] \, \mathbf{e}'_1 = \mathbf{u}'_1, \ldots, [\mathbf{A}_0 | \mathbf{A}_1 + H(\mathsf{ID})\mathbf{G}] \, \mathbf{e}'_d = \mathbf{u}'_d.$$

A naive approach for the scheme to work correctly is that we use each $\mathbf{e}'_\ell$ in each time period. However, the modification makes the scheme too inefficient since the number of secret keys d has to be at least larger than the maximum time period and results in super-polynomial. To reduce the size, we set $\mathbf{u} - \tilde{\mathbf{u}}_\mathsf{T}$ as a subset sum of $\mathbf{u}'_1, \ldots, \mathbf{u}'_d$ so that non-revoked users can produce well-formed decryption keys with smaller d. The resulting decryption key is a concatenation of the corresponding subset sum of $\mathbf{e}'_1, \ldots, \mathbf{e}'_d$ and the key update $\tilde{\mathbf{e}}$. The simulator utilizes a Gaussian sampling algorithm to create $d - 1$ secret key elements $\mathbf{e}'_1, \ldots, \mathbf{e}'_d$ except $\mathbf{e}'_{\ell^*}$ for ID^* and a key update $\tilde{\mathbf{e}}$ for T^* along with their corresponding syndrome vectors, then answers decryption key queries for $(\mathsf{ID}^*, \mathsf{T})$ such that $\mathsf{T} \neq \mathsf{T}^*$. The remaining syndrome vector $\mathbf{u}'_{\ell^*}$ is directly fixed. If $\mathbf{e}'_{\ell^*}$ is not used to answer Q decryption key queries, the approach goes well.

For the above construction to become a provably secure practical RIBE scheme whose adversary is allowed to query Q decryption keys, there are the following three requirements: (1) the number of secret keys d is at most polynomially bounded, (2) a subset sum of $\mathbf{u}_1, \ldots, \mathbf{u}_d$ produces distinct vectors whose number is larger than the maximum time period, (3) there is at least one secret key $\mathbf{e}'_{\ell^*}$ that is not used to answer arbitrary Q decryption key queries. Therefore, we use CFFs so that the resulting scheme satisfies all the above requirements.

2   Preliminaries

Notation, "Probabilistic polynomial-time" is abbreviated as "PPT". We denote $[a, b]$ by a set $\{a, a+1, \ldots, b\}$ for any integers $a, b \in \mathbb{N}$ such that $a \leq b$. We sometimes write $[d]$ as $[1, d]$ for simplicity. Let a bold capital $\mathbf{A}$ and a bold lower $\mathbf{a}$ denote a matrix and a column vector respectively. Let $\mathbf{A}^T$ and $\mathbf{a}^T$ denote their transposes. If we write $(y_1, y_2, \ldots, y_m) \leftarrow \mathcal{A}(x_1, x_2, \ldots, x_n)$ for an algorithm $\mathcal{A}$ having n inputs and m outputs, it means to input $x_1, x_2, \ldots, x_n$ into $\mathcal{A}$ and to get the resulting output $y_1, y_2, \ldots, y_m$. We write $(y_1, y_2, \ldots, y_m) \leftarrow \mathcal{A}^{\mathcal{O}}(x_1, x_2, \ldots, x_n)$ to indicate that an algorithm $\mathcal{A}$ that is allowed to access an oracle $\mathcal{O}$ takes $x_1, x_2, \ldots, x_n$ as input and outputs $(y_1, y_2, \ldots, y_m)$. If $\mathcal{X}$ is a set, we write $x \xleftarrow{\$} \mathcal{X}$ to mean the operation of picking an element x of $\mathcal{X}$ uniformly at random. We use λ as a security parameter. For sufficiently large λ, a function $\mathsf{negl} : \mathbb{R} \to \mathbb{R}$ is negligible if $\mathsf{negl}(\lambda) < 1/p(\lambda)$ for any polynomial $p(\lambda)$. Let X and Y be two random variables taking values in some finite set Ω. Statistical distance is defined as $\Delta(X; Y)$, as $\Delta(X; Y) := \frac{1}{2} \sum_{s \in \Omega} |\Pr[X = s] - \Pr[Y = s]|$. For sets of random variables X and Y, we say that X and Y are statistically close if $\Delta(X; Y)$ is negligible.

Cover Free Families. We define a cover free family (CFF), which is a core building block in our construction, as follows.

Definition 1 (Cover Free Families [19]). *Let α, d, Q be positive integers, and $\mathcal{F} := \{\mathcal{F}_\mu\}_{\mu \in [\alpha]}$ be a family of subsets of $[d]$, where every $|\mathcal{F}_\mu| = w$. $\mathcal{F}$ is said to be w-uniform Q-cover-free if it holds that $\bigcup_{j=1}^{Q} \mathcal{F}_{i_j} \not\supseteq \mathcal{F}_{i_{Q+1}}$ for any $\mathcal{F}_{i_1}, \mathcal{F}_{i_2}, \ldots, \mathcal{F}_{i_{Q+1}} \in \mathcal{F}$ such that $\mathcal{F}_{i_k} \neq \mathcal{F}_{i_\ell}$ for any distinct $k, \ell \in [Q + 1]$.*

Lemma 1 ([25]). *There is a deterministic polynomial time algorithm CFF.Gen that, on input of positive integers α and Q, returns $d \in \mathbb{N}$ and a family $\mathcal{F} = \{\mathcal{F}_\mu\}_{\mu \in [\alpha]}$, such that $\mathcal{F}$ is Q-cover free over $[d]$ and w-uniform, where $d \leq 16Q^2 \log \alpha$ and $w = d/4Q$.*

KUNode Algorithm. To reduce costs of a revocation process, we use a binary tree structure and apply the following KUNode algorithm as in the previous RIBE schemes [7,28,34]. KUNode(BT, RL, T) takes as input a binary tree BT, a revocation list RL, and a time period $\mathsf{T} \in \mathcal{T}$, and outputs a set of nodes. When η is a non-leaf node, then we write η_L and η_R as the left and right child of η, respectively. When η is a leaf node, Path(BT, η) denotes the set of nodes on the path from η to the root. Each user is assigned to a leaf node. If a user who is assigned to η is revoked on a time period $\mathsf{T} \in \mathcal{T}$, then $(\eta, \mathsf{T}) \in \mathsf{RL}$. KUNode(BT, RL, T) is executed as follows. It sets $\mathcal{X} := \emptyset$ and $\mathcal{Y} := \emptyset$. For any $(\eta_i, \mathsf{T}_i) \in \mathsf{RL}$, if $\mathsf{T}_i \leq \mathsf{T}$ then it adds Path(BT, η_i) to $\mathcal{X}$ (i.e., $\mathcal{X} := \mathcal{X} \cup \mathsf{Path}(\mathsf{BT}, \eta_i)$). Then, for any $\eta \in \mathcal{X}$, if $\eta_L \notin \mathcal{X}$, then it adds η_L to $\mathcal{Y}$. If $\eta_R \notin \mathcal{X}$, then it adds η_R to $\mathcal{Y}$. Finally, it outputs $\mathcal{Y}$ if $\mathcal{Y} \neq \emptyset$. If $\mathcal{Y} = \emptyset$, then it adds root to $\mathcal{Y}$ and outputs $\mathcal{Y}$.

Lattices. An m-dimensional integer lattice is an additive discrete subgroup of $\mathbb{Z}^m$. For positive integers q, n, m, a matrix $\mathbf{A} \in \mathbb{Z}_q^{n \times m}$, and a vector $\mathbf{u} \in \mathbb{Z}_q^m$, the m-dimensional integer (shifted) lattices $\Lambda_q^\perp(\mathbf{A})$ and $\Lambda_q^\mathbf{u}(\mathbf{A})$ are defined as $\Lambda_q^\perp(\mathbf{A}) := \{\mathbf{e} \in \mathbb{Z}^m : \mathbf{Ae} = \mathbf{0} \bmod q\}$, $\Lambda_q^\mathbf{u}(\mathbf{A}) := \{\mathbf{e} \in \mathbb{Z}^m : \mathbf{Ae} = \mathbf{u} \bmod q\}$. The lattice $\Lambda_q^\mathbf{u}(\mathbf{A})$ is a shift of the lattice $\Lambda_q^\perp(\mathbf{A})$; if $\mathbf{t} \in \Lambda_q^\mathbf{u}(\mathbf{A})$ then $\Lambda_q^\mathbf{u}(\mathbf{A}) = \Lambda_q^\perp(\mathbf{A}) + \mathbf{t}$. Let $\mathbf{T_A} \in \mathbb{Z}^{m \times m}$ be a basis of a lattice $\Lambda_q^\perp(\mathbf{A})$. Then $\mathbf{T_A} \in \mathbb{Z}^{m \times m}$ is also a basis of a lattice $\Lambda_q^\perp(\mathbf{HA})$ for a full rank $\mathbf{H} \in \mathbb{Z}_q^{n \times n}$.

Matrix Norms. For a vector $\mathbf{u}$, we let $\|\mathbf{u}\|$ denote its L_2 norm. For a matrix $\mathbf{R} \in \mathbb{Z}^{k \times m}$, we define the following three norms:

- $\|\mathbf{R}\|$ denotes the L_2 length of the longest column of $\mathbf{R}$.
- $\|\mathbf{R}\|_{\mathsf{GS}} = \|\tilde{\mathbf{R}}\|$ where $\tilde{\mathbf{R}}$ is the Gram-Schmidt orthogonalization of $\mathbf{R}$.
- $\|\mathbf{R}\|_2$ is defined as $\|\mathbf{R}\|_2 = \sup_{\|\mathbf{x}\|=1} \|\mathbf{Rx}\|$.

Note that $\|\mathbf{R}\|_{\mathsf{GS}} \le \|\mathbf{R}\| \le \|\mathbf{R}\|_2 \le \sqrt{k}\|\mathbf{R}\|$ and that $\|\mathbf{R} \cdot \mathbf{S}\|_2 \le \|\mathbf{R}\|_2 \cdot \|\mathbf{S}\|_2$.

Gaussian Distributions. Let $\mathcal{D}_{\Lambda,\sigma,\mathbf{c}}$ denote the discrete gaussian distribution over Λ with center $\mathbf{c}$ and a parameter σ. If $\mathbf{c} = \mathbf{0}$, we omit the subscript and denote $\mathcal{D}_{\Lambda,\sigma}$. We summarize some basic properties of discrete Gaussian distributions.

Lemma 2 ([20]). *Let Λ be an m-dimensional lattice. Let $\mathbf{T}$ be a basis for Λ, and suppose $\sigma \ge \|\mathbf{T}\|_{\mathsf{GS}} \cdot \omega(\sqrt{\log m})$. Then $\Pr[\|\mathbf{x}\| > \sigma\sqrt{m} : \mathbf{x} \leftarrow \mathcal{D}_{\Lambda,\sigma}] \le \mathsf{negl}(m)$.*

Lemma 3 ([20]). *Let n and q be positive integers with q prime, and let $m \ge 2n \log q$. Then for all but a $2q^{-n}$ fraction of all $\mathbf{A} \in \mathbb{Z}_q^{n \times m}$ and for any $\sigma \ge \omega(\sqrt{\log m})$, the distribution of $\mathbf{u} = \mathbf{Ae} \bmod q$ is statistically close to uniform over $\mathbb{Z}_q^n$ where $\mathbf{e} \leftarrow \mathcal{D}_{\mathbb{Z}^m,\sigma}$. Furthermore, the conditional distribution of $\mathbf{e}$ given $\mathbf{Ae} = \mathbf{u} \bmod q$ is exactly $\mathcal{D}_{\Lambda_q^\mathbf{u}(\mathbf{A}),\sigma}$.*

Sampling Algorithms

Lemma 4. *Let $n, m, q > 0$ be positive integers with q prime. There are probabilistic polynomial time algorithms such that*

- [13]: SampleGaussian$(\mathbf{T}, \sigma) \to \mathbf{e}$
  a randomized algorithm that, given a basis $\mathbf{T}$ for an m-dimensional lattice Λ and a parameter $\sigma \ge \|\mathbf{T}\|_{\mathsf{GS}} \cdot \omega(\sqrt{\log m})$ as inputs, then outputs $\mathbf{e}$ which is distributed according to $\mathcal{D}_{\Lambda,\sigma}$.
- [4,5,29]: TrapGen$(q, n, m) \to (\mathbf{A}, \mathbf{T_A})$
  a randomized algorithm that, when $m \ge 2n\lceil\log q\rceil$, outputs a full rank matrix $\mathbf{A} \in \mathbb{Z}_q^{n \times m}$ and a basis $\mathbf{T_A} \in \mathbb{Z}^{m \times m}$ for $\Lambda_q^\perp(\mathbf{A})$ such that $\mathbf{A}$ is statistically close to uniform and $\|\mathbf{T_A}\|_{\mathsf{GS}} = O(\sqrt{n \log q})$ with overwhelming probability in n.
- [14]: SampleLeft$(\mathbf{A}, \mathbf{F}, \mathbf{u}, \mathbf{T_A}, \sigma) \to \mathbf{e}$
  a randomized algorithm that, given a full rank matrix $\mathbf{A} \in \mathbb{Z}_q^{n \times m}$, a matrix $\mathbf{F} \in \mathbb{Z}_q^{n \times m}$, a vector $\mathbf{u} \in \mathbb{Z}_q^n$, a basis $\mathbf{T_A}$ for $\Lambda_q^\perp(\mathbf{A})$, and a Gaussian parameter $\sigma > \|\mathbf{T_A}\|_{\mathsf{GS}} \cdot \omega(\sqrt{\log m})$ as inputs, then outputs a vector $\mathbf{e} \in \mathbb{Z}_q^{2m}$ sampled from a distribution that is statistically close to $\mathcal{D}_{\Lambda_q^\mathbf{u}(\mathbf{A}|\mathbf{F}),\sigma}$.

- [1]: SampleRight($\mathbf{A}, \mathbf{G}, \mathbf{R}, \mathbf{u}, \mathbf{T_G}, \sigma$) → e *where* $\mathbf{F} = \mathbf{AR} + \mathbf{G}$
  a randomized algorithm that, given full rank matrices $\mathbf{A}, \mathbf{G} \in \mathbb{Z}_q^{n \times m}$, *a matrix*
  $\mathbf{R} \in \mathbb{Z}^{m \times m}$, *a vector* $\mathbf{u} \in \mathbb{Z}_q^n$, *a basis* $\mathbf{T_G}$ *of* $\Lambda_q^\perp(\mathbf{G})$, *and a Gaussian parame-*
  ter $\sigma > \|\mathbf{T_G}\|_{\mathsf{GS}} \cdot \|\mathbf{R}\| \cdot \omega(\sqrt{\log m})$ *as inputs, then outputs a vector* $\mathbf{e} \in \mathbb{Z}_q^{2m}$
  sampled from a distribution that is statistically close to $\mathcal{D}_{\Lambda_q^u(\mathbf{A}|\mathbf{F}),\sigma}$.
- [29]: *Let* $m > n\lceil\log q\rceil$. *Then there is a fixed full rank matrix* $\mathbf{G} \in \mathbb{Z}_q^{n \times m}$
  such that the lattice $\Lambda_q^\perp(\mathbf{G})$ *has a publicly known basis* $\mathbf{T_G} \in \mathbb{Z}_q^{m \times m}$ *with*
  $\|\mathbf{T_G}\|_{\mathsf{GS}} \leq \sqrt{5}$.

We sometimes call $\mathbf{G}$ a gadget matrix that enables us to reduce several parameters. We use SampleGaussian($\mathbf{T}, \sigma$) only for sampling a distribution $\mathcal{D}_{\mathbb{Z}^m,\sigma}$. For the purpose, we always use a standard basis for $\mathbb{Z}^m$ as $\mathbf{T}$. Hence, we omit the basis and write SampleGaussian(σ) throughout the paper.

To obtain a lower bound of σ, we will use the following fact.

Lemma 5 ([1]). *Let* $\mathbf{R}$ *be a* $m \times m$ *matrix chosen at random from* $\{-1, 1\}^{m \times m}$. *Then there is a universal constant* C *such that* $\Pr[\|\mathbf{R}\| > C\sqrt{m}] < e^{-m}$.

Randomness Extraction

Lemma 6 ([1]). *Suppose that* $m > (n + 1)\log_2 q + \omega(\log n)$ *and that* $q > 2$ *is prime. Let* $\mathbf{R}$ *be an* $m \times k$ *matrix chosen uniformly in* $\{-1, 1\}^{m \times k}$ *where* $k = k(n)$ *is polynomial in* n. *Let* $\mathbf{A}$ *and* $\mathbf{B}$ *be matrices chosen uniformly in* $\mathbb{Z}_q^{n \times m}$ *and* $\mathbb{Z}_q^{n \times k}$ *respectively. Then, for all vectors* $\mathbf{e} \in \mathbb{Z}_q^m$, *the distribution* $(\mathbf{A}, \mathbf{AR}, \mathbf{R}^T\mathbf{e})$ *is statistically close to the distribution* $(\mathbf{A}, \mathbf{B}, \mathbf{R}^T\mathbf{e})$.

Encoding Identities as Matrices

Definition 2. *Let* q *be a prime and* n *be a positive integer. We say that a function* $H : \mathbb{Z}_q^n \to \mathbb{Z}_q^{n \times n}$ *is a full-rank difference (FRD) map if:*

1. *for all distinct* $\mathbf{u}, \mathbf{v} \in \mathbb{Z}_q^n$, *the matrix* $H(\mathbf{u}) - H(\mathbf{v}) \in \mathbb{Z}_q^{n \times n}$ *is full rank,*
2. H *is computable in polynomial time in* $n \log q$.

Learning with Errors (LWE). For $\alpha \in (0, 1)$ and an integer $q > 2$, let $\bar{\Psi}_\alpha$ denote the probability distribution over $\mathbb{Z}_q$ obtained by choosing $x \in \mathbb{R}$ according to the normal distribution with mean 0 and standard deviation $\alpha/2\sqrt{\pi}$, then output $\lfloor qx \rceil$. The security of our RIBE scheme is reduced to the following LWE assumption.

Assumption 1 (Learning with Errors (LWE) Assumption [32]). For integers $n, m = m(n)$, $\alpha \in (0, 1)$ such that a prime $q = q(n) > 2$ and $\alpha q > 2\sqrt{n}$, define the distribution: $\mathbf{A} \xleftarrow{\$} \mathbb{Z}_q^{n \times m}, \mathbf{s} \xleftarrow{\$} \mathbb{Z}_q^n, \mathbf{x} \xleftarrow{\$} \bar{\Psi}_\alpha^m, \mathbf{v} \xleftarrow{\$} \mathbb{Z}_q^m$. We assume that for any PPT algorithm $\mathcal{A}$ (with output in $\{0, 1\}$), $Adv_{\mathcal{A}}^{LWE} := |\Pr[\mathcal{A}(\mathbf{A}, \mathbf{A}^T\mathbf{s} + \mathbf{x}) = 1] - \Pr[\mathcal{A}(\mathbf{A}, \mathbf{v}) = 1]|$ is negligible in the security parameter n.

Regev [32] showed that (through a quantum reduction) the LWE problem is as hard as approximating the worst-case GapSVP to $\tilde{O}(n/\alpha)$ factors. Peikert [31], Brakerski et al. [13] showed analogous results through classical reductions.

3   B-DKER RIBE

$\mathcal{M}$, $\mathcal{I}$, and $\mathcal{T}$ denote sets of plaintexts, IDs, and time-periods, respectively. Throughout this paper, we consider a single bit scheme, i.e., $\mathcal{M} := \{0, 1\}$.

An RIBE scheme Π consists of seven-tuple algorithms (SetUp, PKG, KeyUp, DKG, Enc, Dec, Revoke) defined as follows:

- (PP, MK, RL, st) $\leftarrow$ SetUp(λ, N): A probabilistic algorithm for setup. It takes a security parameter λ and the number of users N as input and outputs a public parameter PP, a master secret key MK, an initial revocation list RL $= \emptyset$ and a state st.
- (SK$_{\text{ID}}$, st) $\leftarrow$ PKG(PP, MK, ID, st): An algorithm for private key generation. It takes PP, MK, an identity ID $\in \mathcal{I}$, and st as input and outputs a secret key SK$_{\text{ID}}$ and updated state information st.
- KU$_\text{T}$ $\leftarrow$ KeyUp(PP, MK, T, RL, st): An algorithm for key update generation. It takes PP, MK, a time-period T $\in \mathcal{T}$, a current revocation list RL, and state st as input, and then outputs a key update KU$_\text{T}$.
- DK$_{\text{ID,T}}$ or $\perp$ $\leftarrow$ DKG(PP, SK$_{\text{ID}}$, KU$_\text{T}$): A probabilistic algorithm for decryption key generation. It takes PP, SK$_{\text{ID}}$ and KU$_\text{T}$ as input and then outputs a decryption key DK$_{\text{ID,T}}$ at T or $\perp$ if ID has been revoked by T.
- CT$_{\text{ID,T}}$ $\leftarrow$ Enc(PP, ID, T, M): A probabilistic algorithm for encryption. It takes PP, ID $\in \mathcal{I}$, and T $\in \mathcal{T}$, and a plaintext $M \in \mathcal{M}$ as input and then outputs a ciphertext CT$_{\text{ID,T}}$.
- M or $\perp$ $\leftarrow$ Dec(PP, DK$_{\text{ID,T}}$, CT$_{\text{ID,T}}$): A deterministic algorithm for decryption. It takes PP, DK$_{\text{ID,T}}$ and CT$_{\text{ID,T}}$ as input and then outputs M or $\perp$.
- RL $\leftarrow$ Revoke(PP, ID, T, RL, st): An algorithm for revocation. It takes (ID, T) $\in \mathcal{I} \times \mathcal{T}$, the current revocation list RL, and a state st as input and then outputs an updated revocation list RL.

In the above model, we assume that Π meets the following correctness property: For all security parameter $\lambda \in \mathbb{N}$, all (PP, MK, RL, st) $\leftarrow$ SetUp(λ, N), all $M \in \mathcal{M}$, all ID $\in \mathcal{I}$, all T $\in \mathcal{T}$, if ID has not been revoked by T $\in \mathcal{T}$, it holds that $M =$ Dec(DKG(PP, PKG(PP, MK, ID, st), KeyUp(PP, MK, T, RL, st)), Enc(PP, ID, T, M)).

Throughout this paper, we consider the following security notion called *indistinguishability from random against selective chosen plaintext attacks and Q-bounded decryption key exposure* (IND-sRID-Q-CPA). That is, we define indistinguishability from random against CPA adversaries taking into account *Q-bounded DKER*, which is a weaker notion than original (unbounded) DKER [34]. Q-bounded DKER guarantees that the RIBE scheme is secure even if at most Q decryption keys per user leaked, whereas unbounded DKER allows any number of decryption-key leakage. In our security model, a CPA adversary is allowed to obtain at most Q decryption keys of the target user ID*, and tries to distinguish between the challenge ciphertext and a random element in the ciphertext space. Therefore, our security model also implies anonymity.

Definition 3 (IND-sRID-Q-CPA). *For any a-priori fixed Q $(:= poly(\lambda))$, an RIBE scheme Π is said to satisfy IND-sRID-Q-CPA security if for all PPT adversaries $\mathcal{A}$, $Adv_{\Pi,\mathcal{A}}^{IND\text{-}Q\text{-}CPA}(\lambda, N)$ is negligible in λ. For a PPT adversary $\mathcal{A}$, we define $\mathcal{A}$'s advantage against IND-sRID-Q-CPA security by $Adv_{\Pi,\mathcal{A}}^{IND\text{-}Q\text{-}CPA}(\lambda) := |\Pr[Exp_{\Pi,\mathcal{A}}^{IND\text{-}Q\text{-}CPA}(\lambda) = 1] - 1/2|$, where $Exp_{\Pi,\mathcal{A}}^{IND\text{-}Q\text{-}CPA}(\lambda)$ is defined by the following experiment:*

$$Exp_{\Pi,\mathcal{A}}^{IND\text{-}Q\text{-}CPA}(\lambda) : (ID^*, T^*, state_1) \leftarrow \mathcal{A}(find, \lambda)$$
$$(PP, MK, RL, st) \leftarrow SetUp(\lambda, N)$$
$$(M^*, state_2) \leftarrow \mathcal{A}^{\mathcal{O}}(find, PP, state_1)$$
$$CT_0 \leftarrow Enc(PP, ID^*, T^*, M^*), \quad CT_1 \xleftarrow{\$} \mathcal{C}_\lambda, \quad b \xleftarrow{\$} \{0,1\}$$
$$b' \leftarrow \mathcal{A}^{\mathcal{O}}(guess, CT_b, state_2)$$
$$Return\ 1\ if\ b' = b;\ otherwise,\ return\ 0$$

where $\mathcal{C}_\lambda$ is a ciphertext space which is determined by the security parameter λ. Here, $\mathcal{O}$ is a set of oracles $\{PKG(\cdot), KeyUp(\cdot), Revoke(\cdot,\cdot), DKG(\cdot,\cdot)\}$ defined as follows.

$PKG(\cdot)$: *For a query $ID \in \mathcal{I}$, it stores and returns $PKG(PP, MK, ID, st)$.*
$KeyUp(\cdot)$: *For a query $T \in \mathcal{T}$, it stores and returns $KeyUp(PP, MK, T, RL, st)$.*
$Revoke(\cdot,\cdot)$: *For a query $(ID, T) \in \mathcal{I} \times \mathcal{T}$, it updates a revocation list RL by running $Revoke(PP, ID, T, RL, st)$.*
$DKG(\cdot,\cdot)$: *For a query $(ID, T) \in \mathcal{I} \times \mathcal{T}$, it returns $DKG(PP, SK_{ID}, KU_T)$ and stores it unless it is $\perp$.*

$\mathcal{A}$ is allowed to access the above oracles with the following restrictions.

1. *$KeyUp(\cdot)$ and $Revoke(\cdot,\cdot)$ can be queried at a time period which is later than or equal to that of all previous queries.*
2. *$Revoke(\cdot,\cdot)$ cannot be queried at a time period T after issuing T to $KeyUp(\cdot)$.*
3. *If ID^* was issued to $PKG(\cdot)$ at T', then (ID^*, T) must be issued to $Revoke(\cdot,\cdot)$ such that $T' \leq T \leq T^*$.*
4. *$DKG(\cdot,\cdot)$ cannot be queried at T before issuing T to $KeyUp(\cdot)$.*
5. *(ID^*, T^*) cannot be issued to $DKG(\cdot,\cdot)$.*
6. *If (ID^*, T)'s such that $T \neq T^*$ were issued to $DKG(\cdot,\cdot)$ more than Q times, then (ID^*, T) must be issued to $Revoke(\cdot,\cdot)$ such that $T \leq T^*$.*

4   Construction

In this section, we show the construction of our lattice-based B-DKER RIBE scheme that utilizes CFFs.

- SetUp(λ, N): On input a security parameter λ and a maximal number N of users, set the parameters q, n, m, σ, α. Then, use the TrapGen(q, n, m) algorithm to select $\mathbf{A}_0 \in \mathbb{Z}_q^{n \times m}$ with a basis $\mathbf{T}_{\mathbf{A}_0}$ for $\Lambda_q^\perp(\mathbf{A}_0)$. Select

$\mathbf{A}_1, \mathbf{A}_2 \xleftarrow{\$} \mathbb{Z}_q^{n \times m}$ and $\mathbf{u} \leftarrow \mathbb{Z}_q^n$. Choose an FRD map H as in Definition 2. Run $(w, d, \mathcal{F}) \xleftarrow{\$} \mathsf{CFF.Gen}(|\mathcal{T}|, Q)$ and finally output

$$\mathsf{PP} := (H, \mathbf{A}_0, \mathbf{A}_1, \mathbf{A}_2, \mathbf{u}), \quad \mathsf{MK} := \mathbf{T}_{\mathbf{A}_0},$$

st $:=$ BT, and RL $:= \emptyset$.

- PKG(PP, MK, ID, st): Parse st as BT. Randomly choose an unassigned leaf η from BT, and store ID $\in \mathbb{Z}_q^n$ in the leaf η. For each node $\theta \in \mathsf{Path}(\mathsf{BT}, \eta)$, perform the following steps: Recall $\{\mathbf{u}'_{\theta,\ell}\}_{\ell \in [d]}$ if it was defined. Otherwise, choose $\mathbf{u}'_{\theta,1}, \ldots, \mathbf{u}'_{\theta,d} \xleftarrow{\$} \mathbb{Z}_q^n$ and store them in θ. For every $\ell \in [d]$, sample $\mathbf{e}'_{\theta,\ell} \leftarrow \mathsf{SampleLeft}(\mathbf{A}_0, \mathbf{F}_{\mathsf{ID}}, \mathbf{u}'_{\theta,\ell}, \mathbf{T}_{\mathbf{A}_0}, \sigma)$ where $\mathbf{F}_{\mathsf{ID}} = \mathbf{A}_1 + H(\mathsf{ID})\mathbf{G} \in \mathbb{Z}_q^{n \times m}$. Finally output

$$\mathsf{SK}_{\mathsf{ID}} = \left(\left\{ \theta, \{\mathbf{e}'_{\theta,\ell}\}_{\ell \in [d]} \right\}_{\theta \in \mathsf{Path}(\mathsf{BT}, \eta)} \right).$$

- KeyUp(PP, MK, T, RL, st): For each node $\theta \in \mathsf{KUNode}(\mathsf{BT}, \mathsf{RL}, \mathsf{T})$, perform the following steps: Recall $\{\mathbf{u}'_{\theta,\ell}\}_{\ell \in [d]}$ if it was defined. Otherwise, choose $\mathbf{u}'_{\theta,1}, \ldots, \mathbf{u}'_{\theta,d} \xleftarrow{\$} \mathbb{Z}_q^n$ and store them in θ. Sample $\tilde{\mathbf{e}}_\theta \leftarrow \mathsf{SampleLeft}(\mathbf{A}_0, \mathbf{F}_{\mathsf{T}}, \tilde{\mathbf{u}}_\theta, \mathbf{T}_{\mathbf{A}_0}, \sigma)$ where $\mathbf{F}_{\mathsf{T}} = \mathbf{A}_2 + H(\mathsf{T})\mathbf{G}$ and $\tilde{\mathbf{u}}_\theta = \mathbf{u} - \sum_{\ell \in \mathcal{F}_{\mathsf{T}}} \mathbf{u}'_{\theta,\ell}$. Output

$$\mathsf{KU}_{\mathsf{T}} = \left(\{\theta, \tilde{\mathbf{e}}_\theta\}_{\theta \in \mathsf{KUNode}(\mathsf{BT}, \mathsf{RL}, \mathsf{T})}, \mathcal{F}_{\mathsf{T}} \right),$$

where for simplicity we here assume $\mathcal{F}_{\mathsf{T}}$ is a d-bit string such that ℓ-th bit is one for $\ell \in \mathcal{F}_{\mathsf{T}}$ and other bits are zero.

- DKG(PP, SK$_{\mathsf{ID}}$, KU$_{\mathsf{T}}$): Parse $\mathsf{SK}_{\mathsf{ID}}$ and KU_{T} as $\left\{ \theta, \left\{ \mathbf{e}'_{\theta,\ell} \right\}_{\ell \in [d]} \right\}_{\theta \in \Theta_{\mathrm{SK}}}$ and $\{\theta, \tilde{\mathbf{e}}_\theta\}_{\theta \in \Theta_{\mathrm{KU}}}$, respectively. Output $\perp$ if $\Theta_{\mathrm{SK}} \cap \Theta_{\mathrm{KU}} = \emptyset$. Otherwise, for some $\theta \in \Theta_{\mathrm{SK}} \cap \Theta_{\mathrm{KU}}$, compute $\mathbf{e}_\theta = \sum_{\ell \in \mathcal{F}_{\mathsf{T}}} \mathbf{e}'_{\theta,\ell}$ and output $\mathsf{DK}_{\mathsf{ID}, \mathsf{T}} = (\mathbf{e}_\theta, \tilde{\mathbf{e}}_\theta)$.

- Enc(PP, ID, T, M): To encrypt a bit $M \in \{0, 1\}$, it runs the following steps: Set $\mathbf{F}_{\mathsf{ID}, \mathsf{T}} = [\mathbf{A}_0 | \mathbf{F}_{\mathsf{ID}} | \mathbf{F}_{\mathsf{T}}] \in \mathbb{Z}_q^{n \times 3m}$. Choose $\mathbf{s} \xleftarrow{\$} \mathbb{Z}_q^n$ and $\mathbf{R}_{\mathsf{ID}}, \mathbf{R}_{\mathsf{T}} \xleftarrow{\$} \{-1, 1\}^{m \times m}$. Choose noise $x \leftarrow \bar{\Psi}_\alpha$ and a noise vector $\mathbf{y} \leftarrow \bar{\Psi}_\alpha^m$ and set $\mathbf{z}_{\mathsf{ID}} = \mathbf{R}_{\mathsf{ID}}^T \mathbf{y} \in \mathbb{Z}_q^m$, $\mathbf{z}_{\mathsf{T}} = \mathbf{R}_{\mathsf{T}}^T \mathbf{y} \in \mathbb{Z}_q^m$. Set

$$c_0 = \mathbf{u}^T \mathbf{s} + x + M \left\lfloor \frac{q}{2} \right\rfloor \in \mathbb{Z}_q, \quad \mathbf{c} = \mathbf{F}_{\mathsf{ID}, \mathsf{T}}^T \mathbf{s} + \begin{bmatrix} \mathbf{y} \\ \mathbf{z}_{\mathsf{ID}} \\ \mathbf{z}_{\mathsf{T}} \end{bmatrix} \in \mathbb{Z}_q^{3m}.$$

Output the ciphertext $\mathsf{CT}_{\mathsf{ID}, \mathsf{T}} := (c_0, \mathbf{c}) \in \mathbb{Z}_q \times \mathbb{Z}_q^{3m}$.

- Dec(PP, DK$_{\mathsf{ID}, \mathsf{T}}$, CT$_{\mathsf{ID}, \mathsf{T}}$): It runs the following steps: Parse $\mathbf{c}$ as $\begin{bmatrix} \mathbf{c}_0 \\ \mathbf{c}_1 \\ \mathbf{c}_2 \end{bmatrix}$ where $\mathbf{c}_i \in \mathbb{Z}_q^m$. Compute $c' = c_0 - \mathbf{e}_\theta^T \begin{bmatrix} \mathbf{c}_0 \\ \mathbf{c}_1 \end{bmatrix} - \tilde{\mathbf{e}}_\theta^T \begin{bmatrix} \mathbf{c}_0 \\ \mathbf{c}_2 \end{bmatrix} \in \mathbb{Z}_q$. Compare c' and $\lfloor \frac{q}{2} \rfloor$ treating them as integers in $\mathbb{Z}$. If they are close, i.e., if $|c' - \lfloor \frac{q}{2} \rfloor| < \lfloor \frac{q}{4} \rfloor$, output 1, otherwise output 0.

– Revoke($\mathsf{ID}, \mathsf{T}, \mathsf{RL}, \mathsf{st}$): Add $(\mathsf{ID}, \mathsf{T})$ to RL, and output the updated RL.

Parameters and Correctness. We use the following lemma to bound the noise.

Lemma 7 ([1]). *Let* $\mathbf{e}$ *be some vector in* $\mathbb{Z}^m$ *and let* $y \leftarrow \bar{\Psi}_\alpha$. *Then the quantity* $|\langle \mathbf{e}, \mathbf{y} \rangle|$ *when treated as an integer in* $(-q/2, q/2]$ *satisfies* $|\langle \mathbf{e}, \mathbf{y} \rangle| \leq \|\mathbf{e}\| q\alpha \cdot \omega(\sqrt{\log m}) + \|\mathbf{e}\|\sqrt{m}/2$.

We have during decryption,

$$w = c_0 - \mathbf{e}_\theta^T \begin{bmatrix} \mathbf{c}_0 \\ \mathbf{c}_1 \end{bmatrix} - \tilde{\mathbf{e}}_\theta^T \begin{bmatrix} \mathbf{c}_0 \\ \mathbf{c}_2 \end{bmatrix} = M \left\lfloor \frac{q}{2} \right\rfloor + \underbrace{x - \mathbf{e}_\theta^T \begin{bmatrix} \mathbf{y} \\ \mathbf{R}_{\mathsf{ID}}^T \mathbf{y} \end{bmatrix} - \tilde{\mathbf{e}}_\theta^T \begin{bmatrix} \mathbf{y} \\ \mathbf{R}_{\mathsf{T}}^T \mathbf{y} \end{bmatrix}}_{\text{error term}}.$$

Then, the error term can be bounded as follows.

Lemma 8. *The norm of the error term is bounded by* $wq\sigma m\alpha \cdot \omega(\sqrt{\log m}) + O(w\sigma m^{3/2})$ *with high probability.*

Proof. Let $\mathbf{e}_\theta = (\mathbf{e}_{\theta,1}|\mathbf{e}_{\theta,2})$ and $\tilde{\mathbf{e}}_\theta = (\tilde{\mathbf{e}}_{\theta,1}|\tilde{\mathbf{e}}_{\theta,2})$ with $\mathbf{e}_{\theta,1}, \mathbf{e}_{\theta,2}, \tilde{\mathbf{e}}_{\theta,1}, \tilde{\mathbf{e}}_{\theta,2} \in \mathbb{Z}^m$. Then the error term is

$$x - \mathbf{e}_\theta^T \begin{bmatrix} \mathbf{y} \\ \mathbf{R}_{\mathsf{ID}}^T \mathbf{y} \end{bmatrix} - \tilde{\mathbf{e}}_\theta^T \begin{bmatrix} \mathbf{y} \\ \mathbf{R}_{\mathsf{T}}^T \mathbf{y} \end{bmatrix} = x - (\mathbf{e}_{\theta,1} + \tilde{\mathbf{e}}_{\theta,1} + \mathbf{R}_{\mathsf{ID}}\mathbf{e}_{\theta,2} + \mathbf{R}_{\mathsf{T}}\tilde{\mathbf{e}}_{\theta,2})^T \mathbf{y}.$$

From Lemma 2, we have $\|\mathbf{e}_{\theta,\ell}'\| \leq \sigma\sqrt{2m}$ and $\|\tilde{\mathbf{e}}_\theta\| \leq \sigma\sqrt{2m}$ with high probability. The former bounds imply that $\|\mathbf{e}_\theta\| \leq \sum_{\ell \in \mathcal{F}_\mathsf{T}} \|\mathbf{e}_{\theta,\ell}'\| \leq w\sigma\sqrt{2m}$. Here, we use the fact that CFF is w-uniform. By Lemma 5, $\|\mathbf{R}_{\mathsf{ID}}\| \leq O(\sqrt{m})$ and $\|\mathbf{R}_\mathsf{T}\| \leq O(\sqrt{m})$ with high probability. Then, $\|\mathbf{e}_{\theta,1} + \tilde{\mathbf{e}}_{\theta,1} + \mathbf{R}_{\mathsf{ID}}\mathbf{e}_{\theta,2} + \mathbf{R}_\mathsf{T}\tilde{\mathbf{e}}_{\theta,2}\| \leq \|\mathbf{e}_{\theta,1}\| + \|\tilde{\mathbf{e}}_{\theta,1}\| + \|\mathbf{R}_{\mathsf{ID}}\mathbf{e}_{\theta,2}\| + \|\mathbf{R}_2\tilde{\mathbf{e}}_{\theta,2}\| \leq O(w\sigma m)$. Then, by Lemma 7, the error term is bounded by

$$|x| + \left|(\mathbf{e}_{\theta,1} + \tilde{\mathbf{e}}_{\theta,1} + \mathbf{R}_{\mathsf{ID}}\mathbf{e}_{\theta,2} + \mathbf{R}_2\tilde{\mathbf{e}}_{\theta,2})^T \mathbf{y}\right| \leq w\sigma m q\alpha \cdot \omega(\sqrt{\log m}) + O(w\sigma m^{3/2}).$$

$\square$

Now, for the scheme to work correctly, the following conditions should hold, taking n to be the security parameter:

– the error term is less than $q/5$ with high probability, i.e., $\alpha < [w\sigma m \cdot \omega(\sqrt{\log m})]^{-1}$ and $q = \Omega(w\sigma m^{3/2})$,
– that TrapGen can operate, i.e., $m > 2n \log q$,
– that σ is sufficiently large for SampleLeft and SampleRight, i.e., $\sigma > \|\mathbf{T}_\mathsf{G}\|_{\mathrm{GS}} \cdot \|\mathbf{R}_{\mathsf{ID}}\| \cdot \omega(\sqrt{\log m}) = \sqrt{m} \cdot \omega(\sqrt{\log m})$,
– that Regev's reduction applies, i.e., $q > 2\sqrt{n}/\alpha$,

Hence, we set the parameters (q, m, σ, α) as follows:

$$m = 2n^{1+\delta}, \qquad\qquad q = wm^2 \cdot \omega(\sqrt{\log n}),$$
$$\sigma = \sqrt{m} \cdot \omega(\sqrt{\log n}), \qquad \alpha = \left[wm^{3/2} \cdot \omega(\sqrt{\log n})\right]^{-1},$$

and round up m to the nearest larger integer and q to the nearest larger prime. Here we assume that δ is such that $n^\delta > \lceil \log q \rceil = O(\log n)$.

5   Security

In this section, we prove the security of our scheme in Sect. 4.

Theorem 1. *If the LWE assumption holds and the underlying CFF is Q-cover-free and w-uniform, then the proposed RIBE scheme in Sect. 4 with the parameters set as above is IND-sRID-Q-CPA secure. In particular, if there exists an adversary $\mathcal{A}$ attacking IND-sRID-Q-CPA security of the RIBE scheme, then there exists an adversary $\mathcal{B}$ against the LWE assumption with advantage $Adv_{\mathcal{B}}^{LWE} \geq \frac{1}{w} Adv_{\Pi,\mathcal{A}}^{IND-Q-CPA}(\lambda) - \mathsf{negl}(\lambda)$.*

Due to the page limitation, we omit some detailed discussion of the following proof. Especially, we focus on the part that differs from Chen et al.'s proof [16].

Proof. The proof proceeds in a sequence of games where the first game is the same as IND-sRID-Q-CPA game. In the last game, the challenge ciphertext is a uniform random element in the ciphertext space, hence, the advantage of a PPT adversary $\mathcal{A}$ is zero. Let E_i denote the event that $\mathcal{A}$ wins the game, i.e., $b' = b$, in **Game** i. Then, $\mathcal{A}$'s advantage in **Game** i is $\left| \Pr[E_i] - \frac{1}{2} \right|$.

Let ID^* denote the challenge identity. The simulator $\mathcal{B}$ guesses an adversarial type among the following two types:

- **Type-I adversary:** ID^* will be revoked before T^*. Hence, $\mathcal{A}$ may issue a secret key extraction query for $\mathsf{SK}_{\mathsf{ID}^*}$ or decryption key queries $\mathsf{DK}_{\mathsf{ID}^*,\mathsf{T}}$ for $\mathsf{T} \neq \mathsf{T}^*$ more than Q times.
- **Type-II adversary:** ID^* will not be revoked before T^*. Hence, $\mathcal{A}$ may issue decryption key queries $\mathsf{DK}_{\mathsf{ID}^*,\mathsf{T}}$ for $\mathsf{T} \neq \mathsf{T}^*$ at most Q times.

$\mathcal{B}$ guesses the types of the adversary with probability $1/2$. If the guess is not correct, $\mathcal{B}$ aborts the game and output a random bit. We separate the description of **Game** 2 against the Type-I and Type-II adversary. Other games are the same for both types of the adversary.

Game^{real}: This is the original IND-sRID-Q-CPA game between an adversary $\mathcal{A}$ against our scheme and an IND-RID-Q-CPA challenger.

Game 0: The game is the same as **Game**^{real} except that at the beginning of the game, the challenger guesses an index $\ell^* \in \mathcal{F}_{\mathsf{T}^*}$ such that the secret key element $\mathbf{e}'_{\theta,\ell^*}$ is not used to answer the first Q decryption key queries $\mathsf{DK}_{\mathsf{ID}^*,\mathsf{T}}$ by $\mathcal{A}$, and assume that the guess is right. If the guess is not correct, $\mathcal{B}$ aborts the game and output a random bit.

Obviously, the challenger's guess is right with probability $1/w$. In other words, the reduction loss is w, which is polynomial in the security parameter. Note that in the rest of the proof, the challenger knows the index ℓ^*. The guess is crucial to answer ID's decryption keys in **Game** 2 against the Type II adversary.

Game 1: In **Game** 0, the PP contains random matrices $\mathbf{A}_0, \mathbf{A}_1, \mathbf{A}_2$ in $\mathbb{Z}_q^{n \times m}$. At the challenge phase, the challenger generates a ciphertext $\mathsf{CT}_{\mathsf{ID}^*,\mathsf{T}^*}$. We let $\mathbf{R}_{\mathsf{ID}^*}$ and $\mathbf{R}_{\mathsf{T}^*}$ denote random matrices generated for the creation of the challenge ciphertext. As the proof of Agrawal et al. [1], **Game** 1 is the same as **Game** 0 except that we change the creations of $\mathbf{A}_1$ and $\mathbf{A}_2$ in the PP. The challenger chooses $\mathbf{R}_{\mathsf{ID}^*}$ and $\mathbf{R}_{\mathsf{T}^*}$, which will be used to create the challenge ciphertext $\mathsf{CT}_{\mathsf{ID}^*,\mathsf{T}^*}$, at the setup phase and construct matrices $\mathbf{A}_1$ and $\mathbf{A}_2$ as

$$\mathbf{A}_1 \leftarrow \mathbf{A}_0 \mathbf{R}_{\mathsf{ID}^*} - H(\mathsf{ID}^*)\mathbf{G} \quad \text{and} \quad \mathbf{A}_2 \leftarrow \mathbf{A}_0 \mathbf{R}_{\mathsf{T}^*} - H(\mathsf{T}^*)\mathbf{G}.$$

The remainder of the game is unchanged. In $\mathcal{A}$'s view, **Game** 1 and **Game** 0 are statistically indistinguishable from Lemma 6.

Game 2: In **Game** 1, $\{\mathbf{u}'_{\theta,\ell}\}_{\ell \in [d]}$ are independently random vectors in $\mathbb{Z}_q^n$, and the challenger samples $\{\mathbf{e}'_{\theta,\ell}\}_{\ell \in [d]}$ and $\tilde{\mathbf{e}}_\theta$ using SampleLeft. **Game** 2 is the same as **Game** 1 except that, for each node θ, we change the distributions of $\{\mathbf{u}'_{\theta,\ell}\}_{\ell \in [d]}$, the secret key $\{\mathbf{e}'_{\theta,\ell}\}_{\ell \in [d]}$ for ID^*, and the key update $\tilde{\mathbf{e}}_\theta$ for T^* so that $\mathcal{B}$ can create the keys without using the trapdoor $\mathbf{T}_{\mathbf{A}_0}$. In this game, the distributions differ against the type of adversaries. We use **Game** 2-I and **Game** 2-II to denote the games.

Type-I Adversary: The modification of **Game** 2-I is similar to Chen et al.'s one [16]. By definition, the challenger should answer $\mathsf{SK}_{\mathsf{ID}^*}$ and $\mathsf{DK}_{\mathsf{ID}^*,\mathsf{T}}$ queries only for the nodes $\theta \in \mathsf{Path}(\eta^*)$, where η^* is a randomly selected leaf which ID^* will be assigned to. By definition of Type-I adversary, since ID^* will be revoked before T^*, the challenger should answer $\mathsf{KU}_{\mathsf{T}^*}$ queries only for the nodes $\theta \notin \mathsf{Path}(\eta^*)$. Hence, there are no nodes θ that the challenger should answer key queries for both ID^* and T^*. Then, in **Game** 2-I, we change the distributions as follows:

– Sample independently random $\mathbf{e}'_{\theta,\ell} \leftarrow$ SampleGaussian(σ) and set $\mathbf{u}'_{\theta,\ell} = [\mathbf{A}_0|\mathbf{F}_{\mathsf{ID}^*}]\mathbf{e}_{\theta,\ell}$ for $\ell \in [d]$ and $\theta \in \mathsf{Path}(\eta^*)$,
– Sample $\tilde{\mathbf{e}}_\theta \leftarrow$ SampleGaussian(σ) and set $\tilde{\mathbf{u}}_\theta = [\mathbf{A}_0|\mathbf{F}_{\mathsf{T}^*}]\tilde{\mathbf{e}}_\theta$ for $\theta \notin \mathsf{Path}(\eta^*)$. Set $\mathbf{u}'_{\theta,\ell}$ for $\ell \in [d]\backslash\{\ell^*\}$ as independently random vectors in $\mathbb{Z}_q^n$. Then, set $\mathbf{u}'_{\theta,\ell^*} = \mathbf{u} - \tilde{\mathbf{u}}_\theta - \sum_{\ell \in \mathcal{F}_{\mathsf{T}^*}\backslash\{\ell^*\}} \mathbf{u}'_{\theta,\ell}$.

Although we use ℓ^*, which the challenger guessed in **Game** 0, to create $\{\mathbf{u}'_{\theta,\ell}\}_{\ell \in [d]}$ for $\theta \notin \mathsf{Path}(\eta^*)$, the role can be replaced by any $\ell \in \mathcal{F}_{\mathsf{T}^*}$. Then, the challenger responds to $\mathcal{A}$'s key queries as follows:

– $\mathsf{SK}_{\mathsf{ID}}$ queries for $\mathsf{ID} \neq \mathsf{ID}^*$ and KU_{T} queries for $\mathsf{T} \neq \mathsf{T}^*$ are unchanged,
– answers $\mathsf{SK}_{\mathsf{ID}^*}$ queries using the above $\left\{\mathbf{e}'_{\theta,\ell}\right\}_{\ell \in [d]}$,
– answers $\mathsf{KU}_{\mathsf{T}^*}$ queries using the above $\tilde{\mathbf{e}}_\theta$,
– answers $\mathsf{DK}_{\mathsf{ID},\mathsf{T}}$ queries by using the above $\mathsf{SK}_{\mathsf{ID}}$ and KU_{T}.

Notice that we do not use the trapdoor $\mathbf{T}_{\mathbf{A}_0}$ to create $\mathsf{SK}_{\mathsf{ID}^*}$ and $\mathsf{KU}_{\mathsf{T}^*}$.

As Chen et al. [16], we can show that **Game** 2-I is statistically indistinguishable from **Game** 1 with high probability. In **Game** 1, $\{\mathbf{u}'_{\theta,\ell}\}_{\ell \in [d]}$ are independently random vectors in $\mathbb{Z}_q^n$, and since $\{\mathbf{e}'_{\theta,\ell}\}_{\ell \in [d]}$ for ID^* and $\tilde{\mathbf{e}}_\theta$ for T^* are sampled from $\mathbf{e}_{\theta,\ell} \leftarrow$ SampleLeft$(\mathbf{A}_0, \mathbf{F}_{\mathsf{ID}^*}, \mathbf{u}'_{\theta,\ell}, \mathbf{T}_{\mathbf{A}_0}, \sigma)$ and $\tilde{\mathbf{e}}_\theta \leftarrow$ SampleLeft$(\mathbf{A}_0, \mathbf{F}_{\mathsf{T}^*}, \tilde{\mathbf{u}}_\theta, \mathbf{T}_{\mathbf{A}_0}, \sigma)$ where $\tilde{\mathbf{u}}_\theta = \mathbf{u} - \sum_{\ell \in \mathcal{F}_{\mathsf{T}^*}} \mathbf{u}'_{\theta,\ell}$, the distributions are statistically close to $\mathcal{D}_{\Lambda_q^{\mathbf{u}'_{\theta,\ell}}([\mathbf{A}_0|\mathbf{F}_{\mathsf{ID}^*}]),\sigma}$ and $\mathcal{D}_{\Lambda_q^{\tilde{\mathbf{u}}_\theta}([\mathbf{A}_0|\mathbf{F}_{\mathsf{T}^*}]),\sigma}$, respectively. In **Game 2-I**, $\{\mathbf{e}_{\theta,\ell}\}_{\ell\in[d]}$ for ID^* and $\tilde{\mathbf{e}}_\theta$ for T^* are sampled from $\mathcal{D}_{\mathbb{Z}^{2m},\sigma}$ from the property of SampleGaussian. Hence, by Lemma 3, the distribution of each $\{\mathbf{u}'_{\theta,\ell}\}_{\ell\in[d]}$ and $\tilde{\mathbf{u}}_\theta$ in **Game 2-I** is statistically close to uniform over $\mathbb{Z}_q^n$, respectively. Furthermore, the conditional distribution of each $\{\mathbf{e}'_{\theta,\ell}\}_{\ell\in[d]}$ and $\tilde{\mathbf{e}}_\theta$ given $\{\mathbf{u}'_{\theta,\ell}\}_{\ell\in[d]}$ and $\tilde{\mathbf{u}}_\theta$ is statistically close to $\mathcal{D}_{\Lambda_q^{\mathbf{u}'_{\theta,\ell}}([\mathbf{A}_0|\mathbf{F}_{\mathsf{ID}^*}]),\sigma}$ and $\mathcal{D}_{\Lambda_q^{\tilde{\mathbf{u}}_\theta}([\mathbf{A}_0|\mathbf{F}_{\mathsf{T}^*}]),\sigma}$, respectively. Hence, **Game 2-I** is statistically indistinguishable from **Game 1** in $\mathcal{A}$'s view.

Type-II adversary. The modification of **Game 2-II** is the most technical part of this paper. In this game, the distributions of $\mathbf{u}'$, $\{\mathbf{e}'_{\theta,\ell}\}_{\ell\in[d]}$, and $\tilde{\mathbf{e}}_\theta$ for $\theta \notin \mathsf{Path}(\eta^*)$ are the same as **Game 2-I**, however, we change the distributions of those for $\theta \in \mathsf{Path}(\eta^*)$. As opposed to the case of **Game 2-I**, the challenge ID^* will not be revoked in the challenge time period T^*. Since there are nodes θ which the simulator should create both the secret key $\{\mathbf{e}_{\theta,\ell}\}_{\ell\in[d]}$ for ID^* and the key update $\tilde{\mathbf{e}}_\theta$ for T^*, the previous approach is insufficient. In **Game 2-II**, we change the distributions for $\theta \in \mathsf{Path}(\eta^*)$ as follows:

- Sample independently random $\mathbf{e}'_{\theta,\ell} \leftarrow \mathsf{SampleGaussian}(\sigma)$ and set $\mathbf{u}'_{\theta,\ell} = [\mathbf{A}_0|\mathbf{F}_{\mathsf{ID}^*}]\mathbf{e}'_{\theta,\ell}$ for $\ell \in [d]\setminus\{\ell^*\}$,
- Sample $\tilde{\mathbf{e}}_\theta \leftarrow \mathsf{SampleGaussian}(\sigma)$ and set $\tilde{\mathbf{u}}_\theta = [\mathbf{A}_0|\mathbf{F}_{\mathsf{T}^*}]\tilde{\mathbf{e}}_\theta$. It immediately means that $\mathbf{u}'_{\theta,\ell^*} = \mathbf{u} - \tilde{\mathbf{u}}_\theta - \sum_{\ell\in\mathcal{F}_{\mathsf{T}^*}\setminus\{\ell^*\}}\mathbf{u}'_{\theta,\ell}$.

Then, the challenger responds to $\mathcal{A}$'s key queries as follows:

- $\mathsf{SK}_{\mathsf{ID}}$ queries for $\mathsf{ID} \neq \mathsf{ID}^*$ and KU_{T} queries for $\mathsf{T} \neq \mathsf{T}^*$ are unchanged,
- answers $\mathsf{KU}_{\mathsf{T}^*}$ queries using the above $\tilde{\mathbf{e}}_\theta$,
- answers $\mathsf{DK}_{\mathsf{ID},\mathsf{T}}$ queries for $\mathsf{ID} \neq \mathsf{ID}^*$ by using the above $\mathsf{SK}_{\mathsf{ID}}$ and KU_{T},
- answers $\mathsf{DK}_{\mathsf{ID}^*,\mathsf{T}}$ queries using the above $\{\mathbf{e}'_{\theta,\ell}\}_{\ell\in[d]}$ and KU_{T}.

The challenger can respond to all key queries by $\mathcal{A}$ using the key creation algorithms. Although the challenger can create all the other keys, it cannot create the secret key element $\mathbf{e}'_{\theta,\ell^*}$ for ID^*. However, it does not matter since the maximum number of $\mathsf{DK}_{\mathsf{ID}^*,\mathsf{T}}$ queries by $\mathcal{A}$ is bounded up to Q times by the definition of Type II adversary. Moreover, thanks to the property of CFFs and the guess ℓ^* in **Game 0**, we know that $\mathbf{e}_{\theta,\ell^*}$ is not used to respond to $\mathsf{DK}_{\mathsf{ID}^*,\mathsf{T}}$ queries. As in **Game 2-I**, **Game 2-II** is statistically indistinguishable from **Game 1** in $\mathcal{A}$'s view by Lemma 3.

Game 3: In **Game 2**, a matrix $\mathbf{A}_0$ is generated by TrapGen and its trapdoor $\mathbf{T}_{\mathbf{A}_0}$ is used to respond to $\mathcal{A}$'s key queries for $\mathsf{ID} \neq \mathsf{ID}^*$ and $\mathsf{T} \neq \mathsf{T}^*$. **Game 3** is the same as **Game 2** except that we sample $\mathbf{A}_0$ as a random matrix in $\mathbb{Z}_q^{n\times m}$. From the property of TrapGen, matrices generated by the algorithm are statistically close to random matrices in $\mathbb{Z}_q^{n\times m}$. Hence, the distributions of PP between **Game 2** and **Game 3** are statistically indistinguishable. Observe that

$$[\mathbf{A}_0|\mathbf{F}_{\mathsf{ID}}] := [\mathbf{A}_0|\mathbf{A}_1 + H(\mathsf{ID})\mathbf{G}] = [\mathbf{A}_0|\mathbf{A}_0\mathbf{R}_{\mathsf{ID}^*} + (H(\mathsf{ID}) - H(\mathsf{ID}^*))\,\mathbf{G}],$$
$$[\mathbf{A}_0|\mathbf{F}_{\mathsf{T}}] := [\mathbf{A}_0|\mathbf{A}_2 + H(\mathsf{T})\mathbf{G}] = [\mathbf{A}_0|\mathbf{A}_0\mathbf{R}_{\mathsf{T}^*} + (H(\mathsf{T}) - H(\mathsf{T}^*))\,\mathbf{G}].$$

Due to the property of gadget matrix, we know a trapdoor $\mathbf{T_G}$ which is also a trapdoor for $(H(\mathsf{ID}) - H(\mathsf{ID}^*))\mathbf{G}$ and $(H(\mathsf{T}) - H(\mathsf{T}^*))\mathbf{G}$ if $\mathsf{ID} \neq \mathsf{ID}^*$ and $\mathsf{T} \neq \mathsf{T}^*$, since $H(\mathsf{ID}) - H(\mathsf{ID}^*)$ and $H(\mathsf{T}) - H(\mathsf{T}^*)$ in $\mathbb{Z}_q^{n \times n}$ are full rank. Since the trapdoor is public, one may think that it can be used by anyone, however, the knowledge of secret $\mathbf{R}_{\mathsf{ID}^*}$ and $\mathbf{R}_{\mathsf{T}^*}$ are required to use SampleRight.

Then, the challenger responds to $\mathcal{A}$'s key queries as follows:

- SK$_{\mathsf{ID}^*}$ queries and KU$_{\mathsf{T}^*}$ queries are unchanged,
- answers SK$_{\mathsf{ID}}$ queries for $\mathsf{ID} \neq \mathsf{ID}^*$ by $\mathbf{e}'_{\theta,\ell}$ where $\mathbf{e}'_{\theta,\ell} \leftarrow$ SampleRight$(\mathbf{A}_0, \mathbf{G}, \mathbf{R}_{\mathsf{ID}^*}, \mathbf{u}'_{\theta,\ell}, \mathbf{T_G}, \sigma)$,
- answers KU$_{\mathsf{T}}$ queries for $\mathsf{T} \neq \mathsf{T}^*$ by $\tilde{\mathbf{e}}_\theta$ where $\tilde{\mathbf{e}}_\theta \leftarrow$ SampleRight$(\mathbf{A}_0, \mathbf{G}, \mathbf{R}_{\mathsf{T}^*}, \tilde{\mathbf{u}}_\theta, \mathbf{T_G}, \sigma)$,
- answers DK$_{\mathsf{ID},\mathsf{T}}$ queries by using the above SK$_{\mathsf{ID}}$ and KU$_{\mathsf{T}}$.

Due to the property of SampleRight, the distributions of $\mathbf{e}'_{\theta,\ell}$ and $\tilde{\mathbf{e}}_\theta$, which are the differences from **Game** 2, are statistically close to $\mathcal{D}_{\Lambda_q^{\mathbf{u}'_{\theta,\ell}}([\mathbf{A}_0|\mathbf{F}_{\mathsf{ID}^*}]),\sigma}$ and $\mathcal{D}_{\Lambda_q^{\tilde{\mathbf{u}}_\theta}([\mathbf{A}_0|\mathbf{F}_{\mathsf{T}^*}]),\sigma}$. As a result, **Game** 3 is statistically indistinguishable from **Game** 2 in $\mathcal{A}$'s view.

Game^{final}: **Game**^{final} is the same as **Game** 3 except that the challenge ciphertext CT$_{\mathsf{ID}^*,\mathsf{T}^*}$ is always chosen as a random independent element in the ciphertext space $\mathbb{Z}_q \times \mathbb{Z}_q^{3m}$. Since the challenge ciphertext is always a fresh random element in the ciphertext space, $\mathcal{A}$'s advantage in this game is zero.

If there exists a PPT adversary $\mathcal{A}$ to distinguish between **Game**^{final} and **Game** 3, then there exists another adversary $\mathcal{B}$ to solve LWE problem. Therefore, $\left| \Pr[E_3] - \frac{1}{2} \right| = \left| \Pr[E_3] - \Pr[E_{final}] \right| \leq Adv_{\mathcal{B}}^{LWE}$. Since the proof is the standard technique of lattice-based cryptography, we omit it.

Thus, we complete the proof. □

6 Discussion

To conclude this paper, we give some further comments and open questions of this research.

Key Re-randomization. As mentioned in the introduction, the key re-randomization property is crucial for constructing all the previous (pairing-based) DKER RIBE schemes. One may think that lattice-based RIBE schemes can be easily modified to support the key re-randomization property with $\mathbf{T}_{[\mathbf{A}_0|\mathbf{F}_{\mathsf{ID}}]}$, which is a short basis of $\Lambda_q^\perp([\mathbf{A}_0|\mathbf{F}_{\mathsf{ID}}])$, as secret keys or $\mathbf{T}_{[\mathbf{A}_0|\mathbf{F}_{\mathsf{T}}]}$, which is a short basis of $\Lambda_q^\perp([\mathbf{A}_0|\mathbf{F}_{\mathsf{T}}])$, as key updates. These bases are used to support delegation in the context of hierarchical IBE [2,14]. Indeed, the bases enable any users of RIBE scheme to re-randomize their decryption keys and the scheme to be decryption key exposure resistant. However, the approach is not applicable to the RIBE setting. If a user ID has his own secret key $\mathbf{T}_{[\mathbf{A}_0|\mathbf{F}_{\mathsf{ID}}]}$, he can produce the well-formed decryption key $\mathbf{e}$ such that $[\mathbf{A}_0|\mathbf{F}_{\mathsf{ID}}|\mathbf{F}_{\mathsf{T}}]\mathbf{e} = \mathbf{u}$ for any time periods T without key updates. Hence, KGC cannot revoke any users. For the same reason, constructing lattice-based revocable hierarchical IBE is a major open problem that seems very hard to be solved.

Insecurity of Cheng-Zhang's RIBE Scheme [17]. Cheng and Zhang claimed that their proposed RIBE scheme with the subset difference (SD) method is the first adaptively secure one with smaller key updates. However, there are critical bugs in their security proof, i.e., Game 3 in the proof of their Theorem 1. Here, we follow the notation from [17], e.g., id and t. In their Game 3, the simulator aborts the game if $h_{id^*} = 0$, where $h_{()}$ is a certain function, to answer secret key extraction queries. In addition, the simulator also aborts the game if $h_{id^*} \neq 0$ to create a challenge ciphertext. Hence, the game never ends. Note that the same holds for the target time period t^*.

One may think that Chen et al.'s Gaussian sampling technique [16], which we also used, can be used to fix the bugs. However, it is not the case. Furthermore, Cheng-Zhang's RIBE scheme is not secure even in the selective security model. The difficulty comes from the SD method which they used to revoke users. The SD method is another subset cover framework and it enables us to reduce the size of key updates. Notice that the subset cover framework which Chen et al. [16] and we used in this paper is the CS method. If we modify Cheng-Zhang's RIBE scheme in the selective security model, the secret key e' and the key update $\tilde{e}$ satisfy the following equations:

$$[A_0|A_1 + H(id)G] e' = u' \quad \text{and} \quad [A_0|A_2 + H(t)G] \tilde{e} = \tilde{u}.$$

The main difference between the SD method and the CS method is the restriction of syndrome vectors u' and $\tilde{u}$. In the security proof, the simulator should create both the secret key e' for the target id^* and the key update $\tilde{e}$ for the target t^*. As opposed to the CS method case, if we use the SD method, the simulator should create both e' and $\tilde{e}$ for the same syndrome vector $u' = \tilde{u}$ even without DKER. Since we cannot create the keys by using the trapdoor T_G, we try to create them by using a Gaussian sampling algorithm. Once the simulator uses a Gaussian sampling algorithm to sample e' for the target id^*, then the corresponding syndrome vector $u' = \tilde{u}$ is fixed. Therefore, the simulator cannot create $\tilde{e}$ for the target t^* by using a Gaussian sampling algorithm. Therefore, a construction of lattice-based RIBE with the SD method even in the selective security model and even without DKER is an interesting open problem.

Gadget Matrix. If we do not use CFFs in our scheme, i.e., $w = d = 1$, then the scheme is an RIBE scheme without DKER. However, our parameters are better than Chen et al.'s [16]. Notice that q and σ in our scheme are smaller than those in [16]. The improvement stems from the gadget matrix G due to Micciancio and Peikert [29], hence it is not the technical contribution of this paper.

Semi-adaptive Security. If we replace the hash function $F_{ID} = A_1 + H(ID)G$ of Agrawal et al. [1] by that of adaptively secure schemes [6,10,11,14,20,24,38–40], our scheme achieves semi-adaptive security[3], where an adversary issues the

---

[3] Notice that we do not have to replace $F_T = A_2 + H(T)G$ by adaptively secure ones. Since the maximum time period is polynomially bounded, $|\mathcal{T}|$ security loss enables us to guess the target time period T^*. Indeed, Seo-Emura [34] constructed adaptively secure DKER RIBE scheme by combining the Waters IBE [37] for ID and the Boneh-Boyen IBE [8] for T.

target $(\mathsf{ID}^*, \mathsf{T}^*)$ in advance of any key queries. What is required to prove the security of lattice-based RIBE is trapdoors that can sample short vectors $\mathbf{e}'_{\theta,\ell}$ for $\mathsf{ID} \neq \mathsf{ID}^*$ and $\tilde{\mathbf{e}}$ for $\mathsf{T} \neq \mathsf{T}^*$ according to discrete Gaussian distributions, where all the lattice-based IBE schemes have. However, it is insufficient to construct adaptively secure RIBE even without DKER. In the RIBE setting, we have to set all $\mathbf{u}'_{\theta,\ell}$ in advance of any key queries, then we use $\mathbf{F}_{\mathsf{ID}^*}$, or equivalently ID^*, for the computations. It means that the simulator has to know ID^* at that time. To avoid the obstacle, we should develop new lattice-based RIBE constructions, which are different from Chen et al.'s [16], or it may be equivalent to new lattice-based fuzzy IBE constructions, which are different from Agrawal et al.'s [3].

One may think that adaptively secure IBE is more than enough to construct semi-adaptively secure RIBE. However, we do not know how to construct semi-adaptively secure lattice-based IBE that is more efficient than adaptively secure ones. We think that the construction should be an interesting open problem in this research topic.

Anonymous (B-)DKER RIBE. Our scheme is the first anonymous (B-)DKER RIBE that is resilient to decryption key exposure. As in lattice-based IBE schemes (e.g., [1]) and Chen et al.'s RIBE scheme [16], since pairing-based anonymous IBE [12] does not support the key re-randomization property, an existing anonymous RIBE scheme [15] is insecure if an adversary is allowed to query even a single decryption key. Since the spirit of our construction is the use of distinct $\tilde{\mathbf{u}}$'s for each time period and the concrete construction with CFFs, we did not use specific techniques for lattices. Therefore, we believe that our approach enables one to construct pairing-based anonymous B-DKER RIBE.

Acknowledgement. We would like to thank Shantian Cheng and Juanyang Zhang for their sincere discussion with us. We would like to thank Shuichi Katsumata for his helpful comments. Atsushi Takayasu was (during the submission) and Yohei Watanabe is supported by a JSPS Fellowship for Young Scientists. This research was supported by JST CREST Grant Number JPMJCR14D6, Japan, JSPS KAKENHI Grant Number JP14J08237 and JP17K12697.

References

1. Agrawal, S., Boneh, D., Boyen, X.: Efficient lattice (H)IBE in the standard model. In: Gilbert, H. (ed.) EUROCRYPT 2010. LNCS, vol. 6110, pp. 553–572. Springer, Heidelberg (2010). doi:10.1007/978-3-642-13190-5_28
2. Agrawal, S., Boneh, D., Boyen, X.: Lattice basis delegation in fixed dimension and shorter-ciphertext hierarchical IBE. In: Rabin, T. (ed.) CRYPTO 2010. LNCS, vol. 6223, pp. 98–115. Springer, Heidelberg (2010). doi:10.1007/978-3-642-14623-7_6
3. Agrawal, S., Boyen, X., Vaikuntanathan, V., Voulgaris, P., Wee, H.: Functional encryption for threshold functions (or Fuzzy IBE) from lattices. In: Fischlin, M., Buchmann, J., Manulis, M. (eds.) PKC 2012. LNCS, vol. 7293, pp. 280–297. Springer, Heidelberg (2012). doi:10.1007/978-3-642-30057-8_17
4. Ajtai, M.: Generating hard instances of the short basis problem. In: Wiedermann, J., van Emde Boas, P., Nielsen, M. (eds.) ICALP 1999. LNCS, vol. 1644, pp. 1–9. Springer, Heidelberg (1999). doi:10.1007/3-540-48523-6_1

5. Alwen, J., Peikert, C.: Generating shorter bases for hard random lattices. Theory Comput. Syst. **48**(3), 535–553 (2011)
6. Apon, D., Fan, X., Liu, F.: Fully-secure lattice-based IBE as compact as PKE. IACR Cryptology ePrint Archive 2016, 125 (2016)
7. Boldyreva, A., Goyal, V., Kumar, V.: Identity-based encryption with efficient revocation. In: Ning, P., Syverson, P.F., Jha, S. (eds.) CCS 2008, pp. 417–426. ACM (2008)
8. Boneh, D., Boyen, X.: Efficient selective identity-based encryption without random oracles. J. Cryptology **24**(4), 659–693 (2011)
9. Boneh, D., Franklin, M.K.: Identity-based encryption from the Weil pairing. SIAM J. Comput. **32**(3), 586–615 (2003)
10. Boyen, X.: Lattice mixing and vanishing trapdoors: a framework for fully secure short signatures and more. In: Nguyen, P.Q., Pointcheval, D. (eds.) PKC 2010. LNCS, vol. 6056, pp. 499–517. Springer, Heidelberg (2010). doi:10.1007/978-3-642-13013-7_29
11. Boyen, X., Li, Q.: Towards tightly secure lattice short signature and id-based encryption. In: Cheon, J.H., Takagi, T. (eds.) ASIACRYPT 2016. LNCS, vol. 10032, pp. 404–434. Springer, Heidelberg (2016). doi:10.1007/978-3-662-53890-6_14
12. Boyen, X., Waters, B.: Anonymous hierarchical identity-based encryption (Without Random Oracles). In: Dwork, C. (ed.) CRYPTO 2006. LNCS, vol. 4117, pp. 290–307. Springer, Heidelberg (2006). doi:10.1007/11818175_17
13. Brakerski, Z., Langlois, A., Peikert, C., Regev, O., Stehlé, D.: Classical hardness of learning with errors. In: Boneh, D., Roughgarden, T., Feigenbaum, J. (eds.) STOC 2013, pp. 575–584. ACM (2013)
14. Cash, D., Hofheinz, D., Kiltz, E., Peikert, C.: Bonsai trees, or how to delegate a lattice basis. J. Cryptology **25**(4), 601–639 (2012)
15. Chen, J., Lim, H.W., Ling, S., Su, L., Wang, H.: Anonymous and adaptively secure revocable IBE with constant size public parameters. CoRR abs/1210.6441 (2012)
16. Chen, J., Lim, H.W., Ling, S., Wang, H., Nguyen, K.: Revocable identity-based encryption from lattices. In: Susilo, W., Mu, Y., Seberry, J. (eds.) ACISP 2012. LNCS, vol. 7372, pp. 390–403. Springer, Heidelberg (2012). doi:10.1007/978-3-642-31448-3_29
17. Cheng, S., Zhang, J.: Adaptive-ID secure revocable identity-based encryption from lattices via subset difference method. In: Lopez, J., Wu, Y. (eds.) ISPEC 2015. LNCS, vol. 9065, pp. 283–297. Springer, Cham (2015). doi:10.1007/978-3-319-17533-1_20
18. Emura, K., Seo, J.H., Youn, T.: Semi-generic transformation of revocable hierarchical identity-based encryption and its DBDH instantiation. IEICE Trans. **99–A**(1), 83–91 (2016)
19. Erdös, P., Frankl, P., Füredi, Z.: Families of finite sets in which no set is covered by the union of r others. Isr. J. Math. **51**(1), 79–89 (1985)
20. Gentry, C., Peikert, C., Vaikuntanathan, V.: Trapdoors for hard lattices and new cryptographic constructions. In: Dwork, C. (ed.) STOC 2008, pp. 197–206. ACM (2008)
21. Goldwasser, S., Lewko, A., Wilson, D.A.: Bounded-collusion IBE from key homomorphism. In: Cramer, R. (ed.) TCC 2012. LNCS, vol. 7194, pp. 564–581. Springer, Heidelberg (2012). doi:10.1007/978-3-642-28914-9_32

22. Heng, S.-H., Kurosawa, K.: k-Resilient identity-based encryption in the standard model. In: Okamoto, T. (ed.) CT-RSA 2004. LNCS, vol. 2964, pp. 67–80. Springer, Heidelberg (2004). doi:10.1007/978-3-540-24660-2_6

23. Ishida, Y., Watanabe, Y., Shikata, J.: Constructions of CCA-secure revocable identity-based encryption. In: Foo, E., Stebila, D. (eds.) ACISP 2015. LNCS, vol. 9144, pp. 174–191. Springer, Cham (2015). doi:10.1007/978-3-319-19962-7_11

24. Katsumata, S., Yamada, S.: Partitioning via non-linear polynomial functions: more compact IBEs from ideal lattices and bilinear maps. In: Cheon, J.H., Takagi, T. (eds.) ASIACRYPT 2016. LNCS, vol. 10032, pp. 682–712. Springer, Heidelberg (2016). doi:10.1007/978-3-662-53890-6_23

25. Kumar, R., Rajagopalan, S., Sahai, A.: Coding constructions for blacklisting problems without computational assumptions. In: Wiener, M. (ed.) CRYPTO 1999. LNCS, vol. 1666, pp. 609–623. Springer, Heidelberg (1999). doi:10.1007/3-540-48405-1_38

26. Lee, K.: Revocable hierarchical identity-based encryption with adaptive security. IACR Cryptology ePrint Archive 2016, 749 (2016)

27. Lee, K., Lee, D.H., Park, J.H.: Efficient revocable identity-based encryption via subset difference methods. IACR Cryptology ePrint Archive 2014, 132 (2014)

28. Libert, B., Vergnaud, D.: Adaptive-ID secure revocable identity-based encryption. In: Fischlin, M. (ed.) CT-RSA 2009. LNCS, vol. 5473, pp. 1–15. Springer, Heidelberg (2009). doi:10.1007/978-3-642-00862-7_1

29. Micciancio, D., Peikert, C.: Trapdoors for lattices: simpler, tighter, faster, smaller. In: Pointcheval, D., Johansson, T. (eds.) EUROCRYPT 2012. LNCS, vol. 7237, pp. 700–718. Springer, Heidelberg (2012). doi:10.1007/978-3-642-29011-4_41

30. Nguyen, K., Wang, H., Zhang, J.: Server-aided revocable identity-based encryption from lattices. In: Foresti, S., Persiano, G. (eds.) CANS 2016. LNCS, vol. 10052, pp. 107–123. Springer, Cham (2016). doi:10.1007/978-3-319-48965-0_7

31. Peikert, C.: Public-key cryptosystems from the worst-case shortest vector problem: extended abstract. In: Mitzenmacher, M. (ed.) STOC 2009, pp. 333–342. ACM (2009)

32. Regev, O.: On lattices, learning with errors, random linear codes, and cryptography. In: Gabow, H.N., Fagin, R. (eds.) STOC 2005, pp. 84–93. ACM (2005)

33. Seo, J.H., Emura, K.: Revocable hierarchical identity-based encryption. Theor. Comput. Sci. **542**, 44–62 (2014)

34. Seo, J.H., Emura, K.: Revocable identity-based cryptosystem revisited: security models and constructions. IEEE Trans. Inf. Forensics Secur. **9**(7), 1193–1205 (2014)

35. Seo, J.H., Emura, K.: Revocable hierarchical identity-based encryption via history-free approach. Theor. Comput. Sci. **615**, 45–60 (2016)

36. Watanabe, Y., Emura, K., Seo, J.H.: New revocable IBE in prime-order groups: adaptively secure, decryption key exposure resistant, and with short public parameters. In: Handschuh, H. (ed.) CT-RSA 2017. LNCS, vol. 10159, pp. 432–449. Springer, Cham (2017). doi:10.1007/978-3-319-52153-4_25

37. Waters, B.: Efficient identity-based encryption without random oracles. In: Cramer, R. (ed.) EUROCRYPT 2005. LNCS, vol. 3494, pp. 114–127. Springer, Heidelberg (2005). doi:10.1007/11426639_7

38. Yamada, S.: Adaptively secure identity-based encryption from lattices with asymptotically shorter public parameters. In: Fischlin, M., Coron, J.-S. (eds.) EUROCRYPT 2016. LNCS, vol. 9666, pp. 32–62. Springer, Heidelberg (2016). doi:10.1007/978-3-662-49896-5_2

39. Yamada, S.: Asymptotically compact adaptively secure lattice IBEs and verifiable random functions via generalized partitioning techniques. IACR Cryptology ePrint Archive 2017, 096 (2017)
40. Zhang, J., Chen, Y., Zhang, Z.: Programmable hash functions from lattices: short signatures and IBEs with small key sizes. In: Robshaw, M., Katz, J. (eds.) CRYPTO 2016. LNCS, vol. 9816, pp. 303–332. Springer, Heidelberg (2016). doi:10.1007/978-3-662-53015-3_11

Searchable Encryption

Dynamic Searchable Symmetric Encryption with Physical Deletion and Small Leakage

Peng Xu[1(✉)], Shuai Liang[1], Wei Wang[2], Willy Susilo[3], Qianhong Wu[4], and Hai Jin[1]

[1] Services Computing Technology and System Lab,
Cluster and Grid Computing Lab, School of Computer Science and Technology,
Huazhong University of Science and Technology, Wuhan 430074, China
{xupeng,hjin}@mail.hust.edu.cn, 850328459@qq.com
[2] Cyber-Physical-Social Systems Lab, School of Computer Science and Technology,
Huazhong University of Science and Technology, Wuhan 430074, China
viviawangww@gmail.com
[3] School of Computing and Information Technology, Institute of Cybersecurity
and Cryptology, University of Wollongong, Wollongong, Australia
wsusilo@uow.edu.au
[4] School of Electronic and Information Engineering, Beihang Univerisity,
Beijing, China
qianhong.wu@buaa.edu.cn

Abstract. *Dynamic Searchable Symmetric Encryption* (DSSE) allows a client not only to search over ciphertexts as the traditional searchable symmetric encryption does, but also to update these ciphertexts according to requirements, e.g., adding or deleting some ciphertexts. It has been recognized as a fundamental and promising method to build secure cloud storage. In this paper, we propose a new DSSE scheme to overcome the drawbacks of previous schemes. The biggest challenge is to realize the physical deletion of ciphertexts with small leakage. We employ both logical and physical deletions, and run physical deletion in due course to avoid extra information leakage. Our instantiation achieves noticeable improvements throughout all following aspects: search performance, storage cost, functionality, and information leakage when operating its functions. We also demonstrate its provable security under adaptive attacks and practical performance according to experimental results.

1 Introduction

Symmetric-key encryption with keyword search (or *searchable symmetric encryption*, SSE for short) allows clients to upload their keyword searchable ciphertexts to a server, and then delegate keyword search to the server and retrieve files of an expected keyword. A secure SSE scheme can keep the privacy of keywords not only to outside attackers but also to the server. The details are as follows: for all keywords of a file, a client respectively generates the corresponding keyword searchable ciphertexts and the encrypted file in symmetric-key setting, and stores these ciphertexts in the server; to retrieve the files of an expected keyword, the

© Springer International Publishing AG 2017
J. Pieprzyk and S. Suriadi (Eds.): ACISP 2017, Part I, LNCS 10342, pp. 207–226, 2017.
DOI: 10.1007/978-3-319-60055-0_11

client delegates a keyword search token to the server, and then the server finds out all matching keyword searchable ciphertexts, decrypts out their encrypted file identifiers, and returns the corresponding encrypted files of these identifiers to the client; finally, the client decrypts out these files. Since the encryption of files can be separately processed with an independent symmetric-key encryption scheme, SSE only focuses on the generation of keyword searchable ciphertexts. Hence, unless the clear statement, all encryptions or ciphertexts are searchable in this paper.

In the past decade, most of researches on SSE focus on improving security, accelerating search performance or searching with multiple keywords. Until 2012, Kamara *et al.* [1] first proposed a *dynamic SSE* (DSSE) scheme (called KPR'12 in our paper) by constructing hidden chains to connect all searchable ciphertexts of the same keyword. With a keyword search trapdoor, these hidden chains will be partially disclosed and guide the server to efficiently find out all matching ciphertexts. In addition, KPR'12 can add new ciphertexts to their corresponding chains or delete old ciphertexts from these chains. Clearly, DSSE is more flexible than the traditional SSE both in theory and practice.

But The KPR'12 scheme causes significant information leakage in updating ciphertexts. Specifically, when adding or deleting ciphertexts, it will leak some information of the corresponding chains, e.g., the number of ciphertexts in a chain. These leakage information makes the server having a noticeable advantage to guess keywords. In 2013, Kamara *et al.* [2] modified their previous work by sharply increasing the size of searchable ciphertexts. Technically, this new DSSE scheme (called KP'13 in our paper) generates secure vectors for all keywords, where each vector is of size linear with the number of all files, and then constructs a tree structure for these vectors to accelerate search performance. Since each keyword is contained only by a part of files in practice, these vectors contain many redundancies. Hence, KP'13 takes a high storage complexity.

In 2014, Cash *et al.* [3] proposed a DSSE scheme (called CJJ'14) by applying private counters to constructing hidden relationships among all keyword searchable ciphertexts. Technically, each keyword has a private counter which is initiated as "1"; to generate a searchable ciphertext of a keyword, the current value of the corresponding counter will be taken as input, and after the generation, the counter will be added with "1"; when receiving a keyword search trapdoor, the server can efficiently find out all matching ciphertexts by traversing all possible values of a counter. CJJ'14 is more convenient than KPR'12 and KP'13. But it cannot physically delete ciphertexts. In other words, only logical deletion is achieved by taking extra storage to remember the deleted ciphertexts. When searching a keyword, the deleted ciphertexts will not be taken into account even if they contain the keyword. Hence, its storage complexity will consistently increase with the total number of both adding or deleting operations. This disadvantage also appears in the work of [4].

Rough comparisons of the above DSSE schemes are listed in Table 1 (the exact comparisons will be given in Sect. 7). The summary is that no previous work is good at all aspects of search complexity, storage complexity, functionality,

Table 1. Rough comparisons. **Search** is to find out the files containing a queried keyword. **AddFile** is to add all keyword searchable ciphertexts of a new file. **AddKeyword** is to add a new keyword searchable ciphertext of an existing file. **DeleteFile** is to delete all keyword searchable ciphertexts of an existing file. **DeleteKeyword** is to delete a keyword searchable ciphertext of an existing file. Information leakage denotes the information leaked by running previous functions.

Scheme	Search complexity	Storage complexity	Functions				Information leakage
			AddFile	AddKeyword	DeleteFile	DeleteKeyword	
KPR'12 [1]	Low	Normal	Achieved	Failed	Physical	Failed	Large
KP'13 [2]	Normal	High	Achieved	Failed	Physical	Failed	Normal
CJJ'14 [3]	Low	Low	Achieved	Achieved	Failed	Logical	Small
Ours	Low	Low	Achieved	Achieved	Physical	Physical	Small

and information leakage. Hence, we are interested in proposing a new DSSE scheme to complete this work.

1.1 Our Main Ideas

Before introducing our main ideas, some basic concepts are needed. In the paradigmatic application of DSSE, each file has an unique identifier and several keywords. It is common to let file-keyword pair (id, w) denote that the file with identifier id has keyword w. Suppose database DB consists of all such pairs, which are derived from the application.

For each pair in DB, our scheme will generate three kinds of searchable ciphertexts, called K1, K2, and K3, respectively. The three kinds of ciphertexts are used to accordingly achieve functions **Search**, **DeleteFile**, and **DeleteKeyword**, respectively. Taking pair (id, w) as an example, Fig. 1 shows the generated three ciphertexts, including their hidden relationships. All K1 ciphertexts of the same keyword construct a hidden chain relationship, like the chain of keyword w in Fig. 2; all K2 ciphertexts of the same file identifier also construct a hidden chain relationship, like the chain of identifier id in Fig. 2; no hidden relationship among K3 ciphertexts is needed.

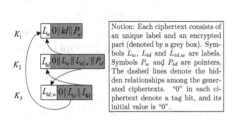

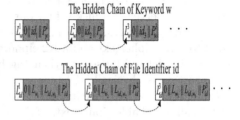

Fig. 1. The generated ciphertexts for pair (id, w)

Fig. 2. The generated hidden chain relationship among ciphertexts, where $P_w^1 = L_w^2$, $P_w^2 = L_w^3$, $P_{id}^1 = L_{id}^2$, and $P_{id}^2 = L_{id}^3$

When searching a keyword with the corresponding keyword search token, function **Search** finds out the hidden chain of the keyword, and follows the guidance of the chain to rapidly find out all matching K1 ciphertexts. By decrypting these matching ciphertexts, function **Search** finally obtains some file identifiers, which refer to the files containing the queried keywords. However, our chains among K1 ciphertexts have some differences with that of KPR'12. One difference is that we do not generate the deterministic heads for all possible chains when initializing a DSSE scheme as KPR'12 did. On the contrary, the head of a chain in our DSSE scheme is dynamically generated when the keyword corresponding to the chain is the first time to be used. So we do not take extra storage for any chain's deterministic head.

When adding a new keyword searchable ciphertext of an existing file with identifier id (let w' be the new keyword), function **AddKeyword** generates three above mentioned ciphertexts of pair (id, w'). The generated K1 ciphertext will be linked to the end of the w''s chain, and similarly the K2 ciphertext will be linked to the end of the id's chain. Summarily, our idea is to link the new generated ciphertexts to the end of chains. This idea is inspired by the drawback of KPR'12 that linking ciphertexts to the middle of chains causes some impact on the old ciphertexts in the chains, i.e. extra information leakage. In addition, we just need to support function **AddKeyword**, since function **AddFile** can be achieved by executing function **AddKeyword** multiple times.

The biggest challenge in our work is to realize the physical deletion with small leakage when running functions **DeleteKeyword** and **DeleteFile**. Roughly, both functions need to delete some ciphertexts from chains. If the deletion is physical, some operations after the deletion are necessary to repair the broken chains. For example, suppose that the second ciphertext in the hidden chain of keyword w in Fig. 2 is physically deleted. To repair the broken chain, values L_w^1 and L_w^3 must be known, and then set $P_w^1 = L_w^3$. These operations leak the fact that the ciphertexts with labels L_w^1 and L_w^3 are in the same chain with the ciphertext with label L_w^2. In the worst case, all ciphertexts in a chain will be leaked. To overcome this challenge, our idea is to employ both logical and physical deletions, and run physical deletion in due course to avoid extra information leakage. The details are as follows.

First, our K3 ciphertexts are used to support function **DeleteKeyword**. When deleting all searchable ciphertexts of a file-keyword pair (id, w), a delete token allows server to quickly find out the matching K3 ciphertext and then decrypt out two indices. Referring to Fig. 1, these two indices respectively correspond to a K1 ciphertext and a K2 ciphertext. Then the K1 and K2 ciphertexts are logically deleted by setting their tag bits to be "1". Finally, that matching K3 ciphertext is physically deleted.

Second, our K2 ciphertexts are used to support function **DeleteFile**. When deleting all searchable ciphertexts of a file with identifier id, a delete token allows the server to find out the hidden chain of id. Following this chain, all matching K2 ciphertexts can be rapidly found. Referring to Fig. 1, each matching K2 ciphertext can be decrypted out two indices, and these indices allow server to find out all related K1 and K3 ciphertexts. Finally, all found K1 ciphertexts are logically deleted by setting their tag bits to be "1", and all found K2 and K3 ciphertexts are physically deleted.

Third, our above ideas show the physical deletion of K2 and K3 ciphertexts and the logical deletion of K1 ciphertexts. Hence, our final goal is to physically delete the K1 ciphertexts. This work is elegantly achieved when the search process is rebooted per keyword according to our extra design. Then all logically deleted K1 ciphertexts of the queried keyword will be physically deleted, and the corresponding chain will be repaired. Summarily, we do the physical deletion of the K1 ciphertexts by function **Search**, not by function **DeleteFile** as previous schemes did. This method does not cause extra information leakage, since the inherent information leakage of function **Search** is enough for repairing a broken chain caused by the physical deletion.

1.2 Our Contributions

Compared with KPR'12, we extend the definition of DSSE by additionally defining functions **AddKeyword** and **DeleteKeyword**. As a result, the new DSSE definition consists of five protocols that are **Setup, AddKeyword, DeleteFile, DeleteKeyword**, and **Search**. A client runs protocol **Setup** to generate searchable ciphertexts, which will be stored in a server. The other protocols allow the client to delegate the corresponding operations to the server. We also extend the traditional security definition, which is called indistinguishability under adaptively chosen keyword attacks (IND-CKA2). In our new security definition, a more powerful adversary is modeled. Specifically, in either a real or an ideal attack game, an adversary is allowed to make a polynomial number of adaptive operations to engage in protocols **AddKeyword, DeleteFile, DeleteKeyword**, or **Search**.

Before proposing our complete DSSE scheme, we construct two basic DSSE schemes to help the understanding of our ideas. The first one shows how to construct the hidden chains among searchable ciphertexts, add new searchable ciphertexts to the corresponding chains, and search a keyword according to the guidance of the corresponding chain. The second one shows how to employ both logical and physical deletions to delete all searchable ciphertexts of a file. From these two basic DSSE schemes, we construct our complete DSSE scheme provably IND-CKA2 secure in the *random oracle* (RO) model. The two basic DSSE schemes are also of independent interest in the applications in which limited functionalities are sufficient.

We make thorough comparisons between our complete DSSE scheme and the related KPR'12, KP'13, and CJJ'14 schemes. The comparisons show that our scheme has noticeable advantages in all aspects of search complexity, storage complexity, functionality, and information leakage. Finally, we show the practicality of our scheme with extensive experimental results in executing its main functions.

1.3 Organization of the Remainder

Sections 2 and 3 respectively define some symbols, two common data structures, DSSE and its IND-CKA2 security. Sections 4 and 5 respectively show our two basic DSSE schemes. Section 6 proposes our complete DSSE scheme and its provable IND-CKA2 security. In Sect. 7, we exactly compare our complete DSSE scheme with some previous schemes, and then show the practice of our scheme by numerical results. The other related works on SSE are reviewed in Sect. 8. Section 9 concludes this paper.

2 Defining Symbols and Data Structures

We let symbol $k \in \mathbb{N}$ denote the security parameter. The set of all binary strings of length $n \in \mathbb{N}$ is denoted as $\{0,1\}^n$, and the set of all finite binary strings denoted as $\{0,1\}^*$. We write $x \xleftarrow{\$} \mathcal{X}$ to represent an element x being sampled uniformly at random from the set $\mathcal{X}$. The output x of an algorithm $\mathbf{A}$ is denoted by $x \leftarrow \mathbf{A}$. $|\mathcal{X}|$ represents the size of set $\mathcal{X}$ or the total number of members in set $\mathcal{X}$. $\mathcal{W}$ denotes the keyword space. Each file is denoted by an unique identifier. $\mathcal{ID}$ is the set of all the file identifiers. (id, w) is a file-keyword pair, where $w \in \mathcal{W}$ and $id \in \mathcal{ID}$. DB is a database or a set of different (id, w) pairs. $|DB|$ is the total number of the pairs in DB (or the size of DB). $DB(w)$ is the set of the file identities that pair with keyword $w \in \mathcal{W}$ in DB. Similarly, $DB(id)$ is a set of the keywords that pair with file $id \in \mathcal{ID}$ in DB. If pair $(id, w) \in DB$ holds, $|DB(id, w)| = 1$, otherwise $|DB(id, w)| = 0$. Symbol $||$ denotes the concatenation of strings.

Our schemes will employ two standard data structures *List* and *Dictionary*. When $\mathcal{T}$ is a *List*, $|\mathcal{T}|$ denotes the total number of records in $\mathcal{T}$. There are four operations on dictionary $\mathcal{D}$. We define them as follows:

- **Creat**($\mathcal{T}$): Take a list $\mathcal{T}$ of label-data pairs as input (where each label is unique), and return a dictionary $\mathcal{D}$;
- **Get**($\mathcal{D}, L$): Take a dictionary $\mathcal{D}$ and a label L as inputs, return the corresponding data D if $(L, D) \in \mathcal{D}$, otherwise return $NULL$;
- **Update**($\mathcal{D}, (L, D)$): Take a dictionary $\mathcal{D}$ and a label-data pair (L, D) as inputs, insert (L, D) into $\mathcal{D}$ if L does not exist in $\mathcal{D}$, otherwise update the original data of label L into the new data D, and finally return $\perp$;
- **Remove**($\mathcal{D}, L$): Take a dictionary $\mathcal{D}$ and a label L as inputs, delete record (L, D) from $\mathcal{D}$ and return $\perp$;

Note that the dictionary algorithm **Creat**($\mathcal{T}$) is history-independent [3]. It means that for any list $\mathcal{T}$ the distribution of $\mathcal{D} \leftarrow$ **Creat**($\mathcal{T}$) depends only on the records of $\mathcal{T}$ not on the members' order in $\mathcal{T}$. In addition, the time complexity of algorithm **Get** is $O(1)$.

3   Defining DSSE and Its Security

To simplify the description of our DSSE concept, we generalize several algorithms defined in KPR'12, and then add two new protocols **AddKeyword** and **DeleteKeyword**. We also make the following assumptions: (1) All file identifiers will never be re-used; (2) The searchable ciphertexts of the same file-keyword pair will never be re-added; (3) Keyword space $\mathcal{W}$ and set $\mathcal{ID}$ have $\mathcal{W} \bigcap \mathcal{ID} = \emptyset$.

Definition 1 (DSSE). *A DSSE scheme consists of the following five protocols between a client and a server:*

- **Setup***: The client takes a security parameter and a database DB as inputs, generates an initial encrypted database EDB, some secret parameters like secret keys, and sends EDB to the server. The server stores EDB.*
- **AddKeyword***: To add the searchable ciphertexts of a new file-keyword pair (id, w), the client takes the file-keyword pair and his secret parameters as inputs, generates and sends the corresponding searchable ciphertexts to the server. The server takes the encrypted database EDB as input, and inserts these ciphertexts into EDB.*
- **DeleteFile***: To delete all searchable ciphertexts of a file with identifier id, the client takes the file's identifier and his secret parameters as inputs, generates and sends a delete token to the server. The server takes the encrypted database EDB as input, deletes all corresponding searchable ciphertexts from EDB.*
- **DeleteKeyword***: To delete the searchable ciphertexts of a file-keyword pair (id, w), the client takes the file-keyword pair and his secret parameters as inputs, generates and sends a delete token to the server. The server takes the encrypted database EDB as input, deletes the corresponding searchable ciphertexts from EDB.*
- **Search***: To find out the files containing an expected keyword w, the client takes the keyword and his secret parameters as inputs, generates and sends a search token to the server. The server takes the encrypted database EDB as input, outputs the file identifiers which means that the corresponding files contain the keyword.*

The IND-CKA2 security of a DSSE scheme defines two games: a real game **Real**$_\mathcal{A}$ between an adversary $\mathcal{A}$ and a challenger and an ideal game **Ideal**$_{\mathcal{A},\mathcal{S}}$ between the adversary $\mathcal{A}$ and a simulator $\mathcal{S}$. In game **Real**$_\mathcal{A}$, the challenger sets up a real DSSE scheme, and the adversary $\mathcal{A}$ adaptively engages in every protocol of DSSE by querying the challenger. On the contrary, in game **Ideal**$_{\mathcal{A},\mathcal{S}}$, the simulator $\mathcal{S}$ sets up a simulated DSSE scheme. It means that $\mathcal{S}$ never knows the real database DB chosen by $\mathcal{A}$, and it only takes leakage functions as inputs to simulate the functions of the challenger. If $\mathcal{A}$ cannot distinguish games **Real**$_\mathcal{A}$ and **Ideal**$_{\mathcal{A},\mathcal{S}}$, we say that the DSSE scheme is IND-CKA2 secure. Moreover, the smaller the leakage, the stronger the IND-CKA2 security.

Definition 2 (IND-CKA2 Security). *Let* **DSSE** $=$ (**Setup**, **AddKeyword**, **DeleteFile**, **DeleteKeyword**, **Search**) *be a DSSE scheme, $\mathcal{A}$ be a stateful* *adversary, $\mathcal{S}$ be a stateful simulator, and $(\mathcal{L}_{Setup}, \mathcal{L}_{AddKeyword}, \mathcal{L}_{DeleteFile}, \mathcal{L}_{DeleteKeyword}, \mathcal{L}_{Search})$ be stateful leakage functions. Consider the following probabilistic experiments:*

- **Real**$_\mathcal{A}(k)$: *$\mathcal{A}$ chooses DB. A challenger runs* **Setup** *to generate some secret parameters and the encrypted database EDB of DB. $\mathcal{A}$ receives EDB and makes a polynomial number of adaptive operations to engage in protocol* **AddKeyword**, **DeleteFile**, **DeleteKeyword** *or* **Search**. *For each query, the challenger returns the corresponding result such as the searchable ciphertexts that will be added to EDB, a token to delete all searchable ciphertexts of a file, a token to delete the searchable ciphertexts of a file-keyword pair or a* search *token. Finally, $\mathcal{A}$ returns one bit b as the output of this experiment.*
- **Ideal**$_{\mathcal{A},\mathcal{S}}(k)$: *$\mathcal{A}$ chooses DB. Given $\mathcal{L}_{Setup}$, $\mathcal{S}$ simulates and sends EDB to $\mathcal{A}$. $\mathcal{A}$ makes a polynomial number of adaptive operations to engage in protocols* **AddKeyword**, **DeleteFile**, **DeleteKeyword** *or* **Search**. *For each query, $\mathcal{S}$ is with the corresponding leakage $\mathcal{L}_{AddKeyword}$, $\mathcal{L}_{DeleteFile}$, $\mathcal{L}_{DeleteKeyword}$ or $\mathcal{L}_{Search}$, then returns an appropriate result such as the searchable ciphertexts that will be added to EDB, a token to delete all searchable ciphertexts of a file, a token to delete the searchable ciphertexts of a file-keyword pair or a* search *token. Finally, $\mathcal{A}$ returns one bit b as the output of this experiment.*

If $|Pr[\textbf{Real}_\mathcal{A}(k) = 1] - Pr[\textbf{Ideal}_{\mathcal{A},\mathcal{S}}(k) = 1]|$ is negligible, we say that **DSSE** *is IND-CKA2 secure with leakage functions $(\mathcal{L}_{Setup}, \mathcal{L}_{AddKeyword}, \mathcal{L}_{DeleteFile}, \mathcal{L}_{DeleteKeyword}, \mathcal{L}_{Search})$.*

4   Our Basic DSSE Scheme D-I

Our basic DSSE scheme D-I only consists of protocols **Setup**, **AddKeyword**, and **Search**. Given a database DB, protocol **Setup** shows the generation of K1 ciphertexts, so that all ciphertexts of the same keyword are connected by a hidden chain. To add the K1 ciphertext of a new file-keyword pair, protocol **AddKeyword** connects the new generated ciphertext to the end of the corresponding chain. With a keyword search trapdoor, protocol **Search** shows how to quickly find out the related file identifiers. Let $\mathbf{F} : \{0,1\}^k \times \{0,1\}^* \rightarrow \{0,1\}^k$ be a key-based pseudo-random function. Let $\mathbf{H} : \{0,1\}^* \rightarrow \{0,1\}^{2k}$ be a cryptographic hash functions. The basic scheme D-I is shown in Fig. 3.

In protocol **Setup**, each keyword w has a pointer parameter P_w, and each K1 ciphertext is a label-data pair. When generating the K1 ciphertext for a file-keyword pair (id, w), the generated label L_w is equal to $\mathbf{F}_{k_1}(w)$ if it is the first time to generate a ciphertext for keyword w, otherwise it is equal to P_w, and the data D_w is the encryption of file identifier id and a new value of P_w. With the same method, all K1 ciphertexts of the same keyword are connected by a hidden chain, since the value of P_w encrypted by the former one of any two neighboring ciphertexts in a chain is equal to the label of the latter one. In addition, the final value of P_w is privately recorded by the client at the end of protocol **Setup**. This value will be used in protocol **AddKeyword** to generate

★ Protocol **Setup**$((k, DB), NULL)$:
  – Client: Take k and DB as inputs, randomly choose two secret keys $\mathcal{K} = (k_1, k_2)$, initialize two empty lists $\mathcal{T}_P$ and $\mathcal{T}_W$, and do the following steps:
    1. For each keyword w in DB, initialize pointer parameter $P_w = NULL$;
    2. For each file-keyword pair $(id, w) \in DB$
      (a) If $P_w = NULL$, set label $L_w = \mathbf{F}_{k_1}(w)$, otherwise set $L_w = P_w$; Set $\{R, P_w\} \xleftarrow{\$} \{0,1\}^{2k}$;
      (b) Generate a K1 ciphertext $(L_w, D_w = (D_{w,1} = (\mathbf{H}(\mathbf{F}_{k_2}(w), R) \oplus (id||P_w)), D_{w,2} = R))$, and add this ciphertext to $\mathcal{T}_W$ in the lexicon order;
    3. For each keyword w in DB, add tuple (w, P_w) into $\mathcal{T}_P$; Generate dictionaries $\mathcal{D}_P \leftarrow \mathbf{Creat}(\mathcal{T}_P)$ and $\mathcal{D}_W \leftarrow \mathbf{Creat}(\mathcal{T}_W)$; Keep $\mathcal{K}$ and $\mathcal{D}_P$ secret, and send the encrypted database $EDB = \mathcal{D}_W$ to the server;
  – Server: Store EDB.
★ Protocol **AddKeyword**$((\mathcal{K}, \mathcal{D}_P, id, w), EDB)$:
  – Client: Take $\mathcal{K} = (k_1, k_2)$, $\mathcal{D}_P$ and a file-keyword pair (id, w) as inputs, retrieve $P_w \leftarrow \mathbf{Get}(\mathcal{D}_P, w)$ according to w, and do the following steps:
    1. If $P_w = NULL$, set $L_w = \mathbf{F}_{k_1}(w)$, otherwise set $L_w = P_w$; Set $\{R, P_w\} \xleftarrow{\$} \{0,1\}^{2k}$;
    2. Generate a K1 ciphertext $(L_w, D_w = (D_{w,1} = (\mathbf{H}(\mathbf{F}_{k_2}(w), R) \oplus (id||P_w)), D_{w,2} = R))$, run algorithm $\mathbf{Update}(\mathcal{D}_P, (w, P_w))$, and send the ciphertext (L_w, D_w) to the server;
  – Server: Take $EDB = \mathcal{D}_W$ and (L_w, D_w) as inputs, and run algorithm $\mathbf{Update}(\mathcal{D}_W, (L_w, D_w))$.
★ Protocol **Search**$((\mathcal{K}, w), EDB)$:
  – Client: Take $\mathcal{K} = (k_1, k_2)$ and a keyword w as inputs, generate and send a search token $ST_w = (\mathbf{F}_{k_1}(w), \mathbf{F}_{k_2}(w))$ to the server;
  – Server: Take $EDB = \mathcal{D}_W$ and $ST_w = (\mathbf{F}_{k_1}(w), \mathbf{F}_{k_2}(w))$ as inputs, initialize an empty set $\mathcal{I}$, set $L_w = \mathbf{F}_{k_1}(w)$, and do the following steps:
    1. Retrieve data $D_w \leftarrow \mathbf{Get}(\mathcal{D}_W, L_w)$ according to L_w; If $D_w = NULL$, return $\mathcal{I}$ and abort;
    2. Parse $D_w = (D_{w,1}, D_{w,2})$, and decrypt out $id||P_w = D_{w,1} \oplus \mathbf{H}(\mathbf{F}_{k_2}(w), D_{w,2})$;
    3. Add id to $\mathcal{I}$, set $L_w = P_w$, and go to step 1).

Fig. 3. Our basic DSSE scheme D-I

a new K1 ciphertext of keyword w. Specifically, this value is taken as the label of this new ciphertext. Hence, it can be connected to the end of the corresponding chain.

When receiving a keyword search trapdoor $ST_w = (\mathbf{F}_{k_1}(w), \mathbf{F}_{k_2}(w))$, protocol **Search** matches value $\mathbf{F}_{k_1}(w)$ with all K1 ciphertexts' labels to find out the hidden chain head of keyword w, and applies value $\mathbf{F}_{k_2}(w)$ to decrypt out a file identifier and a pointer value. The file identifier corresponds to a file containing the queried keyword, and the pointer value guides the server to find out the next matching ciphertext. So on and so forth, all file identifiers related to the queried keyword can be found.

5   Our Basic DSSE Scheme D-II

Our basic DSSE scheme D-II only consists of protocols **Setup**, **DeleteFile**, and **Search**. Given a database DB, protocol **Setup** applies the same idea as the first basic DSSE scheme to generate the K1 and K2 ciphertexts. It generates the hidden chains respectively to connect all K1 ciphertexts of the same keyword and all K2 ciphertexts of the same file identifier. It is worth noting that each

K1 ciphertext in this scheme contains a tag bit with the initial value "0". When a tag bit is equal to "1", it means that the corresponding K1 ciphertext is logically deleted. To delete all searchable ciphertexts (including the K1 and K2 ciphertexts) of a file, protocol **DeleteFile** shows the physical deletion of all related K2 ciphertexts and the logical deletion of all related K1 ciphertexts.

★ Protocol **Setup**$((k, DB), NULL)$:
- Client: Take k and DB as inputs, randomly choose two k-bit secret keys $\mathcal{K} = (k_1, k_2)$, initialize two empty lists $\mathcal{T}_W$ and $\mathcal{T}_F$, and do the following steps:
  1. For each file identifier id or keyword w in DB, initialize pointer parameter $P_{id} = NULL$ or $P_w = NULL$;
  2. For each file-keyword pair $(id, w) \in DB$
     (a) If $P_w = NULL$, set label $L_w = \mathbf{F}_{k_1}(w)$, otherwise set $L_w = P_w$; Set $\{R, P_w\} \xleftarrow{\$} \{0, 1\}^{2k}$;
     (b) Generate a K1 ciphertext $(L_w, D_w = (D_{w,1} = (\mathbf{H}(\mathbf{F}_{k_2}(w), R) \oplus (0||id||P_w)), D_{w,2} = R))$, and add this ciphertext into $\mathcal{T}_W$ in the lexicon order;
     (c) If $P_{id} = NULL$, set label $L_{id} = \mathbf{F}_{k_1}(id)$, otherwise set $L_{id} = P_{id}$; Set $\{R, P_{id}\} \xleftarrow{\$} \{0, 1\}^{2k}$;
     (d) Generate a K2 ciphertext $(L_{id}, D_{id} = (D_{id,1} = (\mathbf{G}(\mathbf{F}_{k_2}(id), R) \oplus (L_w||P_{id})), D_{id,2} = R))$, and add this ciphertext to $\mathcal{T}_F$ in the lexicon order;
  3. Generate dictionaries $\mathcal{D}_W \leftarrow \mathbf{Creat}(\mathcal{T}_W)$ and $\mathcal{D}_F \leftarrow \mathbf{Creat}(\mathcal{T}_F)$;
  4. Keep the privacy of $\mathcal{K}$, and send the encrypted database $EDB = (\mathcal{D}_W, \mathcal{D}_F)$ to the server;
- Server: Store EDB.
★ Protocol **DeleteFile**$((\mathcal{K}, id), EDB)$:
- Client: Take $\mathcal{K} = (k_1, k_2)$ and a file identifier id as inputs, generate and send a delete token $DT_{id} = (\mathbf{F}_{k_1}(id), \mathbf{F}_{k_2}(id))$ to the server.
- Server: Take $EDB = (\mathcal{D}_W, \mathcal{D}_F)$ and $DT_{id} = (\mathbf{F}_{k_1}(id), \mathbf{F}_{k_2}(id))$ as inputs, set $L_{id} = \mathbf{F}_{k_1}(id)$, and do the following steps:
  1. Retrieve data $D_{id} \leftarrow \mathbf{Get}(\mathcal{D}_F, L_{id})$ according to L_{id}; If $D_{id} = NULL$, return $\perp$ and abort;
  2. Parse $D_{id} = (D_{id,1}, D_{id,2})$, decrypt out $L_w||P_{id} = D_{id,1} \oplus \mathbf{G}(\mathbf{F}_{k_2}(id), D_{id,2})$, and run algorithm **Remove**$(\mathcal{D}_F, L_{id})$;
  3. Retrieve data $D_w \leftarrow \mathbf{Get}(\mathcal{D}_W, L_w)$ according to the decrypted L_w, parse $D_w = (D_{w,1}, D_{w,2})$, set the tag bit of D_w to be "1" by computing $D_{w,1} = D_{w,1} \oplus (1||0^{2k})$, run algorithms **Update**$(\mathcal{D}_W, (L_w, D_w = (D_{w,1}, D_{w,2})))$ and **Remove**$(\mathcal{D}_F, L_{id})$, and set $L_{id} = P_{id}$, and go to step 1).
★ Protocol **Search**$((\mathcal{K}, w), EDB)$:
- Client: Take $\mathcal{K} = (k_1, k_2)$ and a keyword w as inputs, generate and send a search token $ST_w = (\mathbf{F}_{k_1}(w), \mathbf{F}_{k_2}(w))$ to the server.
- Server: Take $EDB = (\mathcal{D}_W, \mathcal{D}_F)$ and $ST_w = (\mathbf{F}_{k_1}(w), \mathbf{F}_{k_2}(w))$ as inputs, initialize an empty set $\mathcal{I}$, a temporary label-data pair $(L_w^t = NULL, D_w^t = NULL)$ and a temporary pointer $P_w^t = NULL$, set $L_w = \mathbf{F}_{k_1}(w)$, and do the following steps:
  1. Retrieve data $D_w \leftarrow \mathbf{Get}(\mathcal{D}_W, L_w)$ according to L_w; If $D_w = NULL$, return $\mathcal{I}$ and abort;
  2. Parse $D_w = (D_{w,1}, D_{w,2})$, and decrypt out $T||id||P_w = D_{w,1} \oplus \mathbf{H}(\mathbf{F}_{k_2}(w), D_{w,2})$, where T denotes the tag bit of D_w;
  3. If $L_w^t = NULL$, set $L_w^t = L_w$, $D_w^t = D_w$, $P_w^t = P_w$ and $L_w = P_w$, and go to step 1);
  4. If $T = 1$, parse $D_w^t = (D_{w,1}^t, D_{w,2}^t)$, update $D_{w,1}^t = D_{w,1}^t \oplus (0^{k+1}||(P_w^t \oplus P_w))$, and run algorithms **Update**$(\mathcal{D}_W, (L_w^t, D_w^t = (D_{w,1}^t, D_{w,2}^t)))$ and **Remove**$(\mathcal{D}_W, L_w)$;
  5. If $T = 0$, add the decrypted file identifier id to $\mathcal{I}$, and set $L_w^t = L_w$, $D_w^t = D_w$ and $P_w^t = P_w$;
  6. Set $L_w = P_w$, and go to step 1).

Fig. 4. Our basic DSSE scheme D-II

With a keyword search trapdoor, protocol **Search** not only shows how to quickly find out the related file identifiers as the first basic DSSE scheme does, but also shows how to physically delete the K1 ciphertexts that contain the queried keyword and have their tag bits equaling to "1". Let $\mathbf{F} : \{0,1\}^k \times \{0,1\}^* \rightarrow \{0,1\}^k$ be a key-based pseudo-random function. Let $\mathbf{H} : \{0,1\}^* \rightarrow \{0,1\}^{2k+1}$ and $\mathbf{G} : \{0,1\}^* \rightarrow \{0,1\}^{2k}$ be two cryptographic hash functions. The basic scheme D-II is shown in Fig. 4.

In protocol **DeleteFile**, a delete token $DT_{id} = (\mathbf{F}_{k_1}(id), \mathbf{F}_{k_2}(id))$ allows the server to match value $\mathbf{F}_{k_1}(id)$ with all K2 ciphertexts' labels and find out a matching ciphertext. Then the server applies value $\mathbf{F}_{k_2}(id)$ to decrypt the matching ciphertext and gets a label L_w and a pointer P_{id}. The label L_w corresponds to a K1 ciphertext of id, and the server sets the tag bit of the K1 ciphertext to be "1". In addition, the pointer P_{id} guides the server to quickly find out the next matching K2 ciphertext. So on and so forth, all K1 and K2 ciphertexts of id can be found, and the server physically deletes the found K2 ciphertexts and logically deletes the found K1 ciphertexts. The logically deleted K1 ciphertexts will be physically deleted by protocol **Search**. When searching a keyword, protocol **Search** can quickly find out all matching K1 ciphertexts as the first basic DSSE scheme does. If the tag bit of a matching K1 ciphertext is equal to "1", the server physically deletes this ciphertext, and repairs the corresponding chain relationship among the remaining K1 ciphertexts.

6   Our Complete DSSE Scheme

The above two basic DSSE schemes respectively show our following main ideas: (1) Constructing the hidden chains to connect all searchable ciphertexts of the same keyword to accelerate the search performance; (2) Saving the storage complexity by dynamically generating chain heads; (3) Adding the new generated searchable ciphertext at the end of the corresponding chain; (4) Employing both logical and physical deletions to delete the expected searchable ciphertexts, specially, running physical deletion in due course.

Note that the above last two main ideas are used to avoid extra information leakage. In this section, we extend the above two basic schemes to construct our complete DSSE scheme. It consists of protocols **Setup, AddKeyword, DeleteFile, DeleteKeyword,** and **Search**. Since **DeleteKeyword** is newly achieved by this scheme, it makes other protocols having some differences compared with the above two basic DSSE schemes. But this scheme has exactly the same protocol **Search** as the basic scheme D-II. Hence, this protocol will not be shown in this section. Let $\mathbf{F} : \{0,1\}^k \times \{0,1\}^* \rightarrow \{0,1\}^k$ be a key-based pseudo-random function. Let $\mathbf{H} : \{0,1\}^* \rightarrow \{0,1\}^{2k+1}$ and $\mathbf{G} : \{0,1\}^* \rightarrow \{0,1\}^{3k+1}$ be two cryptographic hash functions. Our complete DSSE scheme is shown in Figs. 5 and 6.

★ Protocol **Setup**$((k, DB), NULL)$:
  - Client: Take a security parameter k and a database DB as inputs, randomly choose two k-bit secret keys $\mathcal{K} = (k_1, k_2)$, initialize four empty lists $\mathcal{T}_P$, $\mathcal{T}_W$, $\mathcal{T}_F$ and $\mathcal{T}_{F,W}$, and do the following steps:
    1. For each file identifier id or keyword w in DB, initialize pointer parameter $P_{id} = NULL$ or $P_w = NULL$;
    2. For each keyword w in DB and each $id \in DB(w)$
       (a) If $P_w = NULL$, set label $L_w = \mathbf{F}_{k_1}(w)$, otherwise set $L_w = P_w$; Set $\{R, P_w\} \overset{\$}{\leftarrow} \{0,1\}^{2k}$;
       (b) Generate a K1 ciphertext $(L_w, D_w = (D_{w,1} = (\mathbf{H}(\mathbf{F}_{k_2}(w), R) \oplus (0||id||P_w)), D_{w,2} = R))$, and add this ciphertext to $\mathcal{T}_W$ in the lexicon order; Set label $L_{id,w} = \mathbf{F}_{k_1}(id, w)$;
       (c) If $P_{id} = NULL$, set label $L_{id} = \mathbf{F}_{k_1}(id)$, otherwise set $L_{id} = P_{id}$; Set $\{R, P_{id}\} \overset{\$}{\leftarrow} \{0,1\}^{2k}$;
       (d) Generate a K2 ciphertext $(L_{id}, D_{id} = (D_{id,1} = (\mathbf{G}(\mathbf{F}_{k_2}(id), R) \oplus (0||L_w||L_{id,w}||P_{id})), D_{id,2} = R))$, and add this ciphertext to $\mathcal{T}_F$ in the lexicon order; Set $R \overset{\$}{\leftarrow} \{0,1\}^k$;
       (e) Generate a K3 ciphertext $(L_{id,w}, D_{id,w} = (D_{id,w,1} = (\mathbf{H}(\mathbf{F}_{k_2}(id, w), R) \oplus (0||L_{id}||L_{id})), D_{id,w,2} = R))$, and add this ciphertext to $\mathcal{T}_{F,W}$ in the lexicon order;
    3. For each keyword w in DB, add tuple (w, P_w) to $\mathcal{T}_P$; For each file identifier id in DB, add tuple (id, P_{id}) to $\mathcal{T}_P$; Generate dictionaries $\mathcal{D}_P \leftarrow \mathbf{Creat}(\mathcal{T}_P)$, $\mathcal{D}_W \leftarrow \mathbf{Creat}(\mathcal{T}_W)$, $\mathcal{D}_F \leftarrow \mathbf{Creat}(\mathcal{T}_F)$ and $\mathcal{D}_{F,W} \leftarrow \mathbf{Creat}(\mathcal{T}_{F,W})$;
    4. Keep $\mathcal{K}$ and $\mathcal{D}_P$ secret, and send the encrypted database $EDB = (\mathcal{D}_W, \mathcal{D}_F, \mathcal{D}_{F,W})$ to the server;
  - Server: Store EDB.
★ Protocol **AddKeyword**$((\mathcal{K}, \mathcal{D}_P, id, w), EDB)$:
  - Client: Take $\mathcal{K} = (k_1, k_2)$, $\mathcal{D}_P$ and a file-keyword pair (id, w) as inputs, retrieve $P_w \leftarrow \mathbf{Get}(\mathcal{D}_P, w)$ according to w, and do the following steps:
    1. If $P_w = NULL$, set label $L_w = \mathbf{F}_{k_1}(w)$, otherwise set $L_w = P_w$; Set $\{R, P_w\} \overset{\$}{\leftarrow} \{0,1\}^{2k}$;
    2. Generate a K1 ciphertext $(L_w, D_w = (D_{w,1} = (\mathbf{H}(\mathbf{F}_{k_2}(w), R) \oplus (0||id||P_w)), D_{w,2} = R))$, and run algorithm $\mathbf{Update}(\mathcal{D}_P, (w, P_w))$; Set label $L_{id,w} = \mathbf{F}_{k_1}(id, w)$; Retrieve $P_{id} \leftarrow \mathbf{Get}(\mathcal{D}_P, id)$ according to id;
    3. If $P_{id} = NULL$, set label $L_{id} = \mathbf{F}_{k_1}(id)$, otherwise set $L_{id} = P_{id}$; Set $\{R, P_{id}\} \overset{\$}{\leftarrow} \{0,1\}^{2k}$;
    4. Generate a K2 ciphertext $(L_{id}, D_{id} = (D_{id,1} = (\mathbf{G}(\mathbf{F}_{k_2}(id), R) \oplus (0||L_w||L_{id,w}||P_{id})), D_{id,2} = R))$, and run algorithm $\mathbf{Update}(\mathcal{D}_P, (id, P_{id}))$; Set $R \overset{\$}{\leftarrow} \{0,1\}^k$;
    5. Generate a K3 ciphertext $(L_{id,w}, D_{id,w} = (D_{id,w,1} = (\mathbf{H}(\mathbf{F}_{k_2}(id, w), R) \oplus (0||L_w||L_{id})), D_{id,w,2} = R))$;
    6. Send ciphertexts $(L_w, D_w, L_{id}, D_{id}, L_{id,w}, D_{id,w})$ to the server;
  - Server: Take $EDB = (\mathcal{D}_W, \mathcal{D}_F, \mathcal{D}_{F,W})$ and $(L_w, D_w, L_{id}, D_{id}, L_{id,w}, D_{id,w})$ as inputs, run algorithms $\mathbf{Update}(\mathcal{D}_W, (L_w, D_w))$, $\mathbf{Update}(\mathcal{D}_F, (L_{id}, D_{id}))$ and $\mathbf{Update}(\mathcal{D}_{F,W}, (L_{id,w}, D_{id,w}))$.

Fig. 5. Our complete DSSE scheme (Part I)

In this scheme, protocol **Setup** newly achieves generation of the K3 ciphertexts. In other words, protocol **Setup** generates three kinds of searchable ciphertexts, i.e. K1, K2, and K3, for each file-keyword pair (id, w). Figure 1 shows the generated K1, K2, and K3 ciphertexts of a file-keyword pair, and their hidden relationship.

The K3 ciphertexts are used to realize protocol **DeleteKeyword**. When deleting all searchable ciphertexts of a file-keyword pair (id, w), the generated delete token $DT_{id,w} = (\mathbf{F}_{k_1}(id, w), \mathbf{F}_{k_2}(id, w))$ of protocol **DeleteKeyword** allows the server to find out the matching K3 ciphertext by matching value

★ Protocol **DeleteFile**$((\mathcal{K}, id), EDB)$:
- Client: Take $\mathcal{K} = (k_1, k_2)$ and a file identifier id as inputs, generate and send a delete token $DT_{id} = (\mathbf{F}_{k_1}(id), \mathbf{F}_{k_2}(id))$ to the server.
- Server: Take $EDB = (\mathcal{D}_W, \mathcal{D}_F, \mathcal{D}_{F,W})$ and $DT_{id} = (\mathbf{F}_{k_1}(id), \mathbf{F}_{k_2}(id))$ as inputs, set label $L_{id} = \mathbf{F}_{k_1}(id)$, and do the following steps:
  1. Retrieve data $D_{id} \leftarrow \mathbf{Get}(\mathcal{D}_F, L_{id})$ according to L_{id}; If $D_{id} = NULL$, return $\perp$ and abort;
  2. Parse $D_{id} = (D_{id,1}, D_{id,2})$, and decrypt out $T||L_w||L_{id,w}||P_{id} = D_{id,1} \oplus \mathbf{G}(\mathbf{F}_{k_2}(id), D_{id,2})$, and run algorithm **Remove**$(\mathcal{D}_F, L_{id})$, where T denotes the tag bit of D_{id};
  3. If $T = 0$, retrieve $D_w \leftarrow \mathbf{Get}(\mathcal{D}_W, L_w)$ according to the decrypted L_w, parse $D_w = (D_{w,1}, D_{w,2})$, set the tag bit of D_w to be "1" by computing $D_{w,1} = D_{w,1} \oplus (1||0^{2k})$, run algorithms **Update**$(\mathcal{D}_W, (L_w, D_w = (D_{w,1}, D_{w,2})))$ and **Remove**$(\mathcal{D}_{F,W}, L_{id,w})$; Set $L_{id} = P_{id}$, and go to step 1).
★ Protocol **DeleteKeyword**$((\mathcal{K}, id, w), EDB)$:
- Client: Take secret keys $\mathcal{K} = (k_1, k_2)$ and a file-keyword pair (id, w) as inputs, generate and send a delete token $DT_{id,w} = (\mathbf{F}_{k_1}(id, w), \mathbf{F}_{k_2}(id, w))$ to the server;
- Server: Take $EDB = (\mathcal{D}_W, \mathcal{D}_F, \mathcal{D}_{F,W})$ and $DT_{id,w} = (\mathbf{F}_{k_1}(id, w), \mathbf{F}_{k_2}(id, w))$ as inputs, set $L_{id,w} = \mathbf{F}_{k_1}(id, w)$ and do the following steps:
  1. Retrieve data $D_{id,w} \leftarrow \mathbf{Get}(\mathcal{D}_{F,W}, L_{id,w})$ according to $L_{id,w}$; If $D_{id,w} = NULL$, return $\perp$ and abort;
  2. Parse $D_{id,w} = (D_{id,w,1}, D_{id,w,2})$, decrypt out $T||L_w||L_{id} = D_{id,w,1} \oplus \mathbf{H}(\mathbf{F}_{k_2}(id, w), D_{id,w,2})$, and run algorithm **Remove**$(\mathcal{D}_{F,W}, L_{id,w})$;
  3. Retrieve data $D_w \leftarrow \mathbf{Get}(\mathcal{D}_W, L_w)$ according to the decrypted label L_w, parse $D_w = (D_{w,1}, D_{w,2})$, set the tag bit of D_w to be "1" by computing $D_{w,1} = D_{w,1} \oplus 1||0^{2k}$, and run algorithm **Update**$(\mathcal{D}_W, (L_w, D_w = (D_{w,1}, D_{w,2})))$;
  4. Retrieve data $D_{id} \leftarrow \mathbf{Get}(\mathcal{D}_F, L_{id})$ according to the decrypted label L_{id}, parse $D_{id} = (D_{id,1}, D_{id,2})$, set the tag bit of D_w to be "1" by computing $D_{id,1} = D_{id,1} \oplus 1||0^{3k}$, and run algorithm **Update**$(\mathcal{D}_F, (L_{id}, D_{id} = (D_{id,1}, D_{id,2})))$.
★ Protocol **Search**$((\mathcal{K}, w), EDB)$ is same as the basic scheme D-II.

Fig. 6. Our complete DSSE scheme (Part II)

$\mathbf{F}_{k_1}(id, w)$ with all K3 ciphertexts' labels, and then the server applies value $\mathbf{F}_{k_2}(id, w)$ to decrypt the matching K3 ciphertext, and gets labels L_w and L_{id}. These two labels respectively correspond to the K1 and K2 ciphertexts of the file-keyword pair (id, w). Finally, the server physically deletes the matching K3 ciphertext, and logically deletes the corresponding K1 and K2 ciphertexts by setting their tag bits to be "1".

It is different with the second basic DSSE scheme that some K2 ciphertexts could have been logically deleted before the execution of protocol **DeleteFile**. Hence, protocol **DeleteFile** in this scheme has two ways to delete K2 ciphertexts. For example, suppose to delete the K2 ciphertext of label L_{id} in protocol **DeleteFile**, the sever decrypts this ciphertext to obtain a tag bit and two labels L_w and $L_{id,w}$. If the tag bit is equal to "0", the server finds out the corresponding K1 and K3 ciphertexts according to those two labels, then physically deletes the K2 and K3 ciphertexts and logically deletes the K1 ciphertext. Otherwise, the server only physically deletes the k2 ciphertext, since the corresponding K1 and K3 ciphertexts have been logically or physically deleted by a previous execution of protocol **DeleteKeyword**.

In addition, protocol **AddKeyword** has the same essence with protocol **Setup** to generate searchable ciphertexts. But protocol **AddKeyword** takes only one file-keyword pair as input. Contrarily, protocol **Setup** takes a lot of file-keyword pairs as inputs.

Summarily, our complete DSSE scheme shows all of our main ideas introduced in Sect. 1.1. The most contributive and novel work in our scheme should be the hybrid of logical and physical deletion of searchable ciphertexts, so that the deletion function only causes small information leakage compared with schemes KPR'12, KP'13, and CJJ'14.

6.1   Provable IND-CKA2 Security

According to the IND-CKA2 security definition, the security proof of our complete DSSE scheme requires us to construct a simulator $\mathcal{S}$. This simulator only takes leakage functions as inputs, and simulates our scheme by responding the following requirements of adversary $\mathcal{A}$. When $\mathcal{A}$ chooses a database DB to engage in protocol **Setup**, $\mathcal{S}$ takes leakage function $\mathcal{L}_{Setup}$ as input, and simulates an encrypted database EDB. When $\mathcal{A}$ chooses a new file-keyword pair to engage in protocol **AddKeyword**, $\mathcal{S}$ takes leakage function $\mathcal{L}_{AddKeyword}$ as input, and simulates the corresponding searchable ciphertexts. When $\mathcal{A}$ chooses a file to engage in protocol **DeleteFile**, $\mathcal{S}$ takes leakage function $\mathcal{L}_{DeleteFile}$ as input, and simulates the corresponding delete token. When $\mathcal{A}$ chooses an old file-keyword pair to engage in protocol **DeleteKeyword**, $\mathcal{S}$ takes leakage function $\mathcal{L}_{DeleteKeyword}$ as input, and simulates the corresponding delete token. When $\mathcal{A}$ chooses a keyword to engage in protocol **Search**, $\mathcal{S}$ takes leakage function $\mathcal{L}_{Search}$ as input, and simulates the corresponding search token.

All the above simulated data will be sent to $\mathcal{A}$. Moreover they must be indistinguishable with real ones in the view of $\mathcal{A}$. To meet the above requirements, we have to assume that the hash functions and the pseudo-random function in our scheme are random oracles. $\mathcal{S}$ controls the responses of these oracles, and makes the above forgeries indistinguishable with the real ones in the view of $\mathcal{A}$.

We define the leakage functions for all proposed protocols. When defining the leakage functions, the most complex work is to define the leakage caused by the linkage of some protocols' instances. In this paper, we apply a new idea to define the leakage functions. This idea makes the definitions more clear. For all ciphertexts generated by protocol **Setup**, let $Old(id, w)$ denote the set of ciphertexts that were generated for file-keyword pair (id, w), let $Old(id)$ denote the set of ciphertexts generated for file id, and let $Old(w)$ denote the set of ciphertexts generated for keyword w. For all ciphertexts generated by protocol **AddKeyword**, let $New(id, w)$ denote the set of ciphertexts generated for file-keyword pair (id, w), let $New(id)$ denote the set of ciphertexts generated for file id, and let $New(w)$ denote the set of ciphertexts generated for keyword w. The leakage functions are $\mathcal{L}_{Setup} = |DB|$, $\mathcal{L}_{AddKeyword} = New(id, w)$, $\mathcal{L}_{DeleteFile} = (Old(id), New(id))$, $\mathcal{L}_{DeleteKeyword} = (Old(id, w), New(id, w))$, and $\mathcal{L}_{Search} = (DB(w), Old(w), New(w))$, respectively.

It is clear that most of above leakage functions are defined as the set of some related ciphertexts. This method is easy to imply the leakage caused by the linkage of some protocols' instances. For example, when running protocol **AddKeyword** to add a file-keyword pair (id, w), one can decide that whether keyword w has been searched by a previous instance of protocol **Search**. This leakage is contained in our definitions. In other words, if the leakage $\mathcal{L}_{AddKeyword} = New(id, w)$ of an instance of protocol **AddKeyword** has some common ciphertexts with the leakage $\mathcal{L}_{Search} = (DB(w), Old(w), New(w))$ of an instance of protocol **Search**, it means that keyword w has been searched by the latter instance. In addition, this example also allows one to decide whether file-keyword pair (id, w) has been deleted by a previous instance of protocol **DeleteFile** or **DeleteKeyword**. This leakage is also contained in our definitions by the similar reason. In general, given two instances of our proposed protocols, the leakage caused by their linkage is implied in our definitions. Finally, we have Theorem 1 whose proof can be found in the full version.

Theorem 1. *Suppose hash functions* **H** *and* **G** *and key-based pseudo-random function* $\mathbf{F}_{k_1}$ *are respectively modeled as three random oracles. Our complete DSSE scheme is IND-CKA2 secure with leakage functions* $(\mathcal{L}_{Setup}, \mathcal{L}_{AddKeyword}, \mathcal{L}_{DeleteFile}, \mathcal{L}_{DeleteKeyword}, \mathcal{L}_{Search})$ *in the RO model, where* $\mathcal{L}_{Setup} = |DB|$, $\mathcal{L}_{AddKeyword} = New(id, w)$, $\mathcal{L}_{DeleteFile} = (Old(id), New(id))$, $\mathcal{L}_{DeleteKeyword} = (Old(id, w), New(id, w))$, *and* $\mathcal{L}_{Search} = (DB(w), Old(w), New(w))$.

7   Comparisons and Experiments

In this section, we make thorough comparisons between our complete DSSE scheme and the related schemes KPR'12, KP'13, and CJJ'14 in Table 2. We also conduct extensive experiments to evaluate the performance of our scheme. Table 2 shows the following advantages of our scheme: (1) the lowest search complexity, which is linear with the total number of files Containing The Queried Keyword; (2) The Lowest Storage Complexity, Which Is Linear With The Size Of Database Db (Or The Total Number Of File-Keyword Pairs In Database Db); (3) The Smallest Leakage To Run Protocol **Setup**, Which Only Contains the size of database DB; (4) the same leakage with schemes KPR'12, KP'13, and CJJ'14 to run protocol **Search**; (5) the same leakage with scheme CJJ'14 to run protocol **AddKeyword**; (6) the smaller leakage to run protocol **DeleteFile** than that of KPR'12; (7) the same leakage (at the worst case) with scheme CJJ'14 to run protocol **DeleteKeyword**. Hence, our DSSE scheme not only supports all functions mentioned in Table 1, but also has the lowest search and storage complexities, and the smallest leakages in most cases.

We coded our complete DSSE scheme and tested its performance on a simulated database DB of millions file-keyword pairs. The input security parameter is of binary size 80 bits. All hash and pseudo-random functions are implemented by running hash function SHA-256. The practical implementation of a DSSE scheme consists of two kinds of time-intensive operations: cryptographic computations and system actions (e.g., network transmission and file system access).

Table 2. Exact comparisons

Scheme	Search complexity	Storage complexity	Leakage functions				
			$\mathcal{L}_{Setup}$	$\mathcal{L}_{Search}$	$\mathcal{L}_{AddKeyword}$	$\mathcal{L}_{DeleteFile}$	$\mathcal{L}_{DeleteKeyword}$
KPR'12 [1]	$O(\lvert DB(w)\rvert)$	$O(\lvert DB\rvert + \lvert W\rvert)$	$\lvert W\rvert, \lvert DB\rvert$	①	×	③	×
KP'13 [2]	$O(\lvert DB(w)\rvert\cdot log\,\lvert \mathcal{ID}\rvert)$	$O(\lvert W\rvert\cdot\lvert \mathcal{ID}\rvert)$	$\lvert W\rvert\cdot\lvert \mathcal{ID}\rvert$	①	×	④	×
CJJ'14 [3]	$O(\lvert DB(w)\rvert)$	$O(\lvert DB\rvert)$	$\lvert DB\rvert$	①	②	×	⑤ at the worst case
Ours	$O(\lvert DB(w)\rvert)$	$O(\lvert DB\rvert)$	$\lvert DB\rvert$	①	②	④	⑤

① : $DB(w)$, $Old(w)$, and $New(w)$. ② : $New(id, w)$. ③ : $Old(id)$, $New(id)$ and a part of $DB(w)$ where $w \in DB(id)$.
④ : $Old(id)$ and $New(id)$. ⑤ : $Old(id, w)$ and $New(id, w)$. × : means that the operation cannot be achieved.
All symbols have been defined in Sects. 2 and 6.1.

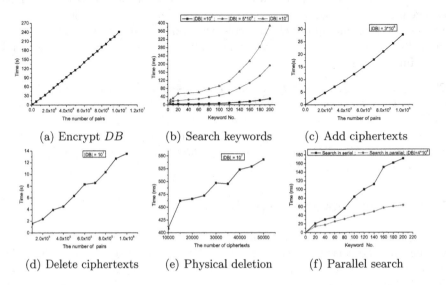

(a) Encrypt DB (b) Search keywords   (c) Add ciphertexts

(d) Delete ciphertexts   (e) Physical deletion   (f) Parallel search

Fig. 7. All tests and their results

To separate cryptographic costs from system costs, we built a test framework excluding network transmission and disk access. In other words, all data are stored in memory. Most of tests were implemented in a PC with Intel CPU 2.4 GHz (Core i5) and Ubuntu system by a single thread. Only the final test is a parallel search with a 4-core processor.

To simulate a database DB with millions file-keyword pairs, we chose 200 commonly used keywords from Google Search Engine. We supposed that each file had no more than 20 keywords, and each file identifier was randomly generated. We paired each keyword with some file identifiers according to this keyword's frequency. Finally, all simulated file-keyword pairs were collected in a database DB.

Figure 7(a) shows the time cost of our complete DSSE scheme to generate an encrypted database EDB for the above simulated database DB, where $\lvert DB\rvert$ is between 10^6 and 10^7. This process contains generating searchable ciphertexts and constructing a self-balancing binary search tree (or AVL tree) for these ciphertexts. For example, the time cost to encrypt DB with size 10^7 is about 241 s. From this experiment result, we can find that the time cost per file-keyword pair is an amortized value: it is determined by taking the complete execution time of experiment and dividing by the number of file-keyword pairs.

Figure 7(b) shows the time cost of our complete DSSE scheme to search each keyword over different scaled DBs. Recall that our protocol **Search** includes the process to physically delete the K1 ciphertexts with the tag bit equaling "1". We show this process in Fig. 7(e). In Fig. 7(b), the line with triangles shows the time costs when $|DB| = 10^6$, the line with circles shows the time costs when $|DB| = 5 \times 10^6$, and the line with rectangles shows the time costs when $|DB| = 10^7$.

Figure 7(c) shows the time cost of our complete DSSE scheme to add the searchable ciphertexts of several file-keyword pairs. This process excludes the generation of searchable ciphertexts, since this part is similar with the process to encrypt a database. So it only contains the process to rebalance the AVL tree according to these new added ciphertexts. We have a group of experiments to add the searchable ciphertexts of the different number (between 10^5 and 10^6) of pairs to a database with the original size $|DB| = 3 \times 10^6$.

Figure 7(d) shows the time cost of our complete DSSE scheme to delete the searchable ciphertexts of several file-keyword pairs. We have a group of experiments to delete the searchable ciphertexts of different number (between 10^5 and 10^6) of pairs from a database with the original size $|DB| = 10^7$.

Figure 7(e) shows the time cost of physical deletion when one searches a keyword in our complete DSSE scheme. Recall that all K1 ciphertexts of the same keyword are applied to construction of the hidden chain relationship. Suppose some of them have the tag bit equaling "1". These ciphertexts will be physically deleted when their associated keywords are searched. This process contains to repair a broken chain and rebalance the original AVL tree of the searchable ciphertexts. For different number (between 10^4 and 5×10^4) of ciphertexts with the tag bit equaling "1", we tested the time cost to physically delete them from a database with the original size $|DB| = 10^7$.

Both in Fig. 7(d) and (e), some singular points indicate that the time cost is not strictly linear with the number of deleted ciphertexts. These singular points are caused by the operations to rebalance the AVL tree of searchable ciphertexts. Comparatively, when different nodes are deleted in an AVL tree, the time costs to rebalance the AVL tree are also different.

Finally, Fig. 7(f) shows the time cost of parallel search in our complete DSSE scheme. We simulated four databases with the same number of file-keyword pairs, and generated their encrypted databases. The total size of all databases is $|DB| = 4 \times 10^6$. The line with circles shows the time cost to search each keyword in parallel with a 4-core processor, and the line with rectangles shows the time cost to search each keyword in the serial mode.

8   Other Related Works

SSE was first introduced by Song *et al.* in [5]. Their instantiated scheme takes search time linear with the total binary size of ciphertexts. A number of efforts [6–8] follow this line and refine Song *et al.*'s original work. The SSE scheme due to Curtmola *et al.* [9] has been proven to be semantically secure against an adaptive adversary. It allows search to be processed in logarithmic time.

In addition to the above efforts devoted to either provable security or better search performance, attention has recently been paid to achieve versatile SSE schemes. Waters *et al.* [10] showed practical applications of SSE and employed it to realize secure and searchable audit logs. Several works in SSE are complex queries for conjunctive [11,12] or disjunctive [13,14] keyword combinations. The works in [9,15] extended SSE to a multi-sender scenario. Recent results [16,17] achieved efficiency improvements for these complex queries. The works in [18,19] supported fuzzy keyword searching. The schemes in [20–23] solved the problem of multi-keyword ranked search and multi-dimensional range query over encrypted cloud data. Lu [24] improved the search performance of range queries by constructing indices. Boldyreva *et al.* [25] first studied symmetric encryption primitive with order preserving and provided an instance with provable security. Chase *et al.* [26] first studied the searchable symmetric encryption of structured data.

In addition to the previously introduced DSSE schemes in [1–3], Naveed *et al.* [27] proposed a DSSE scheme to trade storage for performance by scattering the stored blocks using hashing instead of encrypting the indices. This work leaks keyword frequency like [1]. Emilet *et al.* [4] proposed a hierarchical index structure using oblivious *random access memory* (RAM) to achieve more secure and effective dynamic ciphertext updates with small leakage. This work is not efficient in practice because of a large number of communication rounds and expensive storage costs on the server side [28]. Hahn *et al.* [29] constructed visible relationships to group all searchable ciphertexts of the same keyword, when keywords are at the first time to be searched. According to those groups, the performance to repeatedly search the same keyword will be significantly improved. This method can also be applied in KPR'12, KP'13, and CJJ'14 to accelerate their performance to repeatedly search the same keyword. But the first-time search performance per keyword of [29] is linear with the total number of ciphertexts. Hence, its search complexity is the highest one comparably.

9   Conclusion

In this paper, we proposed a new DSSE scheme to simultaneously support fast keyword search, low storage complexity, versatile functions, and small leakage when implementing these functions. Our scheme has the search complexity linear with the number of searchable ciphertexts containing the queried keyword, and has the storage complexity linear with the size of original database. Compared with previous works, our scheme has the most versatile functions. In addition to search a keyword, it allows a client to (1) add the searchable ciphertexts of a new file-keyword pair, (2) delete the searchable ciphertexts of a file, and (3) delete the searchable ciphertexts of a file-keyword pair. In most cases, our scheme has the smallest leakage compared with previous works. Furthermore, our scheme is proven IND-CKA2 secure, which excludes possible vulnerabilities in design. The most contributive and novel work in our scheme is to achieve physical deletion with small leakage.

Acknowledgement. The paper is partly supported by the National Natural Science Foundation of China under grant no. 61472156, the National Program on Key Basic Research Project (973 Program) under grant no. 2014CB340600, and the Natural Science Foundation of China under grant no. 61672083 and 61370190.

References

1. Kamara, S., Papamanthou, C., Roeder, T.: Dynamic searchable symmetric encryption. In: ACM CCS 2012, pp. 965–976. ACM (2012)
2. Kamara, S., Papamanthou, C.: Parallel and dynamic searchable symmetric encryption. In: Sadeghi, A.-R. (ed.) FC 2013. LNCS, vol. 7859, pp. 258–274. Springer, Heidelberg (2013). doi:10.1007/978-3-642-39884-1_22
3. Cash, D., Jaeger, J., Jarecki, S., Jutla, C., Krawczyk, H., Ros, M.C., Steiner, M.: Dynamic searchable encryption in very-large databases: data structures and implementation. In: NDSS (2014)
4. Stefanov, E., Papamanthou, C., Shi, E.: Practical dynamic searchable encryption with small leakage. In: NDSS (2014)
5. Song, D., Wagner, D., Perrig, A.: Practical techniques for searches on encrypted data. In: IEEE SP 2000, pp. 44–55. IEEE (2000)
6. Agrawal, R., Kiernan, J., Srikant, R., Xu, Y.: Order preserving encryption for numeric data. In: Proceedings of the 2004 ACM SIGMOD International Conference on Management of Data, pp. 563–574. ACM (2004)
7. Chang, Y.-C., Mitzenmacher, M.: Privacy preserving keyword searches on remote encrypted data. In: Ioannidis, J., Keromytis, A., Yung, M. (eds.) ACNS 2005. LNCS, vol. 3531, pp. 442–455. Springer, Heidelberg (2005). doi:10.1007/11496137_30
8. Goh, E.J.: Secure Indexes. Cryptography ePrint Archive, Report 2003/216 (2003)
9. Curtmola, R., Garay, J., Kamara, S., Ostrovsky, R.: Searchable symmetric encryption: improved definitions and efficient constructions. In: ACM CCS 2006, pp. 79–88. ACM (2006)
10. Waters, B.R., Balfanz, D., Durfee, G., Smetters, D.K.: Building an encrypted and searchable audit log. In: NDSS 2004, vol. 4, pp. 5–6 (2004)
11. Golle, P., Staddon, J., Waters, B.: Secure conjunctive keyword search over encrypted data. In: Jakobsson, M., Yung, M., Zhou, J. (eds.) ACNS 2004. LNCS, vol. 3089, pp. 31–45. Springer, Heidelberg (2004). doi:10.1007/978-3-540-24852-1_3
12. Byun, J.W., Lee, D.H., Lim, J.: Efficient conjunctive keyword search on encrypted data storage system. In: Atzeni, A.S., Lioy, A. (eds.) EuroPKI 2006. LNCS, vol. 4043, pp. 184–196. Springer, Heidelberg (2006). doi:10.1007/11774716_15
13. Boneh, D., Waters, B.: Conjunctive, subset, and range queries on encrypted data. In: Vadhan, S.P. (ed.) TCC 2007. LNCS, vol. 4392, pp. 535–554. Springer, Heidelberg (2007). doi:10.1007/978-3-540-70936-7_29

14. Li, M., Yu, S., Cao, N.: Authorized private keyword search over encrypted data in cloud computing. In: IEEE ISDCS 2011, pp. 383–392. IEEE (2011)
15. Jarecki, S., Jutla, C., Krawczyk, H., Rosu, M.C., Steiner, M.: Outsourced symmetric private information retrieval. In: ACM CCS 2013, pp. 875–888. ACM (2013)
16. Katz, J., Sahai, A., Waters, B.: Predicate encryption supporting disjunctions, polynomial equations, and inner products. In: Smart, N. (ed.) EUROCRYPT 2008. LNCS, vol. 4965, pp. 146–162. Springer, Heidelberg (2008). doi:10.1007/978-3-540-78967-3_9
17. Cash, D., Jarecki, S., Jutla, C., Krawczyk, H., Roşu, M.-C., Steiner, M.: Highly-scalable searchable symmetric encryption with support for boolean queries. In: Canetti, R., Garay, J.A. (eds.) CRYPTO 2013. LNCS, vol. 8042, pp. 353–373. Springer, Heidelberg (2013). doi:10.1007/978-3-642-40041-4_20
18. Li, J., Wang, Q., Wang, C., Cao, N., Ren, K., Lou, W.: Fuzzy keyword search over encrypted data in cloud computing. In: IEEE INFOCOM 2010, pp. 1–5. IEEE (2010)
19. Wang, B., Yu, S., Lou, W., Hou, Y.T.: Privacy-preserving multi-keyword fuzzy search over encrypted data in the cloud. In: IEEE INFOCOM 2014, pp. 2112–2120. IEEE (2014)
20. Shi, E., Bethencourt, J., Chan, T.H.: Multi-dimensional range query over encrypted data. In: IEEE SP 2007, pp. 350–364. IEEE (2007)
21. Wang, C., Cao, N., Li, J., Lou, W.J.: Secure ranked keyword search over encrypted cloud data. In: IEEE ICDCS 2010, pp. 253–262. IEEE (2010)
22. Wang, C., Cao, N., Ren, K., Lou, W.: Enabling secure and efficient ranked keyword search over outsourced cloud data. IEEE Trans. Parallel Distrib. Syst. 23(8), 1467–1479 (2012). IEEE
23. Cao, N., Wang, C., Li, M., Ren, K., Lou, W.J.: Privacy-preserving multi-keyword ranked search over encrypted cloud data. IEEE Trans. Parallel Distrib. Syst. 25(1), 222–233 (2014). IEEE
24. Lu, Y.: Privacy-preserving logarithmic-time search on encrypted data in cloud. In: NDSS (2012)
25. Boldyreva, A., Chenette, N., Lee, Y., O'Neill, A.: Order-preserving symmetric encryption. In: Joux, A. (ed.) EUROCRYPT 2009. LNCS, vol. 5479, pp. 224–241. Springer, Heidelberg (2009). doi:10.1007/978-3-642-01001-9_13
26. Chase, M., Kamara, S.: Structured encryption and controlled disclosure. In: Abe, M. (ed.) ASIACRYPT 2010. LNCS, vol. 6477, pp. 577–594. Springer, Heidelberg (2010). doi:10.1007/978-3-642-17373-8_33
27. Naveed, M., Prabhakaran, M., Gunter, C.: Dynamic searchable encryption via blind storage. In: IEEE SP 2014, pp. 639–654. IEEE (2014)
28. Bosch, C., Hartel, P., Jonker, W., et al.: A survey of provably secure searchable encryption. ACM Comput. Surv. 47(2) (2014). Article no. 18
29. Hahn, F., Kerschbaum, F.: Searchable encryption with secure and efficient updates. In: ACM CCS 2014, pp. 310–320. ACM (2014)

Multi-user Cloud-Based Secure Keyword Search

Shabnam Kasra Kermanshahi$^{(\boxtimes)}$, Joseph K. Liu, and Ron Steinfeld

Faculty of Information Technology, Monash University, Melbourne, Australia
{shabnam.kasra,joseph.liu,ron.steinfeld}@monash.edu

Abstract. We propose a *multi-user* Symmetric Searchable Encryption
(SSE) scheme based on the single-user Oblivious Cross Tags (OXT) protocol (Cash et al., CRYPTO 2013). The scheme allows any user to perform a search query by interacting with the server and any $\theta - 1$ 'helping'
users, and preserves the privacy of database content against the server
even assuming leakage of up to $\theta - 1$ users' keys to the server (for a
threshold parameter θ), while hiding the query from the $\theta - 1$ 'helping
users'. To achieve the latter query privacy property, we design a new distributed key-homomorphic pseudorandom function (PRF) that hides the
PRF input (search keyword) from the 'helping' key share holders. By distributing the utilized keys among the users, the need of constant online
presence of the data owner to provide services to the users is eliminated,
while providing resilience against user key exposure.

Keywords: Multi-user · Cloud storage · Searchable encryption · Query
privacy

1 Introduction

Nowadays, outsourcing data (in any form such as email, backups, financial and so
forth) to off-site hosts known as Cloud has become a common trend. However,
confidentiality of the sensitive data is a major concern [12,21,24,27]. Data is
visible to the cloud and those who have the access to the cloud storage. Although
it seems that encryption of data can be a straightforward solution, search through
the encrypted data is a big challenge. In particular, with such straightforward
approaches, the user has to download and decrypt the data first to perform the
search, due to the fact that the data is not readable by the cloud server. This
communication and computation can make such approaches impractical in many
applications.

Recently, several Searchable Encryption (SE) schemes have been proposed
to address the mentioned problem [9,11,13,33]. SE technique enables the data
owner to encrypt the data while the ability of the server to search the data
is retained. In general, based on the utilized encryption technique (symmetric or public key), searchable encryption schemes can be categorized into two
category: Symmetric Searchable Encryption (SSE) (e.g. [39,42]) and Asymmetric Searchable Encryption (ASE) (e.g. [25,26,38]). There exists other features

© Springer International Publishing AG 2017
J. Pieprzyk and S. Suriadi (Eds.): ACISP 2017, Part I, LNCS 10342, pp. 227–247, 2017.
DOI: 10.1007/978-3-319-60055-0_12

to distinguish SE schemes such as structure (single-writer/single-reader, single-writer/multi-reader, multi-writer/single-reader and multi-writer/ multi-reader) or functionalities (ranked keyword query, range query, phrase query, etc.). Focus of this research is on the single-writer/multi-reader SSE scheme that we call it Multi-client. Our multi-client SSE protocol is inspired by symmetric searchable encryption (SSE) protocol of Cash et al. [9] called OXT. Although the designers of OXT suggested to distribute the Master-key to the clients to make their protocol useful for multi-client setting, this straightforward solution increases the likelihood of Master-key exposure and is not resilient to client key exposure; exposure of any single client's key (e.g. by key loss or collusion of this client with the server or unauthorized users) exposes the whole database contents. Later on, a multi-client extension of OXT was proposed [8] using a different approach. In order to search through the server, each client has to refer to the data owner and get the search token. Although this fixes the key loss resilience problem, this approach has several functionality limitations. First, it requires per-query interaction with the data owner. Thus, the data owner must be available all the time. Second, there is no query privacy for clients against the data owner.

In this paper we present a multi-user SSE which has query privacy against both data owner and the other key share holders. In addition, once the data owner performed the EDBSetup phase, it is not necessary to be involved in protocol unless for key update and revocation. At the same time, our protocol is resilient against key exposure of up to $\theta - 1$ client keys. A search is performed by a client via interaction with the server and $\theta - 1$ 'helping' users.

1.1   Our Contributions

As mentioned earlier, our generic design is inspired by OXT protocol of Cash et al. [9]. The contributions of our multi-user SSE can be summarized as followed;

1. Privacy of database content against server resilient against exposure of up to $\theta - 1$ users' keys. More precisely, by considering that the data owner does not collude with server, our multi-user SSE is secure by the size of considered threshold, θ. That is, server is unable to learn any information by colluding with any coalition smaller than θ.

   It is worth to note that the leakage profile (leakage to server) of our multi-user SSE is the same as OXT [9].

2. Our most advanced result is preserving query privacy both against data owner and the other key share holders. This goal has been achieved by designing a new primitive named Randomizable distributed Key-homomorphic PRF. Moreover, using distributed Key-homomorphic PRFs enables data owner to distribute the PRF Key Shares between desirable clients (Key Share Holders) without further interactions. More precisely, clients would be able to carry out the search without per-query interaction with data owner which in turn leads to two more nice features. First, online presence of data owner at all the time is not required. Second, queries performed by clients are not monitored by the data owner. Moreover, due to the inherent property of the threshold secret sharing (explained in Sect. 2.2), in our multi-user SSE scheme, Data owner is able to revoke the key shares from up to $\theta - 1$ of key share holders.

Remark. In the current related works [9,20,34] if data owner decide to update the encryption key a substantial amount of cost would be added to the system in terms of computations performed for encryption of the database using the new key, bandwidth for uploading EDB (Encrypted DataBase) as well as transferring required information to the considered clients. We could achieve more efficient solution which enable data owner to update the encryption key as well as EDB by sending the corresponding key material to the server.

1.2   Related Works

Followed by the first Symmetric Searchable Encryption (SSE) proposed by Song et al. [33] several SSE schemes have been proposed (e.g. [7,10,11,13–17,19,22, 23,29,31]). In early stage most of the works were in single-writer/single-reader setting. However, single-user setting is not beneficial for cloud storage as usually enterprise cloud servers serve multiple users. Multi-user searchable encryption was pioneered by Curtmola et al. [13] for symmetric setting. In their scheme, single-user searchable encryption is transformed to the multi-user one by sharing the utilized key for encryption of the database. In this scheme, key revocation is not considered, thus beside of search ability of the revoked users, collusion with the server is another drawback. Moreover, using broadcast encryption for handling the search queries make it impractical (inefficiency).

In order to manage search ability of the users, the proposed scheme by Bao et al. [2] applies a trusted third party called User Manager (UM). Although it seems that their scheme could handle the key revocation issue, using such a trusted party is not common in cloud storage. The proposed schemes in [14,40, 41] suffer from similar problem.

The proposed work by Popa et al. [28] could overcome the need to the trusted administration, however it is inefficient due to unavoidable network bandwidth overhead and storage overhead. Although the proposed scheme by Tang et al. [35] could improve the Popa's scheme from security perspective, similar to Multi-user searchable encryption schemes in [18,37] did not explain how to revoke a user.

Several searchable encryption schemes have been proposed using Public key structure in order to provide Multi-user setting [1,3,4,6,32,36], however, they have limited applications in practice due to the cost of public key solutions. Thus, investigation of the cons and pros of the mentioned works is out of the scope of this paper.

Motivated by the SSE protocol of Cash et al. [9], Jarecki et al. [20] and Sun et al. [34] proposed multi-user SSE schemes.

Although Sun's scheme could improve the communication overhead by avoiding per-query interaction between data owner and clients which exists in the Jarecki's scheme, Data owner still involved in the token generation process. In addition, the search keywords are predetermined and restricted by the data owner. More importantly, user enrollment and revocation remained unconsidered in the mentioned works.

2   Preliminaries

In this section, the required preliminaries are provided.

2.1   Notations

Frequently used notations and terminologies in this paper are listed in Table 1.

Table 1. Notations and Terminologies

Notation	Description
λ	A security parameter
id_i	The document identifier of the i-th document
W_{id_i}	A list of keywords contained in the i-th document
$DB = (id_i, W_{id_i})_{i=1}^d$	A database consisting of a list of document identifier and keyword-set pairs
$DB[w] = \{id : w \in W_{id}\}$	The set of identifiers of documents that contain keyword w
$W = \bigcup_{i=1}^d W_{id_i}$	The keyword set of the database
θ	Threshold
sterm	The least frequent term among queried terms (or keywords) in a search query
xterm	Other queried terms in a search query (i.e., the queried terms excluding sterm)

2.2   Threshold Secret Sharing

This subsection reviews the secret sharing scheme proposed by Shamir [30] briefly. The idea is to divide the secret $k \in \mathbb{Z}_p$ (for a prime $p > N$) into N pieces such that knowledge of at least θ pieces (threshold) allows recovering k. More precisely, this scheme consists of two main algorithms *Share* and *Recon* as followed.

- Share: This algorithm inputs a secret $k \in \mathbb{Z}_p$ and outputs the corresponding key shares $k_1 \in \mathbb{Z}_p, ..., k_N \in \mathbb{Z}_p$.
- Recon: Reconstruct the secret using any subset $W = \{i_1, ..., i_\theta\} \subset [N]$ of size θ by computing $k = \sum_{j=1}^{\theta} \lambda_{ij}.k_{ij} \pmod{p}$, where $\lambda_{ij} \in \mathbb{Z}_p$ are reconstruction coefficients.

2.3   Pseudorandom Functions (PRFs)

In this subsection, we review Pseudorandom Functions.

Key Homomorphic Pseudorandom Functions. Let $\mathcal{F} : \mathcal{K} \times \mathcal{X} \to \mathcal{Y}$ be an efficiently computable function where $(K, \oplus)$ and $(\mathcal{Y}, \otimes)$ are groups. Tuple $(\mathcal{F}, \oplus, \otimes)$ is a key homomorphic PRF if the following properties hold [5]:

1. $\mathcal{F}$ is a secure pseudorandom function.
2. For every $k_1, k_2 \in \mathcal{K}$ and every $x \in \mathcal{X}$, $\mathcal{F}(k_1, x) \otimes \mathcal{F}(k_2, x) = \mathcal{F}(k_1 \oplus k_2, x)$.

Constructing key homomorphic PRFs in the random oracle model is straightforward. Let G be a finite cyclic group of prime order q and let $H_1 : \mathcal{X} \to G$ be a hash function modeled as a random oracle. Define the function $F_{DDH} : Z_q \times \mathcal{X} \to G$ as $F_{DDH}(k, x) \leftarrow H_1(x)^k$ and observe that $F_{DDH}(k_1 + k_2, x) = F_{DDH}(k_1, x).F_{DDH}(k_2, x)$.

Distributed PRF. A distributed PRF mainly consists of five algorithm; S$etup$, Key $sharing$, P$artial$ $evaluation$, C$ombine$, and E$valuation$ with the following properties [5].

- S$etup$: This algorithm inputs security parameter κ and outputs public parameters pp.
- Key $sharing$ $\mathcal{K} \to \mathcal{K}^{\mathcal{N}}$: This algorithm generates key shares $(k_1, ..., k_N) \in \mathcal{K}^{\mathcal{N}}$ of the considered master key $(k_0 \in_r \mathcal{K})$ using $S = (\theta, N)$ threshold secret sharing scheme proposed by Shamir [30] which is explained in Subsect. 2.2.
- P$artial$ $evaluation$: The function $\mathcal{F} : \mathcal{K} \times \mathcal{X} \to \mathcal{Y}$ takes a key share and an input point and outputs a partial evaluation of the E$valuation$ function f.
- C$ombine$: The algorithm $G : 2^{[N]} \times \mathcal{Y}^{\theta} \to \mathcal{Y}$ inputs a subset $W \subset [N]$ of size θ and θ partial evaluations on key shares in the set W and outputs a value in $\mathcal{Y}$.
- E$valuation$: The function $f : \mathcal{K} \times \mathcal{X} \to \mathcal{Y}$ maps a key and an input to the space of outputs.

The distributed PRF is initialized by a trusted third party who runs S$etup(1^{\kappa})$ to obtain the public parameters pp, samples the master secret key $mk = k_0$ uniformly from $\mathcal{K}$, and performs Key $sharing(k_0)$ to obtain a tuple $(k_1, ..., k_N)$. The key share k_i is distributed as the secret key for each key share holder i along with public parameters pp. A client who wants to compute the evaluation function using k_0 on input x sends x to $\theta - 1$ key share holders $(i_1, ..., i_{\theta-1})$. Each key share holder i responds to the client with $\mathcal{F}(k_i, x)$. then the client locally computes $f(k_0, x)$ by computing $G(W, \mathcal{F}(k_{i_1}, x), ..., \mathcal{F}(k_{i_\theta}, x))$.

Correctness. By considering pp as the output of S$etup(1^{\kappa})$, k_0 sampled uniformly from $\mathcal{K}$, and $(k_1, ..., k_N)$ the key share output by Key $sharing(k_0)$. For every subset $W = i_1, ..., i_{\theta} \subset [N]$ of size θ, and for every input x, a distributed PRF is correct if $f(k_0, x) = G(W, \mathcal{F}(k_{i_1}, x), ..., \mathcal{F}(k_{i_\theta}, x))$.

Security. The E$valuation$ function f should remain pseudorandom even when the adversary is given $\theta - 1$ key shares $(k_{i_1}, ..., k_{i_{\theta-1}})$ for indices $i_1, ..., i_{\theta-1}$ of its choice. The adversary is also given an oracle $\mathcal{O}$ that performs arbitrary partial evaluations: it takes (i, x) as input and returns $\mathcal{F}(k_i, x)$. The adversary should be unable to distinguish the function from random at point x where did not query the oracle $\mathcal{O}$. We formalize this intuition through an experiment between a challenger and an adversary $\mathcal{A}$. For $b \in \{0, 1\}$ the challenger in $Expt_b^{dPRF}$ operates as follows.

1. Given security parameter κ, the challenger runs S$etup(1^{\kappa})$ and publishes public parameters pp to the adversary. The challenger then samples a k_0 uniformly from $\mathcal{K}$ and runs Key $sharing(k_0)$ to obtain $(k_1, ..., k_N)$.

2. The adversary specifies a set $C^* = i_1, ..., i_{\theta-1}$, and the challenger responds with the corresponding key shares $k_{i_1}, ..., k_{i_{\theta-1}}$.
3. The adversary (adaptively) sends key share queries $x_1, ..., x_Q \in \mathcal{X}$ to the challenger, and for each query x_j (here $j \in [1, Q]$) the challenger responds with $\mathcal{F}(k_i, x_j)$ for each $i \notin C^*$.
4. The adversary submits a challenge query $x^* \in \mathcal{X} \setminus \{x_1, .., x_Q\}$ to the challenger. If $b = 0$, the challenger samples and returns a uniformly random $y \in \mathcal{Y}$ to the adversary. If $b = 1$, the challenger responds with $f(k_0, x^*)$.
5. The adversary can adaptively issue more key share queries (step 3) and challenge queries (step 4), to which the challenger responds appropriately, so long as the set of all challenge queries and the set of all key share queries are disjoint.
6. The adversary outputs a bit $b' \in \{0, 1\}$.

Let W_b denote the probability that $\mathcal{A}$ outputs 1 in experiment $Expt_b^{dPRF}$. A distributed PRF Π is secure if for all efficient adversaries $\mathcal{A}$ the quantity $Adv^{dPRF}[\Pi, \mathcal{A}] := |W_0 - W_1|$ is negligible.

2.4   OXT

In this subsection, the proposed protocol by Cash et al. [9] called Oblivious Cross Tags (OXT) is reviewed. This protocol consists of three main sub-protocols; EDB generation, Token generation, and Search which are reviewed in Algorithms 1, 2 and 3, respectively.

EDBSetup(λ, DB): Given security parameter λ and DB $= (id_i, W_i)_{i=1}^d$ and the defined PRFs in Algorithm 1, generates the encrypted database EDB.

TokenGeneration($(\bar{w} = (w_1, ..., w_n)$, EDB)): If client wants to make a query q over EDB, search tokens are required. Algorithm 2 generates search tokens based on the given query.

Search(Tok_q, EDB, XSet): inputs the search token $Tok_q = $ (stag, xtoken[1], xtoken[2], $\cdots$) for a query q and (EDB, XSet), then outputs the search result $ERes$ as shown in Algorithm 3.

DecResult ($ERes$, K): This algorithm inputs the encrypted search result $ERes$ and the utilized key, then outputs the documents identifier id.

T-Set Instantiation. Cash et al. in [9] instantiate a T-set as a hash table with B buckets of size S each. The $TSetSetup(T)$ procedure sets the parameters B and S depending on the total number $N = \Sigma_{w \in W} |T[w]|$ of tuples in T in such a way so that (1) the probability of an overflow of any bucket after storing N elements in this hash table is a sufficiently small constant; and (2) the total size $B.S$ of the hash table is O(N). Details can be referred to the full paper.

Algorithm 1. EDB Setup Algorithm

Input: λ, DB
Output: EDB , XSet
1: **function** EDBSetup(λ, DB)
2:     Initialize $\mathbf{T} \leftarrow \emptyset$ indexed by keywords W.
3:     Select key K_S for PRF F. Select keys K_X, K_I, K_Z for PRF F_p with range $\mathbb{Z}_p^*$.
4:     EDB$\leftarrow \{\}$
5:     **for** $w \in$ W **do**
6:         Initialize $\mathbf{t} \leftarrow \{\}$; and let $K_e \leftarrow F(K_S, w)$.
7:         **for** id $\in$ DB(w) **do**
8:             Set a counter $c \leftarrow 1$
9:             Compute xid $\leftarrow F_p(K_I, \text{id})$, $z \leftarrow F_p(K_Z, w||c)$; $y \leftarrow \text{xid}z^{-1}$, $e \leftarrow \text{Enc}(K_e, \text{id})$.
10:            Set xtag $\leftarrow g^{F_p(K_X, w) \cdot \text{xid}}$ and XSet $\leftarrow$ XSet $\cup$ {xtag}
11:            Append (y, e) to $\mathbf{t}$ and $c \leftarrow c + 1$.
12:        **end for**
13:        $\mathbf{T}[w] \leftarrow \mathbf{t}$
14:    **end for**
15:    Set (TSet, K_T) $\leftarrow$ TSet.Setup($\mathbf{T}$) and let EDB(1) = (TSet, XSet).
16:    **return** EDB = (EDB(1), XSet), $K = (K_S, K_X, K_I, K_Z)$, pp
17: **end function**

Algorithm 2. Token Generation Algorithm

Input: q $= (w_1 \wedge \cdots \wedge w_n)$, EDB.
Output: Result $Tok_{\mathbf{q}}$.
1: **function** TokenGeneration(($\bar{w} = (w_1, \ldots, w_n)$), EDB))
2:     Client's input is $(K_S, K_X, K_I, K_Z, K_T)$ and $\bar{w}$.
3:     Computes stag $\leftarrow$ TSet.GetTag(K_T, w_1).
4:     Client sends stag to the server.
5:     **for** $c = 1, 2, \ldots$ until the server stops **do**
6:         **for** $i = 2, \ldots, m$ **do**
7:             xtoken$[c, i] \leftarrow g^{F_p(K_Z, w_1||c) \cdot F_p(K_X, w_i)}$
8:         **end for**
9:         xtoken$[c] \leftarrow$ (xtoken$[c, 2], \ldots,$ xtoken$[c, m]$)
10:    **end for**
11:    $Tok_{\mathbf{q}} \leftarrow$ (stag, xtoken)
12:    **return** $Tok_{\mathbf{q}}$
13: **end function**

Algorithm 3. Search Algorithm

Input: $Tok_{\mathbf{q}} =$ (stag, xtoken[1], xtoken[2], $\cdots$), EDB, XSet
Output: ERes
1: **function** SEARCH($Tok_{\mathbf{q}}$, EDB, XSet)
2:     R $\leftarrow \{\}$
3:     **for** stag $\in stags$ **do**
4:         $c \leftarrow 1; \ell \leftarrow F(\text{stag}, c)$
5:         **while** $\ell \in$ EDB **do**
6:             $(e, y) \leftarrow$ EDB$[\ell]$
7:             **if** xtoken$[c, i]^y \in$ XSet for all i **then**
8:                 $R \leftarrow R \cup \{e\}$
9:             **end if**
10:            $c \leftarrow c + 1; \ell \leftarrow F(\text{stag}, c)$
11:        **end while**
12:    **end for**
13:    **return** ERes
14: **end function**

3   Syntax of Multi-user SSE

Our multi-user SSE construction Π_{mu} consists of five phases $\Pi_{mu} = (EDBSetup_{mu}, KeySharing_{mu}, TokenGen_{mu}, Search_{mu}, Retrieve_{mu})$ as defined below. We point out the following main differences from the syntax of single-user SSE [9]. For client key loss resilience, the $KeySharing_{mu}$ algorithm allows the Master key K to be split into client key shares $K_1, \ldots, K_N$ using a threshold secret sharing scheme, such that any θ key shares can reconstruct K, for a threshold parameter θ. The $TokenGen_{mu}$ protocol allows a client to compute a search token for a query by interaction with $\theta - 1$ other 'helping' key share holders.

- $EDBSetup_{mu}$: Data owner runs the algorithm $EDBSetup_{mu}$ where takes the security parameter λ and the database DB as the inputs and outputs the encrypted database EDB along with the master key K and the set of public parameters pp.

- $KeySharing_{mu}$: Data owner performs this algorithm which inputs pp, master key K, a threshold parameter θ, and the number of desired key share holders N, and outputs the generated key shares $(K_1, ..., K_N) \in \mathcal{K}^{\mathcal{N}}$ of the considered master key.

- $TokenGen_{mu}$: The $TokenGen_{mu}$ protocol runs by θ key share holders $(i_1, \ldots, i_\theta) \in [N]$. Key share holder i_1 who aim to do the search on EDB starts the protocol by taking the query q, public parameters pp and the key share K_{i_1} as inputs. The $\theta - 1$ other key share holders i_j where $j \in [2, \theta]$ input their key shares K_{i_j}. By the end of this protocol the Key share holder i_1 outputs the search token Tok_q whereas the remaining involving key share holders output $\perp$.

- $Search_{mu}$: This is a protocol between the Key share holder $i_1 \in [N]$ and server where i_1 inputs the search token Tok_q along with pp and server inputs pp and EDB. By the end of this protocol the Key share holder i_1 outputs the encrypted result $ERes$ whereas server outputs $\perp$.

- $Retrieve_{mu}$: This is a protocol between the Key share holder i_1 and $\theta - 1$ other key share holders $(i_2, ..., i_\theta) \in [N]$ where $(pp, ERes, K_{i_1})$ are the inputs of i_1 and the $\theta - 1$ other key share holders i_j input (pp, K_{i_j}) (where $j \in [2, \theta]$). Finally, the Key share holder i_1 outputs Res which is the identifiers of the documents containing the issued query whereas the remaining involving key share holders output $\perp$.

4   Security Definitions of Multi-user SSE

In this section, we give security definitions of our multi-user searchable encryption based on two different viewpoints; Privacy against Server and Query Privacy against other Key Share holders.

4.1   Privacy Against Server

The given semantic security definitions is similar to [9]. The security definition of our multi-user searchable encryption, here Π, is parametrized by a leakage function $\mathcal{L}$ (knowledge about the database and queries gained by the server through interaction with a secure scheme).

Indeed, security shows how the server's view in an adaptive attack (database and queries are selected by the server) can be simulated using only the output of $\mathcal{L}$. For algorithms $\mathcal{A}$ and $\mathcal{S}$, we define a real experiment $\mathbf{Real}_{\mathcal{A}}^{\Pi}(\lambda)$ and an ideal experiment $\mathbf{Ideal}_{\mathcal{A},\mathcal{S}}^{\Pi}(\lambda)$ as follows:

$\mathbf{Real}_{\mathcal{A}}^{\Pi}(\lambda)$: $\mathcal{A}(1^{\lambda})$ chooses a database DB and a subset of corrupted clients $(j_1, ..., j_{\theta-1})$. However, this non-adaptive attacker is not allowed to interact with the clients. The experiment samples a k_0 uniformly from $\mathcal{K}$ and runs $Key\ sharing(k_0)$ to obtain $(k_1, ..., k_N)$. Then, responds with the corresponding key shares $k_{j_1}, ..., k_{j_{\theta}-1}$ as the exposed key shares to the attacker. Afterwards, the experiment runs $(mk, pp, \text{EDB}, \text{XSet}) \leftarrow \text{EDBSetup}(1^{\lambda}, \text{DB})$ and returns $(pp, \text{EDB}, \text{XSet})$ along with C (the list of key share holders, $|C| = N$) to $\mathcal{A}$. Then $\mathcal{A}$ repeatedly chooses a query $q[i]$. Then, the experiment runs the algorithm $TokenGen$ on input $k_{i_1}, ..., k_{i_{\theta}}$, and returns Search tokens to $\mathcal{A}$. Eventually, the experiment outputs the bit that $\mathcal{A}$ returns.

$\mathbf{Ideal}_{\mathcal{A},\mathcal{S}}^{\Pi}(\lambda)$: By setting a counter $i = 0$ and an empty list $\mathbf{q}$ the game is initialized. $\mathcal{A}(1^{\lambda})$ chooses a DB, a query list q and a subset of corrupted clients $(j_1, ..., j_{\theta-1})$. The experiment responds with simulated key shares $k_{j_1}, ..., k_{j_{\theta}-1}$ as the exposed key shares to the attacker. Afterwards, the experiment runs $(pp, \text{EDB}, \text{XSet}) \leftarrow \mathcal{S}(\mathcal{L}(\text{DB}))$ and gives $(pp, \text{EDB}, \text{XSet})$ to $\mathcal{A}$. $\mathcal{A}$ then repeatedly chooses a search query q. To respond, the experiment records this query as $\mathbf{q}[i]$, increments i and gives the output of $\mathcal{S}(\mathcal{L}(\text{DB}, \mathbf{q}))$ to $\mathcal{A}$, where $\mathbf{q}$ consists of all previous queries in addition to the latest query issued by $\mathcal{A}$. Eventually, the experiment outputs the bit that $\mathcal{A}$ returns.

Definition 1 (Security). *The protocol Π is called $\mathcal{L}$-semantically-secure against adaptive attacks if for all adversaries $\mathcal{A}$ there exists an efficient algorithm $\mathcal{S}$ such that* $|\Pr[\mathbf{Real}_{\mathcal{A}}^{\Pi}(\lambda) = 1] - \Pr[\mathbf{Ideal}_{\mathcal{A},\mathcal{S}}^{\Pi}(\lambda)]| \leq \text{negl}(\lambda)$.

Definition 2 (Leakage). *Similar to [9] we define $\mathcal{L}(\text{DB}, \mathbf{q})$, for $\text{DB} = (\text{id}_i, W_i)_{i=1}^{d}$ and $\mathbf{q} = (\Phi, \mathbf{s}, \mathbf{x}_1, ..., \mathbf{x}_n)$, as a tuple $(N, \Phi, \bar{\mathbf{s}}, \text{SP}, XP, \text{RP}, \text{IP})$ formed as follows:*

- $N = \sum_{i=1}^{d} |W_i|$ *is the total number of appearances of keywords in documents (here d indicated the number of documents).*
- $\bar{\mathbf{s}} \in \mathbb{N}^T$ *is the equality pattern of the sterms $\mathbf{s}$, indicating which queries have the same sterms. It is calculated as an array of integers, such that each integer represents one sterm.*
- SP *is the size pattern of the queries, i.e. the number of documents matching the sterm in each query,* $\text{SP}[i] = |\text{DB}(\mathbf{s}[i])|$.
- XP *The vector XP has $\text{XP}[i]$ set to the number of x-terms in the i-th query.*

- $RP[i] = DB[s[i]] \cap DB[x[i]]$, *is the results pattern of the queries, which are the indices of documents matching the entire conjunction.*
- IP *is the conditional intersection pattern, which is a 4-dimensional table defined as follows:*

$$IP[i, j, \alpha, \beta] = \begin{cases} DB(s[i]) \cap DB(s[j]) & \text{if } i \neq j, \alpha \neq \beta, \\ & \text{and } \mathbf{x}_\alpha[i] = \mathbf{x}_\beta[j], \\ \emptyset & \text{otherwise,} \end{cases}$$

4.2   Query Privacy Against Other Key Share Holders

Query privacy is a new property for hiding the search keywords of a client from the other $\theta - 1$ 'helper' key share holders (in our construction, this means that the search query input of PRF is hidden from the 'helper' key share holders).

Indeed, this security shows the compromised clients' view in an adaptive attack (key share holders and queries are selected by the compromised 'helper' clients). For algorithms $\mathcal{A}$ and $\mathcal{S}$, we define a *Query Privacy Game* as follows:

Query Privacy Game: $\mathcal{A}(1^\lambda)$ chooses a set of $i_1, ..., i_\theta$ of key share holders, where i_1 is the client making a query and $i_2, \dots, i_\theta$ are the 'helping' key share holders. Then $\mathcal{S}$ samples a K_0 uniformly from $\mathcal{K}$ and runs $Key\ sharing(K_0)$ to obtain $(K_1, ..., K_N)$, and returns $K_{i_2}, ..., K_{i_{\theta-1}}$ to $\mathcal{A}$. Then $\mathcal{A}$ chooses a pair of keyword queries (x_0, x_1). In order to respond, $\mathcal{S}$ chooses a random bit $b \in_r \{0, 1\}$ and runs $TokenGen_{mu}$ protocol with searching client's input ($q = x_b, pp, K_{i_1}$) and 'helper' client inputs ($K_{i_2}, \dots, K_{i_\theta}$). $\mathcal{S}$ returns the protocol view of the 'helping' share holders $i_2, \dots, i_\theta$ to $\mathcal{A}$. Then, $\mathcal{A}$ outputs a bit b' which is also outputs by the algorithm $\mathcal{S}$. As a result, $Adv(A) = Pr(b = b') - \frac{1}{2}$.

Definition 3 (Query Privacy). *The protocol Π is called Query private if for all adversaries $\mathcal{A}$ in Query Privacy Game $Adv(A) \leq \text{negl}(\lambda)$.*

5   Randomizable Key Homomorphic Distributed PRFs

As a tool for our multi-user SSE, we defined a special type of distributed PRF which makes the input point blind from key share holders and unblind it during performing $Evaluation$ algorithm.

5.1   Definition

Our Randomizable Distributed PRF (RDPRF) mainly consists of seven algorithm; $Setup$, $Key\ sharing$, $Rand$, $Partial\ evaluation$, $Combine$, $UnRand$, and $Evaluation$ with the following properties. Note that except $Rand$ and $UnRand$ the rest of the mentioned algorithms are similar to the ones proposed by Boneh et al. [5] (refer to Sect. 2.3).

- $Setup$: This algorithm inputs security parameter κ (for the rest of this paper, we skip the definition of κ) and outputs master-key mk and public parameters pp.
- $Key\ sharing\ (pp, (mk, N)) \rightarrow \mathcal{K}^{\mathcal{N}}$: This algorithm generates key shares $(k_1, ..., k_N) \in \mathcal{K}^{\mathcal{N}}$ of the considered master key. Here, N is the number of key share holders, $\mathcal{K}$ is the key domain and $\mathcal{K}^{\mathcal{N}}$ is the domain of key shares.
- $Rand$: The function $Rand(x, pp) \rightarrow z$ randomize the input point $x \in \mathcal{K}$ by a uniformly random value $r \in \mathcal{R}$.
- $Partial\ evaluation$: The function $\mathcal{F} : \mathcal{K} \times \mathcal{X} \rightarrow \mathcal{Y}$ takes a key share and an input point and outputs a partial evaluation of the $Evaluation$ function f.
- $Combine$: The algorithm $G : 2^{[N]} \times \mathcal{Y}^{\theta} \rightarrow \mathcal{Y}$ inputs a subset $W \subset [N]$ of size θ (threshold) and θ partial evaluations on key shares in the set W and outputs a value in $\mathcal{Y}$.
- $UnRand$: The function $UnRand(\mathcal{F}(k, z), r)$ inputs the randomized distributed PRF (RDPRF) under key k and the utilized random value r and outputs the unradomized DPRF using the inverse of r.
- $Evaluation$: The function $f : \mathcal{K} \times \mathcal{X} \rightarrow \mathcal{Y}$ maps a key and an input to the space of outputs.

5.2 PRF Evaluation Protocol

Algorithm 4 must be performed for all of the utilized PRFs. The idea is to make the clients able to search through the database without interaction with data owner. More precisely, online presence of data owner at all the time is not required. In addition, Algorithm 4 enables the client to hide the considered keyword for search from the other key share holders.

Assume that a client wants to evaluate a PRF such as $PRF(k_0, x)$. Thus, client sends a short message containing x to each key share holder and by receiving at least θ responses from them, client would be able to evaluate the mentioned PRF using PRF Evaluation Protocol.

Algorithm 4. PRF Evaluation protocol

Input: Key share holders list $C = i_1, i_2, ..., i_N$, $(k_{i_1}, ..., k_{i_\theta})$, x, and θ
Output: $Y = PRF(k_0, x)$
  function PRFEVAL(k_0, x)
    $Y \leftarrow \{\}$
    client $\mathcal{C}$ picks random $r \in \mathbb{Z}_p^*$
    client $\mathcal{C}$ computes $z \leftarrow Rand(x, pp)$
    $j \leftarrow 1$
    for $j = 1, ..., \theta$ **do**
      while $i_j \in C$ **do**
        client $\mathcal{C}$ send z to i_j
        i_j computes $y_{i_j} = \mathcal{F}(k_{i_j}, z)$
        i_j sends y_{i_j} to $\mathcal{C}$
        $j \leftarrow j + 1$
      end while
      client $\mathcal{C}$ performs $y \leftarrow Combine(W, y_{i_1}, ..., y_{i_\theta})$
    end for
    client $\mathcal{C}$ compute $y \leftarrow Unrand(y, r)$
    return Y
  end function

Algorithm 4 is inspired by the proposed key homomorphic PRFs by Boneh et al. [5] (refer to Sect. 2.3). However, it would not leak any information such as the considered keyword to other key share holders.

Correctness. By considering pp as the output of $Setup(1^\lambda)$, k_0 sampled uniformly from $\mathcal{K}$, and $(k_1, ..., k_N)$ the key share output by $Key\ sharing(k_0)$. For every subset $W = i_1, ..., i_\theta \subset [N]$ of size θ, and for every input x, RDPRF is correct if $f(k_0, x) = UnRand(G(W, \mathcal{F}(k_{i_1}, z), ..., \mathcal{F}(k_{i_\theta}, z)))$.

PRF Security Definition of RDPRF. The $Evaluation$ function f should remain pseudorandom even when the adversary is given $\theta - 1$ key shares $(k_{i_1}, ..., k_{i_{\theta-1}})$ for indices $i_1, ..., i_{\theta-1}$ of its choice. The adversary is also given an oracle $\mathcal{O}$ that performs arbitrary partial evaluations: it takes (i, x) as input and returns $\mathcal{F}(k_i, x)$. The adversary should be unable to distinguish the function from random at point x where did not query the oracle $\mathcal{O}$. Note that, Q indicates the total number of issued queries; $Q = Q_1 + Q_2$, where Q_1 and Q_2 are the number of queries made in Query-1 phase and Query-2 phase, respectively. We formalize this intuition through an experiment between a challenger and an adversary $\mathcal{A}$. For $b \in \{0, 1\}$ the challenger in $Expt_b^{dPRF}$ operates as follows.

- Setup. Given security parameter κ, the algorithm works as follows:
    Step 1: the challenger runs $Setup(1^\lambda)$ and publishes public parameters pp to the adversary.
    Step 2: The challenger then samples a k_0 uniformly from $\mathcal{K}$ and runs $Key\ sharing(k_0)$ to obtain $(k_1, ..., k_N)$.
    Step 3: The adversary specifies a set of key share holders $C^* = i_1, ..., i_{\theta-1}$.
    Step 4: The challenger responds with the corresponding key shares $k_{i_1}, ..., k_{i_{\theta-1}}$.
- Query-1. The adversary (adaptively) sends partial evaluation queries $x_1, ..., x_{Q_1} \in \mathcal{X}$ to the challenger, and for each query x_j the challenger responds with $\mathcal{F}(k_i, x_j)$ for each $i \notin C^*$.
- Challenge. The adversary submits a challenge query $(x_1^*, ..., x_m^*) \in \mathcal{X} \setminus \{x_1, .., x_Q\}$ to the challenger. The challenger picks a random bit $b \in \{0, 1\}$. If $b = 0$, the challenger samples $y_i = f(k_0, x_i^*)$ for all $i \neq j$ and randomly choose $j \in_r (1, ..., m)$ and returns $(y_1, ..., y_m)$ to the adversary except the value of y_j is replaced with a uniformly random $y \in \mathcal{Y}$.

    If $b = 1$, $\forall i \in \{1, ..., m\}$ the challenger responds with $y_i = f(k_0, x_i^*)$.
- Query-2. The adversary can adaptively issue more key share queries (step 3) while partial evaluation queries $x_{Q_1}, ..., x_{Q_1+Q_2} \in \mathcal{X}$ and challenge queries (step 4), to which the challenger responds appropriately, so long as the set of all challenge queries and the set of all key share queries are disjoint.
- Guess. The adversary outputs a bit $b' \in \{0, 1\}$.

Let W_b denote the probability that $\mathcal{A}$ outputs 1 in experiment $Expt_b^{dPRF}$. A distributed PRF Π is secure if for all efficient adversaries $\mathcal{A}$ such that $W_b \leq \frac{1}{2} + \frac{1}{2}\frac{Q}{M} + \epsilon$.

Query Privacy Security of RDPRF. The query privacy security of the Randomizable Key Homomorphic Distributed PRF shows for each $x \in \mathcal{X}$, the output of $Rand(x, r)$ is uniform on the domain of the distributed PRF, $\mathcal{X}$, when r is uniform in the input space $\mathbb{Z}_p^*$.

5.3   Concrete Construction of RDPRF

- S*etup*:
  - Choose prime p.
  - Choose $\mathcal{K} = \mathbb{Z}_p^*$ as the key domain.
  - Choose a cyclic group G of prime order p.
  - Choose master key $k_0 \in_r \mathcal{K}$.
  - Define $S = (\theta, N)$ threshold secret sharing scheme proposed by Shamir [30] (refer to Sect. 2.2).
  - Output $mk = k_0$.
  - Output $pp = <G, p, S, \mathcal{K}, H>$ where $H : \mathcal{X} \to G|\{1\}$ is a cryptographic hash function which maps the PRF domain $\mathcal{X} : \{0, 1\}^*$ to its range, $G|\{1\}$, using a randomizer $r \in_r \mathcal{R}$ where $\mathcal{R} = \mathbb{Z}_p^*$.
- K*ey sharing* $(pp, (mk, N)) \to \mathcal{K}^{\mathcal{N}}$: On input $mk = k_0$, an integer N and threshold secret sharing scheme S outputs key shares $k_1, ..., k_N$.
- R*and*(x, pp): Picks up a uniformly random value $r \in_r \mathbb{Z}_p^*$ and outputs r and $z = H(x)^r$.
- P*artial evaluation* (k_i, z): given a key share $k_i \in \mathbb{Z}_p^*$ and an input point $z \in G$ this algorithm returns $y_i = \mathcal{F}(k_i, z)$ where in fact $y_i = z^{k_i}$ is an element of group G.
- C*ombine* $(W, \{y_{i_1}, ..., y_{i_\theta}\})$: for any $W = \{i_1, ..., i_\theta\} \subset [N]$ of size θ and corresponding partial evaluations $\{y_{i_1}, ..., y_{i_\theta}\}$ this algorithm outputs $f(k, z) = z^k = z^{\sum_{j=1}^{\theta} \lambda_{i_j} \cdot k_{i_j}} = \Pi_{j=1}^{\theta}(y_{i_j})^{\lambda_{i_j}}$.
- U*nRand* $(\mathcal{F}(k, z), r)$: this algorithm inputs $y_r = \mathcal{F}(k, z) = H(x)^{rk}$ and the related random value r then outputs the unrandomized value $y = y_r^{r^{-1} \pmod{p}}$.
- C*valuation*(k, x): given a secret k and an input x this algorithm outputs $f(k, x) = H(x)^k$.

Theorem 1. *Suppose the hash function H is random oracle then RDPRF is a secure randomizable key homomorphic distributed PRF that satisfies PRF security if DDH assumption holds and satisfies query privacy unconditionally.*

Please refer to the full version for the proof of this Theorem.

6   Our Construction

In this section, we present an extension of OXT [9] for the multi-user symmetric searchable encryption setting. The proposed extension supports key revocation

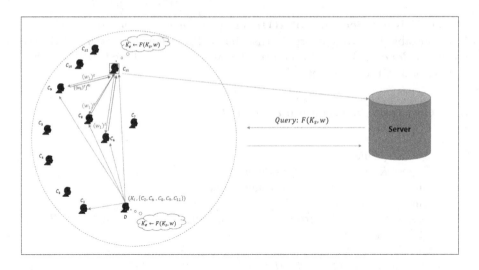

Fig. 1. Instantiation of Multi-user SSE

while preserves full functionality of OXT. Our multi-user SSE construction consists of five algorithm

$$\Pi = (EDBSetup_{mu}, KeySharing_{mu}, TokenGen_{mu}, Search_{mu}, Retrieve_{mu})$$

In the proposed construction $\mathsf{EDBSetup}_{mu}$ algorithm is similar to the ones in OXT [9] except for the utilized PRFs which are distributed key-homomorphic PRFs (refer to Sect. 2.3). In order to enable several clients to access same database, Data owner runs $\mathsf{Key\ Sharing}_{mu}$ algorithm which inputs the utilized PRF keys and outputs the corresponding key shares by performing Shamir's scheme [30] explained in Subsect. 2.2. Then, the generated key shares are distributed to the desired clients along with the list of legitimate key share holders' identity. Let D to be a data owner who outsources an encrypted database EDB to a remote server S such that S cannot learn anything more than what predicted as the leakage profile. Moreover, authorized clients (Key Share holders) such as $i_1, i_2, ..., i_N$ are allowed to carry out the search through EDB. Figure 1 illustrates one example of our construction in the static mode.

To perform a search over EDB, a client needs to run $\mathsf{TokenGen}_{mu}$ protocol as defined in Algorithm 5. Given the query q, this algorithm first performs $PRFEvaluationProtocol$ (4) and then generates the search tokens, Tok_q. One of the main contributions of this paper is hiding the searched keywords from other key share holders when the search token is generated collaboratively. This is achieved by defining another primitive called Randomizable Key Homomorphic Distributed PRFs (refer to Sect. 5).

$Search_{mu}$ protocol is similar to $Search_{OXT}$ as defined in Algorithm3. Once the client sent the search token Tok_q to the server, server do the search over EDB and outputs the encrypted result $ERes$.

Finally, $Retrieve_{mu}$ protocol as described in Algorithm 6 should performed in order to extract the identifiers of the documents containing the searched keyword.

Algorithm 5. TokenGen Protocol

Input: $q = (w_1 \wedge \cdots \wedge w_n)$, EDB.
Output: Result Tok_q.
  function TokenGen$((\bar{w} = (w_1, \ldots, w_n),$ EDB$))$
    Client's input is $(K_S, K_X, K_I, K_Z, K_T)$ and $\bar{w}$.
    Computes stag $\leftarrow$ TSet.GetTag(K_T, w_1).
    Client sends stag to the server.
    for $c = 1, 2, \ldots$ until the server stops client **do**
      for $i = 2, \ldots, m$ **do**
        performs PRF Evaluation Protocol on inputs $(i_1, ..., i_0)$ *and* $(K_{i_1}, ..., K_{i_0})$
        to compute $X = F_p(K_Z, w_1 || c)$ *and* $Y_i = F_p(K_X, w_i)$
        xtoken$[c, i] \leftarrow g^{X \cdot Y_i}$
      end for
      xtoken$[c] \leftarrow ($xtoken$[c, 2], \ldots,$ xtoken$[c, m])$
    end for
    $Tok_q \leftarrow ($stag, xtoken$)$
    return Tok_q
  end function

Algorithm 6. Client Search Result Retrieval Protocol

Input: R, w_1 , EDB.
Output: Result id.
  function Retrieval$((e, id))$
    $id \leftarrow \{\}$
    Client performs PRF Evaluation Protocol for $k_e \leftarrow PRF(k_s, w_1)$
    for $i = 1, 2, \ldots$ until the server stops **do**
      if $e_i \in R$ **then**
        compute $id_i \leftarrow Dec(k_e, e_i)$
        $id \leftarrow id \cup id_i$
      end if
    end for
    return id_i
  end function

---

7 Security Analysis

In this section, we state the security of our multi-user SSE protocol against dishonest server and dishonest/compromised key share holder, respectively. We refer the reader to the full version for proofs.

Theorem 2. *Let $\mathcal{L}$ be the leakage function defined in Sect. 4.2. Then, our multi-user SSE protocol is $\mathcal{L}$-semantically-secure against adaptive server, if OXT [9] is secure and DDH assumption holds.*

Theorem 3. *Our multi-user SSE protocol Π_{mu} is query-private, as defined in Definition 3.*

8   Performance Comparison

Since our multi-user protocol and the proposed protocol by Sun et al. [34] are under the framework of OXT [9], in this section we compare our protocol with them in terms of communication and computation overhead. The communication overhead between the data owner and the server during EDBSetup phase is the same in all of them as well as the communication between client and the server. However, in our multi-user SSE client who wants to search over EDB requires to communicate with at least $\theta - 1$ (θ is the threshold) key share holders in order to generate the search token.

Due to the use of ABE the Sun's protocol has storage overhead and some computational cost to the data owner. Moreover, the data owner should compute an extra exponentiation for the PRF calculation during the setup phase, totally introducing $(2\sum_{w\in W} |DB[w]| + |W|)$ exponentiation operations for the whole database.

For a conjunctive query, e.g., $Q = (w_1 \wedge w_2 \wedge \cdots \wedge w_m)$ performed by a client, we assume that the associated keywords belong to the client's authorized keyword set $\mathbf{w}$, i.e., $w_i \in \mathbf{w}$ for $i \in [m]$. Table 2 summarizes the computation and communication of our Multi-user SSE protocol besides of OXT [9] and Sun's multi-client protocol [34].

To perform the search as described above, the client in our Multi-user SSE does not require to refer to the data owner. However, it has to interact with key share holders to generate the search token where the user needs to compute $((m - 1) + |DB(w_1)|)(2exp + 1inv)$. Note that the two exponentiations and an inversion here are required for $Rand$ and $UnRand$ functions in PRF Evaluation protocol. In contrast, the user in OXT [9] requires per-query interaction with the data owner to get the search token. Thus, the data owner needs to compute $((m - 1).|DB(w_1)|)$ exponentiations.

In Sun's protocol, the client needs to get secret information from the data owner at the beginning, where the data owner needs to computes 3 exponentiations and generates an attribute-related secret key for each client, and then the client is able to perform the searches at the cost of $(m + 1)$ additional exponentiations to the generation of xtoken.

Table 2. Computational and communication cost

Conjunctive query $Q = (w_1 \wedge w_2 \wedge \cdots \wedge w_m)$, where $w_i \in \mathbf{w}$			
Reference	Data owner's comp. cost	Clients' comp. cost	Communication cost
Cash et al. [9]	$\|DB[w_1]\|(m - 1) \cdot exp$	N/A	$l(1 + (m - 1).\|DB(w_1)\|)$
Sun et al. [34]	$3 \cdot exp$	$(\|DB[w_1]\|(m - 1) + (m + 1)) \cdot exp$	$l(1 + (m - 1).\|DB(w_1)\|) + 3\,l_{RSA}$
Our multi-user SSE	N/A	$\|DB[w_1]\|m \cdot exp + m \cdot inv$	$l(m.(1 + \|DB(w_1)\|))$

exp: the exponentiation operation on the group; $| \cdot |$: the size of a finite set or group, e.g., $|\mathbb{G}|$; $\mathbf{w}$: the authorized keyword set for a client.

Since our Multi-user SSE is the enhanced version of OXT [9], we can estimate the extra cost of computation and communication over OXT in the mentioned scenario (by assuming $1inv \leq 1exp$) as followed;

$$Overhead\ ratio\ for\ computation\ = 1 + \frac{(2exp + 1inv)((m-1) + |DB(w_1)|)}{(1exp)((m-1).|DB(w_1)|)}$$

$$\leq 1 + 3(\frac{((m-1) + |DB(w_1)|)}{((m-1).|DB(w_1)|)})$$

$$\leq 1 + 3(\frac{1}{(m-1)} + \frac{1}{|DB(w_1)|})$$

And the communication overhead for the user is;

$$Overhead\ ratio\ for\ communication\ = 1 + \frac{l((m-1)|DB(w_1)|)}{l(1 + (m-1).|DB(w_1)|)}$$

$$= 1 + (\frac{1}{(m-1)} + \frac{1}{|DB(w_1)|})$$

Here, l indicates the length of Xtoken.

9   Further Extension

In this section we are going to discuss about two extensions of our work as described below which will be addressed in more details in the extended version of this document.

First, lets consider the condition that the master key is leaked, Data owner should update the encrypted database using a new key to prevent any extraction of the information by unauthorized entity. Thus, Data owner sends a keying materials to the server for updating the encrypted database. It is assumed that the server do the update honestly and removes the keying materials after finishing the update. Data owner runs $Update$ algorithm as described below.

$Update(EDB, \Delta_E, \Delta_T)$: Server run this algorithm which inputs the encrypted database, EDB, along with two keying materials (Δ_E, Δ_T) for the update of $XSet$ and $TSet$, respectively. Then, for each $i = 1, ..., |t|$ sent by Data owner to Server, it computes $TSet' = H(F(stag, i))^{\Delta_T}$. Moreover, in order to update $XSet$ for each $xtag_i \in XSet$ for $i \in [1, |XSet|]$ this algorithm raise it to Δ_E and computes $xtag_i = (g^{F_p(K_X, w) \cdot xid})^{\Delta_E}$ and update $XSet$ to $XSet'$. Finally, this algorithm outputs $EDB' = (XSet', TSet')$ and server deletes Δ_E, Δ_T and the old EDB.

Although it seems this method adds some computation overhead to the server, it is still inexpensive in terms of communication in compare with the traditional techniques such as re-encryption by Data owner and re-uploading it to the server.

Second, there are two degrees of collusion between server and the key share holders; Passive and Active. The weaker one is passive collusion where the Server exposes $\theta - 1$ (here θ indicates the threshold) of key shares of the valid key share holders. Since our scheme inherited a security property from Shamir's secret sharing scheme (refer to Sect. 2.2), having any subset of key shares smaller than the threshold will not reveal any information about the actual key. Thus, this passive collusion do not help the curious server to gain any knowledge about the key. Moreover, in this condition it is assumed that the server does not communicate with the key share holders, thus cannot be involved in TokenGen protocol. As a result, it is not possible for the server to gain any knowledge about the search keyword.

The stronger assumption is Active collusion where Server exposes a subset of key shares (smaller than threshold) and also can control those $\theta - 1$ the mentioned key share holders in the token generation process. Similar to the passive collusion, the curious server is not able to gain any knowledge about the key using the key shares less than the considered threshold. However, in this case it is possible for the server to find out about the search tokens till Data owner identify and revoke the compromised key share holders. Ideally, in this active server attack, server should not learn anything about EDB beyond the search tokens for the search queries. Achieving this security can be provided in the future work.

Beside of what mentioned above, it is worth to note that although the proposed construction provides a single-writer/multi-reader architecture in the static mode, it can provide a limited version of multi-writer/multi-reader setting in dynamic scenario.

10   Conclusions

In this paper we proposed a novel multi-user symmetric searchable encryption scheme. In fact, we chose to enhance the OXT protocol proposed by Cash et al. [9] from single writer/single reader structure to single writer/multi reader one. Our construction is query private against all of the others involving entities including Data owner, Server, and key share holders. In order to make the search keyword hidden from the other share holders during the token generation process, we defined a new distributed key homomorphic PRF.

The security and efficiency of our multi-user SSE have been analyzed from different aspects. We left some of the open problems to be addressed in the future works while some ideas for database update and key revocation are provided.

References

1. Abdalla, M., Bellare, M., Catalano, D., Kiltz, E., Kohno, T., Lange, T., Malone-Lee, J., Neven, G., Paillier, P., Shi, H.: Searchable encryption revisited: consistency properties, relation to anonymous IBE, and extensions. In: Shoup, V. (ed.) CRYPTO 2005. LNCS, vol. 3621, pp. 205–222. Springer, Heidelberg (2005). doi:10.1007/11535218_13
2. Bao, F., Deng, R.H., Ding, X., Yang, Y.: Private query on encrypted data in multi-user settings. In: Chen, L., Mu, Y., Susilo, W. (eds.) ISPEC 2008. LNCS, vol. 4991, pp. 71–85. Springer, Heidelberg (2008). doi:10.1007/978-3-540-79104-1_6
3. Bellare, M., Boldyreva, A., ONeill, A.: Deterministic and efficiently searchable encryption. In: Menezes, A. (ed.) CRYPTO 2007. LNCS, vol. 4622, pp. 535–552. Springer, Heidelberg (2007). doi:10.1007/978-3-540-74143-5_30

4. Boneh, D., Crescenzo, G., Ostrovsky, R., Persiano, G.: Public key encryption with keyword search. In: Cachin, C., Camenisch, J.L. (eds.) EUROCRYPT 2004. LNCS, vol. 3027, pp. 506–522. Springer, Heidelberg (2004). doi:10.1007/978-3-540-24676-3_30

5. Boneh, D., Lewi, K., Montgomery, H., Raghunathan, A.: Key homomorphic PRFs and their applications. In: Canetti, R., Garay, J.A. (eds.) CRYPTO 2013. LNCS, vol. 8042, pp. 410–428. Springer, Heidelberg (2013). doi:10.1007/978-3-642-40041-4_23

6. Boneh, D., Waters, B.: Conjunctive, subset, and range queries on encrypted data. In: Vadhan, S.P. (ed.) TCC 2007. LNCS, vol. 4392, pp. 535–554. Springer, Heidelberg (2007). doi:10.1007/978-3-540-70936-7_29

7. Bösch, C., Tang, Q., Hartel, P., Jonker, W.: Selective document retrieval from encrypted database. In: Gollmann, D., Freiling, F.C. (eds.) ISC 2012. LNCS, vol. 7483, pp. 224–241. Springer, Heidelberg (2012). doi:10.1007/978-3-642-33383-5_14

8. Cash, D., Jaeger, J., Jarecki, S., Jutla, C.S., Krawczyk, H., Rosu, M., Steiner, M.: Dynamic searchable encryption in very-large databases: data structures and implementation. In: NDSS (2014)

9. Cash, D., Jarecki, S., Jutla, C., Krawczyk, H., Roşu, M.-C., Steiner, M.: Highly-scalable searchable symmetric encryption with support for boolean queries. In: Canetti, R., Garay, J.A. (eds.) CRYPTO 2013. LNCS, vol. 8042, pp. 353–373. Springer, Heidelberg (2013). doi:10.1007/978-3-642-40041-4_20

10. Chang, Y.-C., Mitzenmacher, M.: Privacy preserving keyword searches on remote encrypted data. In: Ioannidis, J., Keromytis, A., Yung, M. (eds.) ACNS 2005. LNCS, vol. 3531, pp. 442–455. Springer, Heidelberg (2005). doi:10.1007/11496137_30

11. Chase, M., Kamara, S.: Structured encryption and controlled disclosure. In: Abe, M. (ed.) ASIACRYPT 2010. LNCS, vol. 6477, pp. 577–594. Springer, Heidelberg (2010). doi:10.1007/978-3-642-17373-8_33

12. Chu, C., Zhu, W.T., Han, J., Liu, J.K., Xu, J., Zhou, J.: Security concerns in popular cloud storage services. IEEE Pervasive Comput. 12(4), 50–57 (2013)

13. Curtmola, R., Garay, J.A., Kamara, S., Ostrovsky, R.: Searchable symmetric encryption: improved definitions and efficient constructions. In: ACM CCS 2006, pp. 79–88 (2006)

14. Dong, C., Russello, G., Dulay, N.: Shared and searchable encrypted data for untrusted servers. In: Atluri, V. (ed.) DBSec 2008. LNCS, vol. 5094, pp. 127–143. Springer, Heidelberg (2008). doi:10.1007/978-3-540-70567-3_10

15. Goh, E.: Secure indexes. IACR Cryptology ePrint Archive 2003:216 (2003)

16. Golle, P., Staddon, J., Waters, B.: Secure conjunctive keyword search over encrypted data. In: Jakobsson, M., Yung, M., Zhou, J. (eds.) ACNS 2004. LNCS, vol. 3089, pp. 31–45. Springer, Heidelberg (2004). doi:10.1007/978-3-540-24852-1_3

17. Hore, B., Mehrotra, S., Canim, M., Kantarcioglu, M.: Secure multidimensional range queries over outsourced data. VLDB J. 21(3), 333–358 (2012)

18. Hwang, Y.H., Lee, P.J.: Public key encryption with conjunctive keyword search and its extension to a multi-user system. In: Takagi, T., Okamoto, T., Okamoto, E., Okamoto, T. (eds.) Pairing 2007. LNCS, vol. 4575, pp. 2–22. Springer, Heidelberg (2007). doi:10.1007/978-3-540-73489-5_2

19. Islam, M.S., Kuzu, M., Kantarcioglu, M.: Access pattern disclosure on searchable encryption: ramification, attack and mitigation. In: NDSS (2012)

20. Jarecki, S., Jutla, C.S., Krawczyk, H., Rosu, M., Steiner, M.: Outsourced symmetric private information retrieval. In: ACM CCS 2013, pp. 875–888. ACM (2013)

21. Jiang, T., Chen, X., Li, J., Wong, D.S., Ma, J., Liu, J.K.: Towards secure and reliable cloud storage against data re-outsourcing. Future Gener. Comp. Syst. **52**, 86–94 (2015)

22. Kerschbaum, F., Sorniotti, A.: Searchable encryption for outsourced data analytics. In: Camenisch, J., Lambrinoudakis, C. (eds.) EuroPKI 2010. LNCS, vol. 6711, pp. 61–76. Springer, Heidelberg (2011). doi:10.1007/978-3-642-22633-5_5

23. Kuzu, M., Islam, M.S., Kantarcioglu, M.: Efficient similarity search over encrypted data. In: 2012 IEEE International Conference Data Engineering, pp. 1156–1167 (2012)

24. Liang, K., Au, M.H., Liu, J.K., Susilo, W., Wong, D.S., Yang, G., Phuong, T.V.X., Xie, Q.: A DFA-based functional proxy re-encryption scheme for secure public cloud data sharing. IEEE Trans. Inf. Forensics Secur. **9**(10), 1667–1680 (2014)

25. Liang, K., Huang, X., Guo, F., Liu, J.K.: Privacy-preserving and regular language search over encrypted cloud data. IEEE Trans. Inf. Forensics Secur. **11**(10), 2365–2376 (2016)

26. Liang, K., Su, C., Chen, J., Liu, J.K.: Efficient multi-function data sharing and searching mechanism for cloud-based encrypted data. In: ASIACCS, pp. 83–94 (2016)

27. Liang, K., Susilo, W., Liu, J.K.: Privacy-preserving ciphertext multi-sharing control for big data storage. IEEE Trans. Inf. Forensics Secur. **10**(8), 1578–1589 (2015)

28. Popa, R.A., Zeldovich, N.: Multi-key searchable encryption. IACR Cryptology ePrint Archive 2013:508 (2013)

29. Raykova, M., Cui, A., Vo, B., Liu, B., Malkin, T., Bellovin, S.M., Stolfo, S.J.: Usable, secure, private search. IEEE Secur. Priv. **10**(5), 53–60 (2012)

30. Shamir, A.: How to share a secret. Commun. ACM **22**(11), 612–613 (1979)

31. Shen, E., Shi, E., Waters, B.: Predicate privacy in encryption systems. In: Reingold, O. (ed.) TCC 2009. LNCS, vol. 5444, pp. 457–473. Springer, Heidelberg (2009). doi:10.1007/978-3-642-00457-5_27

32. Shi, E., Bethencourt, J., Chan, T.H.H., Song, D., Perrig, A.: Multi-dimensional range query over encrypted data. In: 2007 IEEE Symposium on Security and Privacy (SP 2007), pp. 350–364, May 2007

33. Song, D.X., Wagner, D., Perrig, A.: Practical techniques for searches on encrypted data. In: 2000 IEEE Symposium on Security and Privacy, SP 2000 Proceedings, pp. 44–55 (2000)

34. Sun, S.-F., Liu, J.K., Sakzad, A., Steinfeld, R., Yuen, T.H.: An efficient non-interactive multi-client searchable encryption with support for boolean queries. In: Askoxylakis, I., Ioannidis, S., Katsikas, S., Meadows, C. (eds.) ESORICS 2016. LNCS, vol. 9878, pp. 154–172. Springer, Cham (2016). doi:10.1007/978-3-319-45744-4_8

35. Tang, Q.: Nothing is for free: security in searching shared and encrypted data. IEEE Trans. Inf. Forensics Secur. **9**(11), 1943–1952 (2014)

36. Waters, B.R., Balfanz, D., Durfee, G., Smetters, D.K.: Building an encrypted and searchable audit log. In: NDSS 2004 (2004)

37. Wu, X., Xu, L., Zhang, X.: Poster: a certificateless proxy re-encryption scheme for cloud-based data sharing. In: ACMCCS, pp. 869–872. ACM (2011)

38. Xhafa, F., Wang, J., Chen, X., Liu, J.K., Li, J., Krause, P.: An efficient PHR service system supporting fuzzy keyword search and fine-grained access control. Soft Comput. **18**(9), 1795–1802 (2014)

39. Yang, X., Lee, T., Liu, J.K., Huang, X.: Trust enhancement over range search for encrypted data. In: IEEE Trustcom, pp. 66–73 (2016)

40. Yang, Y., Lu, H., Weng, J.: Multi-user private keyword search for cloud computing. In: CloudCom 2011, pp. 264–271 (2011)
41. Zhao, F., Nishide, T., Sakurai, K.: Multi-user keyword search scheme for secure data sharing with fine-grained access control. In: Kim, H. (ed.) ICISC 2011. LNCS, vol. 7259, pp. 406–418. Springer, Heidelberg (2012). doi:10.1007/978-3-642-31912-9_27
42. Zuo, C., Macindoe, J., Yang, S., Steinfeld, R., Liu, J.K.: Trusted boolean search on cloud using searchable symmetric encryption. In: IEEE Trustcom, pp. 113–120 (2016)

Fuzzy Keyword Search and Access Control over Ciphertexts in Cloud Computing

Hong Zhu[1], Zhuolin Mei[1(✉)], Bing Wu[1], Hongbo Li[1], and Zongmin Cui[2]

[1] School of Computer Science and Technology,
Huazhong University of Science and Technology, Wuhan, Hubei, China
meizhuolin@gmail.com
[2] School of Information Science and Technology, Jiujiang University,
Jiujiang, Jiangxi, China

Abstract. With the rapid development of cloud computing, more and more data owners are motivated to outsource their data to cloud for various benefits. Due to serious privacy concerns, sensitive data should be encrypted before being outsourced to the cloud. However, this results that effective data utilization becomes a very challenging task, such as keyword search over ciphertexts. Although many searchable encryption methods have been proposed, they only support exact keyword search. In our paper, we propose a method which could support both the fuzzy keyword search and access control over ciphertexts. Our proposed method achieves fuzzy keyword search and access control through algorithm design and Ciphertext-Policy Attribute-based Encryption. We present word pattern which can be used to balance the search efficiency and privacy. The experimental results demonstrate the efficiency of our method.

Keywords: Fuzzy keyword search · Access control · Encryption

1 Introduction

With the rapid development of cloud computing, more and more sensitive information are being centralized into the cloud, such as emails, personal health records, government documents, etc. By outsourcing data to the cloud, data owners can enjoy various advantages, such as high quality data storage service and maintenance [10]. However, the cloud is not fully trusted by the data owners. Thus, the privacy of sensitive data in the cloud naturally becomes a primary concern of data owners. To mitigate the concern, sensitive data is usually encrypted-before-outsourcing to prevent from unauthorized access [8]. Since the data is encrypted, the searching of documents which contains specific keywords becomes rather difficult.

To solve the problem above, many searchable encryption methods have been proposed, e.g. [1,12,14]. However, they only support exact keyword matching. Misspelled keywords in the query will result in wrong or no matching. Very recently, a few works [4,8,10,11,15,16] extend the exact keyword matching to

© Springer International Publishing AG 2017
J. Pieprzyk and S. Suriadi (Eds.): ACISP 2017, Part I, LNCS 10342, pp. 248–265, 2017.
DOI: 10.1007/978-3-319-60055-0_13

approximate keyword matching, also known as fuzzy keyword search. According to the techniques adopted in these fuzzy keyword search methods, they could be classified into two classes: (1) Wildcard based fuzzy keyword search methods [10,11,16]; (2) Locality-Sensitive Hashing (LSH) [6] and Bloom Filter (BF) [3] based fuzzy keyword search methods [4,8,15]. In wildcard based methods, data owner has to build an expanded index which covers all the possible misspelling keywords. It leads to a very large index and low search efficiency. In LSH and BF based methods, the search is very efficient. However, these methods may miss out some correct search results, because the adopted technique, Locality-Sensitive Hashing, only maps the similar items to the same hash value with a possibility. Additionally, the above fuzzy keyword search methods do not support access control, which is an important requirement of data sharing in cloud computing.

In this paper, we propose a fuzzy keyword search method supporting access control (FKS-AC) over ciphertexts. Compared with wildcard based methods [10,11,16], FKS-AC is more efficient. Compared with LSH and BF based methods [4,8,15], FKS-AC can accurately obtain all the search results without missing a result. The contributions are as follows:

(1) We propose a method which supports both the fuzzy keyword search and access control.
(2) We present word pattern and construct a fuzzy keyword search algorithm. By utilizing word pattern, the search efficiency and privacy can be balanced.
(3) We implement our method. The experimental results show that our method is efficient.

The reminder of this paper is organized as follows: Sect. 2 is the preliminaries. Section 3 is word pattern. Section 4 is the construction of FKS-AC. Section 5 shows the experiment results. Section 6 is the security analysis. Section 7 is the related work.

2 Preliminaries

A ciphertext-policy attribute based encryption (CP-ABE) [2] consists of five algorithms: *Setup, Encrypt, KeyGen, Delegate* and *Decrypt*.

- *Setup*(λ) $\rightarrow$ (PK, MK). The setup algorithm takes the security parameter λ as input, and outputs a public key PK and a master key MK.
- *Encrypt*(PK, M, P) $\rightarrow$ CT. The encryption algorithm takes the public key PK, a message M, and a policy P as input. The algorithm encrypts M and outputs a ciphertext CT.
- *KeyGen*(MK, S) $\rightarrow$ SK. The key generation algorithm takes the master key MK and an attribute set S as input. It outputs a private key SK.
- *Delegate*($SK, \widetilde{S}$) $\rightarrow$ $\widetilde{SK}$. The delegate algorithm takes as input a secret key SK for the attributes in S and a set $\widetilde{S} \subseteq S$. It outputs a secret key $\widetilde{SK}$ for the attributes in $\widetilde{S}$.

- $Decrypt(PK, CT, SK) \rightarrow M$. The decryption algorithm takes as input the public key PK, a ciphertext CT (CT contains a policy P), and a private key SK (SK contains the attribute set S). If S satisfies P, then the algorithm decrypts CT and outputs M.

There are some facts related to groups with efficiently computable bilinear maps which are used in CP-ABE [2]. Let G_0 and G_1 be two multiplicative cyclic groups of prime order p. Let g be a generator of G_0 and e be a bilinear map, $e : G_0 \times G_0 \rightarrow G_1$. The bilinear map e has two properties. (1) Bilinearity: For all $u, v \in G_0$ and $a, b \in Z_p$, we have $e(u^a, v^b) = e(u, v)^{ab}$. (2) Non-degeneracy: $e(g, g) \neq 1$. G_0 is a bilinear group if the group operation in G_0 and the bilinear map $e : G_0 \times G_0 \rightarrow G_1$ are both efficiently computable. Note that the map e is symmetric and $e(g^a, g^b) = e(g, g)^{ab} = e(g^b, g^a)$.

Definition 1 Edit distance [9]. *Edit distance is a method to quantitatively measure the word similarity. The edit distance $ed(w, w')$ between two words w and w' is the number of operations (substitution, deletion, insertion) required to transform one word into the other. Substitution changes one character to another in a word. Deletion deletes one character from a word. Insertion inserts one character into a word.*

3   Word Pattern

In this section, we propose word pattern, word pattern function, and character-appearing order. The word pattern could be used to balance the search efficiency and security. The word pattern function is used to compute the word pattern. The character-appearing order provides the correct way to perform fuzzy keyword search.

Definition 2 *Word pattern function $F_M(w^\circ, i)$ is defined as below*

$$F_M(w^\circ, i) = \begin{cases} (H_M(c^i_{w^\circ}) - H_M(c^{|w^\circ|}_{w^\circ})) \bmod sp, i = 1 \\ (H_M(c^i_{w^\circ}) - H_M(c^{i-1}_{w^\circ})) \bmod sp, 1 < i \leq |w^\circ| \end{cases}$$

H_M *is a hash function, $c^i_{w^\circ}$ is the ith character in w° (w° denotes a keyword w or a searched word w') and sp is a positive integer.*

Definition 3 *$M_{w^\circ} = (F_M(w^\circ, 1), F_M(w^\circ, 2), \ldots, F_M(w^\circ, |w^\circ|))$ is the word pattern of w°. $m^i_{w^\circ} = F_M(w^\circ, i)$ is the word pattern value of the ith character in w°, where $i = 1, \ldots, |w^\circ|$.*

Let S_{char} denote the character set which is used to spell all the keywords, and $|S_{char}|$ denote the number of characters in S_{char}. According the Definition 2, a word pattern value corresponds to average $|S_{char}|^2 \bmod sp$ two-contiguous characters. Given a word pattern value, one can not know the word pattern value is obtained by calculating which two-contiguous characters. Data owner could use sp to balance the privacy (keyword privacy and searched word privacy) and search efficiency: (1) Smaller sp means there are more characters who have the same word pattern value. Thus, when decreasing sp, the security could be enhanced. However, different two-contiguous characters who have the same word pattern value would affect the efficiency of fuzzy keyword search (see Sect. 4.5). (2) Larger sp means there are fewer characters who have the same word pattern value. Thus, when increasing sp, the search efficiency could be improved, but the security decreases.

Definition 4 *Given a word* $w^\circ = c_{w^\circ}^1 c_{w^\circ}^2 \ldots c_{w^\circ}^{|w^\circ|}$, *for* $\forall i < j$ $(i, j \in [1, |w^\circ|])$, *the character-appearing order of* w° *is that* $c_{w^\circ}^i$ *is before* $c_{w^\circ}^j$.

When keywords and searched words have been encrypted, it is difficult to measure the word similarity according to edit distance. Fortunately, we find a method to compute $ed(w, w')$ according to $|w \cap w'|_O$ (see Theorem 2 in Sect. 4.4), where $|w \cap w'|_O$ is the maximal number of characters which are the same in w and w' in the character-appearing order of w and w'. For example, $w = cat$ is a keyword, and $w' = acat$ is a searched word. It is easy to compute $|w \cap w'|_O = 3$.

4 Fuzzy Keyword Search Supporting Access Control

In our scheme, the cloud is considered to be "honest-but-curious" [4,10,11,15]. Thus the cloud would honestly follow the designated protocols and procedures to fulfill the service provider's role, while it may analyze the information stored and processed on the cloud in order to learn additional information about its customers. In our scheme, first data owner builds indexes for documents and encrypts documents using a secure encryption method, such as AES. Next, the data owner stores the encrypted documents and indexes on the cloud. Then, the data owner distributes secret keys to users according to their identifiers. A user uses his/her secret key to generate trapdoors for the searched words and sends the trapdoors to the cloud for fuzzy keyword search. Upon receiving the trapdoors, the cloud server performs fuzzy keyword search and replies with the encrypted documents which contain the searched words.

4.1 System Setup

The data owner defines a character set S_{char} and an attribute set S_{attr}. S_{char} contains all the characters which are used to spell keywords. For example, $S_{char} = \{a, b, \ldots, z, \ A, B, \ldots, Z, -, +, /, \ldots\}$. S_{attr} contains all the attributes. For example, for a school, the attribute set is $S_{attr} = \{computerScience, student, professor, \ldots\}$. Next, the data owner runs the algorithm *Setup* [2]. *Setup* takes the security parameter λ as input. It outputs the public key PK and master key MK. The public key PK is $G_0, g, h = g^\beta, f = g^{1/\beta}, e(g, g)^\alpha$ and the master key MK is β, g^α, where G_0 is a bilinear group of prime order p with generator g, α and β are randomly chosen from Z_p. Then, the data owner chooses a hash function H_M and a positive integer sp to construct the word pattern function F_M. Finally, the data owner publishes F_M and PK, but keeps MK secretly.

4.2 Building Index

For each document $\mathcal{D}$, the data owner defines a document policy p_D. p_D consists of two kinds of policies. One is error-tolerance policy and the other is access control policy. For each keyword of $\mathcal{D}$, the data owner defines an error-tolerance policy, which limits the maximal typos that a user would make when searching the keyword. Additionally, the data owner defines an access control policy which represents who has the privilege to search the keywords of $\mathcal{D}$. In this section, we describe these policies respectively and show how to generate the index Idx_D for $\mathcal{D}$.

Before describing the policies, we want to explain the threshold gate in detail. In our method, error-tolerance policy, access control policy and document policy can be transformed into tree structures. In these tree structures, each internal node is associated with a threshold gate and each leaf is associated with a character (or an attribute). If an internal node is associated with the threshold gate $T(n, m)$, it means that: (1) The internal node has m children. (2) $T(n, m)$ returns true iff there are at least n children who return true. (3) A leaf returns true iff the character (or attribute) associated with the leaf matches the character (or attribute) in the query of a user. Note that, (1) "OR" could be represented as $T(1, m)$, and (2) "AND" could be represented as $T(m, m)$.

Error-tolerance Policy. For each keyword w of the document $\mathcal{D}$, the data owner defines the maximal error-tolerance value e_w and an error-tolerance policy p_{et}^w: $ed(w', w) \leq e_w$, where w' denotes the searched word. p_{et}^w could be represented as a three-level tree T_{pet}^w (as shown in Fig. 1 (a)). The root of T_{pet}^w is composed of the threshold gate $T(1, e_w + 1)$. The root has $e_w + 1$ children, which are numbered from 1 to $e_w + 1$. The tth child is composed of the threshold gate $T(|w| - e_w + t - 1, |w|)$, where $t = 1, \ldots, e_w + 1$. For each subtree of T_{pet}^w, L_i is the ith leaf of the subtree and L_i is associated with c_w^i (the ith character in w and i indicates the character-appearing order). Threshold gates $T(|w| - e_w + t - 1, |w|)$ $(t = 1, \ldots, e_w + 1)$ could be used to determine whether a searched word w' satisfies $ed(w, w') \leq e_w$. Specifically, the cloud uses $T(|w| - e_w + t - 1, |w|)$ to perform fuzzy keyword search: If $|w| \geq |w'|$, the cloud chooses the threshold gate in which $t = 1$; If $|w'| - |w| > 0$, the cloud chooses the threshold gate in which $t = |w'| - |w| + 1$ (see Sect. 4.4).

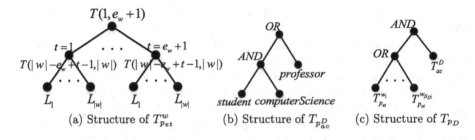

(a) Structure of T_{pet}^w (b) Structure of $T_{p_{ac}^D}$ (c) Structure of T_{p_D}

Fig. 1. Tree structures of error-tolerance, access control and document policies

Access Control Policy. For each document $\mathcal{D}$, the data owner defines an access control policy p_{ac}^D. p_{ac}^D could be represented as a tree, denoted by $T_{p_{ac}^D}$. Internal nodes in $T_{p_{ac}^D}$ are composed of threshold gates and the leaves are associated with attributes. Figure 1 (b) shows the tree structure of the access control policy $p_{ac}^D=professor$ OR $(student$ AND $computerScience)$. For this access control policy p_{ac}^D, it is true iff the user is a professor or a student of computer science. By setting such access control policies, our method could realize the access control.

Document Policy. For each document $\mathcal{D}$, after constructing the access control policy and error-tolerance policies, the data owner constructs a document policy p_D. Suppose that: (1) $\{p_{et}^{w_1}, p_{et}^{w_2}, \dots | w_1, w_2, \dots \in S_{w_D}\}$ is the set of all the error-tolerance policies of keywords in $\mathcal{D}$, where S_{w_D} is the keyword set of $\mathcal{D}$; (2) p_{ac}^D is the access control policy of $\mathcal{D}$. The formal description of p_D is $p_D = (p_{et}^{w_1} \vee \dots \vee p_{et}^{w_{|S_{w_D}|}}) \wedge p_{ac}^D$, where $|S_{w_D}|$ is the total of keywords in S_{w_D}. Because the policies $p_{et}^{w_1}, \dots, p_{et}^{w_{|S_{w_D}|}}$ and p_{ac}^D could be represented as trees $T_{p_{et}}^{w_1}, \dots, T_{p_{et}}^{w_{|S_{w_D}|}}$ and $T_{p_{ac}^D}$, respectively, the policy p_D could be represented as T_{p_D}, as shown in Fig. 1 (c).

Index Generation. For each document $\mathcal{D}$, the data owner runs the algorithm $Encrypt(PK, ID_D||0^l, T_{p_D})$ [2] to generate the index, where PK is the public key, ID_D is the identifier of $\mathcal{D}$, T_{p_D} is the document policy of $\mathcal{D}$. The data owner appends l 0s to the identifier ID_D, denoted by $ID_D||0^l$. In this way, the cloud could check whether a decryption is valid [13]. If a decryption outputs a plaintext that there are l 0s at the end of the plaintext, then the decryption is valid. Otherwise, it is invalid. After running $Encrypt(PK, ID_D||0^l, T_{p_D})$, the data owner could obtain the ciphertext $CT = (T_{p_D}, \tilde{C} = (ID_D||0^l)e(g,g)^{\alpha s}, C = h^s, \forall y \in Y : C_y = g^{q_y(0)}, C_y{}' = H(f(y))^{q_y(0)})$, where T_{p_D} (as shown in Fig. 1 (c)) is the tree structure of p_D, Y is the set of leafs in T_{p_D}, $f(y)$ is the function which returns the character or attribute associated with y, $q_y(0)$ is an integer associated with y, and H is a hash function (details of $Encrypt$ can be found in [2]).

In the CP-ABE method [2], the characters associated with the leafs of subtrees $T_{p_{et}}^{w_i}$ in T_{p_D} are required to be stored in plaintext. Specifically, the leafs of the subtree $T_{p_{et}}^{w_i}$ are associated with the plaintexts of characters $c_{w_i}^1, \dots, c_{w_i}^{|w_i|}$. In order to protect the privacy of keywords in indexes, data owner should transform the tree T_{p_D} into a new tree $T_{p_D}^*$ by replacing the characters $c_{w_i}^1, \dots, c_{w_i}^{|w_i|}$ with the tuples $\langle 1, F(w_i, 1) \rangle, \dots, \langle |w_i|, F(w_i, |w_i|) \rangle$. In these tuples, the first elements indicate the character-appearing orders, and the second elements are the word pattern values. Then, the data owner could construct the index Idx_D by using the ciphertext CT.

$$Idx_D = (T_{p_D}^*, \tilde{C} = (ID_D||0^l)e(g,g)^{\alpha s}, C = h^s,$$
$$\quad w_i \in S_{w_D} : e_{w_i},$$
$$\quad\quad y_k \in Y(T_{P_{et}}^{w_i}) \text{ and } y_k \text{ is the leaf of the } t\text{th subtree of } T_{P_{et}}^{w_i} :$$
$$\quad\quad\quad C_{y_k} = g^{q_{y_k}(0)}, C_{y_k}{}' = H(f(y_k))^{q_{y_k}(0)}, i, t, k, F_M(w_i, k),$$
$$\quad\quad y \in Y(T_{p_{ac}^D}) :$$
$$\quad\quad\quad C_y = g^{q_y(0)}, C_y{}' = H(f(y))^{q_y(0)})$$

e_{w_i} denotes the maximal error-tolerance value of w_i, $char(y_k)$ denotes the character which is associated with the leaf node y_k, $f(y_k)$ (or $f(y)$) is the function which returns the character (or attribute) associated with the leaf y_k (or y), $Y(T_{p_{et}}^{w_i})$ is the set of leafs of $T_{p_{et}}^{w_i}$ ($i = 1, ..., w_{|S_{w_D}|}$), $Y(T_{p_{ac}^D})$ is the set of leafs of $T_{p_{ac}^D}$.

For simplicity, in the following paragraphs, we use the notation $\widehat{C_{c_{w_i}^k}}$ to denote $(C_{y_k} = g^{q_{y_k}(0)}, C_{y_k}{}' = H(f(y_k))^{q_{y_k}(0)})$. $\widehat{C_{c_{w_i}^k}}$ is the **ciphertext component** corresponding to the kth character $c_{w_i}^k$ in the keyword w_i.

We observe that different documents may have the same keywords, and their indexes have the same word patterns. Thus, these indexes are vulnerable to the statistical attacks. To prevent such attacks, the data owner could randomize the keywords and word patterns. For each keyword $w_i = c_{w_i}^1...c_{w_i}^{|w_i|}$ in $\mathcal{D}$, the data owner chooses (1) an integer a_{1w_i} ($a_{1w_i} \geq 0$) randomly, (2) a_{1w_i} characters randomly, denoted by $\eta_1, ..., \eta_{a_{1w_i}}$, (3) a_{1w_i} positions in w_i randomly, and then put $\eta_1, ..., \eta_{a_{1w_i}}$ at these positions. For simplicity, we use the notation w_i^R to denote the randomized w_i. Then, the data owner computes the word pattern and character-appearing order of w_i^R. For each artificial character η_i, the data owner chooses two random values $(C_{\eta_i}, C_{\eta_i}{}')$ as the ciphertext component of η_i, s.t. $|C_{\eta_i}| = |C_{y_j}|$ and $|C_{\eta_i}{}'| = |C_{y_j}{}'|$, where $(C_{y_j}, C_{y_j}{}')$ is the ciphertext component of $c_{w'}^j$ and $c_{w'}^j$ is a character randomly chosen from the keyword w_i. According to the method [2], C_{y_j} and $C_{y_j}{}'$ are computationally indistinguishable from random values. Thus, according to the word pattern values and ciphertext components, attackers cannot distinguish which character is a real character or an artificial character. Thus the index Idx_D can prevent the statistical attacks.

4.3   Trapdoor Generation

For each user u, the data owner runs the algorithm $KeyGen$ to generate the secret key. In our method, the algorithm $KeyGen$ takes as input the master key MK and $S_{char} \cup S_{attr_u}$ (S_{char} is the character set which is used to spell all the keywords of documents, and S_{attr_u} is the attribute set distributed to u by the data owner). It outputs the secret key SK_u for u. $KeyGen$ [2] first randomly chooses a number γ from Z_p, a number γ_c from Z_p for each character $c \in S_{char}$, and a number γ_a from Z_p for each attribute $a \in S_{attr_u}$. Then, $KeyGen$ [2] computes the secret key as $SK_u = (D = g^{(\alpha+\gamma)/\beta}, \forall c \in S_{char} : D_c = g^\gamma \cdot H(c)^{\gamma_c}, D_c{}' = g^{\gamma_c}; \forall a \in S_{attr_u} : D_a = g^\gamma \cdot H(a)^{\gamma_a}, D_a{}' = g^{\gamma_a})$. Finally, the data owner distributes the secret key SK_u to the user u. For simplicity, in the following paragraphs, we use the notation $\overline{D_c}$ to denote $(D_c = g^\gamma \cdot H(c)^{\gamma_c}, D_c{}' = g^{\gamma_c})$. $\overline{D_c}$ is the **secret key component** corresponding to the character c.

The trapdoor generation for a searched word $w' = c_{w'}^1 ... c_{w'}^{|w'|}$ is as follows. According to the above description, in the secret key SK_u of u, there are secret key components for all the characters. Thus, for each character in w', u could find a corresponding secret key component. Then, u could generate a trapdoor $Td_{w'}$ for w'. The trapdoor $Td_{w'}$ is the tuple $\langle Td_{char}, Td_{attr} \rangle$, where $Td_{char} = $

$\{\langle \overline{D_{c_{w'}^i}}, i, F(w', i)\rangle | i = 1, \ldots, |w'|\}$ ($\overline{D_{c_{w'}^i}}$ is the secret key component for the ith character $c_{w'}^i$ of w'), and $Td_{attr} = \{(D_a, D_a') | a \in S_{attr_u}\}$.

For the character c, the secret key component $\overline{D_c}$ in different trapdoors are always the same. Thus, these trapdoors are vulnerable to the statistical attacks. To prevent such attacks, u could run the delegate algorithm *Delegate* [2] to generate new secret keys before each search. Then, for each search, u uses a new secret key to generate trapdoor. We also observe that if the searched words are the same, their word patterns in the trapdoors are the same. Thus, the trapdoors are vulnerable to the statistical attacks, which may leak users' search privacy. To prevent such attacks, users could use the same randomization method in Sect. 4.2 to randomize their trapdoors. Finally, u sends the trapdoor $Td_{w'}$ to the cloud to perform fuzzy keyword search.

4.4   Theorem and Property for FKS-AC

Before describing our fuzzy keyword search algorithm in Sect. 4.5, we want to give some theorems and properties in this section. These theorems and properties are the basis of our method.

Theorem 1 *w is a keyword and w' is a searched word. e_w ($e_w \geq 0$) is the maximal error-tolerance value of w. If $ed(w, w') \leq e_w$, then there is $|w| - e_w \leq |w'| \leq |w| + e_w$, where $|w|$ and $|w'|$ denote the number of characters in w and w' respectively.*

Theorem 1 is the necessary condition of $ed(w, w') \leq e_w$ and it is easy to be proofed. Some keywords in indexes, which do not meet users' search requests, can be filtered out efficiently using Theorem 1.

Theorem 2 *w is a keyword and w' is a searched word. e_w ($e_w \geq 0$) is the maximal error-tolerance value of w. $ed(w, w') \leq e_w$ iff $|w \cap w'|_O \geq |w_{\max}| - e_w$ ($|w_{\max}| = |w|$ if $|w| \geq |w'|$; Otherwise, $|w_{\max}| = |w'|$).*

Proof (1) we proof "if $ed(w, w') \leq e_w$, then there is $|w \cap w'|_O \geq |w_{\max}| - e_w$" in the following two cases.

Case 1: $w_{\min}$ could be transformed into $w_{\max}$ only by using substitutions and insertions.

We suppose $|w_{\max} \cap w_{\min}|_O = n$. As $ed(w_{\max}, w_{\min}) \leq e_w$, we can suppose $ed(w_{\max}, w_{\min}) = e_w - k$, where k ($0 \leq k \leq e_w$) is an integer. According to Definition 1 in Sect. 2, after one operation (substitution or insertion), the word $w_{\min}$ could be transformed into a new word $w_{\min + 1}$. $w_{\min + 1}$ satisfies $ed(w_{\max}, w_{\min + 1}) = ed(w_{\max}, w_{\min}) - 1$ and $|w_{\max} \cap w_{\min + 1}|_O = n + 1$. Thus, it is easy to know that, after $e_w - k$ operations (substitutions and insertions), the word $w_{\min}$ could be transformed into a new word $w_{\min + (e_w - k)}$. $w_{\min + (e_w - k)}$ satisfies $ed(w_{\max}, w_{\min + (e_w - k)}) = ed(w_{\max}, w_{\min}) - (e_w - k) = 0$ (note that $ed(w_{\max}, w_{\min}) = e_w - k$) and $|w_{\max} \cap w_{\min + (e_w - k)}|_O = n + (e_w - k)$. According to Definition 1, $ed(w_{\max}, w_{\min + (e_w - k)}) = 0$ means $w_{\max} = w_{\min + (e_w - k)}$. Thus, we have $|w_{\max} \cap w_{\min + (e_w - k)}|_O = |w_{\max}|$. Because $|w_{\max} \cap w_{\min + (e_w - k)}|_O =$

$|w_{\max}|$ and $|w_{\max} \cap w_{\min+(e_w-k)}|_O = n + (e_w - k)$, we have the conclusion $|w_{\max}| = n + (e_w - k)$. Then, as $|w_{\max} \cap w_{\min}|_O = n$ and $0 \le k \le e_w$, there is $|w_{\max} \cap w_{\min}|_O \ge |w_{\max}| - e_w$. Namely, we have $|w \cap w'|_O \ge |w_{\max}| - e_w$.

Case 2: Substitutions, insertions and deletions are required to transform $w_{\min}$ into $w_{\max}$.

To transform $w_{\min}$ into $w_{\max}$, substitutions and insertions can change the value of $|w_{\max} \cap w_{\min}|_O$, but deletions can not. Thus, if substitutions, insertions and deletions are required to transform $w_{\min}$ into $w_{\max}$, the conclusion $|w_{\max} \cap w_{\min}|_O \ge |w_{\max}| - e_w$ in Case 1 is still correct. Namely, we have $|w \cap w'|_O \ge |w_{\max}| - e_w$.

(2) We proof "if $|w \cap w'|_O \ge |w_{\max}| - e_w$, then there is $ed(w, w') \le e_w$".

As $|w_{\max}| \ge |w_{\min}| \ge |w_{\max} \cap w_{\min}|_O$ and $|w_{\max} \cap w_{\min}|_O \ge |w_{\max}| - e_w$, we have $|w_{\max}| \ge |w_{\min}| \ge |w_{\max}| - e_w$. As $|w_{\max} \cap w_{\min}|_O \ge |w_{\max}| - e_w$, there are at least $|w_{\max}| - e_w$ characters are the same in $w_{\min}$ and $w_{\max}$. Namely, there are at most e_w characters are different in $w_{\min}$ and $w_{\max}$. Thus, to transform $w_{\min}$ into $w_{\max}$, the total of operations is no greater than e_w. Thus, we can know that the edit distance between $w_{\min}$ and $w_{\max}$ is no greater than e_w. Thus, we have the conclusion $ed(w, w') \le e_w$.

Theorem 2 is the sufficient and necessary condition of $ed(w, w') \le e_w$. Thus, by using Theorem 2, our method could correctly perform fuzzy keyword search. According to Theorem 2, it is easy to know that the thresholds in the error-tolerance policy p_{et}^w should be set to $T(|w_{\max}| - e_w, |w|)$. According to Theorem 1, if w and w' satisfy $ed(w, w') \le e_w$, then there are $|w_{\max}| = |w|, |w| + 1, \ldots, |w| + e_w$. Thus, thresholds in the error-tolerance policy p_{et}^w are $T(|w| - e_w, |w|), T(|w| - e_w + 1, |w|), \ldots, T(|w|, |w|)$. For simplicity, these threshold gates could be written as $T(|w| - e_w + t - 1, |w|)$, where $t = 1, 2, \ldots, e_w + 1$. When $|w| \ge |w'|$, it is obvious that the threshold gate in which $t = 1$ could be used to test whether $ed(w, w') \le e_w$. When $|w'| > |w|$, it requires at least $|w'| - |w|$ deletions to transform w' into w. Then, at most $e_w - (|w'| - |w|)$ operations are left which could be used to transform w' into w. Thus, there are at least $|w| - [e_w - (|w'| - |w|)]$ characters should be the same in w and w'. If one uses $T(|w| - e_w + t - 1, |w|)$ to test whether $ed(w, w') \le e_w$, then there is $|w| - [e_w - (|w'| - |w|)] = |w| - e_w + t - 1$. Thus, we can compute $t = |w'| - |w| + 1$. Namely, if $|w'| > |w|$, the threshold gate in which $t = |w'| - |w| + 1$ could be used to test whether $ed(w, w') \le e_w$ (see Sect. 4.2).

A secret key component can be used to decrypt a ciphertext component, iff they have the correct corresponding relationship.

Definition 5 *Corresponding relationship*. In an index Idx_D, $\widehat{C_{c_w^i}}$ is a ciphertext component, which corresponds to the ith character c_w^i in w. In a trapdoor $Td_{w'}$, $\overline{D_{c_{w'}^j}}$ is a secret key component, which corresponds to the jth character $c_{w'}^j$ in w'. A corresponding relationship is the tuple $\langle \widehat{C_{c_w^i}}, \overline{D_{c_{w'}^j}} \rangle$. If $c_w^i = c_{w'}^j$, $\langle \widehat{C_{c_w^i}}, \overline{D_{c_{w'}^j}} \rangle$ is correct. Otherwise, it is wrong.

As keywords in indexes and searched words in trapdoors have been hidden to protect the privacy, it is difficult to find out the correct corresponding relationships. According to the algorithm $Decrypt$ [2], if there are not **enough** correct corresponding relationships, the indexes cannot be correctly decrypted to obtain the identities of documents. "enough" means $|w \cap w'|_O \geq |w_{\max}| - e_w$ (see Theorem 2).

The following properties could be used to help the cloud to efficiently find out the corresponding relationships which may be correct. $A \xrightarrow{p} B$ denotes, if there is A, then there is B with the probability p. According to Sect. 3, it is easy to know that $p = 1/(|S_{char}|^2/sp)$. Note that, if the superscript value v of m_w, c_w (or $m_{w'}$, $c_{w'}$) is greater than $|w|$ (or $|w'|$), then v is set to $v \bmod |w|$ (or $v \bmod |w'|$).

(1) $m_w^{i+1} = m_{w'}^{j+1} \xrightarrow{p} c_w^i = c_{w'}^j$ and $c_w^{i+1} = c_{w'}^{j+1}$

(2) $(m_w^{i+1} + m_w^{i+2} + ... + m_w^{i+k}) \bmod sp = m_{w'}^{j+1} \xrightarrow{p} c_w^i = c_{w'}^j$ and $c_w^{i+k} = c_{w'}^{j+1}$

(3) $m_w^{i+1} = (m_{w'}^{j+1} + m_{w'}^{j+2} + ... + m_{w'}^{j+k}) \bmod sp \xrightarrow{p} c_w^i = c_{w'}^j$ and $c_w^{i+1} = c_{w'}^{j+k}$

(4) $(m_w^{i+1} + m_w^{i+2} + ... + m_w^{i+k}) \bmod sp = (m_{w'}^{j+1} + m_{w'}^{j+2} + ... + m_{w'}^{j+t}) \bmod sp \xrightarrow{p} c_w^i = c_{w'}^j$ and $c_w^{i+k} = c_{w'}^{j+t}$

By utilizing these properties, it is not difficult to design a optimization method to find out the corresponding relationships which may be correct. On the one hand, as different two-contiguous characters may share the same word pattern value, it is inevitable to find out wrong corresponding relationships, which may reduce the search efficiency. On the other hand, as wrong corresponding relationships and correct relationships can not be distinguished, it increases the security.

4.5 Fuzzy Keyword Search with Access Control

In this section, we first illustrate the algorithm $Decrypt$. Then, we give the Fuzzy Keyword Search Algorithm with Access Control (FKSAAC).

Iff a user's attributes and the searched word in his/her trapdoor match the index of a document, the cloud can definitely find out enough and correct corresponding relationships by using the property (1)-(4). Then, the algorithm $Decrypt$ can recover the value $e(g,g)^{\gamma s}$ by using the correct corresponding relationships (details can be found in [2]). Finally, the cloud can compute

$$\frac{\tilde{C}}{e(C,D)/e(g,g)^{\gamma s}} = \frac{(ID_D||0^l)e(g,g)^{\alpha s}}{e(h^s, g^{(\alpha+\gamma)/\beta})/e(g,g)^{\gamma s}} = ID_D||0^l.$$

FKSAAC takes as input the trapdoor $Td_{w'}$ of a searched word w' and the index Idx_D of an encrypted document $\mathcal{D}$. Iff (1) w' satisfies $ed(w_i, w') \leq e_{w_i}$ (represented by an error-tolerance policy of $\mathcal{D}$), where w_i is one of the keywords in $\mathcal{D}$, and (2) attributes in $Td_{w'}$ satisfy the access control policy of $\mathcal{D}$, FKSAAC outputs ID_D of $\mathcal{D}$. Otherwise, FKSAAC outputs false. The algorithm FKSAAC is given below.

Step 1. For each subtree $T_{p_{et}}^{w_i}$ (it represents the keyword w_i) in $T_{p_D}^*$, FKSAAC computes $|w_i|$ according to the number of ciphertext components in Idx_D. Then, FKSAAC computes $|w'|$ according to the number of secret key components in $Td_{w'}$. If $|w_i| - e_{w_i} \lesssim |w'|$ or $|w'| \lesssim |w_i| + e_{w_i}$ (see Theorem 1), FKSAAC aborts the keyword w_i and then executes **Step 1** to test the next keyword in Idx_D. Otherwise, FKSAAC computes $|w'| - |w_i|$: (1) If $|w'| - |w_i| \leq 0$, FKSAAC extracts ciphertext components from Idx_D s.t. these ciphertext components are associated with the value $t = 1$; (2) If $|w'| - |w_i| > 0$, FKSAAC extracts ciphertext components from Idx_D s.t. these ciphertext components are associated with the value $t = |w'| - |w| + 1$ (see Theorem 2).

Step 2. FKSAAC extracts the word pattern of w_i from the index Idx_D and the word pattern of w' from the trapdoor $Td_{w'}$. Then, FKSAAC finds which secret key component of an attribute in $Td_{w'}$ corresponds to which ciphertext component of an attribute in Idx_D (these relationships about attributes are easy to be obtained, because they are stored in plaintext). Next, FKSAAC calculates a set (denoted by S) of combinations according to the properties in Sect. 4.4. In each combination, there are $|w_{\max}| - e_w$ corresponding relationships (see Theorem 2). For each combination in S, FKSAAC extracts the corresponding relationships in it. Then FKSAAC runs the algorithm *Decrypt* to try to decrypt Idx_D by using these corresponding relationships about characters and the relationships about attributes: (1) If *Decrypt* outputs $ID_D||0^l$, FKSAAC returns ID_D; (2) If *Decrypt* outputs $\perp$, FKSAAC tests the next combination in S. If all the outputs of *Decrypt* are $\perp$, FKSAAC executes **Step 1** to test the next keyword in Idx_D.

Step 3. FKSAAC returns false.

The cloud runs FKSAAC to test all the indexes of encrypted documents, and then returns the encrypted documents whose identities have been retrieved to the user u.

5 Experiments

In our experiments, we compare our method FKS-AC with Li's method, Fuzzy Keyword Search over Encrypted Data in Cloud Computing (FKS) [10], and Wang's method, Privacy-Preserving Multi-Keyword Fuzzy Search over Encrypted Data in the Cloud (PPMKFS) [15]. We also do the comparison works of FKS-AC when choosing different values as sp (sp is the parameter in the word pattern function F_M).

The algorithms in FKS-AC are constructed in bilinear groups. We implement FKS-AC using Java Pairing-Based Cryptography Library (JPBC) version 2.0.0, which supports the calculations in bilinear groups. In the experiments of FKS-AC, the character set S_{char} is $\{a, b, \ldots, z, A, B, \ldots, Z, -\}$, the attribute set S_{attr} is $\{a_1, a_2, a_3\}$ and the access control policies are "a_1 AND a_2", "a_1 AND a_3", "a_2 AND a_3", "a_1 OR a_2", etc. In order to compare FKS-AC, PPMKFS and FKS fairly (as PPMKFS and FKS do not support access control, the cloud has to test all the indexes for fuzzy search), we suppose the data owner distributes all the attributes a_1, a_2 and a_3 to users. Then, users have the privilege to search all the documents. Thus, the cloud also has to test all the indexes of documents after receiving a trapdoor from a user.

Our experiments run on a win7 computer with four 2.80 GHz CPUs and 4 G RAM. We randomly extract 400 distinct keywords from the documents in ACM Digital Library. In these keywords, the minimal, maximal and average number of characters are 3, 14 and 8, respectively. The documents is 1000 in total. Each document has 5 keywords, which are randomly chosen from these 400 keywords. Given a keyword w, its maximal error-tolerance value is e_w. In the experiments of FKS-AC and FKS, we set (1) $e_w = 1$, if $|w| \leq 5$; (2) $e_w = 2$, if $5 < |w| \leq 10$; (3) $e_w = 3$, if $|w| > 10$. To generate a searched word w', we randomly chooses e_w characters as typos, and insert them into w. Thus, the number of characters in w' is $|w| + e_w$ ($|w'| = 4, 5, \ldots, 17$). However, we set $e_w = 1$ whether w is a long keyword or not in the experiments of PPMKFS. This is because that, the number of typos allowed by PPMKFS is fixed when LSH family has been chosen.

5.1 The Time of Index Generation

Experimental results. Figure 2 shows the index generation times of FKS-AC, FKS and PPMKFS. Their index generation times are linear to the number of documents. FKS and PPMKFS are more efficient than FKS-AC.

Analysis of the results. As FKS-AC, FKS and PPMKFS generate index per document, thus the times of index generation are linear to the number of documents. The index generation of FKS is constructed on AES. As AES is a symmetric encryption method and the computing overhead is very low, FKS is very efficient. PPMKFS is constructed on LSH and BF (LSH and BF consist of hash functions). The computing overhead of LSH and BF is much less than AES. Thus, the index generation of PPMKFS is more efficient than FKS. In order to support access control, FKS-AC is constructed on CP-ABE. As CP-ABE is an asymmetric encryption method and requires complicated calculations, FKS-AC spends more time building indexes.

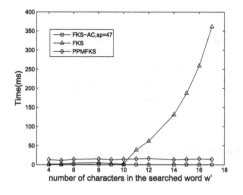

Fig. 2. The time of building indexes

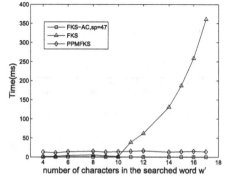

Fig. 3. The time of generating trapdoors

Note that, the data owner generates indexes before outsourcing documents to the cloud. Index generation could be seen as the initialization work before providing the service of fuzzy keyword search. Thus, we think the low efficiency of index generation of FKS-AC could be tolerated.

5.2 The Time of Trapdoor Generation

Experimental results. As shown in Fig. 3, FKS-AC is the most efficient, and the trapdoor generation times of FKS-AC and PPMKFS are constant. Compared with FKS-AC and PPMKFS, FKS costs more time for trapdoor generation.

Analysis of the results. In FKS-AC, trapdoor is generated on user client. A user only puts some secret key components together according to the character-appearing order of w', and then computes the word pattern of w'. Thus, the trapdoor generation of FKS-AC is very efficient. In PPMKFS, trapdoor is generated by data owner. The data owner generates the trapdoor for a user by executing LSH and BF. As LSH and BF consist of dozens of hash functions, the trapdoor generation of PPMKFS is slower than FKS-AC. In FKS, the trapdoor is generated on user client. Before generating a trapdoor for a searched word, the user should first generate a fuzzy keyword set. However, a long searched word necessitates to issue a large fuzzy keyword set. The size of fuzzy keyword set is $O(|w'|^{e_{w'}})$ ($e_{w'} = 1$ if $w' \leq 5$; $e_{w'} = 2$ if $5 < w' \leq 10$; $e_{w'} = 3$ if $w' > 10$). Thus, when $|w'|$ increases, the size of fuzzy keyword set increases rapidly. Then, the user encrypts each word in the fuzzy keyword set, and their ciphertexts are as the trapdoor of the searched word. Thus, the efficiency of trapdoor generation of FKS is very low.

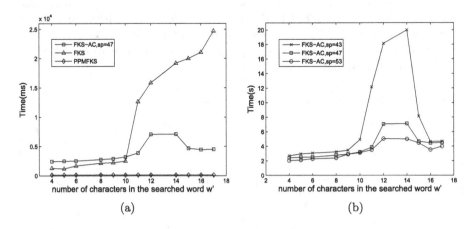

Fig. 4. The average time of fuzzy search

5.3 The Time of Fuzzy Keyword Search

Experimental results. From Fig. 4 (a), we can see that PPMKFS is the most efficient. FKS is nearly the same as FKS-AC when $|w'| < 10$. FKS-AC is more efficient than FKS when $|w'| > 10$. Figure 4 (b) shows that the search efficiency of FKS-AC could be improved by increasing sp.

Analysis of the results. As PPMKFS performs fuzzy search only by multiplying two groups of bit vectors (one group of vectors is a trapdoor, and the other is the index of a document), PPMKFS is very efficient. However, the search result of PPMKFS is not accurate. This is because PPMKFS is based on BF and LSH. Both BF and LSH introduce false positives (a false positive is that, a document should not be in the search result, but it is). Additionally, LSH introduces false negatives (a false negative is that, a document should be in the search result, but it is not). Compared with PPMKFS, FKS and FKS-AC are accurate methods and do not introduce any false positives or false negatives.

In FKS, the size of trapdoor grows rapidly when $|w'|$ increases. When using the trapdoor of a long searched word to search a long keyword (the size of the index and trapdoor are very large), one has to compare each encrypted item in the trapdoor and each encrypted item in the index. Specifically, the time of fuzzy keyword search is $O(T \times |w|^{e_w} \times |w'|^{e_{w'}})$, where T is the time for one comparison between two encrypted items. Thus, the computing overhead of fuzzy search in FKS increases rapidly and inevitably results a long search time.

If the searched word is long, FKS-AC should do more calculations in bilinear groups. Thus, the search time of FKS-AC increases when $|w'|$ increases. Recall that, FKS-AC computes a set of combinations and try to decrypt indexes using the combinations in the set (see the algorithm FKSAAC in Sect. 4.5). Wrong combinations in the set would reduce the search efficiency of FKS-AC. When the searched word w' is very similar to a keyword w, but the typos in w' exceeds e_w, then all the combinations found by FKS-AC are wrong combinations. As the cloud does not know which combinations are wrong, all these wrong combinations will be used to try to decrypt the index. Thus, the search efficiency decreases. For example, when using $w' = consttructionn$ to search $w_1 = construction$, the search is efficient. When using the same w' to search $w_2 = contributions$, the search may be inefficient. When $|w'| = 12$ or 14, there are many such keywords like w_1 and w_2 (e.g. "adaptation" and "adsorption", "Automation" and "Automobiles", etc.). Thus, the search time of FKS-AC increases a lot when $|w'| = 12$ and 14. From Fig. 4 (b), we can see that, the search efficiency increases with the value of sp. This is because larger sp could help the cloud to find corresponding relationships more accurate. Thus, the search efficiency increases when sp increases.

6 Security Analysis

We proof that FKS-AC is secure under the Known Ciphertext Model [15]. Under this model, adversary can only access the encrypted documents, indexes, submitted trapdoors, search results, word patterns of keywords and searched words.

If the adversary records all the information he/she can access, the adversary can build up access patterns. Thus, in the known ciphertext model, nothing beyond the access patterns and the search results should be leaked. We adapt the notations in [15] for our proofs.

- *Search Pattern* (π): Let $Q = \{w_1', \ldots, w_n'\}$ be the set of searched words for n consecutive queries, then π be a binary matrix s.t. $\pi[i,j] = 1$ if $w_i' \in S_{w_i,e_{w_i}}$ and $w_j' \in S_{w_i,e_{w_i}}$, otherwise $\pi[i,j] = 0$ ($S_{w_i,e_{w_i}}$ is the set of w_i' satisfying $ed(w_i, w_i') \leq e_{w_i}$).
- *Access Pattern* (A_p): Let $D(w_i')$ ($w_i' \in S_{w_i,e_{w_i}}$) be a set that contains the identities of documents which contain the keyword w_i. Let $T = \{T_1, \ldots, T_n\}$ be the trapdoors for the query set $Q = \{w_1', \ldots, w_n'\}$. Then, *Access Pattern* for the n trapdoors is defined as $\{A_p(T_1) = D(w_1'), \ldots, A_p(T_n) = D(w_n')\}$.
- *History* (H_n): Let D be the document set and $Q = \{w_1', \ldots, w_n'\}$ be the searched words for n consecutive queries. Then, $H_n = (D, Q)$ is defined as a n-query *History*.
- *Trace* (γ): Let $C = \{C_1, \ldots, C_l\}$ be the set of encrypted documents, $id(C_i)$ be the identity of C_i, $|C_i|$ be the size of C_i, P_{w_i} be the word pattern of w_i, $P_{w_i'}$ be the word pattern of w_i', $S_p(H_n)$ be the *Search Pattern* of H_n and $A_p(H_n)$ be the *Access Pattern* of H_n. Then, $\gamma(H_n) = \{(id(C_1), \ldots, id(C_l)), (|C_1|, \ldots, |C_l|), (P_{w_1}, \ldots, P_{w_n}), (P_{w_1'}, \ldots, P_{w_n'}), S_p(H_n), A_p(H_n)\}$ is defined as the trace of H_n. *Trace* is the maximum amount of information that a data owner allows to leak to an adversary.
- *View* (V): Let $C = \{C_1, \ldots, C_l\}$ be the set of encrypted documents, $id(C_i)$ be the identity of C_i, I be the set of indexes of C, $P_w = (P_{w_1}, \ldots, P_{w_n})$ be the set of word patterns of keywords, $P_{w'} = (P_{w_1'}, \ldots, P_{w_n'})$ be the set of word patterns of searched words, and $T = \{T_1, \ldots, T_n\}$ be the set of trapdoors. Then, $V(H_n) = \{(id(C_1), \ldots, id(C_l)), C, I, P_w, P_{w'}, T\}$ is defined as the view of H_n. *View* is the information that is accessible to an adversary.

We adopt a similar simulation based proof, which is widely used in [5,8,15]. Intuitively, given two histories with the same trace, if the adversary cannot distinguish which of them is generated by the simulator, the adversary cannot learn additional information about the index, trapdoors and the encrypted documents beyond the search result and the access pattern [15].

Theorem 3 *FKS-AC is secure under the known ciphertext model.*

Proof The notation S denotes the simulator, which can simulate a view V^* indistinguishable from an adversary's view $V(H_n) = \{(id(C_1), \ldots, id(C_l)), C, I, P_w, P_{w'}, T\}$. To achieve this, the simulator S does the followings:

(1) Identities of documents are available in the trace. Thus, S can copy these identities, that is, $\{id(C_1)^* = id(C_1), \ldots, id(C_l)^* = id(C_l)\}$. As identity lists of the adversary's view V and the simulated view V^* are the same, they are computationally indistinguishable.

(2) S chooses l random values $\{C_1{}^*, \ldots, C_l{}^*\}$, s.t. $|C_1{}^*| = |C_1|, \ldots, |C_l{}^*| = |C_l|$. The documents are encrypted by using a secure encryption scheme (e.g. AES) of the data owner's choosing. Thus, the outputs of the secure encryption scheme is computationally indistinguishable from random values. Hence, $C_i{}^*$ and C_i are computationally indistinguishable.

(3) S runs the algorithm *Setup* to obtain a public key PK and a master key MK. Then, S runs the algorithm *KeyGen* to obtain a secret key SK.

(4) S constructs n consecutive queries $Q^* = \{w_1'^*, \ldots, w_n'^*\}$, the word patterns $P_{w'^*} = (P_{w_1'^*}, \ldots, P_{w_n'^*})$, and the trapdoors $T^* = \{T_1{}^*, \ldots, T_n{}^*\}$. For each $w_i' \in Q$, $1 \le i \le n$, S generates the searched word $w_i'^*$ randomly, s.t. $|w_i'^*| = |w_i'|$. Then, S computes the word pattern of $w_i'^*$. As $w_i'^*$ is generated randomly, the word pattern of $w_i'^*$ is computationally indistinguishable from random values. Note that, the searched word w_i' may have typos, and additionally, w_i' has been inserted several random characters at random positions for randomization purpose (see Sect. 4.3). Thus, the word patterns of $w_i'^*$ and w_i' are computationally indistinguishable. According to the characters in $w_i'^*$, S generates the trapdoor T_i^* for $w_i'^*$ by utilizing the secret key components in SK. As SK is indistinguishable from random values [2], the trapdoor T_i^* generated by utilizing SK is indistinguishable from random values. For the same reason, the trapdoor T_i for w_i' is also indistinguishable from random values. Hence, the trapdoors T_i^* and T_i are computationally indistinguishable.

(5) For each $C_i{}^*$, S sets an empty set $Set_{C_i^*}$, where $1 \le i \le l$. According to the access pattern A_p, if $id(C_i)$ could be retrieved by using the word w_j', then S adds $w_j'^*$ to $Set_{C_i^*}$, where $1 \le j \le n$. The set $Set_{C_i^*}$ is as the keyword set of the encrypted document $C_i{}^*$. Next, S constructs the document policy for $C_i{}^*$ by using the keywords in $Set_{C_i^*}$, and runs the algorithm *Encrypt* to generate the index $I_{C_i^*}$ for $C_i{}^*$. The ciphertext generated by *Encrypt* is as the index $I_{C_i^*}$ of $C_i{}^*$. As the ciphertext is indistinguishable from random values [2], the index $I_{C_i^*}$ is indistinguishable from random values. For the same reason, the index I_{C_i} generated by running *Encrypt* is also indistinguishable from random values. Thus I_{C_i} and $I_{C_i^*}$ are computationally indistinguishable. Then, we can know that the index set I for $\{C_i | 1 \le i \le l\}$ and I^* for $\{C_i{}^* | 1 \le i \le l\}$ are computationally indistinguishable.

Since each item of V and V^* are computationally indistinguishable, FKS-AC satisfies the security definition presented in Theorem 3.

7   Related Work

Li et al. [10] first propose a searchable encryption method supporting fuzzy keyword search. For each keyword, data owner use the wildcard technique to build a fuzzy keyword set which contains all the possible misspellings. The index and trapdoor are built on the set. To perform a fuzzy search, the cloud checks whether there is intersection between the index and the trapdoor. To limit the size of the set, Liu et al. [11] propose a method which is based on a predefined dictionary.

The dictionary is as a filter to delete the meaningless words in a user's search. However, this method requires that a user should know much about the filed he/she queries. Kuzu et al. [8] propose a generic similarity search method based on Bloom Filter (BF) [3] and Locality-Sensitive Hashing (LSH) [7]. A LSH function hashes close items to the same hash value with higher probability than the items that are far apart. Thus the similarity of the keywords could be measured by using LSH functions. According the hash values of keywords, the data owner builds indexes using BF. Thus, the indexes could support fuzzy keyword search. In [15], Wang et al. propose a multi-keyword fuzzy search method. This method is also based on BF and LSH. However, as LSH can not hash close items to the same hash value with the probability one hundred per cent, LSH would introduce false negatives. Namely, the limitation in LSH inevitably results the in inaccurate search results.

Acknowledgment. The authors would like to thank anonymous reviewers for their constructive comments. This work is partly supported by the Jiangxi Provincial Natural Science Foundation of China (No. 20161BAB202036).

References

1. Attrapadung, N., Libert, B.: Functional encryption for inner product: achieving constant-size ciphertexts with adaptive security or support for negation. In: Nguyen, P.Q., Pointcheval, D. (eds.) PKC 2010. LNCS, vol. 6056, pp. 384–402. Springer, Heidelberg (2010). doi:10.1007/978-3-642-13013-7_23

2. Bethencourt, J., Sahai, A., Waters, B.: Ciphertext-policy attribute-based encryption. In: 2007 IEEE Symposium on Security and Privacy (SP 2007), pp. 321–334. IEEE (2007)

3. Bloom, B.H.: Space/time trade-offs in hash coding with allowable errors. Commun. ACM **13**(7), 422–426 (1970)

4. Chuah, M., Hu, W.: Privacy-aware bedtree based solution for fuzzy multi-keyword search over encrypted data. In: 2011 31st International Conference on Distributed Computing Systems Workshops, pp. 273–281. IEEE (2011)

5. Curtmola, R., Garay, J., Kamara, S., Ostrovsky, R.: Searchable symmetric encryption: improved definitions and efficient constructions. In: ACM Conference on Computer and Communications Security, pp. 895–934 (2006)

6. Gionis, A., Indyk, P., Motwani, R., et al.: Similarity search in high dimensions via hashing. In: VLDB, vol. 99, pp. 518–529 (1999)

7. Indyk, P., Motwani, R.: Approximate nearest neighbors: towards removing the curse of dimensionality. In: Proceedings of the Thirtieth Annual ACM Symposium on Theory of Computing, pp. 604–613. ACM (1998)

8. Kuzu, M., Islam, M.S., Kantarcioglu, M.: Efficient similarity search over encrypted data. In: 2012 IEEE 28th International Conference on Data Engineering, pp. 1156–1167. IEEE (2012)

9. Levenshtein, V.: Binary codes capable of correcting spurious insertions and deletions of ones. Prob. Inf. Transm. **1**(1), 8–17 (1965)

10. Li, J., Wang, Q., Wang, C., Cao, N., Ren, K., Lou, W.: Fuzzy keyword search over encrypted data in cloud computing. In: INFOCOM, 2010 Proceedings IEEE, pp. 1–5. IEEE (2010)

11. Liu, C., Zhu, L., Li, L., Tan, Y.: Fuzzy keyword search on encrypted cloud storage data with small index. In: 2011 IEEE International Conference on Cloud Computing and Intelligence Systems, pp. 269–273. IEEE (2011)

12. Shen, E., Shi, E., Waters, B.: Predicate privacy in encryption systems. In: Reingold, O. (ed.) TCC 2009. LNCS, vol. 5444, pp. 457–473. Springer, Heidelberg (2009). doi:10.1007/978-3-642-00457-5_27

13. Shi, E., Bethencourt, J., Chan, T.H., Song, D., Perrig, A.: Multi-dimensional range query over encrypted data. In: 2007 IEEE Symposium on Security and Privacy (SP 2007), pp. 350–364. IEEE (2007)

14. Sun, W., Wang, B., Cao, N., Li, M., Lou, W., Hou, Y.T., Li, H.: Privacy-preserving multi-keyword text search in the cloud supporting similarity-based ranking. In: Proceedings of the 8th ACM SIGSAC Symposium on Information, Computer and Communications Security, pp. 71–82. ACM (2013)

15. Wang, B., Yu, S., Lou, W., Hou, Y.T.: Privacy-preserving multi-keyword fuzzy search over encrypted data in the cloud. In: IEEE INFOCOM 2014-IEEE Conference on Computer Communications, pp. 2112–2120. IEEE (2014)

16. Wang, J., Ma, H., Tang, Q., Li, J., Zhu, H., Ma, S., Chen, X.: Efficient verifiable fuzzy keyword search over encrypted data in cloud computing. Comput. Sci. Inf. Syst. **10**(2), 667–684 (2013)

Secure and Practical Searchable Encryption: A Position Paper

Shujie Cui[(⊠)], Muhammad Rizwan Asghar,
Steven D. Galbraith, and Giovanni Russello

The University of Auckland, Auckland, New Zealand
scui379@aucklanduni.ac.nz,
{r.asghar,s.galbraith,g.russello}@auckland.ac.nz

Abstract. Searchable Encryption (SE) makes it possible for users to outsource an encrypted database and search operations to cloud service providers without leaking the content of data or queries to them. A number of SE schemes have been proposed in the literature; however, most of them leak a significant amount of information that could lead to inference attacks. To minimise information leakage, there are a number of solutions, such as Oblivious Random Access Memory (ORAM) and Private Information Retrieval (PIR). Unfortunately, existing solutions are prohibitively costly and impractical. A practical scheme should support not only a lightweight user client but also a flexible key management mechanism for multi-user access.

In this position paper, we briefly analyse several leakage-based attacks, and identify a set of requirements for a searchable encryption system for cloud database storage to be secure against these attacks while ensuring usability of the system. We also discuss several possible solutions to fulfil the identified requirements.

1 Introduction

Cloud computing is a successful paradigm offering users virtually unlimited data storage and computational power at very attractive costs. Despite its merits, cloud computing raises privacy issues to users. Once the data is outsourced, it is exposed not only to third party intruders but also to careless or even potentially malicious Cloud Service Providers (CSPs). Standard encryption can protect the content of the outsourced data. However, it also prevents users from searching on encrypted data. If standard encryption is used, there is a trivial solution to perform search on encrypted data: if a particular piece of data is needed, the user has to download all the content to its local (trusted) environment, decrypt the data, and perform the search operation. If the database is very large, this trivial solution does not scale well. The matter becomes more complicated in multi-user settings, where multiple users could access the same data set.

The concept of Searchable Encryption (SE) provides a promising solution to protect outsourced data from unauthorised accesses by CSPs or external adversaries. Encrypted data is tagged with encrypted keywords (also called

© Springer International Publishing AG 2017
J. Pieprzyk and S. Suriadi (Eds.): ACISP 2017, Part I, LNCS 10342, pp. 266–281, 2017.
DOI: 10.1007/978-3-319-60055-0_14

search tokens) in such a way that a CSP, which is given an encrypted search term, can check whether a record has keyword(s) that satisfies the search term. Such schemes allow the CSP to perform encrypted search on encrypted data without leaking the content of the query and the data.

Since the seminal paper by Song *et al.* [45], many SE schemes have been proposed. A long line of works, such as [2, 7, 9, 10, 14, 18, 20, 22, 23, 25, 29, 30, 35, 38, 44, 45, 47, 50, 53, 54, 56, 57], focus on investigating SE with complex functionality (*e.g.*, multi-keyword search, range queries, rank search, and fuzzy search) and improved performance. Although these schemes are secure under some cryptographic assumptions, we will see that the CSP is still potentially able to learn about the data by observing patterns in the results of insert, delete or update operations. For instance, the CSP is able to see which encrypted data is accessed by a given query by looking at the matching records (referred to as *access pattern leakage*). By comparing the matched records, the CSP can also infer if two or more queries are equivalent or not (referred to as *search pattern leakage*). Moreover, the CSP can simply log the number of matched records or files returned by each query (referred to as *size pattern leakage*).

When an SE scheme supports insert and delete operations, it is referred to as a *dynamic* SE scheme. Dynamic SE schemes might leak extra information if they do not support *forward privacy* and *backward privacy* properties. Forward privacy means that the CSP can not learn if newly inserted data or updated data matches previously executed queries. Backward privacy means that the CSP can not learn if deleted or stale data matches new queries. Supporting forward and backward privacy is fundamental to limit the power of the CSP to collect information on how the data evolves over time. Only a few of the existing schemes [5, 6, 10, 47] support forward privacy, but no scheme is able to support both forward and backward privacy simultaneously.

Some recent works [8, 27, 32, 34, 58] have shown that even a minor leakage could be exploited to learn sensitive information and break a scheme. In particular, given the plaintext of a small number of queries (*e.g.*, data, search habit or preference of users), a malicious CSP could recover a large fraction of the data and queries. Unfortunately, the majority of the existing SE solutions, such as [2, 7, 9, 10, 14, 18, 20, 22, 23, 25, 29, 30, 35, 38, 44, 45, 47, 50, 53, 54, 56, 57], are vulnerable to these attacks due to the leakage of search, access and size patterns, and lack of forward and backward privacy.

Privacy-sensitive applications, such as electronic healthcare systems, impose stringent security requirements when it comes to data outsourcing. The first step to meet those requirements is to minimise information leakage that could lead to inference attacks. Oblivious Random Access Memory (ORAM) [21, 36, 46] and Private Information Retrieval (PIR) [12, 13, 55] are two possible techniques to minimise information leakage. However, existing ORAM and PIR schemes are prohibitively costly and impractical. We are concerned with practical solutions where users can get the required data efficiently without incurring high storage, communication and computation overheads. Moreover, in multi-user settings, users could join or leave the system at any time, ideally without affecting the rest of the users. Unfortunately, neither ORAM nor PIR cover these aspects. Therefore, an important problem is to develop secure and practical SE schemes for privacy-sensitive applications. In this paper, we first define a set of requirements towards a secure cloud database. Then, we provide an extensive classification of the existing literature based on these requirements. Furthermore, we provide some research directions and possible approaches to ensure confidentiality without compromising on functionality and a practical user experience.

2   Requirements and Challenges

The recent proposed attacks on SE schemes, such as [8,34,58], put the outsourced data at risk. Almost all the attacks recover the data by leveraging private information leaked by size, search and access patterns. To minimise information leakage, the size, search and access patterns must be hidden from the CSP. In this section, for each pattern, we first briefly describe the typical attacks, and then we identify the requirements and challenges for protecting it. For a practical solution, a flexible key management mechanism is needed for applications requiring multi-user access. We also identify the requirements and challenges to manage the keys, but without leaking private information.

Size Pattern. The number of matched records for each query is called the size pattern or the frequency information [8,27,34,45]. In particular, we say *Size Pattern Privacy (SzPP)* is achieved if the CSP is unable to learn the number of matched records of a query on encrypted data. In most of the existing SE schemes, there are two kinds of frequency information leakages. The first kind is a leakage from the encrypted data stored in the database; we call this *static frequency information*. For instance, in CryptDB [38], the searchable data is only protected with deterministic encryption (the outer layer encryptions are peeled off to support search operations). That is, the same data in the database has the same ciphertext. The frequency information in the database is exposed to the CSP directly. With the knowledge of publicly available information, like census data and hospital statistics, Naveed *et al.* [34] successfully recover more than 60% of patient records from electronic medical databases based on static frequency information without executing any search operation. In contrast, some other schemes [2] use semantically secure primitives to encrypt the data. In such schemes, the static frequency information is protected since all the encrypted data has different ciphertexts. However, after performing a query, the CSP could still count the number of matched records; we call this *dynamic frequency information*. With the knowledge of the frequency information of keywords in plaintext, attackers could recover the queries easily based on the number of matched records, which is called a *count attack* in [8].

Clearly, semantically secure encryption is not sufficient to protect the dynamic frequency information if the search operation is performed by the CSP. Protection against the count attack is required.

Access Pattern. We say that an SE scheme achieves *Access Pattern Privacy (APP)* if the CSP is unable to infer if two (or more) result sets contain the same data or not. A formal definition is given in [14]. A typical instance of access pattern based attack is the *file injection attack* introduced in [58], which is also referred to as the *chosen-document attack* in [8]. Technically, an active malicious CSP sends files with keywords of its choice, such as emails, to users who then encrypt and upload them to the CSP. Afterwards, the CSP tracks these injected files and checks if they match queries. Since all the keywords in these files are known to the CSP, given enough injected files, the CSP could recover the keywords included in queries. Specifically, the keywords included in the matched but not included in the unmatched injected files are the possible searched keywords.

ORAM is a primitive intended for hiding storage access patterns. However, it is difficult to get a practical SE scheme that is based on ORAM technique. We now explain the two main obstacles to using traditional ORAM in SE schemes. First, in ORAM, the store address of required data is known to users before fetching. However, in SE schemes, the CSP first needs to search over the database and get matched records or indexes of matched files. It is impractical to store all the addresses on the user side, especially for applications with thousands of users and resource-constrained devices. Second, despite significant recent improvements [16,19,40], ORAM incurs huge bandwidth, latency and storage overheads, making it impractical for SE schemes. According to the study by Naveed [33], the naive approach, downloading the whole database and search locally for each query, is even more efficient than ORAM.

PIR is another approach to hide the access pattern. It allows users to retrieve the data without leaking which data is retrieved to the CSP. Specifically, in PIR-based SE schemes, such as [15,42], the CSP returns a much larger data set than required to the user. Although the access pattern is unknown to the CSP, the user has to perform some computation locally to extract the matched data. It is clear that the communication and computation overheads on the user are also huge in this approach.

Although both the ORAM and PIR techniques can protect the access pattern from the CSP, they may leak information to users. In an application with fine-grained access control policies, users should only get what they are allowed to learn. However, all the existing ORAM and PIR approaches do not ensure that all the returned data is authorised to the user. Therefore, a more practical method to protect the access pattern without leaking information to users should be proposed.

Search Pattern. We say *Search Pattern Privacy (SPP)* is achieved if the CSP is not able to distinguish if two (or more) encrypted queries feature the same keywords or not. In [32], Liu *et al.* show that given the search habit of users, the searched keywords could be recovered based on the search pattern. In [8], Cash *et al.* illustrate that given the plaintext of a small number of queries, the plaintext of other queries cou ld be recovered easily if the adversary knows the search pattern. It is not trivial to protect the search pattern since it can be inferred not only from the encrypted queries, but also from the access and size patterns.

To protect the search pattern, first we should use a semantically secure encryption algorithm for the search tokens, which makes same queries look different once encrypted. Recall that to protect the static frequency information, it is also necessary to encrypt the data with a semantically secure algorithm. If both the query and the data are semantically secure, to the best of our knowledge, the only solutions in the literature use complex cryptographic primitives such as pairings or homomorphic encryptions. These primitives tend to be much slower than traditional symmetric encryption. So these methods do not scale well when processing the search operation over millions of records. A more efficient approach to test equality between semantically secure encrypted data is needed.

Furthermore, even if the encrypted queries are semantically secure, the CSP could still infer the search pattern by looking at the access pattern. That is, by looking at the physical locations of the encrypted data returned by a search, the CSP can infer that two queries are equivalent if the same result sets are returned, since generally only the same query gets exactly the same result set.

However, even if the matched data for all queries are different in terms of the storage location and ciphertext, the search pattern can still be inferred from the size pattern. If the database is static then equivalent queries will always return the same number of matched records or files. This fact can be used by the CSP to mount an attack: Although it is not always true that the two queries are logically equivalent when their result sets have the same size, it is true that they are different queries when their result set sizes are different.

Therefore, to conceal the search pattern, it is necessary to make the size, storage location and ciphertext of the search results variable even if the same query is executed twice.

Forward and Backward Privacy. Generally speaking, forward and backward privacy mean the CSP will learn nothing if it repeats a previously executed query (using the original search tokens) over newly added or updated data, or executes a new query over data that was supposed to have been deleted or updated. If the SE scheme cannot ensure forward and backward privacy, the CSP could recover all the queries with the file injection attack by executing all the previous queries again over the newly injected files. Similarly, if the CSP learns the plaintext of deleted files or records, then the queries could also be recovered by checking if they match deleted data.

To protect the search and access patterns, it is, in fact, necessary to also ensure forward and backward privacy. Recall that the storage locations and ciphertexts of searched data must be updated to protect the search and access patterns. However, if the CSP could execute the previous queries over the updated data and get a new set of matched data, it will infer the search pattern by comparing the result set of a new query with the result sets of previous queries. Likewise, the CSP can also infer the search pattern by caching the database and executing all the new queries over it.

Forward privacy is achieved in [5,6,10,47]. Unfortunately, all of these proposals require the user to store a set of the latest keys, which will be used to encrypt queries. In multi-user settings, where multiple users could read and write to the database according to the access control policies, if one of the users inserts or updates a new record or file, the keys have to be updated, and then the new keys would have to be distributed to other users. Otherwise, with the stale keys, the other users cannot get the correct result set. These key management issues are impractical for multi-user applications. A more flexible approach is needed. Moreover, to ensure data confidentiality, backward privacy should also be guaranteed.

Key Management. Another issue with existing SE schemes is to have a very flexible key management mechanism for multi-user access. Many schemes, like [14], encrypt the data and queries with a key shared among all the users. Consequently, all the queries and search results issued by one user could be decrypted by all the other authorised users. Even worse, when one user is revoked, the single key has to be changed and the data has to be re-encrypted with the new key. In other schemes, such as [7,52], the keys are only known to the data owner. The users have to send the query and search result to the data owner to get the search tokens and cleartext results, which means that the data owner represents a bottleneck in the system. Both of these options are impractical in modern organisations, since a large number of users may access the data concurrently, or they may join and leave their position at any time. We call all such schemes *Single User (SU)*.

In a *Multi-User (MU)* scheme, users can submit queries to search or update the data uploaded by other users according to the access control policies, and no key regeneration and data re-encryption are needed for user revocation. Almost all the existing MU SE schemes, such as [2,3,17,31,39,51], are based on proxy-encryption techniques. Basically, in these schemes, instead of sharing a single encryption key among all the users, each user has a unique key to encrypt data and queries. Moreover, the CSP stores another key for each user, with which the CSP could perform the equality check between the query and data encrypted by different users. However, all these schemes leak the search pattern since their query encryption algorithms are deterministic. Moreover, in [2,17], if a malicious user colludes with the CSP, they can recover all the data by putting their keys together. The schemes introduced in [3,31,39,51] include several pairing operations, making the search operations computationally intensive. A more secure and practical MU key management mechanism is needed.

3   Literature Review

Since the seminal paper by Song *et al.* [45], many searchable schemes have been proposed and research in this area has been extended in several directions. In this section, we categorise the approaches presented in the literature based on information leakage and key management, and summarise their limitations.

Only several recent works tried to partially address the issue of information leakage. In [35], Naveed *et al.* achieve SzPP. The basic idea is to divide each document into a set of blocks. When a document is requested, a larger set of blocks will be downloaded and decrypted by the client, which aggravates the

Table 1. A comparison of searchable encryption schemes.

Schemes	Search pattern privacy	Access pattern privacy	Size pattern privacy	Forward privacy	Backward privacy	Key management
Hang et al. [23]	×	×	×	×	×	○
Ferretti et al. [18]	×	×	×	×	×	○
Popa et al. [38]	×	×	×	×	×	●
Sarfraz et al. [44]	×	×	×	×	×	●
Sun et al. [50]	×	×	×	×	×	○
Yang et al. [56]	×	×	×	×	×	●
Asghar et al. [2]	×	×	×	×	×	●
Bao et al. [3]	×	×	×	×	×	●
Popa et al. [39]	×	×	×	×	×	●
Tang [51]	×	×	×	×	×	●
Kiayias et al. [31]	×	×	×	×	×	●
Curtmola et al. [14]	×	×	×	Static	Static	○
Jarecki et al. [28]	×	×	×	Static	Static	○
Kamara et al. [30]	×	×	×	×	×	○
Kamara et al. [29]	×	×	×	×	×	○
Hahn et al. [22]	×	×	×	×	×	○
Cao et al. [7]	✓	×	×	Static	Static	○
Wang et al. [52]	✓	✓	✓	Static	Static	○
Ishai et al. [26]	✓	✓	✓	Static	Static	○
Naveed et al. [35]	×	×	✓	×	×	○
Samanthula et al. [43]	✓	✓	✓	×	×	○
Stefanov et al. [47]	×	×	×	✓	×	○
Rizomiliotis et al. [41]	×	×	×	✓	×	○
Bost [5]	×	×	×	✓	×	○
Our objectives	✓	✓	✓	✓	✓	●

✓ and × indicate that the property is achieved or not, respectively.
○ represents a Single User (SU) scheme. ● represents a Multi-User (MU) scheme. *Static* means the scheme does not support insert, update, or delete operations.

computational and storage overheads on the client side. Moreover, it fails to achieve SPP and APP, since the same query requests the same block set.

Samanthula et al. [43] present a query processing framework that supports complex queries. A homomorphic encryption algorithm is used to encrypt the data in their scheme. Thus, it supports more complex queries when compared to other schemes, and achieves SPP, APP, and SzPP. However, this scheme is single user and does not scale well for databases with a large number of attributes.

Cao *et al.* [7] design a scheme that supports a multi-keyword ranked search. The scheme ensures SPP by hiding the trapdoor linkability. Wang *et al.* [52] propose a public multi-keyword searchable encryption scheme based on Paillier [37], which achieves SPP, APP, and SzPP. More recently, in [26], Ishai *et al.* protect both the search and access patterns combining a PIR technique with a B-tree data structure. Although these three schemes provide different index structures for speeding up the search, the constructions are static and do not support insert, update, and delete operations.

In [47], Stefanov *et al.* design a dynamic sub-linear searchable construction based on an ORAM-like hierarchical structure and achieve forward privacy. Similarly, Rizomiliotis *et al.* [41] propose another dynamic ORAM-based scheme that achieves forward privacy and sub-linear search. More recently, the dynamic SE scheme introduced by Bost [5] also achieves forward privacy. Instead of using an ORAM-like structure, this scheme relies on a trapdoor permutation. However, it only ensures forward privacy until a new query is issued. A CSP could still learn if the new file contains the keywords searched previously, by comparing the access pattern of a new query with those of previous queries. Moreover, all these three schemes fail to ensure backward privacy.

Several works have concentrated on supporting multi-user access and simplifying key management. Curtmola *et al.* [14] introduce a multi-user (MU) scheme by combining a single user SE scheme with a broadcast encryption scheme, where only the authorised user can issue queries with the key received from the data owner. However, each time a user is revoked, the data owner has to generate a new key. Even worse, the data stored on the cloud server is encrypted with the key shared among all the users, which means the revoked users can still recover all the data if they collude with the cloud server. The MU SE scheme given by Jarecki *et al.* [28] has the same problem. That is, the data security against revoked users is achieved based on the assumption that there is no collusion between the cloud server and revoked users; otherwise, the key has to be updated and the data has to be re-encrypted with the new key. Moreover, in their scheme, the data owner has to be online to generate search tokens for all the authorised users.

Hang *et al.* [23] and Ferretti *et al.* [18] present two different collusion-resistant mechanisms that support multi-user access to the outsourced data. Although they support approaches to avoid key sharing among users, in both, after user revocation, it is necessary to generate a new key and re-encrypt the data.

CryptDB [38] is a multi-user scheme where each user has her own password, which is managed by a proxy between the user and the database server. Sarfraz *et al.* [44] revisit CrtypDB and also design a MU scheme with a fine-grained access control. Instead of assigning the keys to users, both [38,44] store them in a proxy. Since the users never know the underlying encryption key, they do not require to refresh the key when revoking a user. The problem is that these two mechanisms require the proxy to be online for performing operations on behalf of the users. As a result, the proxy represents a single point of failure: an attacker who compromises the proxy will gain access to all the logged-in users' keys and data.

Sun *et al.* [50] utilise a Ciphertext-Policy Attribute-Based Encryption (CP-ABE) [4] mechanism to achieve a scalable SE scheme that supports multi-user read and write operations without sharing any key. However, for user revocation, the data has to be re-encrypted with a new access structure and secret keys of all the other users need to be updated with a new attribute set. Strictly speaking, this scheme is also a SU scheme.

In the literature, only the proxy-based encryption schemes, such as [2,3,31, 39,51,56], can support multi-user access, where each user has her own key and does not require any re-encryption when an authorised user is revoked.

Many other works also investigated approaches to increase search efficiency [14,22,30], or data integrity and reliability in the setting where the CSP is totally untrusted [11,49]. Unfortunately, as shown in Table 1, none of the reviewed approaches are able to limit information leakage and support multi-user access.

4   Possible Solutions and Future Research

In this section, we propose several possible solutions and outline future research directions to meet the requirements and address the challenges to minimise information leakage and achieve a flexible key management.

Size Pattern. If the search operation is performed by the CSP, it is inevitable that the CSP could count the matched records or files. As mentioned in [8, 14], introducing a set of dummy data into the database is an effective way to protect the size pattern without leaking private information to users. Basically, the dummy data should look exactly like the real data and even should match queries. In this way, the search result for each query will include a random amount of dummy data. Consequently, the size pattern is protected from the CSP. However, to ensure a lightweight overhead on the user end, it should be easy for users to filter out the dummy data before decrypting.

Furthermore, the amount of dummy data should be controllable since it affects the security level and performance of the system. The higher the percentage of dummy data with respect to real data, the harder for the CSP to infer the real size pattern. However, this also implies that more data should be searched by the CSP and more dummy data should be filtered out by the user for each query. The study by Cash *et al.* in [8] suggests that 1.6 is the minimum ratio between dummy and real data to resist against count attacks. A thorough security analysis for identifying a right balance between real and dummy data for achieving a sustainable level of security and performance should be investigated.

Another possible solution could be dividing the database into partitions and distributing these partitions over multiple non-colluding CSPs. For each query, each single CSP searches over its partition independently. Using this approach, each CSP only gets a small part of the search result. The total number of matched records is unknown to all the CSPs if they do not put their sub-results together.

Access Pattern. In the access pattern based attacks, the key point is that the CSP knows which injected records match the query and which do not. Therefore, to resist such attacks, we need to make storage locations of the injected data untraceable for the CSP. In fact, this can be achieved by generating and uploading dummy data when uploading real data. If the dummy and real encrypted data are indistinguishable to the CSP, it cannot learn if the search result contains the injected data or dummy data. Even so, the set of data injected at different time points is still distinguishable for the CSP. A technique that makes the data inserted at different times untraceable is to shuffle the database after executing each query, as we explain in the next sections.

Search Pattern. To protect the search pattern, first of all, the encrypted queries should be semantically secure. Moreover, we should break the link between the search pattern and access and size patterns. That is, we should ensure that the CSP will always see a new set of data being matched even if a query equivalent to the previous one is executed.

To break the link between the access and search patterns, the only choice is to shuffle the physical locations of the searched data after executing each query. Moreover, for making the data untraceable, the corresponding ciphertext should be re-randomised prior to moving to new locations. Even with the ORAM technique, the access pattern is protected by changing the data location and re-randomising its ciphertext. In this way, the CSP is unable to infer the search pattern from the access pattern, since the access patterns for all the queries are different. Note that the scheme is secure against file injection attacks, because the shuffling and re-randomisation operations make all the data untraceable whenever they are inserted.

To break the link between the size pattern and search pattern, when dummy data is introduced to hide the real size pattern, one possible solution is to ensure that the responses to all queries have a constant size. However, this potentially requires a huge number of dummy records (possibly exponentially many) if the database has large variability in its frequency information. A more practical solution is to vary the result size of each query. To do this, some of the dummy data should be deleted or updated, or some new dummy data should be inserted between any two queries. This ensures that the number of matched dummy records are different even if the same query is executed again. Alternatively, as mentioned in Sect. 2, if the database is divided into partitions and stored on multiple CSPs, the matched data together with a set of unmatched data in each partition should be re-randomised and moved across CSPs after executing each query. Due to the re-randomisation and re-location of the data, each CSP will only see a one-time match. That is, a CSP does not learn whether the data ever matched previous queries, or will match future queries.

In summary, to resist leakage-based attacks, a number of dummy records should be introduced and updated after executing each query, and the searched records should be re-randomised and shuffled after executing each query. All these operations affect the performance of the system. The fact is that there is always a trade-off between security and performance. It is impossible to achieve a higher level security without sacrificing performance. However, we aim to design a lightweight client for the user. It is impractical to ask the user to perform these operations. Basically, the dummy records increase the storage, bandwidth and computation overheads on the user end. From a security point of view, these operations should be hidden from the CSP. Otherwise, the CSP could learn more useful information and recover the data and queries. Inevitably, a third entity, or more entities should be involved to guarantee security and achieve efficiency. Specifically, the following two models can be considered:

- **Combining a Private Cloud with the CSP.** According to the latest report by Rightscale [1], the hybrid cloud computing approach is getting more popular among large enterprises. This model combines the public cloud service with a private cloud platform owned by the organisation. The private cloud could be considered as a trusted entity, because it is inherently managed by the organisation, where the sensitive data can be stored and executed without an extra layer of security. However, due to its limited storage and computational power, the bulk of the operations and storage should be delegated to the public CSP. To minimise information leakage, the private cloud could be leveraged to perform the shuffle, re-randomisation and dummy data refreshment operations after executing each query.
- **Combining Multiple CSPs.** The third entity could also be an untrusted public CSP. In fact, the idea of utilising multiple CSPs to reduce the load on users is already integrated into the ORAM technique. In [48], Stefanov and Shi have introduced a 2-cloud oblivious storage system that achieves APP and significantly reduced the bandwidth cost between the client and the CSP. Recently, Hoang *et al.* [24] also proposed a distributed encrypted data structure for SE schemes that could be deployed on two non-colluding CSPs. Their proposal achieves much higher security than traditional SE schemes. Unfortunately, both [24,48] suffer from the same problem as faced by traditional ORAM techniques. That is, an encrypted search operation is not considered and they can only protect the file access pattern. Moreover, in [48], the shuffle operation is performed before returning the data to users, which increases the latency on the user side.

  We could employ at least two non-colluding CSPs. However, we should also consider the search operation performed on index structures, and aim to achieve the index access pattern privacy. Specifically, one CSP stores the encrypted data and performs the search operation, and after executing each query, first it returns the result set to the user, and then sends the searched data to another CSP for shuffling, re-randomising and dummy data refreshing. In this case, the CSP that performs the queries never knows how the searched data is updated, and the CSP that performs rest of the operations cannot execute the query and never knows which of the records are matched. If the CSPs never collude together, all the patterns are protected from them. However, the cooperation between CSPs should be carefully designed, and the approaches to resist against the collusion between the CSPs should also be investigated.

To ensure a high level of security, it is possible to shuffle all the data in the database. However, this degrades the system performance. Although these operations do not affect the end-to-end latency from the user's point of view, the next query cannot be executed until the shuffle, re-randomisation, and dummy data refreshment operations have been finished. Hence, it affects the throughput of the system and should be completed efficiently. The more data is shuffled and re-randomised, the more difficult it is for the CSPs to infer the access pattern, but it is worse in terms of the system performance. It is an interesting research direction to investigate the required amount of data that should be shuffled and re-randomised for achieving a sustainable level of security and performance.

Forward and Backward Privacy. To achieve both forward and backward privacy, first of all, we should ensure the CSP cannot execute previous queries over newly added data or execute new queries over deleted data. Furthermore, to achieve SPP and APP, it is also necessary to ensure that the CSP cannot repeat the previous query after shuffling and re-randomising, or execute a new query over the snapshot of the data before shuffling and re-randomising. Therefore, not only the newly added data but also the shuffled and re-randomised data should include a new element (say a nonce) that should make them unmatched with the previous queries.

Likewise, a new query should include an element that makes it unmatched with stale (deleted or modified) data. However, the new queries must match with the latest data. To this end, the element included in the latest data should be stored somewhere and used to encrypt new queries, as done in [5,6,10,47]. It is impractical to store the new element on the user side in multi-user settings. One possible solution is for a third entity to store and manage these query elements. In this case, all the queries should first be sent to the third entity and re-encrypted with the element included in the latest data. Moreover, the element should be updated when re-randomising the searched data. It is an open problem to achieve both forward and backward privacy in an efficient manner.

Index Structure. To achieve sub-linear search time, a number of works have investigated special index structures to narrow down the search range, such as the inverted index given in [14], the ORAM-like hierarchical structure designed in [47], the red-black tree based structure proposed by Kamara et al. [29], and the B-tree based scheme introduced in [26]. Unfortunately, the CSP could learn the search, access and size patterns from searching the index structure.

To improve search efficiency with minimised leakage, these index structures need to be redesigned. First, dummy data should be inserted into the structure to hide the size pattern. Second, both the encrypted nodes and queries should be semantically secure to hide the search pattern. Finally, to protect patterns and ensure forward and backward privacy, the searched nodes should be shuffled and re-randomised after executing each query.

However, it may be infeasible or inefficient to perform those operations on the proposed index structures. For instance, in the inverted index structure, encrypted linked lists are used to accelerate the searching. To hide the search and access patterns, the linked lists should be shuffled and re-randomised after executing each query. However, the shuffle operation will upset the linkability between nodes, and then the CSP cannot get the correct matched indexes.

Therefore, one potential future work would be to investigate new sub-linear data structures that support equality check between semantically secure encrypted data and can be shuffled and re-randomised efficiently without leaking sensitive information.

Key Management. The existing proxy encryption based key management approaches, including [2,3,17,31,39,51], could be used to ensure efficient user registration and revocation in multi-user settings. However, to ensure SPP, the query encryption should be replaced with a semantically secure primitive, and the equality check operation in these schemes should be changed accordingly. Moreover, as mentioned in [17], the third party could be leveraged to secure against collusion attacks between a user and the CSP. Meanwhile, an approach to avoid expensive pairing operations by making use of the third entity should be investigated.

Towards a more secure cloud database, there are many other security issues to be addressed, such as the accountability of the search result when the CSP is assumed to be totally untrusted and the access control for fine-grained access. Certainly, there is a long way to go to ensure confidentiality and privacy of the outsourced data.

5 Concluding Remarks

In this paper, we investigated the state of the art of SE schemes and some challenges for achieving a secure outsourced database. Almost all the existing SE schemes are vulnerable to inference attacks due to sensitive information leakage, which makes them unusable for privacy-sensitive applications. Based on these attacks, we identify a set of requirements for a cloud database that could be secure against them and ensure an efficient and practical user searching experience. We also briefly reviewed possible solutions to meet these requirements. To achieve a better balance between the security level and performance of the system, we finally outlined several future research directions. These directions will be developed in future work by the authors.

References

1. Rightscale 2016 state of the cloud report. https://www.rightscale.com/lp/state-of-the-cloud. Last Accessed 3 July 2016
2. Asghar, M.R., Russello, G., Crispo, B., Ion, M.: Supporting complex queries and access policies for multi-user encrypted databases. In: Juels, A., Parno, B. (eds.) CCSW 2013, pp. 77–88. ACM (2013)
3. Bao, F., Deng, R.H., Ding, X., Yang, Y.: Private query on encrypted data in multi-user settings. In: Chen, L., Mu, Y., Susilo, W. (eds.) ISPEC 2008. LNCS, vol. 4991, pp. 71–85. Springer, Heidelberg (2008). doi:10.1007/978-3-540-79104-1_6
4. Bethencourt, J., Sahai, A., Waters, B.: Ciphertext-policy attribute-based encryption. In: S&P 2007, pp. 321–334. IEEE Computer Society (2007)
5. Bost, R.: $\sum o\varphi o\varsigma$: Forward secure searchable encryption. In: Weippl, E.R., Katzenbeisser, S., Kruegel, C., Myers, A.C., Halevi, S. (eds.) SIGSAC 2016, pp. 1143–1154. ACM (2016)

6. Bost, R., Fouque, P., Pointcheval, D.: Verifiable dynamic symmetric searchable encryption: optimality and forward security. IACR Cryptology ePrint Archive **2016**, 62 (2016)

7. Cao, N., Wang, C., Li, M., Ren, K., Lou, W.: Privacy-preserving multi-keyword ranked search over encrypted cloud data. IEEE Trans. Parallel Distrib. Syst. **25**(1), 222–233 (2014)

8. Cash, D., Grubbs, P., Perry, J., Ristenpart, T.: Leakage-abuse attacks against searchable encryption. In: Ray, I., Li, N., Kruegel, C. (eds.) SIGSAC 2015, pp. 668–679. ACM (2015)

9. Cash, D., Jaeger, J., Jarecki, S., Jutla, C.S., Krawczyk, H., Rosu, M., Steiner, M.: Dynamic searchable encryption in very-large databases: data structures and implementation. In: NDSS 2014. The Internet Society (2014)

10. Chang, Y.-C., Mitzenmacher, M.: Privacy preserving keyword searches on remote encrypted data. In: Ioannidis, J., Keromytis, A., Yung, M. (eds.) ACNS 2005. LNCS, vol. 3531, pp. 442–455. Springer, Heidelberg (2005). doi:10.1007/11496137_30

11. Cheng, R., Yan, J., Guan, C., Zhang, F., Ren, K.: Verifiable searchable symmetric encryption from indistinguishability obfuscation. In: Bao, F., Miller, S., Zhou, J., Ahn, G. (eds.) ASIA CCS 2015, pp. 621–626. ACM (2015)

12. Chor, B., Kushilevitz, E., Goldreich, O., Sudan, M.: Private information retrieval. J. ACM **45**(6), 965–981 (1998)

13. Crescenzo, G., Cook, D., McIntosh, A., Panagos, E.: Practical private information retrieval from a time-varying, multi-attribute, and multiple-occurrence database. In: Atluri, V., Pernul, G. (eds.) DBSec 2014. LNCS, vol. 8566, pp. 339–355. Springer, Heidelberg (2014). doi:10.1007/978-3-662-43936-4_22

14. Curtmola, R., Garay, J.A., Kamara, S., Ostrovsky, R.: Searchable symmetric encryption: improved definitions and efficient constructions. In: Juels, A., Wright, R.N., di Vimercati, S.D.C. (eds.) CCS 2006, pp. 79–88. ACM (2006)

15. Dautrich, J., Ravishankar, C.V.: Combining ORAM with PIR to minimize bandwidth costs. In: Park, J., Squicciarini, A.C. (eds.) CODASPY 2015, pp. 289–296. ACM (2015)

16. Devadas, S., Dijk, M., Fletcher, C.W., Ren, L., Shi, E., Wichs, D.: Onion ORAM: a constant bandwidth blowup oblivious RAM. In: Kushilevitz, E., Malkin, T. (eds.) TCC 2016. LNCS, vol. 9563, pp. 145–174. Springer, Heidelberg (2016). doi:10.1007/978-3-662-49099-0_6

17. Dong, C., Russello, G., Dulay, N.: Shared and searchable encrypted data for untrusted servers. In: Atluri, V. (ed.) DBSec 2008. LNCS, vol. 5094, pp. 127–143. Springer, Heidelberg (2008). doi:10.1007/978-3-540-70567-3_10

18. Ferretti, L., Pierazzi, F., Colajanni, M., Marchetti, M.: Scalable architecture for multi-user encrypted SQL operations on cloud database services. IEEE Trans. Cloud Comput. **2**(4), 448–458 (2014)

19. Garg, S., Mohassel, P., Papamanthou, C.: TWORAM: efficient oblivious RAM in two rounds with applications to searchable encryption. In: Robshaw, M., Katz, J. (eds.) CRYPTO 2016. LNCS, vol. 9816, pp. 563–592. Springer, Heidelberg (2016). doi:10.1007/978-3-662-53015-3_20

20. Goh, E.: Secure indexes. IACR Cryptology ePrint Archive 2003, 216 (2003)

21. Goldreich, O., Ostrovsky, R.: Software protection and simulation on oblivious RAMs. J. ACM **43**(3), 431–473 (1996)

22. Hahn, F., Kerschbaum, F.: Searchable encryption with secure and efficient updates. In: Ahn, G., Yung, M., Li, N. (eds.) SIGSAC 2014, pp. 310–320. ACM (2014)

23. Hang, I., Kerschbaum, F., Damiani, E.: ENKI: access control for encrypted query processing. In: Sellis, T.K., Davidson, S.B., Ives, Z.G. (eds.) SIGMOD 2015, pp. 183–196. ACM (2015)
24. Hoang, T., Yavuz, A.A., Guajardo, J.: Practical and secure dynamic searchable encryption via oblivious access on distributed data structure. In: Schwab, S., Robertson, W.K., Balzarotti, D. (eds.) ACSAC 2016. pp. 302–313. ACM (2016)
25. Hwang, Y.H., Lee, P.J.: Public key encryption with conjunctive keyword search and its extension to a multi-user system. In: Takagi, T., Okamoto, T., Okamoto, E., Okamoto, T. (eds.) Pairing 2007. LNCS, vol. 4575, pp. 2–22. Springer, Heidelberg (2007). doi:10.1007/978-3-540-73489-5_2
26. Ishai, Y., Kushilevitz, E., Lu, S., Ostrovsky, R.: Private large-scale databases with distributed searchable symmetric encryption. In: Sako, K. (ed.) CT-RSA 2016. LNCS, vol. 9610, pp. 90–107. Springer, Cham (2016). doi:10.1007/978-3-319-29485-8_6
27. Islam, M.S., Kuzu, M., Kantarcioglu, M.: Access pattern disclosure on searchable encryption: ramification, attack and mitigation. In: NDSS 2012. The Internet Society (2012)
28. Jarecki, S., Jutla, C.S., Krawczyk, H., Rosu, M., Steiner, M.: Outsourced symmetric private information retrieval. In: Sadeghi, A., Gligor, V.D., Yung, M. (eds.) SIGSAC 2013, pp. 875–888. ACM (2013)
29. Kamara, S., Papamanthou, C.: Parallel and dynamic searchable symmetric encryption. In: Sadeghi, A.-R. (ed.) FC 2013. LNCS, vol. 7859, pp. 258–274. Springer, Heidelberg (2013). doi:10.1007/978-3-642-39884-1_22
30. Kamara, S., Papamanthou, C., Roeder, T.: Dynamic searchable symmetric encryption. In: Yu, T., Danezis, G., Gligor, V.D. (eds.) CCS 2012, pp. 965–976. ACM (2012)
31. Kiayias, A., Oksuz, O., Russell, A., Tang, Q., Wang, B.: Efficient encrypted keyword search for multi-user data sharing. In: Askoxylakis, I., Ioannidis, S., Katsikas, S., Meadows, C. (eds.) ESORICS 2016. LNCS, vol. 9878, pp. 173–195. Springer, Cham (2016). doi:10.1007/978-3-319-45744-4_9
32. Liu, C., Zhu, L., Wang, M., Tan, Y.: Search pattern leakage in searchable encryption: attacks and new construction. Inf. Sci. **265**, 176–188 (2014)
33. Naveed, M.: The fallacy of composition of oblivious RAM and searchable encryption. IACR Cryptology ePrint Archive 2015, 668 (2015)
34. Naveed, M., Kamara, S., Wright, C.V.: Inference attacks on property-preserving encrypted databases. In: Ray, I., Li, N., Kruegel, C. (eds.) SIGSAC 2015, pp. 644–655. ACM (2015)
35. Naveed, M., Prabhakaran, M., Gunter, C.A.: Dynamic searchable encryption via blind storage. In: SP 2014, pp. 639–654. IEEE Computer Society (2014)
36. Ostrovsky, R.: Efficient computation on oblivious RAMs. In: Ortiz, H. (ed.) STOC 1990, pp. 514–523. ACM (1990)
37. Paillier, P.: Public-key cryptosystems based on composite degree residuosity classes. In: Stern, J. (ed.) EUROCRYPT 1999. LNCS, vol. 1592, pp. 223–238. Springer, Heidelberg (1999). doi:10.1007/3-540-48910-X_16
38. Popa, R.A., Redfield, C.M.S., Zeldovich, N., Balakrishnan, H.: CryptDB: protecting confidentiality with encrypted query processing. In: Wobber, T., Druschel, P. (eds.) SOSP 2011, pp. 85–100. ACM (2011)
39. Popa, R.A., Zeldovich, N.: Multi-key searchable encryption. IACR Cryptology ePrint Archive 2013, 508 (2013)
40. Ren, L., Fletcher, C.W., Kwon, A., Stefanov, E., Shi, E., van Dijk, M., Devadas, S.: Constants count: practical improvements to oblivious RAM. In: Jung, J., Holz, T. (eds.) USENIX Security 2015, pp. 415–430. USENIX Association (2015)

41. Rizomiliotis, P., Gritzalis, S.: ORAM based forward privacy preserving dynamic searchable symmetric encryption schemes. In: Ray, I., Wang, X., Ren, K., Kerschbaum, F., Nita-Rotaru, C. (eds.) CCSW 2015, pp. 65–76. ACM (2015)
42. Rompay, C., Molva, R., Önen, M.: Multi-user Searchable Encryption in the Cloud. In: Lopez, J., Mitchell, C.J. (eds.) ISC 2015. LNCS, vol. 9290, pp. 299–316. Springer, Cham (2015). doi:10.1007/978-3-319-23318-5_17
43. Samanthula, B.K., Jiang, W., Bertino, E.: Privacy-preserving complex query evaluation over semantically secure encrypted data. In: Kutyłowski, M., Vaidya, J. (eds.) ESORICS 2014. LNCS, vol. 8712, pp. 400–418. Springer, Cham (2014). doi:10.1007/978-3-319-11203-9_23
44. Sarfraz, M.I., Nabeel, M., Cao, J., Bertino, E.: Dbmask: Fine-grained access control on encrypted relational databases. In: Park, J., Squicciarini, A.C. (eds.) CODASPY 2015, pp. 1–11. ACM (2015)
45. Song, D.X., Wagner, D., Perrig, A.: Practical techniques for searches on encrypted data. In: S&P 2000, pp. 44–55. IEEE Computer Society (2000)
46. Stefanov, E., van Dijk, M., Shi, E., Fletcher, C.W., Ren, L., Yu, X., Devadas, S.: Path ORAM: an extremely simple oblivious RAM protocol. In: Sadeghi, A., Gligor, V.D., Yung, M. (eds.) SIGSAC 2013, pp. 299–310. ACM (2013)
47. Stefanov, E., Papamanthou, C., Shi, E.: Practical dynamic searchable encryption with small leakage. In: NDSS 2013, vol. 71, pp. 72–75 (2014)
48. Stefanov, E., Shi, E.: Multi-cloud oblivious storage. In: Sadeghi, A., Gligor, V.D., Yung, M. (eds.) SIGSAC 2013, pp. 247–258. ACM (2013)
49. Sun, W., Liu, X., Lou, W., Hou, Y.T., Li, H.: Catch you if you lie to me: efficient verifiable conjunctive keyword search over large dynamic encrypted cloud data. In: INFOCOM 2015, pp. 2110–2118. IEEE (2015)
50. Sun, W., Yu, S., Lou, W., Hou, Y.T., Li, H.: Protecting your right: attribute-based keyword search with fine-grained owner-enforced search authorization in the cloud. In: INFOCOM 2014, pp. 226–234. IEEE (2014)
51. Tang, Q.: Nothing is for free: security in searching shared and encrypted data. IEEE Trans. Inf. Forensics Secur. 9(11), 1943–1952 (2014)
52. Wang, B., Song, W., Lou, W., Hou, Y.T.: Inverted index based multi-keyword public-key searchable encryption with strong privacy guarantee. In: INFOCOM 2015, pp. 2092–2100. IEEE (2015)
53. Wang, B., Yu, S., Lou, W., Hou, Y.T.: Privacy-preserving multi-keyword fuzzy search over encrypted data in the cloud. In: INFOCOM 2014, pp. 2112–2120. IEEE (2014)
54. Wang, B., Hou, Y., Li, M., Wang, H., Li, H.: Maple: scalable multi-dimensional range search over encrypted cloud data with tree-based index. In: Moriai, S., Jaeger, T., Sakurai, K. (eds.) ASIA CCS 2014, pp. 111–122. ACM (2014)
55. Williams, P., Sion, R.: Usable PIR. In: NDSS 2008. The Internet Society (2008)
56. Yang, Y., Liu, J.K., Liang, K., Choo, K.-K.R., Zhou, J.: Extended proxy-assisted approach: achieving revocable fine-grained encryption of cloud data. In: Pernul, G., Ryan, P.Y.A., Weippl, E. (eds.) ESORICS 2015. LNCS, vol. 9327, pp. 146–166. Springer, Cham (2015). doi:10.1007/978-3-319-24177-7_8
57. Yavuz, A.A., Guajardo, J.: Dynamic searchable symmetric encryption with minimal leakage and efficient updates on commodity hardware. In: Dunkelman, O., Keliher, L. (eds.) SAC 2015. LNCS, vol. 9566, pp. 241–259. Springer, Cham (2016). doi:10.1007/978-3-319-31301-6_15
58. Zhang, Y., Katz, J., Papamanthou, C.: All your queries are belong to us: the power of file-injection attacks on searchable encryption. In: USENIX Security 2016, pp. 707–720. USENIX Association (2016)

Cryptanalysis

Fault Attacks on XEX Mode with Application to Certain Authenticated Encryption Modes

Hassan Qahur Al Mahri[✉], Leonie Simpson, Harry Bartlett, Ed Dawson, and Kenneth Koon-Ho Wong

Queensland University of Technology, George Street, Brisbane 4000, Australia
hassan.mahri@hdr.qut.edu.au,
{lr.simpson,h.bartlett,e.dawson,kk.wong}@qut.edu.au

Abstract. The XOR-Encrypt-XOR (XEX) block cipher mode was introduced by Rogaway in 2004. XEX mode uses nonce-based secret masks (L) that are distinct for each message. The existence of secret masks in XEX mode prevents the application of conventional fault attack techniques, such as differential fault analysis. This work investigates other types of fault attacks against XEX mode that either eliminate the effect of the secret masks or retrieve their values. Either of these outcomes enables existing fault attack techniques to then be applied to recover the secret key. To estimate the success rate and feasibility, we ran simulations for ciphertext-only fault attacks against 128-bit AES in XEX mode. The paper discusses also the relevance of the proposed fault attacks to certain authenticated encryption modes based on XEX, such as OCB2, OTR, COPA, SHELL and ElmD. Finally, we suggest effective countermeasures to provide resistance to these fault attacks.

Keywords: Side channel analysis · Fault attack · Authenticated encryption · Block cipher mode · XEX

1 Introduction

In 2004, Rogaway [17] described a new block cipher mode called XOR-Encrypt-XOR (XEX) that can be used with any block cipher. XEX is a nonce-based mode in which each message uses a different nonce. A sequence of secret masks Δ_i (also known as offsets) is obtained from the encryption of the nonce. A different mask from this sequence is XOR-ed with each message block both before and after the underlying block cipher algorithm is applied. If the mode does not apply the last XOR operation with the secret mask, then it is called XE mode.

XEX/XE modes can be used to provide Authenticated Encryption (AE) (i.e. provide simultaneously confidentiality and integrity assurance) with the benefit that the plaintext message is processed only once. This is an attractive feature of AE modes. The drawback of such modes is that the security depends on both the key (K) and the mask (L); revealing either of them will breach the security of the AE mode as a whole [14,17].

© Springer International Publishing AG 2017
J. Pieprzyk and S. Suriadi (Eds.): ACISP 2017, Part I, LNCS 10342, pp. 285–305, 2017.
DOI: 10.1007/978-3-319-60055-0_15

Fault attacks [7] are active attacks that induce an error during the operation of a cryptographic system to extract information about internal values, such as the secret key or any secret variable. The first paper that used fault attacks against cryptographic protocols was published by Boneh et al. [7] to attack RSA. Since then, fault attacks have been widely used to attack many encryption schemes including DES [4] and AES [6,16].

Different physical means can be used to induce a fault into a cryptosystem, including supplying a voltage glitch, clock tampering, inducing a laser beam or radiating an electromagnetic field. The induced fault can flip a bit, skip the execution of an instruction or destroy a memory cell.

The most powerful fault analyses are Differential Fault Analysis (DFA) and Statistical Fault Analysis (SFA). Differential Fault Analysis [4] requires some input to be encrypted twice; with a fault being induced in the last rounds of the second run. After that, the difference between the correct and faulty ciphertexts is used to retrieve the secret key. On the other hand, SFA [12] does not require correct and faulty ciphertext pairs. It requires only a collection of faulty ciphertexts to recover the correct key. However, SFA is not directly applicable unless two conditions are met: the inputs to the block cipher are different from each other, and the faulty ciphertexts are the direct outputs of the block cipher [11].

In XEX mode, the nonce-based masks act as a barrier to conventional fault attack methods. For DFA where two identical block cipher inputs are required to produce a pair of correct/faulty ciphertexts, such as [4,5,22], XOR-ing different nonce-based masks with the plaintext blocks prevents this. For SFA where each block cipher output is XOR-ed with a different secret mask, we do not have direct access to the block cipher outputs. Thus, neither DFA nor SFA can be applied directly. This research is motivated by this fact.

To the best of our knowledge, the most relevant recent work investigating fault attacks on XEX-based modes is by Dobraunig et al. [11]. This work is significant as it demonstrated the practical relevance of statistical fault attacks introduced in [12] to authenticated encryption modes. The work targeted, amongst others, the XEX-based AE modes, such as OCB, OTR, COPA, SHELL and ElmD [3]. Fault attacks on XEX-based modes in [11] require access to parts of the mode where the block cipher output is either known or XOR-ed with a constant-based secret mask. These attacks are not applicable when the masks are not constant-based. The authors performed fault-injection experiments on three real hardware platforms. They showed that the key can be recovered with a couple of faulty ciphertexts. Note that all the listed XEX-based modes in [11] use constant-based masks with the exception of OCB. Although OCB uses nonce-based masks, the attack targeted the XE part, not the XEX part, where the output of the block cipher was accessible.

In this paper, we take a different approach by targeting the XEX part that uses nonce-based secret masks. We propose fault techniques to either skip the masking effect or retrieve the value of the secret mask L. In either case, conventional fault attack techniques [4,12] can then be used to recover the secret key. In the worst case, the entire key can be retrieved with a single additional fault as described in [1,15,18,21]. In addition, if XEX is used as an AE mode, an attacker can breach the AE security by constructing forged messages [14,17]. Unlike previous fault attacks on XEX-based modes, we stress that our approach targets the part of the mode where a direct application of existing fault attack techniques is not possible.

We ran several simulations on a PC to demonstrate the effectiveness of our attacks and to calculate their success rates. The simulations use 128-bit AES as the underlying block cipher operating in XEX mode. We did not perform hardware experiments in this work. However, we consider the fault models in this paper are well documented in the literature and have been shown to be practical in certain research papers, such as [2,19,20]; so can be applied as outlined in this paper.

We then investigated the applicability of our proposed techniques to certain authenticated encryption modes, including candidates in the ongoing CAESAR competition [3], such as COPA, ELmD, SHELL and OTR. Our attacks show that the masking function is a point of vulnerability. Hence, efficient alternative constructions for the mask updating function are suggested as countermeasures.

This paper is organised as follows: Sect. 2 defines the notation used and briefly describes the AES and XEX schemes. Section 3 describes an approach to eliminate the barrier posed by the nonce-based secret masks in XEX mode. The next section shows fault attacks on the last rounds of AES to retrieve the secret masks given ciphertext pairs only. Section 5 verifies the relevance of our proposed approaches to certain authenticated encryption modes and Sect. 6 investigates mechanisms to avoid the proposed fault attacks. The last section draws a conclusion. A practical example of a fault attack, experimental results and figures are presented in Appendices A, B and C respectively.

2   Preliminaries

2.1   Basic Notations

The following notation will be used consistently throughout this paper:

K	: k-bit key used for the block cipher and mask initialisation
n	: the block length in bits of the block cipher
N	: the nonce that is changed for each message
m	: the number of blocks in the plaintext message
$M[i]$	: the ith block in the plaintext message
$C[i]$	: the ith block in the corresponding ciphertext message
$E(.)$	: the block cipher encryption function under the key K
$s_{jk}^{i,(r),(o)}$	: the (j,k) byte in the encryption state of plaintext $M[i]$ after the operation o of round r where $j,k \in \{0,1,2,3\}$
$K_{jk}^{(r)}$	: the (j,k) byte in the subkey of round r where $j,k \in \{0,1,2,3\}$
L_{jk}	: the (j,k) byte in a nonce-based secret value where $j,k \in \{0,1,2,3\}$
sbox[.]	: the AES substitution box that replaces a byte by another byte
sbox^{-1}[.]	: the inverse of the sbox[.] operation
$|X|$	: the length of the string X in bits

$\text{msb}_c(X)$: the most significant c bits of X provided that $|X| \geq c$
$\ll$: logical left shift operation
$\gg$: logical right shift operation
$\wedge$: bitwise-and operation
$\oplus$: bitwise-exclusive-OR operation

2.2 AES Description

In this section, we briefly describe the Advanced Encryption Standard (AES), and refer the reader to [8] for more technical details.

AES is a 128-bit symmetric block cipher that allows three key sizes: 128-bit, 192-bit and 256-bit. AES is an iterated cipher that consists of a number of similar rounds. The number of rounds in AES is 10, 12 or 14 depending on the key size respectively. Each round in AES consists of four fundamental operations:

- **SubBytes** (SB): This operation is a non-linear substitution that replaces each byte in the internal state $s_{ij}^{(r),(o)}$ with another according to a fixed 8×8 s-box.
- **ShiftRow** (SR): This operation changes the order of bytes within the same state where certain bytes are shifted cyclically-left by a certain number of steps.
- **MixColumn** (MC): This is a linear transformation of the four bytes in each column of the state matrix.
- **AddRoundKey** (AK): The state matrix is combined with a round key by a bitwise XOR operation.

AES does not apply the MixColumn operation in the last round. The internal state after each operation for a plaintext block $M[i]$ is written as $s_{jk}^{i,(r),(o)}$ and organised as a matrix of 4×4 bytes where $0 \leq j < 4$ and $0 \leq k < 4$. For example, $s_{00}^{1,(9),(AK)}$ is the first byte of the encryption state of block $M[1]$ after AddRoundKey operation of round 9.

2.3 The Design of XEX Mode

Rogaway [17] introduced a mode of operation for block ciphers known as XEX. The underlying block cipher can be any symmetric block cipher. XEX mode is a nonce-based scheme where every plaintext message uses a different nonce (N). The nonce is encrypted to obtain a secret value $L = E(N)$. This secret value is used to obtain a sequence of secret masks $\{\Delta_i\}$ so that Δ_i is used during the processing of the ith message block $M[i]$. For efficiency of implementation, every new mask Δ_{i+1} should be easily calculated from the previous one Δ_i. XEX mode uses a single key for both the block encryption operation and initialisation of the sequence of masking values.

In the example proposed in [17], Rogaway suggests a doubling masking technique, where new masks are obtained as $\Delta_{i+1} = 2\Delta_i$. If Δ_0 starts with L, the doubling masking technique results in a series of masking values: $L, 2L, 2^2L, 2^3L$, $\dots, 2^{m-1}L$. Each message block uses a different mask that is XOR-ed both before and after the underlying block cipher algorithm is applied, as shown in Fig. 1(a).

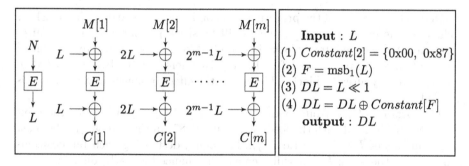

Fig. 1. (a) The most common masking of XEX mode. (b) timing-resistant implementation of doubling masking technique.

The mask multiplication is performed in the finite field $\mathbb{F}_{2^n}$ by multiplying two input polynomials and finding the reminder modulo a primitive polynomial. When $n = 128$ and the finite field $\mathbb{F}_{2^{128}}$ is constructed using the commonly used primitive polynomial $f(x) = x^{128} + x^7 + x^2 + x + 1$, the doubling is as follows:

$$2L = \begin{cases} L \ll 1 & \text{if } \mathrm{msb}_1(L) = 0 \\ (L \ll 1) \oplus 0^{120}10000111 & \text{if } \mathrm{msb}_1(L) = 1 \end{cases} \quad (1)$$

and can be calculated as shown in Fig. 1(b). We note that this choice of finite field is used in Rogaway's paper [17] and has also been adopted in other designs such as COPA, ELmD, SHELL and OTR.

3   Eliminating the Masks in XEX Mode

This section presents two approaches to eliminate the effect of the secret masks, effectively converting the XEX mode to ECB mode.

3.1   Stuck-At-Zero Fault Attack

The duration of an injected fault can be permanent or transient. Permanent fault means that certain bits are disturbed permanently for the entire operation of a hardware platform, whereas transient faults change the value of certain bits temporarily. In addition to duration, the location of a fault can be either precise: affecting a certain bit in an internal register, or random.

Our fault model assumes that the fault will occur in a j-bit block anywhere in the secret mask register L except the last byte. The fault clears the block permanently, and could be performed using any practical physical means. That is, the j-bit in L, where $0 \leq j \leq 120$, will be stuck at 'zero' value permanently. We consider this fault model to be feasible using sophisticated technology, such as laser fault injection system and note that several research papers adopt this fault model (see fault attacks against AES in [6] and ACORN in [10]).

Due to the features of the primitive polynomial used in the doubling masking technique, the entire masking value L will be stuck permanently at zero after only a few faulted plaintext blocks in a multi-block message. If only one bit of L is faulted, L will reach zero after 128 blocks whereas if one byte is faulted, L will be zero only after 16 blocks. Therefore, the effect of masks in XEX mode is avoided.

The location of the j-bits cannot be between $121 \le j \le 127$ since these bit positions are XOR-ed with the feedback value (0x87) in the case where the most significant bit of L is 1 (see Eq. (1)). Therefore, destroying such bit positions will not zero the mask L, but will increase the chance for mask collision.

Assuming a permanent fault is not necessary, the attacker can inject transient stuck-at-zero faults. This fault model has been shown to be feasible using low-budget equipment in [20]. The attacker can force certain bits of L to be 0 for few consecutive blocks. In case a byte is faulted, 16 consecutive set-to-zero faults are required to be induced to any of the first 15 bytes of L.

3.2   Skipping an Instruction Fault Attack

Assuming transient/permanent stuck-at-zero faults are not applicable or consume more time/cost, L can also be overcome in software implementations using a more efficient and easy to set-up fault model. L can be overcome using skipping an instruction, i.e. an instruction is not executed. An instruction can be skipped by applying glitch attacks [6]. This fault model was investigated and proved practical in [19].

One way to eliminate the effect of masks in XEX mode is to skip the execution of instruction (2) in Fig. 1(b) for 128 consecutive blocks. This step will cause the doubling mechanism to always choose $double[0]$ and not $double[1]$ provided that the value of F is zero before the fault injections. Thus after 128 blocks, the entire 128-bit L will be zero and L will be stuck to zero during the processing of all following blocks.

The chance that F is 0 before a fault injection is 50%. In case F was 1, we can repeat the attack a second time with another set of 128 consecutive blocks, but now with a better chance that this carry flag F is zero.

Another more effective way to overcome the masks is to omit the execution of instruction (4) (see Fig. 1(b)) for 128 consecutive blocks, regardless of the value of the carry flag F, as in the previous approach. This approach guarantees that the mask L will be stuck at a value of zero for all following plaintext blocks.

Note that this approach is implementation-dependant. That is, the attacker needs to have knowledge of the implementation to successfully overcome L.

3.3   Security Implication for Mask Elimination

Forcing the masks in XEX mode to zero reduces XEX mode to ECB mode. As a result, if the mode is used as an AE mode, this will enable attackers to breach the integrity assurance mechanism of the mode. In addition, the secret key can be recovered using additional faults. One extra fault injection can completely recover the key as described in [1,15,18,21].

These proposed fault attacks are easy and efficient due to the particular form of the primitive polynomial used to define the finite field. Since the polynomial is sparse and the feedback path is from bits all located in the final byte of L, the attacks work effectively. This work demonstrates the weakness of this commonly used polynomial with respect to fault attacks. Section 6 suggests different primitive polynomials that avoid these fault attacks.

4   A Ciphertext only Attack to Reveal Secret Mask L

In this section, we describe an approach to obtain the value of L under the stricter requirement of using ciphertext blocks only. For this section, we consider AES as the underlying block cipher used in XEX mode.

The challenge with attacking AES in XEX mode rather than the ECB mode is that the block cipher output is XOR-ed with a mask prior to generating the ciphertext. That is, the attacker does not have direct access to the output of the encryption. In addition, masks are guaranteed to be different from each other. A ciphertext-only statistical fault attack has been used previously to determine the secret key in AES encryption [12], but this attack requires a collection of ciphertext bytes that share the same subkey byte. Therefore, the statistical fault attack cannot be applied directly to obtain the secret key from AES in XEX mode. We show, however, that the relationship between the masks used in the doubling masking mechanism enables us to adapt this attack to reveal the initial mask value L. From this, it is then straightforward to find the secret key, completely breaking the security of the cipher. In fact, we note that the key bits can be determined using the same ciphertext bytes used to reveal the mask L.

As a first step toward retrieving L, we collect several masks that share certain mask bytes only. From Eq. (1) and Fig. 1(b), we note that the doubling operation used in XEX mode causes the secret mask $L = (L_{00}, L_{01}, ..., L_{33})$ to shift by one bit to the left for each block in the message. Moreover, we note that the only bits of L that are potentially changed in this process are those in the final byte, L_{33}, of L. Thus, after eight shifts, all of the bytes in the original mask L - except for L_{00} and L_{33} - will appear again in $2^8 L$, but shifted a whole byte to the left. Likewise, all but three bytes of L will appear in $2^{16} L$ and the original byte L_{32} appears a total of fifteen times as:

$$\left\{ \begin{array}{l} L_{32}, (2^8 L)_{31}, (2^{16} L)_{30}, (2^{24} L)_{23}, (2^{32} L)_{22}, (2^{40} L)_{21}, (2^{48} L)_{20}, (2^{56} L)_{13}, \\ (2^{64} L)_{12}, (2^{72} L)_{11}, (2^{80} L)_{10}, (2^{88} L)_{03}, (2^{96} L)_{02}, (2^{104} L)_{01}, (2^{112} L)_{00} \end{array} \right\}$$

before being shifted out of L. In addition, Eq. (1) can be used to show that:

- there is a one-to-one relation between the values of $(2^8 L)_{33}$ and L_{00}.
- the value of $(2^8 L)_{32}$ depends only on L_{00} and L_{33} such that L_{33} can be determined uniquely from L_{00} and $(2^8 L)_{32}$.

The first of these results effectively gives us a sixteenth copy of L_{32} from the mask byte $(2^{120}L)_{33}$. In total (for a sufficiently long message), we can have up to sixteen copies of L_{32}, as shown in Fig. 3 in Appendix C. (We have denoted $(2^{120}L)_{33}$ as L'_{32} in this figure.)

In some situations, 16 repetitions of the same byte are not sufficient to determine the byte's value with high probability. One way to overcome this problem is to increase the number of repetitions by using two bytes rather than one. For example, if we use the byte L_{32} and the byte $(2^8 L)_{32}$, then each byte will repeat 16 times. In addition to these 32 repetitions, we can calculate the value of the byte $(2^{128}L)_{32}$ since we know both $(2^{120}L)_{33}$ and $(2^{120}L)_{00}$. This new byte $(2^{128}L)_{32}$ will also repeat another 16 times. In summary, each of the two bytes L_{32} and $(2^8 L)_{32}$ will repeat 16 times and the combination of the two will repeat 16 more times. At the end, we have 48 occurrences depending only on 16 bits. The same concept applies if we take three bytes or more. In the case of three bytes (24 bits), we can have 96 repetitions in total.

In the following experiments, we consider two fault models as in [12]. The first model (we refer as fault model A) assumes that the attacker has a perfect control on the faulty byte. The fault induces a constant value. The second fault model (fault model B) assumes that the injected fault causes a bias to the targeted byte. Let e be error uniformly distributed in $[0, 255]$. The two fault models are as follows:

A. *Stuck-at-zero* with probability 1:

$$s_{jk}^{i,(r),(o)} \quad = \quad s_{jk}^{i,(r),(o)} \quad \text{AND} \quad 0 \quad \text{with probability 1.}$$

B. *Stuck-at-zero* with probability 1/2:

$$s_{jk}^{i,(r),(o)} \quad = \quad \begin{cases} s_{jk}^{i,(r),(o)} \quad \text{AND} \quad 0 \quad \text{with probability} \quad 1/2 \\ s_{jk}^{i,(r),(o)} \quad \text{AND} \quad e \quad \text{with probability} \quad 1/2 \end{cases}$$

We will apply a fault attack to the internal state s at rounds 8 and 9 of the AES encryption operation. As addressed in [2], these fault models are possible, but for accurate value/location fault injections, high technical skills and high cost might be needed. However, [2] emphasises that the inability to inject only the desired fault does not imply the inability to induce the fault. In either case, our paper outlines the vulnerability of the XEX mode if these faults are possible.

4.1   Fault Model A at Round 9

Suppose that a fault is injected on a certain byte at the end of round 9 $(s_{jk}^{i,(9),(AK)})$. For example, a fault is induced on the byte $s_{00}^{i,(9),(AK)}$ for the first and second plaintext blocks $(i \in \{1, 2\})$ as shown in Fig. 4 in Appendix C.

The injected faults cause the two specified bytes to take a constant value. The faulty bytes will be identical during propagation in the SubBytes, ShiftRow and AddRoundKey operations of round 10 as follows:

$$s_{00}^{1,(10),(SR)} = s_{00}^{1,(10),(SB)} = \text{sbox}[s_{00}^{1,(9),(AK)}]$$

$$s_{00}^{2,(10),(SR)} = s_{00}^{2,(10),(SB)} = \text{sbox}[s_{00}^{2,(9),(AK)}]$$

$$C[1]_{00} = s_{00}^{1,(10),(SR)} \oplus K_{00}^{10} \oplus L_{00}$$

$$C[2]_{00} = s_{00}^{2,(10),(SR)} \oplus K_{00}^{10} \oplus (2L)_{00}$$

$$C[1]_{00} \oplus C[2]_{00} = L_{00} \oplus (2L)_{00} = (3L)_{00}$$

When we XOR $C[1]_{00}$ and $C[2]_{00}$, the two bytes $s_{00}^{1,(10),(SR)}$ and $s_{00}^{2,(10),(SR)}$ cancel each other since they are identical, and we obtain the value of $(3L)_{00}$. Note that our attack is based on the XOR of two consecutive blocks to obtain $(3L)_{00}$ and there is no need to find the subkey byte (K_{00}^{10}).

Repeating the above experiment for blocks $i \in \{9, 10\}$ will retrieve the byte $(2^8 L)_{00} \oplus (2^9 L)_{00} = (2^8 3L)_{00}$ which is equivalent to $(3L)_{01}$ (the second byte of $3L$). Similarly, block $i \in \{17, 18\}$ will enable us to determine the third byte of $3L$, and so on. Thus, by inducing faults in 32 blocks of a cipher in XEX mode we can retrieve the whole $3L$ mask, and consequently, we can easily obtain the original mask L. (To determine the final byte $(3L)_{33}$ it is necessary to adjust for the known value of $(3L)_{00}$.)

4.2 Fault Model A at Round 8

Assume that the fault is injected on a full diagonal at the end of round 8. For example, we inject a fault to the state $s_{jk}^{i,(8),(AK)}$ where $i \in \{1, 2\}$ as shown in Fig. 5 in Appendix C. The diagonal consists of four bytes that can have jk indexes as: $\{00, 11, 22, 33\}$, $\{01, 12, 23, 30\}$, $\{02, 13, 20, 31\}$ or $\{03, 10, 21, 32\}$. Injecting faults to a full diagonal seems infeasible; however, in software implementation running on 32-bit CPUs, a fault to one instruction can distribute to four bytes (see for example [9]).

In this case, we have one MixColumn operation. Hence, we need to know one full column of the internal state in order to reverse the MixColumn operation. Again the injected faults make the four bytes in the diagonal a constant value and they will remain identical through round 9 and 10. XOR-ing the ciphertext blocks will retrieve four bytes of $3L$ mask. For instance, if faults are injected into the diagonal $\{00, 11, 22, 33\}$, then the bytes $\{(3L)_{00}, (3L)_{13}, (3L)_{22}, (3L)_{31}\}$ will be retrieved.

Repeating the experiment with another faulty diagonal for plaintext blocks $i \in \{9, 10\}$, will retrieve four bytes of the mask $2^8(3L)$. However, note that these retrieved bytes are each shifted one byte to the left of the bytes in the mask $3L$. Hence, four diagonal fault injections can retrieve the original mask L completely. That is, in total, we need 8 faulty blocks where each block has a faulty diagonal.

4.3 Fault Model B at Round 9

Unlike fault model A, the fault induced by fault model B does not give a fixed output. Thus, we need to collect several faulty bytes that share the same mask byte and apply a statistical fault analysis with a distinguisher in order to predict the correct value for this mask byte from all possible hypothetical values. As discussed in Sect. 4, with reference to Fig. 3 in Appendix C, the position of the target byte will move through the various locations in the mask $2^{i-1}L$ as subsequent blocks of the message are processed, so we will need to fault different bytes of the AES encryption operation for different message blocks. For our attack, we will use the hamming weight distinguisher, which chooses the hypothetical mask value that minimises the average hamming weight for the faulty stuck bytes.

Retrieving One Byte. As in Sects. 4.1 and 4.2, we aim to obtain information on the content of the mask $2^i 3L$. If we retrieve $2^i 3L$ completely, then we can easily calculate the original mask L.

Suppose that a fault is injected on a certain byte at the end of round 9 $(s_{jk}^{i,(9),(AK)})$. The byte index (jk) will vary depending on the value of the block index (i). The attack is performed in four steps as follows:

1. Collect ciphertext bytes that share two mask bytes $\{(2^i L)_{32}, (2^{i+8}L)_{32}\}$. At the beginning of Sect. 4 we have seen that a maximum of 48 faulty ciphertext bytes can be collected that share two mask bytes.
2. Collect another 48 faulty ciphertext bytes that share two mask bytes $\{(2^{i+1}L)_{32}, (2^{i+9}L)_{32}\}$ from blocks consecutive to the blocks in step 1. The index of each faulty byte in the first set is the same as the index of the corresponding faulty byte in the second set.
3. XOR the two faulty ciphertext bytes in each pair from consecutive blocks to eliminate the shared subkey byte and obtain only two mask bytes $\{(2^i 3L)_{32}, (2^{i+8}3L)_{32}\}$, and their continued mask $\{(2^{i+128}3L)_{32}\}$.
4. Use the hamming weight distinguisher to predict the correct value for $\{(2^i 3L)_{32}, (2^{i+8}3L)_{32}\}$ and their continued mask $\{(2^{i+128}3L)_{32}\}$ from 2^{16} possible candidates.

An example of this process is presented in greater detail in Appendix A.

Retrieving All Bytes. Extending this attack to determine the remaining mask bytes requires careful manipulation of the fault injections. The timing of consecutive fault injections is critical to the success of the attack. If the process to recover a byte after a fault injection is still in progress, injecting a subsequent fault will cause multiple faults in the internal state. This makes the attack impractical. However, allowing a delay after recovering the first byte before injecting the subsequent fault results in the first retrieved mask byte being shifted out of the internal state. The retrieved byte is no longer useful.

All of the bytes in a mask can be obtained by performing fifteen consecutive iterations of fault injections with the appropriate timing as discussed above. This means that any internal state contains at most two faulty bytes. Most modern devices come with 16-bit or 32-bits registers which makes faulting two bytes at a time feasible. This approach is discussed in detail at the end of Appendix A.

We simulate the proposed fault attacks in Sect. 4.3 using 128-bit AES. The attacks are developed in C on a standard desktop computer. We compute the success rate over 1000 iterations using different plaintext messages and nonces. We find that 96 faulty ciphertext bytes are enough to allow one byte in the secret mask to be retrieved with a success rate of 99.9%. Under the same conditions, the attack can be extended to recover the entire 128-bit secret mask with a success rate of 99.2%. For details of these simulations refer to Appendix B.

5 Application to Authenticated Encryption Modes

We examined AE schemes that use the doubling masking technique including the candidates of the ongoing CAESAR competition: OTR, COPA, ELmD and SHELL; and other AE modes, such as ISO 19772 OCB2 [17]. All of these AE block cipher modes use the masking technique of XEX/XE mode.

A summary of the relevance of our techniques against the secret masks in these authenticated encryption modes is presented in Table. 1. The ($\checkmark$) mark indicates that the fault attack technique in the corresponding section of our paper can be applied to the mode, whereas the ($\times$) mark indicates that our technique can not be applied. Note that attacks in Sect. 4 cannot be applied to OTR as OTR is XE-based and not XEX-based.

The ($*$) symbol in Table. 1 indicates that the secret mask in these modes can be retrieved more effectively by direct application of SFA [11] than our technique in Sect. 4 since the masks are constant-based. Note that our attack is directly applicable to OCB2 whereas attacks in [11] are not.

Table 1. Summary of our attacks on secret masks in certain AE modes.

AE mode	Classification	Mask type	Our fault attack technique	
			Sect. 3	Sect. 4
COPA	XEX	Constant-based	$\checkmark$	$\checkmark^*$
ELmD	XEX	Constant-based	$\checkmark$	$\checkmark^*$
SHELL	XEX	Constant-based	$\checkmark$	$\checkmark^*$
OCB2	XEX	Nonce-based	$\checkmark$	$\checkmark$
OTR	XE	Nonce-based	$\checkmark$	$\times$

6 Countermeasures

The success of the fault attacks we have presented depends on the properties of the primitive polynomial used to construct the finite field for updating mask values in XEX mode. The polynomial used in Sect. 2.3 (also adopted by OCB2, COPA, ELmD, SHELL and OTR) is sparse and the feedback is obtained only from bits located in the final byte. Changing the mask updating function is one approach to prevent our attacks. We outline two alternative techniques for the mask updating function so that the proposed attack are not applicable.

The technique in the CAESAR candidate, OCB3, is an alternative option for updating masks which makes our attacks irrelevant. In OCB3 [13], although OCB3 still uses the doubling mechanism, masks depend on an index and each mask is XOR-ed with the prior one which prevents the repetition of mask bytes.

Another approach to preclude our attacks is to use a different function for incrementing masks. Krovetz and Rogaway [13] investigate several maximal 128-bit Linear Feedback Shift Registers (LFSRs); their internal states could be used as secret masks. An example of an efficient maximal LFSRs that has performance comparable to the doubling masking is:

$$S(X, Y) = (Y, (X \ll 1) \oplus (X \gg 1) \oplus (Y \wedge 148))$$

where $|X| = |Y| = 64$. This LFSR does not include the most significant bit of the previous mask to increment the next one and does not allow repetition of mask bytes. Thus, using this LFSR for incrementing masks will avoid our attack.

7   Conclusion

The masking technique in XEX mode acts as a barrier to the fault attack methods commonly used to recover the secret key of the underlying block cipher. This paper presented different fault attack techniques against the generic XEX mode for block ciphers by targeting the secret masks used.

Firstly, we demonstrated three fault attack methods that convert XEX mode into ECB mode by forcing the secret mask L to zero. Injecting a permanent fault into a bit (or a byte) anywhere in the register containing the secret mask L, except for the final byte, will overcome the masking barrier after only 128 (resp. 16) blocks. This can also be achieved using transient faults on a few consecutive message blocks. For software implementations of XEX mode, we demonstrated that L can be eliminated through skipping instruction faults.

Secondly, instead of eliminating L, we provided a detailed ciphertext-only attack to retrieve L. The polynomial used in the doubling masking technique allows repetition of mask bytes. We used SFA with a collection of faulty ciphertext blocks to retrieve L bytes. Finding the secret mask enables retrieving the key using the same faulty blocks.

Thirdly, we verified the ciphertext-only attacks to retrieve L through simulations. In the case of fault model B, we found that the success rate of retrieving one byte of L is 99.9%, and that of retrieving the entire mask is 99.2%.

In addition, we identified certain authenticated encryption modes that are susceptible to our proposed fault attack techniques. These modes all used XEX with a primitive polynomial that makes them vulnerable to our attack.

Our work demonstrates that it is the mask updating function that makes XEX vulnerable to these fault attacks. Hence, an efficient solution to preclude these attacks is to change this primitive polynomial used for updating the mask.

Appendix A: Practical Example for a Fault Attack Using Fault Model B

Retrieving One Byte. We demonstrate the fault attack in Sect. 4.3 with the following example:

Steps [1–2]. We first collect ($2 \times 48 = 96$) faulty bytes in which 48 bytes share the two mask bytes $\{L_{32}, (2^8 L)_{32}\}$, and the other 48 bytes share their consecutive mask bytes $\{(2L)_{32}, (2^9 L)_{32}\}$. These 96 bytes can be obtained using three sets: A, B and G, where each set contains 32 consecutive blocks (see Fig. 6). Set A shares the two mask bytes $\{L_{32}, (2L)_{32}\}$, set B shares $\{(2^8 L)_{32}, (2^9 L)_{32}\}$ and set G shares $\{(2^{128} L)_{32}, (2^{129} L)_{32}\}$. Remember that the mask bytes $(2^{128} L)_{32}$ and $(2^{129} L)_{32}$ are continued masks of $\{L_{32}, (2^8 L)_{32}\}$ and $\{2L_{32}, (2^9 L)_{32}\}$ respectively.

The targeted block indexes in each set are:

Set A:

$$i \in \left\{ \begin{array}{l} 1, 9, 17, 25, 33, 41, 49, 57, 65, 73, 81, 89, 97, 105, 113, 121, \\ 2, 10, 18, 26, 34, 42, 50, 58, 66, 74, 82, 90, 98, 106, 114, 122 \end{array} \right\}$$

Set B:

$$i \in \left\{ \begin{array}{l} 9, 17, 25, 33, 41, 49, 57, 65, 73, 81, 89, 97, 105, 113, 121, 129, \\ 10, 18, 26, 34, 42, 50, 58, 66, 74, 82, 90, 98, 106, 114, 122, 130 \end{array} \right\}$$

Set G:

$$i \in \left\{ \begin{array}{l} 129, 137, 145, 153, 161, 169, 177, 185, 193, 201, 209, 217, 225, 233, 241, 249 \\ 130, 138, 146, 154, 162, 170, 178, 186, 194, 202, 210, 218, 226, 234, 242, 250 \end{array} \right\}$$

The index (jk) of the faulty ciphertext byte corresponds to each block in every row of all sets A, B and G is:

$$jk \in \left\{ 32, 31, 30, 23, 22, 21, 20, 13, 12, 11, 10, 03, 02, 01, 00, 33 \right\}$$

However, to target each ciphertext byte, we inject a fault to its corresponding internal state byte $s_{jk'}^{i,(9),(AK)}$ where $k' = (k + j) \mod 4$. The faulty ciphertext byte indexes are not the same as the targeted internal byte indexes because of the last ShiftRow operation.

Step 3. XOR-ing two ciphertext bytes of the same index jk from two consecutive blocks will give the following result:

$$
\begin{aligned}
C[i+1]_{jk} &= s_{jk}^{i+1,(10),(SR)} \oplus K_{jk}^{10} \oplus 2^i L_{jk} \\
&= 2^i L_{jk} \oplus K_{jk}^{10} \oplus s_{jk'}^{i+1,(10),(SB)} \\
&= 2^i L_{jk} \oplus K_{jk}^{10} \oplus \mathrm{sbox}[s_{jk'}^{i+1,(9),(AK)}] \\
C[i+2]_{jk} &= 2^{i+1} L_{jk} \oplus K_{jk}^{10} \oplus \mathrm{sbox}[s_{jk'}^{i+2,(9),(AK)}] \\
C[i+1]_{jk} \oplus C[i+2]_{jk} &= (2^i 3L)_{jk} \oplus \mathrm{sbox}[s_{jk'}^{i+1,(9),(AK)}] \oplus \mathrm{sbox}[s_{jk'}^{i+2,(9),(AK)}]
\end{aligned}
$$

where $k' = (k+j) \mod 4$. We calculate the value of $(C[i+1]_{jk} \oplus C[i+2]_{jk})$ from every two consecutive blocks in each set. This yields the following equations:

Set A:

$$C[i+1]_{jk} \oplus C[i+2]_{jk} = (3L)_{32} \oplus \mathrm{sbox}[s_{jk'}^{i+1,(9),(AK)}] \oplus \mathrm{sbox}[s_{jk'}^{i+2,(9),(AK)}]$$

Set B:

$$C[i+1]_{jk} \oplus C[i+2]_{jk} = (2^8 3L)_{32} \oplus \mathrm{sbox}[s_{jk'}^{i+1,(9),(AK)}] \oplus \mathrm{sbox}[s_{jk'}^{i+2,(9),(AK)}]$$

Set G:

$$C[i+1]_{jk} \oplus C[i+2]_{jk} = (2^{128} 3L)_{32} \oplus \mathrm{sbox}[s_{jk'}^{i+1,(9),(AK)}] \oplus \mathrm{sbox}[s_{jk'}^{i+2,(9),(AK)}]$$

where the value of $(2^{128} 3L)_{32}$ is uniquely determined by the values of $(3L)_{32}$ and $(2^8 3L)_{32}$, as discussed previously. Each set gives 16 values for $(C[i+1]_{jk} \oplus C[i+2]_{jk})$, and in total 48 values.

The sbox in AES is resistant against differential analysis. Thus, knowing the XOR of $\mathrm{sbox}[s_{jk'}^{i+1,(9),(AK)}]$ and $\mathrm{sbox}[s_{jk'}^{i+2,(9),(AK)}]$ neither uniquely determines $s_{jk'}^{i+1,(9),(AK)}$ nor $s_{jk'}^{i+2,(9),(AK)}$. However, the injected faults will bias the faulty internal bytes to the all-zero byte. We, therefore, proceed by assuming that one of the faulty bytes is zero, namely that $s_{jk'}^{i+2,(9),(AK)} = 0$. This assumption is valid 50% of the time only. We then apply our statistical distinguisher to the value of $s_{jk'}^{i+1,(9),(AK)}$ that is determined by this assumption.

Step 4. For each of the 2^{16} candidates for $(3L)_{32}$ and $(2^8 3L)_{32}$, compute the value for $s_{jk'}^{i+1,(9),(AK)}$ in sets A, B and G. By completing this step, we will have 48 values for $s_{jk'}^{i+1,(9),(AK)}$ for each of the 2^{16} candidates. Use the hamming weight distinguisher to predict the correct value for $(3L)_{32}$ and $(2^8 3L)_{32}$ and their continued mask $(2^{128} 3L)_{32}$.

Retrieving All Bytes. This attack requires a message of at least 3722 full blocks encrypted using 128-bit AES in XEX mode. Note that this attack does not require all the 3722 blocks to be faulted. The steps to retrieve the entire mask L (see Fig. 7 in Appendix C) are as follows:

1. For blocks ($1 \leq i \leq 250$), perform the fault attack, as in Sect. 4.3 and the example at the beginning of this appendix, on certain blocks (shown as orange bytes in Fig. 7) to retrieve the two mask bytes $\{(3L)_{32}, (2^8 3L)_{32}\}$ and their continued byte $(2^{128} 3L)_{32}$.
   Note that the byte $(2^{128} 3L)_{32}$ continues to appear as $(2^{136} 3L)_{31}$, $\cdots$, $(2^{240} 3L)_{00}$, $(2^{248} 3L)_{33}$.
2. For blocks $(1 + 248j) \leq i \leq (250 + 248j)$ where $j \in \{1, \ldots, 15\}$, perform the same attack in step 1. Each iteration is shown in Fig. 7 as successive coloured bytes as yellow, blue, pink, $\ldots$, lime.
   Each iteration retrieves extra bytes and starts just after the previous one.

3. Work backwards to calculate the mask bytes and begin with the last faulty block (shown as lime in Fig. 7). Use Eq. (1) during the transition from one iteration of faults to the previous iteration. For example, we can calculate $(2^{3464}3L)_{33}$ (grey byte) from $(2^{3464}3L)_{00}$ (pink byte) and $(2^{3472}3L)_{32}$ (lime byte). That is, the byte retrieved in the last iteration is not lost.
4. Repeat this approach working backward every 250-block iteration until we retrieve the entire $2^{128}3L$.
   Note that any internal state contains at most two faulty bytes.
5. Compute the original mask L from $2^{128}3L$ using the primitive polynomial.

Appendix B: Experimental Results

We ran a simulated experiment to retrieve one byte of a secret mask given faulty ciphertexts only and using the attack method in Sect. 4.3 cis extended to retrieve the entire L mask. The experiment uses 128-bit AES as the underlying block cipher. We implemented this using the C language and the GNU GCC compiler run on a desktop computer.

To simulate fault model B, we used the pseudo-random C function $rand()$ and the AES with different input messages to determine when the fault should occur. In either case, we used one bit of the output to determine when the stuck-at-zero action occurs. These generated faults are injected to AES in XEX mode.

Retrieving One Byte. As a preliminary step, we performed several sub-experiments with different numbers of faulty bytes to determine how many faulty bytes are needed to obtain a high success rate. We started with 2 faulty bytes that share one mask byte and increase by 2 for every following iteration till the number of faulty bytes is 32 such that every targeted block has only one faulty byte. For each iteration, we computed the success rate over 1000 simulations using different plaintext messages and nonces. We performed these experiments twice: one run uses faults generated from the $rand()$ function and the second uses faults from the output of AES in XEX mode.

Secondly, we computed the success rate for the attack using 96 faulty bytes, as described in Sect. 4.3 and Appendix A. This approach provides the hamming weight distinguisher with 48 faulty bytes that share only two mask bytes.

The results of this experiment are presented in Table 2 for the number of faulty bytes ranging from 2 to 32 and lastly 96. Note that the success rates in both columns are close to each other. Note also that only the last row provides a high success rate of at least 99.9%.

Finally, we evaluated the success rate to retrieve one mask byte considering a more relaxed injection probabilities (p) to bias the faulty byte towards zero. Figure 2 compares the success rate and data complexity for $p \in \{0.5, 0.375, 0.25\}$. Note that the success rate is about 0.96 when $p = 0.5$ and about 0.87 when $p = 0.375$ in case of (1 faulty byte/block), and these probabilities increase to

Table 2. Success rate of fault attacks using fault model B at round 9.

Number of faulty bytes	Success Rate (1000 iterations) *rand()* as PRF	Success Rate (1000 iterations) AES as PRF
2	0.280	0.289
4	0.233	0.238
6	0.405	0.377
8	0.467	0.472
10	0.528	0.556
12	0.637	0.631
14	0.673	0.703
16	0.753	0.744
18	0.787	0.790
20	0.821	0.839
22	0.873	0.861
24	0.885	0.888
26	0.909	0.901
28	0.930	0.929
30	0.940	0.936
32	0.957	0.956
96	0.999	0.999

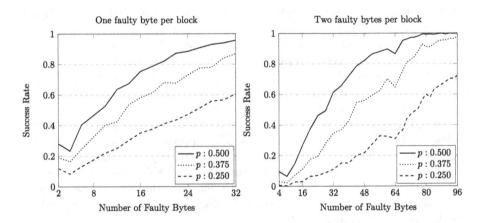

Fig. 2. Success rate to determine one mask byte for different probabilities.

0.999 and 0.975 respectively in case of (2 faulty bytes/block). That is, for low injection probabilities, if an attacker is able to fault more bytes per block, the success rate will increase.

Retrieve the Whole Mask. We performed an experiment to demonstrate the success rate of retrieving the entire secret mask $2^{128}3L$ as discussed in Sect. 4.3 and Appendix A. Each byte is retrieved using 96 faulty bytes. The success rate is also computed over 1000 different plaintext messages each of length 3722 blocks and each with a different nonce. We found that the success rate to retrieve every bit in the mask $2^{2144}3L$ is 99.2% when using AES as the pseudo-random function, and 99.3% when using the *rand()* function.

Appendix C: Figures

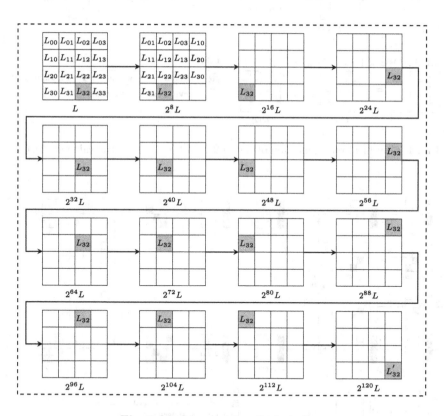

Fig. 3. Masks containing the byte L_{32}.

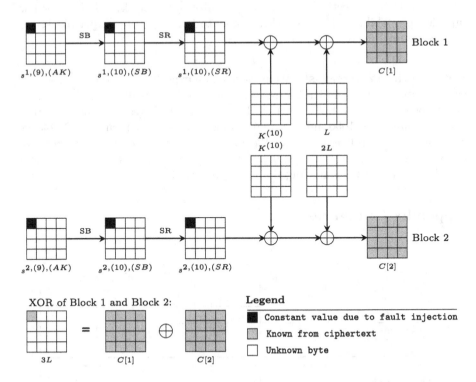

Fig. 4. Graphical representation of round 9 attack to retrieve the value of $(3L)_{00}$.

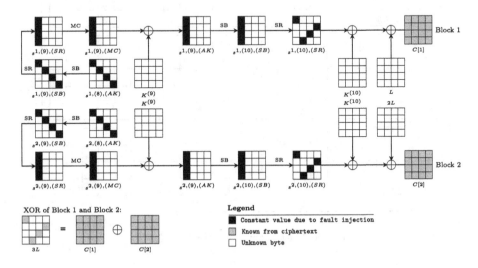

Fig. 5. Graphical representation of round 8 attack to retrieve four bytes in L.

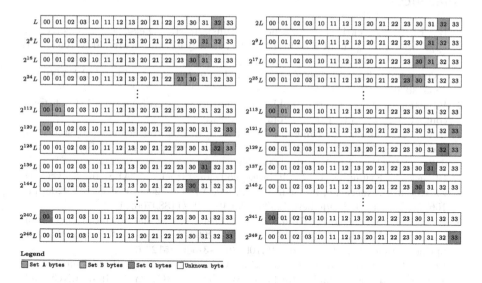

Fig. 6. Mask bytes targeted according to the position of faulty bytes.

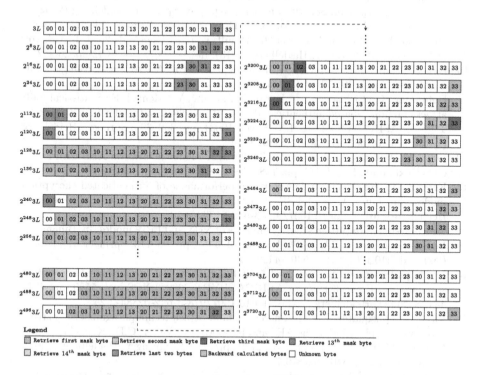

Fig. 7. Technique to retrieve all bytes of $2^{128}3L$. (Color figure online)

References

1. Bar-El, H., Choukri, H., Naccache, D., Tunstall, M., Whelan, C.: The sorcerer's apprentice guide to fault attacks. IACR Cryptology ePrint Archive 2004, 100 (2004)
2. Barenghi, A., Breveglieri, L., Koren, I., Naccache, D.: Fault injection attacks on cryptographic devices: theory, practice, and countermeasures. Proc. IEEE **100**(11), 3056–3076 (2012)
3. Bernstein, D.J.: Cryptographic competitions: CAESAR (2014). http://competitions.cr.yp.to/caesar-submissions.html
4. Biham, E., Shamir, A.: Differential fault analysis of secret key cryptosystems. In: Kaliski, B.S. (ed.) CRYPTO 1997. LNCS, vol. 1294, pp. 513–525. Springer, Heidelberg (1997). doi:10.1007/BFb0052259
5. Blömer, J., Krummel, V.: Fault based collision attacks on AES. In: Breveglieri, L., Koren, I., Naccache, D., Seifert, J.-P. (eds.) FDTC 2006. LNCS, vol. 4236, pp. 106–120. Springer, Heidelberg (2006). doi:10.1007/11889700_11
6. Blömer, J., Seifert, J.-P.: Fault based cryptanalysis of the advanced encryption standard (AES). In: Wright, R.N. (ed.) FC 2003. LNCS, vol. 2742, pp. 162–181. Springer, Heidelberg (2003). doi:10.1007/978-3-540-45126-6_12
7. Boneh, D., DeMillo, R.A., Lipton, R.J.: On the importance of checking cryptographic protocols for faults. In: Fumy, W. (ed.) EUROCRYPT 1997. LNCS, vol. 1233, pp. 37–51. Springer, Heidelberg (1997). doi:10.1007/3-540-69053-0_4
8. Daemen, J., Rijmen, V.: The Design of Rijndael: AES - The Advanced Encryption Standard. Information Security and Cryptography. Springer, Heidelberg (2002)
9. Dehbaoui, A., Mirbaha, A.-P., Moro, N., Dutertre, J.-M., Tria, A.: Electromagnetic glitch on the AES round counter. In: Prouff, E. (ed.) COSADE 2013. LNCS, vol. 7864, pp. 17–31. Springer, Heidelberg (2013). doi:10.1007/978-3-642-40026-1_2
10. Dey, P., Rohit, R.S., Adhikari, A.: Full key recovery of ACORN with a single fault. J. Inf. Sec. Appl. **29**, 57–64 (2016)
11. Dobraunig, C., Eichlseder, M., Korak, T., Lomné, V., Mendel, F.: Statistical fault attacks on nonce-based authenticated encryption schemes. In: Cheon, J.H., Takagi, T. (eds.) ASIACRYPT 2016. LNCS, vol. 10031, pp. 369–395. Springer, Heidelberg (2016). doi:10.1007/978-3-662-53887-6_14
12. Fuhr, T., Jaulmes, É., Lomné, V., Thillard, A.: Fault attacks on AES with faulty ciphertexts only. In: FDTC, pp. 108–118. IEEE Computer Society (2013)
13. Krovetz, T., Rogaway, P.: The software performance of authenticated-encryption modes. In: Joux, A. (ed.) FSE 2011. LNCS, vol. 6733, pp. 306–327. Springer, Heidelberg (2011). doi:10.1007/978-3-642-21702-9_18
14. Minematsu, K.: Improved security analysis of XEX and LRW modes. In: Biham, E., Youssef, A.M. (eds.) SAC 2006. LNCS, vol. 4356, pp. 96–113. Springer, Heidelberg (2007). doi:10.1007/978-3-540-74462-7_8
15. Mukhopadhyay, D.: An improved fault based attack of the advanced encryption standard. In: Preneel, B. (ed.) AFRICACRYPT 2009. LNCS, vol. 5580, pp. 421–434. Springer, Heidelberg (2009). doi:10.1007/978-3-642-02384-2_26
16. Piret, G., Quisquater, J.-J.: A differential fault attack technique against SPN structures, with application to the AES and KHAZAD. In: Walter, C.D., Koç, Ç.K., Paar, C. (eds.) CHES 2003. LNCS, vol. 2779, pp. 77–88. Springer, Heidelberg (2003). doi:10.1007/978-3-540-45238-6_7
17. Rogaway, P.: Efficient instantiations of tweakable blockciphers and refinements to modes OCB and PMAC. In: Lee, P.J. (ed.) ASIACRYPT 2004. LNCS, vol. 3329, pp. 16–31. Springer, Heidelberg (2004). doi:10.1007/978-3-540-30539-2_2

18. Saha, D., Mukhopadhyay, D., Chowdhury, D.R.: A diagonal fault attack on the Advanced Encryption Standard. IACR Cryptology ePrint Archive 2009, 581 (2009)
19. Schmidt, J., Herbst, C.: A practical fault attack on square and multiply. In: FDTC, pp. 53–58. IEEE Computer Society (2008)
20. Skorobogatov, S.P., Anderson, R.J.: Optical fault induction attacks. In: Kaliski, B.S., Koç, K., Paar, C. (eds.) CHES 2002. LNCS, vol. 2523, pp. 2–12. Springer, Heidelberg (2003). doi:10.1007/3-540-36400-5_2
21. Tunstall, M., Mukhopadhyay, D., Ali, S.: Differential fault analysis of the advanced encryption standard using a single fault. In: Ardagna, C.A., Zhou, J. (eds.) WISTP 2011. LNCS, vol. 6633, pp. 224–233. Springer, Heidelberg (2011). doi:10.1007/978-3-642-21040-2_15
22. Yen, S., Joye, M.: Checking before output may not be enough against fault-based cryptanalysis. IEEE Trans. Comput. **49**(9), 967–970 (2000)

How to Handle Rainbow Tables
with External Memory

Gildas Avoine[1,2,5], Xavier Carpent[3], Barbara Kordy[1,5],
and Florent Tardif[4,5(✉)]

[1] INSA Rennes, Rennes, France
[2] Institut Universitaire de France, Paris, France
[3] University of California, Irvine, Irvine, USA
[4] University of Rennes 1, Rennes, France
[5] IRISA, UMR 6074, Rennes, France
florent.tardif@irisa.fr

Abstract. A cryptanalytic time-memory trade-off is a technique that aims to reduce the time needed to perform an exhaustive search. Such a technique requires large-scale precomputation that is performed once for all and whose result is stored in a fast-access internal memory. When the considered cryptographic problem is overwhelmingly-sized, using an external memory is eventually needed, though. In this paper, we consider the rainbow tables – the most widely spread version of time-memory trade-offs. The objective of our work is to analyze the relevance of storing the precomputed data on an external memory (SSD and HDD) possibly mingled with an internal one (RAM). We provide an analytical evaluation of the performance, followed by an experimental validation, and we state that using SSD or HDD is fully suited to practical cases, which are identified.

Keywords: Time memory trade-off · Rainbow tables · External memory

1 Introduction

A cryptanalytic time-memory trade-off (TMTO) is a technique introduced by Martin Hellman in 1980 [14] to reduce the time needed to perform an exhaustive search. The key-point of the technique resides in the precomputation of tables that are then used to speed up the attack itself. Given that the precomputation phase is much more expensive than an exhaustive search, a TMTO makes sense in a few scenarios, e.g., when the adversary has plenty of time for preparing the attack while she has a very little time to perform it, the adversary must repeat the attack many times, or the adversary is not powerful enough to carry out an exhaustive search but she can download precomputed tables. Problems targeted by TMTOs mostly consist in retrieving the preimage of a hashed value or, similarly, recovering a cryptographic key through a chosen plaintext attack.

Related Work. Since Hellman's seminal work, numerous variants, improvements, analyses, and successful attacks based on a TMTO have been published.

© Springer International Publishing AG 2017
J. Pieprzyk and S. Suriadi (Eds.): ACISP 2017, Part I, LNCS 10342, pp. 306–323, 2017.
DOI: 10.1007/978-3-319-60055-0_16

There exist so two major variants: the *distinguished points* [12] introduced by Ron Rivest and the *rainbow tables* [24] proposed by Philippe Oechslin. According to Lee and Hong [20], the rainbow tables outperform the distinguished points, though. As a consequence, we focus on the rainbow tables only, although most of our results might apply to other approaches as well. It is also worth noting that there exist time-memory-data trade-offs [8,13,17], which are particularly (but not only) relevant for attacking stream ciphers. We do not consider this particular family in this work.

Several algorithm-based improvements of the original rainbow table method have been suggested. They reduce either the average running time of the attack or the memory requirement, which are actually directly related to each other. In practice, any, even tiny gain can have a significant impact. Important improvements published so far include the checkpoints [5], the fingerprints [1], the delta-encoding storage [2], and the heterogeneous tables [3,4]. For more details about the analysis of TMTOs and their variants, we refer the reader to [7,15,16,19].

Technology-related enhancements have also been suggested, for example on the implementation of TMTOs on specialized devices such as GPUs or FPGAs [10,21,23,25]. GPU indeed provide a lot of parallel processing power at very affordable prices, and were therefore considered as a support of the rainbow scheme, but as far as hash function are involved, they are mainly used, e.g. in commercial products, to perform exhaustive searches. However, improvements benefiting from the technological advances in data storage have not yet been addressed so much. Most scientific articles published so far assume that the tables fit into the internal memory (RAM). In such a case, accessing the memory is fast enough to be neglected in the evaluation of the TMTO performance. As a consequence, only the computational cost of the cryptographic function to be attacked is considered in the analytic formulas [24]. Nevertheless, implemented tools, e.g., OphCrack [29] and RainbowCrack [27], deal with large-space problems that tend to outweigh the available internal memory. The tools must then use both the internal memory and some external memory. The algorithms used to balance the tables between the memories are poorly documented. To the best of our knowledge, only Kim, Hong, and Park [18] and Spitz [28] formally address this issue. In their article, Kim et al. explain which algorithms the existing tools use.

Finally, examples of successful attacks based on TMTO include (but are not limited to) breaking A5/1 [9] and LILI-128 [26], cracking Windows LM-Hash passwords [24] and Unix passwords [22], recovering keys from Texas Instruments' digital signature transponders [11] and from Megamos Crypto vehicle immobilizers [30].

Contribution. Storing rainbow tables in an external memory has been ignored up to now because this approach was considered impractical with mechanical hard disk drives (HDD). Indeed, HDDs are efficient in sequential reads but perform poorly when random accesses to the disk are required. TMTOs rely mostly on random accesses to the precomputed tables. However, storage devices improve a lot these years. In particular, solid state drives (SSD) are much faster than

HDDs and, although they are still expensive, their price has already decreased significantly. SSDs provide smaller latencies than HDDs because they do not have mechanical parts.

In this paper, we study the behavior of the rainbow tables when they do not fit in RAM. We consider two algorithms. The first one, provided by Lee and Hong in [20], consists in storing the tables in an external memory (Lee and Hong consider the SSD case only) and then filling the RAM with as many table rows as possible; the memory is then emptied and refilled with the subsequent rows. The second algorithm, which we suggest, consists in keeping the tables in the external memory and performing direct accesses to that memory. RAM is very fast but also very expensive, and its size is still quite limited today. SSD is slower but reasonably priced. Finally, HDD is slow but also very cheap. We analyze the relevance of storing the precomputed data on an external memory (SSD and HDD) possibly mingled with an internal one (RAM). We provide an analytical evaluation of the performance, followed by an experimental validation, and we state that using SSD or HDD is fully suited to practical cases, which are identified in the following sections.

2   Primer on Rainbow Tables

2.1   Mode of Operation

Let $h \colon A \to B$ be a one-way function, defined as being a function that is easy to compute but practically impossible to invert. Such a function is typically a cryptographic hash function. Given the image y in B of a value in A, the problem we want to solve is to find the preimage of y, i.e., x in A satisfying $h(x) = y$. The only way to solve the problem consists in picking values in A until the equation holds. This approach is called a *brute force* or an *exhaustive search* if the set A is exhaustively visited. The attack is practical if the set A is not too large. Providing a numerical upper bound is difficult because it depends on the running time of h, on the available processing resources, and on the time that can be devoted to the attack. Roughly speaking, an academic team can today easily perform 2^{48} cryptographic operations during a single day, using a cluster of CPUs. Nonetheless, if the attack is expected to be repeated many times, e.g., to crack passwords, then restarting the computations from scratch every time is cumbersome. A TMTO consists in performing heavy precomputations once, to make the subsequent attacks less resource-consuming.

2.2   Precomputations

Building Tables. The objective of the precomputations is to build *tables*, which is done by computing *matrices* first. As depicted in Fig. 1, a matrix consists of a series of chains built by iterating alternatively h and *reduction* functions $r_i \colon B \to A$, such that r_i maps any point in B to an arbitrary point in A, in an efficient and uniformly distributed fashion. The *starting points* of the chains are

$$
\begin{array}{llllll}
S_1 = X_{1,1} & \xrightarrow{r_1 \circ h} X_{1,2} & \xrightarrow{r_2 \circ h} \cdots & \xrightarrow{r_{t-2} \circ h} X_{1,t-1} & \xrightarrow{r_{t-1} \circ h} & X_{1,t} = E_1 \\
S_2 = X_{2,1} & \xrightarrow{r_1 \circ h} X_{2,2} & \xrightarrow{r_2 \circ h} \cdots & \xrightarrow{r_{t-2} \circ h} X_{2,t-1} & \xrightarrow{r_{t-1} \circ h} & X_{2,t} = E_2 \\
\vdots & \vdots & \ddots & \vdots & & \vdots \\
S_j = X_{j,1} & \xrightarrow{r_1 \circ h} X_{j,2} & \xrightarrow{r_2 \circ h} \cdots & \xrightarrow{r_{t-2} \circ h} X_{j,t-1} & \xrightarrow{r_{t-1} \circ h} & X_{j,t} = E_j \\
\vdots & \vdots & \ddots & \vdots & & \vdots \\
S_m = X_{m,1} & \xrightarrow{r_1 \circ h} X_{m,2} & \xrightarrow{r_2 \circ h} \cdots & \xrightarrow{r_{t-2} \circ h} X_{m,t-1} & \xrightarrow{r_{t-1} \circ h} & X_{m,t} = E_m
\end{array}
$$

Fig. 1. Matrix computed from m starting points.

chosen arbitrarily and the chains are of fixed length t, which defines the *ending points*. This process stops when the number of chains with different ending points is deemed satisfactory. A *table* then consists of the first and last columns of the matrix, and the remaining intermediary values are discarded. A table is said *rainbow* if the reduction functions r_i, for $1 \leq i \leq t - 1$, are all different, while a single reduction function used all along the table leads to classical Hellman-like tables. Rainbow tables are then usually filtered to remove duplicated ending points: such tables are called *clean* rainbow tables [2,4] or *perfect rainbow tables* [6,24]. Similarly, we have clean matrices.

Maximum Size. A table of *maximal size* is obtained when the starting points fully cover the set A. Given that the functions r_i are not injective, many chains collide, though, and the number of rows in a clean rainbow table is consequently much smaller than N. Let t be the chain length, then the *maximum* number of rows in a table is provided by Oechslin in [24]:

$$
m_{\max} = \frac{2N}{t+1}. \tag{1}
$$

Success Rate. The success rate of a clean rainbow table is the probability P for a random value in A to appear in the associated matrix:

$$
P = 1 - \left(1 - \frac{m}{N}\right)^t \approx 1 - e^{\frac{mt}{N}}. \tag{2}
$$

We observe that the maximum probability is obtained when $m = m_{\max}$, and the maximum probability consequently tends towards 86% when t tends to infinity. To increase this success rate, several tables can be used. For instance, for $\ell = 4$ tables, the success rate is greater than 99.9%.

2.3 Attack

Procedure. Given $y \in B$, the attack consists in retrieving $x \in A$, such that $h(x) = y$. To do so, a chain starting from y is computed and the check whether the generated value matches one of the ending points from the table is performed at each iteration.

Given that the reduction functions are different in every column, the attack procedure is quadratic with respect to the chain length. It is also worth noting that the process is applied to the ℓ tables, and the optimal order of search is to go through each table at the same pace. This means that the right-most unvisited column of each table is explored, then the process is iterated until the left-most columns are reached.

Once a matching ending point is found, the corresponding starting point stored in the table is used to recompute the chain until reaching y. If the latter does not belong to the rebuilt chain, then we say that a *false alarm* occurred. False alarms exist because the reduction functions r_i are not injective. Then, the process goes on, until y is found in a column more on the left or the tables have been fully explored.

Evaluation. The analytic formula to evaluate the number of h-operations that are required on average to recover a preimage is given by Avoine, Oechslin, and Junod in [6]:

$$T \approx \gamma \frac{N^2}{M^2}, \tag{3}$$

where γ is a small factor that depends on $c = \frac{mt}{N}$ (the matrix stopping constant) and ℓ (the number of tables), and $M = m\ell$. See e.g. Theorem 2 in [20].

3 Performance of the Algorithms

3.1 Terminology and Assumptions

Rainbow tables can be stored in either internal memory (RAM) or external memory (e.g., SSD or HDD). An alternative is to use two complementary memories, e.g., RAM & SSD or RAM & HDD to benefit from the advantages of both of them.

The attack presented in Sect. 2, possibly combined with practical improvements, works on a single internal or external memory. It consists in performing direct lookups into the memory for matching ending points. We refer to it as Algo$_{DLU}$ (for Direct Look Up). The software Ophcrack [29] employs Algo$_{DLU}$ in the case when only RAM is used. Kim, Hong, and Park analyze in [18] another algorithm, hereafter denoted Algo$_{STL}$, that is used by RainbowCrack [27] and rcracki-mt [32]. Note that tables are generated the same way, regardless of the algorithm used for the attack. A same set of table can thus be used for Algo$_{DLU}$ or Algo$_{STL}$ interchangeably.

We describe below these algorithms and analyze their performance, taking both computation time and access time into account. In the rest of this paper, Algo$_{DLU/RAM}$, Algo$_{DLU/SSD}$, and Algo$_{DLU/HDD}$ refer to Algo$_{DLU}$ using respectively RAM, SSD, or HDD only. The same holds for Algo$_{STL/SSD}$ and Algo$_{STL/HDD}$ which refer to Algo$_{STL}$ using SSD and HDD respectively in addition to the RAM (RAM-only Algo$_{STL}$ is not meaningful).

The model used throughout this paper is the following. The attack (excluding the precomputation phase) is performed on a single computer with access to RAM and external memory (SSD or HDD). We denote τ_F the time (seconds) taken for the CPU to compute an iteration of h. For the external memory, we use two parameters – τ_S and τ_L – which revolve around the concept of *page* which is the smallest amount of external memory that can be addressed by the system. The seek time τ_S (seconds) corresponds to the time taken to read a single random page. The sequential read time τ_L (seconds) is the time to read a page during the read of many consecutive pages.

When the tables fit in RAM, the costs of a memory access and of an h-operation are of the same order of magnitude, i.e., a few hundred CPU cycles. However, the number of memory accesses grows linearly with the length of the table, while the number of h-computations is quadratic. Consequently, when the table is wide enough, the memory access time can be neglected (i.e., $\tau_S = \tau_L = 0$), and the attack time is equal to T multiplied by the cost of a single h-operation.

3.2   Algo$_{DLU}$

The algorithm Algo$_{DLU}$ is the attack described in Sect. 2.3. Its performance is provided in Theorem 1.

Theorem 1. Algo$_{DLU}$ *'s average wall-clock time is* $T_{DLU} = \gamma \frac{N^2}{M^2} \tau_F + \frac{N}{m} \log_2 m \tau_S$.

Proof. The first term of T_{DLU} is the portion of the time used by computations. The second term corresponds to the overhead of seeking data in the memory. As already stated in [6], the attack performs $\frac{N}{m}$ lookups on average in order to find a preimage. Each lookup requires $\log_2 m$ seeks in the memory if a dichotomic search is performed. Finally, each seek costs τ_S seconds on average.

We now look at the case where the memory that is used is RAM. In such a case, the algorithm Algo$_{DLU/RAM}$ is based on the assumption that the tables entirely reside in RAM, and no external memory is used. It takes advantage of fast RAM accesses given that we assume the RAM access time is negligible. In this case, the previous theorem is simplified and leads to Corollary 1.

Corollary 1. Algo$_{DLU/RAM}$ *'s average wall-clock time is* $T_{RAM} = \gamma \frac{N^2}{M^2} \tau_F$.

3.3   Algo$_{STL}$

The algorithm Algo$_{STL}$, described by Kim, Hong, and Park in [18], significantly differs from the other algorithm, mainly because the attack starts with computing all the t possible chains from the value y in B whose preimage is looked for. The tables are then loaded in RAM according to the following procedure. Given the k-th table table$_k$ ($1 \leq k \leq \ell$), containing m ordered pairs (starting point, ending point), a *sub-table* of table$_k$ is a table that contains m/s ordered pairs belonging to table$_k$. In Algo$_{STL}$, tables are stored in an external memory (SSD or HDD) and each of them is partitioned into s non-overlapping sub-tables of a given size. Each of the s sub-tables are loaded into RAM, one at a time, which explains the acronym of the algorithm: Sub-Table Loading. For each sub-table loaded, the t possible chains are used to discover matching endpoints and discard false alarms, as it is done in Algo$_{DLU/RAM}$.

The efficiency of Algo$_{STL}$ is investigated in [18] and summarized in Theorems 2 and 3. The proofs are provided in [18].

Theorem 2. Algo$_{STL}$'s average wall-clock time is

$$T_{STL} = L \cdot \tau_L + F \cdot \tau_F, \tag{4}$$

where $L = \frac{mP}{c\beta}, F = \delta\frac{N^2}{L^2}, \delta \approx \frac{P^3}{\beta^2}\left(\frac{1}{2(1-e^{-c})} + \frac{1}{6} - \frac{c}{48}\right)$, and where $c = \frac{mt}{N} < 2$, β is the number of table entries (starting point – ending point pair) per page, and $P = 1 - e^{-c\ell}$ is the total probability of success.

Theorem 3. In optimal configuration, that is when the memory is of optimal size for a given problem, Algo$_{STL}$'s average wall-clock time is

$$T_{STL}^* = \frac{3}{2^{\frac{2}{3}}}\tau_L^{\frac{2}{3}}\tau_F^{\frac{1}{3}}\delta^{\frac{1}{3}}N^{\frac{2}{3}}, \tag{5}$$

and the memory associated to this situation corresponds to

$$m = \left(\beta\frac{\tau_F}{\tau_L}\right)^{\frac{1}{3}}\left(\frac{1}{1 - e^{-c}} + \frac{1}{3} - \frac{c}{24}\right)^{\frac{1}{3}}cN^{\frac{2}{3}}.$$

Compared with [18], note that we changed the notations $\bar{R}_{tc}$ to δ, $\bar{R}_{tc}$ to γ, $\bar{c}$ to c, and $\bar{R}_{ps}$ to P, for consistency with the other algorithms and other notations in the literature. Also note that the definition of $\bar{R}_{tc}$ (δ) is inconsistent in [18] – sometimes multiplied by a factor of β^2. We chose to stick with the approximation used in Theorem 2, which corresponds to Proposition 5 in [18].

Algo$_{STL}$ has an optimal amount of memory at which it operates. This is because $T = O\left(m + \frac{1}{m^2}\right)$. Beyond a certain threshold, the decrease of the F factor fails to compensate for the increase of the L factor. This behavior is further commented on in Sect. 5.

The value s (number of sub-tables per table) is thoroughly discussed in [18]. If s is too small, sub-tables are very large, and when the search ends, it is likely that significant time was wasted loading the last sub-table. If s is too big, read operations are done on a small amount of memory, which is sub-optimal. As stated in [18] however, the value of s has relatively little impact on the efficiency of Algo$_{STL}$, provided it is "reasonable" (ranging from 45 to 100 in the examples discussed in [18]). In what follows, we assume such a reasonable s is used.

4   Algorithm Constants

The algorithms analyzed in this paper rely on the τ_S, τ_L and τ_F parameters heavily. These are machine-specific constants which can only be determined experimentally. We measured these values for the configuration used in our experimental validation of $\mathsf{Algo}_{\mathsf{DLU}}$, presented in Sect. 6.

4.1   Experimental Setup

The measurements have been done on a single machine with an Intel E5-1603 v3 CPU clocked at 2.8 GHz, and with 32 GB of RAM available. It uses Intel SSD DC-3700 external memory with a capacity of 400 GB, which is separated from the disk containing the operating system.

The Intel SSD use Non-Volatile Memory Express technology, so-called NVMe, which is an interface that provides smaller latencies, by connecting the SSD directly via PCI-Express to the processor and memory instead of going through an intermediate controller. This also allows for better stability in measurements.

4.2   Determination of Values for τ_S, τ_L and τ_F

The time measurements are made with the processor's internal time stamp counter, via the RDTSC instruction. This instruction is constant with respect to the power management re-clocking, and is synchronized across all cores on this CPU model. The processor does not have dynamic over-clocking, i.e., *Turbo Boost* capabilities, so the time stamp counter always increments 2.8 billion times per seconds. This allows for accurate measurements up to nanosecond precision.

Computation Time τ_F. We use the MD5 hash function as the one-way function h. We assume that, during the execution of the TMTO, the CPU is warmed-up, i.e., it is running at its nominal frequency, which is expected in usual conditions. In this case, the time taken by successive applications of h is constant. We have estimated the time τ_F taken by a single application of h by averaging over the measurement of 10^6 applications of h, which gives $\tau_F = 1.786 \cdot 10^{-7}$ s.

Sequential Block Read Time τ_L. In the context of external memory model with sub-tables loading, the constant τ_L refers to the time taken to read a page on disk during a sequential read of many blocks. The sub-tables are typically chosen to reach the maximal read throughput of the disk, with sizes in the order of the dozen or hundreds of megabytes. We note that, since disk have usually better performance in sequential reads than in random access, we should have $\tau_L \ll \tau_S$.

We measured the time to load 1000 arbitrary random data files, of size ranging from 10 to 500 MB, in a RAM allocated array. We obtained $\tau_L = 4.59 \cdot 10^{-6}$ s with a standard deviation $\sigma = 0.73 \cdot 10^{-6}$ s. For reference, the same test on a 5400 rpm HDD gave us $\tau_L = 20.99 \cdot 10^{-6}$ s with $\sigma = 7.65 \cdot 10^{-6}$ s.

Single Block Read Time τ_S. We measured the time taken by successive single-page reads of values at random positions in at least 1 GB files. Each read has been measured separately. The value obtained, averaged over 500 measurements, is $\tau_S = 149.6 \cdot 10^{-6}$ s, $\sigma = 20.7 \cdot 10^{-6}$ s, which is indeed much larger than τ_L. On HDD, we obtained $\tau_S = 7.41 \cdot 10^{-3}$ s and $\sigma = 3.79 \cdot 10^{-3}$ s.

5 Analysis

This section compares the two algorithms described in Sect. 3 on different memory types and aims to characterize which of them has better performance depending on various parameters.

Analysis of $\mathsf{Algo}_{\mathsf{STL}}$ and comparison between $\mathsf{Algo}_{\mathsf{STL/HDD}}$ and $\mathsf{Algo}_{\mathsf{DLU/RAM}}$ was previously done in [18]. However, this comparison is limited in several ways. Most importantly, it only accounts for $\mathsf{Algo}_{\mathsf{STL}}$ in optimal configuration, that is with a fixed memory size. Furthermore, it only considers two data points of memory for $\mathsf{Algo}_{\mathsf{DLU/RAM}}$ and one for $\mathsf{Algo}_{\mathsf{STL/HDD}}$, and does not study $\mathsf{Algo}_{\mathsf{DLU/HDD}}$. The conclusion drawn in [18] is that $\mathsf{Algo}_{\mathsf{STL}}$ is superior for large problems, but the comparison is inconclusive for smaller problems.

In the analysis presented in the current paper, we overcome the aforementioned limitations and also study the case of the SSD memory. We base our comparison on the "Small Search Space Example" given in [18], on which $\mathsf{Algo}_{\mathsf{DLU/RAM}}$ and $\mathsf{Algo}_{\mathsf{STL/HDD}}$ have been compared. The problem space corresponds to passwords of length 7 over a 52-character alphabet (standard keyboard), which gives $N = 52^7 = 2^{39.903}$. The other parameters are $P = 0.999$, $\ell = 4$, $c = 1.7269$, $\delta = 0.73662/\beta^2$, $\gamma = 8.3915$, 16 bytes per chain ($\beta = 256$ for 4 KB pages). For τ_F, τ_L, τ_S, we use values obtained experimentally – see Sect. 4 for details on the methodology – instead of those given in [18]. The reason is that in [18], τ_S was not provided and the constants emanated from a different machine.

5.1 Comparing $\mathsf{Algo}_{\mathsf{STL}}$ and $\mathsf{Algo}_{\mathsf{DLU}}$

Figure 2(a) presents the average wall-clock time for the three algorithms for varying amount of memory available when a SSD is used. Note that $\mathsf{Algo}_{\mathsf{DLU/RAM}}$ is presented at a somewhat unfair advantage since it uses RAM instead of external memory, and is only represented in Fig. 2(a) for completeness.

The main conclusions are the following: (1) The cost of $\mathsf{Algo}_{\mathsf{STL}}$ stops decreasing beyond a certain amount of memory available. This is due to the fact that the time taken for loading increasing amount of chains in RAM is not made up for by the decrease in computation. It is assumed that the optimal amount of external memory is used when possible, even when more is available. This also means that $\mathsf{Algo}_{\mathsf{STL}}$ has an inherent minimal average search time which can never be improved regardless of the memory available. $\mathsf{Algo}_{\mathsf{DLU}}$ has no such threshold. (2) The area (in terms of the external memory amount) where $\mathsf{Algo}_{\mathsf{STL}}$ is more efficient than $\mathsf{Algo}_{\mathsf{DLU}}$ is very small.

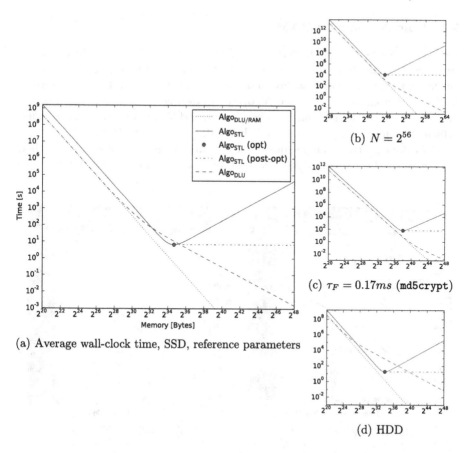

(b) $N = 2^{56}$

(c) $\tau_F = 0.17ms$ (md5crypt)

(a) Average wall-clock time, SSD, reference parameters

(d) HDD

Fig. 2. Average wall-clock time, depending on the memory available.

We can further elaborate that the curves for T_{STL} and T_{DLU} do not intersect if Algo$_{DLU}$ is always more efficient, otherwise they intersect at two points (possibly only one point in a degenerated case). Whether there are 0 or 2 (and the positions of these) intersections depends on problem parameters (N, M, c, ℓ) and machine parameters (β, τ_F, τ_L, τ_S). To illustrate this, Fig. 2 shows the effect of changing some parameters, with all other parameters left untouched.

- Fig. 2(b): When $N = 2^{56}$ the algorithm Algo$_{DLU}$ is superior throughout.
- Fig. 2(c): The md5crypt function is 955 times slower than MD5. When used, it gives $\tau_F = 0.171$ ms, and Algo$_{DLU}$ is again superior throughout.
- Fig. 2(d): Using a hard disk drive instead of SSD implies $\tau_S = 7.41$ ms and $\tau_L = 20.99\,\mu$s. Expectedly, Algo$_{DLU}$ suffers from longer seek time, and Algo$_{STL}$ dominates on a larger area (but not globally).

5.2   Comparison with RAM

Figure 3 presents regions, in terms of RAM and external memory available, in which each algorithm, completed with naive online brute-force and dictionary methods, is the most efficient. Formulas for average wall-clock time described in Sect. 3 were used for Algo$_{STL}$ and Algo$_{DLU}$. An average of $\frac{N}{2}\tau_F$ is used for online brute-force, and the dictionary method is assumed to dominate as long as it has sufficient memory available, i.e., $16N$ bytes (MD5 hashes are 16 bytes).

It is difficult to conclude unequivocally on Algo$_{STL}$ and Algo$_{DLU}$, as their respective performances highly depend on parameters. It can however be

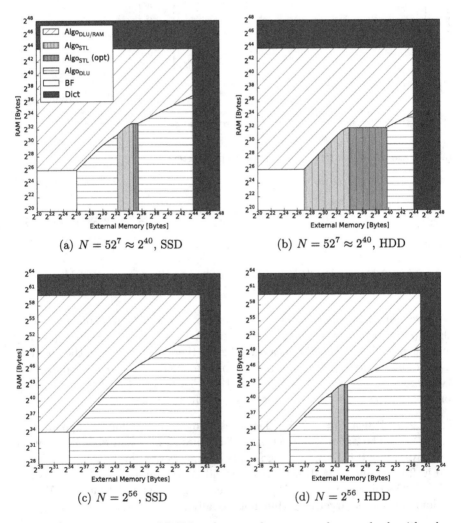

(a) $N = 52^7 \approx 2^{40}$, SSD

(b) $N = 52^7 \approx 2^{40}$, HDD

(c) $N = 2^{56}$, SSD

(d) $N = 2^{56}$, HDD

Fig. 3. Regions, in terms of RAM and external memory, where each algorithm has minimum time, in four different scenarios.

observed that (1) $\mathsf{Algo}_{\mathsf{DLU}}$ typically outperforms $\mathsf{Algo}_{\mathsf{STL}}$ on large problems, and when h is expensive; and (2) the seek time is of crucial importance for $\mathsf{Algo}_{\mathsf{DLU}}$, which performs poorly compared to $\mathsf{Algo}_{\mathsf{STL}}$ on devices (such as hard disk) with slow seek time but high sequential read performance.

5.3   HDD and SSD

Figure 4 compares the performances of $\mathsf{Algo}_{\mathsf{DLU}}$ and $\mathsf{Algo}_{\mathsf{STL}}$ on SSD and HDD. The dashed line represents points where SSD memory and HDD memory are equal. Nowadays, HDD memory is cheaper than SSD, which corresponds to the region above this line.

5.4   Discussion

Conclusion of the Comparisons. The various comparisons done in this section show that many parameters influence the choice of the algorithm and memory type to use, and it is difficult to make a simple judgment as to which is best. These parameters include problem parameters (N, M, c, ℓ) and machine/technology parameters $(\beta, \tau_F, \tau_L, \tau_S)$. A few observation can be made however.

- $\mathsf{Algo}_{\mathsf{DLU}}$ performs better on larger problem spaces than $\mathsf{Algo}_{\mathsf{STL}}$.
- $\mathsf{Algo}_{\mathsf{DLU}}$ performs better on slower hash functions than $\mathsf{Algo}_{\mathsf{STL}}$.
- $\mathsf{Algo}_{\mathsf{STL}}$ handles better than $\mathsf{Algo}_{\mathsf{DLU}}$ the use of slower memories such as HDD.
- In many scenarios, a large portion of where $\mathsf{Algo}_{\mathsf{STL}}$ is most appropriate is *not* in its optimal configuration.
- In some scenarios, the region where $\mathsf{Algo}_{\mathsf{STL}}$ is most appropriate is also close to the typical memory size.

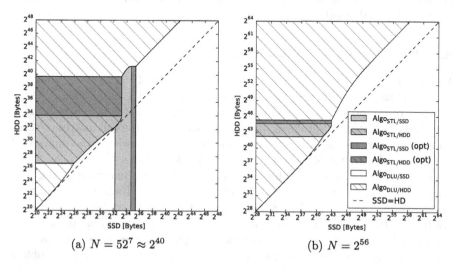

(a) $N = 52^7 \approx 2^{40}$ (b) $N = 2^{56}$

Fig. 4. Regions, in terms of SSD and HDD memory, where each algorithm has minimum time.

Limits of the Analysis. First of all, our results and observations are based on the measures given in Sect. 4. Using a particularly fast or slow HDD, for instance, might influence the results in a non-negligible way. Likewise, using clusters of many disks to reach high quantities of memory might affect τ_S and τ_L enough that the conclusions would be different.

Furthermore, the analysis is based on Sect. 3, and does not consider optimizations such as checkpoints [1,5], endpoint truncation [1,20], and prefix/suffix or compressed delta encoding for chain storage [2]. Likewise, it does not consider optimizations exploiting the architecture, such as loading sub-tables while computing chains in $\mathsf{Algo_{STL}}$.

Including these optimizations would make the analysis much more complex, and we believe that taking them into consideration would not change our conclusions. While some optimizations might favor one algorithm more than the other, it is very unlikely that the frontiers between regions of best performance would shift significantly.

6   Experimentation

We have set up experiments in order to validate the analytical results described in Sects. 3 and 5. The formulas established in Sect. 3 assume that $\mathsf{Algo_{DLU/SSD}}$ and $\mathsf{Algo_{DLU/HDD}}$ do not use RAM at all. We show that, in reality, these algorithms actually do use RAM because operating systems use cache techniques to speed up lookups. Thus, a value read from an external memory is temporarily saved in cache to prevent (to some extent) from accessing the external memory again to get the same value. As a consequence, the results provided in Sect. 3 correspond to upper bounds in practice. We refine the formulas to take the caching effect into account, and we then show that the refined formulas describe more accurately the experimental results.

6.1   Parameters and Methodology

We have conducted the experiments on two problems of size $N = 2^{31}$ and 2^{36}, using the MD5 hash function for a number of columns $t \in \{100, 200, \ldots, 900\}$. The size of the problems allowed us to precompute the matrices in a reasonable time frame. For the 2^{36}-problem, the precomputation of the full matrix took 5 h on 400 processor cores. Sorting the ending points and removing the duplicated ones required a couple of days due to the network latencies.

For each problem, $\ell = 4$ tables were computed with a matrix stopping constant of $c = 1.92$ ($m = 0.96 m_{\mathrm{max}}$), giving $P \approx 0.999$. Each (starting point, ending point) pair is stored on 8 and 16 bytes for $N = 2^{31}$ and $N = 2^{36}$ respectively. The tables are clean and ordered with respect to the ending points.

To evaluate the average running time of $\mathsf{Algo_{DLU}}$, we average the measured attack time for the hashes of 1000 randomly-generated values in the problem space. The timings were based on the processor timestamp counter (RDTSC). In order to keep the experiments independent, the environment is reset before each tests. Indeed there are side effects to be expected due to the way the operating system handles files, some of which also affect the measurements themselves. We discuss them in the subsequent sections.

6.2   Paging and Caching Mechanisms

For every access to data stored on external memory, the full page containing the data is actually returned to the operating system. Since the 60 s, the *paging mechanism* is based on 4 KB pages in most operating systems and external memories [31].

Due to the *caching mechanism*, the data is not fetched directly from the external memory every time we perform a lookup. Instead, the page containing the data is first copied from the external memory to the internal memory, and only then it can be read. Such a mechanism allows the system to speed up memory accesses: as long as the internal memory is not reclaimed for another use, the content of the page remains in it. This means that, if the same page is accessed again, it can be retrieved directly from the internal memory instead of waiting for the external memory.

If several lookups are performed on values that are located close enough in the external memory, then only the earliest lookup will require accessing the external memory. This phenomenon happens when a lookup is performed in the dichotomic search. As a consequence, at some point, every external memory access fetches elements that are located in the same page. Taking paging and caching mechanisms into account, Theorem 1 can be refined to yield Theorem 4.

Theorem 4. *Given β (starting points, ending points) pairs per page. Taking the paging and caching mechanisms into account, Algo$_{\mathsf{DLU}}$'s average wall-clock time is*

$$T_{\mathsf{DLU}} = \gamma \frac{N^2}{M^2}\tau_F + \frac{N}{m}\left(\log_2 m - \log_2 \beta\right) \cdot \tau_S. \tag{6}$$

Proof. The loading of pages instead of single values corresponds to a dichotomic search tree that is $\log_2 \beta$ levels shallower. Thus, each lookup consists in $\log_2 m - \log_2 \beta$ page loads instead of $\log_2 m$.

6.3   Reducing the Caching Impact

To get proper experimental results and bypass the operating system's built-in caching mechanism, we use a cache eviction technique and restrain the internal memory allocated to the program.

Every page that remains in memory after each experiment needs to be reset to a blank state. We use the `madvise` system call to tell the kernel that no additional pages are required. Although the kernel could ignore the setting and keep the pages in memory anyway, it did not seem to happen in our experiments. Alternative methods exist, such as requesting a cache drop, but they might affect the experiments by wiping data needed by the operating system.

We also restrain the internal memory that the program can use to a few megabytes, using the `cgroup` kernel subsystem. Software limitation was used instead of physically limiting the internal memory because physical limitation may cause the operating system to starve for memory, which would greatly affect the results.

6.4   Experimental Results

As expected, our implementation of $\mathsf{Algo}_{\mathsf{DLU/RAM}}$, which mainly depends on τ_F, follows closely the curve given by Corollary 1.

The experimental results concerning $\mathsf{Algo}_{\mathsf{DLU}}$ are presented in Fig. 5. The dashed curves are computed from the revised formula for $\mathsf{Algo}_{\mathsf{DLU}}$, provided by Eq. (6). For each problem, we give the timings when the RAM is restrained (line with dots) and when it is not (line with triangles).

Some caching can still be noticed on the curves, but trying to restrain RAM even further resulted in failures which could be explained by the fact that there is no distinction for the OS between file caching and the caching of the executable itself. Thus, we have to overprovision the RAM to be certain that the program itself does not starve during the execution. Nevertheless, we observe that the experimental curve is below the analytic dashed-line curve. This confirms that Eq. (6) is a more accurate upper bound to the practical wall-clock time of $\mathsf{Algo}_{\mathsf{DLU}}$ than the formula of Theorem 1.

Finally, we remark that even though we have restrained RAM drastically, we can notice the gain in time due to the caching done by the OS. The zones concerning $\mathsf{Algo}_{\mathsf{DLU}}$ in Fig. 2 would therefore have smaller areas, in practice. The impact of the native caching operated by the OS is difficult to predict with exact precision, though.

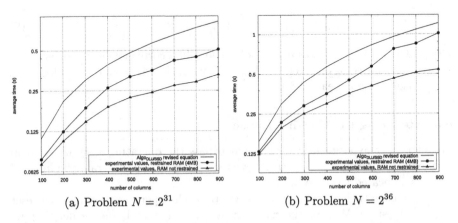

(a) Problem $N = 2^{31}$ (b) Problem $N = 2^{36}$

Fig. 5. TMTO attack average online running time per column, on 1000 hashed values

7 Conclusion

In this paper, we have studied the use of external memory for time-memory trade-offs based on rainbow tables. The use of external memory is motivated by large problems for which precomputed tables are too big to fit in RAM. Two approaches were compared: the first one relying on the classical Algo$_{STL}$ algorithm which takes advantage of RAM by processing sub-tables in internal memory; and the second, based on the Algo$_{DLU}$ algorithm, which uses the standard RAM-based rainbow table algorithm directly on external memory (we are not aware of public implementations or analyses of Algo$_{DLU}$ on external memory).

We evaluate the two algorithms and compare their efficiency on different memory types and different problem parameters. Conclusions are subject to parameters, but several major observations are made. Algo$_{DLU}$ performs better than Algo$_{STL}$ on larger problem spaces, slower hash functions, and faster memories. At the very least, it is not the case that Algo$_{STL}$ is unequivocally more efficient on larger problems, contrarily to what was previously thought.

Costs of the various memory types were not considered formally in our analysis because of the great variability in prices and setups. Very roughly speaking, we can observe that nowadays, a gigabyte of RAM costs between 5 and 20 times more than a gigabyte of SSD, which itself costs between 3 and 8 times more than a gigabyte of HDD. Such prices and comparisons might help an implementer make an educated decision regarding the memory type to use.

We implemented Algo$_{DLU}$ and validated its efficiency analysis (analysis and validation of Algo$_{STL}$ was previously done in [18]). It shows that the analysis is close, but in fact pessimistic due to caching in RAM. Exploiting the RAM in addition to external memory might give an extra edge to Algo$_{DLU}$. Optimizations on Algo$_{STL}$ might exist as well, such as computing chains and loading tables in parallel. Analysis of such optimizations, along with other algorithmic optimizations on rainbow tables and other trade-off variants might be an interesting continuation of this work.

Acknowledgments. This work has been partly supported by the COST Action IC1403 (Cryptacus). Xavier Carpent was supported, in part, by a fellowship of the Belgian American Educational Foundation.

References

1. Avoine, G., Bourgeois, A., Carpent, X.: Analysis of rainbow tables with fingerprints. In: Foo, E., Stebila, D. (eds.) ACISP 2015. LNCS, vol. 9144, pp. 356–374. Springer, Cham (2015). doi:10.1007/978-3-319-19962-7_21
2. Avoine, G., Carpent, X.: Optimal storage for rainbow tables. In: Lee, H.-S., Han, D.-G. (eds.) ICISC 2013. LNCS, vol. 8565, pp. 144–157. Springer, Cham (2014). doi:10.1007/978-3-319-12160-4_9
3. Avoine, G., Carpent, X.: Heterogeneous rainbow table widths provide faster cryptanalyses. In: ACM Asia Conference on Computer and Communications Security - ASIACCS 2017, ASIA CCS 2017, Abu Dhabi, UAE, pp. 815–822. ACM, April 2017

4. Avoine, G., Carpent, X., Lauradoux, C.: Interleaving cryptanalytic time-memory trade-offs on non-uniform distributions. In: Pernul, G., Ryan, P.Y.A., Weippl, E. (eds.) ESORICS 2015. LNCS, vol. 9326, pp. 165–184. Springer, Cham (2015). doi:10.1007/978-3-319-24174-6_9

5. Avoine, G., Junod, P., Oechslin, P.: Time-memory trade-offs: false alarm detection using checkpoints. In: Maitra, S., Veni Madhavan, C.E., Venkatesan, R. (eds.) INDOCRYPT 2005. LNCS, vol. 3797, pp. 183–196. Springer, Heidelberg (2005). doi:10.1007/11596219_15

6. Avoine, G., Junod, P., Oechslin, P.: Characterization and improvement of time-memory trade-off based on perfect tables. ACM Trans. Inf. Syst. Secur. 11(4), 17:1–17:22 (2008)

7. Barkan, E.P.: Cryptanalysis of ciphers and protocols. Ph.D. thesis, Technion - Israel Institute of Technology, Haifa, Israel, March 2006

8. Biryukov, A., Mukhopadhyay, S., Sarkar, P.: Improved time-memory trade-offs with multiple data. In: Preneel, B., Tavares, S. (eds.) SAC 2005. LNCS, vol. 3897, pp. 110–127. Springer, Heidelberg (2006). doi:10.1007/11693383_8

9. Biryukov, A., Shamir, A., Wagner, D.: Real time cryptanalysis of A5/1 on a PC. In: Goos, G., Hartmanis, J., Leeuwen, J., Schneier, B. (eds.) FSE 2000. LNCS, vol. 1978, pp. 1–18. Springer, Heidelberg (2001). doi:10.1007/3-540-44706-7_1

10. Bitweasil: Cryptohaze (2012). http://cryptohaze.com/. Accessed 19 Apr 2017

11. Bono, S., Green, M., Stubblefield, A., Juels, A., Rubin, A., Szydlo, M.: Security analysis of a cryptographically-enabled RFID device. In: USENIX Security Symposium - USENIX 2005, Baltimore, Maryland, USA, pp. 1–16. USENIX, July–August 2005

12. Denning, D.E.: Cryptography and Data Security, p. 100. Addison-Wesley, Boston (1982)

13. Dunkelman, O., Keller, N.: Treatment of the initial value in time-memory-data tradeoff attacks on stream ciphers. Inf. Process. Lett. 107(5), 133–137 (2008)

14. Hellman, M.: A cryptanalytic time-memory trade off. IEEE Trans. Inf. Theory IT 26(4), 401–406 (1980)

15. Hoch, Y.Z.: Security analysis of generic iterated hash functions. Ph.D. thesis, Weizmann Institute of Science, Rehovot, Israel, August 2009

16. Hong, J., Jeong, K.C., Kwon, E.Y., Lee, I.-S., Ma, D.: Variants of the distinguished point method for cryptanalytic time memory trade-offs. In: Chen, L., Mu, Y., Susilo, W. (eds.) ISPEC 2008. LNCS, vol. 4991, pp. 131–145. Springer, Heidelberg (2008). doi:10.1007/978-3-540-79104-1_10

17. Hong, J., Sarkar, P.: New applications of time memory data tradeoffs. In: Roy, B. (ed.) ASIACRYPT 2005. LNCS, vol. 3788, pp. 353–372. Springer, Heidelberg (2005). doi:10.1007/11593447_19

18. Kim, J.W., Hong, J., Park, K.: Analysis of the rainbow tradeoff algorithm used in practice. IACR Cryptology ePrint Archive (2013)

19. Kim, J.W., Seo, J., Hong, J., Park, K., Kim, S.-R.: High-speed parallel implementations of the rainbow method in a heterogeneous system. In: Galbraith, S., Nandi, M. (eds.) INDOCRYPT 2012. LNCS, vol. 7668, pp. 303–316. Springer, Heidelberg (2012). doi:10.1007/978-3-642-34931-7_18

20. Lee, G.W., Hong, J.: Comparison of perfect table cryptanalytic tradeoff algorithms. Des. Codes Crypt. 80(3), 473–523 (2016)

21. Lu, J., Li, Z., Henricksen, M.: Time-memory trade-off attack on the GSM A5/1 stream cipher using commodity GPGPU - (extended abstract). In: Malkin, T., Kolesnikov, V., Lewko, A.B., Polychronakis, M. (eds.) ACNS 2015. LNCS, vol. 9092, pp. 350–369. Springer, Cham (2015). doi:10.1007/978-3-319-28166-7_17

22. Mentens, N., Batina, L., Preneel, B., Verbauwhede, I.: Cracking Unix passwords using FPGA platforms. SHARCS - Special Purpose Hardware for Attacking Cryptographic Systems, February 2005

23. Mentens, N., Batina, L., Preneel, B., Verbauwhede, I.: Time-memory trade-off attack on FPGA platforms: UNIX password cracking. In: Bertels, K., Cardoso, J.M.P., Vassiliadis, S. (eds.) ARC 2006. LNCS, vol. 3985, pp. 323–334. Springer, Heidelberg (2006). doi:10.1007/11802839_41

24. Oechslin, P.: Making a faster cryptanalytic time-memory trade-off. In: Boneh, D. (ed.) CRYPTO 2003. LNCS, vol. 2729, pp. 617–630. Springer, Heidelberg (2003). doi:10.1007/978-3-540-45146-4_36

25. Jean-Jacques, Q., Francois-Xavier, S., Rouvroy, G., Jean-Pierre, D., Jean-Didier, L.: A cryptanalytic time-memory tradeoff: first FPGA implementation. In: Glesner, M., Zipf, P., Renovell, M. (eds.) FPL 2002. LNCS, vol. 2438, pp. 780–789. Springer, Heidelberg (2002). doi:10.1007/3-540-46117-5_80

26. Saarinen, M.-J.O.: A time-memory tradeoff attack against LILI-128. In: Daemen, J., Rijmen, V. (eds.) FSE 2002. LNCS, vol. 2365, pp. 231–236. Springer, Heidelberg (2002). doi:10.1007/3-540-45661-9_18

27. Shuanglei, Z.: Rainbowcrack (2017). http://project-rainbowcrack.com/. Accessed 19 Apr 2017

28. Spitz, S.: Time memory tradeoff implementation on Copacobana. Master's thesis, Ruhr-Universität Bochum, Bochum, Germany, June 2007

29. Tissières, C., Oechslin, P.: Ophcrack (2016). http://ophcrack.sourceforge.net/. Accessed 19 Apr 2017

30. Verdult, R., Garcia, F.D., Ege, B.: Dismantling megamos crypto: wirelessly lock-picking a vehicle immobilizer. In: Proceedings of the 22nd USENIX Security Symposium - USENIX 2013, Washington, DC, USA, pp. 703–718, August 2013

31. Weisberg, P., Wiseman, Y.: Using 4KB page size for virtual memory is obsolete. In: Proceedings of the IEEE International Conference on Information Reuse and Integration - IRI 2009, Las Vegas, Nevada, USA, pp. 262–265, August 2009

32. Westergaard, M., Nobis, J., Shuanglei, Z.: Rcracki-mt (2014). http://tools.kali.org/password-attacks/rcracki-mt. Accessed 19 Apr 2017

Improved Factoring Attacks on Multi-prime RSA with Small Prime Difference

Mengce Zheng[1,2]([⊠]), Noboru Kunihiro[2], and Honggang Hu[1]

[1] Key Laboratory of Electromagnetic Space Information, CAS,
University of Science and Technology of China, Hefei, China
hghu2005@ustc.edu.cn
[2] The University of Tokyo, Tokyo, Japan
zheng@it.k.u-tokyo.ac.jp, kunihiro@k.u-tokyo.ac.jp

Abstract. In this paper, we study the security of multi-prime RSA with small prime difference and propose two improved factoring attacks. The modulus involved in this variant is the product of r distinct prime factors of same bit-size. Zhang and Takagi (ACISP 2013) showed a Fermat-like factoring attack on multi-prime RSA. In order to improve the previous result, we gather more information about the prime factors to derive r simultaneous modular equations. The first attack is based on combining r equations to solve one multivariate modular equation by a generic lattice approach. Since the equation form is similar to multi-prime Φ-hiding problem, we propose the second attack by applying the optimal linearization technique. We also show that our attacks can achieve better bounds in the experiments.

Keywords: Cryptanalysis · Multi-prime RSA · Small prime difference · Factoring attack · Lattice · Linearization technique

1 Introduction

1.1 Background

RSA [20] is a famous public key cryptosystem that has been widely used in various settings. However, the original RSA is not fit for some constrained environments. Since people need faster and more efficient RSA encryption/decryption processes, several variants have been proposed and surveyed [3]. In this paper, we focus on a variant called multi-prime RSA. It is described as follows.

Key Generation. Generate r distinct primes $p_1, p_2, \ldots, p_r$ of same bit-size and modulus $N = \prod_{i=1}^{r} p_i$. Pick a random number that is coprime to $\varphi(N) = \prod_{i=1}^{r}(p_i - 1)$ as the public key e and compute the corresponding private key $d = e^{-1} \bmod \varphi(N)$.

Encryption. Transform the message string into an integer $M \in \mathbb{Z}_N$ and compute the ciphertext as $C = M^e \bmod N$.

© Springer International Publishing AG 2017
J. Pieprzyk and S. Suriadi (Eds.): ACISP 2017, Part I, LNCS 10342, pp. 324–342, 2017.
DOI: 10.1007/978-3-319-60055-0_17

Decryption. Compute $M_i = C^{d_i} \bmod p_i$ for $d_i = d \bmod (p_i - 1)$, $1 \le i \le r$. Combine M_i's by the Chinese Remainder Theorem to obtain the plaintext $M = C^d \bmod N$.

This variant modifies the modulus to $N = p_1 p_2 \cdots p_r$ for $r \ge 3$. It was patented by Compaq [5], using a modulus of the form $N = p_1 p_2 p_3$. We then discuss the performance of multi-prime RSA. The advantage is the efficiency when using Chinese Remainder Theorem in its decryption process. From [3], we know that the asymptotic speedup over the standard RSA is approximately $\frac{r^2}{4}$. Moreover, ordinary attacks such as small private exponent attack and partial key exposure attack are less effective as r increases. But r should not be unrestrictedly large because of the Elliptic Curve Method [18]. Since factoring a multi-prime RSA modulus using ECM is much easier with increasing r, one might choose $r = 3$, 4 and 5 for most settings. Generally speaking, multi-prime RSA with appropriate r might be a practical alternative for reducing the decryption costs.

Without loss of generality, we have $p_1 < p_2 < \cdots < p_r$ and $\frac{1}{2} N^{\frac{1}{r}} < p_1 < N^{\frac{1}{r}} < p_r < 2 N^{\frac{1}{r}}$. The second one indicates that the prime factors are balanced, which means that they are roughly of same bit-size. The prime difference Δ is defined as $\Delta := \max_{i \neq j} |p_i - p_j| = p_r - p_1 = N^\gamma$ for $0 < \gamma < \frac{1}{r}$. The security of multi-prime RSA has been investigated for small private exponent [4,13,14] and for small prime difference [1,22,25,26].

Prime difference was introduced by de Weger [11] to show that one can find an enhanced small private exponent attack with small prime difference. As for multi-prime RSA, it is also applied to obtain some improvements. Thereafter we review some related previous attacks. Suppose that N is a multi-prime RSA modulus with r prime factors. Let $e \approx N$ be a valid public key and $d = N^\delta$ be its corresponding private key.

Bahig-Bhery-Nassr [1]. Given the prime difference $\Delta = N^\gamma$ and the public key (N, e), then multi-prime RSA is insecure if γ and d satisfy

$$2d^2 + 1 < \frac{N^{\frac{2}{r} - \gamma}}{6r}.$$

Zhang-Takagi [25,26]. Given the prime difference $\Delta = N^\gamma$ and the public key (N, e), then d can be probabilistically found in time polynomial in $\log N$ if γ and δ satisfy

$$\delta < 1 - \sqrt{1 + \gamma - \frac{2}{r}}.$$

The bound was later refined to

$$\delta < 1 - \sqrt{1 + 2\gamma - \frac{3}{r}} \text{ for } \gamma \ge \frac{3}{2r} - \frac{1+\delta}{4},$$

$$\delta < \frac{3}{r} - \frac{1}{4} - 2\gamma \text{ for } \gamma < \frac{3}{2r} - \frac{1+\delta}{4}.$$

They also presented a Fermat-like factoring attack for

$$\gamma < \frac{1}{r^2}.$$

Takayasu-Kunihiro [22]. Given the prime difference $\Delta = N^\gamma$ and the public key (N, e), then d can be probabilistically found in time polynomial in $\log N$ if γ and δ satisfy

$$\delta < 1 - \sqrt{1 + 2\gamma - \frac{3}{r}} \text{ for } \frac{3}{2}(\frac{1}{r} - \frac{1}{4}) \le \gamma < \frac{1}{r},$$

$$\delta < 1 - \frac{2}{3}(\sqrt{(7 + 8\gamma - \frac{12}{r})(1 + 2\gamma - \frac{3}{r})} - 1 - 2\gamma + \frac{3}{r}) \text{ for } \gamma < \frac{3}{2}(\frac{1}{r} - \frac{1}{4}).$$

Notice that the condition $\frac{3}{2r} - \frac{1+\delta}{4}$ in Zhang-Takagi attack degenerates to $-\frac{\delta}{4}$ for $r = 6$, and the condition $\frac{3}{2}(\frac{1}{r} - \frac{1}{4})$ in Takayasu-Kunihiro attack degenerates to 0 for $r = 4$. Thus, Zhang-Takagi attack and Takayasu-Kunihiro attack depend on δ with $\gamma < \frac{1}{r}$ for larger r. In such cases, factoring attacks with quite small γ are much more effective without any restriction on δ. The distinction is the dependence on the private exponent and this is also the advantage of factoring attacks.

1.2 Our Contribution

In this paper, we aim to factor the multi-prime RSA modulus with small prime difference. More concretely, N can be factored in polynomial time under which condition when given the multi-prime RSA modulus N that is the product of r distinct primes and its prime difference N^γ.

Let $x_i = p_i - p$ for $i = 1, 2, \ldots, r$ with $|x_i| = |p_i - p| < p_r - p_1 = N^\gamma$ for $p = [N^{\frac{1}{r}}]$. At ACISP 2013, Zhang and Takagi [25] solved x_i from each equation and computed prime factors by $p_i = x_i + p$. In our opinion, they only made use of partial information about prime factors with prime difference. In contrast, we transform the knowledge of all balanced prime factors with prime difference into the following modular equations.

$$\begin{cases} x_1 + p = 0 \bmod p_1, \\ x_2 + p = 0 \bmod p_2, \\ \quad\vdots \\ x_r + p = 0 \bmod p_r. \end{cases}$$

Our factoring problem is somewhat similar to multi-prime Φ-hiding problem introduced by Kiltz et al. [16] because of the modular equation form. The definition of multi-prime Φ-hiding problem is given. Let $N = p_1 \cdots p_r$ be a composite integer (of unknown factorization) with r distinct prime factors of same bit-size. Given N and a prime e, decide whether e divides p_i for $1 \le i \le r - 1$ or not.

In order to solve multi-prime Φ-hiding problem, one can try to solve the following simultaneous equations and then conclude that e is Φ-hidden in N or not.

$$\begin{cases} ex_1 + 1 = 0 \bmod p_1, \\ ex_2 + 1 = 0 \bmod p_2, \\ \quad\vdots \\ ex_{r-1} + 1 = 0 \bmod p_{r-1}. \end{cases}$$

There exist some differences between these two problems. In Φ-hiding problem, since it is not necessary to know the exact values of the unknowns but enough to know if the equations can be solved, one can perform a linearization on the product $\prod_{i=1}^{r-1}(ex_i+1)$ and then decide if $\prod_{i=1}^{r-1}(ex_i+1) = 0 \bmod p_1p_2\cdots p_{r-1}$ can be solved. Thus, it is like a "decision"-form problem. Our factoring problem is like a "search"-form one because we must extract the value of every unknown variable. In our optimized method, we can transform the factoring problem into a "decision"-form problem and then apply the optimal linearization technique.

Another difference is that we do not have $ex_r + 1 = 0 \bmod p_r$ in Φ-hiding problem. This special feature can be applied to improve the bound [24]. However we can not directly use the same technique to solve the factoring problem.

Our improvements are based on two ideas. The first one is a direct method by gathering all the equations together to solve an r-variate modular equation. The drawback of this method is that the running time is exponential in r. So we provide an optimized method by combining fewer equations. Inspired by Tosu and Kunihiro [23], we can benefit from the optimal linearization technique with fewer unknowns and less cost. Thus, we will obtain a great speedup and efficient performance in the practical implementation.

We show that multi-prime RSA modulus with small prime difference can be efficiently factored in the following cases due to various r's.

– For $r \leq 6$, we have

$$\gamma < \frac{2}{r(r+1)}.$$

– For $r \geq 7$ and an optimal l, we have

$$\gamma < \frac{2}{l+1}\left(\frac{1}{r}\right)^{\frac{l+1}{l}}.$$

– For much larger r and the base of natural logarithm e, we have

$$\gamma < \frac{2}{er(\log r + 1)}.$$

2 Preliminaries

2.1 Lattice Based Method

We briefly introduce lattice based method including the LLL algorithm [17], Coppersmith's technique [6–8], Howgrave-Graham's lemma [15] and Coron's reformulation [9,10].

The technique is to construct a set of polynomials modulo R sharing the common roots and then reduce them to the equations over the integers. After transforming known parameters into constructed polynomials' coefficients that form a lattice basis matrix with dimension w. One can compute some short lattice vectors whose norm is expected to be sufficiently small by the LLL algorithm. Eventually, one can solve the desired roots. The LLL algorithm proposed by Lenstra, Lenstra and Lovász [17] is practically used for finding approximately small lattice vectors.

Lemma 1. *Let $\mathcal{L}$ be a lattice with determinant $\det(\mathcal{L})$. The LLL algorithm outputs a reduced basis $(\boldsymbol{v}_1, \boldsymbol{v}_2, \ldots, \boldsymbol{v}_w)$ in polynomial time, and for $1 \leq i \leq w$, the reduced basis vectors satisfy*

$$\|\boldsymbol{v}_1\|, \|\boldsymbol{v}_2\|, \ldots, \|\boldsymbol{v}_i\| \leq 2^{\frac{w(w-1)}{4(w+1-i)}} \det(\mathcal{L})^{\frac{1}{w+1-i}}.$$

The following lemma presented by Howgrave-Graham [15] helps us to judge whether the roots of a modular equation are also roots over the integers. To a given polynomial $g(x_1, \ldots, x_n) = \sum a_{i_1,\ldots,i_n} x_1^{i_1} \cdots x_n^{i_n}$, its norm is defined as $\|g(x_1, \ldots, x_n)\|^2 := \sum |a_{i_1,\ldots,i_n}|^2$.

Lemma 2. *Let $g(x_1, \ldots, x_n) \in \mathbb{Z}[x_1, \ldots, x_n]$ be an integer polynomial that is a sum of at most m monomials. Suppose that*

1. *$\|g(x_1 X_1, \ldots, x_n X_n)\| \leq \frac{R}{\sqrt{m}}$,*
2. *$g(x_1^{(0)}, \ldots, x_n^{(0)}) = 0 \bmod R$ for $|x_1^{(0)}| \leq X_1, \ldots, |x_n^{(0)}| \leq X_n$.*

Then we have $g(x_1^{(0)}, \ldots, x_n^{(0)}) = 0$ over the integers.

The above fundamental lemmas give us the final condition, which is roughly $\det(\mathcal{L}) < R^w$. Some RSA cryptanalytic applications [2,8,12] are derived from such lattice based method. But Boneh and Durfee [2] have noted that solving multivariate equations is heuristic because the polynomials derived from lattice reduction algorithms are not guaranteed to be algebraically independent. In order to extract the exact roots in practice, we rely on the following assumption.

Assumption 1. *The polynomials derived from the LLL algorithm in lattice based method are algebraically independent. Furthermore, the solution can be efficiently found by Gröbner basis computations.*

Our improved attacks can be reduced to solving multivariate linear equations that was studied by Herrmann and May [12].

Lemma 3. *Let $\epsilon > 0$ and let N be a sufficiently large composite integer (of unknown factorization) with a divisor $p \geq N^\beta$. Furthermore, let $f(x_1, \ldots, x_n) \in \mathbb{Z}[x_1, \ldots, x_n]$ be a linear polynomial in n variables. Under Assumption 1, we can find solutions $(x_1^{(0)}, \ldots, x_n^{(0)})$ of the equation $f(x_1, \ldots, x_n) = 0 \bmod p$ with $|x_1^{(0)}| \leq N^{\eta_1}, \ldots, |x_n^{(0)}| \leq N^{\eta_n}$ if*

$$\sum_{i=1}^{n} \eta_i \leq 1 - (n+1)(1-\beta) + n(1-\beta)^{\frac{n+1}{n}} - \epsilon.$$

The time complexity is polynomial in $\log N$ and $(e/\epsilon)^n$.

The lattice based algorithm was later improved by Lu et al. [19] and Takayasu and Kunihiro [21]. Since the cryptanalysis is based on approximations, we neglect the lower order terms and remove ϵ in our methods for simplicity.

2.2 Some Notations

We introduce the following notations for our methods.

- p denotes the value of rounding $N^{\frac{1}{r}}$ to the nearest integer and it is mentioned above as $p = [N^{\frac{1}{r}}]$.
- σ_i^k denotes the elementary symmetric polynomial in k variables $y_1, \ldots, y_k$ of degree i and it is defined by $\sigma_i^k := \sum_{\lambda \subset \{1,2,\ldots,k\}, |\lambda|=i} \left(\prod_{j \in \lambda} y_j \right)$.
- Q_k denotes the product of k prime factors that are chosen from $p_1, p_2, \ldots, p_r$ and hence Q_k is a divisor of N.
- Q'_k denotes the numerical value of the left side after solving the equation and hence Q'_k is a multiple of Q_k.

3 Improved Factoring Attacks

3.1 The Direct Method

As mentioned before, we gather all the equations together to solve an r-variate modular equation. More concretely, we present the following factoring attack.

Proposition 1. *Let $N = p_1 \cdots p_r$ be a multi-prime RSA modulus for $p_1 < \cdots < p_r$ and $p_r - p_1 = N^\gamma$ for $0 < \gamma < \frac{1}{r}$. Then under Assumption 1, N can be factored in time polynomial in $\log N$ but exponential in r if*

$$\gamma < \frac{2}{r(r+1)}.$$

Our approach utilizes the equation form of multi-prime Φ-hiding problem. Let e be the inverse of p modulo N, namely $e = p^{-1} \bmod N$. Then $y_i + p = 0 \bmod p_i$ can be rewritten as $ey_i + 1 = 0 \bmod p_i$ and we obtain

$$\begin{cases} ey_1 + 1 = 0 \bmod p_1, \\ \quad \vdots \\ ey_r + 1 = 0 \bmod p_r. \end{cases}$$

Combining all equations together gives us

$$\prod_{i=1}^{r}(ey_i + 1) = \sum_{i=1}^{r} e^i \sigma_i^r + 1 = 0 \bmod N.$$

We have $e = p^{-1} \bmod N$ that is equivalent to $ep = 1 \bmod N$. It can be reduced to $\sum_{i=1}^{r} e^i \sigma_i^r + ep = 0 \bmod N$ and further

$$\sum_{i=1}^{r} e^{i-1} \sigma_i^r + p = 0 \bmod N.$$

Regarding each σ_i^r as a new variable makes $\sum_{i=1}^{r} e^{i-1}\sigma_i^r + p$ a linear equation. We then figure out each η_i of $|\sigma_i^r| < N^{\eta_i}$ for $i = 1, \ldots, r$ and apply Lemma 3 with $\beta = 1$. It is not hard to know that $\eta_i = i\gamma$ for $1 \le i \le r$. Thus, the final condition is $\sum_{i=1}^{r} i\gamma < 1$, which can be simplified to

$$\gamma < \frac{2}{r(r+1)}.$$

After solving the linear equation, we obtain the values of $\sigma_1^r, \ldots, \sigma_r^r$. Then we extract $x_1, \ldots, x_r$ by solving $x^r - \sigma_1^r x^{r-1} + \cdots + (-1)^r \sigma_r^r = 0$ over the integers. Finally, we compute the prime factors $p_1, \ldots, p_r$ for $p_i = x_i + p$. The full description of the algorithm is given in Appendix A.1.

The running time depends on reducing the basis matrix and extracting the common roots. The LLL algorithm can output the desired polynomials in time polynomial in $\log N$ but exponential in r. This may be a drawback due to large r and forces us to find more efficient method. The Gröbner basis computation for finding the common roots is usually polynomial time in practice. Additionally, one can obtain more polynomials derived from the LLL algorithm and hence the Gröbner basis computation is suggested rather than resultant computation.

3.2   The Optimized Method

As described in the direct method, we still solve the factoring problem in the view of a "search"-form problem. Its drawback is that the time complexity is exponential in r. Consequently, the factoring attack becomes less efficient for larger r.

When considering taking fewer equations to form one modular equation, we have some interesting observations. We randomly choose k ($2 \le k \le r - 1$) equations and obtain a new equation $F(y_1, \ldots, y_k) = 0 \bmod Q_k$. Fortunately, it is enough to know the numerical value Q_k' of the left side and not necessary to know exact values of $y_1, \ldots, y_k$. Then, computing the greatest common divisor $\gcd(Q_k', N)$ gives us all combinations of k prime factors that indicate every prime factor.

In fact, the factoring problem is refined to become of "decision"-form. Thus, we can employ the optimal linearization similar to the technique proposed by

Tosu and Kunihiro [23] when solving multi-prime Φ-hiding problem. The idea is to examine all possible linearization cases to find the optimal setting when it can be efficiently solved. We present the optimized factoring attack below.

Proposition 2. *Let $N = p_1 \cdots p_r$ be a multi-prime RSA modulus for $p_1 < \cdots < p_r$ and $p_r - p_1 = N^\gamma$ for $0 < \gamma < \frac{1}{r}$. Then under Assumption 1, N can be factored in time polynomial in $\log N$ with an optimal l if*

$$\gamma < \frac{2}{l+1} \left(\frac{1}{r}\right)^{\frac{l+1}{l}}.$$

We consider combining k equations and performing a linearization of l ($2 \leq l \leq k$) variables. Note that the parameters k and l need to be decided later. First, we have $(y_1 + p)(y_2 + p) \cdots (y_k + p) = 0 \bmod Q_k$. It can be rewritten as $\sum_{i=0}^{k} p^{k-i} \sigma_i^k = 0 \bmod Q_k$. The expansion is

$$\sigma_k^k + p\sigma_{k-1}^k + p^2\sigma_{k-2}^k + \cdots + p^k = 0 \bmod Q_k.$$

Then, we apply a linearization for the case of l variables. Let $t_1, \ldots, t_{l+1}$ be the integers satisfying $t_1 = k > t_2 > \cdots > t_{l+1} = 0$. We obtain

$$p^{k-t_1} u_1 + p^{k-t_2} u_2 + \cdots + p^{k-t_l} u_l + p^k = 0 \bmod Q_k,$$

where $u_i := \sum_{j=t_{i+1}+1}^{t_i} p^{t_i - j} \sigma_j^k$ for $1 \leq i \leq l$. For $|y_i| < N^\gamma$, $p \approx N^{\frac{1}{r}}$ and $\gamma < \frac{1}{r}$, we know that the bound is $|u_i| < N^{\frac{t_i - t_{i+1} - 1}{r} + (t_{i+1}+1)\gamma}$. In other words, we have

$$\eta_i = \frac{t_i - t_{i+1} - 1}{r} + (t_{i+1}+1)\gamma.$$

Thus, we can find the roots of the linear equation by Lemma 3 with $\beta = \frac{k}{r}$ and above η_i if $\sum_{i=1}^{n} \eta_i < 1 - (l+1)(1 - \beta) + l(1 - \beta)^{\frac{l+1}{l}}$.
Then we have

$$\gamma < \frac{l \cdot \left(\frac{k+1}{r} + (1 - \frac{k}{r})^{\frac{l+1}{l}} - 1\right)}{l + \sum_{i=2}^{l} t_i}.$$

The above bound reaches its maximum by setting $(t_1, t_2, t_3, \ldots, t_l)$ to be $(k, l-1, l-2 \ldots, 1)$. The condition now is

$$\gamma < \frac{2}{l+1} \left(\frac{k+1}{r} + (1 - \frac{k}{r})^{\frac{l+1}{l}} - 1\right).$$

We can further optimize k to obtain the best bound on γ by calculating the derivative on k. It can be verified that $k = r - 1$ is the most suitable choice. Thus, we derive the condition

$$\gamma < \frac{2}{l+1} \left(\frac{1}{r}\right)^{\frac{l+1}{l}}.$$

It means that we need to solve

$$u_1 + p^{r-l}u_2 + \cdots + p^{r-2}u_l + p^{r-1} = 0 \bmod Q_{r-1}.$$

The optimal value of l can be discovered by numerical computation. For each positive integer $r \leq 10$, the optimal cases are $l = 2$ for $r = 3, 4, 5$, and $l = 3$ for $r = 6, 7, 8, 9, 10$. To be specific, we show the final equations need to be solved in our optimized method as follows.

– For $r = 3, 4, 5$, that is

$$u_1 + p^{r-2}u_2 + p^{r-1} = 0 \bmod Q_{r-1}.$$

– For $r = 6, 7, 8, 9, 10$, that is

$$u_1 + p^{r-3}u_2 + p^{r-2}u_3 + p^{r-1} = 0 \bmod Q_{r-1}.$$

As analyzed in [23], we set $l \approx \log r$ for much larger r and the condition is approximated

$$\gamma < \frac{2}{er(\log r + 1)},$$

where e is the base of natural logarithm. Therefore, we also present the factoring attack for much larger r.

Proposition 3. *Let $N = p_1 \cdots p_r$ be a multi-prime RSA modulus for $p_1 < \cdots < p_r$ and $p_r - p_1 = N^\gamma$ for $0 < \gamma < \frac{1}{r}$. Then under Assumption 1, N can be factored in time polynomial in $\log N$ for much larger r if*

$$\gamma < \frac{2}{er(\log r + 1)}.$$

After solving the modular equation, we obtain the values of $u_1, \ldots, u_l$. Then we know all combinations of $r - 1$ prime factors by $\gcd(Q'_{r-1}, N)$. Finally, we compute each prime factor by $\frac{N}{\gcd(Q'_{r-1}, N)}$.

Note that we can find all prime factors by solving the linear equation once because every combination (or product) of $r - 1$ prime factors is equivalent to each other. Using $l \approx \log r$ implies that our method works in time polynomial in $\log N$ and r.

3.3   Discussions

Compare with the direct method, we have two improvements in our optimized method. Firstly, we decrease the number of unknown variables and significantly improve the practical performance for larger r. Secondly, we can achieve a better bound for much larger r at the same time. But for $r \leq 6$, the direct method offers a higher bound and hence the factoring attack is still in polynomial time.

Note that the unknown variables u_i's in the optimized method are quite unbalanced. So we make further improvement by applying better lattice constructions proposed by Takayasu and Kunihiro [21]. Here we omit the complicated analysis and show another advantage. For $r \leq 10$, the optimal l is always 2. It means that the final equation we need to solve in the optimized method is $u_1 + p^{r-2}u_2 + p^{r-1} = 0 \bmod Q_{r-1}$. Thus, we further reduce the running time of the optimized factoring attack. The full description of the optimized algorithm and detailed lattice construction are given in Appendix A.2.

Table 1 shows the comparison of upper bound on γ due to above factoring attacks for $r \leq 10$. The fourth column provides the results using better lattice construction that is discussed above. It is visible that our methods are superior.

Table 1. The comparison of upper bound on γ due to above factoring attacks

r	Section 3.1	Section 3.2	Section 3.3	Zhang-Takagi [25]
3	**0.1666**	0.1283	—	0.1111
4	**0.1000**	0.0833	0.0835	0.0625
5	**0.0666**	0.0596	0.0608	0.0400
6	**0.0476**	0.0458	0.0474	0.0277
7	0.0357	0.0373	**0.0387**	0.0204
8	0.0277	0.0312	**0.0327**	0.0156
9	0.0222	0.0267	**0.0282**	0.0123
10	0.0181	0.0232	**0.0248**	0.0100

3.4 Experimental Results

We now state some experimental results to show the practical performance of our methods. These experiments are carried out under Sage 7.3 running on a laptop with Intel Core i7 CPU 2.70 GHz and 8 GB RAM. The numbers we used are chosen uniformly at random and Assumption 1 is found to hold for the experiments.

During the experiments, we collect many polynomials satisfying our requirements. In other words, we obtain enough sufficiently short vectors after running the LLL algorithm. Hence, we extract the common roots by Gröbner basis computation and finally attain the factorization of multi-prime RSA modulus.

We provide the experimental results on two attacks according to Sects. 3.1 and 3.2 (actually refined by Sect. 3.3), namely the γ_{e1}-column and γ_{e2}-column, respectively. The γ_{zt}-column provides the experimental bound of Zhang-Takagi method. The results about the comparison are showed in Table 2.

We firstly comment the experiments for $r = 3$. We reduce a 220-dimensional lattice for the direct method while we use a lattice whose dimension is 300 for the optimized method. A 1536-bit multi-prime RSA modulus can be successfully factored by a 174-bit prime difference by the direct method. While using the

Table 2. The experimental results of upper bound on γ

r	γ_{zt}	γ_{e1}	γ_{e2}
3	0.1109	0.1132	0.1120
4	0.0620	—	0.0750
5	0.0396	—	0.0533
6	0.0275	—	0.0337
7	0.0202	—	0.0286

optimized method, a 172-bit difference leads to the factorization of a 1536-bit modulus. Thus, we conclude that the direct method performs better for $r = 3$ with roughly similar lattice setting. On the other hand, we observe that the optimized method runs much faster, which is predicted above.

For $4 \leq r \leq 7$, we use the optimized method with lattices whose dimension is around 300 since it is more efficient. We carry out experiments for much smaller moduli with almost the same lattice setting and they work much better. We also do experiments for moduli of the same size with various lattice dimensions for $r = 3, 4$. The results become better as the lattice dimension increases. So the lattice dimension may be a critical limitation that influences the practical performance of lattice based methods. The optimized bounds for $4 \leq r \leq 7$ showed in the γ_{e2}-column are those observed in the experiments with much smaller moduli. More details are given in Appendix B.

4   Conclusions

Factoring attack works better than small private exponent attack on multi-prime RSA with much smaller prime difference, and the former removes the restriction on the private exponents. We further upgrade the insecure bound on the prime difference and propose improved factoring attacks based on lattice approach and the optimal linearization technique.

To summarize, our factoring attacks make significant improvements by taking full knowledge of the small prime difference. We combine more equations rather than only one equation to solve the factoring problem. Furthermore, applying the optimal linearization technique on unknown variables helps us to reduce the time cost and obtain better results.

For our factoring attacks on multi-prime RSA modulus with r primes, solving an r-variate linear equation constructed by r simultaneous modular equations is preferred for $r \leq 6$. And solving an l-variate (l depends on r) linear equation constructed by $r - 1$ equations is preferred for $r \geq 7$. Both factoring attacks can be done in polynomial time.

Acknowledgments. The first author is supported by China Scholarship Council Grant No. 201606340061. This research was partially supported by JST CREST Grant Number JPMJCR14D6, Japan and JSPS KAKENHI Grant Number 16H02780, and National Natural Science Foundation of China (Grant Nos. 61522210, 61632013), 100 Talents Program of Chinese Academy of Sciences, and the Fundamental Research Funds for the Central Universities in China (Grant No. WK2101020005).

A   Algorithms

A.1   The Direct Method

Algorithm 1. The direct method (Sect. 3.1)

Input: Multi-prime RSA modulus N with r and small prime difference N^γ.
Output: The factorization $N = p_1 \cdots p_r$.
1: Compute $p = [N^{\frac{1}{r}}]$ and $e = p^{-1} \bmod N$.
2: Construct the linear modular equation with unknown variables σ_i^r:

$$\sigma_1^r + e^1\sigma_2^r + \cdots + e^{r-1}\sigma_r^r + p = 0 \bmod N.$$

3: Figure out η_i's that are related to the bounds N^{η_i} on σ_i^r for $1 \le i \le r$:

$$|\sigma_i^r| < N^{i\gamma}.$$

4: Extract each σ_i^r by applying Lemma 3.
5: Solve $x^r - \sigma_1^r x^{r-1} + \cdots + (-1)^r \sigma_r^r = 0$ over the integers.
6: Set $p_i = p + x_i$ in increasing order with roots x_i for $1 \le i \le r$.

A.2   The Optimized Method

In Takayasu-Kunihiro lattice construction, we carefully work out the selection of polynomials by considering the sizes of root bounds. For example, we deal with $u_1 + p^{r-2}u_2 + p^{r-1} = 0 \bmod Q_{r-1}$ in our optimized method. We use $u_2^{i_2}(u_1 + p^{r-2}u_2 + p^{r-1})^{i_1}N^{\max\{t-i_1,0\}}$ as the shift polynomials with positive integers m and t that will be optimized later. The indexes i_1 and i_2 satisfy $0 \le i_1 + i_2 \le m$ and $0 \le \gamma_1 i_1 + \gamma_2 i_2 \le \beta t$ in order to select as many helpful polynomials as possible and to let the basis matrix be triangular.

Thus, the shift polynomials modulo p^t have the common roots for u_1 and u_2. We span a lattice by the coefficient vectors of above shift polynomials and the equations are derived from the reduced LLL basis vectors. The small roots can be easily recovered by Gröbner basis computation.

Algorithm 2. The optimized method (Sect. 3.2)

Input: Multi-prime RSA modulus N with r and small prime difference N^γ.
Output: The factorization $N = p_1 \cdots p_r$.

1: Compute $p = [N^{\frac{1}{r}}]$.
2: Choose an optimal l according to r.
3: Construct the linear modular equation with unknown variables u_i:

$$u_1 + p^{r-l}u_2 + \cdots + p^{r-2}u_l + p^{r-1} = 0 \bmod Q_{r-1}.$$

4: Figure out η_i's that are related to the bounds N^{η_i} on σ_i^r for $1 \le i \le l$ with known $(t_1, t_2, t_3, \ldots, t_l, t_{l+1}) = (r-1, l-1, l-2 \ldots, 1, 0)$:

$$|u_i| < N^{\frac{t_i - t_{i+1} - 1}{r} + (t_{i+1}+1)\gamma}.$$

5: Extract each u_i by using Takayasu-Kunihiro lattice construction.
6: Compute $Q'_{r-1} = u_1 + p^{r-l}u_2 + \cdots + p^{r-2}u_l + p^{r-1}$ with roots $\{u_1, \ldots, u_l\}$.
7: Set $p_i = N/\gcd(Q'_{r-1}, N)$ in increasing order for $1 \le i \le r$.

B   More Details About the Experimental Results

More graphs about the experimental results are showed below. Firstly, as showed in Figs. 1 and 2, upper bound on γ gets better when the lattice dimension increases. For the direct method, upper bound on γ remains stable when the lattice dimension is between 50 and 170. For the optimized method, the value is between 60 and 300.

We then show the experimental results for $r = 3$ using the direct method in Fig. 3. As the size of the modulus increases, γ finally arrives around 0.113. This value is beyond the asymptotic bound $\frac{1}{9}$ of previous Zhang-Takagi method.

The remaining graphs are related to the experiments for $3 \le r \le 7$ with various moduli using the optimized method. The lattice dimension of each experiment is set around 300. From Figs. 4, 5, 6, 7 and 8, we find that upper bound on γ is higher for smaller modulus and then goes to a lower value. Also it will finally arrive at a certain value that may be determined by the lattice dimension.

Another observation is that these lattices whose dimension is around 300 seem less effective for moduli with larger bit-size. To be specific, it is less effective for the moduli of greater than 500-bit when $r = 3$. The critical bit-size is 700-bit for $r = 4, 5$ and 1000-bit for $r = 6, 7$. Thus, we guess that the lattices used in our experiments are effective for the prime factor of less than 160-bit. To obtain desired upper bounds, we need to apply some lattices with huge dimension.

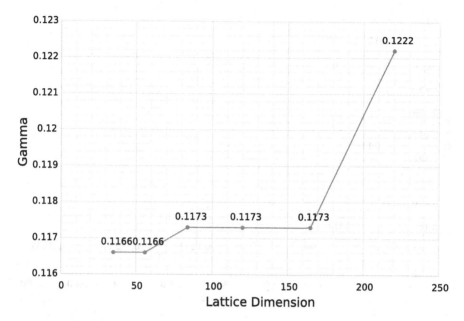

Fig. 1. The experimental results of upper bound on γ with various lattice dimensions and the same bit-size moduli for $r = 3$ using the direct method

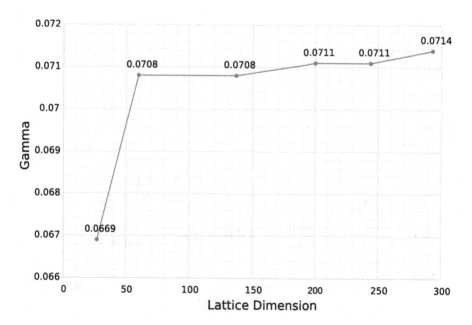

Fig. 2. The experimental results of upper bound on γ with various lattice dimensions and the same bit-size moduli for $r = 4$ using the optimized method

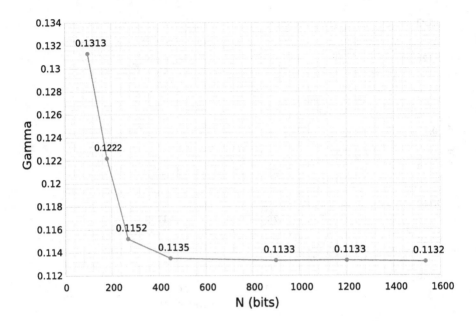

Fig. 3. The experimental results of upper bound on γ with various moduli for $r = 3$ using the direct method

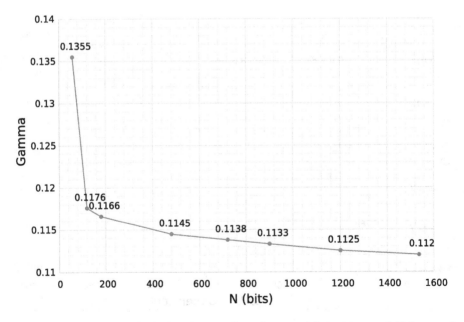

Fig. 4. The experimental results of upper bound on γ with various moduli for $r = 3$ using the optimized method

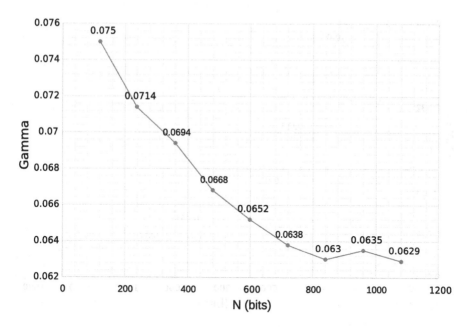

Fig. 5. The experimental results of upper bound on γ with various moduli for $r = 4$ using the optimized method

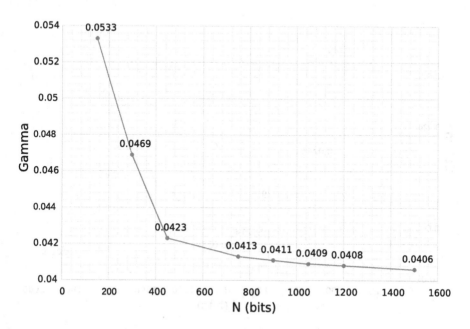

Fig. 6. The experimental results of upper bound on γ with various moduli for $r = 5$ using the optimized method

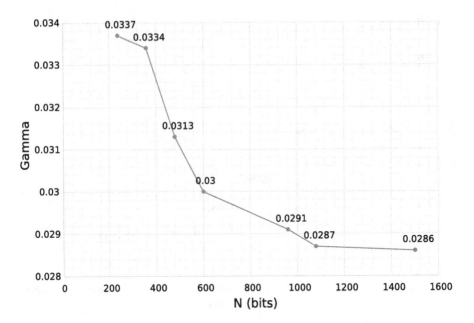

Fig. 7. The experimental results of upper bound on γ with various moduli for $r = 6$ using the optimized method

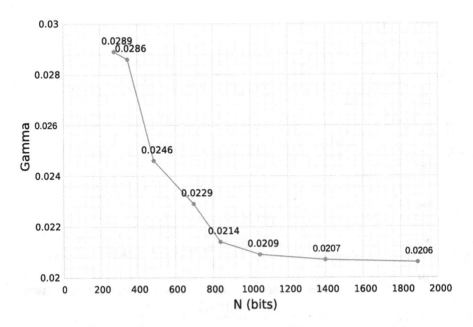

Fig. 8. The experimental results of upper bound on γ with various moduli for $r = 7$ using the optimized method

References

1. Bahig, H.M., Bhery, A., Nassr, D.I.: Cryptanalysis of multi-prime RSA with small prime difference. In: Chim, T.W., Yuen, T.H. (eds.) ICICS 2012. LNCS, vol. 7618, pp. 33–44. Springer, Heidelberg (2012). doi:10.1007/978-3-642-34129-8_4
2. Boneh, D., Durfee, G.: Cryptanalysis of RSA with private key d less than $N^{0.292}$. IEEE Trans. Inf. Theory **46**(4), 1339–1349 (2000)
3. Boneh, D., Shacham, H.: Fast variants of RSA. CryptoBytes **5**(1), 1–9 (2002)
4. Ciet, M., Koeune, F., Laguillaumie, F., Quisquater, J.J.: Short private exponent attacks on fast variants of RSA. Technical report, UCL Crypto Group Technical Report Series CG-2002/4, Université Catholique de Louvain (2002)
5. Collins, T., Hopkins, D., Langford, S., Sabin, M.: Public key cryptographic apparatus and method, US Patent#5,848,159 (1997)
6. Coppersmith, D.: Finding a small root of a bivariate integer equation; factoring with high bits known. In: Maurer, U. (ed.) EUROCRYPT 1996. LNCS, vol. 1070, pp. 178–189. Springer, Heidelberg (1996). doi:10.1007/3-540-68339-9_16
7. Coppersmith, D.: Finding a small root of a univariate modular equation. In: Maurer, U. (ed.) EUROCRYPT 1996. LNCS, vol. 1070, pp. 155–165. Springer, Heidelberg (1996). doi:10.1007/3-540-68339-9_14
8. Coppersmith, D.: Small solutions to polynomial equations, and low exponent RSA vulnerabilities. J. Cryptology **10**(4), 233–260 (1997)
9. Coron, J.-S.: Finding small roots of bivariate integer polynomial equations revisited. In: Cachin, C., Camenisch, J.L. (eds.) EUROCRYPT 2004. LNCS, vol. 3027, pp. 492–505. Springer, Heidelberg (2004). doi:10.1007/978-3-540-24676-3_29
10. Coron, J.-S.: Finding small roots of bivariate integer polynomial equations: a direct approach. In: Menezes, A. (ed.) CRYPTO 2007. LNCS, vol. 4622, pp. 379–394. Springer, Heidelberg (2007). doi:10.1007/978-3-540-74143-5_21
11. De Weger, B.: Cryptanalysis of RSA with small prime difference. Appl. Algebra Eng. Commun. Comput. **13**(1), 17–28 (2002)
12. Herrmann, M., May, A.: Solving linear equations modulo divisors: on factoring given any bits. In: Pieprzyk, J. (ed.) ASIACRYPT 2008. LNCS, vol. 5350, pp. 406–424. Springer, Heidelberg (2008). doi:10.1007/978-3-540-89255-7_25
13. Hinek, M.J.: On the security of multi-prime RSA. J. Math. Cryptology **2**(2), 117–147 (2008)
14. Hinek, M.J., Low, M.K., Teske, E.: On some attacks on multi-prime RSA. In: Nyberg, K., Heys, H. (eds.) SAC 2002. LNCS, vol. 2595, pp. 385–404. Springer, Heidelberg (2003). doi:10.1007/3-540-36492-7_25
15. Howgrave-Graham, N.: Finding small roots of univariate modular equations revisited. In: Darnell, M. (ed.) Cryptography and Coding 1997. LNCS, vol. 1355, pp. 131–142. Springer, Heidelberg (1997). doi:10.1007/BFb0024458
16. Kiltz, E., O'Neill, A., Smith, A.: Instantiability of RSA-OAEP under chosen-plaintext attack. In: Rabin, T. (ed.) CRYPTO 2010. LNCS, vol. 6223, pp. 295–313. Springer, Heidelberg (2010). doi:10.1007/978-3-642-14623-7_16
17. Lenstra, A.K., Lenstra, H.W., Lovász, L.: Factoring polynomials with rational coefficients. Math. Ann. **261**(4), 515–534 (1982)
18. Lenstra Jr., H.W.: Factoring integers with elliptic curves. Ann. Math. **126**(3), 649–673 (1987)
19. Lu, Y., Zhang, R., Peng, L., Lin, D.: Solving linear equations modulo unknown divisors: revisited. In: Iwata, T., Cheon, J.H. (eds.) ASIACRYPT 2015. LNCS, vol. 9452, pp. 189–213. Springer, Heidelberg (2015). doi:10.1007/978-3-662-48797-6_9

20. Rivest, R.L., Shamir, A., Adleman, L.: A method for obtaining digital signatures and public-key cryptosystems. Commun. ACM **21**(2), 120–126 (1978)

21. Takayasu, A., Kunihiro, N.: Better lattice constructions for solving multivariate linear equations modulo unknown divisors. In: Boyd, C., Simpson, L. (eds.) ACISP 2013. LNCS, vol. 7959, pp. 118–135. Springer, Heidelberg (2013). doi:10.1007/978-3-642-39059-3_9

22. Takayasu, A., Kunihiro, N.: General bounds for small inverse problems and its applications to multi-prime RSA. In: Lee, J., Kim, J. (eds.) ICISC 2014. LNCS, vol. 8949, pp. 3–17. Springer, Cham (2015). doi:10.1007/978-3-319-15943-0_1

23. Tosu, K., Kunihiro, N.: Optimal bounds for multi-prime Φ-hiding assumption. In: Susilo, W., Mu, Y., Seberry, J. (eds.) ACISP 2012. LNCS, vol. 7372, pp. 1–14. Springer, Heidelberg (2012). doi:10.1007/978-3-642-31448-3_1

24. Xu, J., Hu, L., Sarkar, S., Zhang, X., Huang, Z., Peng, L.: Cryptanalysis of multi-prime Φ-hiding assumption. In: Bishop, M., Nascimento, A.C.A. (eds.) ISC 2016. LNCS, vol. 9866, pp. 440–453. Springer, Cham (2016). doi:10.1007/978-3-319-45871-7_26

25. Zhang, H., Takagi, T.: Attacks on multi-prime RSA with small prime difference. In: Boyd, C., Simpson, L. (eds.) ACISP 2013. LNCS, vol. 7959, pp. 41–56. Springer, Heidelberg (2013). doi:10.1007/978-3-642-39059-3_4

26. Zhang, H., Takagi, T.: Improved attacks on multi-prime RSA with small prime difference. IEICE Trans. Fundam. Electron. Commun. Comput. Sci. **97**(7), 1533–1541 (2014)

Efficient Compilers for After-the-Fact Leakage: From CPA to CCA-2 Secure PKE to AKE

Suvradip Chakraborty[1], Goutam Paul[2([⊠])], and C. Pandu Rangan[1]

[1] Department of Computer Science and Engineering, Indian Institute
of Technology Madras, Chennai, India
suvradip1111@gmail.com, prangan55@gmail.com
[2] Cryptology and Security Research Unit (CSRU), R. C. Bose Centre
for Cryptology and Security, Indian Statistical Institute, Kolkata, India
goutam.paul@isical.ac.in

Abstract. The goal of leakage-resilient cryptography is to construct cryptographic algorithms that are secure even if the adversary obtains side-channel information from the real world implementation of these algorithms. Most of the prior works on leakage-resilient cryptography consider leakage models where the adversary has access to the leakage oracle before the challenge-ciphertext is generated (before-the-fact leakage). In this model, there are generic compilers that transform any leakage-resilient CPA-secure public key encryption (PKE) scheme to its CCA-2 variant using Naor-Yung type of transformations. In this work, we give an efficient *generic compiler* for transforming a leakage-resilient CPA-secure PKE to leakage-resilient CCA-2 secure PKE in presence of *after-the-fact split-state* (bounded) *memory* leakage model, where the adversary has access to the leakage oracle even after the challenge phase. The *salient* feature of our transformation is that the leakage rate (defined as the ratio of the amount of leakage to the size of secret key) of the transformed after-the-fact CCA-2 secure PKE is same as the leakage rate of the underlying after-the-fact CPA-secure PKE, which is $1 - o(1)$.

We then present another generic compiler for transforming an after-the-fact leakage-resilient CCA-2 secure PKE to a leakage-resilient authenticated key exchange (AKE) protocol in the bounded after-the-fact leakage-resilient eCK (BAFL-eCK) model proposed by Alawatugoda et al. (ASIACCS'14). To the best of our knowledge, this gives the *first* compiler that transform any leakage-resilient CCA-2 secure PKE to an AKE protocol in the leakage variant of the eCK model.

Keywords: After-the-fact leakage · Bounded memory leakage · Split-state · Authenticated key exchange · Leakage-resilient exponentiation

1 Introduction and Related Works

Most of the real-world attacks on a cryptosystem target the physical implementation of the device in which it is implemented. Such "physical attacks" are usually

© Springer International Publishing AG 2017
J. Pieprzyk and S. Suriadi (Eds.): ACISP 2017, Part I, LNCS 10342, pp. 343–362, 2017.
DOI: 10.1007/978-3-319-60055-0_18

based on the *side-channel information* about the internals of the cryptographic device, which the adversary may get via myriads of side-channel attacks like timing measurements, power analysis, fault injection attacks, electromagnetic measurements, microwave attacks, memory attacks and many more [18,20,21]. Leakage-resilient cryptography was introduced to deal with this problem from a theoretical standpoint. It guarantees the security of the cryptosystems even in the face of side-channel attacks and analyzes the effectiveness of side-channel countermeasures in a mathematically rigorous way. The broad idea is that in addition to the usual interfaces with which the adversary can interact with the cryptographic primitive, he/she can choose arbitrary leakage functions (subject to some technical constraints) and get back the result of applying these functions on the secret state of the system.

Based on the restrictions on the leakage functions, various leakage models have evolved in the literature over the past decade. In their pioneering work named "physically observable cryptography", Micali and Reyzin [25] put up a comprehensive framework to model side-channel attacks called *only computation leaks information* (OCLI). Their axiom relies on the assumption that leakage happens as a result of computation and there is no leakage in the absence of computation. Inspired by the "cold-boot attack" Halderman [18], Akavia and Goldwasser [1] formalized the notion of "bounded memory leakage" model. This model removes the restriction that leakage only happens from computation. Instead it allows the adversary to learn any arbitrary information about the secret state of the system stored in memory, with the only restriction that the amount of leakage is bounded. A generalization of the above model called the continuous leakage model was proposed by Dodis et al. [13] and Brakerski et al. [8]. This model places no bound on the overall size of the leakage. The secret key of the cryptosystem is refreshed periodically (erasing the old one) keeping the public key same, and the adversary can obtain bounded leakage in between any two successive key refreshes.

After-The-Fact Leakage. Most of the prior formulations of leakage-resilient PKE [1,8,27–29] considered leakage before the challenge ciphertext is made available to the adversary. So, even if one bit of the secret key leaks in the post-challenge phase, the security of the previously encrypted messages may not be guaranteed. This severely restricts the meaning and applicability of this security notion and also the resulting constructions. However, this seems to be a necessary restriction, as otherwise an adversary may design a leakage function by simply encoding the decryption function along with the challenge ciphertext and the two messages (submitted in the challenge phase) to leak exactly the bit that we are trying to hide using encryption.

Halevi and Lin [19] proposed the *first* meaningful security notion of after-the-fact leakage(AFL) in the context of PKE schemes. Since achieving security against after-the-fact leakage in its full generality is impossible, they considered the *split-state* leakage restriction, where it is assumed that the secret key is split into two parts (in general can be multiple) and each of them is stored in separate memory locations. The adversary can get leakages from each of this memory locations, but independently of each other. Then they showed how to construct an AFL-CPA-secure PKE scheme under their new security model. The leakage rate (defined as the ratio of the leakage tolerated by the scheme to the size of the secret key) of their construction approached $1 - o(1)$ under appropriate choice of parameters. Later, Dziembowski and Faust [15] gave a construction of a AFL-CCA-2 secure PKE scheme in the continuous leakage model under the split-state assumption, with the further restriction that leakage only happens from computation (OCLI axiom). The leakage rate tolerated by their construction is also far from the optimal $1 - o(1)$ rate obtained by the CPA-secure construction of Halevi and Lin [19]. Zhang et al. [34] proposed a generic transformation from AFL-CPA-secure PKE scheme to a AFL-CCA-2-secure PKE scheme. Their transformation preserves the leakage rate of the AFL-CPA-secure PKE scheme, and hence achieves a leakage rate of $1 - o(1)$. However, the main drawback of their transformation is that it is very *inefficient* since it uses simulation-sound non-interactive zero-knowledge proof system, which is far from practical. Fujisaki et al. [16] constructed a multiple-challenge CCA-secure PKE that simultaneously tolerates post-challenge secret key and sender-randomness leakage in the split-state leakage model. However, in their construction that randomness is also split into two parts, unlike ours, where we consider only the secret key to be spitted, and *not* the randomness. Also, the scheme of [16] cannot support split-state decryption as defined in [19] and also in this work. Hence, the two approaches are incomparable.

Leakage-resilient AKE. Authenticated Key Exchange (AKE) protocols allow two parties to jointly compute a unique shared secret key and also to mutually authenticate each other with the assurance that the shared key is known only to them. In our work, we consider the case of 2-party AKE setting. The traditional security models for AKE protocols [7,9,12,22–24,30,31] do not incorporate the possibility of side-channels and hence the AKE protocols analyzed in these models may be completely insecure in the face of side-channel attacks.

Alwen et al. [6] gave the first construction of leakage-resilient AKE (LR-AKE) protocol in the RO model. However, the protocol requires three passes and also does not capture after-the-fact leakage. Later, Moriyama and Okamoto [26] proposed a two-pass (one round) LR-AKE protocol by extending the eCK model to the setting of bounded memory leakage introduced in [1]. However, it also does not capture after-the-fact leakage. In the context of key exchange, after-the-fact leakage was first modeled by Alawatugoda et al. [4] in both the bounded and continuous leakage setting. They also gave somewhat generic constructions of LR-AKE protocols in their new models [4,5]. Unfortunately, both these protocols have been shown insecure in their respective models in the subsequent works (see [32,33]). Recently, Chen et al. [11] gave a generic framework for constructing LR-AKE protocols in the presence of after-the-fact leakage in the bounded memory leakage model (they called their model challenge-dependent eCK (CLR-eCK) model).

1.1   Our Contributions

In this work we continue the study of after-the-fact leakage in the context of CCA-2 secure public key encryption (PKE) schemes and authenticated key exchange (AKE) protocols. Our contributions are two-fold and described below.

1. As our *first* contribution, we give a *generic compiler* from a AFL-CPA-secure PKE scheme to a AFL-CCA-2 secure PKE scheme. The *salient* feature of our compiler is that it *preserves the leakage rate* in the CPA to CCA transformation mentioned above. In other words, the amount of leakage than can be tolerated by our AFL-CCA-2 secure PKE scheme is the *same* as the amount of leakage tolerated by the underlying AFL-CPA secure PKE scheme. Besides, our compiler is also much more *efficient* than the compiler proposed in [34]. So, on one hand our AFL-CCA-2 secure PKE scheme achieves the optimal leakage rate of $1 - o(1)$, and on the other hand is much more efficient than the state-of-the-art AFL-CCA-2 secure PKE constructions.

2. As our *second* contribution, we propose a *generic compiler* from AFL-CCA-2 secure PKE scheme to an after-the-fact leakage-resilient AKE protocol in the BAFL-eCK security model (which is leakage analogue of the eCK model for AKE protocols) proposed in [4]. Note that such a compiler from a CCA-2 secure PKE to a eCK-secure AKE protocol in the standard (non-leakage) model was already proposed by Alawatugoda [2]. They left such a transformation in the context of leakage as a future open problem. Our compiler from AFL-CCA-2 secure PKE scheme to BAFL-eCK secure AKE protocol can be seen as a leakage-resilient implementation of the compiler presented in [2], and hence we solve the above open problem.

1.2   Organization

The rest of the paper is organized as follows. In Sect. 2, we provide the necessary preliminaries required for our constructions. In Sect. 3 we give the security model for after-the-fact leakage resilient CCA-2 secure (AFL-CCA-2) PKE in split-state state (Sect. 3.1) and present our compiler from CPA to CCA-2 secure PKE in the same model (Sect. 3.2). In Sect. 4, we present our generic compiler from CCA-2 secure PKE in the above model to a BAFL-eCK-secure AKE in the standard model. Finally Sect. 5 concludes the paper.

2   Preliminaries

In this section, we provide some basic notations, definitions and tools needed throughout the paper.

2.1   Notations

Throughout this work, we denote the security parameter by κ. We assume that all the algorithms take as input (implicitly) the security parameter represented in unary, i.e., 1^κ. For an integer $n \in \mathbb{N}$, where $\mathbb{N}$ denotes the set of natural numbers, we use the notation $[n]$ to denote the set $[n] \stackrel{\text{def}}{=} \{1, \ldots, n\}$. For a randomized function f, we write $f(x; r)$ to denote the unique output of f on input x with random coins r. We write $f(x)$ to denote a random variable for the output of $f(x; r)$, over the random coins r. For a set S, we let U_S denote the uniform distribution over S. For an integer $r \in \mathbb{N}$, let U_r denote the uniform distribution over $\{0, 1\}^r$, the bit strings of length r. For a distribution or random variable X, we denote by $x \leftarrow X$ the action of sampling an element x according to X. For a set S, we write $s \stackrel{\$}{\leftarrow} S$ to denote sampling s uniformly at random from the S. A function μ is negligible iff $\forall c \in \mathbb{N}$, $\exists n_0 \in \mathbb{N}$ such that $\forall n \geq n_0$, $\mu(n) < n^{-c}$. We sometimes use $\text{negl}(\kappa)$ to denote the set of negligible functions $\mu(\kappa)$. We denote an ensemble $\mathcal{X}$ as a collection of distributions $\{\mathcal{X}_\kappa\}_{\kappa \in \mathbb{N}}$. We sometimes drop the subscript κ when clear from context and write $x \leftarrow \mathcal{X}$ instead of $x \leftarrow \mathcal{X}_\kappa$ to denote sampling an element x from $\mathcal{X}_\kappa$. For two matrices A and B, we denote $A \odot B$ to denote the multiplication of A and B. Let $\mathbb{G}$ be a group of prime order p such that $\log_2(p) \geq \kappa$. Let g be a generator of $\mathbb{G}$, then for a (column/row) vector $A = (A_1, \cdots, A_n) \in \mathbb{Z}_p^n$, we denote by g^A the vector $C = (g^{A_1}, \cdots, g^{A_n})$. Furthermore, for a vector $B = (B_1, \cdots, B_n) \in \mathbb{Z}_p^n$, we denote by C^B the group element $X = \prod_{i=1}^n g^{A_i B_i} = g^{\sum_{i=1}^n A_i B_i}$. We say that F is $(\epsilon_{\text{prf}}, s_{\text{prf}}, q_{\text{prf}})$-secure PRF family, if no adversary of size s_{prf} (when viewed as a circuit) and making q_{prf} oracle queries can distinguish F (instantiated with a random key) from a uniformly random function except with a negligible advantage ϵ_{prf}.

We assume that the reader is familiar with the notions of min-entropy, average conditional min-entropy and randomness extractors. We refer the reader to the full version of our paper [10] for these definitions.

2.2   Leakage-Resilient Storage

We review the definitions of leakage-resilient storage according to Dziembowski and Faust [15]. The idea is to *split* the storage of elements into two parts using a randomized encoding function. As long as leakages from each of its two parts are bounded and independent of each other, no adversary can learn any useful information about the encoded element.

For any $m, n \in \mathbb{N}$, the storage scheme $\Lambda_{\mathbb{Z}_p^*}^{n,m}$ efficiently stores elements $s \in \mathbb{Z}_p^*$ where:

- $\textsf{Encode}_{\mathbb{Z}_p^*}^{n,m}(s) : s_L \stackrel{\$}{\leftarrow} (\mathbb{Z}_p^*)^n \setminus \{(0^n)\}$, and $s_R \leftarrow (\mathbb{Z}_p^*)^{n \times m}$ such that $s_L \odot s_R = s$, where s_L and s_R are interpreted as $(1 \times n)$ and $(n \times m)$ matrices respectively. The function finally outputs (s_L, s_R).
- $\textsf{Decode}_{\mathbb{Z}_p^*}^{n,m}(s_L, s_R) :$ outputs $s_L \odot s_R = s$.

Definition 1 (λ_S-limited adversary). If the amount of leakage obtained by the adversary from each of s_L and s_R is limited to λ_{S_L} and λ_{S_R} bits respectively, the adversary is known as a λ_S-*limited adversary*, where $\lambda_S = (\lambda_{S_L}, \lambda_{S_R})$.

Definition 2 ($\lambda_\Lambda, \epsilon_1$-secure leakage-resilient storage scheme). We say that $\Lambda = (\text{Encode}, \text{Decode})$ is a $(\lambda_\Lambda, \epsilon_1)$-secure leakage-resilient, if for any $s_0, s_1 \xleftarrow{\$} \mathcal{M}$, and any λ_Λ-limited adversary $\mathcal{C}$, the leakage from $\text{Encode}(s_0) = (s_{0_L}, s_{0_R})$ and $\text{Encode}(s_1) = (s_{1_L}, s_{1_R})$ are statistically ϵ_1 close. For an adversary-chosen leakage function $\mathbf{f} = (f_1, f_2)$, and a secret s such that $\text{Encode}(s) = (s_L, s_R)$, the leakage is denoted as $(f_1(s_L), f_2(s_R))$.

Lemma 1 ([15]). *Suppose that* $m < n/20$. *Then* $\Lambda_{\mathbb{Z}_p^*}^{n,m} = (\text{Encode}_{\mathbb{Z}_p^*}^{n,m}(s)$, $\text{Decode}_{\mathbb{Z}_p^*}^{n,m}(s_L, s_R))$ *is* $(\lambda_S, negl(\kappa))$*-secure for some negligible function* negl *and* $\lambda_S = (0.3 \cdot n \log p, 0.3 \cdot n \log p)$.

2.3 Complexity Assumption

The complexity assumption required for our AKE construction is the standard Decisional Diffie-Hellman (DDH) problem. One may refer to the full version of our paper [10] for its description.

2.4 True Simulation Extractable Non-interactive Zero Knowledge Argument System

In this section, we recall the notion of (same-string) *true-simulation extractable non-interactive zero knowledge argument* (tSE-NIZK) first introduced in [14]. This notion is similar to the notion of simulation-sound extractable NIZKs [17] with the difference that the adversary has oracle access to *simulated* proofs only for *true* statements., in contrast to any arbitrary statement as in simulation-sound extractable NIZK proof system.

Let $\Re$ be an efficiently computable binary relation. For pairs $(y, x) \in \Re$, we call y the statement and x the witness. Let $L = \{y \mid \exists x \text{ s.t. } (y, x) \in \Re\}$ be the language consisting of statements in $\Re$. A NIZK argument system consists of three algorithms $(\text{CRSGen}, \text{Prove}, \text{Verify})$ such that: (1) Algorithm CRSGen takes as input 1^κ and generates a common reference string (CRS) crs, a trapdoor TK and an extraction key EK; (2) Algorithm Prove takes as input the statement-witness pair (y, x) and crs and outputs an argument π such that $\Re(y, x) \in 1$; (3) Algorithm Verify takes as input crs, a statement y, and a purported argument π and outputs 1 if the argument is acceptable and 0 otherwise. We require the following properties to hold:

1. **Perfect Completeness:** For all $(y, x) \in \Re$, $(\text{crs}, \text{TK}) \leftarrow \text{CRSGen}(1^\kappa)$, if $\pi \leftarrow \text{Prove}(\text{crs}, (y, x))$, then $\text{Verify}(\text{crs}, x, \pi) = 1$.
2. **Soundness:** For all malicious provers $\mathcal{P}^*$ we have,

$$\Pr\big[\text{Verify}(\text{crs}, y, \pi^*) = 1, y \notin \Re \mid (\text{crs}, \text{TK}) \leftarrow \text{CRSGen}(1^\kappa), (y, \pi^*) \leftarrow \mathcal{P}^*(1^\kappa, \text{crs})\big]$$
$$\leq negl(\kappa).$$

3. **(Composable) Zero-Knowledge:** There exists a PPT simulator Sim such that for all PPT adversaries $\mathcal{A}$, the probability that the experiment below outputs 1 is at most $1/2 + negl(\kappa)$.

(a) *The challenger samples* $(\mathsf{crs}, \mathsf{TK}) \leftarrow \mathsf{CRSGen}(1^\kappa)$, *gives* $(\mathsf{crs}, \mathsf{TK})$ *to* $\mathcal{A}$.

(b) *The adversary* $\mathcal{A}$ *chooses* $(y, x) \in \Re$ *and gives it to the challenger.*

(c) *The challenger samples* $\pi_0 \leftarrow \mathsf{Prove}(y, x, \mathsf{crs})$, $\pi_1 \leftarrow \mathsf{Sim}(y, \mathsf{TK})$, $b \xleftarrow{\$} \{0,1\}$, *and gives* π_b *to* $\mathcal{A}$.

(d) *The adversary* $\mathcal{A}$ *outputs a bit* b' *as a guess for* b; *output 1 if* $b' = b$, *else output 0.*

4. **Strong True-simulation f-Extractability:** We start by defining the simulation oracle $\mathcal{SIM}_{\mathsf{TK}}(.)$. A query to the simulation oracle consists of a statement-witness pair (y, x). The oracle checks if $(y, x) \in \Re$. If true, it outputs a simulated argument $\mathsf{Sim}(\mathsf{TK}, y)$, otherwise it outputs $\bot$. Let f be a fixed efficiently computable function. There exists a PPT algorithm $\mathsf{EXT}(y, \pi, \mathsf{EK})$ such that for all PPT adversaries $\mathcal{P}^*$, we have $\Pr[\mathcal{P}^* \text{ wins}] \leq \mathsf{negl}(\kappa)$ in the following game.

(a) *The challenger samples* $(\mathsf{crs}, \mathsf{TK}, \mathsf{EK}) \leftarrow \mathsf{CRSGen}(1^\kappa)$, *and gives* crs *to* $\mathcal{P}^*$.

(b) $\mathcal{P}^{*\mathcal{SIM}_{\mathsf{TK}}(.)}$ *can adaptively access the simulation oracle* $\mathcal{SIM}_{\mathsf{TK}}(.)$ *as defined above.*

(c) *Finally, the adversary* $\mathcal{P}^*$ *outputs a tuple* (y^*, π^*).

(d) *The challenger runs* $z^* \leftarrow \mathsf{EXT}(y^*, \pi^*, \mathsf{EK})$

(e) $\mathcal{P}^*$ *wins if (a)* $(y^*, \pi^*) \neq (y, \pi)$ *for all pairs* (y, π) *returned by the simulation oracle* $\mathcal{SIM}_{\mathsf{TK}}(.)$; *(b)* $\mathsf{Verify}(\mathsf{crs}, y^*, \pi^*) = 1$ *and (c) for all* x' *such that* $f(x') = z^*$, *we have* $\Re(y^*, x') \in 0$. *(,i.e., the adversary* $\mathcal{P}^*$ *wins if the extractor cannot extract a good value* z^* *on at least one valid witness* x'; *i.e.,* $f(x') = z^*$.*)*

3 CPA to CCA-2 Transformation in the Presence of After-the-fact Leakage

In this section, we present our generic compiler for transforming a leakage-resilient CPA-secure PKE to leakage-resilient CCA-2 secure PKE in the presence of after-the-fact leakage. We first give the security model for after-the-fact CCA-2 secure PKE scheme in Sect. 3.1, followed by the details of our compiler in Sect. 3.2.

3.1 CCA-2 Security in a Split State Model

We consider the *bounded split-state leakage* model similar to [19]. Here the secret key of the cryptosystem is *split* into two parts, and the adversary can obtain leakage from each of these two parts independently, but not a joint leakage from both the secret key components.

Definition 3. (Split state encryption) [19]. A 2-split state encryption scheme $\mathcal{E} = (\mathcal{E}.\mathsf{Gen}, \mathcal{E}.\mathsf{Enc}, \mathcal{E}.\mathsf{Dec})$ has the following structure:

- $\mathcal{E}.\mathsf{Gen}(1^\kappa)$: The key generation algorithm comprises of two subroutines namely, $\mathcal{E}.\mathsf{Gen}_1$ and $\mathcal{E}.\mathsf{Gen}_2$. On input the security parameter 1^κ, the key generation subroutine $\mathcal{E}.\mathsf{Gen}_i$ ($i \in \{1, 2\}$) generates the public-secret key pair, i.e., $(pk_i, sk_i) \leftarrow \mathcal{E}.\mathsf{Gen}_i(1^\kappa, r_i)$ where $r_i \in \{0, 1\}^*$. The public key consists of the pair $pk = (pk_1, pk_2)$ and the secret key consists of the pair $sk = (sk_1, sk_2)$.
- $\mathcal{E}.\mathsf{Enc}_{pk=(pk_1, pk_2)}(m)$: The (randomized) encryption algorithm takes as input a message m, the public key $pk = (pk_1, pk_2)$, and outputs a ciphertext c.
- $\mathcal{E}.\mathsf{Dec}(1^\kappa, c, sk = (sk_1, sk_2))$: The decryption consists of two partial decryption subroutines $\mathcal{E}.\mathsf{Dec}_1$, $\mathcal{E}.\mathsf{Dec}_2$ and a combining subroutine Comb. The decryption subroutine $\mathcal{E}.\mathsf{Dec}_i$ ($i \in \{1, 2\}$) takes as input the ciphertext c and the secret key sk_i and outputs the partial decryption t_i, i.e., $t_i \leftarrow \mathcal{E}.\mathsf{Dec}_i(c, sk_i)$. Finally, Comb takes the ciphertext and the pair (t_1, t_2) to recover the plaintext m, i.e., $m \leftarrow \mathsf{Comb}(c, t = (t_1, t_2))$.

We want the usual *correctness* requirement to hold for the 2-split state encryption scheme $\mathcal{E}$, i.e., $\forall (pk_i, sk_i) \leftarrow \mathcal{E}.\mathsf{Gen}_i(1^\kappa)(i \in \{1, 2\}), \forall m \in \mathcal{M}$, we have, $\mathcal{E}.\mathsf{Dec}\big(sk = (sk_1, sk_2), c = \mathcal{E}.\mathsf{Enc}_{pk}(m)\big) = m$.

We now define the notion of CCA-2 security of PKE schemes in the presence of after-the-fact split-state memory leakage.

Definition 4 (CCA-2 security of split state PKE against after-the-fact leakage ($\ell(\kappa)$)-AFL-CCA-2 security)). Let $\kappa \in \mathbb{N}$ be the security parameter and let $\ell_{\mathsf{pre}}(\kappa)$ and $\ell_{\mathsf{post}}(\kappa)$ be the upper bound on the amounts of memory leakage before and after the challenge phase respectively. A 2-split state PKE $\mathcal{E} = (\mathcal{E}.\mathsf{Gen}, \mathcal{E}.\mathsf{Enc}, \mathcal{E}.\mathsf{Dec})$ is resilient to $\ell(\kappa) = ((\ell_{\mathsf{pre}}(\kappa)), (\ell_{\mathsf{post}}(\kappa)))$ leakage in the split-state model, if for all PPT adversaries $\mathcal{A}$, the probability that the experiment below outputs 1 is at most $\frac{1}{2} + negl(\kappa)$.

1. **Key Generation:** The challenger chooses $r_1, r_2 \in \{0, 1\}^*$ at random and computes $(pk_i, sk_i) \leftarrow \mathcal{E}.\mathsf{Gen}_i(1^\kappa, r_i)$ ($i \in \{1, 2\}$) and sends $pk = (pk_1, pk_2)$ to the adversary.

2. **Pre-challenge Leakage queries:** The adversary makes an arbitrary number of leakage queries $(f_{1,i}^{\mathsf{pre}}, f_{2,i}^{\mathsf{pre}})$ adaptively. Upon receiving the i-th leakage query the challenger sends back $(f_{1,i}^{\mathsf{pre}}(sk_1), f_{2,i}^{\mathsf{pre}}(sk_2))$, provided $\sum_{i=1}^{n(\kappa)} f_{1,i}^{\mathsf{pre}}(sk_1) \leq \ell_{\mathsf{pre}}(\kappa)$ and $\sum_{i=1}^{n(\kappa)} f_{2,i}^{\mathsf{pre}}(sk_2) \leq \ell_{\mathsf{pre}}(\kappa)$, where $n(\kappa)$ denote the number of pre-challenge leakage queries made in this phase.

3. **Pre-challenge Decryption queries:** The adversary $\mathcal{A}$ may ask decryption queries adaptively. The challenger returns the plaintexts m_i corresponding to the queried ciphertexts c_i.

4. **Challenge:** In this phase the challenger chooses $b \xleftarrow{\$} \{0, 1\}$ and computes $c^* = \mathcal{E}.\mathsf{Enc}_{pk}(m_b)$ and gives it to $\mathcal{A}$.

5. **Post-challenge Leakage queries:** The adversary makes an arbitrary number of leakage queries $(f_{1,j}^{\mathsf{post}}, f_{2,j}^{\mathsf{post}})$ adaptively. Upon receiving the j-th leakage query the challenger sends back $(f_{1,j}^{\mathsf{post}}(sk_1), f_{2,j}^{\mathsf{post}}(sk_2))$, provided $\sum_{j=1}^{n'(\kappa)} |f_{1,j}^{\mathsf{post}}(sk_1)| \leq \ell_{\mathsf{post}}(\kappa)$ and $\sum_{j=1}^{n'(\kappa)} |f_{2,j}^{\mathsf{post}}(sk_2)| \leq \ell_{\mathsf{post}}(\kappa)$, where $n'(\kappa)$ denotes the number of post-challenge leakage queries made in this phase.

6. **Post-challenge Decryption queries:** The adversary may continue querying the decryption oracle adaptively with different ciphertexts c_i with the only restriction that $c_i \neq c^*$.

7. **Guess:** Finally, the adversary outputs a bit b' for a guess of the bit b chosen the challenger. If $b' = b$, output 1, else output 0.

We define the advantage of $\mathcal{A}$ as $\mathsf{Adv}_{\mathcal{A}}^{\mathsf{AFL\text{-}CCA\text{-}2}}(\kappa) = |\Pr[b' = b] - \frac{1}{2}|$.

3.2 The Generic Transformation

In this section, we give the generic transformation from after-the-fact leakage-resilient CPA-secure (AFL-CPA) PKE to after-the-fact leakage-resilient CCA-2 secure (AFL-CCA-2) PKE. The main tool we will be using for our transformation is true-simulation extractable NIZK argument system (tSE-NIZK) as defined as Sect. 2.4.

Let $\mathcal{E} = (\mathcal{E}.\mathsf{Gen}, \mathcal{E}.\mathsf{Enc}, \mathcal{E}.\mathsf{Dec})$ be the $\ell(\kappa) = (\ell_{\mathsf{pre}}(\kappa), \ell_{\mathsf{post}}(\kappa))$-leakage-resilient 2-split state CPA-secure PKE from above, and let $\Pi = (\mathsf{CRSGen}, \mathsf{Prove}, \mathsf{Verify})$ be a one-time, strong f-tSE NIZK argument for the relation

$$\mathfrak{R}_{enc} = \{(m, r), (pk, c) \mid c = \mathsf{Enc}_{pk}(m; r)\}$$

where $f(m, r) = m$, i.e., the extractor only requires to extract the message m and not the randomness r of encryption. We show how to construct a leakage-resilient CCA-2 secure PKE $\mathcal{E}' = (\mathcal{E}'.\mathsf{Gen}, \mathcal{E}'.\mathsf{Enc}, \mathcal{E}'.\mathsf{Dec})$ secure against after-the-fact leakage.

1. $\mathcal{E}'.\mathsf{Gen}(1^\kappa)$: Output $\hat{pk} = (pk, \mathsf{crs})$, $\hat{sk} = sk$, where $(pk, sk) \leftarrow \mathcal{E}.\mathsf{Gen}$, and $(\mathsf{crs}, \mathsf{TK}, \mathsf{EK}) \leftarrow \mathsf{CRSGen}(1^\kappa)$.
2. $\mathcal{E}'.\mathsf{Enc}(\hat{pk}, m)$: Output the ciphertext $C = (c, \pi)$, where $c \leftarrow \mathcal{E}.\mathsf{Enc}_{pk}(m; r)$ and $\pi \leftarrow \mathsf{Prove}(\mathsf{crs}, (pk, c), (m, r))$.
3. $\mathcal{E}'.\mathsf{Dec}(sk, C)$: Parse $C = (c, \pi)$. If $\mathsf{Verify}(\mathsf{crs}, (pk, C), \pi) = 1$, output $\mathcal{E}.\mathsf{Dec}(sk, c)$, else output $\perp$.

Theorem 1. *Assume that $\mathcal{E}$ is a $\ell(\kappa) = (\ell_{\mathsf{pre}}(\kappa), \ell_{\mathsf{post}}(\kappa))$-AFL-LR-CPA-secure PKE and Π is a one-time strong f-tSE NIZK argument system for the relation $\mathfrak{R}_{enc}$ where, for any witness (m, r), we define $f(m, r) = m$. Then the scheme $\mathcal{E}'$ defined above is $(\ell_{\mathsf{pre}}(\kappa), \ell_{\mathsf{post}}(\kappa))$-AFL-LR-CCA-2-secure PKE.*

Proof. The proof of this theorem follows via series of games argument. All the games are variant of the original $\ell(\kappa)$-AFL-CCA-2 security game. These games differ in how the challenger ciphertext $C^* = (c^*, \pi^*)$ is generated and the answers to the decryption oracle queries are simulated.

Game 0. This is the original $\ell(\kappa)$-AFL-LR-CCA-2 security game. The challenger correctly generates the public key $\hat{pk} = (pk, \mathsf{crs})$ as in the key generation algorithm and gives it to the adversary. When the adversary submits two challenge messages m_0, m_1, the challenger computes the challenge ciphertext correctly as in the construction. The answers to the decryption queries are also answered correctly. In other words the challenger does the following:

1. Compute $(pk, sk) \leftarrow \mathcal{E}.\mathsf{Gen}$, and $(\mathsf{crs}, \mathsf{TK}, \mathsf{EK}) \leftarrow \mathsf{CRSGen}(1^\kappa)$. Sets the secret key as $\hat{sk} = sk$ and gives the public key $\hat{pk} = (pk, \mathsf{crs})$ to the adversary $\mathcal{A}$.
2. Chooses bit $b \xleftarrow{\$} \{0,1\}$ and compute $c^* \leftarrow \mathcal{E}.\mathsf{Enc}_{pk}(m_b; r)$, $\pi^* \leftarrow \mathsf{Prove}_{\mathsf{crs}}((pk, c^*), (m_b, r))$, and output $C^* = (c^*, \pi^*)$ as challenger ciphertext. Finally give C^* to the adversary.
3. The pre- and post-challenge decryption queries (C_i, π_i) made by $\mathcal{A}$ are answered using $\mathcal{E}'.\mathsf{Dec}(sk, C_i')$.
4. When the adversary asks pre- and post-challenge leakage queries $(f_{1,i}^{\mathsf{pre}}, f_{2,i}^{\mathsf{pre}})$ and $(f_{1,i}^{\mathsf{post}}, f_{2,i}^{\mathsf{post}})$, the challenger returns $(f_{1,i}^{\mathsf{pre}}(sk_1), f_{2,i}^{\mathsf{pre}}(sk_2))$ and $(f_{1,i}^{\mathsf{post}}(sk_1), f_{2,i}^{\mathsf{post}}(sk_2))$ respectively, provided the leakage does not exceed ℓ_{pre} and ℓ_{post} on both the coordinates in the pre- and post-challenge leakage phase.

Game 1. In this game the CRS for Π is generated along with a simulation trapdoor TK and the argument π^* in the challenge ciphertext is simulated using the zero-knowledge simulator $\mathcal{SIM}_{\mathsf{TK}}$. The pre- and post-challenge decryption and leakage queries are answered as in **Game 0**. In other words the challenger does the following:

1. Compute $(pk, sk) \leftarrow \mathcal{E}.\mathsf{Gen}$, and $(\mathsf{crs}, \mathsf{TK}, \mathsf{EK}) \leftarrow \mathsf{CRSGen}(1^\kappa)$. Sets the secret key as $\hat{sk} = sk$ and gives the public key $\hat{pk} = (pk, \mathsf{crs})$ to the adversary $\mathcal{A}$.
2. Chooses bit $b \xleftarrow{\$} \{0,1\}$ and compute $c^* \leftarrow \mathcal{E}.\mathsf{Enc}_{pk}(m_b; r)$, $\pi^* \leftarrow \mathcal{SIM}_{\mathsf{TK}}(pk, c^*)$, and output $C^* = (c^*, \pi^*)$ as challenger ciphertext. Finally give C^* to the adversary.

The decryption and leakage queries are handled in a similar manner as Game 0. The *indistinguishability* of **Game 0** and **Game 1** follows from the *NIZK* property of the tSE-NIZK argument system Π.

Game 2. In this game the CRS for Π is generated together with a simulation trapdoor TK and an extraction trapdoor EK. The challenge ciphertext is simulated using the zero-knowledge simulator similarly as **Game 1**. However the decryption queries are handled in a different manner. The decryption queries $C_i = (c_i, \pi_i)$ are answered by running the extractor on the arguments π_i to extract $f(m_i, r_i) = m_i$. In other words the challenger does the following:

1. Compute $(pk, sk) \leftarrow \mathcal{E}.\mathsf{Gen}$, and $(\mathsf{crs}, \mathsf{TK}, \mathsf{EK}) \leftarrow \mathsf{CRSGen}(1^\kappa)$. Sets the secret key as $\hat{sk} = sk$ and gives the public key $\hat{pk} = (pk, \mathsf{crs})$ to the adversary $\mathcal{A}$.

2. Chooses bit $b \xleftarrow{\$} \{0, 1\}$ and compute $c^* \leftarrow \mathcal{E}.\mathsf{Enc}_{pk}(m_b; r)$, $\pi^* \leftarrow \mathcal{SIM}_{\mathsf{TK}}(pk, c^*)$, and output $C^* = (c^*, \pi^*)$ as challenger ciphertext. Finally give C^* to the adversary.

3. When the adversary queries to the decryption oracle using $C_i = (c_i, \pi_i)$, the challenger runs $\mathsf{EXT}((\hat{pk}, c_i), \pi_i, \mathsf{TK})$ to extract the message m_i.

The answers to the leakage queries are answered similarly as in Game 0. The *indistinguishability* of **Game 1** and **Game 2** follow from the *strong one-time true-simulation extractability* property of the tSE-NIZK argument system Π. The adversary $\mathcal{A}$ sees *only one* simulated proof of a true statement, namely, the argument π^* in the challenge ciphertext $C^* = (c^*, \pi^*)$. Therefore by the strong one-time true simulation extractability property of Π, $\mathcal{A}$ cannot produce any new statement-argument pair $(c_i, \pi_i) \neq (c^*, \pi^*)$ for which the argument π_i verifies but the extractor fails to extract the correct m_i.

Game 3. This is the final game. In which game the challenger changes the way in which the challenge ciphertext c^* is generated. Instead of encrypting the message m_b, the challenger produces the challenge ciphertext as an encryption of 0 (or any fixed message in the message space), i.e., the challenger computes the challenge ciphertext as $C^* = (c^*, \pi^*)$, where $c^* \leftarrow \mathcal{E}.\mathsf{Enc}_{pk}(0; r)$ and $\pi^* \leftarrow \mathcal{SIM}_{\mathsf{TK}}(pk, c^*)$. The decryption queries are still answered using the extraction trapdoor as in Game 2. The leakage queries are answered using the leakage oracle of the AFL-LR-CPA secure scheme $\mathcal{E}$. We show that **Game 2** and **Game 3** are indistinguishable.

Claim. Game 2 and Game 3 are indistinguishable by the $\ell(\kappa) = (\ell_{\mathsf{pre}}(\kappa), \ell_{\mathsf{post}}(\kappa))$-AFL-CPA security of the PKE scheme $\mathcal{E}$.

Proof. If **Game 2** and **Game 3** can be distinguished we can build an adversary $\mathcal{A}'$ against the $\ell(\kappa)$-AFL-CPA secure PKE $\mathcal{E}$. The adversary $\mathcal{A}'$ simulates the execution environment for $\mathcal{A}$ as follows:

1. $\mathcal{A}'$ receives the public key pk^* and computes $(\mathsf{crs}, \mathsf{TK}, \mathsf{EK}) \leftarrow \mathsf{CRSGen}(1^\kappa)$. It then sends the public key $\hat{pk} = (pk^*, \mathsf{crs})$ to $\mathcal{A}$.

2. When $\mathcal{A}$ makes pre- and post-challenge decryption oracle queries $C_i = (c_i, \pi_i)$, $\mathcal{A}'$ uses the extraction trapdoor of the tSE-NIZK argument system Π to simulate the response to these queries, i.e., it computes $\mathsf{EXT}((\hat{pk}, c_i), \pi_i, \mathsf{TK})$ to extract m_i. As already argued above (indistinguishability of Game 1 and Game 2) this properly simulates the decryption oracle responses (except with negligible probability) by the strong one-time true simulation extractability property of Π.

3. When $\mathcal{A}$ makes pre- and post-challenge leakages queries, $\mathcal{A}'$ forwards them to the leakage oracle of the challenger of the $\ell(\kappa)$-AFL-LR-CPA-secure PKE scheme $\mathcal{E}$, and returns back the response to $\mathcal{A}$.

4. When $\mathcal{A}$ makes the challenge query with two messages m_0 and m_1, $\mathcal{A}'$ forwards them to its challenger. It gets back the ciphertext c^* and computes $\pi^* \leftarrow \mathcal{SIM}_{\mathsf{TK}}(pk, c^*)$. Finally, it returns $C^* = (c^*, \pi^*)$ to $\mathcal{A}$.
5. When $\mathcal{A}$ output a bit b', $\mathcal{A}'$ also outputs the same bit b'.

With all but negligible probability, the above represents a proper simulation of the environment for $\mathcal{A}$ by $\mathcal{A}'$. Thus if the advantage of $\mathcal{A}$ is negligible, the advantage of $\mathcal{A}'$ is also negligible. This proves the above claim.

The above claim shows that Game 2 and Game 3 are indistinguishable. Now, note that Game 3 is completely independent of the bit b, and hence the advantage of any adversary in Game 3 is exactly 0. So, by the indistinguishability of the Games 0–3, the advantage of any adversary in Game 0 is $negl(\kappa)$. This concludes the proof of the above theorem.   □

Remark 1. Note that the leakage tolerance of the AFL-LR-CCA-2 secure PKE $\mathcal{E}'$ is *exactly same* as the leakage tolerance of the underlying AFL-LR-CPA-secure PKE $\mathcal{E}$. This is because in Games 2 and 3 the decryption secret key sk is never used for answering the decryption oracle queries. Instead, the extractor trapdoor of the tSE-NIZK is used for simulating the decryption queries and also it is never used in the real scheme. In other words, the decryption oracle responses do not leak any useful information to the adversary, and the leakage that happens from the construction due to adaptive access of the leakage oracle by the adversary is taken care of by the underlying AFL-CPA-secure PKE. This essentially allows us to tolerate the same amount of leakage, namely $\ell = (\ell_{\mathsf{pre}}, \ell_{\mathsf{post}})$ bits of leakage as the underlying CPA-secure scheme $\mathcal{E}$.

4   Compiler for After-the-Fact Leakage-Resilient AKE Protocols

We give a generic framework for designing a bounded after-the-fact leakage eCK-secure (BAFL-eCK) AKE protocol using an arbitrary AFL-LR-CCA-2 secure public key encryption scheme, an arbitrary pseudo-random function and a leakage-resilient storage scheme as defined in Sect. 2.2. We prove the security of our protocol in the *standard* model, assuming the hardness of the DDH problem.

4.1   The Bounded After-the-Fact Leakage-ECK (BAFL-eCK) Model

The BAFL-eCK model, introduced by Alawatugoda et al. [4], can be seen as a (bounded) leakage analogue of the eCK model [23]. Here, the secret key of the cryptosystem is split into n parts and it is assumed that the adversary gets independent leakage from each split. This is modeled by allowing the adversary to send a tuple leakage function $\mathbf{f} = (f_1, \cdots, f_n)$, where the size n of the tuple is protocol-specific (for our purpose $n = 2$, since we consider 2-split state model). The total amount of leakage from each split of the secret key is bounded by the leakage parameters. In particular, if the total leakage bound on the i-th split of the secret key is λ_i, then the condition $\sum |f_i(sk_i)| \leq \lambda_i$ should hold, where

sk_i denote the ith split of the secret key sk. In the BAFL-eCK model it is also assumed that leakage happens as a result of computation following the "Only Computation leaks" (OCLI) axiom [25]. For a key exchange protocol, computation takes place on issuing a Send query. So sending an adversary-chosen adaptive tuple leakage function with the Send query reflects the OCLI premise. Apart from this, the adversary also has all the capabilities of an eCK adversary, namely, it can completely control the communication channel, it can corrupt a party to get its long-terms secret key, reveal the ephemeral/session-specific randomness of a party, and also obtain session keys of sessions run by different parties. Finally, in a "*fresh*" test/challenge session the adversary has to distinguish the session key of that session from a random session key, where freshness is defined as in the eCK model, with one more restriction that the leakage bound of both the parties involved in the test session must be respected. Another notable feature of this model is that the adversary has access to the leakage oracle even *after* the test session (modeling after-the-fact leakage), as long as the bounded and independent leakage assumption holds true. Due to space constraints we refer the reader to [4] and the full version of our paper [10] for detailed description of the BAFL-eCK model.

4.2   Generic BAFL-eCK Secure AKE Protocol in Standard Model

In this section we present a generic construction of BAFL-eCK secure key exchange protocol P using an arbitrary AFL-LR-CCA-2 secure PKE scheme, a LRS encoding scheme and an arbitrary pseudo-random function. We then prove the security of our AKE protocol in the standard model assuming the security of the above primitives and the hardness of the DDH problem. Suppose κ is the security parameter. Let $\mathbb{G}$ denotes a cyclic multiplicative group of prime order p generated by g. The main building blocks used in our construction of the AKE protocol are as follows:

- $\ell(\kappa)$-after-the-fact leakage-resilient 2-split state CCA-2 (AFL-CCA-2) secure PKE $\mathcal{E} = (\mathcal{E}.\mathsf{Gen}, \mathcal{E}.\mathsf{Enc}, \mathcal{E}.\mathsf{Dec})$ with key space $\mathcal{K}$, message space $\mathcal{M}$.
- $\Lambda_{\mathbb{Z}_p^*}^{n,1} = (\mathsf{Encode}_{\mathbb{Z}_p^*}^{n,1}(s), \mathsf{Decode}_{\mathbb{Z}_p^*}^{n,1}(s_L, s_R))$ be a (λ_S, ϵ_1) leakage-resilient storage scheme
- $F : \mathbb{G} \times \{0,1\}^* \rightarrow \mathcal{SK}$ be a $(\epsilon_{\mathsf{prf}}, s_{\mathsf{prf}}, q_{\mathsf{prf}})$-secure PRF family, where $\mathcal{SK}$ denotes the session-key space.

Overview of our Construction. We denote the two protocol participants as U_A and U_B. We assume that U_A is the initiator and U_B is the responder. Alawatugoda [3] gave a generic transformation of a CCA2-secure PKE scheme to an eCK-secure key exchange protocol in the standard model. Our compiler can be viewed as leakage-resilient implementation of the compiler of Alawatugoda [3]. We denote the public-secret key pair of parties U_A and U_B as (pk_{U_A}, sk_{U_A}) and (pk_{U_B}, sk_{U_B}) respectively. We denote (a, A) and (b, B) as the long-term Diffie-Hellman (DH) secret and public keys of U_A and U_B respectively. We also denote (esk_A, epk_A) and (esk_B, epk_B) as the ephemeral secret and public keys of U_A and U_B respectively.

The main idea of the construction of [3] is that it computes epk_A and epk_B as DH public keys and esk_A and esk_B as DH secret keys. It then encrypts the epk_A and epk_B using a CCA-2 secure PKE. The other party who has the secret key can successfully recover epk_A and epk_B respectively. In the session key generation phase both the parties perform *two* DH session key derivation. The first session key derivation involves the ephemeral public and secret keys of both the parties, whereas the second DH session key generation involves the DH long-term keys of both the parties. Finally both the parties use a PRF to derive the final session key.

Our generic AKE construction also follows this simple design strategy. However, the adversarial model is *stronger* than the eCK model. This is because the BAFL-eCK model trivially implies the eCK model, but the other way is not true. In particular, apart from all the information the adversary gets in the eCK model, additionally it also obtains leakage from the secret key of the parties, i.e. both the secret key of the cryptosystem as well as the DH long-term secret key of parties. The leakage that happens from the secret key of the CCA-2 secure PKE can be handled by using a AFL-CCA-2 secure encryption scheme. However, apart from this, the leakage from the DH long-term secret keys also needs to be accounted for. For this, we use *leakage-resilient storage* (LRS) scheme. However, directly using the LRS scheme does not work for our purpose since the secret values in our case are exponents of DH public keys. So we need a way to perform exponentiation in a leakage-resilient fashion. The possibility of leakage-resilient exponentiation was mentioned in [3]. However, no formal derivation was present. Here, we show the leakage-resilient exponentiation operation explicitly and show its correctness.

Leakage-resilient exponentiation. We use the LRS scheme to perform secure exponentiation in the presence of leakage. Suppose that x is the exponent (DH secret key) and we need to compute the DH public key $X = g^x$. We first encode x using the LRS scheme as $(x_L, x_R) \leftarrow \mathsf{Encode}_{\mathbb{Z}_p^*}^{n,1}(x)$, where $x_L \xleftarrow{\$} (\mathbb{Z}_p^*)^n \setminus \{(0^n)\}$, $x_R \leftarrow (\mathbb{Z}_p^*)^{n \times 1} \setminus \{(0^{n \times 1})\}$ such that $x_L \odot x_R = x$. To compute $X = g^x$, we use the two encodings (x_L, x_R), and finally erase x from memory. More precisely, we first compute $X' = g^{x_L} = (g^{x_{L_1}}, g^{x_{L_2}}, \cdots, g^{x_{L_n}})$, and then compute $X = (X')^{x_R} = \prod_{i=1}^{n} g^{x_{L_i} \cdot x_{R_i}} = g^{\sum_{i=1}^{n} x_{L_i} \cdot x_{R_i}} = g^x.$

In our AKE protocol the party U_A chooses $a_L \xleftarrow{\$} (\mathbb{Z}_p^*)^n \setminus \{(0^n)\}$, $a_R \xleftarrow{\$} (\mathbb{Z}_p^*)^{n \times 1} \setminus \{(0^{n \times 1})\}$ and the value of the ephemeral DH exponent a is implicitly set as $a_L \odot a_R$. Party U_B also performs similar operation. In the key generation process if we first choose the long-term DH secret key a it must be securely erased from memory after getting the encoded values a_L and a_R of a. However, in practice secure erasure may not be possible always and some traces of the secret key may be leaked to the adversary. In order to avoid such a vulnerability, two values a_L and a_R are picked at random and we use them as the encodings of

Table 1. Proposed BAFL-eCK secure AKE protocol P

U_A	U_B
Key Generation	
Public parameters: $(\mathbb{G}, p, \langle g \rangle)$	
$a_L \xleftarrow{\$} (\mathbb{Z}_p^*)^n \setminus \{(0^n)\},$	$b_L \xleftarrow{\$} (\mathbb{Z}_p^*)^n \setminus \{(0^n)\},$
$a_R \xleftarrow{\$} (\mathbb{Z}_p^*)^{n \times 1} \setminus \{(0^{n \times 1})\}$	$b_R \xleftarrow{\$} (\mathbb{Z}_p^*)^{n \times 1} \setminus \{(0^{n \times 1})\}$
$A' = g^{a_L}, A = (A')^{a_R} = g^{a_L \cdot a_R} = g^a$	$B' = g^{b_L}, B = (B')^{b_R} = g^{b_L \cdot b_R} = g^b$
$(pk_{U_A}, sk_{U_A}) \leftarrow \mathcal{E}.\mathsf{Gen}(1^\kappa),$	$(pk_{U_B}, sk_{U_B}) \leftarrow \mathcal{E}.\mathsf{Gen}(1^\kappa)$
Session Execution	
$esk_A \xleftarrow{\$} \mathbb{Z}_p^*, epk_A \leftarrow g^{esk_A}$	$esk_B \xleftarrow{\$} \mathbb{Z}_p^*, epk_B \leftarrow g^{esk_B}$
$C_A \leftarrow \mathcal{E}.\mathsf{Enc}_{pk_{U_B}}(epk_A)$	$C_B \leftarrow \mathcal{E}.\mathsf{Enc}_{pk_{U_A}}(epk_B)$
$\xrightarrow{\quad U_A, U_B, C_A \quad}$	
$\xleftarrow{\quad U_B, U_A, C_B \quad}$	
Session Key Generation	
Set sid $= (U_A \| U_B \| C_A \| C_B)$	Set sid $= (U_A \| U_B \| C_A \| C_B)$
$epk_B \leftarrow \mathcal{E}.\mathsf{Dec}_{sk_{U_A}}(C_B),$	$epk_A \leftarrow \mathcal{E}.\mathsf{Dec}_{sk_{U_B}}(C_A),$
$Z'_{A_1} = (B)^{a_L}, Z_{A_1} = (Z'_{A_1})^{a_R},$	$Z'_{B_1} = (A)^{b_L}, Z_{B_1} = (Z'_{B_1})^{b_R},$
$Z_{A_2} = epk_B^{esk_A},$	$Z_{B_2} = epk_A^{esk_B},$
$SK = F(Z_{A_1}, \mathsf{sid}) \oplus F(Z_{A_2}, \mathsf{sid})$	$SK = F(Z_{B_1}, \mathsf{sid}) \oplus F(Z_{B_2}, \mathsf{sid})$

the long-term DH exponent a. In this way, we refrain from using the long-term DH secret key a directly. Note that, this approach is identical to first picking a random element $a \in \mathbb{Z}_p^*$ and then encoding it to obtain a_L and a_R. Thus our approach avoids the vulnerability of exposing the secret DH exponent and hence avoid leaking directly from the exponents a and b. Since the value a is not available to the adversary, it can get only bounded and independent leakage (under split-state assumption) from a_L and a_R respectively. We can then use the security of the LRS scheme to argue security of our AKE protocol.

Thus combined with the security of the AFL-CCA-2 secure encryption, LRS scheme and security of DH key exchange (DDH assumption), we obtain a BAFL-eCK-secure AKE protocol in standard model. The details of the protocol is presented in Table 1.

Correctness: The correctness of the protocol is easy to verify. It is enough to show that $Z_{A_1} = Z_{B_1}$ and $Z_{A_2} = Z_{B_2}$. The correctness of the decrypted values epk_B and epk_A at both the parties U_A and U_B respectively follow from the correctness of the AFL-CCA-2 secure PKE scheme.

We have $Z_{A_1} = (Z'_{A_1})^{a_R} = ((B)^{a_L})^{a_R} = B^{a_L \cdot a_R} = B^a = (g^b)^a = g^{ab}$.
Similarly, $Z_{B_1} = (Z'_{B_1})^{b_R} = ((A)^{b_L})^{b_R} = A^{b_L \cdot b_R} = A^b = (g^a)^b = g^{ab} = Z_{A_1}$.
The value $Z_{A_2} = epk_B^{esk_A} = (g^{esk_B})^{esk_A} = (g^{esk_A})^{esk_B} = epk_A^{esk_B} = Z_{B_2}$.

4.3   Security Proof

In this section we proof the following theorem:

Theorem 2. *If* $\mathcal{E} = (\mathcal{E}.\mathsf{Gen}, \mathcal{E}.\mathsf{Enc}, \mathcal{E}.\mathsf{Dec})$ *is a* $\ell(\kappa)$-*AFL-CCA-2-secure PKE,* $\Lambda_{\mathbb{Z}_p^*}^{n,1}$ *be a* $(\lambda_\Lambda, \epsilon_1)$ *leakage-resilient storage scheme,* F *is a* $(\epsilon_{\mathsf{prf}}, s_{\mathsf{prf}}, q_{\mathsf{prf}})$ *PRF, and the DDH assumption holds in* $\mathbb{G}$ *of prime order* p *generated by* g, *then the above AKE protocol* P *is* $(\ell(\kappa), \lambda_\Lambda)$-*BAFL-eCK-secure. In particular,*

$$\mathsf{Adv}_{\mathsf{P}}^{\mathsf{BAFL\text{-}eCK}}(\mathcal{A})$$
$$\leq n^2 \ell^2 \max \left((2\epsilon_1 + \mathsf{Adv}_{\mathcal{B}}^{\mathsf{DDH}}(\kappa) + \epsilon_{\mathsf{prf}}), (\mathsf{Adv}_{\mathcal{S}}^{\mathsf{AFL\text{-}CCA\text{-}2}}(\kappa) + \epsilon_{\mathsf{prf}}) \right).$$

where n *is the total no. of protocol principles/parties and* ℓ *is the maximum no. of sessions that can be executed by a party concurrently.*

Proof Sketch. We give an overview of our proof here. The detailed proof is given in full version of our paper [10].

According to the freshness condition of the BAFL-eCK model (see Def. 3.2 in [4]) we have to consider the following cases and sub-cases:

1. A partner to the test session *exists*.
   (a) Adversary corrupts both the owner and the partner principals to the test session.
   (b) Adversary corrupts neither the owner nor the partner principal to the test session.
   (c) Adversary corrupts the owner to the test session, but does not corrupt the partner to the test session.
   (d) Adversary corrupts the partner to the test session, but does not corrupt the owner to the test session.
2. A partner to the test session *does not exist*.
   (a) Adversary corrupts the owner to the test session.
   (b) Adversary does not corrupt the owner to the test session.

Case 1(a). In this case, the adversary corrupts both the owner and the peer to the test session. So the adversary knows both the long-term Diffie-Hellman (DH) keys a and b of the parties U_A and U_B respectively. Besides, it also learns the secret keys of the AFL-CCA-2 secure encryption scheme $\mathcal{E}$, namely, sk_{U_A} and sk_{U_B} of U_A and U_B respectively. However, the adversary does not learn the ephemeral secret keys of the test session and its matching session. So, the secrecy of the session key lies in the secrecy of the values Z_{A_2} and Z_{B_2}. Note that the adversary can get both epk_A and epk_B by using the encryption secret keys. So the value $Z_{A_2} = Z_{B_2} = g^{esk_A esk_B}$ is hard to distinguish from a random value by the DDH assumption. In our proof we replace it with a random value. Finally, we replace the session key with a random value from the same space. This change is again oblivious to the adversary by the security of the PRF F used for deriving the final session key. Also note that the leakage queries in this case does not make much sense since the adversary already knows the long-term keys of both the principles. Since the challenger has the secret keys of all the parties it can easily simulate the leakage queries.

Case 1(b). In this case, the adversary learns the ephemeral secret keys esk_A and esk_B of parties U_A and U_B respectively corresponding to the test session and its matching session. The adversary does not know the long-term DH keys and the secret keys of the AFL-CCA-2 secure PKE scheme $\mathcal{E}$. However, the adversary may obtain leakage from both of them via Send queries according to the BAFL-eCK security model. In this case, the challenger knows neither of the long-term secrets of U_A and U_B, so it cannot simulate the leakage queries by itself. Instead the challenger uses the leakage oracle of the AFL-CCA-2 secure PKE scheme and the LRS scheme to respond to the leakage queries. The LRS scheme $\Lambda_{\mathbb{Z}_p^*}^{n,1}$ ensures that even if the adversary obtains bounded leakage from the two encodings of the secret key independently, it cannot learn any information about the secret value. Given that the adversary does not learn any information about the long-term DH keys, the security of the DH shared key $Z_{A_1} = Z_{B_1}$ ensures the secrecy of the session key. In particular, given the DH public keys g^a and g^b, it is hard to distinguish the value $Z_{A_1} = Z_{B_1} = g^{ab}$ from random value by the DDH assumption. Similar to the above case, we then replace this value with a random value. Finally, we replace the session key with a random value from the same space. This change is again oblivious to the adversary by the security of the PRF F used for deriving the final session key.

Case 1(c). In this case the adversary $\mathcal{A}$ learns the long-term DH key of U_A, i.e., $a = a_L \cdot a_R$ and the secret key sk_{U_A}. For party U_B, the adversary learns the ephemeral secret key esk_B. In his case, the challenger knows sk_{U_A} and a, so it can simulate the leakage queries for party U_A by itself. However, for party U_B, it does not know its long-term secret keys. It uses the leakage oracle of the AFL-CCA-2 secure PKE scheme and the LRS scheme to answer leakage queries for U_B. Note that, the adversary can compute the value $Z_{A_1} = Z_{B_1} = g^{ab}$. So the secrecy of the session key in this case depends on the security of the values Z_{A_2} and Z_{B_2}. Also note that the adversary knows the value esk_B. However, the ephemeral public key epk_A is protected by the security of C_A, since the long-term secret key sk_B is not revealed to the adversary $\mathcal{A}$.

Case 1(d). The security in this case is similar to that of Case 1(c). Here the adversary $\mathcal{A}$ learns the long-term DH key of U_B, i.e., $b = b_L \cdot b_R$, the secret key sk_{U_B} and the ephemeral secret key esk_A of party U_A. In this case, challenger uses the leakage oracle of the AFL-CCA-2 PKE scheme and the LRS scheme to answer leakage queries for U_A. As before, the adversary can compute the value $Z_{A_1} = Z_{B_1} = g^{ab}$. So the secrecy of the session key in this case depends on the security of the values Z_{A_2} and Z_{B_2}. The adversary also knows the value esk_A. However, the ephemeral public key epk_B is protected by the security of C_B, since the long-term secret key sk_A is not revealed to the adversary $\mathcal{A}$.

In Case 2, the partner to the test session *does not* exist. By the freshness condition of the BAFL-eCK, the adversary is *not* allowed to corrupt the peer to the test/challenge session. The proof for Case 2(a) is similar to the proof of

Case 1(c). The situation that the ephemeral secret key of the partner to the test session is given to $\mathcal{A}$ is the *same* as the case that the test session has no matching session because $\mathcal{A}$ can decide arbitrary ephemeral key. By a similar argument the proof for Case 2(b) is also similar to the analysis for Case 1(d).

5   Conclusion

In this paper, we proposed two generic compilers for after-the-fact leakage. One is a generic transformation from a leakage-resilient CPA-secure PKE to a leakage-resilient CCA-2-secure PKE in split-state bounded memory leakage model. The salient feature of our transformation is that the leakage tolerance of the transformed CCA-2 secure PKE is exactly same as the leakage tolerance of the underlying CPA-secure PKE and is also efficient. Our second compiler transforms any after-the-fact leakage-resilient CCA-2 secure PKE to a leakage-resilient AKE protocol in the BAFL-eCK model. An interesting open problem would be to design a generic compiler for transforming a CPA-secure PKE to a CCA-2 secure PKE in the presence of after-the-fact leakage, but in non-split state model. We also leave open the problem of constructing a generic compiler for leakage-resilient CPA-secure PKE to a leakage resilient CCA-2 secure PKE in the presence of continuous after-the-fact leakage.

Acknowledgments. We acknowledge the reviewers for their helpful comments. Part of this work was initiated when the first author was visiting R. C. Bose Centre for Cryptology and Security, Indian Statistical Institute, Kolkata during the Summer of 2016. The first and the third author are grateful to the project "Information Security Education and Awareness Program" of Ministry of Information Technology, Government of India.

References

1. Akavia, A., Goldwasser, S., Vaikuntanathan, V.: Simultaneous hardcore bits and cryptography against memory attacks. In: Reingold, O. (ed.) TCC 2009. LNCS, vol. 5444, pp. 474–495. Springer, Heidelberg (2009). doi:10.1007/978-3-642-00457-5_28
2. Alawatugoda, J.: Generic construction of an\ mathrm $\{eCK\}$-secure key exchange protocol in the standard model. Int. J. Inf. Secur., 1–17 (2015)
3. Alawatugoda, J.: Generic transformation of a CCA2-secure public-key encryption scheme to an eCK-secure key exchange protocol in the standard model. Cryptology ePrint Archive, Report 2015/1248 (2015). http://eprint.iacr.org/2015/1248
4. Alawatugoda, J., Stebila, D., Boyd, C.: Modelling after-the-fact leakage for key exchange. In: Proceedings of the 9th ACM Symposium on Information, Computer and Communications Security, pp. 207–216. ACM (2014)
5. Alawatugoda, J., Stebila, D., Boyd, C.: Continuous after-the-fact leakage-resilient eCK-Secure key exchange. In: Groth, J. (ed.) IMACC 2015. LNCS, vol. 9496, pp. 277–294. Springer, Cham (2015). doi:10.1007/978-3-319-27239-9_17
6. Alwen, J., Dodis, Y., Wichs, D.: Leakage-resilient public-key cryptography in the bounded-retrieval model. In: Halevi, S. (ed.) CRYPTO 2009. LNCS, vol. 5677, pp. 36–54. Springer, Heidelberg (2009). doi:10.1007/978-3-642-03356-8_3

7. Bellare, M., Rogaway, P.: Entity authentication and key distribution. In: Stinson, D.R. (ed.) CRYPTO 1993. LNCS, vol. 773, pp. 232–249. Springer, Heidelberg (1994). doi:10.1007/3-540-48329-2_21

8. Brakerski, Z., Kalai, Y.T., Katz, J., Vaikuntanathan, V.: Cryptography resilient to continual memory leakage (2010)

9. Canetti, R., Krawczyk, H.: Analysis of key-exchange protocols and their use for building secure channels. In: Pfitzmann, B. (ed.) EUROCRYPT 2001. LNCS, vol. 2045, pp. 453–474. Springer, Heidelberg (2001). doi:10.1007/3-540-44987-6_28

10. Chakraborty, S., Paul, G., Rangan, C.P.: Efficient compilers for after-the-fact leakage: from CPA to CCA-2 secure PKE to AKE (full version). Cryptology ePrint Archive (2017). http://eprint.iacr.org/2017/451

11. Chen, R., Mu, Y., Yang, G., Susilo, W., Guo, F.: Strongly leakage-resilient authenticated key exchange. In: Sako, K. (ed.) CT-RSA 2016. LNCS, vol. 9610, pp. 19–36. Springer, Cham (2016). doi:10.1007/978-3-319-29485-8_2

12. Cremers, C.: Examining indistinguishability-based security models for key exchange protocols: the case of CK, CK-HMQV, and ECK. In: Proceedings of the 6th ACM Symposium on Information, Computer and Communications Security, pp. 80–91. ACM (2011)

13. Dodis, Y., Haralambiev, K., López-Alt, A., Wichs, D.: Cryptography against continuous memory attacks. In: 2010 51st Annual IEEE Symposium on Foundations of Computer Science (FOCS), pp. 511–520. IEEE (2010)

14. Dodis, Y., Haralambiev, K., López-Alt, A., Wichs, D.: Efficient public-key cryptography in the presence of key leakage. In: Abe, M. (ed.) ASIACRYPT 2010. LNCS, vol. 6477, pp. 613–631. Springer, Heidelberg (2010). doi:10.1007/978-3-642-17373-8_35

15. Dziembowski, S., Faust, S.: Leakage-resilient cryptography from the inner-product extractor. In: Lee, D.H., Wang, X. (eds.) ASIACRYPT 2011. LNCS, vol. 7073, pp. 702–721. Springer, Heidelberg (2011). doi:10.1007/978-3-642-25385-0_38

16. Fujisaki, E., Kawachi, A., Nishimaki, R., Tanaka, K., Yasunaga, K.: Post-challenge leakage resilient public-key cryptosystem in split state model. IEICE Trans. Fundam. Electron. Commun. Comput. Sci. 98(3), 853–862 (2015)

17. Groth, J.: Simulation-sound NIZK proofs for a practical language and constant size group signatures. In: Lai, X., Chen, K. (eds.) ASIACRYPT 2006. LNCS, vol. 4284, pp. 444–459. Springer, Heidelberg (2006). doi:10.1007/11935230_29

18. Halderman, J.A., Schoen, S.D., Heninger, N., Clarkson, W., Paul, W., Calandrino, J.A., Feldman, A.J., Appelbaum, J., Felten, E.W.: Lest we remember: cold-boot attacks on encryption keys. Commun. ACM 52(5), 91–98 (2009)

19. Halevi, S., Lin, H.: After-the-fact leakage in public-key encryption. In: Ishai, Y. (ed.) TCC 2011. LNCS, vol. 6597, pp. 107–124. Springer, Heidelberg (2011). doi:10.1007/978-3-642-19571-6_8

20. Kocher, P., Jaffe, J., Jun, B.: Differential power analysis. In: Wiener, M. (ed.) CRYPTO 1999. LNCS, vol. 1666, pp. 388–397. Springer, Heidelberg (1999). doi:10.1007/3-540-48405-1_25

21. Kocher, P.C.: Timing attacks on implementations of Diffie-Hellman, RSA, DSS, and other systems. In: Koblitz, N. (ed.) CRYPTO 1996. LNCS, vol. 1109, pp. 104–113. Springer, Heidelberg (1996). doi:10.1007/3-540-68697-5_9

22. Krawczyk, H.: HMQV: a high-performance secure Diffie-Hellman protocol. In: Shoup, V. (ed.) CRYPTO 2005. LNCS, vol. 3621, pp. 546–566. Springer, Heidelberg (2005). doi:10.1007/11535218_33

23. LaMacchia, B., Lauter, K., Mityagin, A.: Stronger security of authenticated key exchange. In: Susilo, W., Liu, J.K., Mu, Y. (eds.) ProvSec 2007. LNCS, vol. 4784, pp. 1–16. Springer, Heidelberg (2007). doi:10.1007/978-3-540-75670-5_1

24. Menezes, A., Ustaoglu, B.: Comparing the pre- and post-specified peer models for key agreement. In: Mu, Y., Susilo, W., Seberry, J. (eds.) ACISP 2008. LNCS, vol. 5107, pp. 53–68. Springer, Heidelberg (2008). doi:10.1007/978-3-540-70500-0_5

25. Micali, S., Reyzin, L.: Physically observable cryptography. In: Naor, M. (ed.) TCC 2004. LNCS, vol. 2951, pp. 278–296. Springer, Heidelberg (2004). doi:10.1007/978-3-540-24638-1_16

26. Moriyama, D., Okamoto, T.: Leakage resilient eCK-secure key exchange protocol without random oracles. In: Proceedings of the 6th ACM Symposium on Information, Computer and Communications Security, pp. 441–447. ACM (2011)

27. Naor, M., Segev, G.: Public-key cryptosystems resilient to key leakage. In: Halevi, S. (ed.) CRYPTO 2009. LNCS, vol. 5677, pp. 18–35. Springer, Heidelberg (2009). doi:10.1007/978-3-642-03356-8_2

28. Qin, B., Liu, S.: Leakage-resilient chosen-ciphertext secure public-key encryption from hash proof system and one-time lossy filter. In: Sako, K., Sarkar, P. (eds.) ASIACRYPT 2013. LNCS, vol. 8270, pp. 381–400. Springer, Heidelberg (2013). doi:10.1007/978-3-642-42045-0_20

29. Qin, B., Liu, S.: Leakage-flexible CCA-secure public-key encryption: simple construction and free of pairing. In: Krawczyk, H. (ed.) PKC 2014. LNCS, vol. 8383, pp. 19–36. Springer, Heidelberg (2014). doi:10.1007/978-3-642-54631-0_2

30. Sarr, A.P., Elbaz-Vincent, P., Bajard, J.-C.: A new security model for authenticated key agreement. In: Garay, J.A., Prisco, R. (eds.) SCN 2010. LNCS, vol. 6280, pp. 219–234. Springer, Heidelberg (2010). doi:10.1007/978-3-642-15317-4_15

31. Shoup, V.: On formal models for secure key exchange. Citeseer (1999)

32. Toorani, M.: On continuous after-the-fact leakage-resilient key exchange. In: Proceedings of the Second Workshop on Cryptography and Security in Computing Systems, p. 31. ACM (2015)

33. Yang, Z., Li, S.: On security analysis of an after-the-fact leakage resilient key exchange protocol. Inf. Process. Lett. 116(1), 33–40 (2016)

34. Zhang, Z., Chow, S.S.M., Cao, Z.: Post-challenge leakage in public-key encryption. Theor. Comput. Sci. 572, 25–49 (2015)

Improved Integral Attack on HIGHT

Yuki Funabiki[1]([✉]), Yosuke Todo[2], Takanori Isobe[3], and Masakatu Morii[1]

[1] Kobe University, 1-1 Rokkodai-cho, Nada-ku, Kobe, Hyogo 657-8501, Japan
funabiki@stu.kobe-u.ac.jp, mmorii@kobe-u.ac.jp
[2] NTT Secure Platform Laboratories, 3-9-11 Midori-cho,
Musashino, Tokyo 180-8585, Japan
todo.yosuke@lab.ntt.co.jp
[3] University of Hyogo, 7-1-28 Minatojima-minamimachi,
Chuo-ku, Kobe, Hyogo 650-0047, Japan
takanori.isobe@ai.u-hyogo.ac.jp

Abstract. HIGHT is a lightweight block cipher with 64-bit block length and 128-bit security, and it is based on the ARX-based generalized Feistel network. HIGHT became a standard encryption algorithm in South Korea and also is internationally standardized by ISO/ICE 18033-3. Therefore, many third-party cryptanalysis against HIGHT have been proposed. Especially, impossible differential and integral attacks are applied to reduced-round HIGHT, and the current best attack under the single-key setting is 27 rounds using the impossible differential attack. In this paper, we propose an improved integral attack against HIGHT. We first propose new 19-round integral characteristics by using the propagation of the division property, and they are improved by two rounds compared with previous integral characteristics. Finally, we can attack 28-round HIGHT by appending 9-round key recovery. Moreover, we can attack 29-round HIGHT if the full code book is used, and it improves by two rounds compared with previous best attack.

Keywords: Block cipher · HIGHT · Integral attack · Division property · Partial-sum technique · Bitwise partial-sum technique · Meet-in-the-middle technique

1 Introduction

The lightweight cryptography is one of the most actively discussed topics in the community of symmetric-key cryptographers. The motivation of the lightweight symmetric-key cryptography is to design high-performance and secure symmetric-key ciphers under the area-constraining environments. Such ciphers are expected to be proper for radio frequency identification (RFID), sensor network, and Internet of Things (IoT). Nowadays, a huge number of such ciphers have been proposed, and please refer to [2], where a list of lightweight ciphers is well summarized.

The generalized Feistel network (GFN) is suited to the design of lightweight block ciphers because each F-function is very small. LBlock [23] and TWINE [19]

© Springer International Publishing AG 2017
J. Pieprzyk and S. Suriadi (Eds.): ACISP 2017, Part I, LNCS 10342, pp. 363–383, 2017.
DOI: 10.1007/978-3-319-60055-0_19

Table 1. Comparison of attack results on HIGHT.

Model	Attack	#Rounds	Data	Time	Reference
Single key	Imp. Diff	18	$2^{46.8}$	$2^{109.2}$	[7]
	Imp. Diff	26	2^{61}	$2^{119.53}$	[12]
	Imp. Diff	26	$2^{61.6}$	$2^{114.35}$	[3]
	Imp. Diff	27	2^{58}	$2^{126.6}$	[3]
	Integral	16	2^{42}	2^{51}	[7]
	Integral	22	2^{62}	$2^{118.71}$	[25]
	Integral	22	2^{62}	$2^{102.35}$	[14]
	Integral	26	2^{57}	$2^{120.55}$	[15]
	Integral	28	2^{63}	2^{127}	Sect. 4
	Integral	29	2^{64}	2^{126}	Sect. 5
Related key	Imp. Diff	31	2^{64}	$2^{127.28}$	[12]
	rectangle	32 (full)	$2^{57.84}$	$2^{125.83}$	[10]

are examples of such ciphers. HIGHT, which was proposed by Hong et al. at CHES 2006 [7], is also a lightweight block cipher adopting the GFN. Moreover, HIGHT was standardized by ISO/IEC 18033-3 [8]. HIGHT only consists of three operations, i.e., modular additions over 256, bitwise rotations, and bitwise XOR. Such structure is often called ARX, and HIGHT is regarded as an ARX-based generalized Feistel network. Some ARX-based ciphers have been proposed, but there are many unsolved problems in the security analysis compare with the S-box-based ciphers. Therefore, HIGHT standardized by ISO/IEC is one of the most attractive ARX-based ciphers and is well analyzed.

In the related-key setting, the full HIGHT was already broken using the related-key rectangle attack [10]. On the other hand, impossible differential and integral attacks have been often applied to HIGHT under the single-key setting, but the full HIGHT has not been attacked yet. The current best attack is proposed by Chen using the impossible differential attack and 27-round HIGHT is attacked [3] (Table 1).

In this paper, we propose the current best attack by using the improved integral attacks. The integral attack consists of two parts; an integral characteristic and key recovery. In the integral characteristic, attackers first prepare a set of chosen plaintexts, where the XOR of the part of all corresponding states after several encryption rounds is always 0 for all secret keys. Then, in the key recovery, they guess round keys used in the last several rounds and evaluate whether the XOR of partially decrypted texts is 0 or not. If the correct key is guessed, the XOR is 0 because of the integral characteristic. Therefore, if the XOR is not 0, the guessed round key is discarded.

The integral cryptanalysis on HIGHT was first evaluated by the designers [7]. They showed 12-round integral characteristics with 2^8 chosen plaintexts, and 16-round HIGHT is attacked by using the characteristic. However, the error of this 12-round characteristics was pointed out by Zhang et al., and they showed that the correct integral characteristics with 2^8 chosen plaintexts cover only 11 rounds [25]. Moreover, they improved the 11-round characteristic to 17-round one by using the higher-order integral characteristics. As a result, 22-round HIGHT is attacked by using the 17-round characteristic. Then, the key recovery part is dramatically improved by Sasaki and Wang. They first proposed the meet-in-the-middle technique for the key recovery of the integral attack [14], which is useful to reduce the time complexity. Moreover, they proposed the bitwise partial-sum technique and optimized the key recovery [15]. As a result, 26-round HIGHT is attacked. Note that both improvements use the same 17-round characteristic by Zhang et al.

In this paper, we first show new 19-round integral characteristics, which is improved by two rounds than previous 17-round one. Our new characteristic is found by the propagation of the division property [21]. The division property is a general technique to find integral characteristics and recently applied to a wide range of block ciphers. New 18-round integral characteristics with 2^{63} chosen plaintexts are found by the propagation of the division property, and 18-round characteristics are extended to 19-round ones. Then, we show that 28-round HIGHT can be attacked by using this extended 19-round characteristic. Moreover, we show that 29-round HIGHT can be attacked by using the same characteristic if the full code book is used. Since the previous best attack is up to 27 rounds, our new attacks are the current best attack under the single-key setting.

2   Preliminaries

2.1   Specification of HIGHT

HIGHT is a block-cipher proposed at CHES 2006 by Hong et al. [7]. The block size is 64 bits and the key size is 128 bits. It adopts the type-2 generalized Feistel network with 8 branches and 32 rounds. Please refer to [7] for details. Note that a figure with an incorrect subkey order is showed in [7], and the designers later fixed the problem [1].

Encryption. The 64-bit plaintext and ciphertext are considered as concatenations of 8 bytes and denoted by $P = P_7\|P_6\| \cdots \|P_0$ and $C = C_7\|C_6\| \cdots \|C_0$, respectively. The input of the $(r + 1)$-th round function is represented as $X^r = X_7^r\|X_6^r\| \cdots \|X_0^r$ for $r = 0, 1, \ldots, 32$. At first, the plaintext is loaded into an internal state $X_7^0\|X_6^0\| \cdots \|X_0^0$ as follows.

$$X_0^0 = P_0 \boxplus WK_0, \quad X_1^0 = P_1, \quad X_2^0 = P_2 \oplus WK_1, \quad X_3^0 = P_3,$$
$$X_4^0 = P_4 \boxplus WK_2, \quad X_5^0 = P_5, \quad X_6^0 = P_6 \oplus WK_3, \quad X_7^0 = P_7,$$

where WK_i denotes 8-bit whitening keys for $i = 0, 1, \ldots, 7$. The operation $\boxplus$ denotes addition mod 2^8. Then, the value $X_7^r\|X_6^r\| \cdots \|X_0^r$ is updated as Fig. 1

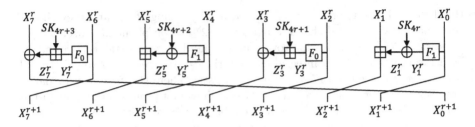

Fig. 1. Round function procedure of HIGHT

for $r = 0, 1, \ldots, 31$, where $F_0(x) = (x \lll 1) \oplus (x \lll 2) \oplus (x \lll 7)$ and $F_1(x) = (x \lll 3) \oplus (x \lll 4) \oplus (x \lll 6)$. The operation about $(x \lll s)$ denotes an s-bit left rotation of an 8-bit value x, and SK_i denotes the i-th 8-bit subkey for $i = 0, 1, \ldots, 127$. The swap of the byte position is omitted in the last round. The internal state between F and the key addition is defined by $Y_1^r, Y_3^r, Y_5^r, Y_7^r$, and the internal state after the key addition is defined by $Z_1^r, Z_3^r, Z_5^r, Z_7^r$. Finally, the ciphertext is generated from X^{32} by applying the post whitening as follows.

$$C_0 = X_0^{32} \boxplus WK_4, \quad C_1 = X_1^{32}, \quad C_2 = X_2^{32} \oplus WK_5, \quad C_3 = X_3^{32},$$
$$C_4 = X_4^{32} \boxplus WK_6, \quad C_5 = X_5^{32}, \quad C_6 = X_6^{32} \oplus WK_7, \quad C_7 = X_7^{32}.$$

Decryption. The decryption process is explained in the similar to the encryption process. This operation is identical to an operation for encryption apart from the following two modifications.

1. All $\boxplus$ operations are replaced by $\boxminus$ operations except for the $\boxplus$ operations connecting SK_i and outputs of F_0, where the operation about $\boxminus$ denotes subtraction mod 2^8.
2. The order in which the keys WK_i and SK_i are applied is reversed.

Key Schedule. The 128-bit master key is considered as a concatenation of 16 bytes and denoted by $K = K_{15} \| K_{14} \| \cdots \| K_0$. In the key schedule, 4 whitening keys for plaintexts are first generated from the master key as $(WK_0, WK_1, WK_2, WK_3) = (K_{12}, K_{13}, K_{14}, K_{15})$, and 4 whitening keys for ciphertexts are generated from the master key as $(WK_4, WK_5, WK_6, WK_7) = (K_0, K_1, K_2, K_3)$. Moreover, the 128 subkeys are generated as

$$\begin{cases} SK_{16 \cdot i + j} = K_{j-i \mod 8} \boxplus \delta_{16 \cdot i + j}, \\ SK_{16 \cdot i + j + 8} = K_{(j-i \mod 8) + 8} \boxplus \delta_{16 \cdot i + j + 8}, \end{cases}$$

where δ_i is a constant.

2.2   Integral Characteristics and Division Property

The integral attack was first proposed by Daemen et al. to evaluate the security of SQUARE [5], and then it was formalized by Knudsen and Wagner [9].

The integral attack consists of two parts; construction of an integral characteristic and key recovery. In this subsection, we focus on the first part, and the second part is described in the next subsection.

The most common integral characteristic exploits the set of chosen plaintexts such that the sum of chosen bits in texts encrypted a certain number of rounds is always 0 for all secret keys. Assume that m-bit encrypted texts hold this characteristic in the target block cipher. Then, since the probability that the ideal block cipher holds this characteristic is 2^{-m}, the distinguishing attack is directly derived from the integral characteristic.

Division Property. The division property, which was recently proposed in [21,22], is a general method to find integral characteristics, and it is defined as follows.

Definition 1 (Division Property [21,22]). *Let $\mathbb{X}$ be a multiset whose elements take a value of $\mathbb{F}_2^n$. When the multiset $\mathbb{X}$ has the division property $\mathcal{D}_{\mathbb{K}}^{1^n}$, where $\mathbb{K}$ denotes a set of m-dimensional vectors whose i-th element takes 0 or 1, it fulfills the following conditions:*

$$\bigoplus_{x \in \mathbb{X}} x^u = \begin{cases} unknown & \text{if there exist } k \in \mathbb{K} \text{ s.t. } u \succeq k, \\ 0 & \text{otherwise,} \end{cases}$$

where $x^u = \prod_{i=1}^n x[i]^{u[i]}$, and $u \succeq k$ if $u[i] \geq k[i]$ for all i. Here, $x[i]$ denotes the i-th bit of x from the least significant bit (lsb).

Todo and Morii showed the propagation rules of the division property for three basic operations; copy, xor, and and [22].

Let $I = \{i_1, i_2, \ldots, i_{|I|}\}$ be the index of active plaintext bits. Then, the division property of such chosen plaintexts becomes $\mathcal{D}_k^{1^n}$, where $k_i = 1$ if $i \in I$ and $k_i = 0$ otherwise. Then, to search for integral characteristics, *division trail* is evaluated.

Definition 2 (Division Trail [24]). *Let us consider the propagation of the division property*

$$\{k\} \stackrel{\text{def}}{=} \mathbb{K}_0 \to \mathbb{K}_1 \to \mathbb{K}_2 \to \cdots \to \mathbb{K}_r,$$

where $\mathcal{D}_{\mathbb{K}_i}$ be the division property after i-round propagation. Moreover, for any vector $k_{i+1}^* \in \mathbb{K}_{i+1}$, there must exist a vector $k_i^* \in \mathbb{K}_i$ such that k_i^* can propagate to k_{i+1}^* by the propagation rule of the division property. Furthermore, for $(k_0, k_1, \ldots, k_r) \in (\mathbb{K}_0 \times \mathbb{K}_1 \times \cdots \times \mathbb{K}_r)$ if k_i can propagate to k_{i+1} for all $i \in \{0, 1, \ldots, r-1\}$, we call $(k_0 \to k_1 \to \cdots \to k_r)$ an r-round division trail.

Let E_k be the target r-round block cipher. Then, if there is no division trail $k_0 \xrightarrow{E_k} k_r = e_i$, the i-th bit of r-round ciphertexts is always balanced. In [21], [20], and [22], all possible division trails are evaluated by using a breadth-first search. Unfortunately, it is practically infeasible to apply this method to block ciphers whose block length exceeds 32 because the size of $\mathbb{K}_i$ is extremely large.

MILP-Aided Propagation Search. A mixed-integer linear programming (MILP) was introduced to cryptanalysis by Mouha et al. in [11]. Then, the MILP has been successfully applied to various cryptanalyses [4,13,17,17,18,24]. The MILP is an optimization or feasibility program where variables are restricted to integers. An MILP model $\mathcal{M}$ consists of variables $\mathcal{M}.var$, constraints $\mathcal{M}.con$, and an objective function $\mathcal{M}.obj$, and the following is an example of MILP.

Example 1.

$$\mathcal{M}.var \leftarrow x, y, z \text{ as binary.}$$
$$\mathcal{M}.con \leftarrow x + 2y + 3z \leq 4 \quad \text{and} \quad x + y \geq 1$$
$$\mathcal{M}.obj \leftarrow \text{maximize } x + y + 2z$$

The answer of the model $\mathcal{M}$ is 3, where $(x, y, z) = (1, 0, 1)$.

MILP solver can solve such optimization program, and it returns *infeasible* if there is no feasible solution. Moreover, if there is no objective function, the MILP solver only evaluates whether this model is feasible or not.

Xiang et al. showed that all division trails are efficiently evaluated by using the MILP in [24], where three division trails for basic operations are modeled as follows.

Proposition 1 (MILP model for COPY). *Let* $a \xrightarrow{COPY} (b_1, b_2, \ldots, b_m)$ *be a division trail of COPY, where one bit is copied to m bits. The following inequalities are sufficient to describe the propagation of the division property for* copy.

$$\begin{cases} \mathcal{M}.var \leftarrow a, b_1, b_2, \ldots, b_m \text{ as binary.} \\ \mathcal{M}.con \leftarrow a = b_1 + b_2 + \cdots + b_m \end{cases}$$

Proposition 2 (MILP model for XOR). *Let* $(a_1, a_2, \ldots, a_m) \xrightarrow{XOR} b$ *be a division trail of XOR, where the XOR of m bits is computed. The following inequalities are sufficient to describe the propagation of the division property for* xor.

$$\begin{cases} \mathcal{M}.var \leftarrow a_1, a_2, \ldots, a_m, b \text{ as binary.} \\ \mathcal{M}.con \leftarrow a_1 + a_2 + \cdots + a_m = b \end{cases}$$

Proposition 3 (MILP model for 2-bit AND). *Let* $(a_1, a_2) \xrightarrow{AND} b$ *be a division trail of AND, where the AND of 2 bits is computed. The following inequalities are sufficient to describe the propagation of the division property for* and.

$$\begin{cases} \mathcal{M}.var \leftarrow a_1, a_2, b \text{ as binary.} \\ \mathcal{M}.con \leftarrow b \geq a_i \text{ for all } i \in \{1, 2\} \end{cases}$$

In [24], an additional constraint $b - a_1 - a_2 \leq 0$ *is used, but it is redundant. Namely, even if the redundant constraint is not used, it does not affect the result of MILP.*

We first create the MILP model for a target block cipher by using Proposition 1, 2, and 3. Then, the division property of plaintexts is constrained according to the index I of active plaintext bits. Moreover, the division property of the i-th bit of ciphertexts is constrained to 1 when the i-th bit of ciphertexts is evaluated, and the division property of the other bits is constrained to 0. If the MILP solver judges that the model is infeasible, the i-th bit of ciphertexts is balanced. Please refer to [24] in detail.

2.3   Key Recovery and Bitwise Partial-Sum Technique

Supposing that κ-bit secret key is involved to evaluate the integral characteristic with $2^{|I|}$ texts from ciphertexts, the trivial key recovery requires $2^{|I|+\kappa}$ time complexity. Ferguson et al. proposed the partial-sum technique to reduce the time complexity in [6]. In this technique, we first store the frequency of ciphertexts into a memory, ciphertexts are partially decrypted by guessing the part of involved keys, and reduce the size of the memory. Since the complexity is the product of the memory size and the partially guessed key size, the attacker can reduce the whole complexity by partial decryption and compressing the data size step by step.

Sasaki and Wang proposed the bitwise partial-sum technique, which improves the complexity of the partial-sum technique for ARX designs [15]. Suppose that n-bit variables X, Y and n-bit unknown key K. Also suppose that 2^{2n} pairs of (X, Y) are given to the attacker, and the goal of the attacker is to compute Z by exhaustively guessing K, where the following two operations are considered.

$$Z = (X \oplus K) \boxplus Y, \qquad Z = (X \boxplus K) \oplus Y.$$

The complexity to compute Z is $2^{2n} \cdot 2^n = 2^{3n}$ operations. The bitwise partial-sum can reduce the complexity to $n \cdot 2^{2n+1}$ by computing Z bit by bit.

In practice, we need to evaluate the complexity for mod subtraction because of analyzing on decryption. At first, n-bit variable $\bar{Y}$ and $\bar{K}$ denote inverse elements corresponding to Y and K, respectively. Then, the following equations can be easily derived.

$$(X \oplus K) \boxminus Y = (X \oplus K) \boxplus \bar{Y}, \qquad (X \boxminus K) \oplus Y = (X \boxplus \bar{K}) \oplus Y.$$

Hence, we can consider that the mod subtraction is equivalent to the mod addition are equivalent as far as guessing all values of $\bar{Y}$ and $\bar{K}$, and use same procedure shown by [15]. The complexities to compute the above equations with the bytewise and bitwise partial-sum is given in Table 2.

Table 2. Summary of the complexity of the bytewise and bitwise partial-sum

Target equation	Bytewise partial-sum	Bitwise partial-sum
$Z = (X \oplus K) \boxminus Y$	2^{3n}	$n \cdot 2^{2n+1}$
$Z = (X \boxminus K) \oplus Y$	2^{3n}	$n \cdot 2^{2n+1}$

3   New Integral Characteristics on HIGHT

3.1   Previous 17-Round Integral Characteristics

Zhang et al. first showed 11-round integral characteristics with 2^8 chosen plaintexts in [25]. Moreover, they extended the characteristics to 17-round ones by using the higher-order integral as

$$(\mathcal{A},\mathcal{A},\mathcal{A},\mathcal{A},\mathcal{A},\mathcal{A},\mathcal{A},\mathcal{C}) \xrightarrow{17R} (\mathcal{U},\mathcal{U},\mathcal{U},\mathcal{U},\mathcal{B}_0,\mathcal{U},\mathcal{U},\mathcal{U}),$$

$$(\mathcal{A},\mathcal{A},\mathcal{A},\mathcal{C},\mathcal{A},\mathcal{A},\mathcal{A},\mathcal{A}) \xrightarrow{17R} (\mathcal{B}_0,\mathcal{U},\mathcal{U},\mathcal{U},\mathcal{U},\mathcal{U},\mathcal{U},\mathcal{U}),$$

where $\mathcal{B}_0$ denotes that the lsb of the byte is balanced [25]. Moreover, $\mathcal{A}$ denotes that every value appears the same number in the multiset, $\mathcal{C}$ denotes that the value is fixed to a constant for all texts in the multiset and $\mathcal{U}$ denotes that the multiset is indistinguishable from one of n-bit random values.

3.2   New Integral Characteristics Based on Division Property

We first propose some new 18-round integral characteristics, which are found by the propagation of the division property. As the unique structure of HIGHT, there are modular constant additions and modular additions of two values. Such additions are represented by the combination of half and full adders, and we generate the MILP model by simulating these adders by three propagation rules.

MILP Model for Modular Additions. We first consider the MILP model for half and full adders. In the half adder, the input is two bits a and b, and the output is the sum s and the carry c. Then, s and c are computed as

$$c = a \wedge b, \qquad s = a \oplus b.$$

In the full adder, the input is three bits a, b, and x, and the output is the sum s and the carry c. Then, s and c are computed as

$$c = (a \wedge b) \oplus (x \wedge (a \oplus b)), \qquad s = a \oplus b \oplus x.$$

halfAdder and fullAdder in Algorithm 1 generates the MILP model of the division property for halfAdder and fullAdder, respectively. Here, halfAdder consists of 6 $\mathcal{M}.vars$ and 5 $\mathcal{M}.cons$, and fullAdder consists of 13 $\mathcal{M}.vars$ and 10 $\mathcal{M}.cons$. Moreover, modAdd in Algorithm 1 shows the MILP model of the division property for modular addition of two n-bit values, where $(6 + 13 \times (n-2) + 1)$ $\mathcal{M}.vars$ and $(5 + 10 \times (n-2) + 1)$ $\mathcal{M}.cons$ are used. Constant round keys are modular added to the state in HIGHT, and modAddConst in Algorithm 1 shows the MILP model of the division property. In the constant addition, corresponding division property is always 0. Therefore, additions of the lsb and msb are simply represented, and it is enough to use halfAdder for additions of other bits. Therefore, $2 + 6 \times (n-2) + 1$ $\mathcal{M}.vars$ and $1 + 5 \times (n-2) + 1$ $\mathcal{M}.cons$ are used.

Algorithm 1. MILP model of division property for modular addition of two values.

1: **procedure** halfAdder($\mathcal{M}, a, b$)	1: **procedure** modAdd($\mathcal{M}, a, b, n$)
2: $\mathcal{M}.var \leftarrow a_s, b_s, a_c, b_c, s, c$ *	2: $(\mathcal{M}, s_1, c_1) = $halfAdder$(\mathcal{M}, a_1, b_1)$
3: $\mathcal{M}.con \leftarrow a = a_s + a_c$	3: **for** $i = 2$ to $n - 1$ **do**
4: $\mathcal{M}.con \leftarrow b = b_s + b_c$	4: $(\mathcal{M}, s_i, c_i) = $fullAdder$(\mathcal{M}, a_i, b_i, c_{i-1})$
5: $\mathcal{M}.con \leftarrow s = a_s + b_s$	5: $\mathcal{M}.var \leftarrow s_n$
6: $\mathcal{M}.con \leftarrow c \geq a_c$ and $c \geq b_c$	6: $\mathcal{M}.con \leftarrow s_n = a_n + b_n + c_{n-1}$
7: **return** $(\mathcal{M}, s, c)$	7: **return** $(\mathcal{M}, s)$
1: **procedure** fullAdder($\mathcal{M}, a, b, x$)	1: **procedure** modAddConst($\mathcal{M}, a, n$)
2: $\mathcal{M}.var \leftarrow a_s, b_s, a_u, b_u, a_v, b_v$ *	2: $\mathcal{M}.var \leftarrow s_1, c_1$
3: $\mathcal{M}.var \leftarrow x_s, x_w, s, c$ *	3: $\mathcal{M}.con \leftarrow a_1 = s_1 + c_1$
4: $\mathcal{M}.con \leftarrow a = a_s + a_u + a_v$	4: **for** $i = 2$ to $n - 1$ **do**
5: $\mathcal{M}.con \leftarrow b = b_s + b_u + b_v$	5: $(\mathcal{M}, s_i, c_i) = $halfAdder$(\mathcal{M}, a_i, c_{i-1})$
6: $\mathcal{M}.con \leftarrow x = x_s + x_w$	6: $\mathcal{M}.var \leftarrow s_n$
7: $\mathcal{M}.con \leftarrow s = a_s + b_s + x_s$	7: $\mathcal{M}.con \leftarrow s_n = a_n + c_{n-1}$
8: $\mathcal{M}.var \leftarrow u, v, w$ *	8: **return** $(\mathcal{M}, s)$
9: $\mathcal{M}.con \leftarrow u \geq a_u$ and $u \geq b_u$	
10: $\mathcal{M}.con \leftarrow v = a_v + b_v$	
11: $\mathcal{M}.con \leftarrow w \geq x_w$ and $w \geq v$	
12: $\mathcal{M}.con \leftarrow c = u + w$	
13: **return** $(\mathcal{M}, s, c)$	

* means each variant are defined as binary.

New 18-Round Integral Characteristics. We implemented an MILP model of the division property for HIGHT. The algorithm to search for integral characteristics is described in Algorithm 2 of Appendix A. To find the longest integral characteristics, we choose one constant bit from 64 plaintext bits, i.e., 64 sets of 2^{63} chosen plaintexts are tried out. As a result, we found six 18-round integral characteristics as

$$\text{IC1} \quad (\mathcal{A}, \mathcal{A}, \mathcal{A}, \mathcal{A}, \mathcal{A}, \mathcal{A}, \mathcal{A}, \mathcal{A}_0) \xrightarrow{18R} (\mathcal{U}, \mathcal{U}, \mathcal{U}, \mathcal{U}, \mathcal{B}_0, \mathcal{U}, \mathcal{U}, \mathcal{U}),$$

$$\text{IC2} \quad (\mathcal{A}, \mathcal{A}, \mathcal{A}, \mathcal{A}_0, \mathcal{A}, \mathcal{A}, \mathcal{A}, \mathcal{A}) \xrightarrow{18R} (\mathcal{B}_0, \mathcal{U}, \mathcal{U}, \mathcal{U}, \mathcal{U}, \mathcal{U}, \mathcal{U}, \mathcal{U}),$$

$$\text{IC3} \quad (\mathcal{A}, \mathcal{A}, \mathcal{A}, \mathcal{A}, \mathcal{A}, \mathcal{A}_0, \mathcal{A}, \mathcal{A}) \xrightarrow{18R} (\mathcal{U}, \mathcal{U}, \mathcal{U}, \mathcal{U}, \mathcal{B}_{1,0}, \mathcal{U}, \mathcal{U}, \mathcal{U}),$$

$$\text{IC4} \quad (\mathcal{A}, \mathcal{A}, \mathcal{A}, \mathcal{A}, \mathcal{A}, \mathcal{A}_1, \mathcal{A}, \mathcal{A}) \xrightarrow{18R} (\mathcal{U}, \mathcal{U}, \mathcal{U}, \mathcal{U}, \mathcal{B}_{1,0}, \mathcal{U}, \mathcal{U}, \mathcal{U}),$$

$$\text{IC5} \quad (\mathcal{A}, \mathcal{A}_0, \mathcal{A}, \mathcal{A}, \mathcal{A}, \mathcal{A}, \mathcal{A}, \mathcal{A}) \xrightarrow{18R} (\mathcal{B}_{1,0}, \mathcal{U}, \mathcal{U}, \mathcal{U}, \mathcal{U}, \mathcal{U}, \mathcal{U}, \mathcal{U}),$$

$$\text{IC6} \quad (\mathcal{A}, \mathcal{A}_1, \mathcal{A}, \mathcal{A}, \mathcal{A}, \mathcal{A}, \mathcal{A}, \mathcal{A}) \xrightarrow{18R} (\mathcal{B}_{1,0}, \mathcal{U}, \mathcal{U}, \mathcal{U}, \mathcal{U}, \mathcal{U}, \mathcal{U}, \mathcal{U}),$$

where $\mathcal{A}_i$ denotes seven bits except for i-th bit are active and i-th bit is constant, and $\mathcal{B}_{1,0}$ denotes that the lsb and the second lsb are balanced[1].

---

[1]   Sun et.al. also independently proposed 18-round integral characteristics in [16]. However, they presented only two characteristics as IC1 and IC2.

3.3   Extended 19-Round Integral Characteristics

We propose how to extend six 18-round integral characteristics to 19-round ones by appending one round to the plaintext side. Especially, we do not need to guess secret keys for extensions from IC1, IC2, IC3 and IC5, and it does not require the use of the full code book. Unfortunately, other two extensions requires guessing the part of secret keys, but we can easily append one round by using the full code book.

Extending IC1 and IC2. We consider the extension from IC1 and IC2, where the round function using F_0 is involved (see Fig. 2). Then, the lsb of the left half of the output is represented as

$$L[0] \oplus (F_0(R) \boxplus SK)[0] = L[0] \oplus F_0(R)[0] \oplus SK[0].$$

When the lsb of the left half of the plaintext takes a value $\mathcal{X} = F_0(R)[0]$, the lsb of the left half of the output is always constant. As a result, we can get two 19-round integral characteristics as

IC1' $(\mathcal{A}^7 \| \mathcal{X}, \mathcal{A}, \mathcal{A}, \mathcal{A}, \mathcal{A}, \mathcal{A}, \mathcal{A}, \mathcal{A}) \xrightarrow{19R} (\mathcal{U}, \mathcal{U}, \mathcal{U}, \mathcal{U}, \mathcal{B}_0, \mathcal{U}, \mathcal{U}, \mathcal{U}),$

IC2' $(\mathcal{A}, \mathcal{A}, \mathcal{A}, \mathcal{A}, \mathcal{A}^7 \| \mathcal{X}, \mathcal{A}, \mathcal{A}, \mathcal{A}) \xrightarrow{19R} (\mathcal{B}_0, \mathcal{U}, \mathcal{U}, \mathcal{U}, \mathcal{U}, \mathcal{U}, \mathcal{U}, \mathcal{U}),$

without guessing any bit of secret key, where $\mathcal{A}^i$ denotes that i bits are active.

Extending IC3 and IC5. We consider the extension from IC3 and IC5, where the round function using F_1 is involved (see Fig. 3). Then, the lsb of the left half of the output is represented as

$$L[0] \boxplus (F_1(R) \oplus SK)[0] = L[0] \oplus F_1(R)[0] \oplus SK[0].$$

When the lsb of the left half of the plaintext takes a value $\mathcal{X} = F_1(R)[0]$, the lsb of the left half of the output is always constant. As a result, we can get two 19-round integral characteristics as

IC3' $(\mathcal{A}, \mathcal{A}, \mathcal{A}, \mathcal{A}, \mathcal{A}, \mathcal{A}, \mathcal{A}^7 \| \mathcal{X}, \mathcal{A}) \xrightarrow{19R} (\mathcal{U}, \mathcal{U}, \mathcal{U}, \mathcal{U}, \mathcal{B}_{1,0}, \mathcal{U}, \mathcal{U}, \mathcal{U}),$

IC5' $(\mathcal{A}, \mathcal{A}, \mathcal{A}^7 \| \mathcal{X}, \mathcal{A}, \mathcal{A}, \mathcal{A}, \mathcal{A}, \mathcal{A}) \xrightarrow{19R} (\mathcal{B}_{1,0}, \mathcal{U}, \mathcal{U}, \mathcal{U}, \mathcal{U}, \mathcal{U}, \mathcal{U}, \mathcal{U}),$

without guessing any bit of secret key.

$L = \mathcal{A} \| \cdots \| \mathcal{A} \| \mathcal{X}$ $R = \mathcal{A} \| \mathcal{A} \| \cdots \| \mathcal{A}$ $L = \mathcal{A} \| \cdots \| \mathcal{A} \| \mathcal{X}$ $R = \mathcal{A} \| \mathcal{A} \| \cdots \| \mathcal{A}$ $L = \mathcal{A} \| \cdots \| \mathcal{X} \| \mathcal{A}$ $R = \mathcal{A} \| \mathcal{A} \| \cdots \| \mathcal{A}$

$\mathcal{A} \| \cdots \| \mathcal{A} \| \mathcal{C}$ $\mathcal{A} \| \mathcal{A} \| \cdots \| \mathcal{A}$ $\mathcal{A} \| \cdots \| \mathcal{A} \| \mathcal{C}$ $\mathcal{A} \| \mathcal{A} \| \cdots \| \mathcal{A}$ $\mathcal{A} \| \cdots \| \mathcal{C} \| \mathcal{A}$ $\mathcal{A} \| \mathcal{A} \| \cdots \| \mathcal{A}$

Fig. 2. IC1, 2   **Fig. 3.** IC3, 5   **Fig. 4.** IC4, 6

Extending IC4 and IC6. We consider the extension from IC4 and IC6 (see Fig. 4). The second lsb is constant in these integral characteristics instead of the lsb. Then, the second lsb of the left half of the output is represented as

$$L[1] \oplus F_1(R)[1] \oplus SK[1] \oplus (L[0] \times (F_1(R)[0] \oplus SK[0])).$$

When the second lsb of the left half of the plaintext takes a value $\mathcal{X} = F_1(R)[1] \oplus (L[0] \times (F_1(R)[0] \oplus SK[0]))$, the output second lsb is constant. Then,

IC4' $(\mathcal{A}, \mathcal{A}, \mathcal{A}, \mathcal{A}, \mathcal{A}, \mathcal{A}, \mathcal{A}^6 \| \mathcal{X} \| A^1, \mathcal{A}) \xrightarrow{19R} (\mathcal{U}, \mathcal{U}, \mathcal{U}, \mathcal{U}, \mathcal{B}_{1,0}, \mathcal{U}, \mathcal{U}, \mathcal{U}),$

IC6' $(\mathcal{A}, \mathcal{A}, \mathcal{A}^6 \| \mathcal{X} \| A^1, \mathcal{A}, \mathcal{A}, \mathcal{A}, \mathcal{A}, \mathcal{A}) \xrightarrow{19R} (\mathcal{B}_{1,0}, \mathcal{U}, \mathcal{U}, \mathcal{U}, \mathcal{U}, \mathcal{U}, \mathcal{U}, \mathcal{U}).$

Unfortunately, these extension requires guessing $SK[0]$ and the full code book.

These integral characteristics could not be detected by MILP-aided tool. In our procedure that how to extend integral characteristics, we have to compose the set of chosen plaintexts which include some non-linear part, represented as $\mathcal{X}$. On the other hand, the division property provide the completely linear and generalized set of chosen plaintexts. As a result, the MILP-aided tool using the division property can find 18-round integral characteristics but cannot find 19-round ones.

4   28-Round Attack on HIGHT Without Full Code Book

4.1   Whitening Key Addition to Integral Characteristics

In Sect. 3.3, we showed new 19-round integral characteristics, but we cannot use each characteristic directly because whitening key is added to plaintexts at first. In this section, we propose how to add the whitening to six 19-round integral characteristics.

First, we add the whitening to IC1' or IC2', where the XOR is used as the addition. Then, the whitening key is linearly involved to the lsb of the left half of the output. Therefore, even if there is the whitening, we can use IC1' without guessing the key.

Next, we add the whitening to IC3' or IC5', where the modular addition is used as the addition. Then, the whitening key is nonlinearly involved to the lsb of the left half of the output. Unfortunately, this requires guessing the whitening key, and the use of the full code book is required to add the whitening. Similarly, the full code book is required to add the whitening to IC4' or IC6'.

As a result, we can add the whitening to IC1' and IC2' without using the full code book. Other four integral characteristics can be added the whitening when the full code book is used. Hereafter, we only use IC1' and IC2' to avoid the use of the full code book in this section.

4.2 Meet-in-the-Middle Technique

Let us consider the integral attack using IC1'. Then, $X_3^{19}[0]$ is balanced and can be written as a linear combination of two variables $X_4^{20}[0]$ and $Z_3^{19}[0]$, where $X_i^r[j]$ denotes the j-th bit of the X_i^r. In the meet-in-the-middle technique [14], each sum is independently computed from ciphertexts, and secret keys satisfying $\bigoplus Z_3^{19}[0] = \bigoplus X_4^{20}[0]$ are recovered by using the computation like the meet-in-the-middle attack. Furthermore, for HIGHT, this concept is extended by exploiting more linearity inside the round function in [15]. Since the complexity for computing $\bigoplus Z_3^{19}[0]$ is much bigger than the one for $\bigoplus X_4^{20}[0]$, we reduce the number of subkeys involved $\bigoplus Z_3^{19}[0]$. We focus on that $Z_3^{19}[0]$ is computed by $SK_{77}[0] \boxplus Y_3^{19}[0]$, and this is represented as $Z_3^{19}[0] = SK_{77}[0] \oplus Y_3^{19}[0]$ because the lsb of the modular addition is a XOR. Therefore, $SK_{77}[0]$ can be removed, namely $\bigoplus X_4^{20}[0] = \bigoplus Y_3^{19}[0]$. Furthermore, by utilizing the linearity of F_0, i.e., $Y_3^{19}[0] = X_3^{20}[7] \oplus X_3^{20}[6] \oplus X_3^{20}[1]$, we can move more subkey bits, and finally get the following equation.

$$\bigoplus (X_4^{20}[0] \oplus X_4^{21}[7] \oplus X_4^{21}[6] \oplus X_4^{21}[1]) = \bigoplus (Z_3^{20}[7] \oplus Z_3^{20}[6] \oplus Z_3^{20}[1]). \quad (1)$$

Unfortunately, 13-byte keys are involved to the right half of Eq. (1), and we cannot append 9 rounds like [15]. Moreover, 14-byte keys are involved when IC2' is used. Alternatively, we attack 28-round HIGHT from the 2-nd round to 29-th round with whitening keys. Then, 12-byte keys and 13-byte keys are involved when IC1' and IC2' are used, respectively. We detail the analyses of the involved keys about each Z_i^r in Table 5 of Appendix B.

We prepare the 28-round HIGHT from the 2-nd to 29-th round and apply IC1' to 19-round between 2-nd and 20-th round. Then, $X_3^{20}[0]$ is balanced, and we finally get the following equation.

$$\bigoplus (X_4^{21}[0] \oplus X_4^{22}[7] \oplus X_4^{22}[6] \oplus X_4^{22}[1]) = \bigoplus (Z_3^{21}[7] \oplus Z_3^{21}[6] \oplus Z_3^{21}[1]). \quad (2)$$

4.3 Attack Procedure

We use the relationship between the whitening key, subkey and master key in Table 3.

Since the computation for the right-hand side of Eq. (2) requires much more complexity than the left-hand side, we only explain the procedure to obtain the right-hand side of Eq. (2) and evaluate the time complexity. The partial decryption for obtaining $\bigoplus (Z_3^{21}[7] \oplus Z_3^{21}[6] \oplus Z_3^{21}[1])$ is shown in Fig. 5. We first describe our procedure with the bytewise partial-sum technique as following steps:

1. The analysis starts from at most 2^{64} ciphertexts of $(C_0, \ldots, C_7)$.
2. K_1 and K_2 are guessed and the data is compressed into 2^{56} texts.
3. K_2 has been already guessed, so K_3 is guessed and the data is converted into 2^{56} texts.

Table 3. Relationship between Whitening key, Subkey and Master key from 1-st to 29-th round

Round	RK_7	RK_5	RK_3	RK_1	Round	RK_7	RK_5	RK_3	RK_1
W	K_{15}	K_{14}	K_{13}	K_{12}	16	K_{12}	K_{11}	K_{10}	K_9
1	K_3	K_1	K_1	K_0	17	K_7	K_6	K_5	K_4
2	K_7	K_6	K_5	K_4	18	K_3	K_2	K_1	K_0
3	K_{11}	K_{10}	K_9	K_8	19	K_{15}	K_{14}	K_{13}	K_{12}
4	K_{15}	K_{14}	K_{13}	K_{12}	20	K_{11}	K_{10}	K_9	K_8
5	K_2	K_1	K_0	K_7	21	K_6	K_5	K_4	K_3
6	K_6	K_5	K_4	K_3	22	K_2	K_1	K_0	K_7
7	K_{10}	K_9	K_8	K_{15}	23	K_{14}	K_{13}	K_{12}	K_{11}
8	K_{14}	K_{13}	K_{12}	K_{11}	24	K_{10}	K_9	K_8	K_{15}
9	K_1	K_0	K_7	K_6	25	K_5	K_4	K_3	K_2
10	K_5	K_4	K_3	K_2	26	K_1	K_0	K_7	K_6
11	K_9	K_8	K_{15}	K_{14}	27	K_{13}	K_{12}	K_{11}	K_{10}
12	K_{13}	K_{12}	K_{11}	K_{10}	28	K_9	K_8	K_{15}	K_{14}
13	K_0	K_7	K_6	K_5	29	K_4	K_3	K_2	K_1
14	K_4	K_3	K_2	K_1	W	K_3	K_2	K_1	K_0
15	K_8	K_{15}	K_{14}	K_{13}					

When Round is W, RK_i denotes the round key corresponding WK. Otherwise, RK_i denotes the round key corresponding SK

4. K_{15} is guessed and the data is compressed into 2^{48} texts.
5. K_3 has been already guessed, so K_4 is guessed and the data is converted into 2^{48} texts.
6. K_8 is guessed and the data is converted into 2^{48} texts.
7. K_{11} is guessed and the data is compressed into 2^{40} texts.
8. K_1 has been already guessed, so K_0 is guessed and the data is converted into 2^{40} texts.
9. K_9 is guessed and the data is converted into 2^{40} texts.
10. K_{12} is guessed and the data is converted into 2^{40} texts.
11. K_7 is guessed and the data is compressed into 2^{32} texts.
12. K_3 has been already guessed, so the data is converted into 2^{32} texts.
13. K_0 has been already guessed, so the data is converted into 2^{32} texts.
14. K_8 has been already guessed, so the data is converted into 2^{32} texts.
15. K_{13} is guessed and the data is compressed into 2^{24} texts.
16. K_4 has been already guessed, so the data is compressed into 2^{16} texts.
17. K_{12} has been already guessed, so the data is compressed into 2^8 texts.
18. K_0 has been already guessed, so the data is compressed into 1 text of Z_3^{21}. Then, we can calculate the value of $\bigoplus(Z_3^{21}[7] \oplus Z_3^{21}[6] \oplus Z_3^{21}[1])$.

This procedure and its time complexity evaluation is summarized in Table 4. Step 11 and 15 requires the dominant time complexity, where 2^{128} round

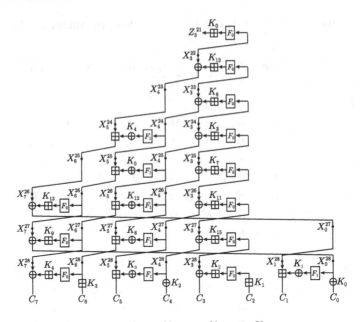

Fig. 5. Partial decryption for $\bigoplus(Z_3^{21}[7] \oplus Z_3^{21}[6] \oplus Z_3^{21}[1])$ on 28-round attack

function computations is used for the bytewise partial sum. We apply the bitwise partial sum to Step 11 and 15 to reduce the complexities. Step 11 starts from 2^{40} texts of $(X_0^{27}, X_3^{26}, X_4^{26}, X_5^{26}, X_7^{27})$, and the goal is obtaining 2^{32} texts of $(X_0^{27}, X_3^{25}, X_5^{26}, X_7^{27})$ with guessing K_7. We then apply the bitwise partial sum to guess K_7. Referring Table 2, its time complexity is reduced to $n \cdot (2^{80+39+1}) = 2^{123}$ round functions, where $n = 8$. In Step 15, we can also reduce the time complexity about 2^{128} to $n \cdot (2^{88+31+1}) = 2^{123}$ round functions, similarly. Finally, the time complexity in the key recovery is estimated by Step 11 and 15 because the complexities of other steps are negligible compared with 2^{123}. Hence, the time complexity of the key recovery is about 2^{124} round functions(RF).

Since only one integral characteristic with one balance bit is used, this key recovery only reduces the 1-bit of information on the master key. Therefore, we finally exhaustively searches 2^{127} master keys. As a result, the whole complexity of our attack is 2^{124} RF $+ 2^{127}$ Enc $\approx 2^{127}$ Enc.

5   29-Round Attack on HIGHT with Full Code Book

When the use of the full code book is acceptable, we can attack 29-round HIGHT, where one round is added to the plaintext side from the 28-round attack. Therefore, while 28-round HIGHT from the 2-nd to 29-th round is attacked in Sect. 4, the natural 29-round HIGHT is attacked.

We briefly describe the overview of our 29-round attack. We first prepare the set of chosen texts for the input of the 2-nd round function such that it brings 19-round integral characteristics, i.e., $X_3^{20}[0]$ is balanced, and it is the same as the 28-round attack. Next, we guess the round key in the 1-st round and whitening keys, and get the set of corresponding plaintexts. Since the set of plaintexts depends on the guessed keys, 29-round attack requires the use of the full code book. Moreover, the position of the guessed keys depends on each characteristic, and Appendix C shows it in detail. Finally, we execute the key recovery that is the same as that for the 28-round attack.

Table 4. Summary of the computation for $\bigoplus(Z_3^{21}[7] \oplus Z_3^{21}[6] \oplus Z_3^{21}[1])$.

Step	Guessed keys	Data size	Texts need to be analyzed	Complexity (bytewise)	Complexity (bitwise)
1	—	2^{64}	$(C_0, C_1, C_2, C_3, C_4, C_5, C_6, C_7)$	2^{64} MA	—
2	K_1, K_2	2^{56}	$(C_0, C_1, X_3^{28}, C_4, C_5, C_6, C_7)$	$2^{16} \cdot 2^{64} = 2^{80}$ RF	—
3	$K_3(, K_2)$	2^{56}	$(C_0, C_1, X_3^{28}, X_4^{28}, X_5^{28}, C_6, C_7)$	$2^{16} \cdot 2^8 \cdot 2^{56} = 2^{80}$ RF	—
4	K_{15}	2^{48}	$(C_0, C_1, X_3^{27}, X_5^{28}, C_6, C_7)$	$2^{24} \cdot 2^8 \cdot 2^{56} = 2^{88}$ RF	—
5	$K_4(, K_3)$	2^{48}	$(C_0, C_1, X_3^{27}, X_5^{28}, X_6^{28}, X_7^{28})$	$2^{32} \cdot 2^8 \cdot 2^{48} = 2^{88}$ RF	—
6	K_8	2^{48}	$(C_0, C_1, X_3^{27}, X_4^{27}, X_5^{27}, X_7^{28})$	$2^{40} \cdot 2^8 \cdot 2^{48} = 2^{96}$ RF	—
7	K_{11}	2^{40}	$(C_0, C_1, X_3^{26}, X_5^{27}, X_7^{28})$	$2^{48} \cdot 2^8 \cdot 2^{48} = 2^{104}$ RF	—
8	$K_0(, K_1)$	2^{40}	$(X_0^{28}, X_0^{27}, X_3^{26}, X_5^{27}, X_7^{28})$	$2^{56} \cdot 2^8 \cdot 2^{40} = 2^{104}$ RF	—
9	K_9	2^{40}	$(X_0^{27}, X_3^{26}, X_5^{27}, X_6^{27}, X_7^{27})$	$2^{64} \cdot 2^8 \cdot 2^{40} = 2^{112}$ RF	—
10	K_{12}	2^{40}	$(X_0^{27}, X_3^{26}, X_4^{26}, X_5^{26}, X_7^{27})$	$2^{72} \cdot 2^8 \cdot 2^{40} = 2^{120}$ RF	—
11	K_7	2^{32}	$(X_0^{27}, X_3^{25}, X_5^{26}, X_7^{27})$	$2^{80} \cdot 2^8 \cdot 2^{40} = 2^{128}$ RF	$n \cdot (2^{80+39+1}) = 2^{123}$ RF
12	(K_3)	2^{32}	$(X_0^{27}, X_3^{24}, X_5^{26}, X_7^{27})$	$2^{88} \cdot 2^0 \cdot 2^{32} = 2^{120}$ RF	—
13	(K_0)	2^{32}	$(X_0^{27}, X_3^{24}, X_5^{25}, X_7^{27})$	$2^{88} \cdot 2^0 \cdot 2^{32} = 2^{120}$ RF	—
14	(K_8)	2^{32}	$(X_0^{27}, X_3^{23}, X_5^{25}, X_7^{27})$	$2^{88} \cdot 2^0 \cdot 2^{32} = 2^{120}$ RF	—
15	K_{13}	2^{24}	$(X_3^{23}, X_5^{25}, X_6^{25})$	$2^{88} \cdot 2^8 \cdot 2^{32} = 2^{128}$ RF	$n \cdot (2^{88+31+1}) = 2^{123}$ RF
16	(K_4)	2^{16}	(X_3^{23}, X_4^{23})	$2^{96} \cdot 2^0 \cdot 2^{24} = 2^{120}$ RF	—
17	(K_{12})	2^8	(X_3^{22})	$2^{96} \cdot 2^0 \cdot 2^{16} = 2^{112}$ RF	—
18	(K_0)	1	$\bigoplus(Z_3^{21}[7] \oplus Z_3^{21}[6] \oplus Z_3^{21}[1])$	$2^{96} \cdot 2^0 \cdot 2^8 = 2^{104}$ RF	—

MA and RF stand for memory access and round function, respectively

We first try to execute 29-round attack using the 19-round integral characteristic IC1'. To prepare the set of plaintexts, we have to guess the value of K_{14} and K_2. Unfortunately, K_{14} is not involved to the key recovery shown in Table 4. Therefore, the complexity of each step always requires 2^8 times, and the time complexity in Step 11 and 15 is over 2^{128} even if the bit-wise partial sum is applied. As a result, we cannot use IC1'. We next try to execute 29-round attack using the 19-round integral characteristic IC3'. Note that the position of balanced byte is the same as that by IC1', i.e., $X_3^{20}[0]$ is balanced. Therefore, we can use the same procedure for the key recovery. To prepare the set of plaintexts, we have to guess the value of K_{15} and K_3, which are already guessed in Step 4 and 3 in the key recovery, respectively. Hence, we add two bytes to the guessed keys in Step 1–2 and one byte to them in Step 3, and the complexity does not change after Step 4. Therefore, even if IC3' is used, the complexity of the key recovery is still 2^{124} RF because the dominant part is in Step 11 and 15. Moreover, when IC4' is used, we have to guess the value of not only K_{15} and K_3 but also the lsb of K_4 and K_{12}, but all additional guessing keys have been already guessed in the key recovery. Therefore, similarly to the key recovery using IC3', the dominant complexity is still 2^{124} RF. Since we can execute the key recovery using both IC3' and IC4' in the same time, 2 bits of information of the master key is recovered. As a result, the whole complexity of our attack is 2^{124} RF $+ 2^{126}$ Enc $\approx 2^{126}$ Enc.

6   Conclusions

In this paper, we first proposed 19-round integral characteristics by using the propagation of the division property. These characteristics are improved by two rounds compared with previous ones. Then, we showed the attack against 28-round HIGHT by appending 9-round key recovery. We attacked 28-round HIGHT with 2^{63} data size and 2^{127} time complexity. Moreover, we showed another attack on 29-HIGHT with 2^{64} data size and 2^{126} time complexity. These attacks are the best known attack against HIGHT under the single-key setting.

A   Detailed MILP Model for HIGHT

In this appendix, the detailed algorithm to search for integral characteristics on HIGHT is described.

As a result of running the Algorithm 2 with our machine (CPU: i5-6500 @ 3.20 GHz, 3.20 GHz/RAM: 8.00 GB/64-bit operating system, x64 base processor), it took about 50 min.

Algorithm 2. MILP model of division property for R-round HIGHT.

1: **procedure** funcF$(\mathcal{M}, x, r_1, r_2, r_3)$
2:     $\mathcal{M}.var \leftarrow y[j], x_1[j], x_2[j], x_3[j]$ for $j \in \{0, 1, \ldots, 7\}$*
3:     **for** $j = 0$ to 7 **do**
4:         $\mathcal{M}.con \leftarrow x[j] = x_1[j] + x_2[j] + x_3[j]$
5:         $\mathcal{M}.con \leftarrow y[j] = x_1[(j - r_1) \bmod 8] + x_2[(j - r_2) \bmod 8] + x_3[(j - r_3) \bmod 8]$
6:     **return** $(\mathcal{M}, y)$
1: **procedure** roundFunc1$(\mathcal{M}, l, r)$
2:     $\mathcal{M}.var \leftarrow x[j], s[j]$ for $j \in \{0, 1, \ldots, 7\}$*
3:     **for** $j = 0$ to 7 **do**
4:         $\mathcal{M}.con \leftarrow r[j] = x[j] + s[j]$
5:     $(\mathcal{M}, y) = \text{funcF}(\mathcal{M}, x, 3, 4, 6)$
6:     $t = \text{modAdd}(\mathcal{M}, l, y, 8)$
7:     **return** $(\mathcal{M}, s, t)$
1: **procedure** roundFunc0$(\mathcal{M}, l, r)$
2:     $\mathcal{M}.var \leftarrow x[j], s[j]$ for $j \in \{0, 1, \ldots, 7\}$*
3:     **for** $j = 0$ to 7 **do**
4:         $\mathcal{M}.con \leftarrow r[j] = x[j] + s[j]$
5:     $(\mathcal{M}, y) = \text{funcF}(\mathcal{M}, x, 1, 2, 7)$
6:     $z = \text{modAddConst}(\mathcal{M}, y, 8)$
7:     $\mathcal{M}.var \leftarrow t[j]$ for $j \in \{0, 1, \ldots, 7\}$*
8:     **for** $j = 0$ to 7 **do**
9:         $\mathcal{M}.con \leftarrow t[j] = l[j] + z[j]$
10:     **return** $(\mathcal{M}, s, t)$
1: **procedure** HIGHT(round R, index I, target bit t)
2:     create MILP model $\mathcal{M}$
3:     $\mathcal{M}.var \leftarrow x_i^0[j]$ for $(i, j) \in \{(0, 0), (0, 1), \ldots, (7, 7)\}$*
4:     **for** $(i, j) = (0, 0)$ to $(7, 7)$ **do**
5:         **if** $8 \times i + j$ is included in I **then** $\mathcal{M}.con \leftarrow x_i^0[j] = 1$
6:         **else** $\mathcal{M}.con \leftarrow x_i^0[j] = 0$
7:     **for** $r = 0$ to $R - 1$ **do**
8:         $(\mathcal{M}, x_1^{r+1}, x_2^{r+1}) = \text{roundFunc1}(\mathcal{M}, x_1^r, x_0^r)$
9:         $(\mathcal{M}, x_3^{r+1}, x_4^{r+1}) = \text{roundFunc0}(\mathcal{M}, x_3^r, x_2^r)$
10:         $(\mathcal{M}, x_5^{r+1}, x_6^{r+1}) = \text{roundFunc1}(\mathcal{M}, x_5^r, x_4^r)$
11:         $(\mathcal{M}, x_7^{r+1}, x_0^{r+1}) = \text{roundFunc0}(\mathcal{M}, x_7^r, x_6^r)$
12:     **for** $(i, j) = (0, 0)$ to $(7, 7)$ **do**
13:         **if** $8 \times i + j = t$ **then** $\mathcal{M}.con \leftarrow x_i^r[j] = 1$
14:         **else** $\mathcal{M}.con \leftarrow x_i^r[j] = 0$
15:     solve this MILP model $\mathcal{M}$
16:     **if** $\mathcal{M}$ is infeasible **then return** the target bit is balanced.
17:     **else return** the target bit is unknown.

* means each variant are defined as binary.

B   Involved Key Size in Key Recovery

In this appendix, the detailed analyses of the involved key size in the calculation of Z_i^r is described.

Table 5. The number of involved key bytes in calculation of Z_i^r

Rounds of Key Recovery	Target	Type of using IC	Involved Key Size	Ignored Keys
20 – 28 R	Z_3^{20}	IC1', IC3', IC4'	13 bytes	K_5, K_6, K_{10}
20 – 28 R	Z_7^{20}	IC2', IC5', IC6'	14 bytes	K_4, K_{12}
21 – 29 R	Z_3^{21}	IC1', IC3', IC4'	**12 bytes**	K_5, K_6, K_{10}, K_{14}
21 – 29 R	Z_7^{21}	IC2', IC5', IC6'	13 bytes	K_7, K_8, K_{12}
22 – 30 R	Z_3^{22}	IC1', IC3', IC4'	13 bytes	K_{10}, K_{13}, K_{14}
22 – 30 R	Z_7^{22}	IC2', IC5', IC6'	13 bytes	K_8, K_{11}, K_{12}
23 – 31 R	Z_3^{23}	IC1', IC3', IC4'	13 bytes	K_5, K_{13}, K_{14}
23 – 31 R	Z_7^{23}	IC2', IC5', IC6'	13 bytes	K_7, K_8, K_{15}
24 – 32 R	Z_3^{24}	IC1', IC3', IC4'	13 bytes	K_4, K_5, K_9
24 – 32 R	Z_7^{24}	IC2', IC5', IC6'	14 bytes	K_7, K_{11}

C   Detailed Addition of Whitening Layer

In this appendix, we described detailed procedure how to add the whitening layer to three 19-round integral characteristics. The first 2-round procedure on HIGHT is shown in Fig. 6. Please refer to Table 3 in order to know the relationship between the round keys and the master keys.

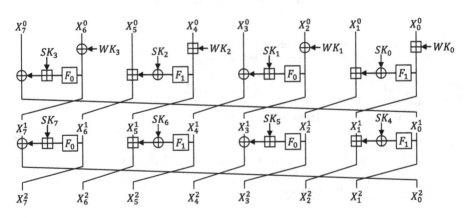

Fig. 6. 1-st and 2-nd round procedure of HIGHT

We consider the extension from IC1' and the lsb of X_0^2 is represented as

$$X_0^2[0] = X_7^1[0] \oplus SK_7[0] \oplus F_0(X_6^1)[0]$$
$$= X_6^0[0] \oplus WK_3[0] \oplus SK_7[0] \oplus F_0(F_1(X_4^0 \boxplus WK_2) \oplus SK_2 \boxplus X_5^0)[0].$$

We can ignore the value of $WK_3[0]$ and $SK_7[0]$ because $X_0^2[0]$ is added linearly by them using XOR. But we cannot ignore that this extension requires guessing the value of K_{14} and K_2 as WK_2 and SK_2, respectively. Next, we consider the extension from IC3'. In case of considering the lsb, we can regard the modular addition as the XOR. So the lsb of X_2^2 is represented as

$$X_2^2[0] = X_1^1[0] \oplus SK_4[0] \oplus F_1(X_0^1)[0]$$
$$= X_0^0[0] \oplus WK_0[0] \oplus SK_4[0] \oplus F_1(F_0(X_6^0 \oplus WK_3) \boxplus SK_3 \oplus X_7^0)[0].$$

This extension requires guessing the value of K_{15} and K_3 as WK_3 and SK_3, respectively. Finally, we consider the extension from IC4' and the second lsb is represented as

$$X_2^2[1] = X_1^1[1] \oplus F_1(X_0^1)[1] \oplus SK_4[1] \oplus (X_1^1[0] \times (F_1(X_0^1)[0] \oplus SK_4[0])),$$

where each X^1 are represented as follows:

$$X_1^1[1] = X_1^0[1] \oplus WK_0[1] \oplus (X_0^0[0] \times WK_0[0])),$$
$$X_1^1[0] = X_1^0[0] \oplus WK_0[0],$$
$$X_0^1 = F_0(X_6^0 \oplus WK_3) \boxplus SK_3 \oplus X_7^0.$$

This extension requires guessing the value of $K_4[0], K_{12}[0], K_{15}$ and K_3 as $SK_4[0], WK_0[0], WK_3$ and SK_3, respectively.

References

1. Agency, K.I.S.: Hight algorithm specification (2009)
2. Biryukov, A., Perrin, L.: Lightweight cryptography lounge (2015). http://cryptolux. org/index.php/Lightweight_Cryptography
3. Chen, J., Wang, M., Preneel, B.: Impossible differential cryptanalysis of the lightweight block ciphers TEA, XTEA and HIGHT. In: Mitrokotsa, A., Vaudenay, S. (eds.) AFRICACRYPT 2012. LNCS, vol. 7374, pp. 117–137. Springer, Heidelberg (2012). doi:10.1007/978-3-642-31410-0_8
4. Cui, T., Jia, K., Fu, K., Chen, S., Wang, M.: New automatic search tool for impossible differentials and zero-correlation linear approximations (2016). http://eprint. iacr.org/2016/689
5. Daemen, J., Knudsen, L., Rijmen, V.: The block cipher Square. In: Biham, E. (ed.) FSE 1997. LNCS, vol. 1267, pp. 149–165. Springer, Heidelberg (1997). doi:10.1007/ BFb0052343
6. Ferguson, N., Kelsey, J., Lucks, S., Schneier, B., Stay, M., Wagner, D., Whiting, D.: Improved cryptanalysis of Rijndael. In: Goos, G., Hartmanis, J., Leeuwen, J., Schneier, B. (eds.) FSE 2000. LNCS, vol. 1978, pp. 213–230. Springer, Heidelberg (2001). doi:10.1007/3-540-44706-7_15

7. Hong, D., et al.: HIGHT: a new block cipher suitable for low-resource device. In: Goubin, L., Matsui, M. (eds.) CHES 2006. LNCS, vol. 4249, pp. 46–59. Springer, Heidelberg (2006). doi:10.1007/11894063_4

8. ISO/IEC: JTC1: ISO/IEC 18033-3: Information technology - security techniques - encryption algorithms - part 3: Block ciphers (2010)

9. Knudsen, L., Wagner, D.: Integral cryptanalysis. In: Daemen, J., Rijmen, V. (eds.) FSE 2002. LNCS, vol. 2365, pp. 112–127. Springer, Heidelberg (2002). doi:10.1007/3-540-45661-9_9

10. Koo, B., Hong, D., Kwon, D.: Related-key attack on the Full HIGHT. In: Rhee, K.-H., Nyang, D.H. (eds.) ICISC 2010. LNCS, vol. 6829, pp. 49–67. Springer, Heidelberg (2011). doi:10.1007/978-3-642-24209-0_4

11. Mouha, N., Wang, Q., Gu, D., Preneel, B.: Differential and linear cryptanalysis using mixed-integer linear programming. In: Wu, C.-K., Yung, M., Lin, D. (eds.) Inscrypt 2011. LNCS, vol. 7537, pp. 57–76. Springer, Heidelberg (2012). doi:10.1007/978-3-642-34704-7_5

12. Özen, O., Varıcı, K., Tezcan, C., Kocair, Ç.: Lightweight block ciphers revisited: cryptanalysis of reduced round PRESENT and HIGHT. In: Boyd, C., González Nieto, J. (eds.) ACISP 2009. LNCS, vol. 5594, pp. 90–107. Springer, Heidelberg (2009). doi:10.1007/978-3-642-02620-1_7

13. Sasaki, Y., Todo, Y.: New impossible dierential search tool from design and cryptanalysis aspects (2016). http://eprint.iacr.org/2016/1181. This paper is accepted in Eurocrypt 2017

14. Sasaki, Y., Wang, L.: Meet-in-the-middle technique for integral attacks against feistel ciphers. In: Knudsen, L.R., Wu, H. (eds.) SAC 2012. LNCS, vol. 7707, pp. 234–251. Springer, Heidelberg (2013). doi:10.1007/978-3-642-35999-6_16

15. Sasaki, Y., Wang, L.: Bitwise partial-sum on HIGHT: A New tool for integral analysis against ARX designs. In: Lee, H.-S., Han, D.-G. (eds.) ICISC 2013. LNCS, vol. 8565, pp. 189–202. Springer, Cham (2014). doi:10.1007/978-3-319-12160-4_12

16. Sun, L., Wang, W., Liu, R., Wang, M.: Milp-aided bit-based division property for ARX-based block cipher. IACR Cryptology ePrint Archive 2016, 1101 (2016). http://eprint.iacr.org/2016/1101

17. Sun, S., Hu, L., Wang, M., Wang, P., Qiao, K., Ma, X., Shi, D., Song, L.: Towards finding the best characteristics of some bit-oriented block ciphers and automatic enumeration of (related-key) differential and linear characteristics with predefined properties (2014). http://eprint.iacr.org/2014/747

18. Sun, S., Hu, L., Wang, P., Qiao, K., Ma, X., Song, L.: Automatic security evaluation and (Related-key) differential characteristic search: application to SIMON, PRESENT, LBlock, DES(L) and other bit-oriented block ciphers. In: Sarkar, P., Iwata, T. (eds.) ASIACRYPT 2014. LNCS, vol. 8873, pp. 158–178. Springer, Heidelberg (2014). doi:10.1007/978-3-662-45611-8_9

19. Suzaki, T., Minematsu, K., Morioka, S., Kobayashi, E.: TWINE: a lightweight block cipher for multiple platforms. In: Knudsen, L.R., Wu, H. (eds.) SAC 2012. LNCS, vol. 7707, pp. 339–354. Springer, Heidelberg (2013). doi:10.1007/978-3-642-35999-6_22

20. Todo, Y.: Integral cryptanalysis on full MISTY1. In: Gennaro, R., Robshaw, M. (eds.) CRYPTO 2015. LNCS, vol. 9215, pp. 413–432. Springer, Heidelberg (2015). doi:10.1007/978-3-662-47989-6_20

21. Todo, Y.: Structural evaluation by generalized integral property. In: Oswald, E., Fischlin, M. (eds.) EUROCRYPT 2015. LNCS, vol. 9056, pp. 287–314. Springer, Heidelberg (2015). doi:10.1007/978-3-662-46800-5_12

22. Todo, Y., Morii, M.: Bit-based division property and application to SIMON family. In: Peyrin, T. (ed.) FSE 2016. LNCS, vol. 9783, pp. 357–377. Springer, Heidelberg (2016). doi:10.1007/978-3-662-52993-5_18

23. Wu, W., Zhang, L.: LBlock: a lightweight block cipher. In: Lopez, J., Tsudik, G. (eds.) ACNS 2011. LNCS, vol. 6715, pp. 327–344. Springer, Heidelberg (2011). doi:10.1007/978-3-642-21554-4_19

24. Xiang, Z., Zhang, W., Bao, Z., Lin, D.: Applying MILP method to searching integral distinguishers based on division property for 6 lightweight block ciphers. In: Cheon, J.H., Takagi, T. (eds.) ASIACRYPT 2016. LNCS, vol. 10031, pp. 648–678. Springer, Heidelberg (2016). doi:10.1007/978-3-662-53887-6_24

25. Zhang, P., Sun, B., Li, C.: Saturation attack on the block cipher HIGHT. In: Garay, J.A., Miyaji, A., Otsuka, A. (eds.) CANS 2009. LNCS, vol. 5888, pp. 76–86. Springer, Heidelberg (2009). doi:10.1007/978-3-642-10433-6_6

Cryptanalysis of Simpira v2

Ivan Tjuawinata$^{(\boxtimes)}$, Tao Huang, and Hongjun Wu

Division of Mathematical Sciences, School of Physical and Mathematical Sciences,
Nanyang Technological University, Singapore, Singapore
S120015@e.ntu.edu.sg, {huangtao,wuhj}@ntu.edu.sg

Abstract. In Asiacrypt 2016, Simpira v2 was proposed as a family of efficient permutations. It combines the AES round function with the Generalized Feistel Scheme (GFS) to construct permutations with arbitrarily large size which is a multiple of 128-bit. In this paper, we study the security of Simpira-3, the 3-block instance of Simpira v2. By applying the truncated differential analysis, we construct 8-round and 9-round distinguishers for Simpira-3 with complexity 2 and 2^{22} respectively. Then, we apply the impossible differential analysis to construct a 9-round impossible differential. Using this impossible differential, we can launch 9- and 10-round partial key recovery attacks on Simpira-3-based block cipher. Lastly, we present a boomerang distinguisher for 10-round Simpira-3 with practical complexity 2^{23}. To the best of our knowledge, this is the first cryptanalysis results on Simpira-3. Our analysis will not affect the security of Simpira.

Keywords: Simpira · Impossible-differential cryptanalysis · Cryptographic permutation

1 Introduction

In the recent development of the symmetric-key cryptographic algorithms, permutation is one of the commonly used building blocks. Permutations can be used to build block ciphers. A well-known result is to use the (iterated) Even-Mansour construction [10,11] with a permutation to construct a block cipher. Permutations can be used to design hash functions. This kind of application can be found in the SHA-3 finalist Keccak [4], JH [21] and Grøstl [12]. It can be used to design authenticated cipher as well. In the recent CAESAR competition, many candidates are based on permutations, such as Ascon [9], ICEPOLE [17,18], NORX [1], Ketje [2] and Keyak [3].

Simpira v2 [14] is a family of permutations proposed by Gueron and Mouha in Asiacrypt 2016. Different from the previous permutations designs, Simpira provides a scalable framework which can process any multiple of the 128-bit AES block size. The Generalized Feistel Structure (GFS) with an F-function that consists of two rounds AES operation is used when the block size is more than 128-bit. The designers also proposed several applications of Simpira v2: a block cipher using Even-Mansour construction, a hash function using Davies-Meyer

© Springer International Publishing AG 2017
J. Pieprzyk and S. Suriadi (Eds.): ACISP 2017, Part I, LNCS 10342, pp. 384–401, 2017.
DOI: 10.1007/978-3-319-60055-0_20

construction, a wide-block encryption scheme and an authenticated encryption scheme. The security of Simpira is 2^{128} for distinguishing attacks. The designers also claim that when the permutation is at least 256-bit, the security of Simpira-based block cipher has 128-bit security. The software performance of Simpira with block number $b \leq 4$ and $b = 6$ is below 1 cycle per byte on the Intel Skylake processor using AES-NI.

Previous work. In [19], Rønjom analysed the invariant subspaces on Simpira v1 [13], the first version of Simpira. It was shown in the analysis that invariant subspaces existed in the even-round of Simpira-4, the 4-block variant of the Simpira family. Dobraunig et al. [8] independently proposed an attack on Simpira-4 which exploited the property of the GFS of Simpira-4. Due to those analysis, the designers of Simpira have updated the design with a different GFS for Simpira-4 as well as the definition of round constant for all the Simpira family. Zong et al. [22] presented the first cryptanalysis results on Simpira v2. They provided a 9-round impossible differential for Simpira-4 and presented a partial key-recovery attack on the 7-round Simpira-4-based block cipher. The complexity of this attack is 2^{57} to recover 256 bits key. For the 8-round case, the complexity is 2^{170} to recover all the key bits.

Our contributions. Considering the instances in the Simpira family, Simpira-1 is the 12-round AES without round-key; Simpira-2 is an application of the standard Feistel network; Simpira-4 has been studied in the previous analysis. But the properties of Simpira-3 have not been thoughtfully analysed in any previous work. In this paper, we give the first analysis on the Simpira-3. The summary of our results are listed below.

- Truncated Differential Analysis:
    8 rounds:
    - Distinguishing attack with 2 queries, 0 probability of false negative and 2^{-96} probability of false positive
    9 rounds:
    - Distinguishing attack with 2^{22} inverse queries, 0.0001 probability of false negative and 0.00003 probability of false positive.
    - Key Recovery attack with 2^{24} decryption queries to recover k_0 and k_2
- Impossible Differential Analysis:
    9 rounds:
    - Key Recovery attack with 2^{50} decryption queries to recover k_0.
    10 rounds:
    - Key Recovery attack with 2^{70} decryption queries to recover k_1.
- Boomerang attack
    10 rounds:
    - Distinguishing attack with 2^{23} queries which distinguishes Simpira-3 from random permutation with failure probability less than 0.1%.
    - Key Recovery attack with 2^{53} encryption queries and 2^{85} decryption queries to recover k_0.

Outline. The rest of the paper is organized as follows. In Sect. 2, we provide the preliminaries for our analysis. In Sect. 3, we present the truncated differential cryptanalysis on Simpira-3. In Sect. 4, we apply the impossible differential attack on Simpira-3. In Sect. 5, we discuss the boomerang attack on Simpira-3. We conclude this paper in Sect. 6.

2   Preliminaries

2.1   Notation

$\oplus$	Bitwise XOR
$\mathcal{P}$	Plaintext space
$\mathcal{C}$	Ciphertext space
$\mathcal{K}$	Key space
S	Intermediate state
$S_j^{[h]}[\ell_1, \cdots, \ell_t]$	State of round h, subblock j, byte $\ell_1, \ell_2, \cdots, \ell_t$
0	Zero difference
$*$	Arbitrary difference

2.2   Description of Simpira

We describe the specification for Simpira-3, the 3-block instance of Simpira, which is the target of our analysis. A complete specification on Simpira v2 can be found in [14]. Simpira-3 is a permutation function that follows the type-1 Generalized Feistel structure (GFS-1) with 3 sub-blocks of size 128 bits each. Figure 1 illustrates how Simpira-3 works in three consecutive rounds $3i, 3i + 1$ and $3i + 2$. Note that we have re-ordered the sub-blocks in rounds $S^{[3i+1]}$ and $S^{[3i+2]}$ for readability. The total number of rounds is 21 for Simpira-3 proposed in [14].

The non-linear function $F_{c,b}$ is a 2 round AES with the first AddRoundKey changed to AddRoundConstant and the second one omitted. The round constant depends on the value of c, b, where c is a counter that is initialized by one and incremented after every evaluation of $F_{c,b}$. We assign the number of blocks as the value of b, which is 3 for Simpira-3. More specifically:

$$F_{(c,b)}(S) = MC \circ SR \circ SB \circ AC \circ MC \circ SR \circ SB(S).$$

Here MC, SR, SB are MixColumn, ShiftRow and SubByte of the AES [6] respectively. AC is AddRoundConstant.

We will omit the index (c, b) of $F_{(c,b)}$ for the remainder of this paper.

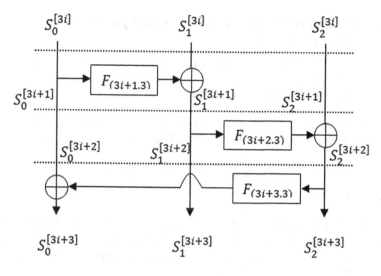

Fig. 1. Round $3i, 3i+1, 3i+2$ of Simpira-3, $0 \le i \le 6$.

2.3 Even-Mansour Construction

In [11], Even and Mansour proposed a way to use a keyless permutation to build a block cipher. Given a permutation π, the block cipher built by the Even-Mansour construction with a single key K is defined to be $E : \mathcal{P} \times \mathcal{K} \to \mathcal{C}$ such that for any plaintext $P \in \mathcal{P}$ and key $K \in \mathcal{K}$,

$$E(P, K) = \pi(P \oplus K) \oplus K.$$

In this paper, we consider the block cipher built from the Even-Mansour construction with the permutation function described in Subsect. 2.2. So the length of P, K and C are all 384 bits each. The security claim given in [14] is the least between 2^{128} and $2^{n/2}$ where $n = 384$. Hence the security claim is 2^{128} while it does not claim any security for the attack with bigger complexity. So we aim for attacks with complexity less than 2^{128}.

3   Truncated Differential Attack on Simpira-3

In this section, we review some basic concepts and properties of Simpira-3. Then we apply the truncated differential cryptanalysis [16] to study the security of Simpira-3.

First, we recall the definition of Super S-Box as defined in [7].

Definition 1. [7] *The AES Super Sbox SS maps a 4-byte array (a_0, a_1, a_2, a_3) to a 4-byte array (b_0, b_1, b_2, b_3) using a 4-byte array key (k_0, k_1, k_2, k_3). It consists of the sequence of four transformations:* SubByte, MixColumn, AddRoundKey *and* SubByte.

By this definition and the commutativity of SubByte and ShiftRow, we can rewrite the definition of $F(S)$ as

$$F(S) = MC \circ SR \circ SS \circ SR(S).$$

The Super SBox has the following property:

Property 1. Fix a key $K = (k_0, k_1, k_2, k_3) \in \mathbb{F}_2^{32}$ and consider non-zero input and output differences $\Delta input, \Delta output \in \mathbb{F}_2^{32}$. Then in average, the equation:

$$SS(x) \oplus SS(x \oplus \Delta input) = \Delta output$$

has one solution for x.

In our analysis, we consider two types of byte difference, either 0 (must be zero) or $*$ (arbitrary value). Let $\Delta S_1, \Delta S_2$ be two 4×4 non-zero matrices with elements from $\{0, *\}$ representing two truncated differential pattern in some state. We say $\Delta S_1 \neq \Delta S_2$ if

$$\{(i,j)|0 \leq i,j \leq 3, \Delta S_1(i,j) = *\} \cap \{(i,j)|0 \leq i,j \leq 3, \Delta S_2(i,j) = *\} = \emptyset.$$

The following observation is made in [22].

Observation 1. *If there exists at least one column of $SR \circ SB(\Delta S)$ to be inactive, then the number of possible values of $\Delta F(S)$ is strictly less than 2^{128}.*

This means that if $SR \circ SB(\Delta S)$ has at least one zero columns, $\Delta F(S)$ will have some pattern that we can recognize.

For the Generalized Feistel structure of 3 sub-blocks, there exists asymmetry between the forward and backward direction. More specifically, in the forward direction, any difference introduced through F will pass through F in each of the following rounds, this is not true for the backward direction. Every time a difference is introduced to a sub-block by F, it will pass through one round untouched before having to go through another F. This leads to a slower diffusion in the backward direction than the forward direction. In our truncated differential cryptanalysis, we will exploit this property to study the inverse permutation.

After searching the possible truncated differential of Simpira-3, the following observation gives the best 8-round truncated differential that we found.

Observation 2 *(8-Round Backward Truncated Differential).* *Let a be a truncated differential pattern such that $SR \circ SB(a)$ has at least one zero column. Then the differential*

$$(0,0,a) \xrightarrow{\text{8R backwards}} (F(a), r, r)$$

has probability 1. This means that if $\Delta S^{[8]} = (0,0,a)$, then with probability 1, we have $\Delta S^{[0]} = (F(a), r, r)$.

Proof. Here we use r to represent the unknown difference in some sub-blocks. For example $F(F(a))$ is not considered as identifiable, so we label it as r. It is easy to see that the following 8-round backwards differential holds with probability 1:

$$(0, 0, a) \to (0, 0, a) \to (0, 0, a) \to (F(a), 0, a) \to (F(a), 0, a)$$
$$\to (F(a), r, a) \to (F(a), r, a) \to (F(a), r, r) \to (F(a), r, r).$$

This characteristic is depicted in Fig. 2.

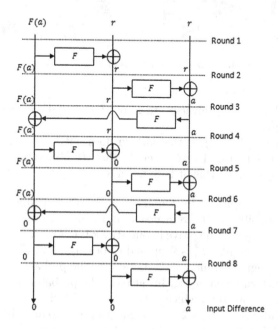

Fig. 2. Backward difference propagation of the 8-round Simpira-3 $(0, 0, a) \xrightarrow{8R} (F(a), r, r)$.

3.1 Distinguishing Attacks on Simpira-3

In this subsection, we describe the distinguishing attack on Simpira-3 based on the truncated differential characteristic we found above. We propose two different distinguishing attacks, one for the 8-round Simpira-3 and another for the 9-round Simpira-3.

8-Round Distinguishing Attack. Suppose that $\varPi$ is a permutation function defined as $\varPi : (\mathbb{F}_2^{128})^3 \to (\mathbb{F}_2^{128})^3$. We will identify if $\varPi$ is an 8-round Simpira-3 or a random permutation using the following procedure.

1. Select a a differential pattern such that $SR \circ SB(a)$ has three zero columns. Possible values of a are depicted in Fig. 3. Choose $C_1, C_2 \in (\mathbb{F}_2^{128})^3$ such that $C_1 \oplus C_2 \in (0, 0, a)$.

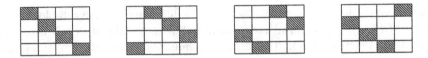

Fig. 3. Four possible pattern of a. Filled cells denote arbitrary differences as long as they are not all zero.

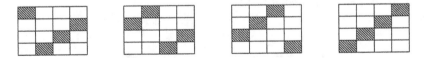

Fig. 4. Respective patterns of $MC^{-1}(F(a))$.

2. Input C_1 and C_2 to the inverse oracle of Π to obtain $P = (p_0^1, p_1^1, p_2^1)$ and $P_2 = (p_0^2, p_1^2, p_2^2)$.
3. Calculate $MC^{-1}(p_0^1 \oplus p_0^2)$. If the pattern does not follow the corresponding pattern depicted in Fig. 4, we conclude that Π is a random permutation. Otherwise, we conclude that it is Simpira-3.

Note that if Π is Simpira-3, by Observation 2, given a difference of pattern $(0, 0, a)$, with probability 1 after 8 inverse rounds, the pattern will be $(F(a), r, r)$. So the probability of a false negative in our attack is 0. On the other hand, if Π is a random permutation, $p_0^1 \oplus p_0^2$ is supposed to be a random 128-bit state. Hence $MC^{-1}(p_0^1 \oplus p_0^2)$ is again a random 128-bit state. The probability that it has the corresponding pattern given in Fig. 4 is at most the probability that the value in the 12 blank cells are all zero, which is $(2^{-8})^{12} = 2^{-96}$. So the probability of our attack giving a false positive is 2^{-96}. Considering the complexity of the attack, we only require 2 inverse queries and negligible processing time and storage.

9-Round Distinguishing Attack. In this attack, we will add a round after the 8-round truncated differential characteristic. Namely $(F(a), 0, a) \rightarrow (0, 0, a)$, which is depicted in Fig. 5.

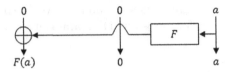

Fig. 5. Round 9 in distinguishing attack.

The details of this 9-round distinguishing attack is given in Appendix A. The complexity of this attack is 2^{22} queries of the inverse permutation.

3.2   Key Recovery Attack on 9-Round Simpira-3

The distinguishing attacks given above can easily be adapted to attack the block cipher constructed by using the Even-Mansour construction with Simpira-3.

Assuming that the encryption scheme follows the (single key) Even-Mansour structure with key $K = (k_0, k_1, k_2)$ and the permutation function being the 9-round Simpira-3, we can use the 9-round truncated differential distinguisher to launch the partial key recovery attack.

The attack is given in the Appendix B. With 2^{24} decryption queries, we are able to recover 256 key bits out of the total 384 key bits.

4   Impossible Differential Attack on Simpira-3

In this section, we will use the impossible differential [5, 15] to analyse the block cipher based on Simpira-3. We remark that the analysis described in this section can be adapted to develop distinguishing attack using a similar method.

The backward truncated differential trail we found in the previous section can be extended to an impossible differential trail in the following observation.

Observation 3 *(9-round Impossible Differential). Let a and b be two truncated differential patterns such that $SR \circ SB(a)$ and $SR \circ SB(b)$ have at least one zero column and the nonzeros of $SR \circ SB(a)$ and $SR \circ SB(b)$ lie in different column. Then the differential:*

$$(b, F(b), r) \xrightarrow{9R} (a, 0, 0)$$

is impossible.

Proof. We can see that the following 1 round forward truncated differential has probability 1.

$$(b, F(b), r) \rightarrow (b, F(b), r).$$

In the backward direction, as discussed in Observation 2, the differential pattern follows the following path:

$$(a, 0, 0) \rightarrow (a, 0, 0) \rightarrow (a, 0, 0) \rightarrow (a, F(a), 0) \rightarrow (a, F(a), 0)$$
$$\rightarrow (a, F(a), r) \rightarrow (a, F(a), r) \rightarrow (r, F(a), r) \rightarrow (r, F(a), r).$$

If the trail is valid, we must have some difference that is in both patterns, $F(b)$ and $F(a)$. Since the nonzero columns of $SR \circ SB(a)$ is completely different from the nonzero columns of $SR \circ SB(b)$, we have $MC^{-1}(F(a)) \neq MC^{-1}(F(b))$. But it is impossible for a non-zero difference to be both in $F(a)$ and $F(b)$. Hence this 9 rounds differential path is an impossible differential. □

For the following attacks, we will consider two families of patterns which are denoted by a and b. The first family, a, is already defined in Figs. 3 and 4. The other family, b, is in fact the complement of a, depicted in Figs. 6 and 7 respectively.

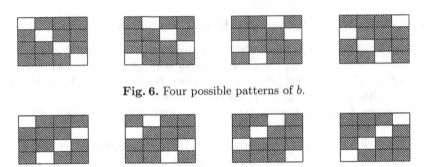

Fig. 6. Four possible patterns of b.

Fig. 7. Patterns of $MC^{-1}(F(b))$ corresponding to Fig. 6.

4.1   Key Recovery Attack on 10-Round Simpira-3

For the key recovery attack for E_K with Π being the 10-round Simpira-3, we use the 9-round impossible differential we described in Observation 3 and then append it with the rotated variant of the round given in Fig. 5 which is $(a, 0, 0) \xrightarrow{1R} (a, F(a), 0)$.

We describe the 10-round attack in the following steps:

1. Let a be the first pattern given in Fig. 3. We also fix b to be the corresponding pattern in Fig. 6. Lastly, let $F(a)$ and $F(b)$ be the MixColumn of the corresponding patterns in Figs. 4 and 7 respectively.
2. Construct 2^{34} ciphertexts differing only in the active cells of $(a, F(a), 0)$. This gives us 2^{67} ciphertext pairs each with difference pattern $(a, F(a), 0)$.
3. Decrypt the 2^{34} ciphertexts to find the corresponding plaintexts. Filter the pairs with plaintext difference $(b, F(b), r)$. This gives us a 64 bit filter. Therefore, we expect to have 2^3 pairs out of the 2^{67} pairs of plaintext with differences pattern $(b, F(b), r)$.
4. For each of the remaining pair, let the ciphertext difference be $(\Delta c_0, \Delta c_1, \Delta c_2)$ and the plaintext difference be $(\Delta p_0, \Delta p_1, \Delta p_2)$. From the impossible differential in Observation 3, the relation $(a, 0, 0) \to (a, F(a), 0)$ in Round 10 must be invalid. This gives a filter of one value of the key bytes $k_1[0, 7, 10, 13]$ (See Step 4 in Appendix B for more details).
5. Repeat this 2^{34} times to filter out all wrong $k_1[0, 7, 10, 13]$.
6. Repeat the whole process for other patterns of $(a, F(a), b, F(b))$ to recover the remaining bytes of k_1.

The reasoning behind the 2^{34} repetition is exactly the same as the reasoning of the repetition done in the 9-round key recovery using truncated differential found in Appendix B. The complexity of this attack is $2^{34} \times 2^{34} \times 4 \approx 2^{70}$ decryption queries and 2^{104} pairs to recover k_1.

We can actually also mount a key recovery attack on 9-round Simpira-3, which can be found in Appendix C.

5   Boomerang Attack on Simpira-3

The boomerang attack, proposed by David Wagner in FSE 1999 [20] is a powerful tool to analyse block ciphers and permutations. To apply the boomerang attack, we need to concatenate two short differential trails to make a longer one.

In our analysis, we apply it to the truncated differential of Simpira-3. We first review the following result from [20] in finding the success probability of the boomerang attack.

Lemma 1. [20] *Let E be an encryption operation that can be decomposed to $E = E_1 \circ E_0$. We further let $\Delta \to \Delta^*$ be a truncated differential characteristic for E_0 and $\nabla \to \nabla^*$ be a truncated differential characteristic for E_1^{-1}. Then a truncated boomerang attack using these two characteristics has success probability p where:*

$$p \approx Pr(\Delta \to \Delta^*) \times Pr(\nabla \to \nabla^*)^2 \times Pr(\Delta^* \to \Delta)$$
$$\times Pr(w \oplus x \oplus y \in \Delta^* | w \in \Delta^*, x, y \in \nabla^*).$$

A slight modification on Observation 3 gives us the following observation:

Observation 4. *Let b be one of the pattern given in Fig. 6. Then the truncated boomerang attack for 9 rounds with:*

- $\Delta = (b, F(b), r) \xrightarrow{1R} \Delta^* = (b, F(b), r)$
- $\nabla = (b, 0, 0) \xrightarrow{8R} \nabla^* = (r, F(b), r)$

has success probability 2^{-32}.

Proof. By Observation 3 we have that $Pr(\Delta \to \Delta^*) = Pr(\nabla \to \nabla^*) = 1$. Furthermore, it is easy to see that $Pr(\Delta^* \to \Delta) = 1$. So the success probability p of this attack is the same as the probability that $\mathbf{w} = (w_0, w_1, w_2) \oplus \mathbf{x} = (x_0, x_1, x_2) \oplus \mathbf{y} = (y_0, y_1, y_2) \in (b, F(b), r)$ given that $\mathbf{w} \in (b, F(b), r), \mathbf{x}, \mathbf{y}, \in (r, F(b), r)$. Now note that this probability is one for the second and third subblock. So we have the success probability, p is:

$$p \approx Pr(\mathbf{w} \oplus \mathbf{x} \oplus \mathbf{y} \in (b, F(b), r) | \mathbf{w} \in (b, F(b), r), \mathbf{x}, \mathbf{y}, \in (r, F(b), r))$$
$$= Pr(w_0 \oplus x_0 \oplus y_0 \in b | w_0 \in b, x_0, y_0 \in r)$$
$$= Pr(z_0 \in b | z_0 \in r)$$
$$= Pr(z_0 \text{ has 4 zeros in the four specific cells})$$
$$= (2^{-8})^4 = 2^{-32}. \qquad \qquad \square$$

5.1   Distinguishing Attack on 10- Rounds Simpira-3

The differences used in our boomerang attack are given below:

- $\Delta = (b, F(b), r)$,
- $\Delta^* = (b, F(b), r)$,

- $\nabla = (b, 0, 0)$,
- $\nabla^* = (r, F(b), r)$,

where b is one of the four patterns described in Fig. 6.

Assume that we are given a permutation function Π and we are asked to identify whether Π is a 10-round Simpira-3 or a random permutation. Again we will use the rotated pattern given in Fig. 5 such that it follows the form for the 10-th round of Simpira-3.

1. Fix a pattern b to be one of the pattern given in Fig. 3 and $F(b)$ be the MixColumn of the corresponding pattern given in Fig. 7.
2. Generate 2^{22} different $P^{(i)}, i = 1, \cdots, 2^{22}$ such that for any $i, j, P^{(i)} \oplus P^{(j)} \in (b, F(b), r)$.
3. Compute $C^{(i)} = \Pi(P^{(i)})$.
4. Generate $d_0^{(i)}$ such that $c_0^{(i)} \oplus d_0^{(i)} \in b$.
5. Compute $\delta = F(c_0^{(i)}) \oplus F(d^{(i)})_0$ and generate $d_1^{(i)} = c_1^{(i)} \oplus \delta$. Lastly, we let $d_2^{(i)} = c_2^{(i)}$. Define $D^{(i)} = (d_0^{(i)}, d_1^{(i)}, d_2^{(i)})$.
6. Compute $Q^{(i)} = \Pi^{-1}(D^{(i)})$.
7. Compute $n = \left| \{ \{i, j\} : i \neq j, Q^{(i)} \oplus Q^{(j)} \in (b, F(b), r) \} \right|$.
8. If $n \geq 1880$, conclude that Π is Simpira-3, otherwise, conclude that Π is a random permutation.

Note that if Π is Simpira, the probability that $Q^{(i)} \oplus Q^{(j)} \in (b, F(b), r)$ is 2^{-32} by Observation 4. On the other hand, this probability is 2^{-64} when Π is a random permutation. With a similar argument in the 9-round truncated differential distinguishing attack, the probabilities of false negative and false positive are 0.0001 and 0.00003 respectively. The complexity of this attack is $2^{22}\Pi$ queries, $2^{22}\Pi^{-1}$ queries and 2^{43} pairs to process.

Here we need to use the actual input value of the state in the last round's F. Hence this distinguisher of the permutation function cannot be applied to distinguish the block cipher using Even-Mansour construction with 10-round Simpira-3 as its permutation function.

Moreover, we can construct a distinguisher for 9-round Simpira-3 and launch a partial key recovery attack for 10-round Simpira-3 based on it. The details are provided in Appendices E and F respectively.

6   Conclusion

In this paper, we described three types of cryptanalysis on Simpira-3, namely truncated differential analysis, impossible differential analysis and boomerang attack. Applying the cryptanalysis techniques, we present the first practical distinguisher for 9-round and 10-round Simpira-3 permutations with complexity 2^{22} and 2^{23} respectively. We also present partial key recovery attacks on the 9-round and 10-round Simpira-3 based block ciphers, which greatly reduce the key space in those instances. We remark that our attacks on Simpira-3 cannot directly extend to Simpira-4 to improve the previous results, as Simpira-4 has a more symmetric structure.

Our attacks provide the first concrete security analysis on Simpira-3. The results confirm that Simpira-3 has a good security margin and we hope that our results will be useful for the future analysis on the Simpira family of permutations.

A   9-Round Truncated Differential Distinguishing Attack

The 9-round truncated differential distinguisher can be done in the following way. We are assuming that we are given a permutation $\Pi : \left(\mathbb{F}_2^{128}\right)^3 \to \left(\mathbb{F}_2^{128}\right)^3$ and we are asked to identify whether Π is a 9-round Simpira-3 or a random function.

1. Fix the pattern a as the last pattern given in Fig. 3 and $F(a)$ as the MixColumn of its corresponding pattern in Fig. 4. In other words, now the non-zero cells of a are in cells $1, 6, 11, 12$ following the numbering of state cells in [6]. Similarly, the possible non-zero cells of $MC^{-1}(F(a))$ are in cells $3, 6, 9, 12$.
2. Fix $c_1 \in \mathbb{F}_2^{128}$, $c_0[0, 1, 2, 4, 5, 6, 8, 10, 11, 13, 14, 15]$ and $c_2[0, 1, \cdots, 11, 13, 14, 15]$.
3. For $i, j = 0, \cdots, 2^8 - 1$, we define $c_0^{(2^8 i + j)}[3, 6, 9, 12] = (i, j, 0, 0)$ and $c_0^{(2^{16} + 2^8 i + j)}[3, 6, 9, 12] = (0, 0, i, j)$. So now we have $c_0^{(i)}$ for $i = 0, \cdots, 2^{17} - 1$.
4. For $i = 0, \cdots, 2^4 - 1$, we define $c_2^{(i)}[12] = i$ and $c_2^{(2^4 + i)}[12] = 2^4 + i$. So now we have $c_2^{(j)}$ for $j = 0, \cdots, 2^5 - 1$.
5. For $i = 0, \cdots, 2^{17} - 1, j = 0, \cdots, 2^5 - 1$, calculate $\Pi^{-1}(c_0^{(i)}, c_1, c_2^{(j)}) = (p_0^{(i,j)}, p_1^{(i,j)}, p_2^{(i,j)})$. From these plaintexts, we can generate 2^{43} plaintext pairs.
6. Count the number of plaintext pairs that have difference pattern $(F(a), r, r)$. Let this number be n. If $n \geq 1880$, conclude that Π is Simpira-3. Otherwise we conclude that Π is a random permutation.

Note that if Π is Simpira-3 and $F(\Delta c_2) = \Delta c_0$, then $\Delta p_0 = F(a)$ with probability 1. So

$$Pr(\Delta p_0 = F(a) | \Pi \text{ is } Simpira - 3 \text{ and } F(\Delta c_2) = \Delta c_0) = Pr(F(\Delta c_2) = \Delta c_0).$$

Now we note that by the choice of our inputs,

$$\{MC^{-1}(\Delta c_0^i)\} = \{\Delta \in \{0, *\}^{4 \times 4}, \Delta[0, 1, 2, 4, 5, 7, 8, 10, 11, 13, 14, 15] = 0\}.$$

Moreover,

$$\{\Delta c_2^j\} = \{\Delta \in \{0, *\}^{4 \times 4}, \Delta[0, 1, 2, 3, 4, 5, 6, 7, 8, 9, 10, 13, 14, 15] = 0\}.$$

By design, $MC^{-1}(F(\Delta c_2^j))$ has the fourth pattern given in Fig. 4. So the probability above equals to the probability that $MC^{-1}(\Delta c_0^i)$ coincides with the value we get from $MC^{-1}(F(\Delta c_2^j))$ which only depends on the value of the 4 values in cells $3, 6, 9, 12$. Hence this probability is 2^{-32}.

Furthermore, if Π is Simpira-3, $F(\Delta c_2) \neq \Delta c_0$ or if Π is a random permutation, Δp_0 can be seen as a random 128-bit state. So we also have that $MC^{-1}(\Delta p_0)$ is also a random 128-bit state. So for this value to be in the $MC^{-1}(F(a))$ pattern, the probability, as discussed before, is 2^{-96}. So now we have that if Π is Simpira-3, then the number of pairs that has ΔP_0 in $F(a)$ pattern follows a binomial distribution with 2^{43} trials and $2^{-32} + 2^{-96}(1 - 2^{-32}) \approx 2^{-32}$ success probability. Let this random variable be denoted by X_1. On the other hand, if Π is a random permutation, then this random variable follows another binomial distribution with 2^{43} trials and 2^{-96} success probability. Let this random variable be denoted by X_2. Then our attack's probability of false negative is

$$\alpha = Pr(n \leq 1779 | n \sim X_1).$$

and our attack's false positive probability is

$$\beta = Pr(n \geq 1880 | n \sim X_2).$$

A simple calculation using the normal approximation of random variables will tell us that $\alpha \approx 0.0001$ and $\beta \approx 0.00003$.

Lastly, for the complexity, our attack complexity is 2^{22} inverse enquiries and 2^{43} comparison.

B   9-Round Key Recovery Using Truncated Differential

1. Select a according to the first pattern given in Fig. 3. $F(a)$ is the difference after MixColumn of the corresponding pattern in Fig. 4.
2. Generate $(c_0^{(i)}, c^1, c_2^{(j)})$ with an analogous method as the one we described in the 9-rounds distinguishing attack in Appendix A.
3. Decrypt $(c_0^{(i)}, c^1, c_2^{(j)})$ to obtain 2^{22} plaintexts $(p_0^{(i,j)}, p_1^{(i,j)}, p_2^{(i,j)})$ and generate 2^{43} plaintext-ciphertext pairs from it, all with the ciphertext differences in the pattern $(F(a), 0, a)$.
4. Out of these 2^{43} pairs, we have a probability 2^{-32} for the corresponding Δp_0 to have difference pattern $F(a)$. When this happens with high probability we have $F(\Delta c_2) = \Delta c_0$. We can expect around 2^{11} pairs that satisfy this. Let the differences in the first and last sub-blocks be $(\Delta c_0^{(i)}, \Delta c_2^{(i)}), i = 1, \cdots, 2^{11}$ with its corresponding ciphertexts being $(c_0^{(i,1)}, c_2^{(i,1)})$ and $(c_0^{(i,2)}, c_2^{(i,2)})$. Due to the linearity of SR and MC, we also have that $SS(SR(\Delta c_2)) = MC^{-1} \circ SR^{-1}(\Delta c_0)$. By Observation 1, we can identify the value of $(c_0^{(i,1)} \oplus k_0, c_2^{(i,1)} \oplus k_2)$ and $(c_0^{(i,2)} \oplus k_0, c_2^{(i,2)} \oplus k_2)$. Note that since the observation only mentions that there is in average one pair of solutions for $(c_0^{(i,1)} \oplus k_0, c_2^{(i,1)} \oplus k_2)$ and $(c_0^{(i,2)} \oplus k_0, c_2^{(i,2)} \oplus k_2)$, there are two possibilities of matching the pair. So for each of the filtered $(\Delta c_0, \Delta c_2)$, we obtain two possible values of $(k_0[0, 5, 10, 15], k_2[0, 7, 10, 13])$. Note that the two possible values that we obtain from $(\Delta c_0^{(i)}, \Delta c_2^{(i)})$ will contain a correct key

$(k_0^*[0, 5, 10, 15], k_2^*[0, 7, 10, 13])$ and $(k_0^*[0, 5, 10, 15] \oplus \Delta_0, k_2^*[0, 7, 10, 13] \oplus \Delta_2)$ where $\Delta_0 = c_0^{(i,1)} \oplus c_0^{(i,2)}$ and $\Delta_2 = c_2^{(i,1)} \oplus c_2^{(i,2)}$.

So a wrong key can be in at least two pairs if the difference in both the first and last sub-blocks in the two pairs are the same. Now a specific difference in the last block can only occur in at most 2^7 different pairs by our choices of c_2. Since we have 2^{11} pairs, we can expect to filter out all the wrong $(k_0[0, 5, 10, 15], k_2[0, 7, 10, 13])$.

5. Repeating the whole process with a as the second, third and last patterns given in Fig. 3 will help us in recovering the other 12 bytes of k_0 and k_2.

Note that here the complexity of each iteration is 2^{22} decryption enquiry and 2^{43} processing of the pairs and there are 4 iterations. So in total, the time complexity is 2^{24} to recover the value of k_0 and k_2.

C   Key Recovery Attack on 9-Round Simpira-3

We define E_K to be the block cipher built by using the Even-Mansour construction with 9-round Simpira-3.

For this key recovery attack, we use a shortened variant of the 9-round impossible differential that we have in Observation 3 where we omit the first round of that trail. Therefore, we need to rotate the whole trail and it changes the input difference pattern from $(F(b), r, b)$ to $(F(b), r, r)$. This 8-round impossible differential can be found in the Appendix D. Based on this differential, we then append one more round, which is the round given in Fig. 5. The attack procedure is given as follows:

1. Let a be the first pattern in Fig. 3, and b be the first pattern given in Fig. 6, which is the complementary of a. Let $F(a)$ and $F(b)$ be the MixColumn of the corresponding patterns in Figs. 4 and 7 respectively.
2. Construct 2^{22} ciphertexts that differ in the active cells of $(F(a), 0, a)$. This provides us with 2^{43} ciphertext pairs with difference pattern $(F(a), 0, a)$.
3. Decrypt the 2^{22} ciphertexts to get 2^{22} plaintexts. For each of the 2^{43} pairs of plaintext, we check if they have difference pattern $(F(b), r, r)$. Since $F(b)$ provides a 32-bit filter, we expect to have 2^{11} pairs of plaintext with difference $(F(b), r, r)$.
4. For each of the remaining pair, let the ciphertext difference be $(\Delta c_0, \Delta c_1, \Delta c_2)$ and the plaintext difference be $(\Delta p_0, \Delta p_1, \Delta p_2)$. From the impossible differential in Appendix D, the relation $(0, 0, a) \to (F(a), 0, a)$ in Round 9 must be invalid. This gives a filter of one value of the key bytes $k_0[0, 7, 10, 13]$ (See Step 4 in Appendix B for more details).
5. Repeat the above procedure for 2^{26} times to detect all wrong possible values of $k_0[0, 7, 10, 13]$.
6. Repeat the whole process for the other 3 patterns of $(a, F(a), b, F(b))$ to recover the remaining bytes of k_0.

For each iteration, we are left with 2^{11} pairs. With 2^{26} iterations, the total number of pairs is 2^{37}. The probability that any wrong key left after the attack is $(1 - 2^{-32})^{2^{37}} < 2^{-32}$. Hence we expect to have only one key remaining after 2^{26} iterations.

In total we have $2^{22} \times 2^{26} \times 4 \approx 2^{50}$ decryption queries and 2^{51} pairs to process to recover the value of k_0.

D   8-Round Impossible Differential Figure

See Fig. 8.

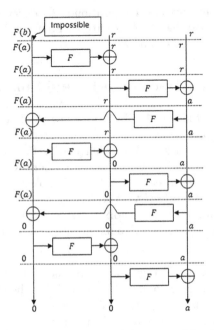

Fig. 8. 8-round impossible differential used for 9-round impossible distinguisher

E   Distinguishing Attack on 9- Rounds Simpira-3

In this case, we will be using the following values:

- $\Delta = (a, F(a), r)$,
- $\Delta^* = (a, F(a), r)$,
- $\nabla = (a, 0, 0)$ and
- $\nabla^* = (r, F(a), r)$

where a is one of the patterns described in Fig. 3.

By the same argument as the one given in Observation 4, it is easy to see that the success probability of this boomerang trail is 2^{-96}.

Assume that we are given a permutation function Π and we are asked to identify whether Π is 10-round Simpira-3 or a random permutation.

1. Fix a pattern a to be one of the pattern given in Fig. 3 and $F(a)$ be `MixColumn` of the corresponding pattern given in Fig. 7.
2. Generate $2^{51}P^{(i)}, i = 1, \cdots, 2^{51}$ such that for any $i, j, P^{(i)} \oplus P^{(j)} \in (a, F(a), r)$.
3. Calculate $C^{(i)} = \Pi(P^{(i)})$.
4. Generate $D^{(i)}$ such that $C^{(i)} \oplus D^{(i)} \in (a, 0, 0)$
5. Calculate $Q^{(i)} = \Pi^{-1}(D^{(i)})$.
6. Compute $n = \left| \{(i,j) | i \neq j, Q^{(i)} \oplus Q^{(j)} \in (a, F(a), r)\} \right|$.
7. If $n \geq 2$, conclude that Π is Simpira-3, otherwise, conclude that Π is a random permutation.

We note that in this attack, if Π is Simpira, the probability that $Q^{(i)} \oplus Q^{(j)} \in (a, F(a), r)$ is 2^{-96} by the observation we made above. This probability becomes 2^{-192} when Π is a random permutation. So by a similar argument in the 9-Rounds Distinguishing attack based on Truncated differential analysis, the probability of false negative and false positive are 0.0001 and 0.00003 respectively. The complexity here is $2^{51}\Pi$ queries, $2^{51}\Pi^{-1}$ queries and 2^{100} pairs to process.

The distinguisher we introduced above in fact can be improved if we are using b instead of a. However, we will be using the distinguisher described here to launch a key recovery attack on 10-rounds Simpira-3 and the complexity of the key recovery attack is the smallest if we use a.

F   10-Round Key Recovery Attack Using Boomerang

As before, let E_K be a block cipher built by using the Even Mansour scheme with 10-round Simpira-3 as its permutation function. For this attack, we will call the active diagonal in each of the pattern given in Fig. 3 as first, second, third and fourth diagonal respectively. So for example, in the first pattern given in Fig. 6, the active diagonals are second, third and fourth diagonal. Similarly, we call the active anti-diagonal in each of the pattern given in Fig. 4 as the first, second, third and fourth anti-diagonal respectively.

The attack goes as follows:

1. Let a be the first pattern given in Fig. 3 and $F(a)$ be the `MixColumn` of the corresponding pattern in Fig. 4.
2. Construct 2^{51} plaintexts $P^{(i)}, i = 1, \cdots, 2^{51}$ such that $\forall i, j, P^{(i)} \oplus P^{(j)} \in (a, F(a), r)$.
3. Calculate $C^{(i)} = (c_0^{(i)}, c_1^{(i)}, c_2^{(i)}) = E_K(P^{(i)})$.
4. For each guess of the value of the first diagonal of k_0, generate $d_0^{(i)}$ such that $d_0^{(i)} \oplus c_0^{(i)} \in a$. Since we guessed the value of the keys in the active cells, we know the exact value of $\delta = F(d_0^{(i)} \oplus c_0^{(i)})$. Generate $d_1^{(i)}$ such that $d_0^{(i)} \oplus c_0^{(i)} = \delta$. Set $d_2^{(i)} = c_2^{(i)}$ and let $D^{(i)} = (d_0^{(i)}, d_1^{(i)}, d_2^{(i)})$.
5. Calculate $Q^{(i)} = E_K^{-1}(D^{(i)})$.

6. Compute $n = \left| \{(i,j) | i \neq j, Q^{(i)} \oplus Q^{(j)} \in (a, F(a), r) \} \right|$. If $n \geq 2$, conclude that the current guess of $k_0[0, 5, 10, 15]$ passes the filter. Otherwise, conclude the current guess is wrong repeat with different guess of the 4-byte subkey.
7. Repeat the whole attack with the other three patterns of a to retrieve the value of k_0 in the other three diagonals.

Note that in this attack, we assume that if our guess key is wrong, then the remaining 9 rounds is a random permutation instead of 9-round Simpira-3 that is discussed in the 9-rounds distinguishing attack. So we use the 9-round distinguishing attack here to decide whether the current guess of key is correct or not. So with failure probability of less than 0.1%, we can recover the value of k_0. For the complexity, for each pattern of a, we recover one diagonal of k_0 with complexity 2^{51} encryption queries and $2^{32} \times 2^{51} = 2^{83}$ decryption queries. Since we repeat the attack four times for four different values of a, the total complexity is 2^{53} encryption queries and 2^{85} decryption queries.

We note here that this attack recovers different subkey from the one recovered in the key recovery attack of 10-round Simpira-3 based on impossible differential attack. The attack described in this subsection recovers the value of k_0 while the previous one recovers the value of k_1.

References

1. Aumasson, J.-P., Jovanovic, P., Neves, S.: NORX v3.0. Submission to CAESAR (2016). http://competitions.cr.yp.to/caesar-submissions.html
2. Bertoni, G., Daemen, J., Peeters, M., Van Assche, G., Van Keer, R.: CAESAR submission: Ketje v2. Submission to CAESAR (2016). http://competitions.cr.yp.to/caesar-submissions.html
3. Bertoni, G., Daemen, J., Peeters, J., Van Assche, G., Van Keer, R.: CAESAR submission: Keyak v2. Submission to CAESAR (2016). http://competitions.cr.yp.to/caesar-submissions.html
4. Bertoni, G., Daemen, J., Peeters, M., Van Assche, G.: Keccak sponge function family main document. Submission to NIST (Round 2) (2009)
5. Biham, E., Biryukov, A., Shamir, A.: Cryptanalysis of Skipjack reduced to 31 rounds using impossible differentials. In: Stern, J. (ed.) EUROCRYPT 1999. LNCS, vol. 1592, pp. 12–23. Springer, Heidelberg (1999). doi:10.1007/3-540-48910-X_2
6. Daemen, J., Rijmen, V.: The Design of Rijndael: AES-the Advanced Encryption Standard. Springer, Heidelberg (2002)
7. Daemen, J., Rijmen, V.: Understanding two-round differentials in AES. In: Prisco, R., Yung, M. (eds.) SCN 2006. LNCS, vol. 4116, pp. 78–94. Springer, Heidelberg (2006). doi:10.1007/11832072_6
8. Dobraunig, C., Eichlseder, M., Mendel, F.: Cryptanalysis of Simpira v1. Cryptology ePrint Archive, Report 2016/244 (2016). http://eprint.iacr.org/2016/244
9. Dobraunig, C., Eichlseder, M., Mendel, F., Schläffer, M.: Ascon v1.2. Submission to CAESAR (2016). http://competitions.cr.yp.to/caesar-submissions.html
10. Dunkelman, O., Keller, N., Shamir, A.: Minimalism in cryptography: the Even-Mansour scheme revisited. In: Pointcheval, D., Johansson, T. (eds.) EUROCRYPT 2012. LNCS, vol. 7237, pp. 336–354. Springer, Heidelberg (2012). doi:10.1007/978-3-642-29011-4_21

11. Even, S., Mansour, Y.: A construction of a cipher from a single pseudorandom permutation. J. Cryptology **10**(3), 151–161 (1997)
12. Gauravaram, P., Knudsen, L.R., Matusiewicz, K., Mendel, F., Rechberger, C., Schläffer, M., Thomsen, S.S.: Grøstl-a SHA-3 candidate. Submission to NIST (2008)
13. Gueron, S., Mouha, N.: Simpira: a family of efficient permutations using the AES round function. Cryptology ePrint Archive, Report 2016/122 (2016). http://eprint. iacr.org/2016/122
14. Gueron, S., Mouha, N.: Simpira v2: a family of efficient permutations using the AES round function. In: Cheon, J.H., Takagi, T. (eds.) ASIACRYPT 2016. LNCS, vol. 10031, pp. 95–125. Springer, Heidelberg (2016). doi:10.1007/978-3-662-53887-6_4
15. Knudsen, L.: DEAL - a 128-bit block cipher. In: NIST AES Proposal (1998)
16. Knudsen, L.R.: Truncated and higher order differentials. In: Preneel, B. (ed.) FSE 1994. LNCS, vol. 1008, pp. 196–211. Springer, Heidelberg (1995). doi:10.1007/ 3-540-60590-8_16
17. Morawiecki, P., Gaj, K., Homsirikamol, E., Matusiewicz, K., Pieprzyk, J., Rogawski, M., Srebrny, M., Wójcik, M.: ICEPOLE v2. submission to CAESAR competition. http://competitions.cr.yp.to/caesar-submissions.html
18. Morawiecki, P., Gaj, K., Homsirikamol, E., Matusiewicz, K., Pieprzyk, J., Rogawski, M., Srebrny, M., Wójcik, M.: ICEPOLE: high-speed, hardware-oriented authenticated encryption. In: Batina, L., Robshaw, M. (eds.) CHES 2014. LNCS, vol. 8731, pp. 392–413. Springer, Heidelberg (2014). doi:10.1007/ 978-3-662-44709-3_22
19. Rønjom, S.: Invariant subspaces in Simpira. Cryptology ePrint Archive, Report 2016/248 (2016). https://eprint.iacr.org/2016/248
20. Wagner, D.: The boomerang attack. In: Knudsen, L. (ed.) FSE 1999. LNCS, vol. 1636, pp. 156–170. Springer, Heidelberg (1999). doi:10.1007/3-540-48519-8_12
21. Wu, H.: The hash function JH. Submission to NIST (2011)
22. Zong, R., Dong, X., Wang, X.: Impossible differential attack on Simpira v2. Cryptology ePrint Archive, Report 2016/1161 (2016). http://eprint.iacr.org/2016/1161

Statistical Integral Distinguisher with Multi-structure and Its Application on AES

Tingting Cui[1,2,4], Ling Sun[1], Huaifeng Chen[1], and Meiqin Wang[1,3(✉)]

[1] Key Laboratory of Cryptologic Technology and Information Security,
Ministry of Education, Shandong University, Jinan 250100, China
mqwang@sdu.edu.cn
[2] Science and Technology on Communication Security Laboratory,
Chengdu 610041, China
[3] State Key Laboratory of Cryptology, P.O. Box 5159, Beijing 100878, China
[4] Nanyang Technological University, Singapore, Singapore

Abstract. Advanced Encryption Standard (AES), published by NIST, is widely used in data encryption algorithms, hash functions, authentication encryption schemes and so on. Studying distinguishing attacks on (reduced round) AES can help designers and cryptanalysts to evaluate the security of target ciphers. Since integral attack is one of the most powerful tool in the field of symmetric ciphers, in this paper, we evaluate the security of AES by integral cryptanalysis. Firstly we put forward a new statistical integral distinguisher with multiple structures on input and integral properties on output, which enables us to reduce the data complexity comparing to the traditional integral distinguishers under multiple structures. As illustrations, we propose a secret-key distinguisher on 5-round AES with secret S-box under chosen-ciphertext mode. Its data, time and memory complexities are $2^{114.32}$ chosen ciphertexts, 2^{110} encryptions and $2^{33.32}$ blocks. This is the best integral distinguisher on AES with secret S-box under secret-key setting so far. Then we present improved known-key distinguishers on 8-round and full 10-round AES-128 with reduced complexities based on Gilbert's work at ASIACRYPT'14. These distinguishers are the best ones according to the time complexity. Moreover, the proposed statistical integral model could be used to proceed known-key distinguishing attacks on other AES-like ciphers.

Keywords: Statistical integral model · Secret S-box · Secret key · Known key · AES

1 Introduction

Advanced Encryption Standard (AES) [8], published by NIST, is widely used in the field of symmetric ciphers. For instances, AES and reduced-round versions of AES are usually used as components for hash functions, authentication encryption schemes and so on. Since the goal of distinguishing attack is to distinguish

© Springer International Publishing AG 2017
J. Pieprzyk and S. Suriadi (Eds.): ACISP 2017, Part I, LNCS 10342, pp. 402–420, 2017.
DOI: 10.1007/978-3-319-60055-0_21

a target cipher from random permutations with some special property, studying the distinguishers on AES can help designers and cryptanalysts to evaluate the security of target cipher, which is meaningful.

In secret-key distinguishing attack, adversary needs to distinguish the target cipher from random permutations without knowing the key and internal states. Such distinguisher can be used in key-recovery attack. Furthermore, reduced round AES are often utilized to design authentication encryptions such as the third-round candidates AES-OTR [20] in CAESAR competition [6]. It is necessary to research the secret-key distinguisher on AES. Beside that, the performances of block ciphers under known key settings need be considered. Block ciphers, because of their security and simplicity, are often adopted as components of hash functions by designers, such as Whirlpool [3] and Photon [13]. Since the attacker can fully control the inter behaviour of a hash function, if a block cipher is used to design hash function, its resistance to known-key attack or chosen-key attack, where the adversaries know the key or can choose the key, should be considered. The first known-key security model is proposed by Knudsen and Rijmen for block cipher in [15] where the secret key is known to the attacker and the goal is to distinguish the block cipher from a random permutation by constructing a set of plaintext/ciphertext pairs satisfying a special property. Such a property is easy to check but impossible to achieve for any random permutation with the same complexity and a non-negligible probability by using oracle accesses to this random permutation and its inverse. Since its establishment, several types of known-key distinguishers have been proposed, such as distinguishers with integral property [1,12,15,21], subspace distinguishers [17,18], (multiple) limited-birthday distinguishers [11,14], and the known-key distinguisher for PRESENT by combining meet-in-the-middle technique and truncated differential [5]. Moreover, the chosen-key distinguishing attack on the full AES-256 has been provided in [4].

Integral attack is an important cryptanalytic technique for symmetric-key ciphers, which was firstly put forward by Daemen et al. in [7], then unified as integral attack by Knudsen and Wagner in [16]. In an integral distinguisher, one fixes a part of plaintext bits and takes all possible values for the other plaintext bits such that the values on partial bits of ciphertext are uniformly distributed, to distinguish an actual cipher from a random permutation. If one additional linear layer is considered, the property will be that the XOR of all possible values of the specific part of ciphertext becomes zero, which is referred as zero-sum property [2]. In order to reduce the data complexity, Wang et al. applied statistical technique on original integral distinguisher and proposed a statistical integral distinguisher at FSE'16 [24], which consists of applying a statistical technique to the original integral distinguisher with the active property. As a result, this statistical integral distinguisher requires less data complexity than that of the original integral distinguisher. However, Wang et al. only considered the case that only one integral property on ciphertext, they didn't discuss the cases that there are several integral properties on ciphertext and multiple structures of data should be used at the same time. These limit the effect of integral attacks on block ciphers, especially for known-key distinguishing attacks.

In this paper, we consider the cases omitted in [24] and use our statistical integral model to improve secret-key and known-key distinguishing attacks on AES with further less data and time complexities.

1.1 Our Contributions

Statistical Integral Distinguisher with Multiple Structures. We propose a statistical integral distinguisher with multiple structures on input and integral properties on output. In some situations of integral attacks such as known-key distinguishing attack on AES, multiple structures of input have to be used where for each structure s input bits take all possible values and the corresponding b t-bit outputs are uniformly distributed respectively. The statistical integral distinguisher in [24] can reduce the data complexity from $\mathcal{O}(2^s)$ to $\mathcal{O}(2^{s-t/2})$ by using one t-bit integral property if only one structure is used. But if there are N_s structures involved, the model in [24] cannot be applied. For the sake of reducing the data requirements for the original integral distinguisher with multiple structures, we construct a new statistical integral distinguisher. In our new distinguisher, the data complexity is

$$\mathcal{O}(\sqrt{N_s/b} \cdot 2^{s-\frac{t}{2}}),$$

while the data complexity of the original distinguisher is

$$\mathcal{O}(N_s \cdot 2^s).$$

In order to verify our theoretical model, we implement the experiments for mini version of AES. It shows that the experimental results are in good accordance with the theoretic results.

Improved Secret-Key Integral Distinguisher on AES. AES is one of the most famous block ciphers. Until 2015, the best secret-key distinguishers on AES were 4 rounds, such as impossible differential, zero-correlation linear hull and integral distinguisher. Then at CRYPTO'16, Sun *et al.* proposed a 5-round distinguisher on AES with secret S-box under chosen-ciphertext mode with integral zero-correlation technique in [23]. But the data complexity of this distinguisher is up to 2^{128}. Recently, Grassi *et al.* put forward a 5-round distinguisher on AES with secret S-box by utilizing a 4-round impossible differential in [9]. The data complexity is $2^{98.2}$. Later, they proposed another one on 5-round AES in [10]. That distinguisher is independent with the details of S-box, MC operation and secret-key, and its data complexity is reduced to 2^{32}. However, it utilizes the property of AES structure and has nothing with the secret-key, this weakness limits it to be used in key recovery attacks. In this paper, we will evaluate the security of AES from the point of integral distinguishing attack. We present a secret-key distinguisher on 5-round AES with secret S-box by adopting our statistical integral model under chosen-ciphertext mode. The data and time complexities are $2^{114.32}$ chosen ciphertexts and 2^{110} encryptions respectively. Its memory requirements are $2^{33.32}$ blocks. This is the best integral distinguisher on AES with secret S-box under secret-key setting so far (Table 1).

Improved Known-Key Distinguishers on AES. We apply the statistical integral distinguisher with multiple structures into the known-key distinguishing attacks on AES. The first known-key distinguisher on AES was proposed by Knudsen and Rijmen in [15], where they gave an integral known-key distinguisher for 7-round AES. At ASIACRYPT'14, Gilbert provided a very important untwisted representation of AES and used this representation to distinguish 8-round AES and the full 10-round AES with the complexity 2^{64} under the known-key model in [12]. Besides the integral known-key distinguishers, the known-key distinguisher with match-in-the-middle technique for 7-round AES was presented in [19], with rebound technique for 8-round AES were provided in [11,14] whose complexities are 2^{48} and 2^{44} 8-round encryptions respectively. In this paper, we take advantage of our statistical integral model to improve known-key distinguisher on 8-round AES and full 10-round AES, whose respective time complexities are $2^{42.61}$ computations and $2^{59.60}$ computations. These distinguishers are the best known-key ones on AES according to the time complexity so far. See Table 2.

Table 1. Summary of secret-key integral distinguishers on AES

Type	Rounds	Data (CC)	Time	Memory	Source
Integral	5	2^{128}	2^{128}	-	[23]
Statistical integral	**5**	$2^{114.32}$	2^{110}	$2^{33.32}$	**Section 4**

CC: Chosen-cipertext

Table 2. Summary of known-key distinguishing attacks on AES

Type	Rounds	Time	Memory	Source
Integral	7	2^{56}	—	[15]
MITM	7	2^{24}	—	[19]
Limited-birthday	8	2^{48}	2^{35} bytes	[11]
Multiple limited-birthday	8	2^{44}	2^{35} bytes	[14]
Integral	8	2^{64}	—	[12]
Statistical integral	**8**	$2^{42.61}$	2^{13} bytes	**Section 5**
Integral	10	2^{64}	—	[12]
Statistical integral	**10**	$2^{59.60}$	$2^{58.84}$ bytes	**Section 5**

MITM: Match-in-the-middle

1.2 Ontline of This Paper

In Sect. 2, some preliminaries are given. Then we present a statistical integral model with multiple structures on input and integral properties on output in Sect. 3. In Sects. 4 and 5, secret-key statistical integral distinguisher and improved known-key distinguishers on AES are put forward respectively. At last, we conclude this paper in Sect. 6.

2   Preliminaries

2.1   Description of AES

AES is a byte-orient Substitution-Permutation Network (SPN). It has three versions, namely AES-128, -192 and -256. The block-size/key-size/total-rounds of these versions are 128/128/10, 128/192/12 and 128/256/14 respectively. Each round function includes 4 components:

- SubBytes (SB): A nonlinear bijective mapping $\mathbb{F}_2^8 \to \mathbb{F}_2^8$ for each byte of state;
- ShiftRows (SR): Left rotate the i-th row by i bytes, where $i = 0, 1, 2, 3$;
- MixColumns (MC): Left multiply with an MDS matrix over the field $GF(2^8)$ on each column;
- AddRoundKey (AK): XOR with a 128 bits subkey.

It is worth noting that there is a whiten key XORed with plaintext before the first round function and the MC operation is omitted in the last round. Since we do not use the key schedule in this paper, we ignore it here.

All in all, $2r$-round AES can be described as follows:

$$AES_{2r} = AK \diamond (SB \diamond SR \diamond MC \diamond AK)^{2r-1} \diamond SB \diamond SR \diamond AK \tag{1}$$

where $A \diamond B$ denotes to implement A operation firstly, then B operation.

In [12], Gilbert proposed a new representation of AES. Firstly he defined two operations T and SC as follows, then built two special byte permutations $P = SR \diamond T \diamond SR^{-1}$ and $Q = SR^{-1} \diamond T \diamond SR \diamond SC$. With these two permutations, Gilbert proposed two transformations $S = Q^{-1} \diamond SB \diamond MC \diamond AK \diamond SB \diamond P^{-1}$ and $R = P \diamond SR \diamond MC \diamond AK \diamond SR \diamond Q$, which operate on columns and rows respectively.

$$T : \begin{pmatrix} a_0 & a_4 & a_8 & a_{12} \\ a_1 & a_5 & a_9 & a_{13} \\ a_2 & a_6 & a_{10} & a_{14} \\ a_3 & a_7 & a_{11} & a_{15} \end{pmatrix} \mapsto \begin{pmatrix} a_0 & a_1 & a_2 & a_3 \\ a_4 & a_5 & a_6 & a_7 \\ a_8 & a_9 & a_{10} & a_{11} \\ a_{12} & a_{13} & a_{14} & a_{15} \end{pmatrix}$$

$$SC : \begin{pmatrix} a_0 & a_4 & a_8 & a_{12} \\ a_1 & a_5 & a_9 & a_{13} \\ a_2 & a_6 & a_{10} & a_{14} \\ a_3 & a_7 & a_{11} & a_{15} \end{pmatrix} \mapsto \begin{pmatrix} a_0 & a_{12} & a_8 & a_4 \\ a_1 & a_{13} & a_9 & a_5 \\ a_2 & a_{14} & a_{10} & a_6 \\ a_3 & a_{15} & a_{11} & a_7 \end{pmatrix}$$

As a result, $2r$-round AES has three equivalent representations:

$$AES_{2r} = AK \diamond SR \diamond Q \diamond (S \diamond R)^{r-1} \diamond S \diamond P \diamond SR \diamond AK, \tag{2}$$

$$AES_{2r} = AK \diamond P^{-1} \diamond SB \diamond R \diamond (S \diamond R)^{r-1} \diamond SB \diamond Q^{-1} \diamond AK, \tag{3}$$

$$AES_{2r} = AK \diamond SB \diamond SR \diamond MC \diamond AES_{2r-2} \diamond AK^{-1} \diamond MC \diamond AK \cdot SB \diamond SR \diamond AK. \tag{4}$$

Throughout this paper, we use $X_{(i)}$ and $X_{(i\sim j)}, i, j = 0, 1, \ldots, 15$ to denote the i-th byte and $i \sim j$-th bytes of state X respectively.

2.2 Brief Description of Known-Key Distinguishers on AES in [12]

In this subsection, we briefly recall the known-key distinguishers for 8-round and 10-round AES proposed by Gilbert at ASIACRYPT'14 [12].

In order to mount a known-key distinguisher for AES_8, Gilbert firstly proposed two integral distinguishers shown in Fig. 1, where $(A_1^j, A_2^j, A_3^j, A_4^j), j = 0, 1, \ldots, 4$, A and C denote uniform distribution on 4 bytes, uniform distribution on 1 bytes and constant respectively. Then given 2^{64} data $\mathcal{Z} = \{R(x, 0, 0, 0) \oplus (y, 0, 0, 0) | x, y \in (0, 1)^{32}\}$, this set $\mathcal{Z}$ can be divided into 2^{32} structures according to different values of x, and each structure takes all 2^{32} values on the first column and constants on other columns. So the set $\mathcal{Z}$ satisfies the first integral distinguisher in Fig. 1. Since R operation is an affine mapping, $R(\mathcal{Z}^{-1}) = \{(x, 0, 0, 0) \oplus R^{-1}(y, 0, 0, 0)\}$ can be divided into 2^{32} structures according to different values of y, thus the set $R(\mathcal{Z}^{-1})$ satisfies the second integral distinguisher in Fig. 1.

Combining with these two integral distinguishers with R operation above, a known-key distinguisher on AES_8 is built that all input and output bytes resulted from 2^{64} middle texts $\mathcal{Z}$ are uniformly distributed. However, for random permutations, the upper bound of the probability satisfying the uniformly distributed property for each byte is $\frac{1}{2^{128}-1}$ with $q \leq N = 2^{64}$ oracle queries.

Furthermore, with the representation of Eq. (3), Gilbert mounted a known-key distinguisher for AES_{10}. This distinguisher is implemented by extending one round on each side based on the distinguisher for AES_8. The same 2^{64} middle texts $\mathcal{Z}$ as for the known-key distinguisher on AES_8 are used. For the corresponding input-output pairs $(p_i, c_i), i = 1, \ldots, 2^{64}$, the adversary can find at least one value (Δ, Γ), where $\Delta, \Gamma \in (0, 1)^{128}$, to make each byte of $R \circ SB(P^{-1}(p_i) \oplus \Delta)$ and $R^{-1} \circ SB^{-1}(Q(c_i) \oplus \Gamma)$ be uniform distribution within time complexity 2^{64}. However, for a random permutation, the upper bound of the probability satisfying the uniformly distributed property for each byte is $2^{-16.5}$ with $q \leq N = 2^{64}$ oracle queries.

Since Gilbert's work is based on the integral distinguisher and uses the active property[1], if we can improve the statistical integral model proposed by Wang et al. in [24], we can further improve Gilbert's work and widely utilize the new method to all AES-like ciphers. With the improved known-key distinguishers, 10-round AES-like ciphers cannot be regarded as ideal random permutations, and the time complexities of new distinguishers are less than previous ones.

---

[1] Active property means that the values on target bits are uniform distributed.

$$
\begin{bmatrix} A_1^0CCC \\ A_2^0CCC \\ A_3^0CCC \\ A_4^0CCC \end{bmatrix} \xrightarrow{S} \begin{bmatrix} A_1^0CCC \\ A_2^0CCC \\ A_3^0CCC \\ A_4^0CCC \end{bmatrix} \xrightarrow{R} \begin{bmatrix} A_1^1 A_1^2 A_1^3 A_1^4 \\ A_2^1 A_2^2 A_2^3 A_2^4 \\ A_3^1 A_3^2 A_3^3 A_3^4 \\ A_4^1 A_4^2 A_4^3 A_4^4 \end{bmatrix} \xrightarrow{S} \begin{bmatrix} A_1^1 A_1^2 A_1^3 A_1^4 \\ A_2^1 A_2^2 A_2^3 A_2^4 \\ A_3^1 A_3^2 A_3^3 A_3^4 \\ A_4^1 A_4^2 A_4^3 A_4^4 \end{bmatrix} \xrightarrow{P \diamond SR \diamond AK} \begin{bmatrix} AAAA \\ AAAA \\ AAAA \\ AAAA \end{bmatrix}
$$

$$
\begin{bmatrix} A_1^0CCC \\ A_2^0CCC \\ A_3^0CCC \\ A_4^0CCC \end{bmatrix} \xrightarrow{S^{-1}} \begin{bmatrix} A_1^0CCC \\ A_2^0CCC \\ A_3^0CCC \\ A_4^0CCC \end{bmatrix} \xrightarrow{R^{-1}} \begin{bmatrix} A_1^1 A_1^2 A_1^3 A_1^4 \\ A_2^1 A_2^2 A_2^3 A_2^4 \\ A_3^1 A_3^2 A_3^3 A_3^4 \\ A_4^1 A_4^2 A_4^3 A_4^4 \end{bmatrix} \xrightarrow{S^{-1}} \begin{bmatrix} A_1^1 A_1^2 A_1^3 A_1^4 \\ A_2^1 A_2^2 A_2^3 A_2^4 \\ A_3^1 A_3^2 A_3^3 A_3^4 \\ A_4^1 A_4^2 A_4^3 A_4^4 \end{bmatrix} \xrightarrow{(AK \diamond SR \diamond Q)^{-1}} \begin{bmatrix} AAAA \\ AAAA \\ AAAA \\ AAAA \end{bmatrix}
$$

Fig. 1. Two integral distinguishers under the new representation of AES in [12]

2.3 Statistical Integral Distinguisher

In this subsection, we recall the statistical integral distinguisher proposed by Wang *et al.* in [24].

Assume that $H : \mathbb{F}_2^n \to \mathbb{F}_2^n$ is a part of a block cipher, its input and output both can be split into two parts as follows:

$$
H : \mathbb{F}_2^r \times \mathbb{F}_2^s \to \mathbb{F}_2^t \times \mathbb{F}_2^u, H(x,y) = \begin{pmatrix} H_1(x,y) \\ H_2(x,y) \end{pmatrix}.
$$

If the first r bits of input are fixed as a constant λ and only the first t bits of output are considered, then the function H can be denoted as T_λ:

$$
T_\lambda : \mathbb{F}_2^s \to \mathbb{F}_2^t, T_\lambda(y) = H_1(\lambda, y).
$$

When y takes over all possible values, the outputs $T_\lambda(y)$ are uniformly distributed, then an integral distinguisher is constructed.

If the adversary only takes $N < 2^s$ different y, sets a counter $V[T_\lambda(y)]$ and initializes this counter as zero, a statistical integral distinguisher can be constructed by investigating the distribution of the statistic as follows:

$$
T = \sum_{i=0}^{2^t-1} \frac{(V[T_\lambda(y)] - N \cdot 2^{-t})^2}{N \cdot 2^{-t}} \tag{5}
$$

For the right key guess (the target cipher), the statistic T follows a χ^2 distribution with mean $\mu_0 = (2^t-1)\frac{2^s-N}{2^s-1}$ and variance $\sigma^2 = 2(2^t-1)(\frac{2^s-N}{2^s-1})^2$, but for the wrong key guess (a random permutation), it follows a χ^2 distribution with mean $\mu_0 = (2^t-1)$ and variance $\sigma^2 = 2(2^t-1)$. The relation of data complexity, type-I error probability α_0 and type-II error probability α_1 is as follows

$$
N = \frac{(2^s-1)(q_{1-\alpha_0} + q_{1-\alpha_1})}{\sqrt{(2^t-1)/2} + q_{1-\alpha_1}} + 1, \tag{6}
$$

3 Statistical Integral Distinguisher with Multiple Structures on Input and Integral Properties on Output

In some integral distinguishers, there are b groups of t output bits with the active property. If we can utilize all properties at the same time, the data complexity can be further reduced. What's more, in some attack settings, N_s structures, i.e. that N_s different λ, should be used together. For these special settings, we construct the new statistical integral distinguisher in this section.

Firstly, we split the input into two parts and output into $b + 1$ parts.

$$H : \mathbb{F}_2^r \times \mathbb{F}_2^s \rightarrow \mathbb{F}_2^t \times \mathbb{F}_2^t \times \ldots \times \mathbb{F}_2^t \times \mathbb{F}_2^u, \ H(x, y) = \begin{pmatrix} H_1(x, y) \\ H_2(x, y) \\ \ldots \\ H_{b+1}(x, y) \end{pmatrix}.$$

Then we use T_λ^i to denote the function H_i where the first r bits of its input are fixed to the value λ and b outputs $H_i, 1 \leq i \leq b$, are considered:

$$T_\lambda^i : \mathbb{F}_2^s \rightarrow \mathbb{F}_2^t, \ T_\lambda^i(y) = H_i(\lambda, y), i = 1, 2, \ldots, b.$$

For a special integral distinguisher, when y iterates all possible values of $\mathbb{F}_2^s$, $T_\lambda^i(y), i = 1, 2, \ldots, b$ are all uniformly distributed with probability one. Furthermore, if we take N_s values for λ, *i.e.* N_s structures and in each structure y iterates all possible values of $\mathbb{F}_2^s$, the integral properties on output are satisfied as well.

Now assume we need $N < 2^s$ values of y under each structure and we use N_s structures which are independent. $T_\lambda^i(y) \in \mathbb{F}_2^t, i = 1, 2, \ldots, b$ are computed for each y and we allocate a counter vector $V_i[T_\lambda^i(y)]$ to store the occurrences of $T_\lambda^i(y)$. Then we investigate the distribution of the following statistic:

$$C = \sum_{\lambda=1}^{N_s} \sum_{i=1}^{b} \sum_{T_\lambda^i(y)=0}^{2^t-1} \frac{(V_i[T_\lambda^i(y)] - N \cdot 2^{-t})^2}{N \cdot 2^{-t}}. \tag{7}$$

The statistic C follows different distributions determined by whether we are dealing with an actual cipher or a random permutation.

Proposition 1. *For sufficiently large N, and t, the statistic $\frac{2^s-1}{2^s-N}C_{cipher}$ (C_{cipher} is the statistic C for cipher) follows a χ^2-distribution with degree of freedom $b \cdot N_s \cdot (2^t - 1)$, which means that C_{cipher} approximately follows a normal distribution with mean and variance*

$$\mu_0 = Exp(C_{cipher}) = b \cdot N_s \cdot (2^t - 1) \frac{2^s - N}{2^s - 1}, \ \sigma_0^2 = Var(C_{cipher}) = 2b \cdot N_s \cdot (2^t - 1)(\frac{2^s - N}{2^s - 1})^2.$$

The statistic C_{random} (C_{random} is the statistic C for randomly drawn permutation) follows a χ^2-distribution with degree of freedom $b \cdot N_s \cdot (2^t - 1)$, which means that C_{random} approximately follows a normal distribution with mean and variance

$$\mu_1 = Exp(C_{random}) = b \cdot N_s \cdot (2^t - 1) \ and \ \sigma_1^2 = Var(C_{random}) = 2b \cdot N_s \cdot (2^t - 1).$$

Proof. Deduced from Proposition 1 in [24], for a randomly drawn permutation, the statistic $\sum_{T_\lambda^i(y)=0}^{2^t-1} \frac{(V_i[T_\lambda^i(y)]-N\cdot 2^{-t})^2}{N\cdot 2^{-t}}$ follows a χ^2-distribution with degree of freedom 2^t-1 for any λ and i. Then the statistic C'_{random} for the randomly drawn permutation

$$C_{random} = \sum_{\lambda=1}^{N_s}\sum_{i=1}^{b}\sum_{T_\lambda^i(y)=0}^{2^t-1} \frac{(V_i[T_\lambda^i(y)]-N\cdot 2^{-t})^2}{N\cdot 2^{-t}}$$

is the sum of $N_s\cdot b$ independent χ^2 statistics with degree of freedom 2^t-1, so the statistic C_{random} follows a χ^2-distribution with degree of freedom $b\cdot N_s\cdot(2^t-1)$. Then for sufficiently large N and t, C_{random} approximately follows a normal distribution with the expected value and variance:

$$Exp(C_{random}) = b\cdot N_s\cdot(2^t-1) \text{ and } Var(C_{random}) = 2b\cdot N_s\cdot(2^t-1).$$

Since the statistic for the cipher $\frac{2^s-1}{2^s-N}\sum_{T_\lambda^i(y)=0}^{2^t-1} \frac{(V_i[T_\lambda^i(y)]-N\cdot 2^{-t})^2}{N\cdot 2^{-t}}$, for any λ and i, follows a χ^2-distribution with degree of freedom 2^t-1 deduced from [24]. Then the statistic $\frac{2^s-1}{2^s-N}C'_{cipher}$ for the cipher

$$\frac{2^s-1}{2^s-N}C_{cipher} = \sum_{\lambda=1}^{N_s}\sum_{i=1}^{b}\frac{2^s-1}{2^s-N}\sum_{T_\lambda^i(y)=0}^{2^t-1} \frac{(V_i[T_\lambda^i(y)]-N\cdot 2^{-t})^2}{N\cdot 2^{-t}}$$

is the sum of $N_s\cdot b$ independent χ^2 statistics with degree of freedom 2^t-1, so the statistic $\frac{2^s-1}{2^s-N}C_{cipher}$ follows a χ^2-distribution with degree of freedom $b\cdot N_s\cdot(2^t-1)$. Then for sufficiently large N and t, C_{cipher} approximately follows a normal distribution with the expected value and variance:

$$Exp(C_{cipher}) = b\cdot N_s\cdot(2^t-1)\cdot\frac{2^s-1}{2^s-N} \text{ and } Var(C_{cipher}) = 2b\cdot N_s\cdot(2^t-1)\cdot(\frac{2^s-1}{2^s-N})^2.$$

$\square$

Corollary 1. *Under the assumption of Proposition 1, for type-I error probability α_0 (the probability to wrongfully discard the cipher), and type-II error probability α_1 (the probability to wrongfully accept a randomly chosen permutation as the cipher), to distinguish a cipher and a random permutation based on b independent t-bit outputs when randomly choosing N_s values for r-bit inputs and N values for s-bit inputs, then the following equation holds.*

$$N = \frac{(2^s-1)(q_{1-\alpha_0}+q_{1-\alpha_1})}{\sqrt{(b\cdot N_s\cdot(2^t-1))/2}+q_{1-\alpha_0}} + 1, \tag{8}$$

where $q_{1-\alpha_0}$ and $q_{1-\alpha_1}$ are the respective quantiles of the standard normal distribution.

Corollary 1 is obtained from the equation about the decision threshold $\tau = \mu_0+\sigma_0 q_{1-\alpha_0} = \mu_1-\sigma_1 q_{1-\alpha_1}$. And the statistic test is also based on the decision threshold τ: if $C \leq \tau$, the test outputs 'cipher'; Otherwise, if the statistic $C > \tau$, the test outputs 'random'. Note that in this statistical method the success probability $Ps = 1 - \alpha_0$, and the relation between α_1 and the advantage of the attack a is $\alpha_1 = 2^{-a}$.

In order to verify the theoretical model in Corollary 1, we implement the experiments for mini version of AES in Appendix A.1. It shows that the experimental results are in good accordance with the theoretic results.

From Eq. (8), we know that the data complexity for the statistical distinguisher is $N \cdot N_s$. For the given values of $n, s, t, \alpha_0, \alpha_1$, the ratio of the data complexity with N_s structures to that with one structure is $\sqrt{N_s}$. It means that more structures will result in high data complexity, so we should avoid to utilize more structures. However, for the known-key integral distinguisher for AES etc., we have to use enough structures to make the plaintexts and the ciphertexts satisfying the desired properties simultaneously. Moreover, if b is increased, the data complexity can be reduced, but as b increases, the time complexity in some situations will be increased accordingly. Thus, we should take the proper value for b according to the time-data tradeoff.

4 Secret-Key Statistical Integral Distinguisher on Reduced 5-Round AES

In this section, we propose a secret-key distinguisher on 5-round AES with our statistical integral model based on the work of Sun et al. in [23]. In this distinguisher, the S-box used in AES is secret.

Firstly, we slightly modify the zero-correlation linear hull for 5-round decryption of AES under chosen-ciphertext mode proposed by Sun et al. in [23] (Lemma 3). Let $V = \{(x_{(i)}) \in F_{2^8}^{16} | x_{(0)} \oplus x_{(13)} = (k_5)_{(0)} \oplus (k_5)_{(13)}\}$, and assume that the input mask $\Gamma_I = (a_{(i)})_{0 \leq i \leq 15}$ and output mask $\Gamma_O^0 = (\beta_{(i)})_{0 \leq i \leq 15}$ satisfy:

$$a_{(i)} = \begin{cases} a, i = 0, 13, \\ 0, otherwise. \end{cases} \qquad \beta_{(j)} = \begin{cases} nonzero, j = \{0, 5, 10, 15\} \\ 0, otherwise. \end{cases}$$

Then the correlation for $\Gamma_I \rightarrow \Gamma_O^0$ on V is always 0. Note that there are three other zero-correlation linear hulls as well, when $j = \{1, 6, 11, 12\}$, $\{2, 7, 8, 13\}$, $\{3, 4, 9, 14\}$. The corresponding output masks are Γ_O^1, Γ_O^2 and Γ_O^3 respectively. One of the four cases is shown in Fig. 2.

With the technique proposed by Sun et al. in [22], these four zero-correlation linear hulls can be transformed into integral ones. Taking the linear hull $\Gamma_I \rightarrow \Gamma_O^0$ as an example, the corresponding integral distinguisher is that if the adversary takes over 2^{120} different values of ciphertexts c satisfying $c_{(0)} \oplus c_{(13)} = (k_5)_{(0)} \oplus (k_5)_{(13)}$, then the values on 4 bytes of plaintext $(p_{(0)}, p_{(5)}, p_{(10)}, p_{(15)})$ are uniformly distributed.

Based on these integral distinguishers, we can implement a statistical integral distinguisher for each candidate $\Delta = (k_5)_{(0)} \oplus (k_5)_{(13)}$, where $s = 120$ and $t = 32$. In order to have the success probability $(1 - \alpha_0)^{2^8} = (1 - \alpha_1)^{2^8} = 95\%$, we set

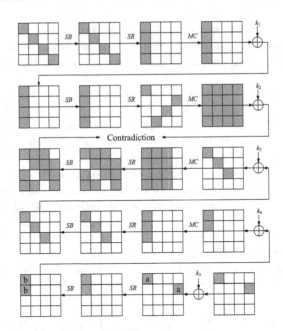

Fig. 2. Zero-correlation linear hull on 5-round AES with secret S-box under secret-key setting. Gray and white cells denote nonzero and zero masks respectively. The two cells with a or b are exactly the same mask.

Algorithm 1. Secret-key statistical integral distinguisher on 5-round AES with secret S-box

---

1 **for** 2^8 *candidates of* Δ **do**
2   Set a counter $V[4][2^{32}]$ and initialize it to zero;
3   **for** N *chosen ciphertext/plaintext pairs* (c,p) **do**
      // Consider those four integrals together.
4   **for** $i \leftarrow 0 \sim 3$ **do**
5   Increment counter $V[i][c^i_{part}]$ by one according to the related 4 bytes $c^i_{part} \in (0,1)^{32}$ of ciphertext c;
6   Calculate the statistic $T_\Delta = \sum_{b=0}^{3} \sum_{z=0}^{2^{32}-1} \frac{(V[b][z] - N \cdot 2^{-32})^2}{N \cdot 2^{-32}}$;
7 **if** *Only one* Δ *such that* $T_\Delta < \tau$ **then**
8   **return** AES;
9 **return** random permution;

$\alpha_0 = \alpha_1 = 0.0002$, then $q_{1-\alpha_0} = q_{1-\alpha_1} \approx 3.54$. Meanwhile, we can use these four integral distinguishers above together within one structure, so $b = 4$ and $N_s = 1$. Thus by Eq. (8), $N = 2^{106.32}$ chosen ciphertexts. The decision threshold is about $\tau \approx 17179212992.15$. As there are 2^8 different values of Δ, the total data complexity of this distinguisher is $N' = 2^{106.32} \times 2^8 = 2^{114.32}$ chosen ciphertexts.

What's more, we can see from Algorithm 1, the main time complexity happens on Step 5, which is about $2^8 \times 2^{106.32} \times 4 \times 1/16 \times 1/5 \approx 2^{110}$ encryptions, if we regard one simple operation as $\frac{1}{16}$ one round encryption. Beside that, memory requirements are about $4 \times 2^{32} \times 10 \approx 2^{37.32}$ bytes $= 2^{33.32}$ blocks.

As far as we know, this distinguisher is the best secret-key integral one on 5-round AES with secret S-box.

5 Improved Known-Key Distinguishers on AES

In this section, we will use our new statistical integral model to reduce the complexities of known-key distinguishers on AES proposed by Gilbert at ASI-ACRYPT'14 in Sects. 5.1 and 5.2.[2] The time complexity is reduced to $2^{42.61}$ in the known-key distinguisher on 8-round AES. For the 10-round AES, the time complexity is reduced to $2^{59.60}$. Compared to all the public known-key distinguishers for 8-round AES, our distinguisher is the best one according to both time and memory complexities. Moreover, our known-key distinguisher on 10-round AES is the best one according to the time complexity.

5.1 Improved Known-Key Distinguisher on 8-Round AES

As described in Subsect. 2.2, the known-key distinguisher for AES_8 is based on the uniformly distributed integral property with 2^{32} structures and each structure takes 2^{32} texts. This integral property can be transformed to a statistical integral property by using Proposition 1. So in our known-key distinguisher on AES_8, we utilize the statistical integral properties on each byte of input and output to distinguish the actual cipher and random permutations. In this way, the required number of structures and texts of one structure can be reduced. The process to distinguish the actual cipher AES_8 from the random permutation is described in Algorithm 2.

Since in the middle of the distinguisher, the numbers of structures before and after R operation should be the same, i.e. that $N = N_s$. By applying Proposition 1 in above case, we have $s = 32$, $t = 8$, $b = 16$ and $N = N_s$. If we set the error probabilities $\alpha_0 = 2^{-128}$ and $\alpha_1 = 2^{-128}$ (the values of α_0 and α_1 can be different and take any suitable values), then $q_{1-\alpha_0} = q_{1-\alpha_1} \approx 13.06$. According to Eq. (8), $N = N_s \approx 2^{20.81}$ and the threshold value $\tau \approx 7478730631.39$.

For the case of AES_8, as $\alpha_0 = 2^{-128}$, the probability to wrongly regard AES_8 as a random permutation is $\alpha_0 + (1-\alpha_0)\alpha_0 \approx 2^{-127}$, which means that the success probability to correctly identify AES cipher is about $(1 - \alpha_0)^2 \approx 1 - 2^{-127}$.

While for the case of random permutation, the adversary can implement encryption and decryption oracle queries to the cipher and random permutation. But statistical integral property (exploiting χ^2 distribution) is different

---

[2] These improved known-key distinguishers on AES in this paper follow the idea in Gilbert' work at ASIACRYPT'14, but we adopt statistical integral method instead of integral method and more delicate processes to reduce the data and time complexities.

Algorithm 2. Improved known-key distinguisher on AES_8

---

1 Initialize the statistic C' and C'' as zero;
2 **for** *all N values of $x \in (0,1)^{32}$* **do**
3   Initialize the counter vector $V[16][2^8]$ to zero;
4   **for** *all N values of $y \in (0,1)^{32}$* **do**
5   Compute 16 bytes of input $p_{(l)}, l = 0, \dots, 15$ from
         $Z = (x, 0, 0, 0) \oplus R(y, 0, 0, 0)$;
6   Increment the corresponding counter $V[l][p_{(l)}]$ by one;
7      $C' = C' + \sum_{l=0}^{15} \sum_{p_{(l)}=0}^{2^8-1} [\frac{(V[l][p_{(l)}] - N \times 2^{-8})^2}{N \times 2^{-8}}]$;

8 **if** $C' > \tau$ **then**
9   return $\perp$; // The distinguishing attack is failed.

10 **for** *all N values of $y \in (0,1)^{32}$* **do**
11   Initialize the counter vector $V[16][2^8]$ to zero;
12   **for** *all N values of $x \in (0,1)^{32}$* **do**
13   Compute 16 bytes of output $c_{(l)}, l = 0, \dots, 15$ from
         $Z = (x, 0, 0, 0) \oplus R(y, 0, 0, 0)$;
14   Increment the corresponding counter $V[l][c_{(l)}]$ by one;
15      $C'' = C'' + \sum_{l=0}^{15} \sum_{c_{(l)}=0}^{2^8-1} [\frac{(V[l][c_{(l)}] - N \times 2^{-8})^2}{N \times 2^{-8}}]$;

16 For AES_8, $C'' \leq \tau$;
17 For any random permutation, $C'' > \tau$.

---

from traditional integral property (utilizing uniform distribution). At the best of times the adversary chooses the data which automatically satisfy the statistical property on the input, but to satisfy the statistical property on the output, the probability is $\alpha_1 = 2^{-128}$. In order to satisfy the statistical properties both on the input and output, the probability to wrongly regard this random permutation as AES cipher is $1 \times \alpha_1 = 2^{-128}$.

To summarize, the advantage to distinguish AES cipher from random permutation is not negligible. The total time complexity of this known-key distinguisher is about $2 \times 2^{41.61} = 2^{42.61}$ computations. The memory requirements are about $16 \times 2^8 \times 2 = 2^{13}$ bytes used for storing the counter vector $V[16][2^8]$.

5.2 Improved Known-Key Distinguisher on 10-Round AES

The statistical integral distinguisher on AES_{10} is based on the distinguishing property of AES_{10} in [12], which is represented according to Eq. (4), see Fig. 3.

Along with the idea within the distinguisher on AES_{10} in [12], in our known-key distinguisher on AES_{10}, we use $N_s < 2^{32}$ structures, each of which takes $N = N_s$ middle texts, to obtain N^2 input/output pairs. For AES cipher, there is one value for (Δ, Γ) to let each byte of $R \circ SB(R^{-1}(input \oplus \Delta))$ and $R^{-1} \circ SB^{-1}(Q(output \oplus \Gamma))$ satisfy the statistical integral property with a high probability. But for any random permutation, the probability to have one solution for (Δ, Γ) to obtain the same property is very low.

However, in above way, the distinguisher has high time complexity. In order to reduce the time complexity, we implement the distinguisher in the following way. As N_s structures are used, we divide them into N_s/n_s groups and each group has n_s structures. Then we compute the statistic value for each group. There is one value (Δ, Γ) to make all the statistics for N_s/n_s groups on both states $Input' = MC \circ SR \circ SB(input \oplus \Delta)$ and $Output' = MC^{-1} \circ SB^{-1} \circ SR^{-1}(output \oplus \Gamma)$ less than the given threshold τ for AES_{10}. However, for the random permutation, even if the attacker can carefully choose the inputs to find one value of Δ to satisfy the statistical property on the state $Input'$ with probability one, the probability to find one value Γ to satisfy the statistical property on the state $Output'$ is very low.

In order to further reduce the time complexity, we focus on statistics on 8-byte states – $Input'_{(0\sim3)}$ and $Output'_{(0\sim3)}$. So we only need to find two 32-bit values for $\Delta' = (\Delta_{(0)}, \Delta_{(5)}, \Delta_{(10)}, \Delta_{(15)})$ and $\Gamma' = (\Gamma_{(0)}, \Gamma_{(7)}, \Gamma_{(10)}, \Gamma_{(13)})$. The detailed process for this known-key distinguisher on AES_{10} is described in Algorithm 3.

In this setting, by applying Proposition 1, $s = 32$, $t = 8$, $b = 1$ and $n_s = 2^8$. If we set the error probabilities $\alpha_0 = 2^{-50}$ and $\alpha_1 = 2^{-10.51}$, then $N = 2^{27.92}$ and $\tau = 64123.53$ according to Eq. (8).

$$
(input) \xleftarrow{(I^*)^{-1}}
\begin{bmatrix} AAAA \\ \diamond AAAA \\ AAAA \\ AAAA \end{bmatrix}
\xleftarrow{(AK \circ SR \circ Q \circ S \circ R \circ S)^{-1}}
\begin{bmatrix} A_1CCC \\ A_2CCC \\ A_3CCC \\ A_4CCC \end{bmatrix}
\xleftarrow{R^{-1}} \overset{\mathcal{R}^{-1}(\mathcal{Z})}{}
\begin{bmatrix} A_1CCC \\ A_2CCC \\ A_3CCC \\ A_4CCC \end{bmatrix} \overset{\mathcal{Z}}{}
\xrightarrow{S \circ R \circ S \circ P \circ SR}
\begin{bmatrix} AAAA \\ AAAA \\ AAAA \\ AAAA \end{bmatrix}
\xrightarrow{F^*} (output)
$$

$$(I^*)^{-1} = (AK \diamond SB \diamond SR \diamond MC)^{-1} \qquad\qquad F^* = MC \diamond AK \diamond SB \diamond SR \diamond AK$$

Fig. 3. Known-key distinguisher for AES_{10}. (A_1, A_2, A_3, A_4) and A denote uniform distribution on 4 bytes and 1 byte respectively. C denotes constant byte.

In Algorithm 3, we filter out the wrong values for $\Delta' = (\Delta_{(0)}, \Delta_{(5)}, \Delta_{(10)}, \Delta_{(15)})$ with the statistics on $Input'_{(0\sim3)}$ one by one. At last, the probability that one wrong Δ' is remained after all $2^{27.92-8}$ filtering processes is about $(2^{32} - 1) \cdot \alpha_1^{4 \times 2^{19.92}} \approx 0$, while the probability that the right candidate Δ cannot pass the filtering process is $1 - (1 - \alpha_0)^{4 \times 2^{19.92}} \approx 2^{-28.08}$.

In the similar way, we filter out the wrong values for $\Gamma' = (\Gamma_{(0)}, \Gamma_{(7)}, \Gamma_{(10)}, \Gamma_{(13)})$ with the statistics for $Output'_{(0\sim3)}$ one by one. Finally, the probability that one wrong Γ' can pass the filtering process is also about 0, while the probability that the right Γ' cannot pass the filtering process is also $2^{-28.08}$. Therefore, for the case of AES_{10}, the probability to correctly identify the AES_{10} cipher is about $(1 - 2^{-28.08})^2 \approx 1 - 2^{-27.08}$.

While for the case of random permutation, at the best of the times the adversary can choose the inputs that there is always at least one value of Δ' remaining after the filtering process, but the probability that there is at least one Γ' surviving after the filtering process is about 0.

Algorithm 3. Improved known-key distinguisher on AES_{10}

---

1 Allocate vectors $V[N][N]$, $V'[N][N]$;

2 **for** *all* N^2 *values of* $(y_i, x_j), 0 \le i, j < N$ **do**

3   Calculate input p and output c from $Z = (x_j, 0, 0, 0) \oplus R(y_i, 0, 0, 0)$ and let
    $V[j][i] = (p_{(0)}, p_{(5)}, p_{(10)}, p_{(15)})$, $V'[i][j] = (c_{(0)}, c_{(7)}, c_{(10)}, c_{(13)})$;

    // Steps 4 ∼ 30 proceed the first group with n_s structures.

4 **for** *all* 2^{16} *values of* $(\Delta_{(0)}, \Delta_{(5)})$ **do**

5   Allocate vectors $V_1[n_s][2^{24}]$;

6   **for** *all* n_s *values of* j *and* N *values of* i **do**

7   Get $(p_{(0)}, p_{(5)}, p_{(10)}, p_{(15)})$ from $V[j][i]$;

8   Compute $W_0 = 2 \cdot SB(p_{(0)} \oplus \Delta_{(0)}) \oplus 3 \cdot SB(p_{(5)} \oplus \Delta_{(5)})$; // $\cdot$ operate
       on F_2^8.

9   Let $V_1[j][W_0, p_{(10)}, p_{(15)}]$ increase one;

10   **for** *all* 2^8 *values of* $\Delta_{(10)}$ **do**

11   Allocate a counter vectors $V_2[n_s][2^{16}]$, and initialize to zero;

12   **for** *all* n_s *values of* j *and all* 2^{24} *values of* $W_0 \| p_{(10)} \| p_{(15)}$ **do**

13   Compute $W_1 = W_0 \oplus (SB(p_{(10)} \oplus \Delta_{(10)}))$;

14   Let $V_2[j][W_1, p_{(15)}] \mathrel{+}= V_1[j][W_0, p_{(10)}, p_{(15)}]$;

15   **for** *all* 2^8 *values of* $\Delta_{(15)}$ **do**

16   Allocate counter vectors $V_3[n_s][2^8]$, and initialize to zero;

17   **for** *all* n_s *values of* j *and all* 2^{16} *values of* $(W_1, p_{(15)})$ **do**

18              $W' = W_1 \oplus (SB(p_{(15)} \oplus \Delta_{(15)}))$, let $V_3[j][W'] \mathrel{+}=$
             $V_2[j][W_1, p_{(15)}]$;

19           $C_1 = \sum_{j=0}^{n_s-1} \sum_{W'=0}^{2^8-1} \frac{(V_3[j][W'] - N \times 2^{-8})^2}{N \times 2^{-8}}$;

20   **if** $C_1 \le \tau$ **then**

21   Put $\Delta' = (\Delta_{(0)}, \Delta_{(5)}, \Delta_{(10)}, \Delta_{(15)})$ into V_k. // About remain
             $2^{32} \cdot \alpha_1$ values.

22 **for** *all values of* $\Delta' \in V_k$ **do**

23   Allocate counter vectors $V_4[n_s][2^8]$, and initialize to zero;

24   **for** *all* n_s *values of* j *and* N *values of* i **do**

25   Get $(p_{(0)}, p_{(5)}, p_{(10)}, p_{(15)})$ from $V[j][i]$ and compute $Input'_1 = SB(p_{(0)} \oplus$
       $\Delta_{(0)}) \oplus 2 \cdot SB(p_{(5)} \oplus \Delta_{(5)}) \oplus 3 \cdot SB(p_{(10)} \oplus \Delta_{(10)}) \oplus SB(p_{(15)} \oplus \Delta_{(15)})$;

26   Increment $V_4[j][Input'_1]$ by one;

27     $C_2 = \sum_{j=0}^{n_s-1} \sum_{W=0}^{2^8-1} \frac{(V_4[j][W] - N \times 2^{-8})^2}{N \times 2^{-8}}$;

28   **if** $C_2 \le \tau$ **then**

29   Put Δ' into $V_{k_1}[\cdot]$. // About $2^{32} \cdot \alpha_1^2$ values are remained.

30 Proceed the similar steps as 22-29 for the other 2 bytes $Input'_{(2 \sim 3)}$. // About 1
    value is remained.

31 Check if this Δ' satisfies the other $N/n_s - 1$ groups of n_s structures;

32 **if** *there is no solution for* Δ' *remained* **then**

33   return $\perp$. // The distinguishing attack is failed.

34 Proceed Steps 4 ∼ 31 with $V'[N][N]$ to compute the distributions on
    $Output'_{(0 \sim 3)}$ by guessing $\Gamma' = (\Gamma_{(0)}, \Gamma_{(7)}, \Gamma_{(10)}, \Gamma_{(13)})$;

35 For AES_{10}, there exists one solution for Γ';

36 For any random permutation, there is no solution for Γ'.

So the success probability of this distinguisher is about $1 - 2^{-27.08}$. The advantage to distinguish AES_{10} from random permutation is not negligible. The time complexity of Steps $2 \sim 3$ is $N \times N = 2^{55.84}$ full round encryptions. Then the time complexity of Steps $4 \sim 9$ is about $2^{16} \times n_s \times N = 2^{51.92}$ memory accesses (MA). Steps $10 \sim 14$ take $2^{16} \times 2^8 \times n_s \times 2^{24} = 2^{56}$ MA, and Steps $15 \sim 21$ require about $2^{32} \times n_s \times 2^{16} = 2^{56}$ MA. Since $\alpha_1 = 2^{-10.51}$, Steps $22 \sim 29$ take $2^{32} \times \alpha_1 \times n_s \times N = 2^{57.41}$ MA and Step 30 needs about $(2^{32} \times \alpha_1^2 + 2^{32} \times \alpha_1^3) \times n_s \times N \approx 2^{46.91}$ MA. After one filter process, the number of candidates for Δ is about 1. Consequently by filtering with other $N/n_s - 1$ groups of structures, the time complexity of Step 31 is $(N/n_s - 1) \times n_s \times N \approx 2^{55.84}$ MA. Then if we roughly set one access to a table is equivalent to one full round encryption, the total complexity from Step $4 \sim 31$ is about $2^{51.92} + 2^{56} + 2^{56} + 2^{57.41} + 2^{46.91} + 2^{55.84} \approx 2^{58.49}$ encryptions. Since Step 34 also takes $2^{58.49}$ encryptions, the total time complexity of the whole attack is about $2^{55.84} + 2 \times 2^{58.49} \approx 2^{59.60}$ full round encryptions. In addition, the dominant memory requirements happen on $V[N][N]$ and $V'[N][N]$, which need about $2 \times 4 \times N \times N = 2^{58.84}$ bytes.

6   Conclusion

In this paper, we propose a statistical integral distinguisher with multiple structures on input and multiple integral properties on output based the work of Wang et al. at FSE'16. With this distinguisher, we give the known-key distinguishing attack on 8-round and full round AES-128 based on the Gilbert's work at ASIACRYPT'14, which are the best known-key distinguishers for AES so far according to the time complexity. Beside that, we present a secret-key statistical integral distinguisher on 5-round AES with secret S-box under chosen-ciphertext mode. This is the best integral distinguisher on AES with secret S-box under secret-key setting. As a future work, we try to apply more statistical techniques into the field of symmetric ciphers and find improved attack on AES and AES-like ciphers.

Acknowledgement. This work has been supported by 973 Program (No. 2013CB834205), NSFC Projects (No. 61133013, No. 61572293), Program for New Century Excellent Talents in University of China (NCET-13-0350), Program from Science and Technology on Communication Security Laboratory of China (No. 9140c110207150c11050).

A   Appendix

A.1   Experiment Results

In order to verify the theoretical model of statistical integral distinguisher in Sect. 3, we implement the distinguishing attack in Sect. 5 on a mini variant of AES with the block size 64-bit denoted as AES* here. The round function of AES* is similar to that of AES, including four operations, *i.e.*, SB, SR, MC and

AK. 64-bit block is partitioned into 16 nibbles and *SB* uses S-box S_0 in LBlock. *SR* is same as that of AES, and the matrix used in *MC* is

$$M = \begin{pmatrix} 1 & 1 & 4 & 9 \\ 9 & 1 & 1 & 4 \\ 4 & 9 & 1 & 1 \\ 1 & 4 & 9 & 1 \end{pmatrix},$$

which is defined over $GF(2^4)$. For the multiplication, each nibble and value in M are considered as a polynomial over $GF(2)$ and then the nibble is multiplied modulo $x^4 + x + 1$ by the value in M. The addition is simply XOR operation. The subkeys are XORed with the nibbles in *AK* operation.

There is similar known-key integral distinguisher for 8-round AES* since its similarity to AES, see Fig. 1. Given a set of data $\mathcal{Z} = \{(x,0,0,0) \oplus R(y,0,0,0)|x \in (0,1)^{16}\}$ for fixed y, *i.e.*, the first column of $\mathcal{Z}$ takes all 2^{16} possible values and other columns are fixed to some constants, after $S \diamond R \diamond S$ operation, each column of output u is active, i.e. that 2^{16} values are uniformly distributed on each column of output. Since $R^{-1}(\mathcal{Z}) = \{R^{-1}((x,0,0,0) \oplus (y,0,0,0))\}$ has 2^{16} structures that each one takes all 2^{16} possible values on the first columns and constants on other columns, after $(S \diamond R \diamond S)^{-1}$ operation, each column of output u is active.

In our experiment, we consider the distributions of four 8-bit values in v including the first and second nibble in each column of v. Here $s = 16, t = 8$ and $b = 4$. If we set $\alpha_0 = 0.2$ and take different values for N and N_s, α_1 and τ can be computed using Eq. (8). By randomly choosing N_s values for y and N values for x, we proceed the experiment to compute the statistics C' for AES* and random permutations. With 2000 times of experiments, we can obtain the empirical error probabilities $\widehat{\alpha_0}$ and $\widehat{\alpha_1}$. The experimental results for $\widehat{\alpha_0}$ and $\widehat{\alpha_1}$ are compared with the theoretical values α_0 and α_1 in Fig. 4.

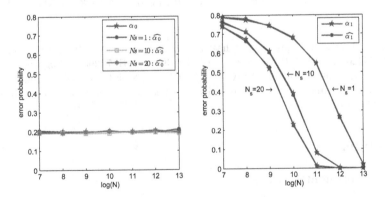

Fig. 4. Experimental results for AES* considering four input bytes. In detail, set the value of α_0 and change the values of N and N_s, the theoretical and empirical α_0 are shown in the left part of figure, corresponding α_1 calculated and tested by Eq. (5) are shown in the right part of figure.

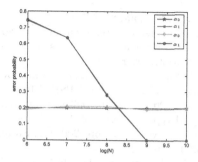

Fig. 5. Experimental results for AES* considering two input and output bytes. In detail, set the theoretical $\alpha_0 = 0.2$ and change the values of N, then the corresponding theoretical α_1 and empirical α_0 and α_1 are calculated and tested by Eq. (5) in this figure

Moreover, we implement the second experiment where we set $b = 4$ including two bytes of u and two bytes of v. We set $\alpha_0 = 0.2$ and let $N = N_s$, the empirical error probabilities are obtained from 1000 times of experiments. The experimental results for $\widehat{\alpha_0}$ and $\widehat{\alpha_1}$ are compared with the theoretical values α_0 and α_1 in Fig. 5.

Figures 4 and 5 show that the test results for the error probabilities are in good accordance with those for theoretical model.

References

1. Aoki, K.: A middletext distinguisher for full CLEFIA-128. In: 2012 International Symposium on Information Theory and its Applications (ISITA), pp. 521–525. IEEE (2012)
2. Aumasson, J., Meier, W.: Zero-sum distinguishers for reduced keccak-f and for the core functions of luffa and hamsi, 2009. Presented at the rump session of Cryptographic Hardware and Embedded Systems- CHES (2009)
3. Barreto, P.S.L.M., Rijmen, V.: Whirlpool. In: van Tilborg, H.C.A., Jajodia, S. (eds.) Encyclopedia of Cryptography and Security, 2nd edn, pp. 1384–1385. Springer, New York (2011)
4. Biryukov, A., Khovratovich, D., Nikolić, I.: Distinguisher and related-key attack on the full AES-256. In: Halevi, S. (ed.) CRYPTO 2009. LNCS, vol. 5677, pp. 231–249. Springer, Heidelberg (2009). doi:10.1007/978-3-642-03356-8_14
5. Blondeau, C., Peyrin, T., Wang, L.: Known-key distinguisher on full PRESENT. In: Gennaro, R., Robshaw, M. (eds.) CRYPTO 2015. LNCS, vol. 9215, pp. 455–474. Springer, Heidelberg (2015). doi:10.1007/978-3-662-47989-6_22
6. CAESAR: Competition for Authenticated Encryption: Security, Applicability, and Robustness. https://competitions.cr.yp.to/caesar.html
7. Daemen, J., Knudsen, L., Rijmen, V.: The block cipher square. In: Biham, E. (ed.) FSE 1997. LNCS, vol. 1267, pp. 149–165. Springer, Heidelberg (1997). doi:10.1007/BFb0052343
8. FIPS 197. Advanced Encryption Standard. Federal Information Processing Standards Publication 197, U.S. Department of Commerce/N.I.S.T (2001)

9. Grassi, L., Rechberger, C., Rønjom, S.: Subspace trail cryptanalysis and its applications to AES - extended version. https://eprint.iacr.org/2016/592

10. Grassi, L., Rechberger, C., Rønjom, S.: A new structural-differential property of 5-round AES. https://eprint.iacr.org/2017/118.pdf

11. Gilbert, H., Peyrin, T.: Super-Sbox cryptanalysis: improved attacks for AES-like permutations. In: Hong, S., Iwata, T. (eds.) FSE 2010. LNCS, vol. 6147, pp. 365–383. Springer, Heidelberg (2010). doi:10.1007/978-3-642-13858-4_21

12. Gilbert, H.: A simplified representation of AES. In: Sarkar, P., Iwata, T. (eds.) ASIACRYPT 2014. LNCS, vol. 8873, pp. 200–222. Springer, Heidelberg (2014). doi:10.1007/978-3-662-45611-8_11

13. Guo, J., Peyrin, T., Poschmann, A.: The PHOTON family of lightweight hash functions. In: Rogaway, P. (ed.) CRYPTO 2011. LNCS, vol. 6841, pp. 222–239. Springer, Heidelberg (2011). doi:10.1007/978-3-642-22792-9_13

14. Jean, J., Naya-Plasencia, M., Peyrin, T.: Multiple limited-birthday distinguishers and applications. In: Lange, T., Lauter, K., Lisoněk, P. (eds.) SAC 2013. LNCS, vol. 8282, pp. 533–550. Springer, Heidelberg (2014). doi:10.1007/978-3-662-43414-7_27

15. Knudsen, L., Rijmen, V.: Known-key distinguishers for some block ciphers. In: Kurosawa, K. (ed.) ASIACRYPT 2007. LNCS, vol. 4833, pp. 315–324. Springer, Heidelberg (2007). doi:10.1007/978-3-540-76900-2_19

16. Knudsen, L., Wagner, D.: Integral cryptanalysis. In: Daemen, J., Rijmen, V. (eds.) FSE 2002. LNCS, vol. 2365, pp. 112–127. Springer, Heidelberg (2002). doi:10.1007/3-540-45661-9_9

17. Lamberger, M., Mendel, F., Rechberger, C., Rijmen, V., Schläffer, M.: Rebound distinguishers: results on the full whirlpool compression function. In: Matsui, M. (ed.) ASIACRYPT 2009. LNCS, vol. 5912, pp. 126–143. Springer, Heidelberg (2009). doi:10.1007/978-3-642-10366-7_8

18. Lamberger, M., Mendel, F., Rechberger, C., Rijmen, V., Schläffer, M.: The rebound attack and subspace distinguishers: application to whirlpool. Cryptology ePrint Archive, Report 2010/198 (2010)

19. Mendel, F., Peyrin, T., Rechberger, C., Schläffer, M.: Improved cryptanalysis of the reduced Grøstl compression function, ECHO permutation and AES block cipher. In: Jacobson, M.J., Rijmen, V., Safavi-Naini, R. (eds.) SAC 2009. LNCS, vol. 5867, pp. 16–35. Springer, Heidelberg (2009). doi:10.1007/978-3-642-05445-7_2

20. Minematsu, K.: AES-OTR (v3.1). https://competitions.cr.yp.to/round3/aesotrv31.pdf

21. Minier, M., Phan, R.C.-W., Pousse, B.: Distinguishers for ciphers and known key attack against Rijndael with large blocks. In: Preneel, B. (ed.) AFRICACRYPT 2009. LNCS, vol. 5580, pp. 60–76. Springer, Heidelberg (2009). doi:10.1007/978-3-642-02384-2_5

22. Sun, B., Liu, Z., Rijmen, V., Li, R., Cheng, L., Wang, Q., Alkhzaimi, H., Li, C.: Links among impossible differential, integral and zero correlation linear cryptanalysis. In: Gennaro, R., Robshaw, M. (eds.) CRYPTO 2015. LNCS, vol. 9215, pp. 95–115. Springer, Heidelberg (2015). doi:10.1007/978-3-662-47989-6_5

23. Sun, B., Liu, M., Guo, J., Qu, L., Rijmen, V.: New insights on AES-like SPN ciphers. In: Robshaw, M., Katz, J. (eds.) CRYPTO 2016. LNCS, vol. 9814, pp. 605–624. Springer, Heidelberg (2016). doi:10.1007/978-3-662-53018-4_22

24. Wang, M., Cui, T., Chen, H., Sun, L., Wen, L., Bogdanov, A.: Integrals go statistical: cryptanalysis of full Skipjack variants. In: Peyrin, T. (ed.) FSE 2016. LNCS, vol. 9783, pp. 399–415. Springer, Heidelberg (2016). doi:10.1007/978-3-662-52993-5_20

Conditional Differential Cryptanalysis for Kreyvium

Yuhei Watanabe[1]([✉]), Takanori Isobe[2], and Masakatu Morii[3]

[1] National Institute of Advanced Industrial Science and Technology, Osaka, Japan
yuhei.watanabe@aist.go.jp
[2] University of Hyogo, Hyogo, Japan
takanori.isobe@ai.u-hyogo.ac.jp
[3] Kobe University, Hyogo, Japan

Abstract. Kreyvium is a NLFSR-based stream cipher which is oriented to homomorphic-ciphertext compression. This is a variant of Trivium with 128-bit security. Designers have evaluated the security of Kreyvium and concluded that the resistance of Kreyvium to the conditional differential cryptanalysis is at least the resistance of Trivium, and even better. However, we consider that this attack is effective due to the structure of Kreyvium. This paper shows conditional differential cryptanalysis for Kreyvium. We propose the method of arrangement of differences and conditions to obtain good higher-order conditional differential characteristics. We use two types of higher-order conditional differential characteristics to find the distinguisher, e.g. the bias of higher-order conditional differential characteristics of keystream and the *neutrality* of keystreams. In the first one, we obtain a distinguisher on Kreyvium with 730 rounds from 20-th order characteristic. In the second one, we obtain a distinguisher on Kreyvium with 899 rounds from 24-th and 25-th order conditional differential characteristic. We experimentally confirm all our attacks. The second one shows that we can obtain the distinguisher on Kreyvium with more rounds than the distinguisher on Trivium. Therefore, Kreyvium has lower security than Trivium for the conditional differential cryptanalysis.

Keywords: Differential cryptanalysis · Conditional differential · Higher-order differential · Distinguisher · Kreyvium

1 Introduction

A fully homomorphic encryption (FHE) scheme is a promising technology for recent cloud-based services such as cloud computing and storage services. However, if FHE schemes are deployed in a straightforward method, the size of ciphertexts becomes very large, and the environment of communication considerably suffers from it. In order to reduce the size of ciphertexts, Cateaut et al.

This work was done when the first and second authors belonged to Kobe University.
J. Pieprzyk and S. Suriadi (Eds.): ACISP 2017, Part I, LNCS 10342, pp. 421–434, 2017.
DOI: 10.1007/978-3-319-60055-0_22

Table 1. Results of the conditional differential cryptanalysis for Trivium and Kreyvium on the single-key setting

Cipher	Round	Evaluation	Type of attack	Reference
Trivium	798	Neutrality	Distinguisher	[6]
	799	Cube attack	Key recovery	[5]
	829	Cube tester	Distinguisher	[9]
Kreyvium	730	Zero sum	Distinguisher	Sect. 4
	899	Neutrality	Distinguisher	Sect. 4

showed an efficient method for compressing ciphertexts by using a symmetric encryption scheme, and investigate the cost of a homomorphic evaluation when several symmetric primitives are used for this purpose [3]. Furthermore, they proposed a new NLFSR-based stream cipher called Kreyvium, and optimized for the usage of FHE. Kreyvium is based on a Trivium, and offers 128-bit security, while Trivium [2] achieves only 80-bit security.

Designers of Kreyvium have evaluated the security of Kreyvium for various attacks which are applied to Trivium. The most successful attacks on Trivium are cube attacks and conditional differential cryptanalysis [1,4–7,9,10]. Dinur et al. proposed cube attacks and showed key recovery attacks for Trivium with 774 rounds by using 29-th order differential characteristic [4]. Aumasson et al. proposed cube testers, and showed a distinguisher for Trivium with 790 rounds by using 30-th order differential characteristic [1]. Stankovski showed cube testers, and showed a distinguisher for Trivium with 806 rounds by using 44-th order differential characteristic [10]. Fouque et al. improved cube attacks, and showed key recovery attacks for Trivium with 799 rounds by using 37-th order differential characteristic [5]. Liu et al. proposed a heuristic algorithm for searching favorable cubes, and showed a distinguisher for Trivium with 839 rounds by using 37-th order differential characteristic [7]. Sarker et al. improved cube testers, and showed a distinguisher for Trivium with 829 rounds by using 27-th order differential characteristic [9]. Knellwolf et al. showed a conditional differential cryptanalysis, and showed a distinguisher for Trivium with 798 rounds by using 24-th and 25-th order conditional differential characteristic [6]. Moreover, they showed a distinguisher for Trivium with 961 rounds on the weak-key setting.

Designers of Kreyvium conclude that the resistance of Kreyvium to these attacks is at least the resistance of Trivium, and even better [3]. The reason is that adversaries have fewer bits forced to be zero than the case of Trivium despite introducing IV bits in two registers simultaneously. In addition, since Kreyvium has two additional XORs per round, they get more involved relations that provide a better resistance against the conditional differential cryptanalysis [6].

1.1 Our Contribution

In this paper, we explore the security of conditional differential cryptanalyses for Kreyvium. Our evaluation starts with the fact that the important factor for finding good conditional differential characteristics is how to arrange differences and conditions in the initial states, not the number of zero in the initial state. Kreyvium supports 128-bit IV whose size is larger than that of Trivium, and is initially loaded into two registers of sizes 84 and 111 bits. We exploit degree of freedom of IV and the structure of Kreyvium to determine appropriate positions of differences and conditions to efficiently prevent the diffusion of differences.

We propose two types of higher-order conditional differential characteristics. The first one observes the bias of higher-order differential characteristics of keystream, i.e. the sum of keystream bits generated by a set of chosen IVs becomes zero. We give a distinguisher on 730-round Kreyvium by using 20-th order conditional differential characteristic with 2^{20} IVs. The second one utilize the *neutrality* of keystreams to find distinguisher as well as Knellwolf et al.'s attack [6], where neutrality means the probability that d-th order conditional differential characteristic equals $(d+1)$-th order conditional differential characteristic. In this case, we obtain a distinguisher on 899-round Kreyvium by using 24-th and 25-th order conditional differential characteristic, whose round is 70 more round than the best attacks of Trivium. Note that all our attacks are experimentally verified. Table 1 summarizes the results of Trivium and our results of Kreyvium. Therefore, we reveal that conditional differential attacks on Kreyvium are much more efficient than Trivium contrary to designer's expectation.

1.2   Paper Organization

This paper is organized as follows. Section 2 explains the description of Kreyvium. In Sect. 3, we describe the conditional differential cryptanalysis for Trivium. In Sect. 4, we propose the conditional differential cryptanalysis for Kreyvium. Section 5 concludes this paper.

2   Description of Kreyvium

Kreyvium, which was proposed by Canteaut et al. in 2016, is a stream cipher for the efficient homomorphic-ciphertext compression [3]. Kreyvium consists of five registers whose size is 93, 84, 111, 128, and 128 bits, respectively. Let $(s_1, s_2, \ldots, s_{93})$, $(s_{94}, s_{95}, \ldots, s_{177})$, $(s_{178}, s_{179}, \ldots, s_{288})$, $(K^*_{127}, K^*_{126}, \ldots, K^*_0)$, and $(IV^*_{127}, IV^*_{126}, \ldots, IV^*_0)$ be states of each register. Kreyvium has 128-bit key and 128-bit initialization vector (IV). Figure 1 shows the structure of Kreyvium. Let k, x, and z be the key and the IV, the keystream, respectively. The algorithm of Kreyvium consists of the key initialization part and the keystream generation part. In the key initialization part, the key and the IV are loaded into registers. The key initialization part initializes them by the update functions. This part is clocked 1152 times. Let t be the number of round Algorithm 1 shows the process of this part. In the keystream generation part, we obtain the keystream from initialized state. Algorithm 2 shows the process of this part.

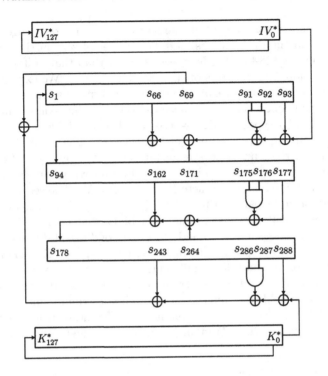

Fig. 1. Kreyvium

3   Conditional Differential Cryptanalysis

Knellwolf et al. showed a conditional differential cryptanalysis for Trivium in 2011 [6]. The conditional differential cryptanalysis is a kind of differential crypt-analyses, and it is well suited for analysis of NLFSR-base ciphers. This attack imposes conditions to prevent differences from spreading and observes a bias of the difference on the keystream bit.

3.1   Overview of Conditional Differential Cryptanalysis

Figure 2 shows the overview of the conditional differential cryptanalysis. Adversaries introduce the difference into the IV and observe the propagation of it. In the key initialization part, they analyze conditions on initial state bits to prevent the propagation of differences. In the end, they obtain the conditional differential characteristic between the initial state and the keystream. When they find a good differential characteristic which appear in the keystream, they can use it as a distinguisher which is able to distinguishing keystreams from random sequence.

Usually, the update function of NLFSR-based stream cipher consists of linear operations and nonlinear operations. Figure 3 shows patterns of the diffusion of differences. If a state bit inputted to the linear operation has a difference, it is

Algorithm 1. Key Initialization

$(s_1, s_2, \ldots, s_{93}) \leftarrow (k_0, k_1, \ldots, k_{92})$

$(s_{94}, s_{95}, \ldots, s_{177}) \leftarrow (x_0, x_1, \ldots, x_{83})$

$(s_{178}, s_{179}, \ldots, s_{288}) \leftarrow (x_{84}, \ldots, x_{127}, 1, \ldots, 1, 0)$

$(K_{127}^*, K_{126}^*, \ldots, K_0^*) \leftarrow (k_0, k_1, \ldots, k_{127})$

$(IV_{127}^*, IV_{126}^*, \ldots, IV_0^*) \leftarrow (x_0, x_1, \ldots, x_{127})$

for $i = 1$ to 1152 do

$\quad t_1 = s_{66} \oplus s_{91} \cdot s_{92} \oplus s_{93} \oplus s_{171} \oplus IV_0^*$

$\quad t_2 = s_{162} \oplus s_{175} \cdot s_{176} \oplus s_{177} \oplus s_{264}$

$\quad t_3 = s_{243} \oplus s_{286} \cdot s_{287} \oplus s_{288} + s_{69} \oplus K_0^*$

$\quad t_4 \leftarrow K_0^*$

$\quad t_5 \leftarrow IV_0^*$

$\quad (s_1, s_2, \ldots, s_{93}) \leftarrow (t_3, s_1, s_2, \ldots, s_{92})$

$\quad (s_{94}, s_{95}, \ldots, s_{177}) \leftarrow (t_1, s_{94}, s_{95}, \ldots, s_{176})$

$\quad (s_{178}, s_{179}, \ldots, s_{288}) \leftarrow (t_2, s_{178}, s_{179}, \ldots, s_{287})$

$\quad (K_{127}^*, K_{126}^*, \ldots, K_0^*) \leftarrow (t_4, K_{127}^*, K_{126}^*, \ldots, K_1^*)$

$\quad (IV_{127}^*, IV_{126}^*, \ldots, IV_0^*) \leftarrow (t_5, IV_{127}^*, IV_{126}^*, \ldots, IV_1^*)$

end for

Algorithm 2. Keystream Generation

for $i = 1$ to N do

$\quad$ output $z \leftarrow s_{66} \oplus s_{93} \oplus s_{162} \oplus s_{177} \oplus s_{243} \oplus s_{288} \oplus K_0^*$

$\quad t_1 = s_{66} \oplus s_{91} \cdot s_{92} \oplus s_{93} \oplus s_{171} \oplus IV_0^*$

$\quad t_2 = s_{162} \oplus s_{175} \cdot s_{176} \oplus s_{177} \oplus s_{264}$

$\quad t_3 = s_{243} \oplus s_{286} \cdot s_{287} \oplus s_{288} \oplus s_{69} \oplus K_0^*$

$\quad t_4 \leftarrow K_0^*$

$\quad t_5 \leftarrow IV_0^*$

$\quad (s_1, s_2, \ldots, s_{93}) \leftarrow (t_3, s_1, s_2, \ldots, s_{92})$

$\quad (s_{94}, s_{95}, \ldots, s_{177}) \leftarrow (t_1, s_{94}, s_{95}, \ldots, s_{176})$

$\quad (s_{178}, s_{179}, \ldots, s_{288}) \leftarrow (t_2, s_{178}, s_{179}, \ldots, s_{287})$

$\quad (K_{127}^*, K_{126}^*, \ldots, K_0^*) \leftarrow (t_4, K_{127}^*, K_{126}^*, \ldots, K_1^*)$

$\quad (IV_{127}^*, IV_{126}^*, \ldots, IV_0^*) \leftarrow (t_5, IV_{127}^*, IV_{126}^*, \ldots, IV_1^*)$

end for

---

surely diffused to output of the update function. If a state bit inputted to the nonlinear operation has the difference, we is not able to know whether output of the update function has a difference without knowledge of values inputted to non linear function. In this case, conditions are imposed to determine the difference of the update bit.

3.2 Higher-Order Differential Characteristics

The attack for Trivium utilizes higher-order conditional differential characteristics. We describe a basic strategy of the analysis for Trivium. Let k and x be a key and IV. Let d be the number of order. Let f be the function of the stream cipher. The d-th differential characteristic of f with respect to $e_1, e_2, \ldots, e_d$ is

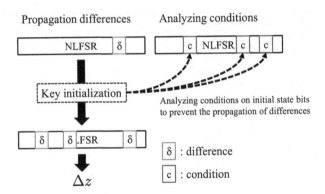

Fig. 2. Overview of conditional differential cryptanalysis in the single-key setting

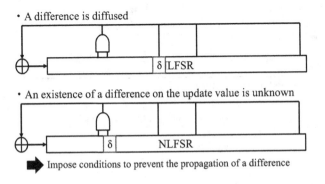

Fig. 3. Patterns of the diffusion of differences

defined as

$$\Delta_{e_1,\ldots,e_d}^{(d)} f(k,x) = \sum_{c \in L(e_1,\ldots,e_d)} f(k, x \oplus c),$$

where $L(e_1,\ldots,e_d)$ is the set of all 2^d linear combinations of $e_1,\ldots,e_d$.

The higher-order conditional differential characteristic $\Delta_{e_1,\ldots,e_d}^{(d)} f(k,x)$ is a characteristic between the initial state and the keystream bit. A distinguisher can be obtained from the bias of $\Delta_{e_1,\ldots,e_d}^{(d)} f(k,x)$. When the IV changes randomly, adversaries observe the bias of $\Delta_{e_1,\ldots,e_d}^{(d)} f(k,x)$. If they find the bias of $\Delta_{e_1,\ldots,e_d}^{(d)} f(k,x)$, they obtain the distinguisher.

Instead of deriving the bias of $\Delta_{e_1,\ldots,e_d}^{(d)} f(k,x)$, adversaries will derive neutral variables for the higher-order conditional differential characteristics. This technique is used in [6]. Let i be the index of the IV, and let e_i be the 1-bit difference at bit position i of x. This attack evaluates a distinguisher by the neutrality of x_i in $\Delta_{e_1,\ldots,e_d}^{(d)} f(k,x)$. This means the probability that $\Delta_{e_1,\ldots,e_d}^{(d)} f(k,x) = \Delta_{e_1,\ldots,e_d}^{(d)} f(k,x \oplus e_i)$ for a random key k. Using a single neutral variable as a distinguisher needs at least two evaluations of $\Delta^{(d)}_{e_1,\ldots,e_d} f(k,x)$. In the case of a d-th order conditional differential characteristic this reveals to 2^{d+1} queries to f. If the neutrality of x_i is p, the resulting distinguishing advantage is $|1/2 - p|$.

Knellwolf et al. obtained the distinguisher for Trivium with 798 rounds and with 961 rounds on the weak-key setting by using 24-th and 25-th order conditional differential characteristic.

4   Conditional Differential Cryptanalysis of Kreyvium

This section shows the conditional differential cryptanalysis for Kreyvium. First of all, we explain our attack strategy, and then we introduce an efficient method to determine appropriate positions of differences and conditions by exploiting degree of freedom of IV and the structure of Kreyvium. Finally we give distinguishers of reduced-round Kreyvium by using higher-order conditional differential characteristics.

4.1   Attack Strategy

In our attack, we utilize higher-order conditional differential characteristics similar to attacks on Trivium. In order to obtain higher-order conditional differential characteristics for NLFSR-based stream ciphers with large number of rounds, we need to properly choose arrangements of differences and conditions in the initial states, and control propagation of differences. In particular, we need to find appropriate positions of differences and conditions to efficiently prevent the diffusion of differences

As mentioned before, an update function of NLFSR-based stream cipher consists of linear operations and nonlinear operations. Figure 4 shows the construction of update functions of Kreyvium. Let S^T be a state of the Kreyvium in round T. Let f_A and f_B be a linear function and nonlinear function, respectively. We define S^T_A and S^T_B for t_1, t_2, and t_3 as a set of bits which is used in f_A and f_B, respectively, where

$$S^T_{A_{t_1}} = \{s_{66}, s_{93}, s_{171}, x_0\},$$

$$S^T_{A_{t_2}} = \{s_{162}, s_{177}, s_{264}\},$$

$$S^T_{A_{t_3}} = \{s_{243}, s_{288}, s_{69}, k_0\},$$

$$S^T_{B_{t_1}} = \{s_{91}, s_{92}\},$$

$$S^T_{B_{t_2}} = \{s_{175}, s_{176}\},$$

$$S^T_{B_{t_3}} = \{s_{286}, s_{287}\}.$$

Then, f_A and f_B for each t are given as

$$f_A(S_{A_{t_1}}^T) = s_{66} \oplus s_{93} \oplus s_{171} \oplus x_0,$$

$$f_B(S_{B_{t_1}}^T) = s_{91} \cdot s_{92},$$

$$f_A(S_{A_{t_2}}^T) = s_{162} \oplus s_{177} \oplus s_{264},$$

$$f_B(S_{B_{t_2}}^T) = s_{175}, s_{176},$$

$$f_A(S_{A_{t_3}}^T) = s_{243} \oplus s_{288} \oplus s_{69} \oplus k_0,$$

$$f_B(S_{B_{t_3}}^T) = s_{286} \cdot s_{287}.$$

The update function of an Kreyvium is given as,

$$(Update) = f_A(S_A^T) \oplus f_B(S_B^T),$$

where the difference of the update value is defined as follows.

$$\Delta(Update) = \Delta f_A(S_A^T) \oplus \Delta f_B(S_B^T)$$

Let us consider how to efficiently prevent the diffusion of differences by exploiting properties of a linear function f_A and nonlinear function f_B.

Linear Function. Since $\Delta f_A(S_A^T)$ is a linear function, output difference of $\Delta f_A(S_A^T)$ is determined from inputs differences. If the number of input bits having a difference are even, these differences are canceled out in $f_A(S_A^T)$, i.e., an output difference of $\Delta f_A(S_A^T)$ becomes zero. Regarding linear function $f_A(S_A^T)$, we try to find *differences* in the initial state which lead to such a event of $\Delta f_A(S_A^T) = 0$.

Nonlinear Function. In the case of $\Delta f_B(S_B^T)$, we are not able to determine an output difference of $\Delta f_B(S_B^T)$ from input differences. However, we can control an output difference of $\Delta f_B(S_B^T)$ by the values of inputs. For example, if only s_{92} has a difference, an output difference of $\Delta f_B(S_{B_{t_1}}^T)$ becomes zero under the condition of $s_{91} = 0$. Thus, we impose conditions to state bits which do not have differences and control the value of $\Delta f_B(S_B^T)$. Regarding nonlinear function $f_B(S_B^T)$, we try to find *conditions of values* in the initial state which lead to such a event of $\Delta f_B(S_B^T) = 0$.

4.2   How to Arrange Differences in Initial State

In order to get an efficient differential characteristic, we determine positions of differences in initial states which prevent the diffusion of differences in linear

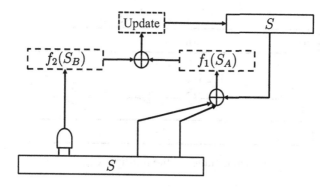

Fig. 4. Construction of the update function of Kreyvium

operations. According to Algorithm 1, state bits of linear operations are given as follows:

$$t_1 : s_{66}, s_{93}, s_{171}$$
$$t_2 : s_{162}, s_{177}, s_{264}$$
$$t_3 : s_{243}, s_{288}, s_{69}.$$

Each bit has following distances,

$$t_1 : 93 - 66 = 27, 171 - 66 = 105, 171 - 93 = 78$$
$$t_2 : 177 - 162 = 15, 264 - 162 = 102, 264 - 177 = 87$$
$$t_3 : 288 - 243 = 45, 243 - 69 = 174, 288 - 69 = 219$$

Interestingly, every distances are multiples of three. Figure 5 shows distances of state bits used for computing t_2. As mentioned before, two differences are XORed, then the result is a zero difference. For example, if s_{66} and s_{93} have differences, the t_1 is given as follows;

$$s_{66} \oplus \Delta s_{66} \oplus s_{93} \oplus \Delta s_{93} = s_{66} \oplus 1 \oplus s_{93} \oplus 1 = s_{66} \oplus s_{93}.$$

In this case, the propagation of differences in the linear function is prevented. If such events happen frequently, we expect to obtain better higher-order differential characteristics. Therefore, *we arrange differences with the distance of multiples of three.*

Next, let us consider that which area in the initial states where differences are inserted is preferable to prevent the diffusion of the differences. In the Kreyvium IV is loaded into registers as follows;

$$(s_{94}, s_{95}, \dots, s_{177}) \leftarrow (x_0, x_1, \dots, x_{83})$$
$$(s_{178}, s_{179}, \dots, s_{288}) \leftarrow (x_{84}, \dots, x_{127}, 1, \dots, 1, 0)$$

We use not only the area of $x_0, x_1, \dots, x_{83}$ but also the area of $x_{84}, \dots, x_{127}$ to arrange differences. According to the algorithm of Kreyvium, in the position of

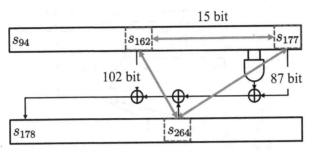

15 bit

Each distance is the multiple of 3

Fig. 5. Distances of state bits (t_2)

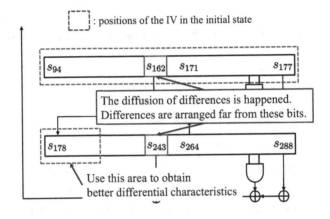

Fig. 6. Concept of the arrangement of differences

s_{162} and s_{243}, a difference is propagated to other states by the update function. Thus, we arrange differences into positions which is far from such bits, namely leftmost bit of the register. Figure 6 shows the concept of the arrangement of differences by exploiting the construction of Kreyvium. Therefore, we divide differences into the register size of 84 and the register size of 111, and arrange differences in bits whose positions are far from s_{162} and s_{243}.

Let j be indices of IV. When d-th order characteristic is used, our attack arranges d-bit differences as follows,

$$j = 3l,$$

where l is $0 \le l \le d/2 - 1$ and $28 \le l \le 28 + (d/2 - 1)$.

4.3   How to Arrange Conditions in Initial State

In the update process of Kreyvium, there are nonlinear operations, namely AND operation, such as $s_{91} \cdot s_{92}$, $s_{175} \cdot s_{176}$, and $s_{286} \cdot s_{287}$. As shown in Sect. 4.1, when

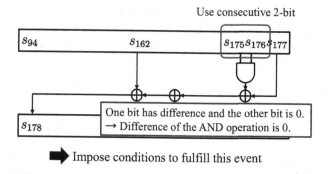

Fig. 7. How to impose conditions to the nonlinear operation

one bit has the difference and the other bit has the condition, we can control the value of the difference of nonlinear operations. Figure 7 shows how to impose conditions to nonlinear operations. Let a and b be state bits. Let Δa be the difference of a. The difference of output of the operation of $a \cdot b$ is $\Delta a \cdot b$ because $(a \oplus \Delta a) \cdot b = ab \oplus \Delta a \cdot b$. If b is zero, $\Delta a \cdot b$ is zero. Moreover, these operations use the consecutive 2 bits of the state, e.g. s_{175} and s_{176}. Therefore, when a bit of state bit except the leftmost bit and the rightmost bit of the register has a difference, we arrange zero values into both the former and later of the state bit. For example, when s_{176} has the difference in the initial state, we impose conditions such as $s_{175} = s_{177} = 0$. Additionally, when the leftmost bit s_{178} has the difference in the initial state, we impose conditions such as $s_{162} = 0$, $s_{176} = 0$, and $s_{177} = 1$ to get $t_2 = 0$ in the first round.

Therefore, for d-th order characteristic, our attack arranges $2(d-1)$-bit conditions in the initial state as follows,

$$j = 3m - 1$$
$$j = 3n + 1$$

where m is $1 \leq l \leq d/2 - 1$ and $29 \leq l \leq 28 + (d/2 - 1)$, and n is $0 \leq n \leq d/2 - 1$ and $28 \leq n \leq 28 + (d/2 - 1)$.

4.4 Distinguisher for Kreyvium

We show the distinguisher of the first output keystream bit by using the higher-order conditional differential characteristic.

As shown in Sect. 3, we obtain higher-order differential characteristics as follows. The d-th differential characteristic of f with respect to $e_1, e_2, \ldots, e_d$ is defined as

$$\Delta_{e_1, \ldots, e_d}^{(d)} f(k, x) = \sum_{c \in L(e_1, \ldots, e_d)} f(k, x \oplus c),$$

where $L(e_1, \ldots, e_d)$ is the set of all 2^d linear combinations of $e_1, \ldots, e_d$.

Zero-Sum Distinguisher. Let us use the parameter of $d = 20$, namely 20-th order conditional differential characteristics. In this case, we arrange 20-bit differences by using the rule in Sect. 4.2 and impose 38-bit conditions obtained in Sect. 4.3 as follows:

$$\text{Differences} : x_j \ \ j = 3l \text{ for } 0 \le l \le 9 \text{ and } 28 \le l \le 37$$
$$\text{Conditions} : x_j \ \ j = 3m - 1 \text{ for } 1 \le m \le 9 \text{ and } 29 \le m \le 37$$
$$j = 3n + 1 \text{ for } 0 \le n \le 9 \text{ and } 28 \le n \le 37$$

Since $x_{84} = s_{178}$ has the difference, we additionally impose $x_{68} = 0$, $x_{82} = 0$, and $x_{83} = 1$. Then we find the bias of $\Delta_{e_1,\ldots,e_d}^{(d)} f(k, x) = 0$ with probability one after 730 key initialization rounds. We actually do experiments with 128 different keys and 2^{10} different IVs, and confirm that our distinguisher works in any pair of key and IVs. We evaluate time complexity of our attack. The bias of $\Delta_{e_1,\ldots,e_d}^{(d)} f(k, x) = 0$ is obtained with probability one in our attack. In random case, this event happen with probability $1/2$. When we perform our distinguisher for N times, the success probability is $1 - (1/2)^N$. Then, time complexity of our attack is given by $N \cdot 2^{20}$. Therefore, we can distinguish Kreyvium from random source up to 730 rounds with time complexity of $N \cdot 2^{20}$ and 2^{20} IVs. If N is 2^{10}, time complexity of our attack is given by 2^{30}. It takes eight hours to find our distinguisher with one CPU core (Intel(R) Core(TM) i7 CPU 4771@ 3.50Ghz).

Neutrality Distinguisher. We evaluate the neutrality of $\Delta_{e_1,\ldots,e_d}^{(d)} f(k, x)$ to find the distinguisher. In this case, we use the parameter of $d = 24$ and $d = 25$, namely 24-th and 25-th order conditional differential characteristics.

First, we arrange 24-bit differences and 48-bit conditions are given as follows:

$$\text{Differences} : x_j \ \ j = 3l \text{ for } 0 \le l \le 11 \text{ and } 28 \le l \le 39$$
$$\text{Conditions} : x_j \ \ j = 3m - 1 \text{ for } 1 \le m \le 11 \text{ and } 29 \le m \le 40$$
$$j = 3n + 1 \text{ for } 0 \le n \le 11 \text{ and } 28 \le n \le 40$$

Since $x_{84} = s_{178}$ has the difference, we additionally impose $x_{68} = 0$, $x_{82} = 0$, and $x_{83} = 1$. In this case, we arrange conditions for $d = 25$ because we use 25-th order conditional differential characteristics in later.

Second, we arrange 25-bit differences and 48-bit conditions are given as follows:

$$\text{Differences} : x_j \ \ j = 3l \text{ for } 0 \le l \le 11 \text{ and } 28 \le l \le 40$$

The arrangement of conditions is similar to the case of 24-bit. In this case, we have 25-bit differences and 51-bit conditions. Then, we have $128 - (25 + 51) = 52$-bit IVs which can be chosen freely. We evaluate the neutrality of 24-th and 25-th order conditional differential characteristics. In our attack, we can evaluate the neutrality by using the constant key because 52-bit IVs can be chosen freely. We do experiments with 492 different keys and 2^7 different IVs, and obtain the average of biases. From the average of bias, we find the bias of neutrality with probability 0.53435 after 899 key initialization rounds. Based on this bias, the number of samples for a distinguishing attack is given by Theorem 1.

Theorem 1 [8]. *Let X and Y be the distributions, and suppose that the event e happens in X with probability p and in Y with probability $p \cdot (1 + q)$. Then for small p and q, $O(\frac{1}{p \cdot q^2})$ samples suffice to distinguish X from Y with a constant probability of success.*

In this case, p and q are given as $p = 1/2$ and $q = 0.03435$. The number of samples is $\frac{1}{pq^2} = 424$. Then, time complexity of our attack is given by $2^{25} \cdot 2^7 \cdot 424 \approx 2^{40.728}$. It takes 32 hours to find our distinguisher with one CPU core (Intel(R) Core(TM) i7 CPU 4771@ 3.50Ghz).

5   Conclusion

This paper showed the conditional differential cryptanalysis for Kreyvium. Our method was inspired by the attack for Trivium. In Kreyvium, the IV is loaded into two registers of sizes 84 and 111 bits. We proposed how to arrange differences and conditions based on this structure. Our arrangement of differences and conditions could obtain good conditional differential characteristics. We proposed two types of higher-order conditional differential characteristics to find the distinguisher, i.e. the bias of higher-order conditional differential characteristics of keystream and the *neutrality* of keystreams. In the first one, the biases were found, and we obtained the distinguisher on Kreyvium with 730 rounds by using 20-th order conditional differential characteristic. In the second one, we found the specific neutrality and obtained the distinguisher on Kreyvium with 899 rounds by using 24-th and 25-th order conditional differential characteristic. As a result, Kreyvium is weak for the conditional differential cryptanalysis compared with Trivium.

Acknowledgments. This work was supported in part by Grant-in-Aid for Scientific Research (C) (KAKENHI 26330155, 17K12698) for Japan Society for the Promotion of Science.

References

1. Aumasson, J.-P., Dinur, I., Meier, W., Shamir, A.: Cube testers and key recovery attacks on reduced-round MD6 and Trivium. In: Dunkelman, O. (ed.) FSE 2009. LNCS, vol. 5665, pp. 1–22. Springer, Heidelberg (2009). doi:10.1007/978-3-642-03317-9_1
2. Cannière, C.: Trivium: a stream cipher construction inspired by block cipher design principles. In: Katsikas, S.K., López, J., Backes, M., Gritzalis, S., Preneel, B. (eds.) ISC 2006. LNCS, vol. 4176, pp. 171–186. Springer, Heidelberg (2006). doi:10.1007/11836810_13

3. Canteaut, A., Carpov, S., Fontaine, C., Lepoint, T., Naya-Plasencia, M., Paillier, P., Sirdey, R.: Stream ciphers: a practical solution for efficient homomorphicciphertext compression. In: Peyrin, T. (ed.) FSE 2016. LNCS, vol. 9783, pp. 313–333. Springer, Heidelberg (2016). doi:10.1007/978-3-662-52993-5_16

4. Dinur, I., Shamir, A.: Cube attacks on tweakable black box polynomials. In: Joux, A. (ed.) EUROCRYPT 2009. LNCS, vol. 5479, pp. 278–299. Springer, Heidelberg (2009). doi:10.1007/978-3-642-01001-9_16

5. Fouque, P.-A., Vannet, T.: Improving key recovery to 784 and 799 rounds of Trivium using optimized cube attacks. In: Moriai, S. (ed.) FSE 2013. LNCS, vol. 8424, pp. 502–517. Springer, Heidelberg (2014). doi:10.1007/978-3-662-43933-3_26

6. Knellwolf, S., Meier, W., Naya-Plasencia, M.: Conditional differential cryptanalysis of Trivium and KATAN. In: Miri, A., Vaudenay, S. (eds.) SAC 2011. LNCS, vol. 7118, pp. 200–212. Springer, Heidelberg (2012). doi:10.1007/978-3-642-28496-0_12

7. Liu, M., Lin, D., Wang, W.: Searching cubes for testing boolean functions and its application to Trivium. In: IEEE International Symposium on Information Theory, ISIT 2015, pp. 496–500 (2015)

8. Mantin, I., Shamir, A.: A practical attack on broadcast RC4. In: Matsui, M. (ed.) FSE 2001. LNCS, vol. 2355, pp. 152–164. Springer, Heidelberg (2002). doi:10.1007/3-540-45473-X_13

9. Sarkar, S., Maitra, S., Baksi, A.: Observing biases in the state: case studies with Trivium and Trivia-SC. Des. Codes Cryptogr. 82(1), 351–375 (2017). http://dx.doi.org/10.1007/s10623-016-0211-x

10. Stankovski, P.: Greedy distinguishers and nonrandomness detectors. In: Gong, G., Gupta, K.C. (eds.) INDOCRYPT 2010. LNCS, vol. 6498, pp. 210–226. Springer, Heidelberg (2010). doi:10.1007/978-3-642-17401-8_16

Digital Signatures

Practical Strongly Invisible and Strongly Accountable Sanitizable Signatures

Michael Till Beck[1], Jan Camenisch[2]([✉]), David Derler[3], Stephan Krenn[4],
Henrich C. Pöhls[5], Kai Samelin[2,6], and Daniel Slamanig[3]

[1] Ludwig-Maximilians-Universität München, Munich, Germany
michael.beck@ifi.lmu.de
[2] IBM Research – Zurich, Rüschlikon, Switzerland
{jca,ksa}@zurich.ibm.com
[3] IAIK, Graz University of Technology, Graz, Austria
{david.derler,daniel.slamanig}@tugraz.at
[4] AIT Austrian Institute of Technology GmbH, Vienna, Austria
stephan.krenn@ait.ac.at
[5] ISL and Chair of IT-Security, University of Passau, Passau, Germany
hp@sec.uni-passau.de
[6] TU Darmstadt, Darmstadt, Germany

Abstract. Sanitizable signatures are a variant of digital signatures
where a designated party (the sanitizer) can update admissible parts
of a signed message. At PKC'17, Camenisch et al. introduced the notion
of *invisible* sanitizable signatures that hides from an outsider which parts
of a message are admissible. Their security definition of invisibility, however, does not consider dishonest signers. Along the same lines, their
signer-accountability definition does not prevent the signer from falsely
accusing the sanitizer of having issued a signature on a sanitized message by exploiting the malleability of the signature itself. Both issues
may limit the usefulness of their scheme in certain applications.

We revise their definitional framework, and present a new construction eliminating these shortcomings. In contrast to Camenisch et al.'s
construction, ours requires only standard building blocks instead of
chameleon hashes with ephemeral trapdoors. This makes this, now even
stronger, primitive more attractive for practical use. We underpin the
practical efficiency of our scheme by concrete benchmarks of a prototype
implementation.

1 Introduction

Digital signatures are an important means to protect the integrity and authenticity of digital data. Ordinary digital signatures are all-or-nothing in the sense

The full version of this paper is available at the IACR Cryptology ePrint Archive.
J. Camenisch and K. Samelin were supported by the EU ERC PERCY, grant
agreement n° 32131. D. Derler, S. Krenn, H. C. Pöhls and D. Slamanig were
supported by EU H2020 project PRISMACLOUD: This project has received funding
from the European Union's Horizon 2020 research and innovation programme under
grant agreement n° 644962.

© Springer International Publishing AG 2017
J. Pieprzyk and S. Suriadi (Eds.): ACISP 2017, Part I, LNCS 10342, pp. 437–452, 2017.
DOI: 10.1007/978-3-319-60055-0_23

that once a message has been signed, it is only possible to verify whether the signature is valid for the entire original message or not. In particular, it is not possible to update (parts of) a signed message in a determined manner without invalidating the signature. However, there are many real-life use cases in which a subsequent modification of the signed data by some designated entity is desired. As an illustrative example consider a patient record that is signed by a medical doctor. The accountant, tasked to charge an insurance company, requires authentic information about the treatments and the patient's insurance number, but not of other parts of the patient record. Clearly, when using conventional digital signatures to guarantee the authenticity of the patient record, far too much information is revealed to the accountant. One solution to avoid such privacy intrusive practices would require the doctor to re-sign only the data relevant for the accountant. However, this would have to be repeated every time a new subset of the record needs to be forwarded to some party that demands authentic information. Especially, this would induce too much overhead to be practical in real scenarios, or may even be impossible due to loss of availability of the doctor for signing subsets from old documents.

Sanitizable signature schemes (SSS) [2] allow for such controlled modifications of signed messages without invalidating the signature. In fact, they are more general than strictly needed by the given example: when signing, the signer determines which blocks $m[i]$ of the message $m = (m[1], m[2], \ldots, m[i], \ldots, m[\ell])$ can be updated (i.e., are flagged *admissible*). Any such admissible block can later be changed to a different bitstring $m[i]' \in \{0,1\}^*$, where $i \in \{1, 2, \ldots, \ell\}$, by a designated party named the *sanitizer*. The sanitizer is represented by a public key. The sanitization process requires the corresponding private key, but does not require the signer's involvement. Sanitization of a message m results in an altered message $m' = (m[1]', m[2]', \ldots, m[i]', \ldots, m[\ell]')$, where $m[i] = m[i]'$ for every non-admissible block, and also a signature σ', which verifies under the given public keys. Hence, authenticity of the message m' is still ensured. Coming back to the above example, playing the role of the sanitizer, a server storing the signed patient records is able to black-out the sensitive parts of a signed patient record, without any additional communication with the doctor, and, in particular, without access to doctor's signing key.

Concrete real-world applications of SSSs include secure routing, privacy-preserving document disclosure, anonymous credentials, group content protection, and blank signatures [2,10–12,17,18,21,31].

Motivation. Recently, the property of invisibility was proposed by Camenisch et al. [13] as a very strong notion of privacy for SSS.[1] Informally, this property guarantees that an outsider cannot even decide which blocks of a signed message are admissible. This property is especially useful, if it must be hidden which parts of a signed message can be changed by a sanitizer. However, their invisibility definition is weak in the sense that it is not possible to query the

---

[1] Their idea dates back to the original paper by Ateniese et al. [2], which name this property "strong transparency" (cf. Pöhls et al. for a discussion [41]). However, they neither provide a formal definition nor a provably secure construction.

sanitization oracle for keys different from the challenged ones. Thus, as soon as the adversary gains access to a sanitization oracle, it may be able to decide this question, which may be too limiting, or surprising, in certain use-cases. This is in particular relevant, if a sanitizer needs to sanitize messages from multiple signers: in one of their application scenarios, a cloud-service is used to outsource some computations. The results, however, need to be signed by the outsourcing party. Using SSSs, the cloud can sanitize a signed message, and input the result of the computation. However, it must remain hidden which computations are outsourced to protect trade secrets. This is precisely captured by the invisibility property. However, if the cloud-service uses the same key pair for multiple clients, Camenisch et al.'s [13] definition is not sufficient. Moreover, their construction does not achieve "strong signer-accountability", as defined by Krenn et al. [35]. Namely, they do not prevent the signer from exploiting the malleability of previously seen sanitized signatures to accuse the sanitizer of having created one particular signature. We stress that this only addresses the signature; the message in question still needs to be issued by the sanitizer at some point. We stress that this limitation is explicitly mentioned by Camenisch et al. [13]. Nonetheless, lacking both properties may lead to some practical issues. For "strong signer-accountability", this was already pointed out by Krenn et al. [35], and thus it is desirable to achieve the strengthened properties.

Contribution. Our contribution is manifold. (1) We present a strengthened invisibility definition dubbed *strong* invisibility, which even protects against dishonest signers. (2) We present a provably secure construction of strongly invisible sanitizable signatures, which (3) also achieves a stronger accountability notion compared to the construction by Camenisch et al. [13]. In particular, we exclude the malleability of the signatures, even for signers. This makes our construction suitable for a broader range of applications. Moreover, (4) our construction does not require chameleon-hashes with ephemeral trapdoors, and can thus be considered simpler than the one in [13], as only standard primitives are required. In more detail, the construction is solely based on unique signatures, labeled CCA2-secure encryption schemes, and collision-resistant chameleon-hashes, paired with a special and novel way to generate randomness for the chameleon-hashes. Finally, (5) to demonstrate that our construction is practical, we have implemented it. The evaluation shows that the primitive is efficient enough for most use-cases.

Related Work and State-of-the-Art. SSSs have been introduced by Ateniese et al. [2], and later most of the current security properties were introduced by Brzuska et al. [8] (with some later refinements due to Gong et al. [30]). Later on, additional properties such as (strong) unlinkability [10,12,26], and non-interactive public accountability [11,12] were introduced. Quite recently, Krenn et al. further refined the security properties to also account for the signatures in analogy to the strong unforgeability of conventional signatures [35].

Invisibility of SSS, formalized by Camenisch et al. [13], prohibits that an outsider can decide which blocks are admissible, dating back to the original ideas by Ateniese et al. [2]. We extend their work, and use the aforementioned results as our starting point for the strengthened definitions. Miyazaki et al. also introduce invisibility of sanitizable signatures [38]. However, they actually address the related, but different [37], concept of redactable signatures [7,22,33,42,43].

Also, several extensions such as limiting the sanitizer to certain values [15,23,34,41], SSSs which allow the signer to add new sanitizers after signing [17,44], SSSs for multi-sanitizer and multi-signer environments [9,12,16], as well as sanitization of signed encrypted data [19,25] have been considered. SSSs have also been used as a tool to make other primitives accountable [40], and to construct other primitives, such as redactable signatures [6,37]. Also, SSSs for data-structures that are more complex than simple lists have been considered [41]. Our results carry over to the aforementioned extended settings with only minor additional adjustments. Implementations of SSSs are also presented, proving that this primitive is practical [11,12,36,39].

Finally, we note that computing on signed messages is a much broader field, and refer to [1,7,20,28,29] for comprehensive overviews of other related primitives.

2   Preliminaries

Let us give our notation, assumptions, and the required building blocks, first. All formal security definitions are given in the full version of this paper.

Notation. The main security parameter is denoted by $\lambda \in \mathbb{N}$. All algorithms implicitly take 1^λ as an additional input. We write $a \leftarrow A(x)$ if a is assigned to the output of algorithm A with input x. If we use external random coins r, we use the notation $a \leftarrow A(x; r)$, where $r \in \{0,1\}^\lambda$. An algorithm is efficient if it runs in probabilistic polynomial time (ppt) in the length of its input. For the remainder of this paper, all algorithms are ppt if not explicitly mentioned otherwise. Most algorithms may return a special error symbol $\bot \notin \{0,1\}^*$, denoting an exception. If S is a set, we write $a \leftarrow S$ to denote that a is chosen uniformly at random from S. For a message $m = (m[1], m[2], \ldots, m[\ell])$, we call $m[i]$ a block, while $\ell \in \mathbb{N}$ denotes the number of blocks in a message m. For a list we require that we have a unique, injective, and efficiently reversible, encoding, mapping the list to $\{0,1\}^*$. In the definitions, we speak of a general message space $\mathcal{M}$ to be as generic as possible. For our instantiations, however, we let the message space $\mathcal{M}$ be $\{0,1\}^*$ to reduce unhelpful boilerplate notation. A function $\nu : \mathbb{N} \to \mathbb{R}_{\geq 0}$ is negligible, if it vanishes faster than every inverse polynomial, i.e., $\forall k \in \mathbb{N}$, $\exists n_0 \in \mathbb{N}$ such that $\nu(n) \leq n^{-k}$, $\forall n > n_0$. For certain security properties we require that values only have one canonical representation, e.g., a "2" is not the same as a "02", even if written as elements of $\mathbb{N}$.

We assume that the reader is familiar with IND-CCA2 secure labeled encryption-schemes, pseudo-random functions, unique strongly-unforgeable digital signatures, and pseudo-random generators. Formal definitions are given in the full version of this paper.

Chameleon-Hashes. The given framework is based upon the work done by Camenisch et al. [13].

Definition 1. *A chameleon-hash* CH *is a tuple of five ppt algorithms* (CHPGen, CHKGen, CHash, CHCheck, CHAdapt), *such that:*

CHPGen. *The algorithm* CHPGen *outputs public parameters of the scheme:* $\mathsf{pp_{ch}} \leftarrow \mathsf{CHPGen}(1^\lambda)$. *For brevity, we assume that* $\mathsf{pp_{ch}}$ *is implicit input to all other algorithms.*

CHKGen. *The algorithm* CHKGen *given the public parameters* $\mathsf{pp_{ch}}$ *outputs the private, and public, keys of the scheme:* $(\mathsf{sk_{ch}}, \mathsf{pk_{ch}}) \leftarrow \mathsf{CHKGen}(\mathsf{pp_{ch}})$.

CHash. *The algorithm* CHash *gets as input the public key* $\mathsf{pk_{ch}}$, *and a message* m *to hash. It outputs a hash* h, *and some randomness* r: $(h, r) \leftarrow \mathsf{CHash}(\mathsf{pk_{ch}}, m)$.[2]

CHCheck. *The deterministic algorithm* CHCheck *gets as input the public key* $\mathsf{pk_{ch}}$, *a message* m, *randomness* r, *and a hash* h. *It outputs a decision* $d \in \{0, 1\}$ *indicating whether the hash* h *is valid:* $d \leftarrow \mathsf{CHCheck}(\mathsf{pk_{ch}}, m, r, h)$.

CHAdapt. *The algorithm* CHAdapt *on input of secret key* $\mathsf{sk_{ch}}$, *the message* m, *the randomness* r, *hash* h, *and a new message* m' *outputs new randomness* r': $r' \leftarrow \mathsf{CHAdapt}(\mathsf{sk_{ch}}, m, m', r, h)$.

The correctness and formal security definitions are given in the full paper.

Definition 2 (Secure Chameleon-Hashes). *We call a chameleon-hash* CH *secure, if it is correct, indistinguishable, collision-resistant, and unique.*

RSA Instance Generator. Let $(n, p, q, e, d) \leftarrow \mathsf{RSAKGen}(1^\lambda)$ be an instance generator which returns an RSA modulus $n = pq$, where p and q are distinct primes, $e > n'$ an integer co-prime to $\varphi(n)$, and $de \equiv 1 \bmod \varphi(n)$. Here, n' is the largest RSA modulus possible w.r.t. λ. It is assumed that e is prime and chosen independently of p and q, while d is calculated from e, and not vice versa.

The Chameleon-Hash by Camenisch et al. [13]. Next, as Construction 1, we restate the construction by Camenisch et al. [13], which is secure, if the one-more RSA-Assumption [4] holds. Now, let CH := (CHPGen, CHKGen, CHash, CHCheck, CHAdapt) as defined in Construction 1. $\mathcal{H}_n : \{0, 1\}^* \to \mathbb{Z}_n^*$, with $n \in \mathbb{N}$, denotes a random oracle. Each n is implicitly required to have λ bits. This is not explicitly checked in the algorithms.

---

[2] The randomness r is also sometimes called "check value" [3].

CHPGen(1^λ): Call RSAKGen with the restriction $e > n'$, and e prime. Return e.
CHKGen(pp_{ch}): Generate p, q using RSAKGen(1^λ). Let $n = pq$. Compute d such that $ed \equiv 1 \bmod \varphi(n)$. Return ($sk_{ch}, pk_{ch}$) = (d, n).
CHash(pk_{ch}, m): Draw $r \leftarrow \mathbb{Z}_n^*$. If external random coins r' is used, one can use the random oracle, i.e., $r \leftarrow \mathcal{H}_n(r')$. Let $h \leftarrow \mathcal{H}_n(m)r^e \bmod n$. Return (h, r).
CHCheck(pk_{ch}, m, r, h'): If $r \notin \mathbb{Z}_n^*$, return 0. Let $h \leftarrow \mathcal{H}_n(m)r^e \bmod n$. Return 1, if $h = h'$, and 0 otherwise.
CHAdapt(sk_{ch}, m, m', r, h): If CHCheck(pk_{ch}, m, r, h) = 0, return $\perp$. If $m = m'$, return r. Let $g \leftarrow \mathcal{H}_n(m)$, $y \leftarrow gr^e \bmod n$, and $g' \leftarrow \mathcal{H}_n(m')$. Return $r' \leftarrow (y(g'^{-1}))^d \bmod n$.

Construction 1. Secure CH

3   Stronger Invisible Sanitizable Signatures

We now present our framework for strongly invisible sanitizable signatures, along with the strengthened security model, and a provably secure construction based on only standard primitives.

3.1   The Framework for Sanitizable Signature Schemes

Subsequently, we introduce the framework for SSSs. The definitions are essentially the ones given by Camenisch et al. [13], which are itself based on existing work [2,8,11,12,30,35]. However, due to our goals, we need to re-define the security experiments. Like Camenisch et al. [13], we do not consider "non-interactive public accountability" [11,12,32], which allows a third party to decide which party is accountable, instead transparency is achieved, which is mutually exclusive to this property. However, it remains elegantly easy to achieve, e.g., by signing the signature again [11,13].

For brevity, we now set some additional notation. This notation is based on existing definitions, making reading more comfortable [8,13]. The variable ADM contains the set of indices of the modifiable blocks, as well as ℓ denoting the total number of blocks in the message m. We write ADM(m) = 1, if ADM is valid w.r.t. m, i.e., ADM contains the correct ℓ and all indices are in m. For example, let ADM = $(\{1, 2, 4\}, 4)$. Then, m must contain four blocks, and all but the third are admissible. If we write $m_i \in$ ADM, we mean that m_i is admissible. MOD is a set containing pairs $(i, m[i]')$ for those blocks that are modified, meaning that $m[i]$ is replaced with $m[i]'$. We write MOD(ADM) = 1, if MOD is valid w.r.t. ADM, meaning that the indices to be modified are contained in ADM. To allow for a compact presentation of our construction, we write $\bar{X}_{n,m}$, with $n \leq m$, for the vector $(X_n, X_{n+1}, X_{n+2}, \ldots, X_{m-1}, X_m)$.

Definition 3 (Sanitizable Signatures).   *A sanitizable signature scheme SSS consists of the ppt algorithms* (SSSPGen, KGen$_{sig}$, KGen$_{san}$, Sign, Sanit, Verify, Proof, Judge) *such that:*

SSSPGen. *The algorithm* SSSPGen, *on input security parameter* λ, *generates the public parameters:* $\mathsf{pp_{sss}} \leftarrow \mathsf{SSSPGen}(1^\lambda)$. *We assume that* $\mathsf{pp_{sss}}$ *is implicitly input to all other algorithms.*

KGen$_{\mathsf{sig}}$. *The algorithm* KGen$_{\mathsf{sig}}$ *takes the public parameters* $\mathsf{pp_{sss}}$, *and returns the signer's private key and the corresponding public key:* $(\mathsf{sk_{sig}}, \mathsf{pk_{sig}}) \leftarrow$ KGen$_{\mathsf{sig}}(\mathsf{pp_{sss}})$.

KGen$_{\mathsf{san}}$. *The algorithm* KGen$_{\mathsf{san}}$ *takes the public parameters* $\mathsf{pp_{sss}}$, *and returns the sanitizer's private key as well as the corresponding public key:* $(\mathsf{sk_{san}}, \mathsf{pk_{san}}) \leftarrow$ KGen$_{\mathsf{san}}(\mathsf{pp_{sss}})$.

Sign. *The algorithm* Sign *takes as input a message* m, $\mathsf{sk_{sig}}$, $\mathsf{pk_{san}}$, *as well as a description* ADM *of the admissible blocks. If* $\mathrm{ADM}(m) = 0$, *this algorithm returns* $\bot$. *It outputs a signature* $\sigma \leftarrow$ Sign$(m, \mathsf{sk_{sig}}, \mathsf{pk_{san}}, \mathrm{ADM})$.

Sanit. *The algorithm* Sanit *takes a message* m, *modification instruction* MOD, *a signature* σ, $\mathsf{pk_{sig}}$, *and* $\mathsf{sk_{san}}$. *It outputs* m' *together with* σ': $(m', \sigma') \leftarrow$ Sanit$(m, \mathrm{MOD}, \sigma, \mathsf{pk_{sig}}, \mathsf{sk_{san}})$ *where* $m' \leftarrow \mathrm{MOD}(m)$ *is message* m *modified according to the modification instruction* MOD.

Verify. *The algorithm* Verify *takes as input the signature* σ *for a message* m *w.r.t. the public keys* $\mathsf{pk_{sig}}$, *and* $\mathsf{pk_{san}}$. *It outputs a decision* $d \in \{1, 0\}$: $d \leftarrow$ Verify$(m, \sigma, \mathsf{pk_{sig}}, \mathsf{pk_{san}})$.

Proof. *The algorithm* Proof *takes as input* $\mathsf{sk_{sig}}$, *a message* m, *a signature* σ, *a set of polynomially many additional message/signature pairs* $\{(m_i, \sigma_i)\}$, *and* $\mathsf{pk_{san}}$. *It outputs a string* $\pi \in \{0, 1\}^*$ *which can be used by the* Judge *to decide which party is accountable given a message/signature pair* (m, σ): $\pi \leftarrow$ Proof$(\mathsf{sk_{sig}}, m, \sigma, \{(m_i, \sigma_i) \mid i \in \mathbb{N}\}, \mathsf{pk_{san}})$.

Judge. *The algorithm* Judge *takes as input a message* m, *a signature* σ, $\mathsf{pk_{sig}}$, $\mathsf{pk_{san}}$, *as well as a proof* π. *Note, this means that once a proof* π *is generated, the accountable party can be derived by anyone for that message/signature pair* (m, σ). *It outputs a decision* $d \in \{\mathsf{Sig}, \mathsf{San}\}$, *indicating whether the message/signature pair has been created by the signer, or the sanitizer:* $d \leftarrow$ Judge$(m, \sigma, \mathsf{pk_{sig}}, \mathsf{pk_{san}}, \pi)$.

Correctness of Sanitizable Signature Schemes. The usual correctness requirements must hold, i.e., every signed and sanitized message/signature pair should verify, while a honestly generated proof on a honestly generated message/signature pair points to the correct accountable party. We refer to Brzuska et al. [8] for a formal definition, which straightforwardly extends to this framework.

3.2 Security of Sanitizable Signature Schemes

Next, we introduce the security model, based on the work done by Camenisch et al. [13], but extended to account for our new insights. In other words, we strengthen their invisibility notion, and achieve *strong* signer-accountability [35].

Due to space requirements, we only sketch the security properties we do not alter. The formal definitions are given in the full version of this paper.

Unforgeability. No one should be able to generate any new signature not seen before without having access to any private keys.

Immutability. Sanitizers must only be able to perform allowed modifications. In particular, a sanitizer must not be able to modify non-admissible blocks.

Privacy. Similar to semantic security for encryption schemes, privacy captures the inability of an attacker to derive any knowledge about sanitized parts.

Transparency. An attacker cannot tell whether a specific message/signature pair has been sanitized or not.

Sanitizer-Accountability. For sanitizer-accountability, a sanitizer should not be able to accuse a signer if the signer is actually not responsible for a given message/signature pair.

Experiment SSig-Accountability$_{\mathcal{A}}^{SSS}(\lambda)$

   $pp_{sss} \leftarrow SSSPGen(1^{\lambda})$
   $(sk_{san}, pk_{san}) \leftarrow KGen_{san}(pp_{sss})$
   $(pk^*, \pi^*, m^*, \sigma^*) \leftarrow \mathcal{A}^{Sanit(\cdot,\cdot,\cdot,\cdot,sk_{san})}(pk_{san})$
      for $i = 1, 2, \ldots, q$ let (m_i', σ_i') and $(m_i, MOD_i, \sigma_i, pk_{sig,i})$
         index the answers/queries from/to Sanit
      return 1, if $Verify(m^*, \sigma^*, pk^*, pk_{san}) = 1 \wedge$
         $\forall i \in \{1, 2, \ldots, q\} : (pk^*, m^*, \sigma^*) \neq (pk_{sig,i}, m_i', \sigma_i') \wedge$
         $Judge(m^*, \sigma^*, pk^*, pk_{san}, \pi^*) = San$
      return 0

Fig. 1. SSS strong signer-accountability

Definition 4 (Strong Signer-Accountability). *An SSS is strongly signer-accountable, if for any ppt adversary $\mathcal{A}$ there exists a negligible function ν such that* $\Pr[SSig\text{-}Accountability_{\mathcal{A}}^{SSS}(\lambda) = 1] \leq \nu(\lambda)$, *where the experiment is defined in Fig. 1.*

3.3   Strong Invisibility of SSSs

Subsequently, we introduce the property of *strong* invisibility. The definition is derived from the one given by Camenisch et al. [13], but allows queries to the sanitization oracle with all adversarially chosen public keys.

In a nutshell, the adversary can query an LoRADM oracle which either makes ADM_0 or ADM_1 admissible in the final signature. Of course, the adversary has to be restricted to $ADM_0 \cap ADM_1$ for sanitization requests for signatures originating from those created by LoRADM, and their derivatives, to avoid trivial attacks with the challenge key. However, compared to the original definition, we do not restrict that the signer public key is the challenge one. Moreover, as in the original definition, the sign oracle can be simulated by querying the LoRADM oracle with $ADM_0 = ADM_1$.

Definition 5 (Strong Invisibility). *An SSS is strongly invisible, if for any ppt adversary $\mathcal{A}$ there exists a negligible function ν such that* $\left| \Pr[SInvisibility_{\mathcal{A}}^{SSS}(\lambda) = 1] - \frac{1}{2} \right| \leq \nu(\lambda)$, *where the corresponding experiment is defined in Fig. 2.*

Experiment $\mathsf{SInvisibility}_{\mathcal{A}}^{\mathsf{SSS}}(\lambda)$
   $\mathsf{pp_{sss}} \leftarrow \mathsf{SSSPGen}(1^\lambda)$
   $(\mathsf{sk_{sig}}, \mathsf{pk_{sig}}) \leftarrow \mathsf{KGen_{sig}}(\mathsf{pp_{sss}})$
   $(\mathsf{sk_{san}}, \mathsf{pk_{san}}) \leftarrow \mathsf{KGen_{san}}(\mathsf{pp_{sss}})$
   $b \leftarrow \{0, 1\}$
   $\mathcal{Q} \leftarrow \emptyset$
   $a \leftarrow \mathcal{A}^{\mathsf{Sanit}'(\cdot,\cdot,\cdot,\cdot,\mathsf{sk_{san}}),\mathsf{Proof}(\mathsf{sk_{sig}},\cdot,\cdot,\cdot,\cdot),\mathsf{LoRADM}(\cdot,\cdot,\cdot,\cdot,\mathsf{sk_{sig}},b)}(\mathsf{pk_{sig}}, \mathsf{pk_{san}})$
      where oracle LoRADM on input of $m, \mathrm{ADM}_0, \mathrm{ADM}_1, \mathsf{pk_{san}'}, \mathsf{sk_{sig}}, b$:
         return $\perp$, if $\mathrm{ADM}_0(m) \neq \mathrm{ADM}_1(m)$
         return $\perp$, if $\mathsf{pk_{san}} \neq \mathsf{pk_{san}'} \wedge \mathrm{ADM}_0 \neq \mathrm{ADM}_1$
         let $\sigma \leftarrow \mathsf{Sign}(m, \mathsf{sk_{sig}}, \mathsf{pk_{san}}, \mathrm{ADM}_b)$
         if $\mathsf{pk_{san}'} = \mathsf{pk_{san}}$, let $\mathcal{Q} \leftarrow \mathcal{Q} \cup \{(m, \sigma, \mathrm{ADM}_0 \cap \mathrm{ADM}_1)\}$
         return σ
      where oracle Sanit' on input of $m, \mathrm{MOD}, \sigma, \mathsf{pk_{sig}'}, \mathsf{sk_{san}}$:
         return $\perp$, if $\mathsf{pk_{sig}'} = \mathsf{pk_{sig}} \wedge \nexists (m, \sigma, \mathrm{ADM}) \in \mathcal{Q} : \mathrm{MOD}(\mathrm{ADM}) = 1$
         let $(m', \sigma') \leftarrow \mathsf{Sanit}(m, \mathrm{MOD}, \sigma, \mathsf{pk_{sig}'}, \mathsf{sk_{san}})$
         if $\mathsf{pk_{sig}'} = \mathsf{pk_{sig}} \wedge \exists (m, \sigma, \mathrm{ADM}') \in \mathcal{Q} : \mathrm{MOD}(\mathrm{ADM}') = 1$,
            let $\mathcal{Q} \leftarrow \mathcal{Q} \cup \{(m', \sigma', \mathrm{ADM}')\}$
         return (m', σ')
   return 1, if $a = b$
   return 0

Fig. 2. SSS strong invisibility

Clearly, our definition implies the invisibility definition by Camenisch et al. [13], and strong invisibility is not implied by any other property.

Definition 6 (Secure SSS). *We call an SSS secure, if it is correct, private, unforgeable, immutable, sanitizer-accountable, strongly signer-accountable, and strongly invisible.*

As mentioned before, we do not consider non-interactive public accountability, unlinkability, or transparency, as essential requirements, as it depends on the concrete use-case whether these properties are required.

3.4   Construction

Our construction is similar to the one by Camenisch et al. [13][3] but contains several improvements. In their paradigm, each block is protected by a chameleon-hash with ephemeral trapdoors under the sanitizer's key, while the hash values are signed by the signer. Then the ephemeral trapdoors for the modifiable blocks are revealed to the sanitizer, who can modify those blocks by computing collisions. Our trick is to mimic chameleon hashes with ephemeral trapdoors by generating a *fresh* chameleon hash key pair for each block, while only the overall message is protected by a chameleon hash under the sanitizer's key. Then we give the secret keys $\mathsf{sk_{ch}^i}$ for which the respective block $m[i]$ is admissible

---

[3] Which, in turn, is based on prior work [8,30,36].

$\mathsf{SSSPGen}(1^\lambda)$: Let $\mathsf{pp}_{ch} \leftarrow \mathsf{CHPGen}(1^\lambda)$. Return $\mathsf{pp}_{sss} = \mathsf{pp}_{ch}$.

$\mathsf{KGen}_{sig}(\mathsf{pp}_{sss})$: Let $(\mathsf{pk}_\Sigma, \mathsf{sk}_\Sigma) \leftarrow \mathsf{KGen}_\Sigma(1^\lambda)$, $\kappa \leftarrow \mathsf{KGen}_{prf}(1^\lambda)$, and return $((\kappa, \mathsf{sk}_\Sigma), \mathsf{pk}_\Sigma)$.

$\mathsf{KGen}_{san}(\mathsf{pp}_{sss})$: Let $(\mathsf{sk}_{ch}, \mathsf{pk}_{ch}) \leftarrow \mathsf{CHKGen}(\mathsf{pp}_{sss})$, $(\mathsf{sk}_\Pi, \mathsf{pk}_\Pi) \leftarrow \mathsf{KGen}_\Pi(1^\lambda)$, and return $((\mathsf{sk}_{ch}, \mathsf{sk}_\Pi), (\mathsf{pk}_{ch}, \mathsf{pk}_\Pi))$.

Construction 2. Secure and transparent SSS - Key Generation

to the sanitizer while the public keys pk_{ch}^i are included in the signature by the signer. To hide whether a given block is sanitizable, each sk_{ch}^i is encrypted; a sanitizable block contains the real sk_{ch}^i, while a non-admissible block encrypts a 0 (0 is assumed to be an invalid sk_{ch}^i). To prohibit the re-use of ciphertexts from different pk_{sig}s, which is exactly the thin line between invisibility and strong invisibility, the signer also needs to put its public key pk_{sig} into the label for each ciphertext. As we show in the proof, this then allows to simulate decryption for all requests when using labeled CCA2-secure encryption. To achieve accountability, as Camenisch et al. [13], we generate additional "tags" for a chameleon-hash (which binds everything together) in a special way, i.e., using PRFs and PRGs. This idea can essentially be tracked back to Brzuska et al. [8]. To achieve strong signer-accountability, we need to resort to *unique* signature schemes, and generate the randomness of the chameleon hash (one can use the one given in Sect. 2) in a special way. Namely, we use the unique signature scheme to sign a random value. The resulting signature is hashed, and used as a randomness source for the outer chameleon-hash. To maintain transparency, the signature is encrypted to the sanitizer, who verifies that the signature is correct upon every sanitization, and does not produce sanitized signatures otherwise. This is necessary, as the definition of CH collision-resistance does not rule out that the adversary can find new colliding hashes for already seen collisions. Our trick prohibits such attacks. In more detail, the proof π needs to also contain the randomness used to generate the chameleon-hash, which is exactly the hashed signature on a public random value. For readability, we split up the construction into three parts. The first part (Construction 2) contains the key generation algorithms. The second part (Construction 3) contains the algorithms for signing, sanitizing, and verifying, while the third part (Construction 4) contains the algorithms for proof generation and the judge.

Theorem 1 (proven in the full version of this paper). *If Π, Σ, and CH, are secure, while PRF, and PRG, are pseudo-random, the construction given in Construction 2–4 is a secure, and transparent, SSS.*

4 Evaluation

To demonstrate the practicality of our scheme, we have implemented our construction in Java. The chameleon-hash CH we implemented is the one presented in Sect. 2. All RSA-moduli for Σ and CH have a fixed bit-length of 2,048 Bit (with balanced primes). Likewise, each e generated (one for Σ, and one for CH)

$\mathsf{Sign}(m, \mathsf{sk}_{\mathsf{sig}}, \mathsf{pk}_{\mathsf{san}}, \mathrm{ADM})$: If $\mathrm{ADM}(m) \neq 1$, return $\bot$. Let $x_0 \leftarrow \{0,1\}^\lambda$, $x_0' \leftarrow \mathsf{Eval}_{\mathsf{prf}}(\kappa, x_0)$, $\tau \leftarrow \mathsf{Eval}_{\mathsf{prg}}(x_0')$, $x_1 \leftarrow \{0,1\}^\lambda$. Further, let

$$\forall i \in \{1, \ldots, \ell\} : (\mathsf{sk}_{\mathsf{ch}}^i, \mathsf{pk}_{\mathsf{ch}}^i) \leftarrow \mathsf{CHKGen}(\mathsf{pp}_{\mathsf{ch}}), (h_i, r_i) \leftarrow \mathsf{CHash}(\mathsf{pk}_{\mathsf{ch}}^i, (i, m[i], \mathsf{pk}_{\mathsf{sig}})),$$
$$\forall j \notin \mathrm{ADM} : \mathsf{sk}_{\mathsf{ch}}^j \leftarrow 0, \text{ and } \forall i \in \{1, \ldots, \ell\} : c_i \leftarrow \mathsf{Enc}_\Pi(\mathsf{pk}_\Pi, \mathsf{sk}_{\mathsf{ch}}^i, \mathsf{pk}_{\mathsf{sig}}).$$

Return $\sigma = (\sigma', x_0, x_1, \widetilde{\mathsf{pk}}_{\mathsf{ch}\,1,\ell}, \widetilde{r}_{0,\ell}, \tau, c_h, \widetilde{c}_{1,\ell}, \widetilde{h}_{0,\ell})$, where

$$\sigma_h \leftarrow \mathsf{Sign}_\Sigma(\mathsf{sk}_\Sigma, x_1), c_h \leftarrow \mathsf{Enc}_\Pi(\mathsf{pk}_\Pi, (m, \sigma_h, \widetilde{r}_{1,\ell}, \tau), \mathsf{pk}_{\mathsf{sig}}), t \leftarrow \mathcal{H}(\sigma_h, x_1, \mathsf{pk}_{\mathsf{sig}}),$$
$$(h_0, r_0) \leftarrow \mathsf{CHash}(\mathsf{pk}_{\mathsf{ch}}, (0, x_0, x_1, \widetilde{\mathsf{pk}}_{\mathsf{ch}\,1,\ell}, m, \tau, \ell, \widetilde{h}_{1,\ell}, c_h, \widetilde{c}_{1,\ell}, \widetilde{r}_{1,\ell}, \mathsf{pk}_{\mathsf{sig}}); t),$$
$$\sigma' \leftarrow \mathsf{Sign}_\Sigma(\mathsf{sk}_\Sigma, (x_0, x_1, \widetilde{\mathsf{pk}}_{\mathsf{ch}\,1,\ell}, \widetilde{h}_{0,\ell}, c_h, \widetilde{c}_{1,\ell}, \mathsf{pk}_{\mathsf{san}}, \mathsf{pk}_{\mathsf{sig}}, \ell))$$

$\mathsf{Verify}(m, \sigma, \mathsf{pk}_{\mathsf{sig}}, \mathsf{pk}_{\mathsf{san}})$: Return 1 if all of the following checks hold, and 0 otherwise:

$$\forall i \in \{1, \ldots, \ell\} : \mathsf{CHCheck}(\mathsf{pk}_{\mathsf{ch}}^i, (i, m[i], \mathsf{pk}_{\mathsf{sig}}), r_i, h_i) = 1 \wedge$$
$$\mathsf{CHCheck}(\mathsf{pk}_{\mathsf{ch}}, (0, x_0, x_1, \widetilde{\mathsf{pk}}_{\mathsf{ch}\,1,\ell}, m, \tau, \ell, \widetilde{h}_{1,\ell}, c_h, \widetilde{c}_{1,\ell}, \widetilde{r}_{1,\ell}, \mathsf{pk}_{\mathsf{sig}}), r_0, h_0) = 1 \wedge$$
$$\mathsf{Verify}_\Sigma(\mathsf{pk}_\Sigma, (x_0, x_1, \widetilde{\mathsf{pk}}_{\mathsf{ch}\,1,\ell}, \widetilde{h}_{0,\ell}, c_h, \widetilde{c}_{1,\ell}, \mathsf{pk}_{\mathsf{san}}, \mathsf{pk}_{\mathsf{sig}}, \ell), \sigma') = 1.$$

$\mathsf{Sanit}(m, \mathrm{MOD}, \sigma, \mathsf{pk}_{\mathsf{sig}}, \mathsf{sk}_{\mathsf{san}})$: Return $\bot$ if $\mathsf{Verify}(m, \sigma, \mathsf{pk}_{\mathsf{sig}}, \mathsf{pk}_{\mathsf{san}}) \neq 1$. Let $(m^\circ, \sigma_h, \widetilde{r}_{1,\ell}^\circ, \tau^\circ) \leftarrow \mathsf{Dec}_\Pi(\mathsf{sk}_\Pi, c_h, \mathsf{pk}_{\mathsf{sig}})$, check whether $\mathsf{Verify}_\Sigma(\mathsf{pk}_\Sigma, x_1, \sigma_h) \neq 1$, and return $\bot$ if so. Further, obtain $(h_0^v, \cdot) \leftarrow \mathsf{CHash}(\mathsf{pk}_{\mathsf{ch}}, (0, x_0, x_1, \widetilde{\mathsf{pk}}_{\mathsf{ch}\,1,\ell}, m^\circ, \tau^\circ, \ell, \widetilde{h}_{1,\ell}, c_h, \widetilde{c}_{1,\ell}, \widetilde{r}_{1,\ell}^\circ, \mathsf{pk}_{\mathsf{sig}}); \mathcal{H}(\sigma_h, x_1, \mathsf{pk}_{\mathsf{sig}}))$ and return $\bot$ if $h_0^v \neq h_0$. Otherwise, obtain

$$\forall i \in \{1, \ldots, \ell\} : \mathsf{sk}_{\mathsf{ch}}^i \leftarrow \mathsf{Dec}_\Pi(\mathsf{sk}_\Pi, c_i, \mathsf{pk}_{\mathsf{sig}}) \text{ and return } \bot, \text{ if } \mathsf{sk}_{\mathsf{ch}}^i = \bot \vee (m[i]' \in \mathrm{MOD} \wedge \mathsf{sk}_{\mathsf{ch}}^i = 0).$$

For each block $m[i]' \in \mathrm{MOD}$, let $r_i' \leftarrow \mathsf{CHAdapt}(\mathsf{sk}_{\mathsf{ch}}^i, (i, m[i], \mathsf{pk}_{\mathsf{sig}}), (i, m[i]', \mathsf{pk}_{\mathsf{sig}}), r_i, h_i)$. If any $r_i' = \bot$, return $\bot$. For each block $m[i]' \notin \mathrm{MOD}$, let $r_i' \leftarrow r_i$. Let $m' \leftarrow \mathrm{MOD}(m)$. Draw $\tau' \leftarrow \{0,1\}^{2\lambda}$. Let

$$r_0' \leftarrow \mathsf{CHAdapt}(\mathsf{sk}_{\mathsf{ch}}, (0, x_0, x_1, \widetilde{\mathsf{pk}}_{\mathsf{ch}\,1,\ell}, m, \tau, \ell, \widetilde{h}_{1,\ell}, c_h, \widetilde{c}_{1,\ell}, \widetilde{r}_{1,\ell}, \mathsf{pk}_{\mathsf{sig}}),$$
$$(0, x_0, x_1, \widetilde{\mathsf{pk}}_{\mathsf{ch}\,1,\ell}, m', \tau', \ell, \widetilde{h}_{1,\ell}, c_h, \widetilde{c}_{1,\ell}, \widetilde{r'}_{1,\ell}, \mathsf{pk}_{\mathsf{sig}}), r_0, h_0).$$

Finally, return $(m', (\sigma', x_0, x_1, \widetilde{\mathsf{pk}}_{\mathsf{ch}\,1,\ell}, \widetilde{r'}_{0,\ell}, \tau', c_h, \widetilde{c}_{1,\ell}, \widetilde{h}_{0,\ell}))$.

Construction 3. Secure and transparent SSS - Main Algortihms

has 2,050 Bit. Σ is a standard RSA-FDH implementation, with the required constraints. We have fixed the output size of $\mathcal{H}$, PRF, and PRG, to 512 and $2 \cdot 512$, respectively, as these sizes turned out to yield the best performance when using 2,048 Bit moduli. $\mathcal{H}$, and PRF, were implemented using SHA-512. $\mathcal{H}_n$ is SHA-512 in counter-mode [5], similar to what is used in existing implementations [14,27]. Π was implemented using the IND-CCA2-secure version of RSA-OAEP (2,048 Bit modulus), paired with a symmetric encrypt-then-MAC cipher-suite (AES/3DES-CBC-MAC). These implementations were taken from the SCAPI-framework [24]. They use 128 Bit encryption keys, and 112 Bit MAC keys.

Proof($\mathsf{sk_{sig}}, m, \sigma, \{(m_i, \sigma_i) \mid i \in \mathbb{N}\}, \mathsf{pk_{san}}$): If any of the following checks holds return $\bot$:

$$\mathsf{Verify}(m, \sigma, \mathsf{pk_{sig}}, \mathsf{pk_{san}}) = 0 \ \vee \ \exists i \in \{1, \ldots, \ell\} \ : \ \mathsf{Verify}(m_i, \sigma_i, \mathsf{pk_{sig}}, \mathsf{pk_{san}}) = 0$$

Otherwise, go through the list of (m_i, σ_i) and find a (non-trivial) colliding tuple of the chameleon-hash with (m, σ), i.e., where it holds that

$$1 = \mathsf{CHCheck}(\mathsf{pk_{ch}}, (0, x_0, x_1, \widetilde{\mathsf{pk}}_{\mathsf{ch}1,\ell}, m, \tau, \ell, \widetilde{h}_{1,\ell}, c_h, \widetilde{c}_{1,\ell}, \widetilde{r}_{1,\ell}, \mathsf{pk_{sig}}), r_0, h_0) \ \wedge$$
$$1 = \mathsf{CHCheck}(\mathsf{pk_{ch}}, (0, x_0, x_1, \widetilde{\mathsf{pk}}_{\mathsf{ch}1,\ell}, m', \tau', \ell, \widetilde{h}'_{1,\ell}, c'_h, \widetilde{c}'_{1,\ell}, \widetilde{r}'_{1,\ell}, \mathsf{pk_{sig}}), r'_0, h'_0) \ \wedge$$
$$(\tau \neq \tau' \ \vee \ m \neq m') \ \wedge \ h_0 = h'_0.$$

Let this signature/message pair be $(\sigma', m') \in \{(m_i, \sigma_i) \mid i \in \mathbb{N}\}$. Return $\pi = ((\sigma', m'), \mathsf{Eval_{prf}}(\kappa, x_0), \mathsf{Sign}_{\Sigma}(\mathsf{sk}_{\Sigma}, x_1))$, where x_0, and x_1, are contained in (σ', m').

Judge($m, \sigma, \mathsf{pk_{sig}}, \mathsf{pk_{san}}, \pi$): Parse π as $((\sigma', m'), v, \sigma_h)$ with $v \in \{0,1\}^{\lambda}$, and return Sig on failure. Return Sig if any of the following checks hold

$$0 = \mathsf{Verify}(m', \sigma', \mathsf{pk_{sig}}, \mathsf{pk_{san}}) \ \vee \ 0 = \mathsf{Verify}(m, \sigma, \mathsf{pk_{sig}}, \mathsf{pk_{san}}) \ \vee$$
$$\mathsf{Verify}_{\Sigma}(\mathsf{pk}_{\Sigma}, x_1, \sigma_h) = 0 \ \vee \ \mathsf{Eval_{prg}}(v) \neq \tau'.$$

With $t' \leftarrow \mathcal{H}(\sigma_h, x_1, \mathsf{pk_{sig}})$, $(h_t, r_t) \leftarrow \mathsf{CHash}(\mathsf{pk_{ch}}, (0, x_0, x_1, \widetilde{\mathsf{pk}}_{\mathsf{ch}1,\ell}, m', \tau', \ell, \widetilde{h}_{1,\ell}, c_h, \widetilde{c}_{1,\ell}, \widetilde{r}'_{1,\ell}, \mathsf{pk_{sig}}); t')$, return San if we have a non-trivial collision satisfying the following checks, and Sig otherwise:

$$h_0 = h'_0 = h_t \ \wedge \ r_t = r_0 \ \wedge$$
$$1 = \mathsf{CHCheck}(\mathsf{pk_{ch}}, (0, x_0, x_1, \widetilde{\mathsf{pk}}_{\mathsf{ch}1,\ell}, m, \tau, \ell, \widetilde{h}_{1,\ell}, \widetilde{c}_{1,\ell}, \mathsf{pk_{sig}}), r_0, h_0) \ \wedge$$
$$1 = \mathsf{CHCheck}(\mathsf{pk'_{ch}}, (0, x'_0, x'_1, \widetilde{\mathsf{pk}'}_{\mathsf{ch}1,\ell'}, m', \tau', \ell', \widetilde{h}'_{1,\ell'}, c'_h, \widetilde{c}'_{1,\ell'}, \mathsf{pk_{sig}}), r'_0, h'_0) \ \wedge$$
$$\widetilde{c}_{1,\ell} = \widetilde{c}'_{1,\ell'} \ \wedge \ x_0 = x'_0 \ \wedge \ x_1 = x'_1 \ \wedge \ \ell = \ell' \ \wedge \ \widetilde{\mathsf{pk}}_{\mathsf{ch}1,\ell} = \widetilde{\mathsf{pk}'}_{\mathsf{ch}1,\ell'} \ \wedge \ \widetilde{h}_{0,\ell} = \widetilde{h}'_{0,\ell'}.$$

Construction 4. Secure and transparent SSS - Accountability

The measurements were performed on a Lenovo W530 with an Intel i7-3470QM@2.70 Ghz, and 16 GiB of RAM. No performance optimization such as CRT were implemented, and only a single thread does the computations. This was done to see the actual lower bound of our construction, i.e., any additional optimization helps. We evaluated our implementation with 32 blocks, wheres 50% were marked as admissible. For sanitization, 50% of the admissible blocks were sanitized, i.e., 8 blocks. We omitted proof generation, and the judge, as they are simple database look-ups, paired with comparisons, and depend on the number of signatures generated. The overall results are depicted in Fig. 3a and b and are based on 200 runs. Parameter generation is also omitted, as this is a one-time setup, i.e., drawing a random prime with 2,050 Bit.

As demonstrated, signing is the most expensive operation. The lion's share is finding suitable primes; the exponentiations within the algorithms only have a negligible overhead, as seen by the runtime of sanitization, and verification. A practical optimization would therefore be to generate the generated keys in

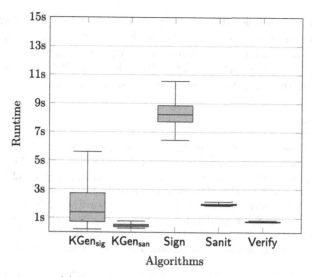

(a) Box-plots of the run-times in ms

	KGen$_{sig}$	KGen$_{san}$	Sign	Sanit	Verify
Min.:	200	285	6'443	1'868	714
25th PCTL:	725	383	7'718	1'907	731
Median:	1'393	468	8'243	1'946	746
75th PCTL:	2'726	547	8'860	2'006	774
90th PCTL:	4'563	667	9'733	2'161	826
95th PCTL:	5'619	782	10'050	2'317	874
Max.:	8'023	1'018	11'327	3'151	998
Average:	2'017	487	8'367	2'002	764
SD:	1'690	139	914	183	52

(b) Percentiles for our implementation in ms

Fig. 3. Performance evaluation results

advance, when no other computation is done, or even in parallel. However, even without these optimization the runtime can be considered practical, also with decent security parameters, and rather expensive RSA-based primitives.

5   Conclusion

We have strengthened the current invisibility definition of sanitizable signatures. Namely, the adversary is now able to query arbitrary keys to the sanitization oracle. We have shown that prohibiting this may lead to serious problems in real-life scenarios. Moreover, we have presented a simplified construction of a strongly invisible, and transparent, sanitizable signature scheme, which is also *strongly* signer-accountable. That is, we even exclude malleability of the signatures. Our construction is also simpler than the construction given by Camenisch et al. [13], as it does not require chameleon hashes with ephemeral trapdoors, i.e., it only requires standard primitives, which are less costly. Our corresponding evaluation shows that this primitive can be considered practical. Still, it remains an open problem how to construct SSSs which are simultaneously unlinkable, and invisible.

References

1. Ahn, J.H., Boneh, D., Camenisch, J., Hohenberger, S., shelat, A., Waters, B.: Computing on authenticated data. In: Cramer, R. (ed.) TCC 2012. LNCS, vol. 7194, pp. 1–20. Springer, Heidelberg (2012). doi:10.1007/978-3-642-28914-9_1
2. Ateniese, G., Chou, D.H., Medeiros, B., Tsudik, G.: Sanitizable signatures. In: Vimercati, S.C., Syverson, P., Gollmann, D. (eds.) ESORICS 2005. LNCS, vol. 3679, pp. 159–177. Springer, Heidelberg (2005). doi:10.1007/11555827_10
3. Ateniese, G., Magri, B., Venturi, D., Andrade, E.R.: Redactable blockchain - or - rewriting history in bitcoin and friends. IACR Cryptology ePrint Archive 2016, 757 (2016)
4. Bellare, M., Namprempre, C., Pointcheval, D., Semanko, M.: The one-more-rsa-inversion problems and the security of chaum's blind signature scheme. J. Cryptol. 16(3), 185–215 (2003). doi:10.1007/s00145-002-0120-1
5. Bellare, M., Rogaway, P.: Random oracles are practical: a paradigm for designing efficient protocols. In: CCS, pp. 62–73 (1993)
6. Bilzhause, A., Huber, M., Pöhls, H.C., Samelin, K.: Cryptographically enforced four-eyes principle. In: ARES, pp. 760–767 (2016)
7. Brzuska, C., et al.: Redactable signatures for tree-structured data: definitions and constructions. In: Zhou, J., Yung, M. (eds.) ACNS 2010. LNCS, vol. 6123, pp. 87–104. Springer, Heidelberg (2010). doi:10.1007/978-3-642-13708-2_6
8. Brzuska, C., Fischlin, M., Freudenreich, T., Lehmann, A., Page, M., Schelbert, J., Schröder, D., Volk, F.: Security of sanitizable signatures revisited. In: Jarecki, S., Tsudik, G. (eds.) PKC 2009. LNCS, vol. 5443, pp. 317–336. Springer, Heidelberg (2009). doi:10.1007/978-3-642-00468-1_18
9. Brzuska, C., Fischlin, M., Lehmann, A., Schröder, D.: Sanitizable signatures: how to partially delegate control for authenticated data. In: BIOSIG, pp. 117–128 (2009)
10. Brzuska, C., Fischlin, M., Lehmann, A., Schröder, D.: Unlinkability of sanitizable signatures. In: Nguyen, P.Q., Pointcheval, D. (eds.) PKC 2010. LNCS, vol. 6056, pp. 444–461. Springer, Heidelberg (2010). doi:10.1007/978-3-642-13013-7_26
11. Brzuska, C., Pöhls, H.C., Samelin, K.: Non-interactive public accountability for sanitizable signatures. In: Capitani di Vimercati, S., Mitchell, C. (eds.) EuroPKI 2012. LNCS, vol. 7868, pp. 178–193. Springer, Heidelberg (2013). doi:10.1007/978-3-642-40012-4_12
12. Brzuska, C., Pöhls, H.C., Samelin, K.: Efficient and perfectly unlinkable sanitizable signatures without group signatures. In: Katsikas, S., Agudo, I. (eds.) EuroPKI 2013. LNCS, vol. 8341, pp. 12–30. Springer, Heidelberg (2014). doi:10.1007/978-3-642-53997-8_2
13. Camenisch, J., Derler, D., Krenn, S., Pöhls, H.C., Samelin, K., Slamanig, D.: Chameleon-hashes with ephemeral trapdoors and applications to invisible sanitizable signatures. IACR Cryptology ePrint Archive 2017, 11 (2017)
14. Camenisch, J., Lehmann, A., Neven, G., Samelin, K.: Virtual smart cards: how to sign with a password and a server. In: Zikas, V., Prisco, R. (eds.) SCN 2016. LNCS, vol. 9841, pp. 353–371. Springer, Cham (2016). doi:10.1007/978-3-319-44618-9_19

15. Canard, S., Jambert, A.: On extended sanitizable signature schemes. In: Pieprzyk, J. (ed.) CT-RSA 2010. LNCS, vol. 5985, pp. 179–194. Springer, Heidelberg (2010). doi:10.1007/978-3-642-11925-5_13

16. Canard, S., Jambert, A., Lescuyer, R.: Sanitizable signatures with several signers and sanitizers. In: Mitrokotsa, A., Vaudenay, S. (eds.) AFRICACRYPT 2012. LNCS, vol. 7374, pp. 35–52. Springer, Heidelberg (2012). doi:10.1007/978-3-642-31410-0_3

17. Canard, S., Laguillaumie, F., Milhau, M.: Trapdoor sanitizable signatures and their application to content protection. In: Bellovin, S.M., Gennaro, R., Keromytis, A., Yung, M. (eds.) ACNS 2008. LNCS, vol. 5037, pp. 258–276. Springer, Heidelberg (2008). doi:10.1007/978-3-540-68914-0_16

18. Canard, S., Lescuyer, R.: Protecting privacy by sanitizing personal data: a new approach to anonymous credentials. In: ASIACCS, pp. 381–392 (2013)

19. Damgård, I., Haagh, H., Orlandi, C.: Access control encryption: enforcing information flow with cryptography. In: Hirt, M., Smith, A. (eds.) TCC 2016. LNCS, vol. 9986, pp. 547–576. Springer, Heidelberg (2016). doi:10.1007/978-3-662-53644-5_21

20. Demirel, D., Derler, D., Hanser, C., Pöhls, H.C., Slamanig, D., Traverso, G.: PRISMACLOUD D4.4: overview of functional and malleable signature schemes. Technical report, H2020 Prismacloud (2015). www.prismacloud.eu

21. Derler, D., Hanser, C., Slamanig, D.: Blank digital signatures: optimization and practical experiences. In: Camenisch, J., Fischer-Hübner, S., Hansen, M. (eds.) Privacy and Identity 2014. IAICT, vol. 457, pp. 201–215. Springer, Cham (2015). doi:10.1007/978-3-319-18621-4_14

22. Derler, D., Pöhls, H.C., Samelin, K., Slamanig, D.: A general framework for redactable signatures and new constructions. In: Kwon, S., Yun, A. (eds.) ICISC 2015. LNCS, vol. 9558, pp. 3–19. Springer, Cham (2016). doi:10.1007/978-3-319-30840-1_1

23. Derler, D., Slamanig, D.: Rethinking privacy for extended sanitizable signatures and a black-box construction of strongly private schemes. In: Au, M.-H., Miyaji, A. (eds.) ProvSec 2015. LNCS, vol. 9451, pp. 455–474. Springer, Cham (2015). doi:10.1007/978-3-319-26059-4_25

24. Ejgenberg, Y., Farbstein, M., Levy, M., Lindell, Y.: SCAPI: the secure computation application programming interface. IACR Cryptology ePrint Archive 2012, 629 (2012)

25. Fehr, V., Fischlin, M.: Sanitizable signcryption: sanitization over encrypted data (full version). IACR Cryptology ePrint Archive, Report 2015/765 (2015)

26. Fleischhacker, N., Krupp, J., Malavolta, G., Schneider, J., Schröder, D., Simkin, M.: Efficient unlinkable sanitizable signatures from signatures with re-randomizable keys. In: Cheng, C.-M., Chung, K.-M., Persiano, G., Yang, B.-Y. (eds.) PKC 2016. LNCS, vol. 9614, pp. 301–330. Springer, Heidelberg (2016). doi:10.1007/978-3-662-49384-7_12

27. Fleischhacker, N., Krupp, J., Malavolta, G., Schneider, J., Schröder, D., Simkin, M.: Efficient unlinkable sanitizable signatures from signatures with re-randomizable keys. In: Cheng, C.-M., Chung, K.-M., Persiano, G., Yang, B.-Y. (eds.) PKC 2016. LNCS, vol. 9614, pp. 301–330. Springer, Heidelberg (2016). doi:10.1007/978-3-662-49384-7_12

28. Ghosh, E., Goodrich, M.T., Ohrimenko, O., Tamassia, R.: Fully-dynamic verifiable zero-knowledge order queries for network data. ePrint 2015, 283 (2015)

29. Ghosh, E., Ohrimenko, O., Tamassia, R.: Zero-Knowledge authenticated order queries and order statistics on a list. In: Malkin, T., Kolesnikov, V., Lewko, A.B., Polychronakis, M. (eds.) ACNS 2015. LNCS, vol. 9092, pp. 149–171. Springer, Cham (2015). doi:10.1007/978-3-319-28166-7_8

30. Gong, J., Qian, H., Zhou, Y.: Fully-secure and practical sanitizable signatures. In: Lai, X., Yung, M., Lin, D. (eds.) Inscrypt 2010. LNCS, vol. 6584, pp. 300–317. Springer, Heidelberg (2011). doi:10.1007/978-3-642-21518-6_21

31. Hanser, C., Slamanig, D.: Blank digital signatures. In: ASIACCS, pp. 95–106 (2013)

32. Höhne, F., Pöhls, H.C., Samelin, K.: Rechtsfolgen editierbarer signaturen. Datenschutz und Datensicherheit **36**(7), 485–491 (2012). doi:10.1007/s11623-012-0165-8

33. Johnson, R., Molnar, D., Song, D., Wagner, D.: Homomorphic signature schemes. In: Preneel, B. (ed.) CT-RSA 2002. LNCS, vol. 2271, pp. 244–262. Springer, Heidelberg (2002). doi:10.1007/3-540-45760-7_17

34. Klonowski, M., Lauks, A.: Extended sanitizable signatures. In: Rhee, M.S., Lee, B. (eds.) ICISC 2006. LNCS, vol. 4296, pp. 343–355. Springer, Heidelberg (2006). doi:10.1007/11927587_28

35. Krenn, S., Samelin, K., Sommer, D.: Stronger security for sanitizable signatures. In: Garcia-Alfaro, J., Navarro-Arribas, G., Aldini, A., Martinelli, F., Suri, N. (eds.) DPM/QASA -2015. LNCS, vol. 9481, pp. 100–117. Springer, Cham (2016). doi:10. 1007/978-3-319-29883-2_7

36. de Meer, H., Pöhls, H.C., Posegga, J., Samelin, K.: Scope of security properties of sanitizable signatures revisited. In: ARES, pp. 188–197 (2013)

37. de Meer, H., Pöhls, H.C., Posegga, J., Samelin, K.: On the relation between redactable and sanitizable signature schemes. In: Jürjens, J., Piessens, F., Bielova, N. (eds.) ESSoS 2014. LNCS, vol. 8364, pp. 113–130. Springer, Cham (2014). doi:10. 1007/978-3-319-04897-0_8

38. Miyazaki, K., Hanaoka, G., Imai, H.: Invisibly sanitizable digital signature scheme. IEICE Trans. **91–A**(1), 392–402 (2008)

39. Pöhls, H.C., Peters, S., Samelin, K., Posegga, J., Meer, H.: Malleable signatures for resource constrained platforms. In: Cavallaro, L., Gollmann, D. (eds.) WISTP 2013. LNCS, vol. 7886, pp. 18–33. Springer, Heidelberg (2013). doi:10. 1007/978-3-642-38530-8_2

40. Pöhls, H.C., Samelin, K.: Accountable redactable signatures. In: ARES, pp. 60–69 (2015)

41. Pöhls, H.C., Samelin, K., Posegga, J.: Sanitizable signatures in XML signature — performance, mixing properties, and revisiting the property of transparency. In: Lopez, J., Tsudik, G. (eds.) ACNS 2011. LNCS, vol. 6715, pp. 166–182. Springer, Heidelberg (2011). doi:10.1007/978-3-642-21554-4_10

42. Samelin, K., Pöhls, H.C., Bilzhause, A., Posegga, J., Meer, H.: Redactable signatures for independent removal of structure and content. In: Ryan, M.D., Smyth, B., Wang, G. (eds.) ISPEC 2012. LNCS, vol. 7232, pp. 17–33. Springer, Heidelberg (2012). doi:10.1007/978-3-642-29101-2_2

43. Steinfeld, R., Bull, L., Zheng, Y.: Content extraction signatures. In: Kim, K. (ed.) ICISC 2001. LNCS, vol. 2288, pp. 285–304. Springer, Heidelberg (2002). doi:10. 1007/3-540-45861-1_22

44. Yum, D.H., Seo, J.W., Lee, P.J.: Trapdoor sanitizable signatures made easy. In: Zhou, J., Yung, M. (eds.) ACNS 2010. LNCS, vol. 6123, pp. 53–68. Springer, Heidelberg (2010). doi:10.1007/978-3-642-13708-2_4

Tightly-Secure Signatures from the Decisional Composite Residuosity Assumption

Xiao Zhang[1,2], Shengli Liu[1,2,3($\boxtimes$)], and Dawu Gu[1]

[1] Department of Computer Science and Engineering,
Shanghai Jiao Tong University, Shanghai 200240, China
{zhangx522,slliu,dwgu}@sjtu.edu.cn
[2] State Key Laboratory of Cryptology, P.O. Box 5159, Beijing 100878, China
[3] Westone Cryptologic Research Center, Beijing 100070, China

Abstract. In this paper, we construct the first *tightly* secure signature scheme against adaptive chosen message attacks (CMA) from the Decisional Composite Residuosity (DCR) Assumption. Moreover, the verification key in our scheme is of constant size. Based on the DCR assumption, we design a one-time secure signature scheme first, then we employ a flat tree structure to obtain a signature scheme that is secure against non-adaptive chosen message attacks (NCMA). By combining the one-time scheme and NCMA-secure scheme, we obtain the final CMA-secure signature scheme with a tight security reduction to the DCR assumption.

1 Introduction

One focus of modern cryptography has been the construction of Digital Signature schemes that can be rigorously proved secure based on computational assumptions. Over the years, many digital signature schemes were proposed, and the securities of the schemes were proved with reductions to the one-wayness of trapdoor permutations [GMR88, Rom90], the RSA assumption [HJK11, HW09], the CDH assumption [Wat05] and the Short Integer Solution (SIS) assumption [CG05a, MP12], etc.

A proof of security for a cryptographic scheme generally proceeds by demonstrating a reduction which shows how a polynomial-time adversary $\mathcal{A}$ "breaking" the scheme can be used to construct a polynomial-time adversary $\mathcal{B}$ "solving" a hardness problem. What we expect is the success probabilities (ϵ_A, ϵ_B) and running time (T_A, T_B) of $\mathcal{A}$ and $\mathcal{B}$ are approximately the same. However, security reductions often suffer from a nontrivial multiplicative security loss L (such that only $\epsilon_A \leq L \cdot \epsilon_B$ can be guaranteed). We call a scheme tightly secure if its security reduction to a hardness problem is tight, i.e., the security loss factor L is a constant number. If the factor L is only related to the security parameter λ, the scheme is called *almost* tightly secure. As to digital signature, security reduction of most of the existing schemes will lose at least a factor q, which is the maximal number of queried signatures. As a consequence, to realize a desired target security level, one has to increase the apparent security level inside the

© Springer International Publishing AG 2017
J. Pieprzyk and S. Suriadi (Eds.): ACISP 2017, Part I, LNCS 10342, pp. 453–468, 2017.
DOI: 10.1007/978-3-319-60055-0_24

construction to compensate for the loose reduction, e.g., key-length recommendations should also take q into account. This inflates the size of data atoms by some polynomial factor, with in turn increases the running time of cryptographic operations by another polynomial factor.

To achieve tight security reduction, the first effort was made by Cramer and Damgard in [CD96], who proposed the use of flat tree structure for signature schemes based on the RSA assumption. In the follow-up papers [CG05a, BMS03], Cramer and Damgard's method was extended to cover Factoring and CDH assumptions, respectively. Later, Hofheinz and Jager [HJ12] proposed a binary tree-based construction from the Decision Linear (DLIN) assumption. More recently, Blazy et al. [BKKP15] gave a new framework for obtaining signatures with a tight security reduction by showing that any Chameleon Hash function can be transformed into a (binary) tree-based signature scheme with tight security. Their instantiations include signature schemes from assumptions like DLOG, RSA, SIS, Factoring. Other than tree-based signature schemes, works on identity-based encryption [CW13, BKP14] imply almost tightly secure signatures based on the k-LIN assumption. In addition, applying algebraic partitioning technique, Hofheinz proposed a tightly secure signature scheme based on DDH in [Hof16b].

The DCR assumption, proposed by Paillier [Pai99], has been widely used in public-key encryption (PKE). Very recently, a PKE with almost tight security reduction to the DCR assumption has been proposed by Hofheiz in [Hof16a]. A natural question is:

Is that possible to design a tightly secure digital signature scheme from the DCR assumption?

In this paper, we answer this question affirmatively.

Table 1. Comparison with existing tightly secure signature schemes

Scheme	Assumption	Reduction loss	Verification key	Signature size
[HJ12]	LIN	$O(1)$	$O(1)$	$O(\lambda)$
[CW13]	k-Lin	$O(\lambda)$	$O(\lambda k^2)$	$O(k)$
[BKP14]	k-Lin	$O(\lambda)$	$O(\lambda k^2)$	$O(k)$
[BKKP15]	DLOG	$O(1)$	$O(1)$	$O(\lambda)$
[BKKP15]	RSA	$O(1)$	$O(1)$	$O(\lambda)$
[BKKP15]	Factoring	$O(1)$	$O(1)$	$O(\lambda)$
[Hof16b]	DDH	$O(\lambda)$	$O(1)$	$O(1)$
Our scheme	DCR	$O(1)$	$O(1)$	$O(\lambda)$

Remark. The verification key of the signature scheme based on RSA (and Factoring) in [BKKP15] consists of at least 6 elements, while the verification key of our scheme has only 3 elements. At the same time, the modulus N used in [BKKP15] cannot be public parameter since the factoring of N is included in the signing key. In our scheme, N can be shared as public parameter by all users.

1.1 Our Contributions

In this paper, we construct tightly secure digital signature schemes from the DCR assumption.

- We construct a one-time signature scheme, which is strongly existentially unforgeable under non-adaptive chosen message attacks (*sot-euf-ncma*) based on the DCR assumption.
- From the one-time signature scheme, we construct a tree-based signature scheme, which is existentially unforgeable under non-adaptive chosen message attacks (*euf-ncma*), with a tight reduction to the DCR assumption.
- We show how to combine the *euf-ncma* secure signature scheme with the *sot-euf-ncma* secure scheme to yield an adaptively secure signature scheme (existentially unforgeable under adaptive chosen message attacks) with a tight reduction to the DCR assumption.

A comparison of our scheme with other several existing tightly secure schemes is demonstrated in Table 1.

2 Preliminaries

2.1 Notations

The security parameter is λ. "PPT" abbreviates "probabilisitic polynomial-time". We denote by $x \xleftarrow{\$} \mathcal{X}$ the process of sampling an element x from a finite set $\mathcal{X}$ uniformly at random. A function $negl : \mathbb{N} \to \mathbb{R}$ is negligible if for any polynomial $p(\lambda)$ it holds that $negl(\lambda) < 1/p(\lambda)$ for all sufficiently large $\lambda \in \mathbb{N}$. Let $[n] = \{1, 2, \ldots, n\}$. By $A := B$ we denote that the value of B is assigned to A. For integers $x, N \in \mathbb{Z}$ with $N > 0$, we define

$$|x|_N = \begin{cases} x \bmod N & \text{if } x \bmod N < N/2 \\ -x \bmod N & \text{if } x \bmod N \geq N/2 \end{cases} \tag{1}$$

such that $0 \leq |x|_N \leq N/2$.

2.2 Groups and Public Parameters

Let $N = PQ$, for distinct safe primes P, Q (i.e., such that $P = 2P' + 1$ and $Q = 2Q' + 1$ for prime $P', Q' > 2^\lambda$). Define

$$\mathbb{G}_1 = \left\{ |x^N|_{N^2} \mid x \in \mathbb{Z}_{N^2}^* \right\} \subseteq \mathbb{Z}_{N^2}^*$$
$$\mathbb{G}_2 = \left\{ |(1+N)^e|_{N^2} \mid e \in \mathbb{Z}_N \right\} \subseteq \mathbb{Z}_{N^2}^*$$
$$\mathbb{G} = \left\{ |y|_{N^2} \mid y \in \mathbb{Z}_{N^2}^* \right\} \subseteq \mathbb{Z}_{N^2}^*$$

Apparently, we have the following facts [Hof16a].

- $\mathbb{G}_1, \mathbb{G}_2, \mathbb{G}$ are well-defined groups with the group operation $a \cdot b = |ab|_{N^2}$;
- The membership in $\mathbb{G}$ can be efficiently decided.
- $\mathbb{G}_1 \cdot \mathbb{G}_2 = \{h_1 \cdot h_2 \mid h_1 \in \mathbb{G}_1, h_2 \in \mathbb{G}_2\} = \mathbb{G}$.

Furthermore, let GGen be a PPT algorithm that on input 1^λ returns descriptions of $\mathbb{G}$, $\mathbb{G}_1$, $\mathbb{G}_2$, and generators g, g_1, g_2 of $\mathbb{G}$, $\mathbb{G}_1$ and $\mathbb{G}_2$ respectively. In other words, par $= (\mathbb{G}, \mathbb{G}_1, \mathbb{G}_2, g, g_1, g_2) \leftarrow$ GGen.

2.3   Decisional Composite Residuosity (DCR) Assumption

In 1999, Paillier presented the Decisional Composite Residuosity (DCR) assumption in [Pai99], Informally speaking, the DCR assumption states that given a RSA modulus N and an integer $z \in Z_{N^2}^*$, it is hard to decide whether z is a N-th residue modulo N^2 or not. Following [DJ01], here we will give a variant of DCR assumption in Definition 1: given an element $z \in \mathbb{G}$, it is hard to decide whether z is in $\mathbb{G}_1$ or a coset of $\mathbb{G}_1$ generated by g_2. This assumption is in fact implied by Paillier's original DCR assumption.

Definition 1 (DCR Assumption). *The DCR Assumption holds relative to* GGen *in group* $\mathbb{G}$ *if for any PPT* $\mathcal{A}$*, the following is negligible:*

$$\mathbf{Adv}_{\mathbb{G},\mathcal{A}}^{dcr}(\lambda) := |\Pr[\mathcal{A}(\mathsf{par}, g_1^r) = 1] - \Pr[\mathcal{A}(\mathsf{par}, g_1^r g_2) = 1]|, \qquad (2)$$

where par$= (N, \mathbb{G}, \mathbb{G}_1, \mathbb{G}_2, g, g_1, g_2) \leftarrow$GGen$(1^\lambda)$, $r \xleftarrow{\$} \mathbb{Z}_{|\mathbb{G}_1|}$.

2.4   Collision-Resistant Hash Function

Definition 2 (Collision-resistant hash function). *A family of collision-resistant hash function* CRHF*, associated with a domain* $\mathcal{X}$ *and a range* $\mathcal{R}$*, consists of two PPT algorithms* (HGen, HEval)*.* HGen(1^λ) *generates a uniformly random function, denoted by* $H : \mathcal{X} \rightarrow \mathcal{R}$*.* HEval$(H, x)$ *produces the value* $H(x)$ *for all* $x \in \mathcal{X}$*. Furthermore, for any PPT algorithm* $\mathcal{A}$*, the following function is negligible:*

$$\mathbf{Adv}_{H,\mathcal{A}}^{cr}(\lambda) := \Pr[x \neq x' \wedge H(x) = H(x') \mid H \leftarrow \mathsf{HGen}(1^\lambda), (x, x') \leftarrow \mathcal{A}(H)].$$

2.5   Signatures

Definition 3 (Signature scheme). *A digital signature scheme with message space* $\mathcal{M}$ *consists of three PPT algorithms* SS $=$ (Gen, Sign, Verify) *with the following properties.*

- *The probabilistic key generation algorithm* Gen(1^λ) *returns the verification/secret key* (vk, sk)*.*
- *The probabilistic signing algorithm* Sign(sk, m) *returns a signature* σ *w.r.t. message* m *in message space* $\mathcal{M}$*.*

– *The deterministic verification algorithm* Verify(vk, m, σ) *returns 1 or 0, where 1 means that σ is a valid signature of message m.*

Definition 4 (*euf-ncma* security). *A digital signature scheme* SS = (Gen, Sign, Verify) *is existentially unforgeable under non-adaptive chosen message attacks (euf-ncma), if for any PPT adversary* $\mathcal{A}$, *the following advantage is negligible:*

$$\mathbf{Adv}_{\mathsf{SS},\mathcal{A}}^{euf\text{-}ncma}(\lambda) := \Pr\left[\begin{array}{c} m^* \notin \mathcal{Q} \\ \wedge\, \mathsf{Verify}(vk, m^*, \sigma^*) = 1 \end{array} \middle| \begin{array}{l} \mathcal{Q} := \{m_1, \cdots, m_q\} \leftarrow \mathcal{A}(1^\lambda) \\ (vk, sk) \leftarrow \mathsf{Gen}(1^\lambda) \\ \sigma_i \leftarrow \mathsf{Sign}(sk, m_i) \text{ for } j \in [q] \\ (m^*, \sigma^*) \leftarrow \mathcal{A}(vk, \sigma_1, \cdots, \sigma_q) \end{array} \right]. \quad (3)$$

If $\mathbf{Adv}_{\mathsf{SS},\mathcal{A}}^{euf\text{-}ncma}(\lambda)$ *is negligible for $q = 1$, then* SS *is one-time existentially unforgeable under non-adaptive chosen message attacks (oteuf-ncma).*

Definition 5 (*euf-cma* security). *A digital signature scheme* SS = (Gen, Sign, Verify) *is existentially unforgeable secure under adaptive chosen message attacks (euf-cma), if for any PPT adversary* $\mathcal{A}$, *the following advantage is negligible:*

$$\mathbf{Adv}_{\mathsf{SS},\mathcal{A}}^{euf\text{-}cma}(\lambda) := \Pr\left[\begin{array}{c} m^* \notin \mathcal{Q} \\ \wedge\, \mathsf{Verify}(vk, m^*, \sigma^*) = 1 \end{array} \middle| \begin{array}{l} (vk, sk) \leftarrow \mathsf{Gen}(1^\lambda) \\ (m^*, \sigma^*) \leftarrow \mathcal{A}^{\mathsf{SignO}}(vk) \end{array} \right], \quad (4)$$

where the oracle SignO(m_i) *runs* $\sigma_i \leftarrow$ Sign(sk, m_i), *and* $\mathcal{Q} = \{m_i\}_{i \in [q]}$ *denotes q queries made by $\mathcal{A}$ to the signing oracle. If* $\mathbf{Adv}_{\mathsf{SS},\mathcal{A}}^{euf\text{-}ncma}(\lambda)$ *is negligible for any PPT adversary $\mathcal{A}$ who has only one access to* SignO, *then* SS *is one-time existentially unforgeable under adaptive chosen message attacks (oteuf-cma).*

If we relax adversary's winning condition from $m^* \notin \mathcal{Q}$ to $(m^*, \sigma^*) \notin \{(m_i, \sigma_i)_{i \in [q]}\}$ in Eq. (4), the *euf-cma* security is improved to *strong euf-cma* security, denoted by *seuf-cma* (and *oteuf-cma* to *soteuf-cma*, respectively). Similarly, if $m^* \notin \mathcal{Q}$ is replaced with $(m^*, \sigma^*) \notin \{(m_i, \sigma_i)_{i \in [q]}\}$ in Eq. (3), the *euf-ncma* security is improved to *strong euf-ncma* security, denoted by *seuf-ncma* (and *oteuf-ncma* to *soteuf-ncma*, respectively).

3 One-Time Signatures Against Non-adaptive Adversaries

In this section, we construct a *soteuf-ncma* secure signature scheme and prove its security with a tight reduction to the DCR assumption.

To setup the system, first call GGen(1^λ) to output par = ($N, \mathbb{G}, \mathbb{G}_1, \mathbb{G}_2, g, g_1, g_2$). Here $N = PQ$ and $\mathbb{G}, \mathbb{G}_1, \mathbb{G}_2$ are defined as in Sect. 2.2 with $|\mathbb{G}_1| = \varphi(N)/4$ and $|\mathbb{G}_2| = N$. Let $pp = (\mathsf{par}, H)$ be the global public parameters, where $H : \{0,1\}^* \rightarrow \{0,1\}^{\ell_H}$ is a collision-resistant hash function. Moreover, $|\mathbb{G}_2| = N > 2^{\ell_H}$. The global public parameters pp serves as implicit input for all algorithms of the following signature scheme.

Our signature scheme OTS consists of three algorithms (OTGen, OTSig, OTVer) described as follows.

- OTGen(1^λ) uniformly chooses $x, y \in \mathbb{G}$, and sets $osk = (x, y)$, $ovk = (X, Y) = (x^N, y^N) \in \mathbb{G}_1^2$. Then it outputs osk and ovk.
- OTSig(osk, M) computes

$$\sigma = |x \cdot y^\kappa|_N \in \{0, \cdots, \lfloor N/2 \rfloor\} \text{ for } \kappa = H(M) \tag{5}$$

and outputs σ.
- OTVer(ovk, M, σ) outputs 1 iff $\sigma^N = X \cdot Y^\kappa$ for $ovk = (X, Y)$ and $\kappa = H(M)$.

Correctness is straightforward. Before presenting security proof, we give a technical lemma as follows.

Lemma 1. *Let* $Z = g_1^r g_2^b$ *for* $r \xleftarrow{\$} \mathbb{Z}_{|\mathbb{G}_1|}$ *and* $b \xleftarrow{\$} \{0, 1\}$ *be a DCR challenge and* $\kappa \in \{0, 1\}^{\ell_H}$. *There exists an algorithm* $\mathcal{T}$ *which takes as inputs* Z, κ *(public parameter pp is an implicit input), and outputs* $\sigma \in \{0, \cdots, \lfloor N/2 \rfloor\}$, $X, Y \in \mathbb{G}^2$, *i.e.,* $(\sigma, X, Y) \leftarrow \mathcal{T}(Z, \kappa)$, *such that*

(i) (X, Y, σ, κ) *satisfies the equation*

$$\sigma^N = X \cdot Y^\kappa. \tag{6}$$

(ii) For each κ, *there exists a unique* σ *such that* (κ, σ) *satisfies (6).*
(iii) If $b = 0$, (X, Y) *is distributed uniformly over* $\mathbb{G}_1^2$.
(iv) If $b = 1$, *then (6) has a unique solution* (κ, σ).

Proof. Algorithm $\mathcal{T}$ can be constructed as follows. It chooses $s, t \xleftarrow{\$} \mathbb{G}_1^2$, sets $X := s^N / Z^\kappa$, $Y := t^N Z$, and $\sigma = |st^\kappa|_N$. A straightforward calculation shows that (6) holds no matter $b = 0$ or $b = 1$.

For (σ, κ) that satisfies (6), assume that there exists another valid output σ' satisfying $\sigma'^N = XY^\kappa = \sigma^N$. Recall that for any $W \in \mathbb{G}_1$, $\sigma^N = W$ has a unique solution $\sigma \in \mathbb{G}$ such that $\sigma \in \{0, \cdots, \lfloor N/2 \rfloor\}$. This fact leads to (ii).

If $b = 0$, (X, Y) is distributed uniformly over $\mathbb{G}_1^2$ due to the fact that s, t are randomly chosen in $\mathbb{G}_1$ and $Z \in \mathbb{G}_1$. This yields (iii).

If $b = 1$, assume that there are two pairs (κ, σ) and (κ', σ') satisfying (6), i.e.,

$$\sigma^N = X \cdot Y^\kappa, \quad \sigma'^N = X \cdot Y^{\kappa'}. \tag{7}$$

According to (ii), for each κ, there exists a unique σ such that (κ, σ) satisfies (6), so all we have to do is to prove $\kappa = \kappa'$. Eq. (7) implies $(\sigma/\sigma')^N = Y^{\kappa-\kappa'}$. For $b = 1$, $Y = t^N Z = t^N g_1^r g_2$, then $(\sigma/\sigma')^N = (t^N g_1^r g_2)^{\kappa-\kappa'}$. Since $(\sigma/\sigma')^N \in \mathbb{G}_1$, we have $g_2^{\kappa-\kappa'} = 1$ hence $\kappa = \kappa'$. So we proved (iv) and complete the proof. $\square$

Theorem 1. *If the DCR assumption holds relative to* GGen *in group* $\mathbb{G}$, *and* H *is collision-resistant, the above signature scheme* OTS *is strongly one-time euf-ncma secure. To be more specific, for any PPT adversary* $\mathcal{A}$, *there exist PPT adversaries* $\mathcal{B}^{DCR}$ *and* $\mathcal{B}^{CRHF}$ *such that*

$$\mathbf{Adv}_{\mathsf{OTS},\mathcal{A}}^{soteuf\text{-}ncma}(\lambda) = \mathbf{Adv}_{\mathsf{OTS},\mathcal{A}}^{oteuf\text{-}ncma}(\lambda) \leq \mathbf{Adv}_{\mathcal{B}^{CRHF}}^{cr}(\lambda) + \mathbf{Adv}_{\mathcal{B}^{DCR}}^{dcr}(\lambda). \tag{8}$$

Proof. $\mathbf{Adv}_{\mathsf{OTS},\mathcal{A}}^{oteuf\text{-}ncma}(\lambda)$ characterizes the probability that $\mathcal{A}$ wins in the *oteuf-ncma* security game. Let $\mathsf{bad}_{\mathsf{coll}}$ be the event that $\mathcal{A}$'s forgery (M^*, σ^*) induces a hash collision, i.e., $\mathcal{A}$ ever queried a message $M(\neq M^*)$ such that $H(M) = H(M^*)$. Therefore,

$$
\begin{aligned}
\mathbf{Adv}_{\mathsf{OTS},\mathcal{A}}^{oteuf\text{-}ncma}(\lambda) &= \Pr\left[\mathcal{A} \text{ wins}\right] \\
&= \Pr\left[\mathcal{A} \text{ wins} \wedge \mathsf{bad}_{\mathsf{coll}}\right] + \Pr\left[\mathcal{A} \text{ wins} \wedge \overline{\mathsf{bad}_{\mathsf{coll}}}\right] \\
&\leq \Pr\left[\mathsf{bad}_{\mathsf{coll}}\right] + \Pr\left[\mathcal{A} \text{ wins} \wedge \overline{\mathsf{bad}_{\mathsf{coll}}}\right]
\end{aligned} \tag{9}
$$

It is easy to see that

$$
\Pr\left[\mathsf{bad}_{\mathsf{coll}}\right] \leq \mathbf{Adv}_{\mathcal{B}^{\mathsf{CRHF}}}^{cr}(\lambda) \tag{10}
$$

where adversary $\mathcal{B}^{\mathsf{CRHF}}$ simulates the *oteuf-ncma* game with $\mathcal{A}$ and outputs such a collision upon $\mathsf{bad}_{\mathsf{coll}}$.

To bound $\Pr\left[\mathcal{A} \text{ wins} \wedge \overline{\mathsf{bad}_{\mathsf{coll}}}\right]$, we construct an adversary $\mathcal{B}^{\mathsf{DCR}}$ as follows. $\mathcal{B}^{\mathsf{DCR}}$ receives as input a DCR challenge $Z = g_1^r g_2^b$ with $r \xleftarrow{\$} \mathbb{Z}_{|\mathbb{G}_1|}$ and $b \xleftarrow{\$} \{0,1\}$. It invokes $\mathcal{A}$, and receives a message M chosen by $\mathcal{A}$. Then $\mathcal{B}^{\mathsf{DCR}}$ invokes algorithm $\mathcal{T}$ in Lemma 1 to obtain $(\sigma, X, Y) \leftarrow \mathcal{T}(Z, H(M))$. It returns $vk := (X, Y)$ and signature σ to $\mathcal{A}$. If $\mathcal{A}$ outputs a forgery (M^*, σ^*), such that $H(M) \neq H(M^*)$ and $\sigma^{*N} = X \cdot Y^{H(M^*)}$, then $\mathcal{B}^{\mathsf{DCR}}$ outputs 1, otherwise 0.

- If $b = 0$, $vk = (X, Y)$ is a correctly distributed verification key by Property *(iii)*. Note that σ is a valid signature for M under vk by Property *(i)* and is unique by Property *(ii)*, thus is correctly distributed. Hence $\mathcal{B}^{\mathsf{DCR}}$ perfectly simulates the *oteuf-ncma* game for $\mathcal{A}$, and $\mathcal{B}^{\mathsf{DCR}}$ outputs 1 as long as $\mathcal{A}$ wins and $\overline{\mathsf{bad}_{\mathsf{coll}}}$ occurs. As a result,

$$
\Pr\left[\mathcal{B}^{\mathsf{DCR}}(Z) = 1 \mid b = 0\right] = \Pr\left[\mathcal{A} \text{ wins} \wedge \overline{\mathsf{bad}_{\mathsf{coll}}}\right]. \tag{11}
$$

- If $b = 1$, the solution $(H(M), \sigma)$ for Eq. (6) is unique according to property *(iv)* of Lemma 1. Note that $\mathsf{bad}_{\mathsf{coll}}$ does not occur, so $M \neq M^*$ implies $H(M) \neq H(M^*)$. Hence, it is impossible for (M^*, σ^*) to pass the verification. As a result, $\mathcal{B}^{\mathsf{DCR}}$ outputs 1 with probability 0, i.e.,

$$
\Pr\left[\mathcal{B}^{\mathsf{DCR}}(Z) = 1 \mid b = 1\right] = 0. \tag{12}
$$

Eqs. (11) and (12) implies that

$$
\begin{aligned}
\mathbf{Adv}_{\mathcal{B}^{\mathsf{DCR}}}^{dcr}(\lambda) &= \left|\Pr\left[\mathcal{B}^{\mathsf{DCR}}(Z) = 1 \mid b = 0\right] - \Pr\left[\mathcal{B}^{\mathsf{DCR}}(Z) = 1 \mid b = 1\right]\right| \\
&= \Pr\left[\mathcal{A} \text{ wins} \wedge \overline{\mathsf{bad}_{\mathsf{coll}}}\right].
\end{aligned} \tag{13}
$$

The combination of (9) (10) and (13) derives (8). Note that our signing algorithm OTSig is deterministic, i.e., $M^* \neq M$ is equivalent to $(M^*, \sigma^*) \neq (M, \sigma)$, thus the above signature scheme OTS is strongly one-time *euf-ncma* secure as well. $\qquad\square$

4 Tightly Secure Signatures Against Non-adaptive Adversaries

This scheme NSIG is based on the one-time signature scheme OTS in Sect. 3, and implicitly includes a binary tree of depth d, which allows us to sign up to 2^d signatures, such that all nodes except the root node can be generated "on the fly". Each node will be associated with a key pair (ovk, osk) of OTS and will be defined by the verification key ovk. This tree will be initialized by generating (ovk_0, osk_0) for the root by invoking OTGen. Define the root node $N_0 := ovk_0$. When signing a message M, the signer picks the leftmost unused leaf N_d, invokes $(ovk_d, osk_d) \leftarrow \mathsf{OTGen}(1^\lambda)$, and defines $N_d := ovk_d = (x_d^N, y_d^N)$. The signer determines the path P from the leaf $N_d = ovk_d$ to the root $N_0 = ovk_0$ and collects all the nodes along the path and all their siblings to a set called S_P. How to obtain set S_P is illustrated in Fig. 1. For each node in S_P, if no key is assigned for the node yet, the signer invokes $(ovk, osk) \leftarrow \mathsf{OTGen}(1^\lambda)$ to assign this node with a freshly generated verification key ovk.

The signer will sign the path in a top-down manner. For each node $N_{i-1} \in \{N_j\}_{j \in [d]}$ along the path P, the signer will generate a signature on its two child nodes using osk_{i-1}, i.e., $\sigma_{i-1} \leftarrow \mathsf{OTSig}(osk_{i-1}, N_i^{\mathrm{left}} || N_i^{\mathrm{right}})$. For the leaf node, compute $\sigma_d \leftarrow \mathsf{OTSig}(osk_d, M)$. Finally, the signer outputs the verification keys of nodes in set S_P and all the one-time signatures $(\sigma_i)_{i \in [d]}$ as the final signature $\sigma = \left((N_{i+1}^{\mathrm{left}} || N_{i+1}^{\mathrm{right}}, \sigma_i)_{i \in \{0,1,\ldots,d-1\}}, \sigma_d \right)$ on M. Furthermore, as a quiet standard technique, we can transform our stateful tree-based scheme into a stateless one by using pseudo-random function. See more details in [Gol86].

This signature scheme consists of three algorithms NSIG = (NGen, NSign, NVerify) as follows. Let $pp = (\mathrm{par}(= N, \mathbb{G}, \mathbb{G}_1, \mathbb{G}_2, g, g_1, g_2), H)$ be the public parameters serving as implicit input for all algorithms of the scheme. We also illustrate the tree in Fig. 1.

- NGen(1^λ): Invoke $(ovk_0, osk_0) \leftarrow \mathsf{OTSig}$, and this defines the root of the tree $N_0 = ovk_0$. Set $sk = osk_0 = (x, y) \in \mathbb{G}_1^2$, $vk = ovk_0 = (X, Y) = (x^N, y^N) \in \mathbb{G}_1^2$ and return (vk, sk).
- NSign(sk, M): Choose the leftmost unused leaf N_d. Determine all nodes $\{N_0, N_1, \ldots, N_d\}$ along the path P from root N_0 to leaf N_d. (Some of them may not be assigned with any value initially.)

  For $i = 0$ to $d - 1$ do
    Find the two child nodes $(N_{i+1}^{\mathrm{left}}, N_{i+1}^{\mathrm{right}})$ of N_i (here N_{i+1} is either N_{i+1}^{left} or N_{i+1}^{right}).
    If N_{i+1}^{left} is not defined, then

$$(ovk_i, osk_i) \leftarrow \mathsf{OTGen}(1^\lambda); \quad N_{i+1}^{\mathrm{left}} := ovk_i;$$

    If N_{i+1}^{right} is not defined, then

$$(ovk_i', osk_i') \leftarrow \mathsf{OTGen}(1^\lambda); \quad N_{i+1}^{\mathrm{right}} := ovk_i';$$

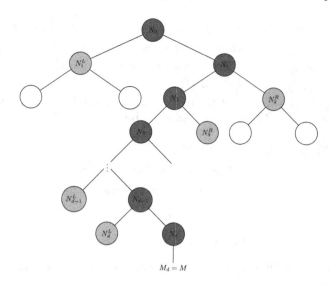

Fig. 1. The tree in the NSIG scheme. The nodes on the path is the blue nodes and their siblings are the light blue ones. All the nodes on the path and their siblings constitute set $S_P = \{N_0, N_1^L, N_1, N_2, N_2^R, N_3, N_3^R, \ldots, N_d^L, N_d\}$. In this signature $\sigma = ((M_0, \sigma_0), (M_1, \sigma_1), \cdots, (M_{d-1}, \sigma_{d-1}), \sigma_d)$, $M_0 = N_1^L \| N_1$, $M_1 = N_2 \| N_2^R$, $M_2 = N_3 \| N_3^R, \ldots, M_{d-1} = N_d^L \| N_d$, $M_d = M$. (Color figure online)

$\sigma_i \leftarrow \mathsf{OTSig}(osk_i, N_{i+1}^{\mathrm{left}} \| N_{i+1}^{\mathrm{right}})$.
$\sigma_d \leftarrow \mathsf{OTSig}(osk_d, M)$.
$\sigma := ((N_{i+1}^{\mathrm{left}} \| N_{i+1}^{\mathrm{right}}, \sigma_i)_{i \in \{0,1,\ldots,d-1\}}, \sigma_d)$.
$\mathrm{Return}(\sigma)$

- $\mathsf{NVerify}(vk, M, \sigma)$: Parse $\sigma = ((M_0, \sigma_0), (M_1, \sigma_1), \cdots, (M_{d-1}, \sigma_{d-1}), \sigma_d)$. Further parse $M_i = (ovk_{i+1} \| ovk_{i+1}')$.
$M_d := M$;
For $i = d$ down to 1 do
  If $\mathsf{OTVer}(ovk_i, M_i, \sigma_i) = 0 \wedge \mathsf{OTVer}(ovk_i', M_i, \sigma_i) = 0$, $\mathrm{Return}(0)$;
If $\mathsf{OTVer}(vk = ovk_0, M_0, \sigma_0) = 0$, $\mathrm{Return}(0)$; Else $\mathrm{Return}(1)$.

The correctness NSIG follows from OTS. We prove the security as follows.

Theorem 2. *If the DCR assumption holds with* GGen, *and* H *is collision-resistant, then* NSIG *is euf-ncma secure. Specifically, for any PPT adversary* $\mathcal{A}$, *there exist PPT adversaries* $\mathcal{B}^{\mathsf{DCR}}$ *and* $\mathcal{B}^{\mathsf{CRHF}}$ *such that*

$$\mathbf{Adv}_{\mathsf{NSIG}, \mathcal{A}}^{euf\text{-}ncma}(\lambda) \leq \mathbf{Adv}_{\mathcal{B}^{\mathsf{CRHF}}}^{cr}(\lambda) + \mathbf{Adv}_{\mathcal{B}^{\mathsf{DCR}}}^{dcr}(\lambda). \tag{14}$$

Proof. In the *euf-ncma* security game, assume adversary $\mathcal{A}$ chooses q messages $(M^{(j)})_{j \in [q]}$, receives q corresponding signatures $(\sigma^{(j)})_{j \in [q]}$ and vk from the challenger, and outputs a forgery (M^*, σ^*). Denote by $N_d^{(1)}, \cdots, N_d^{(q)}$ the q leaves that were used by the challenger in signing q chosen messages $M^{(1)}, \cdots, M^{(q)}$.

For $j \in [q]$, parse $\sigma^{(j)} = \left((M_i^{(j)}, \sigma_i^{(j)})_{i \in \{0,1,\ldots,d-1\}}, \sigma_d^{(j)} \right)$ and $\sigma^* = ((M_i^*,$
$\sigma_i^*)_{i \in \{0,1,\ldots,d-1\}}, \sigma_d^*)$. For $\mathcal{A}$'s forgery, define set $\mathcal{M}^* := \{M_1^*, M_2^*, \ldots, M_{d-1}^*, M^*\}$.
For each message query $M^{(j)}$ from $\mathcal{A}$ and the corresponding signature $\sigma^{(j)}$, define
$\mathcal{M}^{(j)} := \{M_1^{(j)}, M_2^{(j)}, \ldots, M_{d-1}^{(j)}, M^{(j)}\}$.

Let $\mathsf{bad_{coll}}$ be the event that there exists a $k \in [q]$, and an element $m \in \mathcal{M}^{(k)}$
and an element $m^* \in \mathcal{M}^*$ such that $m \neq m^*$ but $H(m) = H(m^*)$. Clearly,

$$
\begin{aligned}
\mathbf{Adv}_{\mathsf{NSIG},\mathcal{A}}^{euf\text{-}ncma}(\lambda) &= \Pr[\mathcal{A} \text{ wins}] \\
&= \Pr\left[\mathcal{A} \text{ wins} \wedge \mathsf{bad_{coll}}\right] + \Pr\left[\mathcal{A} \text{ wins} \wedge \overline{\mathsf{bad_{coll}}}\right] \\
&\leq \Pr\left[\mathsf{bad_{coll}}\right] + \Pr\left[\mathcal{A} \text{ wins} \wedge \overline{\mathsf{bad_{coll}}}\right]
\end{aligned}
\tag{15}
$$

It is easy to see that

$$
\Pr[\mathsf{bad_{coll}}] \leq \mathbf{Adv}_{\mathcal{B}\mathsf{CRHF}}^{cr}(\lambda)
\tag{16}
$$

for an adversary $\mathcal{B}^{\mathsf{CRHF}}$ that simulate $euf\text{-}ncma$ game with $\mathcal{A}$ and outputs any
such collision upon $\mathsf{bad_{coll}}$.

Let $\overline{\mathsf{bad_{coll}}}$ be the event that $\mathsf{bad_{coll}}$ does not occur. To bound
$\Pr\left[\mathcal{A} \text{ wins} \wedge \overline{\mathsf{bad_{coll}}}\right]$, we construct an adversary $\mathcal{B}^{\mathsf{DCR}}$, who simulates the real
$euf\text{-}ncma$ game for $\mathcal{A}$ as follows.

- $\mathcal{B}^{\mathsf{DCR}}$ receives as input a DCR challenge $Z = g_1^r g_2^b$ with $r \xleftarrow{\$} \mathbb{Z}_{|G_1|}$ and
  $b \xleftarrow{\$} \{0,1\}$.
- Denote by $(M^{(1)}, \cdots, M^{(q)})$ the q messages chosen by $\mathcal{A}$, $(N_d^{(1)}, \cdots, N_d^{(q)})$
  the q leftmost leaves that were used in signing the q messages.
- $\mathcal{B}^{\mathsf{DCR}}$ constructs a binary tree of at least q paths in a bottom-up way by using
  the algorithm $\mathcal{T}$ in Lemma 1.
  - $\mathcal{B}^{\mathsf{DCR}}$ computes $\kappa^{(j)} = H(M^{(j)})$ for all $j \in [q]$. Given Z and $\kappa^{(1)}, \cdots, \kappa^{(q)}$,
    each queried leaf node $N_d^{(j)}$ is determined by computing

    $$
    (\sigma_d^{(j)}, X^{(j)}, Y^{(j)}) \leftarrow \mathcal{T}(Z, \kappa^{(j)})
    $$

    and setting $N_d^{(j)} := (X^{(j)}, Y^{(j)})$. $\mathcal{B}^{\mathsf{DCR}}$ records $(N_d^{(j)}, \sigma_d^{(j)})$ and attaches
    the tuple to leaf node $N_d^{(j)}$.
  - For $i = d - 1$ down to 0 do
      For $j = 1$ to q do
          For each node $N_i^{(j)}$ in the i-th level of the j-th path, if $N_i^{(j)}$ is not
    defined,
    do the following steps.
    1. Let $N_{i+1}^{(j)\text{left}}$ and $N_{i+1}^{(j)\text{right}}$ be the left child and right child of $N_i^{(j)}$.
    2. If $N_{i+1}^{(j)\text{right}}$ is not defined[1], choose a random element $R \in \{0,1\}^{\ell_H}$,
       and call $(\tilde{\sigma}^{(j)}, X_{i+1}^{(j)\text{right}}, Y_{i+1}^{(j)\text{right}}) \leftarrow \mathcal{T}(Z, R)$. Define $N_{i+1}^{(j)\text{right}} :=$
       $(X_{i+1}^{(j)\text{right}}, Y_{i+1}^{(j)\text{right}})$.

---

[1] Since the q leaves are the leftmost ones, $N_{i+1}^{(j)\text{left}}$ has already been determined.

3. Compute $\kappa_i^{(j)} = H(N_{i+1}^{(j)\text{left}}||N_{i+1}^{(j)\text{right}})$.
   $(\sigma_i^{(j)}, X_i^{(j)}, Y_i^{(j)}) \leftarrow \mathcal{T}(Z, \kappa_i^{(j)})$.
   Set $N_i^{(j)} := (X_i^{(j)}, Y_i^{(j)})$.

4. $\mathcal{B}^{\text{DCR}}$ records $(N_{i+1}^{(j)\text{left}}, N_{i+1}^{(j)\text{right}}, \sigma_i^{(j)})$ and attaches the tuple to node $N_i^{(j)}$.

- Consequently, the root N_0 is determined by the previous procedure. Suppose $N_0 = (X_0, Y_0)$. $\mathcal{B}^{\text{DCR}}$ defines $vk := (X_0, Y_0)$.
- For each queried message $M^{(j)}$ with $j \in [q]$, $\mathcal{B}^{\text{DCR}}$ computes the corresponding signature as follows. It chooses the path from the root to the j-th leftmost leaf. According to the attachments of the d nodes $N_0^{(j)}, N_1^{(j)}, \ldots, N_d^{(j)}$ on the j-th path, $\mathcal{B}^{\text{DCR}}$ sets $\sigma^{(j)} = ((N_{i+1}^{(j)\text{left}}||N_{i+1}^{(j)\text{right}}, \sigma_i^{(j)})_{i \in \{0,1,\ldots,d-1\}}, \sigma_d^{(j)}))$.
- $\mathcal{B}^{\text{DCR}}$ sends $(vk, \sigma^{(1)}, \ldots, \sigma^{(q)})$ to $\mathcal{A}$.

- After obtaining $\mathcal{A}$'s forgery (M^*, σ^*), $\mathcal{B}^{\text{DCR}}$ outputs 1 if Bad_{coll} does not occur and (M^*, σ^*) is a valid forgery (i.e., it passes the verification).

Now we analyze the probability $\Pr\left[\mathcal{B}^{\text{DCR}}(Z) = 1 \mid b = 0\right]$ and $\Pr[\mathcal{B}^{\text{DCR}}(Z) = 1 \mid b = 1]$. Recall that the value of each node N_i in the tree is generated by $\mathcal{T}(Z, \cdot)$

- If $b = 0$, then $Z = g_1^r$. According to Property (iii) of Lemma 1, $\mathcal{T}(Z, \cdot)$ will output uniform (X, Y). Hence, $vk = N_0 = (X_0, Y_0)$ is randomly distributed over $\mathbb{G}_1 \times \mathbb{G}_1$, just like the output of NGen. Therefore, $\mathcal{B}^{\text{DCR}}$ perfectly simulates vk for $\mathcal{A}$. Moreover, $\mathcal{B}^{\text{DCR}}$ computes the signature of $M^{(j)}$ as $\sigma^{(j)} = ((N_{i+1}^{(j)\text{left}}||N_{i+1}^{(j)\text{right}}, \sigma_i^{(j)})_{i \in \{0,1,\ldots,d-1\}}, \sigma_d^{(j)}))$. Here both $N_{i+1}^{\text{left}} = (X_{i+1}^{\text{left}}, Y_{i+1}^{\text{left}})$ and $N_{i+1}^{\text{right}} = (X_{i+1}^{\text{right}}, Y_{i+1}^{\text{right}})$ are randomly distributed $\mathbb{G}_1 \times \mathbb{G}_1$, since they are outputs of $\mathcal{T}(Z, \cdot)$. Recall that $(\sigma_i^{(j)}, X_i^{(j)}, Y_i^{(j)})$ is generated by $\mathcal{T}(Z, H(N_{i+1}^{(j)\text{left}}||N_{i+1}^{(j)\text{right}}))$, then σ_i is also correctly distributed according to Property (i) and (ii) of Lemma 1.

In this case, $\mathcal{B}^{\text{DCR}}$ perfectly simulates the *euf-ncma* game for $\mathcal{A}$, and

$$\Pr\left[\mathcal{B}^{\text{DCR}}(Z) = 1 \mid b = 0\right] = \Pr\left[\mathcal{A} \text{ wins} \wedge \overline{\text{bad}}_{\text{coll}}\right]. \tag{17}$$

- If $b = 1$, we analyze the valid forgery (M^*, σ^*) of $\mathcal{A}$. First, parse $\sigma^* = ((M_i^*, \sigma_i^*)_{i \in \{0,1,\ldots,d-1\}}, \sigma_d^*)$, and $M_i^* = N_{i+1}^{*\text{left}}||N_{i+1}^{*\text{right}}$. Since the forgery is valid, we have $\text{OTVer}(N_i^{*\text{left}}, M_i, \sigma_i) = 1$ or $\text{OTVer}(N_i^{*\text{right}}, M_i, \sigma_i) = 1$ for $i \in [d]$ (we set $M_d^* = M^*$). If $\text{OTVer}(N_i^{*\text{left}}, M_i, \sigma_i) = 1$, set $N_i^* = N_i^{*\text{left}}$, otherwise set $N_i^* = N_i^{*\text{right}}$. We also have that $\text{OTVer}(N_0 = N_0^*, M_0, \sigma_0) = 1$. Consequently we get the set of nodes along the path forged by $\mathcal{A}$, which is denoted by $\Omega^* = \{N_0^* = N_0, N_1^*, \ldots, N_d^*\}$. Recall that $\mathcal{B}^{\text{DCR}}$ sets up a binary tree by answering $\mathcal{A}$'s q signature queries, where each signature $\sigma^{(j)}$ determines a unique path of the tree. Define set $\Omega^{(j)} = \{N_0^{(j)} = N_0, N_1^{(j)}, \ldots, N_d^{(j)}\}$, which consists of all the nodes along the j-th path. Because the forgery path (determined by $\mathcal{A}$) and the tree (created by $\mathcal{B}^{\text{DCR}}$ with the q paths) share the same root N_0, there must exists a path k and a biggest index δ such that $N_\delta^* \in \Omega^{(k)}$. Suppose that $N_\delta^* = N_\delta^{(k)} = (X, Y)$, then $N_{\delta+1}^* \neq N_{\delta+1}^{(k)}$. We have

$$(\sigma_\delta^{(k)})^N = X \cdot Y^{H(N_{\delta+1}^{(k)\text{left}} || N_{\delta+1}^{(k)\text{right}})}, \quad \text{either } N_{\delta+1}^{(k)} = N_{\delta+1}^{(k)\text{left}} \text{ or } N_{\delta+1}^{(k)} = N_{\delta+1}^{(k)\text{right}}. \quad (18)$$

At the same time, if σ_δ^* is a valid signature, we have

$$\sigma_\delta^{*N} = X \cdot Y^{H(N_{\delta+1}^{*\text{left}} || N_{\delta+1}^{*\text{right}})}, \quad \text{either } N_{\delta+1}^* = N_{\delta+1}^{*\text{left}} \text{ or } N_{\delta+1}^* = N_{\delta+1}^{*\text{right}}. \quad (19)$$

If $\mathsf{Bad_{coll}}$ does not occur, $N_{\delta+1}^* \neq N_{\delta+1}^{(k)}$ implies $H(N_{\delta+1}^{*\text{left}} || N_{\delta+1}^{*\text{right}}) \neq H(N_{\delta+1}^{(k)\text{left}} || N_{\delta+1}^{(k)\text{right}})$. Recall that $(\sigma_\delta^{(k)}, X, Y)$ are output of $\mathcal{T}(Z = g_1^r g_2^b, H(N_{\delta+1}^{(k)\text{left}} || N_{\delta+1}^{(k)\text{right}}))$. Now that $b = 1$, according to Property (iv), equation $\sigma^N = X \cdot Y^\kappa$ has a unique solution (σ, κ). That means Eqs. (18) and (19) cannot hold simultaneously as long as $\mathsf{Bad_{coll}}$ does not occur. As a result,

$$\Pr\left[\mathcal{B}^{\mathsf{DCR}}(Z) = 1 \mid b = 1\right] = 0. \quad (20)$$

Then $\mathcal{B}^{\mathsf{DCR}}$ output 1 with probability 0.

Combining Eqs. (17) and (20), we have

$$\mathbf{Adv}_{\mathcal{B}^{\mathsf{DCR}}}^{dcr}(\lambda) = \left| \Pr\left[\mathcal{B}^{\mathsf{DCR}}(Z) = 1 \mid b = 0\right] - \Pr\left[\mathcal{B}^{\mathsf{DCR}}(Z) = 1 \mid b = 1\right] \right|$$
$$= \Pr\left[\mathcal{A} \text{ wins} \wedge \overline{\mathsf{bad_{coll}}}\right]. \quad (21)$$

Finally, Eq. (14) follows from Eqs. (15), (16) and (21).   □

5   Tightly Secure Signatures Against Adaptive Adversaries

With the $euf\text{-}ncma$ secure NSIG in Sect. 4 and the $oteuf\text{-}ncma$ secure OTS in Sect. 3, we construct an $euf\text{-}cma$ secure ASIG. The construction is inspired by [HJ12]. The key pair (vk, sk) is generated using NSIG. To sign a message M, the signer uses algorithm $\mathcal{T}$ to generate a fresh verification key ovk and a corresponding one-time signature σ for M, then signs ovk with sk of NSIG.

Different from the security reduction in [EGM89], which will lose a factor of q (the number of queried signatures), our reduction is $tight$. The key observation is that our one-time signature scheme is implemented by algorithm $\mathcal{T}$ in Lemma 1, which can strictly exclude the reduction factor $1/q$ resulting from 1-out-q valid forgery match in [EGM89].

Our scheme consists of three algorithms ASIG = (AGen, ASign, AVerify) as follows. Let $pp = (\text{par}(= N, \mathbb{G}, \mathbb{G}_1, \mathbb{G}_2, g, g_1, g_2), H)$ be the public parameters serving as implicit input for all algorithms of the scheme.

- AGen(1^λ): Invoke $(vk_N, sk_N) \leftarrow$ NGen and choose $Z = g_1^r$ for $r \xleftarrow{\$} \mathbb{Z}_{|\mathbb{G}_1|}$. Set $vk := (vk_N, Z)$ and $sk := sk_N$.
- ASig(sk, M): Invoke $(\sigma', X, Y) \leftarrow \mathcal{T}(Z, H(M))$, set $M' = (X, Y)$ and compute $\sigma'' \leftarrow$ NSig(sk, M'). Return $\sigma = (\sigma', \sigma'', X, Y)$.
- AVerify(vk, M, σ): Parse $\sigma = (\sigma', \sigma'', X, Y)$. Set $M' = (X, Y)$ and output 1 if NVerify(vk_N, M', σ'') = 1 and $\sigma'^N = X \cdot Y^{H(M)}$, otherwise 0.

In this scheme, the verification key consists of only three elements in $\mathbb{G}$. The correctness follows from the correctness of NSIG and Property (i) of Lemma 1.

Theorem 3. *If the DCR assumption holds with* GGen, *and* H *is collision-resistant, then* SIG *is euf-cma secure. Specifically, for any PPT adversary* $\mathcal{A}$, *there exist PPT adversaries* $\mathcal{B}^{\mathsf{DCR}}$ *and* $\mathcal{B}^{\mathsf{CRHF}}$ *such that*

$$\mathbf{Adv}_{\mathsf{SIG},\mathcal{A}}^{euf\text{-}cma}(\lambda) \leq 2\mathbf{Adv}_{\mathcal{B}^{\mathsf{CRHF}}}^{cr}(\lambda) + 2\mathbf{Adv}_{\mathcal{B}^{\mathsf{DCR}}}^{dcr}(\lambda). \tag{22}$$

Proof. Given vk, adversary $\mathcal{A}$ adaptively queries q messages and outputs a forgery. Assume $\mathcal{A}$ chooses q messages $M^{(j)}$ and receives the corresponding signatures $\sigma^{(j)} = (\sigma'^{(j)}, \sigma''^{(j)}, X^{(j)}, Y^{(j)})$ for all $j \in [q]$. Finally $\mathcal{A}$ outputs a forgery (M^*, σ^*), with $\sigma^* = (\sigma'^*, \sigma''^*, X^*, Y^*)$.

Let $\mathsf{bad_{coll}}$ be the event that $\mathcal{A}$'s forgery (M^*, σ^*) induces a hash collision, i.e., there exists a queried $M^{(j)}(\neq M^*)$ such that $H(M^{(j)}) = H(M^*)$. We have

$$\begin{aligned}
\mathbf{Adv}_{\mathsf{ASIG},\mathcal{A}}^{euf\text{-}cma}(\lambda) &= \Pr\left[\mathcal{A} \text{ wins}\right] \\
&= \Pr\left[\mathcal{A} \text{ wins} \wedge \mathsf{bad_{coll}}\right] + \Pr\left[\mathcal{A} \text{ wins} \wedge \overline{\mathsf{bad_{coll}}}\right] \\
&\leq \Pr\left[\mathsf{bad_{coll}}\right] + \Pr\left[\mathcal{A} \text{ wins} \wedge \overline{\mathsf{bad_{coll}}}\right] \tag{23}
\end{aligned}$$

Clearly, we have

$$\Pr\left[\mathsf{bad_{coll}}\right] \leq \mathbf{Adv}_{\mathcal{B}^{\mathsf{CRHF}}}^{cr}(\lambda) \tag{24}$$

for an adversary $\mathcal{B}^{\mathsf{CRHF}}$ that simulate *euf-cma* game with $\mathcal{A}$ and outputs such a collision upon $\mathsf{bad_{coll}}$.

Let Reuse be the event that for $\mathcal{A}$'s forgery $(M^*, \sigma^* = (\sigma'^*, \sigma''^*, X^*, Y^*))$, there exists $j \in [q]$ such that $(X^{(j)}, Y^{(j)}) = (X^*, Y^*)$. Let $\overline{\text{Reuse}}$ be the event that Reuse does not occur, i.e., $\forall\, j \in [q]$, $(X^{(j)}, Y^{(j)}) \neq (X^*, Y^*)$. Then

$$\begin{aligned}
\Pr\left[\mathcal{A} \text{ wins} \wedge \overline{\mathsf{bad_{coll}}}\right] &= \Pr[\mathcal{A} \text{ wins} \wedge \overline{\mathsf{bad_{coll}}} \wedge \text{Reuse}] + \Pr[\mathcal{A} \text{ wins} \wedge \overline{\mathsf{bad_{coll}}} \wedge \overline{\text{Reuse}}] \\
&\leq \underbrace{\Pr[\mathcal{A} \text{ wins} \wedge \overline{\mathsf{bad_{coll}}} \wedge \text{Reuse}]}_{(*)} + \underbrace{\Pr[\mathcal{A} \text{ wins} \wedge \overline{\text{Reuse}}]}_{(**)}. \tag{25}
\end{aligned}$$

We will show that $(*)$ is negligible due to the DCR assumption. More precisely, we construct a PPT algorithm $\mathcal{B}^{\mathsf{DCR}}$ which simulate the *euf-cma* game for $\mathcal{A}$ as follows.

$\mathcal{B}^{\mathsf{DCR}}$ is given $Z = g_1^r g_2^b$ where r is random and $b \leftarrow \{0, 1\}$. $\mathcal{B}^{\mathsf{DCR}}$ invokes $(vk_N, sk_N) \leftarrow$ NGen(pp), sets $vk := (vk_N, Z)$ and $sk := sk_N$. It sends vk to $\mathcal{A}$.

When $\mathcal{A}$ queries a message $M^{(j)}$ for signature, $\mathcal{B}^{\mathsf{DCR}}$ uses sk to invoke $\sigma^{(j)} \leftarrow$ $\mathsf{ASig}(sk, M^{(j)})$ and replies $\sigma^{(j)}$ to $\mathcal{A}$. Finally $\mathcal{A}$ outputs a forgery (M^*, σ^*) with $\sigma^* = (\sigma'^*, \sigma''^*, X^*, Y^*)$. If (M^*, σ^*) is valid, no hash collision occurs, and there exists some $j \in [q]$ such that $(X^*, Y^*) = (X^{(j)}, Y^{(j)})$, i.e., $\mathcal{A}$ wins $\wedge$ $\overline{\mathsf{bad}_{\mathsf{coll}}} \wedge \mathsf{Reuse}$ happens, $\mathcal{B}^{\mathsf{DCR}}$ outputs 1.

If $b = 0$, we have $Z = g_1^r$. Then both $vk = (vk_N, Z)$ and $\sigma^{(j)}$ $(j \in [q])$ replied by $\mathcal{B}^{\mathsf{DCR}}$ are correctly distributed. Therefore,

$$\Pr[\mathcal{B}^{\mathsf{DCR}}(Z) = 1 | b = 0] = \Pr[\mathcal{A} \text{ wins} \wedge \overline{\mathsf{bad}_{\mathsf{coll}}} \wedge \mathsf{Reuse}].$$

If $b = 1$, we have $Z = g_1^r g_2$. Due to Property (iv) of Lemma 1, $\sigma'^N = X \cdot Y^{H(M)}$ only has a unique solution $(\sigma'^{(j)}, H(M^{(j)}))$. $M^{(j)} \neq M^*$ and no hash collision imply that $H(M^{(j)}) \neq H(M^*)$. Therefore, $\sigma^{*N} = X \cdot Y^{H(M^*)}$ does not hold, and $\mathcal{A}$'s forgery cannot be valid. Therefore,

$$\Pr[\mathcal{B}^{\mathsf{DCR}}(Z) = 1 | b = 1] = 0.$$

Consequently,

$$\mathbf{Adv}_{\mathcal{B}^{\mathsf{DCR}}}^{dcr}(\lambda) = |\Pr\left[\mathcal{B}^{\mathsf{DCR}}(Z) = 1 \mid b = 0\right] - \Pr\left[\mathcal{B}^{\mathsf{DCR}}(Z) = 1 \mid b = 1\right]|$$
$$= \Pr[\mathcal{A} \text{ wins} \wedge \overline{\mathsf{bad}_{\mathsf{coll}}} \wedge \mathsf{Reuse}]. \tag{26}$$

To show $(**)$ is negligible, we construct an $euf\text{-}ncma$ adversary $\mathcal{B}$ for NSIG as follows.

At the beginning, $\mathcal{B}$ randomly chooses q pairs $(x^{(j)}, y^{(j)}) \in \mathbb{G}_1^2$ as one-time secret keys $osk^{(j)} = (x^{(j)}, y^{(j)})$, and computes $(X^{(j)}, Y^{(j)}) = (x^{(j)N}, y^{(j)N})$ as verification keys $ovk^{(j)}$ of OTS. Then it sends $\{(X^{(j)}, Y^{(j)})\}_{j \in [q]}$ to its own challenger and obtains verification key vk_N and signatures $\{\sigma''^{(j)}\}_{j \in [q]}$.

Next, $\mathcal{B}$ chooses $r \xleftarrow{\$} \mathbb{Z}_{|\mathbb{G}_1|}$, computes $Z = g_1^r$ and sends $vk := (vk_N, Z)$ to adversary $\mathcal{A}$. Note that vk_N is generated by $\mathcal{B}$'s challenger with NGen, therefore vk is correctly distributed.

When $\mathcal{A}$ queries a message $M^{(j)}$, $\mathcal{B}$ uses the secret key $(x^{(j)}, y^{(j)})$ of OTS to generate $\sigma'^{(j)} \leftarrow \mathsf{OTSig}(osk^{(j)}, M^{(j)})$, i.e., $\sigma'^{(j)} = |x^{(j)} \cdot y^{(j)H(M^{(j)})}|_N$, and returns $\sigma^{(j)} = (\sigma'^{(j)}, \sigma''^{(j)}, X^{(j)}, Y^{(j)})$ to $\mathcal{A}$ for all $j \in [q]$. Since $\sigma'^{(j)}$ has the same distribution as that generated by algorithm $\mathcal{T}$ and $\sigma''^{(j)}$ is the output of NSIG, $\mathcal{B}$ simulates the $euf\text{-}cma$ game perfectly for $\mathcal{A}$.

Finally, $\mathcal{A}$ outputs its forgery $\sigma^* = (\sigma'^*, \sigma''^*, X^*, Y^*)$. Then $\mathcal{B}$ outputs $((X^*, Y^*), \sigma''^*)$ as its own forgery. It is obvious that if $\mathcal{A}$'s forgery is valid, and $\nexists j \in [q]$ such that $(X^{(j)}, Y^{(j)}) = (X^*, Y^*)$, i.e., $\mathcal{A}$ wins $\wedge$ $\overline{\mathsf{Reuse}}$ occurs, then $\mathcal{B}$'s forgery is valid. So we have

$$\Pr\left[\mathcal{A} \text{ wins} \wedge \overline{\text{Reuse}}\right] = \mathbf{Adv}_{\mathsf{NSIG},\mathcal{B}}^{euf\text{-}ncma}(\lambda) \leq \mathbf{Adv}_{\mathcal{B}\mathsf{CRHF}}^{cr}(\lambda) + \mathbf{Adv}_{\mathcal{B}\mathsf{DCR}}^{dcr}(\lambda), \quad (27)$$

where the last step of Eq. (27) follows from Theorem 2.

Finally, the combination of (23), (24), (25), (26) and (27) yields (22) and we complete this proof. □

Acknowledgments. The authors are supported by the National Natural Science Foundation of China Grant (Nos. 61672346, 61373153, 61472250). We thank the anonymous reviewers for their comments and suggestions.

References

[BKKP15] Blazy, O., Kakvi, S.A., Kiltz, E., Pan, J.: Tightly-secure signatures from chameleon hash functions. In: Katz, J. (ed.) PKC 2015. LNCS, vol. 9020, pp. 256–279. Springer, Heidelberg (2015). doi:10.1007/978-3-662-46447-2_12

[BKP14] Blazy, O., Kiltz, E., Pan, J.: (Hierarchical) Identity-based encryption from affine message authentication. In: Garay, J.A., Gennaro, R. (eds.) CRYPTO 2014. LNCS, vol. 8616, pp. 408–425. Springer, Heidelberg (2014). doi:10.1007/978-3-662-44371-2_23

[BMS03] Boneh, D., Mironov, I., Shoup, V.: A secure signature scheme from bilinear maps. In: Joye, M. (ed.) CT-RSA 2003. LNCS, vol. 2612, pp. 98–110. Springer, Heidelberg (2003). doi:10.1007/3-540-36563-X_7

[CD96] Cramer, R., Damgård, I.: New generation of secure and practical RSA-based signatures. In: Koblitz, N. (ed.) CRYPTO 1996. LNCS, vol. 1109, pp. 173–185. Springer, Heidelberg (1996). doi:10.1007/3-540-68697-5_14

[CG05a] Catalano, D., Gennaro, R.: Cramer-Damgård signatures revisited: efficient flat-tree signatures based on factoring. In: Vaudenay, S. (ed.) PKC 2005. LNCS, vol. 3386, pp. 313–327. Springer, Heidelberg (2005). doi:10.1007/978-3-540-30580-4_22

[CW13] Chen, J., Wee, H.: Fully, (almost) tightly secure IBE and dual system groups. In: Canetti, R., Garay, J.A. (eds.) CRYPTO 2013. LNCS, vol. 8043, pp. 435–460. Springer, Heidelberg (2013). doi:10.1007/978-3-642-40084-1_25

[DJ01] Damgård, I., Jurik, M.: A generalisation, a simplication and some applications of Paillier's probabilistic public-key system. In: Kim, K. (ed.) PKC 2001. LNCS, vol. 1992, pp. 119–136. Springer, Heidelberg (2001). doi:10.1007/3-540-44586-2_9

[EGM89] Even, S., Goldreich, O., Micali, S.: On-Line/Off-Line digital signatures. In: Brassard, G. (ed.) CRYPTO 1989. LNCS, vol. 435, pp. 263–275. Springer, New York (1990). doi:10.1007/0-387-34805-0_24

[GMR88] Goldwasser, S., Micali, S., Rivest, R.L.: A digital signature scheme secure against adaptive chosen-message attacks. SIAM J. Comput. **17**(2), 281–308 (1988)

[Gol86] Goldreich, O.: Two remarks concerning the Goldwasser-Micali-Rivest signature scheme. In: Odlyzko, A.M. (ed.) CRYPTO 1986. LNCS, vol. 263, pp. 104–110. Springer, Heidelberg (1987). doi:10.1007/3-540-47721-7_8

[HJ12] Hofheinz, D., Jager, T.: Tightly secure signatures and public-key encryption. In: Safavi-Naini, R., Canetti, R. (eds.) CRYPTO 2012. LNCS, vol. 7417, pp. 590–607. Springer, Heidelberg (2012). doi:10.1007/978-3-642-32009-5_35

[HJK11] Hofheinz, D., Jager, T., Kiltz, E.: Short signatures from weaker assumptions. In: Lee, D.H., Wang, X. (eds.) ASIACRYPT 2011. LNCS, vol. 7073, pp. 647–666. Springer, Heidelberg (2011). doi:10.1007/978-3-642-25385-0_35

[Hof16a] Hofheinz, D.: Adaptive partitioning. IACR Cryptology ePrint Archive 2016, 373 (2016)

[Hof16b] Hofheinz, D.: Algebraic partitioning: fully compact and (almost) tightly secure cryptography. In: Kushilevitz, E., Malkin, T. (eds.) TCC 2016. LNCS, vol. 9562, pp. 251–281. Springer, Heidelberg (2016). doi:10.1007/978-3-662-49096-9_11

[HW09] Hohenberger, S., Waters, B.: Realizing hash-and-sign signatures under standard assumptions. In: Joux, A. (ed.) EUROCRYPT 2009. LNCS, vol. 5479, pp. 333–350. Springer, Heidelberg (2009). doi:10.1007/978-3-642-01001-9_19

[MP12] Micciancio, D., Peikert, C.: Trapdoors for lattices: simpler, tighter, faster, smaller. In: Pointcheval, D., Johansson, T. (eds.) EUROCRYPT 2012. LNCS, vol. 7237, pp. 700–718. Springer, Heidelberg (2012). doi:10.1007/978-3-642-29011-4_41

[Pai99] Paillier, P.: Public-key cryptosystems based on composite degree residuosity classes. In: Stern, J. (ed.) EUROCRYPT 1999. LNCS, vol. 1592, pp. 223–238. Springer, Heidelberg (1999). doi:10.1007/3-540-48910-X_16

[Rom90] Rompel, J.: One-way functions are necessary and sufficient for secure signatures. In: Proceedings of the Twenty-Second Annual ACM Symposium on Theory of Computing, pp. 387–394. ACM (1990)

[Wat05] Waters, B.: Efficient identity-based encryption without random oracles. In: Cramer, R. (ed.) EUROCRYPT 2005. LNCS, vol. 3494, pp. 114–127. Springer, Heidelberg (2005). doi:10.1007/11426639_7

Author Index

Printed in the United States
By Bookmasters